Sisterhood
of Saints

DAILY GUIDANCE
AND INSPIRATION

Melanie Rigney

Franciscan
MEDIA
Cincinnati, Ohio

To Wendy—
A longtime sister
& the heart of a
treasured friend!
May you find comfort
that you can pass on
in these pages!
Love,

Cover and book design by Mark Sullivan
Cover image © Fotolia | Matka Wariatka

LIBRARY OF CONGRESS CATALOGING-IN-PUBLICATION DATA
Rigney, Melanie.
Sisterhood of saints : daily guidance and inspiration / Melanie Rigney.
pages cm
Includes bibliographical references and index.
ISBN 978-1-61636-617-9 (alk. paper)
1. Catholic women—Religious life. 2. Christian women saints—Meditations. 3. Christian women saints—Biography. 4. Devotional calendars—Catholic Church. I. Title.
BX2353.R54 2013
282.092'52—dc23
2013009740

ISBN 978-1-61636-617-9

Copyright ©2013, Melanie Rigney. All rights reserved.
Published by Franciscan Media
28 W. Liberty St.
Cincinnati, OH 45202
www.FranciscanMedia.org

Printed in the United States of America.
Printed on acid-free paper.
13 14 15 16 17   5 4 3 2 1

For Mimi Fitzgerald,
who teaches me not to canonize people
here on earth, but to love them as Christ does.

Every saint has a past, and every sinner has a future.
—Oscar Wilde

PREFACE

These women changed my life. I hope they change yours.

What did researching the lives of more than seven hundred women in close to two dozen books and countless websites teach me about the female blesseds and saints of our Church you'll find in these pages?

They weren't perfect, for starters. They fought with their parents, their spouses, their siblings, and their children—not to mention priests, bishops, cardinals, popes, and even their fellow women religious. Sometimes they hurt people, badly.

They were outcasts sometimes as well, because of the way they looked or talked or dressed or because people couldn't see beyond their disabilities. They wondered why God made them that way, and they wondered why God stopped talking to them. Others wondered why God talked to them quite so much, even when they were trying to fix dinner.

They taught people to read and write in spite of persecution and possible arrest. They walked into the poorest of neighborhoods, sometimes with priests, often by themselves, and nursed the untouchables and fed the hungry. They helped people who had given up on themselves, people who had never heard of God or had little use for him if they had.

Some of them were really ordinary—I mean, *really* ordinary. They got married. They had children. They joined an order and received assignments that never put their lives in danger. And while some traveled thousands of miles for God, some never left their hometowns.

Some women crossed battle lines or offered up their lives in wartime. Others battled with inner demons. Some died in horrible ways after torture that had to have been designed by the devil. Others died safely in their beds.

In short, they are women just like you and me.

This book is designed for today's busy woman. For each day, you'll find a short synopsis of the life of the saint or blessed, a paragraph about its relevance to your life today, a snippet from Scripture or the woman's writings, and a challenge. The entries are based on themes in all of our lives, such as caregiving, cleaning, coping with illness or disability, involvement with a faith community, relationships, work, and the like. It should take just ten minutes or so to read the page. Hopefully, the lesson and the challenge will stay with you throughout the day.

You'll find the biggies here, of course, the ones we all know by first name: Mary. Therese. Teresa. Anne. Elizabeth. Monica. Brigid. Catherine. Agnes. Juliana. Hildegard. Lucy. Agnes. But I hope you'll also make some new friends, like Marianne Cope, Eugenie Smet, Agnes Phila, Laura Montoya, and Anna Schaffer. And I hope you'll introduce them to your daughter, your sister, your mother, your grandmother, your friends, your coworkers, your neighbors, and your fellow parishioners, because we can all always use more friends.

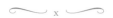

As I said, these women changed my life. Because, you see, no matter how different they were, no matter whether they lived in the first century or the twenty-first, whether they lived in India or Peru or Italy or France or Germany or Mexico or the United States or Canada, they loved God.

Even more importantly, they knew God loves us, through the good times and the bad. They didn't always understand God or the situations he put them in, but they knew he was love. They whispered that to me as they told me their stories.

I hope they change your life too.

ACKNOWLEDGMENTS

Writing this book was a true gift. I thank Mary Carol Kendzia of Franciscan Media, my editor, for believing in me and for her patience, and Lisa Biedenbach for her work on the concept.

Nothing good comes without prayer power. I am humbled by the number of friends who prayed as I was writing this book, and offered the names of their favorite saints and blesseds. While I am sure I will miss many names, special thanks to Philip Kiko, Duffy Kiko, Trudy Harlow Dervan, Fran deVenoge, Sandy Cleva, Karen Audant, Helene Mullaney, Henri Johnson, Meg Gilroy, Adrienne Cleary, Joan Sheppard, and Susan Trainor.

Finally, this book would not have been written without the help of my sister, Maureen Rigney. She did the lion's share of the research behind the quotes or Scripture you'll see on each page. Maureen also listened to me obsess about my favorite saint of the hour (and sometimes, there were several a day) and made more than her share of weekend lunches and dinners so I could commune with these women. I couldn't ask for a better sister.

Blessed Virgin Mary

First century

She stayed with him. In Christ's darkest hours, on Calvary, his mother was there. It must have been incredibly painful for Mary to watch her only son suffer so, and yet she stayed, knowing that his burden was lightened by seeing her face.

Perhaps Mary thought about the angel's visit to her. Perhaps she remembered Jesus's birth in the manger. Perhaps she mourned a little over memories of the wedding at Cana, when she pushed him to feed the people. She knew now there would be no wedding for him. Now, Mary didn't know for sure what God had in store. She only knew that she loved God and her son, and she trusted the Lord.

Sometimes, we forget who's in charge. We fret about the future and nurture past hurts. Mary's example reminds us how much simply being present and attentive can be to those in our lives who are hurting—and of our need to turn over the hard tasks to God.

❧ Inspiration

Then Mary said, "Here am I, the servant of the Lord; let it be with me according to your word." Then the angel departed from her. (Luke 1:38)

❧ Challenge

Just for today, put aside your worrying and your anxiety. Trust in God the way Mary did.

Zdislava of Lemberk

Circa 1220–1252

Some children run away to join the circus. Legend has it that Zdislava ran away to become a hermit when she was seven or so. She later married a wealthy man, and the two clashed over her tireless work with the poor, in particular refugees from the Tatar invasions. Eventually, they reached a point of peace and worked together to found a Dominican convent with which Zdislava was involved for the rest of her life. Pope Paul VI described her as "an example of marital fidelity, a support of domestic spirituality and moral integrity."

Marriage isn't always easy. We come to it from different life experiences, which is why mutual respect and understanding are critical in building a lifelong union. Compromise is important to any relationship, yet we must be mindful that preserving peace with our spouses, children, and others comes second to what God desires.

Inspiration

Each of you, however, should love his wife as himself, and a wife should respect her husband. (Ephesians 5:33)

Challenge

Pray for guidance about how to approach, in a loving yet faithful way, an issue that divides you and your spouse or another important person in your life.

Genevieve of Paris

Circa 422–500

Genevieve was called to be part of the action. She was only fifteen when she left the hill country of France for Paris. While she was there, the city was under siege, and she was instrumental in helping to break a blockade. Later, as Attila the Hun was marching toward the city, it's said that Genevieve assembled a group of women who, through prayer, called on God to save the city. Attila changed his plans.

Isn't amazing, the way God answers our prayers, sometimes in the way we hope and anticipate, sometimes in other ways that serve us even better? Never be afraid to pray for something big or seemingly out of reach.

✞ Inspiration

David built there an altar to the LORD, and offered burnt offerings and offerings of well-being. So the LORD answered his supplication for the land, and the plague was averted from Israel. (2 Samuel 24:25)

✞ Challenge

Genevieve's patronages include women soldiers. Consider writing a letter of thanks to a woman you know in the military; if you don't know one, volunteer an hour at your local USO, VFW, or other service club.

Elizabeth Ann Seton

August 28, 1774–January 4, 1821

Elizabeth is best known as the first native-born American saint and the founder of the American Sisters of Charity, which now consists of more than five thousand religious women ministering through schools, social service centers, and hospitals throughout the world. What you might not know is that she began life as an Episcopalian and converted to Catholicism less than a decade before she was commissioned to found Sisters of Charity. The impetus for her conversion was the strong support and faith of friends with whom she and her family stayed in Italy as her husband was dying. At her canonization in 1975, Pope John Paul II said, "May the dynamism and authenticity of her life be an example in our day, and for generations to come, of what women can and must accomplish, in the fulfillment of their role, for the good of humanity."

What a blessing for Elizabeth and all of us that her husband's friends weren't afraid to talk with her about the strength they found in their faith! It's that kind of real-world evangelization that even the shyest of us can do for God.

Inspiration

Put your heart at His feet. It is the gift He loves most. (St. Elizabeth Ann Seton)

Challenge

Spend some time thinking and praying about why you follow Christ as a Catholic and how that informs the way you interact with non-Catholics.

Genoveva Torres Morales

January 3, 1870–January 5, 1956

To Genoveva, God mattered, and little else. She didn't dwell on the fact that she was orphaned at an early age or that she walked on crutches from age thirteen on because part of one leg had been amputated. She didn't dwell on the fact that her disability kept her from her desire to be a Carmelite nun or on the fact that the Spanish Civil War resulted in the closing of the women's boardinghouses she had founded. She stayed positive and kept going, rebuilding the boardinghouses after the war with the Angelicas, the religious order she helped to found.

It's hard when life kicks us in the pants. We always have a choice—give into bitterness and anger, or pick ourselves up, dust ourselves off, and with God's help, start again.

Inspiration

Even if I must suffer greatly, thanks be to God's mercy, I will not lack courage. (St. Genoveva Torres Morales)

Challenge

Reach out to a friend who's going through a hard time. Offer to pray together for acceptance and serenity. Help him or her where you can in building a new life, whether that means connections in finding a new place to live or a new job, rides to Mass, meals, groceries, or simply a listening ear.

Gertrude the Great

January 6, 1256–November 17, 1302

Gertrude is recognized as an important mystic writer in our Christian faith tradition. While she received religious instruction at a Benedictine monastery from an early age, she also concerned herself with the study of philosophy, literature, and the like. Eventually, she discerned that her time and efforts should be spent on spiritual writing that might serve both theologians and laypeople. Gertrude also is known as one of the early devotees of the Sacred Heart of Jesus.

We fritter away time every day on silly Internet games, trashy novels, insipid television shows, and the like. And while we all need time to relax, like Gertrude, we must be jealous of the hours we have been given here on earth to do God's work.

Inspiration

O Jesus, you who are immensely dear to me, be with me always so that my heart may stay with you and that your love may endure with me with no possibility of division. (St. Gertrude the Great)

Challenge

Resolve not to play your favorite Internet or video game for a week. Spend the time instead with Scripture or a ministry.

Syncletica

316–400

Syncletica is among the best known of the desert mothers, who lived as hermits or in monastic communities in Egypt, Palestine, and Syria in the fourth and fifth centuries. Syncletica grew up in an affluent family and never married; when her parents died, she gave away their wealth to the poor and moved away from the city of Alexandria. Other women came to learn about spirituality from her as word of her piety spread.

Our society encourages the accumulation of stuff—furniture, clothing, trinkets, and other toys we consider essential but that may get in the way of our spiritual development. From Syncletica, we learn that if we have a relationship with God, we have it all.

☙ Inspiration

Oh, how happy should we be, did we but take as much pains to gain heaven and please God, as worldlings do to heap up riches and perishable goods! (St. Syncletica)

☙ Challenge

Take an inventory of one room in your home. What haven't you used in a year? Consider downsizing and donating the excess to a shelter or nonprofit secondhand store. Then consider doing the same with another room.

Lindalva Justo de Oliveira

October 20, 1953–April 9, 1993

Lindalva had only been a nun for about five years when she encountered Augusto da Silva Peixoto at the nursing home where she was assigned. He was only forty-six, younger than the other patients, and he became obsessed with her. Lindalva initially refused to seek another assignment. But after a few months, she asked the authorities for help, and Augusto agreed to improve his behavior. Then, on Good Friday of 1993, he stabbed her forty-four times. Her dying words were, "God protect me."

Lindalva wasn't yet forty when she was murdered. We don't know how many days we will have on this earth. We do know that God asks us to make the most of the time we receive, fearlessly loving and spreading the Good News.

Inspiration

Follow Jesus, who fought until death for the life of sinners, and gave his own life, not as God but as man, for the forgiveness of sins. (Blessed Lindalva Justo de Oliveira)

Challenge

Think about your plans for the day. How can you offer it up for others? Can you take time to pray at lunch? Run an errand for a sick friend? Play a game that that your children love but that might bore you?

Wiltrudis of Bergen

Died circa 986

Wiltrudis founded a Benedictine convent after her husband, Duke Berthold of Bavaria, died in about 947. About ten years before her own death, she became the abbess. She was known both for her piety and for her handicraft talents.

Losing a loved one can leave us at loose ends. All the activities we once enjoyed doing as a couple or as part of a family or group of friends just don't seem the same when we're alone or with different people. Wiltrudis's example reminds us that God has a plan for us as our sorrow heals.

Inspiration

We know love by this, that he laid down his life for us—and we ought to lay down our lives for one another. (1 John 3:16)

Challenge

What activities have you put aside due to the loss or illness of a loved one? Maybe you and your friend or spouse volunteered as docents at a local museum, and you just haven't had the heart to go back. Or perhaps you stopped going to daily Mass because you were taking your mother to chemotherapy, and now her sessions are done. Ask God to show you some ways that you could rechannel those energies for good.

Leonie Françoise de Sales Aviat

September 16, 1844–January 10, 1914

When Leonie was twenty-two, she was ready to become a nun. She had attended school at the Monastery of the Visitation and was well acquainted with the mother superior and chaplain. Yet they both in essence said to her, "Not yet." So Leonie went to work at a factory that manufactured and repaired eyeglasses. It was there that she realized her vocation as a woman religious would be instructing working-class females through the Oblate Sisters of St. Francis de Sales.

"No," "not yet," and other words that indicate our will won't be done are difficult to hear. Leonie's example shows us that when we turn our lives over to God's timing, the result is beautiful.

Inspiration

I ask Our Lord to give you the grace to recognize difficulties and nuisances, not as obstacles, but as a true and efficacious means to make progress along the good and true little path. (St. Leonie Françoise de Sales Aviat)

Challenge

What is it that you want that you know God is steering you away from? It might be a romantic interest, or a growing obsession with an Internet game or with shopping for clothes out of your price range. Pray for the strength and faith to obey.

Tatiana of Rome

Died 235

Tatiana's politically connected father was a Christian, but he hid that fact. Tatiana took a different path, becoming a deaconess. Her work with the sick and the poor drew the attention of Emperor Alexander Severus, who had her arrested. At one point when Tatiana was being tortured, angels were seen circling her, which resulted in eight of her persecutors kneeling down on the spot and converting. She and her father, who had gone public with his belief, were executed together.

It was dangerous to be a Christian in the third century. It's dangerous today as well. Doing God's work often attracts attention, sometimes good, sometimes bad. That doesn't matter. What matters is that we continue to do it, while remaining indifferent to those who would seek to stop us.

Inspiration

And I tell you, everyone who acknowledges me before others, the Son of Man also will acknowledge before the angels of God. (Luke 12:8)

Challenge

Are you practicing your faith in private rather than in public? Is it easier to offer service to complete strangers than to your neighbors or coworkers? Consider ways you may merge these two separate aspects of your life. Keep that special feeling you have after receiving the Eucharist on Sundays going throughout the week.

Marguerite Bourgeoys

April 17, 1620–January 12, 1700

Marguerite felt a call to religious life, but living in a cloister didn't appeal to her. So in her twenties, she joined a group of laywomen who were teaching poor children. Then, ten years later, an opportunity came for her to go to what is now Quebec to help educate children of Native Americans and settlers. There, she used a stable to open Montreal's first school. While the decision to remain uncloistered was challenged repeatedly, Marguerite and her group of teachers were able to continue living among the people they were serving. Today, her Sisters of the Congregation de Notre Dame serve on four continents.

Meeting the poor where they live—in ghettos and barrios and neighborhoods unfamiliar to us—can be uncomfortable. Yet in our work with them, if we present ourselves with dignity and compassion, and offer the same, we can work together on a more level ground.

❧ Inspiration

Teaching is the work most suited to draw down the graces of God if it is done with purity of intention, without distinction between the poor and the rich, between relatives and friends and strangers, between the pretty and the ugly, the gentle and the grumblers, looking upon them all as drops of Our Lord's blood. (St. Marguerite Bourgeoys)

❧ Challenge

Step out of your comfort zone. Offer to tutor a child from a different culture at your parish school, or volunteer with friends at a food pantry or homeless shelter.

Colette

January 13, 1381–March 6, 1447

Colette yearned for a quiet spiritual life, to the point that when she was orphaned at seventeen, she gave away her inheritance. A few years later she became an anchoress, locked in a cell with a single window that looked into a church. During her eight years as an anchoress, she was instructed by St. Francis of Assisi in a vision to return the Order of the Poor Clares to its simpler days of poverty and austerity. She went on to found nearly twenty convents and reinvigorate several others. Colettine nuns work today in ten countries.

That simple life Colette desired turned complicated. She had to deal with those who challenged her mission, just as we do today. But it's about what God wants for us, not what we want for ourselves.

Inspiration

If there be a true way that leads to the everlasting Kingdom, it is most certainly that of suffering, patiently endured. (St. Colette)

Challenge

Ask God what he wants from you. Then listen, no matter how challenging the answer is, and do it, even if it upsets the peaceful, contemplative life you have carved out for yourself—or if it takes you out of a hectic life and into a quiet place.

Nino of Georgia

Circa 280–332

Nino was about forty when she arrived as a slave in what is now the country of Georgia. Her status, however, did not prevent her from sharing her faith and praying over those with medical issues. As a result, Nino came to the attention of the ailing queen, who made a recovery and then converted to Christianity. The pagan king converted as well after he became lost in the dark during a hunting trip and prayed to Nino's God for help. Thereafter, he made Christianity the kingdom's state religion.

Nino didn't worry about her place in society. She simply was herself— a daughter of God—and treated everyone, from the people on the street to the queen, with love and compassion. It's an important lesson in this world today, where too often the face people present to each other is based on political or personal gain.

Inspiration

All who exalt themselves will be humbled, and all who humble themselves will be exalted. (Matthew 23:12)

Challenge

Keep notes today about the tone and facial gestures you use with people. Do you always present the same face? If not, what can you do to change that and show everyone the person God created you to be?

Ita of Limerick

Circa 475–January 15, 570

She's called the foster mother of Ireland's early saints, due to the number of them who passed through the school associated with her community in County Limerick. Legend has it that one of Ita's students asked what God most valued, and her response was true faith, generosity, and simplicity of spirit. Unlike some saints of her time, who traveled about founding more convents, churches, and schools, Ita stayed where she was planted. She and her community helped the poor of their region. A visit by an angel left the young Ita devoted to the Holy Trinity as it dwells in each of us.

Ita's example shows that no one path is right for all of us. We can make a difference in bringing souls to the kingdom, whether we never move away from our own hometown or live a vagabond's life. There's always a place for God's work to be done.

Inspiration

For if those who are nothing think they are something, they deceive themselves. All must test their own work; then that work, rather than their neighbor's work, will become a cause for pride. (Galatians 6:3–4)

Challenge

How are you measuring up in the areas of true faith, generosity, and simplicity of spirit? Select one on which to focus in the coming months.

Lucy Filippini

January 16, 1672–March 25, 1732

Lucy's gift was teaching and teaching others to teach. She worked with a cardinal to develop schools that taught girls about Christ, as well as reading and homemaking skills. Eventually, the pope brought her to Rome to establish schools there. In addition, the organization now known as the Religious Teachers Filippini offered retreats and conferences for women.

Our religious education doesn't end after we get our sacraments or graduate from high school or college. We learn from the Mass readings, from studying Scripture and other religious works, and from taking time out for spiritual instruction. It's important that we continue to drink from the well of knowledge.

Inspiration

The beginning of wisdom is this: Get wisdom,
and whatever else you get, get insight. (Proverbs 4:7)

Challenge

Make a plan to attend a spiritual conference or retreat this year. Ask your pastor or spiritual director for recommendations. Or, sign up for an adult education course or an evening discussion of the sacraments, Scripture, or social justice at your parish. If you can make the time commitment, consider volunteering to be an RCIA sponsor or to teach religious education. Deepen your faith by expanding your knowledge of our Church.

Maria Candida of the Eucharist (Maria Barba)

January 16, 1884–June 12, 1949

Maria said her devotion to the Eucharist began even before her First Communion. After her mother had received the Eucharist, she would beg her for God as well, and her mother would then bend down and breathe on Maria's lips. She became a Carmelite nun when she was thirty-five and spent countless hours in adoration. Maris is best known for the meditation she wrote on the Eucharist. At her beatification in 2004, Pope John Paul II said, "She fell so deeply in love with the Eucharistic Jesus that she felt a constant, burning desire to be a tireless apostle of the Eucharist."

Holy Communion is the most visible, tangible means we have of God sharing his love for us. What a gift we have as Catholics, to celebrate the True Presence of Christ each time we participate in Mass!

Inspiration

How great is the love of God made bread for our souls, who becomes a prisoner for me! (Blessed Maria Candida)

Challenge

Spend time today in adoration before the Blessed Sacrament or, if that is not possible, in quiet contemplation and awe of the gift of eternal life Christ won for us on the cross. Consider committing to attending daily Mass twice in the coming week, and savor the relationship with Christ we have through the Eucharist.

Margaret of Hungary

January 27, 1242–January 18, 1271

Margaret's parents, the king and queen of Hungary, had pledged that their next child would be turned over to God if they were victorious over invading warriors. As a result, Margaret was taken to a convent before she was four years old. It was a good fit. But later, when she was in her late teens, her father changed his mind and sought to arrange a marriage for her that would benefit his kingdom. She refused, and ultimately spent her remaining years in a convent her parents built on an island in the Danube River.

We are taught through the commandments to honor our parents and teach our children to do the same. And yet, there are situations such as Margaret's where our greater obligation, or that of our children, is to God. Knowing when the source of dispute is willfulness or divine inspiration is difficult, but it's important to listen and keep the lines of communication open.

Inspiration

As a father has compassion for his children,

so the LORD has compassion for those who fear him. (Psalm 103:13)

Challenge

What issue is separating you from your children or parents? Pray for guidance so that you may listen and discern God's desire in the situation.

Regina Protmann

1552–January 18, 1613

Regina wasn't wedded to conventional thinking. There were no cloistered convents in her area, so she and two other women moved into a house together and nursed the sick there. The order she founded, the Sisters of St. Catherine of Alexandria, also established schools for girls, which were unusual at the time. "The words 'As God wills' became the motto of her life," Pope John Paul II said at her beatification Mass in 1999.

Regina must have created quite a stir in her part of Prussia by the way she went about service to the sick and to young people. But her actions were grounded in serving God. Similarly, we need not concern ourselves about what people think of our actions if we are acting in God's name.

Inspiration

Do not flee from the world, but instead confront, engage, and embrace it, constantly. Service to the needy and sick humanity shall have precedent over any formal regulation. (Blessed Regina Protmann)

Challenge

What are you not doing for the needy because you're concerned about what people will say? Pray for the strength to focus on God's approval, not other people's, and the courage to carry out his plan for you.

Eustochia Calafato

March 25, 1434–January 20, 1485

Eustochia ran into challenges in the way she wanted to devote her life to Christ. When she first entered a convent in her mid-teens, her brothers threatened to burn it down, so she had to return home. Ultimately, they relented. Then, after more than a decade at the convent, she founded a new community that was regarded as so excessively strict that some friars refused to celebrate Mass there. Ultimately, they were ordered to do so.

Are there some forms of devotion that speak to you but not to your family and friends? Perhaps you lose yourself at adoration, or are filled with the Holy Spirit when you view relics. Or perhaps you're the one who scratches her head when friends talk about venerating the cross during Holy Week. Church-sanctioned practices that draw us closer to Christ feed our souls, whether others understand us or not.

Inspiration

What should I do then? I will pray with the spirit, but I will pray with the mind also; I will sing praise with the spirit, but I will sing praise with the mind also. (1 Corinthians 14:15)

Challenge

Consider spending some time with a spiritual practice—adoration, the rosary, the Divine Office, or another means—that is different from your typical prayer style. Be open to where you are led.

Agnes of Rome

Circa 291–304

Thousands of Christians went to their deaths during Agnes's time, but her example stood out to her contemporaries and down through the ages to us, as well. She was just thirteen when she was beheaded for refusing to sacrifice to the Roman gods. Tradition states that she suffered torture and was sent to a house of prostitution, where she successfully defended her virtue.

Our faith is tested every day of our lives, not as dramatically or publicly as the experience of Agnes and the other early martyrs, but it is tested by those we encounter who do not understand Catholicism or Christianity. Agnes's example inspires us to stand in confidence and with God when our beliefs are questioned or ridiculed.

Inspiration

Christ made my soul beautiful with the jewels of grace and virtue. I belong to him whom the angels serve. (St. Agnes of Rome)

Challenge

Pray for a family member, friend, coworker, or acquaintance who criticizes you for your devotion to the Church. Where appropriate, engage the person in a non-threatening dialogue. So often, non-Catholics' perspectives on Church teachings regarding hot-button issues, such as same-gender marriage, contraception, divorce, homosexuality, abortion, and immigration, are misinformed or incomplete. Preparing a thoughtful defense can also be formation for us.

Laura Vicuna

April 5, 1891–January 22, 1904

It was a less than ideal home situation, to put it mildly. Laura's father died when she was young, and to support her two children, her mother went to work for a wealthy man who agreed to pay for Laura's schooling. The man and her mother began a relationship that Laura did not approve of, and the man became troubled by Laura's growing faith and beat her. Laura contracted a form of tuberculosis and told God she was offering up her life for her mother's. Her mother sought forgiveness at Laura's deathbed.

Have you ever done something that compromised your ethics or morals for or in front of your children? Perhaps you justified it to yourself because your decision meant more money for the family or made you happier, and you told yourself the children wouldn't notice. Ah, but they do. They see everything we do. Better to be right with God and scrimp on toys or dining out than to cut corners on our faith in favor of earthly goods.

✒Inspiration

Mama, I offer my life for you. (Blessed Laura Vicuna)

✒Challenge

Monitor yourself with your children or other young people today. Is God with you at all times in your words and actions? Or do you cut off people in traffic, gossip about family members, complain about the way something inconsequential, such as yard work, was done, or say nothing when a store clerk makes an error in your favor?

Marianne Cope

January 23, 1838–August 9, 1918

Imagine the comments some of Marianne's acquaintances made in 1883 when they learned she was going to Hawaii to help people who suffered from Hansen's disease (leprosy). But Marianne didn't see it that way at all. She declared she wasn't afraid of any disease and got to work. She demanded the removal of a government administrator who abused patients. She successfully lobbied for government funds for a home for the healthy daughters of leprosy patients when no one else would care for them. The king of Hawaii honored her for her acts of benevolence. And despite thirty years of advocating for those with leprosy, she never contracted the disease.

Dealing with the stigma that surrounds some diseases can be as daunting as the illnesses themselves. Have you ever told a trusted friend that you suffer from depression, only to have her tell you to get more sleep or to stop thinking about your problems? Or maybe you have a friend who suffers from lung cancer who is regularly asked how long she smoked. Marianne's example reminds us that it's not about the disease—it's about reflecting God's love to the sick and leaving the judgment to him.

Inspiration

The charity of the good knows no creed and is confined to no one place. (St. Marianne Cope)

Challenge

Spend an afternoon volunteering at a hospital or nursing home, or write a letter or e-mail to a patient advocacy organization thanking the group for its work.

Agnes Tsao Kou Ying

1821–January 25, 1856

Raised in a Catholic family, Agnes married when she was eighteen and was left a widow two years later. She was given refuge by another Catholic widow, and while living there met a priest who invited her to do some missionary work. As a result, Agnes spent the last four years of her short life teaching catechism and life skills in rural China. Then, she was arrested, along with her spiritual mentor and others. The authorities tried to get her to deny her faith, but she refused repeatedly. Finally, after spending three days in a cage so small that she couldn't sit or lie down, Agnes died. She was canonized in 2000 as one of the Martyrs of China.

Teaching seems like such a harmless profession. And yet, it is subversive, especially when it comes to taking Jesus to non-Christian communities. The power of the cross is shown by the efforts to which people will go to attempt to keep Christ out of the lives of others.

Inspiration

Who is to condemn? It is Christ Jesus, who died, yes, who was raised, who is at the right hand of God, who indeed intercedes for us. (Romans 8:34)

Challenge

Pray for the sisters and brothers in teaching orders in countries where being Christian is dangerous or illegal, or consider sending a donation to such a ministry.

Bathild

Died 680

In Old English, Bathild means "bold sword" or "bold spear," and that phrase certainly describes this saint. She was taken into slavery as a child and still managed to distinguish herself to the point that she came to the attention of King Clovis II, who married her. When the king died, their oldest son was only five, so Bathild became regent for several years. During that time, she worked to reduce the slave trade and to reduce the selling of spiritual favors. She spent her final years in one of the monasteries she had founded.

When we are in positions of powerlessness, it's easy to talk about how we'd change things if we were in charge. Bathild's example inspires us to remember the disfranchised when we are in a position to act on their behalf.

Inspiration

Rescue the weak and the needy;

deliver them from the hand of the wicked. (Psalm 82:4)

Challenge

Write down five things you would do for your parish or neighborhood if you were in charge. Maybe you'd see that the fliers and bulletins at the church entrances were tidied up, or that the garbage that tends to accumulate in front of a stop sign got picked up. Then figure out a way you could accomplish one of those things even without formal authority.

Paula of Rome

347–404

Paula was only thirty-two when she was widowed. She didn't want for anything financially—her family was wealthy—but she found riches of a different kind three years later when she met the man who would become St. Jerome. She and one of her daughters studied Hebrew under Jerome, and they chose to accompany him to the Holy Land. In Bethlehem, where she died, she founded two monasteries, one for women and one for men. It is believed she helped Jerome with his studies, in particular the translation of the Latin Vulgate.

Do you believe in soul mates? While by all accounts Paula and her husband had a good relationship (including five children), it appears she found an intellectual connection with Jerome that further opened her soul to God. Losing a spouse to death or divorce causes a fissure in our hearts that God can use for his glory if we allow ourselves to become his servants.

Inspiration

Therefore encourage one another and build up each other, as indeed you are doing. (1 Thessalonians 5:11)

Challenge

Offer up a special prayer for your husband, living or dead, today, or for another special man who has influenced your faith journey.

Angela Merici

March 21, 1474–January 27, 1540

Angela's early life was marked by sorrow. She and her sister were orphaned when Angela was just ten. Then, her sister died suddenly. When Angela was twenty, the uncle who had been caring for her died as well. From that time on, she devoted her life to educating girls in her northern Italian city through the founding of the Ursuline sisters, the first teaching order of women and the first to work outside a cloister. While she was visiting Rome, Pope Clement VII asked her to stay in Rome to expand her work there, but she chose to return home.

We can grow bitter when loss strikes our lives. Or, like Angela, we can use our pain to better the lives of others, with the help of Christ. The choice is ours.

Inspiration

Let your intentions in the fulfillment of your duties be so pure that you reject from your actions every other object but the glory of God and the salvation of souls. (St. Angela Merici)

Challenge

Identify a loss that is still holding a place in your soul. How can you use it to serve others? If you've recently lost a parent to Alzheimer's, it might be helpful to support other people going through your experience. If a pet died after years of friendship, perhaps you can volunteer at the front desk of an animal shelter.

Candelaria of St. Joseph (Susana Paz-Castillo Ramirez)

August 11, 1863–January 31, 1940

Candelaria was doing God's work as a woman religious long before she took her vows. In her early twenties, her mother died, so she was responsible for the care of her siblings as well as some cousins. A few years later, Venezuela was rocked by an earthquake, and Candelaria helped out as a nurse. In 1902, she was part of a small community of women who were nurses at a new hospital in her hometown. That community led to what is now the Venezuelan Carmelite Sisters—and to Candelaria finally taking vows when she was in her fifties.

God calls us to be obedient to him. While we should be respectful of authority figures, we can't let them get in the way of leading souls to the kingdom. If one manner of service is closed to us because permission doesn't come, we must find another way to minister.

Inspiration

Do not fear those who kill the body but cannot kill the soul; rather fear him who can destroy both soul and body in hell. (Matthew 10:28)

Challenge

What are you waiting for? What obstacle, real or imagined, is in the way of doing what God desires? How can you move past it?

Hyacintha Mariscotti

1585–January 30, 1640

Hyacintha became a nun for the wrong reason: the young man she favored chose to marry her younger sister. Hyacintha made it clear to her father that she didn't expect that taking vows would affect her life when she was joining the St. Bernardine community. For her first ten years in the community, she made no lifestyle changes. Finally, her heart and soul were opened to God. She publicly confessed her excesses and drastically simplified her habits. Hyacintha also served as a nurse during an epidemic and established the Oblates of Mary of Sacconi and helped the poor, the elderly, and the imprisoned.

Perhaps you know someone who always has to wear the finest designer clothes, eat at the trendiest restaurants, and take the most expensive vacations. Perhaps that person is you. We learn from Hyacintha that sometimes those extravagances are hiding an internal hurt, one that, in the end, only God can heal.

✒ Inspiration

When I was a child, I spoke like a child, I thought like a child, I reasoned like a child; when I became an adult, I put an end to childish ways. (1 Corinthians 13:11)

✒ Challenge

If you're a shopaholic, resolve to donate to a women's shelter what you would spend on clothing this week. Or, if you're prudent with your money but you know someone who isn't, ask in a loving way what is prompting his or her spending. Listen carefully.

Hildegard Burjan

January 30, 1883–June 11, 1933

Hildegard, a Catholic convert from Judaism, is called the first female politician to be beatified. One of the first female members of Austria's Parliament, she focused on equal wages and caring for the poor and sick. Hildegard was a founder of the sisters of Caritas Socialis in Austria, which provides hospice and other care to women, the elderly, the sick, and children. When she and her husband were expecting a child, a doctor recommended they abort, but Hildegard refused and went on to have their only daughter, Elisabeth. Pope Benedict XVI said of Hildegard when she was beatified in 2012, "She brought together women who want to be the source of God's love."

Politics isn't a dirty word. While our country was founded on the principle of church-state separation, that does not mean Catholics need to be silent on the issues that are important to our faith and our country: Abortion, immigration, same-gender marriage, wise stewardship of natural resources. Speaking up isn't a sin. Staying silent is.

✒ Inspiration

We cannot help people with money and small offerings, rather we must give them the confidence that they are capable of doing something for themselves. (Blessed Hildegard Burjan)

✒ Challenge

What hot-button issue speaks to you? Write a letter or e-mail to the appropriate elected official expressing your viewpoint in a positive way.

Marcella

325–410

Marcella found herself widowed after less than a year of marriage. Her beauty and her place in society brought her suitors, but she chose instead to leave that life behind. She was one of the founders of the "brown dress society," a group of women who spent their days in service to the poor and in worship. Marcella also had a long friendship and correspondence with St. Jerome.

In our consumption-driven society, it's easy to focus on how we look on the outside. Is brown really the new black? What's the new look for spring? Better to focus on the shape of our interior closet and spiritual growth. And we don't have to wait for a department store sale or a bonus at work to do it.

Inspiration

I will praise her for nothing but the virtue which is her own and which is the more noble, because forsaking both wealth and rank she has sought the true nobility of poverty and lowliness. (St. Jerome on St. Marcella)

Challenge

Go through your interior wardrobe. What un-Christlike trappings remain? Pride? Resentment? Anger? Put these castaways into a virtual box and give them away through prayer. Ask God to help you find new things to wear.

Brigid

Circa 451–523

Brigid was nothing if not hospitable. It's said she turned a barrel of beer into enough for eighteen churches; as a child, she gave away butter to the poor and turned water into healing milk. She was also passionate about serving God, founding Ireland's first convent as well as a school of art that was known for its illuminated manuscripts. Along with Patrick, Brigid is a patron saint of Ireland.

Brigid also is said to have been very bashful and modest. Yet she shared her gifts, time, and knowledge freely with those in her monastery and beyond. She provides a good reminder to smile, engage, and trust the Holy Spirit when we are placed in unfamiliar social settings.

Inspiration

"You that are simple, turn in here!"
   To those without sense she says,
"Come, eat of my bread
   and drink of the wine I have mixed.
Lay aside immaturity, and live,
   and walk in the way of insight." (Proverbs 9:4–6)

Challenge

Invite someone at church or in your neighborhood whom you don't know well to have coffee with you and ask about what's going on in the person's life. See where God takes you.

Jeanne de Valois

April 23, 1464–February 4, 1505

Jeanne was forced to marry her second cousin, the Duke of Orleans, for political reasons, but she made the best of the situation for more than twenty years. When her husband ascended to the throne of France, however, he immediately moved to rid himself of her for another woman, saying that Jeanne suffered from a plethora of physical deformities that prevented them from having a true marriage. Again for political reasons, the pope granted the annulment. Jeanne spent her final years in a convent, pursuing her lifelong devotion to the Blessed Virgin.

Holding our heads high amid malicious gossip is difficult. It's also hard when we see ourselves or our love cast aside after years of marriage. But as we learn from Jeanne, even as we defend ourselves and seek to share the truth, all too often, the devil prevails. It's a good reminder that our focus must always be on God, not our earthly disappointments and hurts.

Inspiration

God be praised who has allowed this, that I may serve him better than I have heretofore done. (St. Jeanne de Valois)

Challenge

Spend some time in prayer with the Blessed Virgin, who knows what lies deepest in a woman's heart.

Marie de St. Ignace (Claudine Thévenet)

March 30, 1774–February 3, 1837

Claudine was nineteen when she saw her brothers being executed. They were casualties of the French Revolution. Both called on her to "forgive, as we forgive," requests she never forgot. The institute she founded initially focused on helping poor children and then expanded to the Christian education of girls from wealthier families. Today, the Congregation of the Religious of Jesus and Mary helps young people on five continents.

Perhaps you've experienced the trauma of loved ones dying too young from disease or accidents. Claudine's reaction to her brothers' executions reminds us that our grieving cannot become all-encompassing and prevent us from forging on with God's work. At her beatification Mass in 1981, Pope John Paul II, who also canonized her twelve years later, said Claudine's life "reminds Christians that putting everything on God is worth the effort."

✒ Inspiration

The only preferences I will permit are for the most poor, the most miserable, those who have most defects; those you will love a great deal. (St. Marie de St. Ignace)

✒ Challenge

Journal or scrapbook about the impact someone who's died had on your life, and think about how you can share with others the gift he or she gave you.

Mary of Providence (Eugenie Smet)

March 25, 1825–February 7, 1871

When she was very young, Eugenie became very concerned about the souls in purgatory. She was only twenty-one when she founded the Society of the Helpers of the Holy Souls, which continues today with a goal of having Masses said each day for the holy souls and the defense of human rights.

Sometimes, we focus on this world and heaven, and we lose sight of the passage place that is purgatory. While we don't know what purgatory will look like or how long we'll be there, we do know that we need this intermediate step for purification before we go to spend eternity with God. The *Catechism of the Catholic Church* (1030) assures us that those who die in God's grace and friendship but are less than perfect (and that's all of us), "are indeed assured of their eternal salvation; but after death they undergo purification, so as to achieve the holiness necessary to enter the joy of heaven."

Inspiration

If one of our friends was imprisoned in a house of fire, how we should rush to her assistance. Then think how we should try to deliver the souls in purgatory. (Blessed Mary of Providence)

Challenge

Don't wait for All Souls Day on November 1. Consider offering a daily or Sunday Mass at your parish for your departed relatives. Pray for all those who are going through their final purification before their joyful reunion with God.

Agatha of Catania

Circa 231–251

Agatha could have taken the easy way out and married the Roman consul Quintianus. But she refused, saying she had consecrated her life to God. It is said she suffered unimaginable suffering—time in a house of prostitution, her breasts cut off and her body rolled over live coals before she died.

It's tempting for us to take the easy way out sometimes in our own lives, to join in when friends gossip or to raise our voices when our children push us too far. Agatha's example reminds us to be confident, constant, consistent, and ever-present in our service to God.

❧ Inspiration

My courage and my thought be so firmly founded upon the firm stone of Jesus Christ, that for no pain it may not be changed. (St. Agatha of Catania)

❧ Challenge

Agatha's patronages include breast cancer. Consider signing up for a charity event and making a donation to a group that battles this disease. Or, work with your parish to set up a relationship with a local clinic to provide free or low-cost mammograms for poor women. Or, if you have a friend who is preparing to undergo chemotherapy as a cancer treatment, arrange for people to take him or her to sessions and to provide meals for the family.

Maria Vicenta of Saint Dorothy Chavez Orozco

February 6, 1867–July 30, 1949

Maria Vicenta was a fearless nurse. It was a bout with pleurisy that convinced her God wanted her to do service in that way, and she went on to spend for thirty years as the superior general of the Servants of the Holy Trinity and the Poor, which she founded. Some of her greatest moments came during the Mexican revolution. Even though the hospital where the other sisters were working was turned into a military headquarters, they continued helping the wounded. She and a postulant once were left alone at the hospital and were subjected to death threats by soldiers. The women went on anyway, and when the commander arrived, he reprimanded the men. In the years thereafter, the sisters opened seventeen more medical facilities.

We all like to think we could endure much for Christ, but until we are tested, we just don't know. Maria Vicenta's example of serving amid death threats reminds us of how passionate we can be for Christ when we place ourselves in ministries in which we can lose ourselves.

✿ Inspiration

Blessed is anyone who endures temptation. Such a one has stood the test and will receive the crown of life that the Lord has promised to those who love him. (James 1:12)

✿ Challenge

Are there times the people you are serving—be they family members or strangers—don't appreciate what you are doing for them? Ask for Christ's help in forging on anyway.

Rosalie Rendu (Jeanne Marie Rendu)

September 9, 1786–February 7, 1856

Rosalie was born into the middle class, but her vocation took her to one of the poorest areas of Paris for fifty-four years. She was tireless in her efforts, setting up a home for the elderly, a school, an orphanage, a youth center, and more. In a way reminiscent of the world attention Blessed Teresa of Calcutta later received, students, ambassadors, holy men, even Emperor Napoleon III, came to see what she was doing. The emperor awarded her the Cross of the Legion of Honor.

Rosalie understood that hiding her light under a bushel basket would not have helped the poor. She and her community went into the slums, but they also reached out to people who had the means to help them expand the good they could do. She reminds us that letting others know how they can help our ministry is a gift too.

Inspiration

If you want someone to love you, you must be the first to love; and if you have nothing to give, give yourself. (Blessed Rosalie Rendu)

Challenge

Think today about what you have to give, in time, talent, or treasure, to the marginalized in your community. Then do it.

Josephine Bakhita

Circa 1869–February 8, 1947

Bakhita's life started like many other children amid a loving family in the Sudan. But before she reached the age of ten, she was kidnapped by slave traders. She went through a series of owners, including one who had her tattooed everywhere but her face. One family took her to Venice and bonded her to a convent; Josephine successfully fought to stay there and became a Canossian sister herself, serving for fifty years. She said she was grateful to the slave traders, for otherwise she would not have had an opportunity to become a Christian.

Our life journeys take us to some painful places—the loss of loved ones, illness, physical violence, betrayal. And yet God is there with us every step of the way, offering his healing balm if we have faith and trust enough to accept it.

Inspiration

The Lord has loved me so much: we must love everyone...we must be compassionate! (St. Josephine Bakhita)

Challenge

Each time you are tempted to complain today, stop yourself and offer up a prayer of thanksgiving for how God has helped you through the trials of life. Pray for the faith to believe he will see you through your current struggles as well.

Apollonia

Died circa 249

The anti-Christian mob in Alexandria was going wild, and the authorities were doing nothing to stop it. A man and woman already had been stoned to death. Other Christians were fleeing the city. Then the mob came after Apollonia, striking out or pulling out all her teeth. A fire was begun; the old woman was told she would be burned alive if she didn't renounce her faith. She asked for a moment to think, and then leaped into the flames.

Apollonia faced certain death and chose to expedite the process rather than renounce her faith. You might say she robbed the mob of the opportunity to mistreat her further. And while we are unlikely to find ourselves in this situation, it is helpful to know our Church supports her decision. St. Augustine of Hippo called Apollina's action "pious devotion and ready service."

Inspiration

Be strong and bold; have no fear or dread of them, because it is the LORD your God who goes with you; he will not fail you or forsake you. (Deuteronomy 31:6)

Challenge

Torture of Christians continues today. Consider making a donation or writing a letter of support for an organization that helps persecuted Christians. Get the name of an appropriate one through your parish or diocesan social justice or relief services contact.

Scholastica

Circa 480–543

Scholastica was the twin sister of St. Benedict. We know little about her other than the legend of their last meeting. Both had joined monasteries, and they would visit each other once a year. Scholastica begged Benedict to stay and talk through the morning; her brother said he could not. She then bowed her head in prayer, and a severe storm began. When Benedict scolded Scholastica, her response was, "See, I asked you, and you would not listen to me. So I asked my Lord, and he has listened to me."

We are the most ourselves—good and bad, lecturing and petulant—around our siblings, perhaps because we revert to childhood behavior. But there's also a simple honesty among brothers and sisters. We share a common history and stories. And because of (or in spite of) them, we love unreservedly.

Inspiration

Two are better than one, because they have a good reward for their toil. For if they fall, one will lift up the other; but woe to one who is alone and falls and does not have another to help. (Ecclesiastes 4:9–10)

Challenge

Spend time in person or on the phone with one of your siblings today. Relive memories of your childhood thoughts about God, or talk about where you are on your spiritual journeys today.

Anna Katharina Emmerich

September 8, 1774–February 9, 1824

Anna Katharina came from a large family, and spent little time in school. She was repeatedly rejected by convents because she couldn't bring a big enough dowry. Finally, she was accepted by one but had to leave after nine years when it was closed for political reasons. It was then, when she went to work for a priest and became bedridden, that she received the gift of stigmata of Christ's Passion. In the homily at her beatification, Pope John Paul II said, "We are equally impressed with the new blessed's patience in putting up with physical weakness and her strong character, as well as her unshakable faith."

Blessed John Paul II's praise of Anna Katharina reminds us that faith outweighs our personal flaws which seem at times so overwhelming and that God can use our imperfections and brokenness to help bring other souls to him.

✥ Inspiration

The thief comes only to steal and kill and destroy. I came that they may have life, and have it abundantly. (John 10:10)

✥ Challenge

Make a list of your three top flaws that you believe keep you from Christ's love. Perhaps you're concerned about a temper you have trouble controlling or a disability, such as a hearing or sight impairment. Pray for the reassurance that you are truly loved by God, who rejoices in you just as you are.

Alfonsa Clerici

February 14, 1860–January 14, 1930

Alfonsa may have felt a bit conflicted. She enjoyed her work as a teacher, but she also felt she had a religious vocation. She chose to marry the two by joining the Sisters of the Most Precious Blood and continuing her teaching career. Alfonsa's service included becoming director at the sisters' college where she had received her master's degree.

What joy, to be able to join our passions and do God's work in the most engaged, fulfilling way possible! And we can all do this, whether what speaks to us is taking care of babies, singing, writing, cooking, cleaning—the list is endless.

Inspiration

We have gifts that differ according to the grace given to us: prophecy, in proportion to faith; ministry, in ministering; the teacher, in teaching; the exhorter, in exhortation; the giver, in generosity; the leader, in diligence; the compassionate, in cheerfulness. (Romans 12:6–8)

Challenge

If you had a day with no responsibilities or obligations, what would you do? Reading? Playing with your children? Shopping? How can you put that interest to work for Christ and community?

Catherine de' Ricci

April 23, 1522–February 1, 1590

While this Dominican nun meditated about Christ's passion and the experience of the Blessed Virgin each day, she totally devoted herself to this practice from 12 P.M. Thursday to 3 P.M. Friday for twelve years. During this worship, Catherine went into raptures and sometimes received the stigmata. Initially, her religious community was suspicious of what she was experiencing, but ultimately they came to accept her.

A regular prayer time is essential to our spiritual growth. Unless we build it into our schedule, prayer can become an afterthought, something that is nice to have instead of a soul-feeding essential. We owe it to ourselves and God to make the time for prayer.

Inspiration

So I tell you, whatever you ask for in prayer, believe that you have received it, and it will be yours. (Mark 11:24)

Challenge

Commit to spending fifteen minutes in quiet reflection each day this week at the same time, whether it's in the morning, at lunchtime, or before bedtime. Consider praying the rosary or other familiar prayers to help you center and calm yourself. If your schedule allows, consider praying the Liturgy of the Hours for a day or two.

Emilie d'Oultremont d'Hooghvorst

October 11, 1818–February 22, 1878

Emilie, a young widow with four children, was praying in a Belgian chapel on the day the dogma of the Immaculate Conception was announced in Rome. As she prayed, the Blessed Mother asked her to love Jesus and the Body of Christ with a mother's heart. Emilie was quick to say yes. Less than three years later, she founded the Institute of Sisters of Mary Raparatrix, and made her vows a year later. At the time of Emilie's death, the sisters had a missionary presence in eight countries. Today, they work in nearly two dozen countries on three continents.

God's will comes to us in different ways, but often, it is in those still, quiet moments of prayer. Emilie's story reminds us to listen when we pray, not just to bring our problems and intentions.

Inspiration

My heart felt the need of giving to God all the respect, love, and adoration he deserved. (Blessed Emilie d'Oultremont Hooghvorst)

Challenge

Resolve to take your prayer life into a deeper place. Perhaps that means time in adoration, or reciting the Liturgy of the Hours, or simply adding five minutes of centering prayer before a meal. Be open to discovery.

Piety of the Cross (Tomasa Ortiz Real)

November 12, 1842–February 26, 1916

Piety's vocation got off to a very rocky start. She attempted to enter a cloistered community twice but had to leave both times for health reasons. Then, not long after she and other women founded a community with two locations, there was a dispute, and Piety ended up with only one other sister. A bishop recommended the two of them go on a month-long Salesian retreat to pray about what should come next. During that time, Piety thought further about an earlier prayer experience she had had regarding the Sacred Heart of Jesus, and was inspired to found the Congregation of Salesian Sisters of the Sacred Heart of Jesus, which assists those in need of charity.

The way isn't always clear. Sometimes, we think God is calling us to do something when it turns out our ego or personality or fears, not God, are pushing us in that direction. Piety's example reminds us to take time out to discern God's will and not to rush into things.

Inspiration

I am poor and when I have nothing to give to the poor, I give them my soul, my heart, and my love, since love is worth much more than money offerings. (Blessed Piety of the Cross)

Challenge

Contemplate what Piety said about love being worth more than money. Slow down today and share some love with someone you haven't seen for a while.

Maria Troncatti

February 16, 1883–August 25, 1969

Maria's ministry was in healing. She worked as a Red Cross nurse at a military hospital during World War I. A few years later, as a member of the Daughters of Mary Help of Christians, she began what would be a nearly fifty-year career as a missionary in Ecuador. In addition to providing spiritual and general education, she served as a nurse and, in essence, a doctor for the native people. She died in a plane crash in Ecuador in 1969.

It didn't matter to Maria what people looked like or how much they had or how educated they were. She simply loved them and tried to help fill their spiritual and medical needs. In the same way, we can meet people where they are, and by reflecting Christ, we can provide what they need.

Inspiration

A look at the crucifix gives me life and the courage to work. (Blessed Maria Troncatti)

Challenge

Who among your family or friends is ailing physically? Visit the person, if possible, or call him or her, or mail a card expressing the person's importance in your life. In addition, consider sharing this gratitude with another member of the person's immediate circle.

Cecilia Eusepi

February 17, 1910–October 1, 1928

She called herself a "half-stupid clown." In fact, Cecilia Eusepi titled the life story she was asked to write *The Story of a Clown*, reminiscent of *The Story of a Soul* by St. Thérèse of Lisieux, which had influenced her spiritual journey greatly. Like Thérèse, Cecilia yearned to be a nun—a missionary, to be precise. But that was not to be; tuberculosis forced her to live in the Order of the Servants of Mary before she made her final vows. It is said she died singing hymns to Mary. Pope Benedict XVI said of Cecilia: "She lived with a steadfast faith, showing a great capacity for sacrifice for the salvation of souls."

Cecilia was only sixteen when it became obvious that she would never fulfill her missionary dream. Yet her love for Jesus never wavered. Her example reminds us to embrace whatever God puts before us in life, even if events don't fit into what was our life plan.

✒ Inspiration

It is beautiful to give oneself to Jesus who gave himself to us without reserve. (Blessed Cecilia Eusepi)

✒ Challenge

Make no small plans—or any big ones either—today. Appreciate the gift of life as it comes to you, without complaint.

Geltrude Comensoli

January 18, 1847–February 18, 1903

Even as a child, Geltrude was devoted to the Eucharist. She was seven when she secretly went to church to make her First Communion. When she was in her thirties, she spoke with Pope Leo XIII about establishing an adoration religious institution. He encouraged her to incorporate the work she was already doing to educate young female factory workers. The order Geltrude founded, the Congregation of the Sacramentine Sisters of Bergamo, opened with an hour of adoration, and proceeded to reflect Christ's love and charity to each other and the poor.

Quiet time with the Blessed Sacrament refreshes and rejuvenates us, and prepares us to go out into the world to do our Lord's work. It can be difficult in our busy lives to find even an hour a week or a month to spend in adoration, but when we can, we are richly rewarded.

Inspiration

Jesus Christ lives in our midst to be close to and ready to help us always. (St. Geltrude Comensoli)

Challenge

Make an adoration date with Jesus—and keep it. Offer prayers of thanksgiving or supplication, or sit quietly with your eyes closed, drinking in his love.

Pina Suriano

February 18, 1915–May 19, 1950

Pina felt the call to the religious life at a very young age. But her parents, her mother in particular, opposed the idea because they wanted her to get married. Try as she might to explain her calling, her parents would have none of it, so she did her best to fulfill her longing through involvement in church groups such as Catholic Action, Youth Catholic Action, and the Association of the Daughters of Mary, which she founded. Finally, when she was twenty-five, she received permission to join an order. However, a heart condition kept her from staying. Pina continued to work for Catholic organizations until her death.

Wisdom sometimes comes from the mouths of babes—or those we remember as babes and would prefer not to let grow up. It's important to give young people a warm, safe place to discern God's plan for them, rather than allow our own desires for their lives to override that discernment.

Inspiration

I feel alone and without help, human or divine, abandoned even by the One who is my entire life.... I live in silence and do not answer back; I offer all this up to him. (Blessed Pina Suriano)

Challenge

Where are you playing God in the life of a young person, dismissing his or her future plans as unrealistic? Pray for the grace to listen yourself, and provide gentle, supportive guidance where appropriate.

Jacinta Marto

March 11, 1910–February 20, 1920

We know Jacinta as the youngest of the children who saw the Blessed Virgin at Fatima in 1917. She also may be the one of the three who changed the most as a result of the experience, from a chatty, bubbly girl to a much more introspective child concerned about the souls in need of salvation. Her health was weakened as a result of a flu epidemic, and she endured great pain in her final months.

Growing closer to God doesn't mean we can't laugh or enjoy life. It does mean, however, we become more present to others, as Jacinta did, and become more aware of the effect our words and actions may have on them. We cease to need to be the center of attention for ourselves or others, and give that place to God.

Inspiration

Tell everybody that God grants us graces through the Immaculate Heart of Mary; that people are to ask for them; and that the Heart of Jesus wants the Immaculate Heart of Mary to be venerated at his side. (Blessed Jacinta Marto)

Challenge

Say a rosary and, along with the Mysteries, and contemplate how you have changed spiritually in the past year or two. In what ways would you like to be closer to Christ a year from now? How can you get to that place?

Ascención of the Heart of Jesus (Ascención Nicol y Goñi)

March 14, 1868–February 24, 1940

Ascención taught as a Dominican in her native Spain for nearly thirty years; then, when problems with the government arose, she and some of the other sisters decided it was time to pursue their desire to do missionary work among the poor in faraway lands. They wrote to church authorities in the Americas and Philippines to offer their services and ended up in a remote area of Peru when Ascención was nearly fifty. Out of this service grew the Dominican Missionary Sisters of the Rosary, with nearly eight hundred missionaries in more than twenty countries.

The spark that turned into a flame for Ascención and her companions was lit by reading missionary magazines, something they probably regarded as both formation and relaxation. We can combine those two activities as well, with spiritual magazines, e-newsletters, and movies. It's possible to discover our passion for ministry even as we're being entertained.

☙Inspiration

I cannot explain what the soul feels…. Never have I felt so close to God as in my sixteen months in the mountains. (Blessed Ascención of the Heart of Jesus)

☙Challenge

Set aside time in the next week to read a spiritual magazine or e-newsletter. Make a list of three activities you are inspired to do with family or friends or for the larger community as a result.

Margaret of Cortona

Circa 1247–February 22, 1297

It wasn't the type of life we generally expect a saint to live. Margaret lost her mother when she was young and moved in with a man when she was about seventeen. They had a son. Then, ten years after they had been together, her lover was murdered. Margaret tried to return home with her son, but her stepmother refused to allow it. Margaret and her child ended up in the care of Franciscan friars, and they eventually joined the Third Order of St. Francis and ministered to the poor.

People mess up, and it's especially hard to watch as our children and other young people go down paths we know are likely to lead to heartbreak. Providing gentle guidance when it's needed, and love even when that guidance isn't followed, helps them to start fresh—just as St. Margaret of Cortona did.

Inspiration

The way of salvation is easy; it is enough to love. (St. Margaret of Cortona)

Challenge

What error made by a young person are you finding difficult to forgive? Reread the story of the prodigal son. Which person in the story are you? Which one do you want to be? Pray for the wisdom to forgive, and to welcome that person back into your life.

Maria Adeodata Pisani

December 29, 1806–February 25, 1855

Maria's early home life had all kinds of signs of trouble. Her family was wealthy, but her mother left when Maria was young, unable to cope with her husband's dissolute lifestyle. The child was raised by her paternal grandmother for a time, but then the older woman died, and Maria was sent to a boarding school for girls of the noble class. Her father became involved in a revolt and was deported to Malta, where Maria and her mother eventually moved. Finally, when Maria was nearly twenty-two and had rebuffed marriage offers, she was allowed to become a cloistered Benedictine nun, and became known for her obedience and charities.

So many children these days grow up in single-parent homes, or in dysfunctional families, or they lack the basic necessities of life. Maria's example reminds us that even when parents don't provide a good foundation, it's possible for young people to be grounded by other responsible adults, such as other family members or teachers. God never leaves us behind.

✒ Inspiration

I can do all things through him who strengthens me. (Philippians 4:13)

✒ Challenge

Is there a child in your family or neighborhood who seems to be at risk? If the situation is not so severe that authorities need to be notified, offer to spend an hour a week tutoring him or her, or take part in activities that interest the child. Even a small amount of attention may help the child understand he or she is important to you—and to God.

Teresa Bracco

February 24, 1924–August 28, 1944

Life in Teresa's area of Italy had changed dramatically in the fall of 1943 with clashes between German troops and those who opposed them. Yet it's reported she continued to attend daily Mass and to pray the rosary throughout the day in the ensuing months. Then on August 28, 1944, Teresa and two other young women were seized by soldiers. She so strongly resisted one's rape attempt that he killed her. At her beatification in 1998, Pope John Paul II called on young people to "learn from her clear faith, witnessed to in daily commitment, moral consistency without compromises, and the courage of sacrificing even life if necessary, in order not to betray the values that give it meaning."

Sometimes, the physical world and our inner spiritual lives clash in violent ways. Teresa's example inspires us to be true to God and to our values even in the face of death.

✒ Inspiration

I would rather be killed than give in. (Blessed Teresa Bracco)

✒ Challenge

Consider volunteering at a rape counseling center, perhaps by doing something as simple as taking in cookies for the staff and the violated women. Pray for healing for the victims, and for their abusers, pray that they receive the help they need during their incarcerations.

Walburga

Circa 710–circa 779

Walburga is called the first female author of England and Germany. She penned the life story of her brother, St. Winibald, as well as the story of her other brother, St. Willibald, and his time in Palestine. She was educated from an early age at an abbey. The niece of St. Boniface, Walburga was among those sent to Germany to help him evangelize, and it is said that her prayers on the ship's deck calmed a storm during the voyage.

Walburga was somewhat of a trailblazer, and the strong support of her family in her writing and ministry must have been important to her. Similarly, our own faith journeys and works are made easier when our families are there cheering for us—and we for them.

✒ Inspiration

And whoever does not provide for relatives, and especially for family members, has denied the faith and is worse than an unbeliever. (1 Timothy 5:8)

✒ Challenge

Tell someone in your family or within your parish about how an aspect of the way he or she conducts himself or herself in faith inspires you. Perhaps it's the way your husband helps with bringing parish donations to the food bank or the way your sister can always be counted upon as an RCIA sponsor, no matter what other obligations she has.

Paula Fornes de San Jose de Calasanz

October 11, 1799–February 26, 1889

Paula was the oldest of five children born to a working class family. Her father died when she was ten, and as a result, she went to work early to help her mother support the family and never received a formal education. Perhaps that's why she was determined to see that other girls in Spain had the opportunity to be educated. Paula opened her first school when she was thirty, and upon founding her third school, started what is now known as the Sisters of the Pious Schools. At the time of Paula's death, the order had opened nearly 350 schools across Spain.

When we miss out on an opportunity in life, it's easy to become cynical and bitter. Paula's example reminds us of the joy and happiness that comes from sharing with others what we ourselves may not have.

Inspiration

Make us glad as many days as you have afflicted us,
and as many years as we have seen evil. (Psalm 90:15)

Challenge

Think of something you wish you had had when you were young. Perhaps you longed to have your mother help you learn to make cookies or to have your father read to you. Spend time doing just that with one of your children or another young person in your life.

Matilda of Hackeborn

Circa 1241–1298

Matilda was called "God's nightingale" for her beautiful voice and her service as her convent's choir mistress, among other duties. But life was not always sweet for this mystic. At the convent, she shared with two of the other nuns some of the special revelations Christ had given her, only to find out later they were putting together a book based on what she had said. At first Matilda felt betrayed, then after prayer, she embraced the idea as a way to share Christ's love with others.

Don't we just hate surprises? Not special birthday or Christmas presents, but those events and interactions that catch us totally off guard. We want to be in control of our lives and our destinies. But this desire sets us up for turmoil, because surprises, good and bad, will always be there. The one constant is God. Let's try to turn over more control to him, since he already has it anyway.

✒ Inspiration

For wisdom will come into your heart,

and knowledge will be pleasant to your soul. (Proverbs 2:10)

✒ Challenge

Where and how are people—and God—surprising you this week? Pray for the wisdom to let go and let God.

Hedwig, queen of Poland

1371–July 17, 1399

Hedwig, daughter of the king of Hungary, was forced to marry the prince of Lithuania, Jagiello, before she was a teenager, even though she had fallen in love with the young duke of Austria. As part of the match, Jagiello agreed to convert from paganism. Their work together included renovation of Krakow University. The couple's first child, a daughter, died shortly after her birth, and Hedwig passed away a few days later. In his homily at Hedwig's canonization, Blessed John Paul II said she "inspired religious and cultural cooperation between the nations."

Few women in this country will be presented with an arranged marriage these days. However, our decision to follow Christ can sometimes mean we don't get to follow our hearts. Hedwig's example shows us the good that God can work even when we're guided down a path different from the one we would have selected.

Inspiration

If then there is any encouragement in Christ, any consolation from love, any sharing in the Spirit, any compassion and sympathy, make my joy complete: be of the same mind, having the same love, being in full accord and of one mind. (Philippians 2:1–2)

Challenge

Who in your life is harboring anger because he or she doesn't have the job, the family, or other situation that the person thinks is his or her right? Pray that the Holy Spirit rains down the gift of acceptance on this person.

Maria Sagrario of St. Aloysius Gonzaga

January 8, 1881–August 15, 1936

Maria excelled at the family business. Her father provided pharmaceutical services to Spain's royal family, and Maria was among the first women in Spain to earn a college degree in that challenging discipline. She took over the business after her father's death, but felt a call to the religious life. Maria took final vows with the Discalced Carmelites of Santa Ana and San Jose of Madrid two days before her thirty-ninth birthday. She was prioress when the Spanish Civil War broke out and the convent was threatened by a mob. She sent the sisters to a safe place and went to the home of another sister's parents. Maria was killed when she refused to disclose the location of the other sisters or the convent's valuables.

The discipline and intellect Maria developed in college served her well during her final days. Her example reminds us that our gifts are meant to be used wherever God takes us, not simply on what seems to be the most logical or comfortable path.

✒ Inspiration

Keep your gaze always on our most beloved Jesus, asking him in the depths of his heart what he desires for you, and never deny him anything even if it means going strongly against the grain for you. (Blessed Maria Sagrario of St. Aloysius Gonzaga)

✒ Challenge

Make a list of what you believe are your greatest innate gifts—empathy? A keen mind? A strong body? A sense of humor? Ask God for guidance in how you can best use them today.

Raphaela Maria Porras

March 1, 1850–January 6, 1925

Stories of some female saints include women, such as Clare and Agnes of Assisi, who had the support of their real-life sisters. This is not one of those stories. While Rafaela and her older sister, Delores, became nuns at the same time, trouble began when they were asked to form a new order, Handmaids of the Sacred Heart, and Rafaela was named superior. Eventually, another sister forced Rafaela out of her position as superior. Rafaela spent the next thirty years doing menial tasks without a complaint.

Think of how hurt Rafaela must have been that her own sister undermined her in their community. It is true that those who know us best also know our weak spots best and sometimes choose to exploit them. All we can do is hold our heads high and rise above their treachery with God's help.

Inspiration

Then Jesus said to them, "Prophets are not without honor, except in their hometown, and among their own kin, and in their own house." (Mark 6:4)

Challenge

Do you have a sibling, other relative, or former friend from whom you are estranged? If it is safe for you to do so, write a loving note to the person. If it is not, pray for his or her soul.

Angela de la Cruz

January 30, 1846–March 2, 1932

Angela was so sure of what God wanted her to do with her life that she wouldn't take no for an answer. Even as she was working in a shoe shop, she felt the call to the religious life. One order rejected her due to her poor health; a few years later, another order accepted her, but she had to leave. Her spiritual director counseled her to continue charitable works on her own and helped her develop a spiritual regime while she lived at home. Others liked what she was doing, and Angela eventually founded the Congregation of the Cross, a lay order that works with the sick and homeless, and lives entirely from alms.

Adversity can make us question that small, still voice inside that we believe calls us to be wives, mothers, women religious, nurses, teachers, or other roles in today's world. Angela's example helps us to understand the importance of persevering amid our struggles, and having the courage to follow God's path for us.

Inspiration

The nothing keeps silent, the nothing does not want to be, the nothing suffers all…. The nothing does not impose itself, the nothing does not command with authority, and finally, the nothing in the creature is practical humility. (St. Angela de la Cruz)

Challenge

Spend some quiet time today reflecting on what God is calling you to do, and think about how you can cast doubt and negativity aside in pursuit of that calling.

Katharine Drexel

November 26, 1858–March 3, 1955

The wealthy Drexel family was socially conscious, donating large amounts of money to help the less fortunate. Katharine's passion was the plight of Native Americans. When she was in her early thirties, she met with Pope Leo XIII in Rome and asked for missionaries to staff some of the schools she was financing. His response: She should consider becoming a missionary herself. In 1891, she founded the Sisters of the Blessed Sacrament, which provides religious education within the Native American and African American communities. Katharine opened and supported nearly sixty missions and schools in her lifetime.

It's easy to complain about the world's problems. Katharine's example shows the amazing things that can happen when we take up the cross and follow where God leads.

Inspiration

And here is the passive way—to be filled unto the fullness of God. The passive way—I abandon myself to it, not in a multiplicity of trials, extraordinary penances accomplished, practices of great works—but in peaceful abandonment to the tenderness of Jesus, which I must try to imitate, and by being in constant union with his meek and humble heart. (St. Katharine Drexel)

Challenge

Next time you begin complaining about why your parish, neighborhood, or community isn't doing something about a problem, pray for guidance on how you can become part of the solution.

Cunegund

Died March 3, 1033

Cunegund and her husband, Henry, Duke of Bavaria (who also was canonized), were known for their support of the Church. Their projects included the monastery and cathedral at Bamberg, Germany, said to have been one of Europe's most beautiful in its day. They were criticized for the amount of money they spent on Church-related projects instead of at court. Further gossip, especially about Cunegund's alleged infidelities, plagued them at times, but they remained together. Whether or not they had agreed to a chaste marriage, it is a fact that the couple had no children. After Henry died, Cunegund spent her remaining years in a convent, caring for the sick and taking on the most menial of tasks.

People love to talk, don't they? Yet Henry and Cunegund rose above the rumors. In the same way, we need to focus on the good we see in people and leave the judging to God.

✒ Inspiration

A gossip reveals secrets;

therefore do not associate with a babbler. (Proverbs 20:19)

✒ Challenge

Resolve not to listen to or pass on a single piece of gossip today. If someone begins to share with you a so-called concern about another person, suggest he or she discuss it with that person directly.

Marie-Louise-Elisabeth de Lamoignon (Mother Saint-Louis)

October 3, 1763–March 4, 1825

Marie-Louise, her husband, and their children had a happy home that was torn asunder when her husband was executed during the French Revolution. Ten years later, after the children were grown, Marie-Louise took on as her ministry assistance to poor and abandoned young women, founding the Sisters of Charity of St. Louis. The congregation today is active in ten countries.

Sometimes it seems we are asked to bear more than is humanly possible. Imagine being in your early thirties and losing your husband as nearly everything about the world you know is crumbling around you. Instead of giving up, Marie-Louise focused on what was important: God and raising her children, then her larger ministry.

Inspiration

Let us now plan to work with renewed vigor, to purify us and to hold fast to God. (Blessed Marie-Louise-Elisabeth de Lamoignon)

Challenge

Are your family's financial matters in order if someone should die? How about spiritual matters? On whom would you rely to guide your children's formation if you died? Discuss these arrangements with the appropriate person or people. Make sure your wishes are written down and in a safe place.

Agnes of Bohemia

June 20, 1211–March 6, 1282

Agnes wasn't afraid to say no. A Bohemian princess, she longed for a life devoted to God. However, she received marriage proposals from three kings: Henry VII of Germany, Henry III of England, and Holy Roman Emperor Frederick II. Finally, she appealed to Pope Gregory IX for assistance. She established a Poor Clare monastery a few years later. As this was the first such monastery north of the Alps, Clare of Assisi sent some of her nuns to Agnes and wrote to Agnes of her support for the project.

Peer pressure can be difficult to withstand. Agnes's example reminds us to stand firm when other people's plans and ideas for us run counter to what God is asking of us.

Inspiration

Have nothing to do with anyone who would stand in your way and would seek to turn you aside from fulfilling the vows which you have made to the Most High and from living in that perfection to which the Spirit of the Lord has called you. (St. Clare of Assisi to St. Agnes)

Challenge

What are you doing solely because others expect it of you and not because you feel called to do it? This may include parish or ministry-related activities. Examine what is an obligation versus a passion, and consider where you might need more balance of the two in your life.

Perpetua and Felicity

Died March 7, 203

Perpetua, along with her slave, Felicity, and three others, was imprisoned for being Christian. Perpetua's father, a pagan, pleaded with her to deny her faith, but Perpetua stood firm. During her incarceration, she had a vision of an unbaptized brother who had died young: First he appeared in pain, then at peace. The little group became a family of sorts during their time in prison. Perpetua's child was with them for part of the time, and Felicity gave birth during their imprisonment. None of this prevented the women and their companions from being abused. Ultimately, their throats were slit.

Perpetua, Felicity, and the others built their own faith community while they were in prison. In the same way, we create community in many places—our homes, our parishes, our workplaces. With God at the center, this fellowship can help us through the most difficult of circumstances.

Inspiration

We lie not in our own power but in the power of God. (St. Perpetua)

Challenge

Consider your various communities and how the members of each might benefit from knowing each other. Are there ways in which you can link your communities, perhaps introducing your prayer group friends to your after-Mass doughnut friends? It could be a holy moment of communion.

Rita Amada de Jesus

March 5, 1848–January 6, 1913

Rita was a prayer warrior, even at a young age. And it was a dangerous time to be one in her native Portugal. The government had taken over all Church properties, and closed houses for male and female religious. Rita, however, did not let that shut down her prayer life. She traveled from parish to parish, showing people how to pray, especially how to pray the rosary. Eventually, she was allowed to found an institution called the Sisters of Jesus, Mary, and Joseph and to open a school. Shortly before her death, she was able to send some of the sisters to Brazil.

When we meet with adversity, prayer can be difficult. We wonder where God is, and why he doesn't seem to answer our prayers. Rita took just the opposite tack; while the government was taking an anti-religion stance, she was all the more active, teaching people to pray. We can do the same, especially in our country's difficult political climate.

Inspiration

Blessed are those who are persecuted for righteousness' sake, for theirs is the kingdom of heaven. (Matthew 5:10)

Challenge

Pray the rosary today, after daily Mass or with someone you love. Make today's prayer about community, not about you individually.

Catherine of Bologna (Catherine de Vigri)

September 8, 1413–March 9, 1463

Catherine was a true renaissance woman. This Poor Clare is known for her works of art and her writings, including the *Treatise on the Seven Spiritual Weapons Necessary for Spiritual Warfare.* She was also blessed with visions of the Blessed Virgin and Christ.

Feeding the poor and clothing the hungry are important ministries. But so is the ability to write a moving eulogy or devotion, compose a beautiful hymn, or paint a glorious sunset. The ways in which God gifts us with the talent to touch souls are as infinitesimal as he is.

Inspiration

To combat evil it is necessary: "(1) to be careful always to do good; (2) to believe that we can never achieve anything truly good by ourselves; (3) to trust in God and, for His love, never to fear the battle against evil, either in the world or in ourselves; (4) to meditate frequently on the events and words of Jesus' life, especially His passion and death; (5) to remember that we must die; (6) to keep the benefits of heaven firmly in our minds, (7) to be familiar with Holy Scripture, keeping it in our hearts to guide all our thoughts and actions." (St. Catherine of Bologna)

Challenge

What are your artistic talents? Think of how you can put them to work for God. Alternatively, meditate on Catherine's seven spiritual weapons, and their application in your life.

Anne Marie Eugenie of Jesus

August 25, 1817–March 10, 1898

In her early life, Anne Eugenie wanted for little. Her family had money and was involved in political action, social justice, and intellectual discourse. One thing was lacking for her, however: a faith life. Through the help of friends, she found a relationship with God after her mother's death and her father's business failures. When she was twenty-two, she founded the Religious of the Assumption, which aims to change society through education.

We all know people who don't have an active faith life and seem to get along just fine. We don't always know what's going on for them at home or work or in their souls. Being transparent about the way Christ works in our lives helps others be more open to him when they face a crisis of their own.

✈ Inspiration

I was seized by a longing to devote all my strength or rather all my weakness to the Church which...I saw as alone holding the key to the knowledge and achievement of all that is good. (St. Anne Marie Eugenie of Jesus)

✈ Challenge

Call or visit with a non-churchgoing friend who is struggling. Listen. Offer to pray together, or let the friend know you will be praying for him or her.

Teresa Margaret of the Sacred Heart (Anna Maria Redi)

July 15, 1747–March 7, 1770

"God is love" was the focus of Teresa Margaret's short life. She became a Carmelite nun when she was eighteen and died five years later. She is known for the depth of her prayer life and for her efforts to lead a hidden interior spiritual life, using the Holy Family as her model.

The more we grow in love with God, the more we put away behaviors and thoughts that are displeasing to him and dangerous to us. God loves us no matter what, but the deeper we love him, the happier and more serene we become.

✒ Inspiration

I propose to have no other purpose in all my activities, either interior or exterior, other than the motive of love alone, by constantly asking myself: "Now what am I doing in this action? Do I love God?" If I should notice any obstacle to pure love, I shall take myself in hand and recall that I must seek to return my love for his love. (St. Teresa Margaret)

✒ Challenge

Use St. Teresa Margaret's words to guide your prayers as you move throughout your day. Note the obstacles you encounter, and ask for God's help with them. Try to refrain from turning your interior struggles into public drama wherever possible.

Frances of Rome
1384–March 9, 1440

Frances was less than thrilled when her wealthy parents decided she would be married at the age of twelve. The quiet child, who had wanted to enter a convent, likely was also unhappy at the prospect of leaving her home to live with her in-laws. It turned out, however, that not only did she and Lorenzo have a happy marriage for forty years, but Frances also found a spiritual companion in her sister-in-law, Vanozza. Together, they cared for the sick and poor. Frances also worked tirelessly to assist those who suffered due to plague and famine in Rome, and she later founded what is now called the Oblates of Tor de' Specchi, a group of laywomen who minister to the poor.

Sisters-in-law are special women. They didn't grow up with you like sisters, but there is a unique bond since you share the love of a brother or a husband's brother. Even if you have nothing else in common, this is a marvelous basis on which to begin a friendship.

Inspiration
Let us be friends, Francesca; I will help you to lead the life you desire, and together we shall arrive at the end we have in view. (Vanozza to St. Frances)

Challenge
Call or write your sister-in-law (or other female relative) to see how she is doing. You also may want to tell her how she inspires you.

Dulce Lopes Pontes

May 26, 1914–March 13, 1992

Dulce, sometimes called the Mother Teresa of Brazil, didn't stray far from home to do her ministry. She grew up in Salvador on Brazil's northeast coast and joined the Congregation of the Missionary Sisters of the Immaculate Conception of the Mother of God when she was eighteen. That same year, she founded a Christian workers movement in Salvador. The Charitable Works Foundation of Sister Dulce today is one of the top health institutions in Brazil and is the only one with more than a thousand beds for those who rely on public assistance. Sister Dulce was nominated for the Nobel Peace Prize.

We sometimes think we need to go to the third world or impoverished areas of the United States to minister to the poor and needy. However, like Sister Dulce, all we need to do is look in our own backyards to find people in need of our love and assistance.

Inspiration

There is nothing better that you can do in this world than to totally give yourself to God in the person of the poor and our needy brother. (Blessed Dulce Lopes Pontes)

Challenge

What is the easiest thing you could do today to alleviate suffering among the poor, elderly, or ailing in your town? Visit a nursing home? Make a contribution to a food pantry? Do it.

Giuseppina Catanea (Maria Giuseppina of Jesus Crucified)

February 18, 1894–March 14, 1948

Good health was not one of the blessings Giuseppina received. Before she took her final vows as a cloistered Carmelite, she was paralyzed with tuberculosis of the spine, and then she was miraculously cured through the intercession of St. Francis Xavier. Other ailments she suffered included blindness and hearing issues. Those who knew Giuseppina said she bore it all with a smile.

Having a chronic or a temporary illness can make us cranky and ask where God is and why we have to suffer. That's not a question anyone on earth can answer. We can pray, however, to accept with grace the health problems that beset us, and to gracefully accept help from our caregivers.

✒ Inspiration

Even youths will faint and be weary,
    and the young will fall exhausted;
but those who wait for the LORD shall renew their strength,
    they shall mount up with wings like eagles,
they shall run and not be weary,
    they shall walk and not faint. (Isaiah 40:30–31)

✒ Challenge

Make a note to yourself that the next time you are ill, you will accept the lasagna casseroles, chicken pot pies, and tuna salads that others offer, whether or not you ever take a bite. Allowing others to give is a gift in and of itself.

Louise de Marillac

August 12, 1591–March 15, 1660

Timing is everything. Louise considered becoming a nun when she was young, but instead she got married in her early twenties. Somewhat at loose ends after her husband's death a dozen years later, she met Vincent de Paul. He became her spiritual adviser, and in her early forties, Louise took religious vows. Together, they founded the Daughters of Charity of St. Vincent de Paul.

In today's world, we seek immediate gratification. We want what we want, and we want it now. If it doesn't happen on our timetable, we become discouraged and give up, or impatient. When we turn our lives over to God's timing, we find peace, and we may be pleasantly surprised at what he has in store for us.

✽ Inspiration

Certainly it is the great secret of the spiritual life to abandon to God all that we love by abandoning ourselves to all he wills. (St. Louise de Marillac)

✽ Challenge

Try living in the moment, not mourning the past or anticipating the future, just for a single hour today. That means no "what if," "if only," or "I wish" statements. Afterward, journal about how the experience felt, and think about trying it for two hours the next day.

Angela of Foligno

1248–January 4, 1309

For the first thirty years of her life, Angela likely would have laughed if you'd told her she would be beatified one day. Born into an affluent, non-Christian family, she married at twenty and did not let her husband or children slow down her hard-living, adulterous lifestyle. An earthquake, wars, and other events made her reconsider her life, and she prayed to St. Francis of Assisi for guidance, which he provided. Then she hit rock bottom, with her mother, husband, and children all dying within a few months. She is noted for establishing a non-cloistered community of sisters and for her writings.

The people who lead the wildest, most ungodly lives sometimes are closer to redemption than we think. Angela's story reminds us that no one is beyond the touch of God—or our prayer power.

Inspiration

A divine voice spoke to my soul, saying, "I did not love you as a joke." These words caused me mortal pain for immediately the eyes of my soul were opened and I saw all that he suffered in life and death…and that it was not as a joke but because of perfect and tender love that he loved me. (Blessed Angela of Foligno)

Challenge

Is someone in your family living in a way that has you in despair for his or her salvation? Pray for the person, and keep him or her in your life, letting the person see how God's presence helps you through hard times.

Gertrude of Nivelles

626–March 17, 659

Gertrude's life took a somewhat different path than many of the other saints who were also women religious. Her mother, Itta, built a double monastery after Gertrude's father died, and both women entered it. Gertrude was named as abbess. But after her mother's death, Gertrude cut back on her official duties so that she could spend more time studying Scripture, and she devoted the last three years of her life to that activity and doing penance.

Knowing when it's time to leave a leadership position or other life role is difficult and often humbling. It's hard to believe anyone else can handle, let alone do as well, a ministry or job responsibility at which we've excelled. And yet, we must leave, for our time on earth is limited, and we must help others prepare to carry on after us.

Inspiration

It will not be so among you; but whoever wishes to be great among you must be your servant, and whoever wishes to be first among you must be your slave; just as the Son of Man came not to be served but to serve, and to give his life a ransom for many. (Matthew 20:26–28)

Challenge

In what ministry, parenting group, or other activity have you held the same position for more than three years? Prayerfully consider stepping aside for someone new, and consider what you might do in new service.

Maria Barbara of the Holy Trinity (Barbara Maix)

June 27, 1818–March 17, 1873

Talk about a Holy Spirit moment! Barbara and her companions were in Hamburg, waiting for the ship that would take them to North America. They had been expelled from their native Austria due to the nationalist uprisings that were going on there, and it's easy to imagine the concerns and sadness many must have had about this next stage of their lives and ministry. It was then, as they waited, that Barbara decided it would be Brazil, not North America, where they would go. The Sisters of the Immaculate Heart of Mary continues today to work with underprivileged women there.

Some people would call Barbara's abrupt change of course intuition. Some would call it stupidity. Some would call it risk taking. We would call it obedience and confidence in God's will. We encounter similar opportunities in our own lives all the time. Do we listen?

Inspiration

David said further to his son Solomon, "Be strong and of good courage, and act. Do not be afraid or dismayed; for the LORD God, my God, is with you. He will not fail you or forsake you, until all the work for the service of the house of the LORD is finished." (1 Chronicles 28:20)

Challenge

What big step is God inviting you to take? Take a deep breath, say a prayer, and then take it.

Celestina of the Mother of God (Marianna Donati)

October 26, 1848–March 18, 1925

For Celestina, it was all about God's timing. She was forty-one before she was able to leave home and form what would later become the Daughters of the Poor of St. Joseph Calasanz. Celestina was tireless in her outreach to disadvantaged children and women, and she persevered even when one of the other sisters died about a year after the institute was formed, followed less than two years later by the archbishop who had supported the plan.

It would have been easy for Celestina to simply give up on her dream of a vocation. Instead, she was patient and cared for her father until the time was right to serve God in a more public way. May we all have her wisdom and patience.

Inspiration

For God is not unjust; he will not overlook your work and the love that you showed for his sake in serving the saints, as you still do. And we want each one of you to show the same diligence so as to realize the full assurance of hope to the very end, so that you may not become sluggish, but imitators of those who through faith and patience inherit the promises. (Hebrews 6:10–12)

Challenge

What have you prayed and prayed and prayed for only to feel God isn't listening? He's listening, all right, and giving you an answer. Pray for the strength to hear it—and act upon it.

Maria Josefa of the Heart of Jesus

September 7, 1842–March 20, 1912

Maria Josefa was passionate about caring for the sick, no matter how risky it could be to provide that care. The sisters of the Institute of the Servants of Jesus of Charity, which she founded, nursed people who had cholera, tuberculosis, and other highly contagious diseases. Today, the order's ministries include assisting those with AIDS and providing day-care centers for the elderly and food for the poor.

We weren't all meant to be nurses or doctors or paramedics. We can, however, treat the ill with the respect and dignity we would like. No one deserves to contract AIDS, lung cancer, alcoholism, or other illnesses that carry a stigma in our society.

Inspiration

Don't believe, sisters, that the assistance consists only in giving medicines and food to the sick. There is another type of assistance that must never be forgotten, and it is the assistance of the heart that adjusts and enters in sympathy with the person who suffers and goes to meet his needs. (St. Maria Josefa of the Heart of Jesus)

Challenge

Examine your conscience. Where have you judged or avoided someone who is ill, and why? Pray for guidance in getting beyond your prejudice.

Benedetta Cambiagio Frassinello

October 2, 1791–March 21, 1858

When they were young, Benedetta and her husband, Giovanni, both had considered joining orders. After they married, they agreed to live as brother and sister. They became caregivers for Benedetta's sister through a terminal illness and then decided to join orders. That was not the end of their relationship, however. Benedetta and Giovanni continued to work together to establish schools for at-risk girls. Their projects spawned so much gossip that the pair and other friends moved and established the Benedictine Sisters of Providence near Genoa, which continues to focus on educating young women.

It stings to have others wrongly judge us and our motives. Benedetta's life reminds us of the importance of doing the work God calls us to do, regardless of what others may say.

Inspiration

When he was abused, he did not return abuse; when he suffered, he did not threaten; but he entrusted himself to the one who judges justly. (1 Peter 2:23)

Challenge

Be mindful of judgmental comments people may make about others in your presence. Gently ask them to avoid such statements. If they refuse, change the topic of conversation and excuse yourself.

Darerca

Circa late fourth century–early fifth century

Darerca must have been some kind of spirit-filled mother. She was the sister of Ireland's St. Patrick, and it appears Darerca was married twice. She had numerous children—by some reports, as many as seventeen sons, who all became bishops. We do know that many of her children—perhaps fourteen daughters and sons—became saints.

Think of it: Raising even half as many children as Darerca is reported to have had so that they reflected Christ so much that they found a vocation or served in such a way that others followed them to the degree they became saints. We know the time she would have spent with each child would have been limited, much more than we are able to spend with our children today. Her story inspires us to make our time with children be as God-filled as we can make it.

✒ Inspiration

My child, keep your father's commandment,
  and do not forsake your mother's teaching.
Bind them upon your heart always;
  tie them around your neck.
When you walk, they will lead you;
  when you lie down, they will watch over you;
  and when you awake, they will talk with you. (Proverbs 6:20–22)

✒ Challenge

Talk about God today, in person, via phone, or through e-mail, with at least one of your children or a younger friend. Let him or her know you are praying for his or her continual spiritual formation.

Rafqa Pietra Choboq Ar-Rayès de Himlaya
June 29, 1832–March 23, 1914

Lebanon-born Rafqa had been a nun for more than thirty years when in October 1885, she asked Jesus to let her feel some of his suffering from the passion. She immediately suffered excruciating pains in her head and eyes. Rafqa had no real relief after that. She eventually lost her sight and became paralyzed. Still, she praised God and thanked him for the gift of suffering. At Rafqa's canonization in 2001, Pope John Paul II prayed that she watch in particular over the people of the Middle East and that she intercede with God "to open hearts to the patient quest for new ways to peace and so hasten the advent of reconciliation and harmony."

Can you imagine thanking God for the gift of pain, much less asking him for suffering to begin with? What a place of trust and faith, to be grateful and full of praise no matter what challenge we experience. God is there in both good times and bad, sorrow and joy.

Inspiration
I know that the sickness I have is for the good of my soul and his glory…. The sickness accepted with patience and thanksgiving purifies the soul as the fire purifies gold. (St. Rafqa Pietra Choboq Ar-Rayès de Himlaya)

Challenge
Make a list of your aches and pains and complaints with God. Then burn them, and resolve to say a prayer of thanks when you next think of them today.

Catherine of Sweden

1331–March 24, 1381

Catherine was a devoted daughter of St. Bridget of Sweden. In fact, nineteen-year-old Catherine was in Rome with Bridget when Catherine's husband died back in Sweden, and after that time the mother and daughter were constant companions. After Bridget died, Catherine took over the leadership of the Order of the Holy Savior, which had been founded by her mother, and she gained approval from the rule Catherine had written. The daughter also was a tireless advocate for her mother's canonization; unfortunately, she did not live to see the success of her efforts.

Mothers are special people. They love us like no one else and have seen us at our most vulnerable, from infancy to childhood, through adolescence and adulthood. It's no wonder, then, that the Holy Mother holds a special place in the hearts of Catholics.

✈ Inspiration

Do not speak harshly to an older man, but speak to him as to a father, to younger men as brothers, to older women as mothers, to younger women as sisters—with absolute purity.

…If a widow has children or grandchildren, they should first learn their religious duty to their own family and make some repayment to their parents; for this is pleasing in God's sight. (1 Timothy 5:1–2, 4)

✈ Challenge

Do something nice for your mother or, if that is not possible, offer up some prayers for her.

Margaret Clitherow

Circa 1556–March 25, 1586

Margaret converted to Catholicism when she was eighteen, at a time when Catholics were being persecuted in the aftermath of the establishment of the Church of England. That, however, had no effect on her passion for her newfound faith. Margaret helped hide priests in her home and ultimately was discovered doing so. She refused to enter a plea in court because her children and servants would have been called to testify against her. As a result, Margaret was crushed to death.

Are there times you feel uncomfortable being identified as a Catholic? Perhaps it's when the subject of abortion or contraception funding comes up with friends or coworkers. Christ doesn't call us to run away from controversy, but to stand up for Church teachings and enlighten those who question why we believe what we believe.

Inspiration

Jesu! Jesu! Have mercy on me! (St. Margaret Clitherow)

Challenge

Pray for the people of North Korea and other countries in which Catholics and other Christians are persecuted. Or, spend time studying the *Catechism of the Catholic Church* and other Church resources so that you can explain the Catholic position on today's controversial issues. Church doctrine and dogma begin with Christ and love, not from hatred or a human desire for control over others.

Maria Serafina of the Sacred Heart (Clotilde Micheli)

September 11, 1849–March 24, 1911

Maria knew she was going to found a religious order. The Blessed Virgin told her that before she was eighteen. She just didn't know how long it was going to take. After years of fits and starts, she took her vows with an order when she was nearly forty. She then had an opportunity to found a new order, but it turned out her vision was not aligned with what the local bishop desired. It was shortly before Maria's forty-second birthday when the Sisters of the Angels, Adorers of the Most Holy Trinity, came to be and began working with the poor.

God's timing can be so frustrating sometimes. We believe we know what he wants, but there often are obstacles in getting there. May we remember that "no" does not always mean "never"; it can also mean "Not yet," and "Don't give up too soon."

Inspiration

Be patient, therefore, beloved, until the coming of the Lord. The farmer waits for the precious crop from the earth, being patient with it until it receives the early and the late rains. (James 5:7)

Challenge

Is God frustrating you in some way? Talk with your pastor or spiritual director about what you have discerned is his will for you and how you can be more patient as it unfolds.

Maria Karlowska

September 4, 1865–March 24, 1935

Maria was working at her sister's dressmaking shop in Poznan, Poland, when she first began meeting prostitutes and other girls from poor families. This ministry led her to found what is now known as the Good Shepherd Sisters, which also assists those suffering from sexually transmitted infections. The sisters' combination of catechesis and medical care has led to many conversions and restorations of dignity. At Maria's beatification in 1997, Pope John Paul II said her devotion to Christ spawned "an insatiable hunger for love [that]…will never say 'enough,' will never stop midway."

Maria's willingness to go into the areas where prostitutes lived and worked drew criticism, but she didn't care. For her, it was about easing suffering and carrying God's name. May we remember this as opportunities for ministries outside our comfort zone present themselves.

Inspiration

We must proclaim the Heart of Jesus, that is, so to live from him, in him, and for him, as to become like him and that in our lives he may be more visible than we ourselves. (Blessed Maria Karlowska)

Challenge

Think about a ministry that would make you uncomfortable—not something that would endanger you, but something that might challenge your preconceived notions of people. How could you overcome your feelings to offer help, keeping in mind Maria's "insatiable hunger for love"?

Olympia Bida

1903–January 28, 1952

Olympia was steadfast in her faith amid the Soviet presence in Ukraine. However, her catechization and surreptitious religious services were discovered by authorities, and she was exiled to Siberia with other sisters in her order. She did her best to keep a sense of community among the sisters before a serious illness claimed her. She, Josaphata Hordashevska, and another nun were among those beatified in 2001 as Martyrs of Ukraine.

Following Christ is pretty easy when we're cozy in our own homes, surrounded by people just like us. Keeping the fire burning when our comforts are stripped away is something else. We learn from Olympia the importance that community, even under trying circumstances, plays in our lives.

✒ Inspiration

Let's follow him bravely. Not only when all is well, but even when times are bitter, let us say: Glory to God in all matters. (Blessed Olympia Bida)

✒ Challenge

Build your community where you are today. Arrange a potluck dinner or songfest with your sisters in Christ who you don't see often enough. Ask each woman to share about a time that her life was changed by community support, whether it was in her parish, her college sorority, her neighborhood, or extended family.

Gwladys of Wales

Sixth century

The story of Gwladys and Gwynllyw is the stuff of Hollywood movies. The legend is that Gwynllyw and his men abducted her after her father refused to allow the match. King Arthur came along in support of Gwynllyw—after Arthur agreed not to take Gwladys for himself. It wasn't until their oldest son, Cadoc, convinced them to give up their wild lives that they both converted to Christianity and embraced good works.

If you're a cradle Catholic, stories like this may infuriate you. Why should people live such riotous lives and still, if they are sincere about their conversion, get into heaven, the same as someone who lived a good Christian life from the get-go? Consider that there's a true poverty in a godless lifestyle, and that at some level, those who come to God late may wish they'd had his presence earlier.

✍ Inspiration

But the father said to his slaves, "Quickly, bring out a robe—the best one—and put it on him; put a ring on his finger and sandals on his feet. And get the fatted calf and kill it, and let us eat and celebrate; for this son of mine was dead and is alive again; he was lost and is found!" And they began to celebrate. (Luke 15:22–24)

✍ Challenge

God isn't fair—we should be grateful for that—but he is merciful. Thank him for the times he's welcomed you back after you've made mistakes.

Maria Restituta (Helen Kafka)

May 1, 1894–March 30, 1943

Maria was prescient when she selected Restituta, an early Church martyr, as her religious name. Her own path to martyrdom began when she said no to the Nazis, who came to the hospital where she was working as a surgical nurse and told her to remove the crucifixes she had hung in the rooms of a new wing. That act, and her general attitude about the political climate (she called Hitler a madman), were described as high treason. In the months she spent in prison before her execution, she cared for her fellow inmates.

When the going gets tough as Christians, what do we do? Do we put away the visible signs of Christ in our lives so we don't get persecuted or ridiculed? Maria's brave example reminds us that Christ lives not only in our hearts and souls, but also in the way we show him to the world.

✎Inspiration

I have lived for Christ; I want to die for Christ. (Blessed Maria Restituta)

✎Challenge

Be bold in your faith today. Wear a crucifix or religious medal. Leave some prayer cards in a public place. Say grace out loud if you're having a meal at a restaurant with others.

Juana Maria Condesa Lluch

March 30, 1862–January 16, 1916

Juana came from a wealthy family yet knew from a very early age she wanted to serve God's poor in the same way the Blessed Virgin had in turning over her life to the Lord. Her archbishop told her she was too young when, at eighteen, she came to him with the idea of a congregation devoted to helping struggling factory workers. But four years later, he relented. At her beatification in 2003, Pope John Paul II said Juana's "profoundly Christian youth" prepared her "to dedicate herself totally to the love of God."

People sometimes underestimate our abilities, don't they? We are reminded by Juana's story that when God places something on our heart, we must persevere and press on, respecting authorities but continuing forward with what God desires of us.

✍ Inspiration

And Mary said,
"My soul magnifies the Lord,
    and my spirit rejoices in God my Savior,
for he has looked with favor on the lowliness of his servant.
    Surely, from now on all generations will call me blessed;
for the Mighty One has done great things for me,
    and holy is his name." (Luke 1:46–49)

✍ Challenge

Have you turned your will over to God? Spend some quiet time with the Magnificat (Luke 1:46–54) today, meditating on how you might better emulate Mary.

Margaret Flesch

February 24, 1826–March 25, 1908

When Margaret was young, it was not unusual for orphans in Germany to in essence be auctioned off to the highest bidder, as there was no infra-structure for orphanages or other community care. Margaret decided to do something about this. When she was twenty-five, she and one of her sisters took up residence in an area of their church and took in orphans and cared for them. She worked as a day laborer to provide for her brood and eventually, with help from her pastor and other women, raised enough funds to open a home for the children and the ill. In 1863, Margaret became the first superior general of the Franciscan Sisters of the Blessed Virgin Mary of the Angels.

Margaret's contemporaries probably gave little thought to the plight of the orphans. After all, it was how things had always been done. Her example inspires us to envision how we can serve Christ and our brothers and sisters beyond the way things have always been done.

☙ Inspiration

It is through service to others, lovingly given, that we reach a special fulfillment and union with our Lord. (Blessed Margaret Flesch)

☙ Challenge

Imagine how people living in the margins of society in your commu-nity could have a better life. Then take one small step—volunteer at a food pantry, donate supplies to a free clinic, take cookies to a women's shelter—to make it happen.

Agape, Chionia, and Irene

Died 304

The three sisters went to their deaths because they concealed copies of Scripture and refused to eat food that had been offered in sacrifice to pagan gods. They told the inquisitor they were more fearful of offending God than emperors.

Many other Christians of this time compromised themselves on issues such as these. Perhaps they decided it made more sense to live to fight another day. Perhaps they were fearful. Agape, Chionia, and Irene remind us that cutting corners on our faith isn't appropriate. They also remind us that it's easier to stand strong for Christ with loved ones beside you.

Inspiration

I believe in the living God, and will not by an evil action lose all the merit of my past life. (St. Agape)

Challenge

In what area of your life are you not living your faith? Are you uncomfortable with expectations at work or even within your own home that seem to run counter to your beliefs? For example, are you asked to sign off on false expense reports or timesheets or incomplete tax documents? Or is your spouse's disciplinary style with your children overly harsh? Talk with a sister, or someone who's like a sister to you, about ways to address the problem in a faith-filled manner.

Mary of Egypt

Circa 344–421

God hit Mary like a ton of bricks. A prostitute for seventeen years in Egypt, she went to Jerusalem looking for business. However, a force prevented her from entering the church, not once but three or four times. She prayed to a statue of the Blessed Virgin in the courtyard and followed a voice that told her to cross the Jordan River. There, she received the Eucharist, then went into the desert, where she remained alone for forty-seven years. She died after a priest she had encountered a year earlier returned and offered her the Eucharist on Holy Thursday.

Who says people can't change? With God's help, even the wickedest among us can find new life. Always, we are called to love even the most unlovable among us and to pray for them to come into the Light.

Inspiration

For I will be merciful toward their iniquities,

and I will remember their sins no more. (Hebrews 8:12)

Challenge

Do a small kindness for the wickedest person you know without telling him or her about it. You never know what goodness may sprout from the seed you plant.

Maria Crescentia Hoss

October 20, 1682–April 5, 1744

Just as it was customary for a woman to bring a dowry into a marriage, so it was the usual practice during Maria's time for a dowry to accompany one's entry into a religious order. But Maria's family was too poor to pay a dowry, so the monastery she wished to enter refused her. Eventually, the community was convinced to accept her, but the other nuns continued to treat her poorly until a new superior was named three years later. The mistreatment she suffered inspired her to treat others with kindness and compassion regardless of their financial largesse or poverty.

We are often judged by others in this world by the color of our skin, our gender, our age, our appearance, our financial status—the list goes on and on. Shrugging off those hurts and loving as Christ instructed us is difficult. Yet ultimately, it is the only real way to effect change in our hearts and minds and those of our persecutors.

✏ Inspiration

God wants the convent rich in virtue, not in temporal goods. (St. Maria Crescentia Hoss)

✏ Challenge

Pray for the people who have wronged you, that they may be more considerate of the feelings of others. Then forgive them, fully and sincerely.

Ethelburga of Kent

Died circa 647

Ethelburga's mother, St. Bertha, was a Christian, and her father, King Ethelbert of Kent, was a convert. When Ethelburga became the second wife of King Edwin of Northumbria, it was with the understanding he would at least consider converting. Ultimately, he did so, on Easter Sunday. When her husband died in battle a few years later, Ethelburga returned to Kent and lived in a monastery the rest of her life.

Spouses have such a strong influence on each other's faith journey. It's unlikely Ethelburga nagged Edward every day while he was wrestling with his decision. More likely, she and her confessor, Paulinus, answered his questions and clarified his views, and showed Edward by their actions how Christians live. In the same way, we help spark continual conversion in those we love best or drive them away from the faith. The choice is ours.

✒ Inspiration

So faith comes from what is heard, and what is heard comes through the word of Christ. (Romans 10:17)

✒ Challenge

Set aside time today for one-on-one sharing and prayer with your spouse or a friend who is near and dear to your heart and soul. Grow in faith together.

Juliana of Liege

1193–April 5, 1258

This Belgian nun had the same vision for more than twenty years. It was of a full moon with one dark spot. Eventually, she discerned that it was a sign of the need for a feast honoring Christ in the Eucharist. Juliana began to share the vision with others and made it her goal to have the Feast of Corpus Christi established. The papal bull that accomplished this was issued six years after she died.

We won't see all of our goals and desires accomplished in this world. Like Juliana, we can only do what God asks of us, and leave the rest in his hands, confident in his timing.

Inspiration

Beloved, I do not consider that I have made it my own; but this one thing I do: forgetting what lies behind and straining forward to what lies ahead. I press on toward the goal for the prize of the heavenly call of God in Christ Jesus. (Philippians 3:13–14)

Challenge

Where are you putting your life on a meaningless timetable—kids acing their classes by next year, a promotion at work within three years? Where do you feel despair because that self-imposed timetable isn't being met? Pray for the confidence to let God's will to be done if and as he desires, and stop trying to set deadlines for him.

Josaphata Hordashevska

November 20, 1869–April 7, 1919

Josaphata grew up in what is now Ukraine, and the area had a decided lack of women religious who could live among the people and minister to them. As she was preparing to enter a cloistered order, her spiritual director asked if she would instead serve as the founding member—and superior and directress—of the community-based Congregation of the Sisters Servants of Mary Immaculate. Josaphata prayed for a few days, then said yes, and took on her new duties after two months with another community order. She was just twenty-two. Later, she had to resign from her leadership post because she had not taken her perpetual vows, but she persevered and was reinstated after completing her vows.

Josaphata wasn't afraid to say yes to Christ, even though she was young and had almost no experience as a woman religious. She inspires us to say yes as well, even when God's questions are daunting.

✒ Inspiration

Educate the heart of the people, and serve where the need is greatest. (Blessed Josaphata Hordashevska)

✒ Challenge

Contemplate Josaphata's words. Is there somewhere God is calling you to serve, somewhere that the need is greater than your current ministries?

Julie Billiart

July 12, 1751–April 8, 1816

You couldn't have asked for a more unlikely pair of friends. Julie was partially paralyzed and had the most basic of educations. Françoise was a viscountess who, before the French Revolution, had been presented at the Court of Louis XVI and Marie Antoinette. They both ended up in Amiens and slowly became friends. They were the first two superiors of the Institute of the sisters of Notre Dame, which serves poor children.

We tend to associate with people who are like us in terms of faith, family status, political beliefs, hobbies, interests, age, education, or income. But getting to know someone with whom we seemingly have nothing in common can teach us much. It's an opportunity to share the Good News—or to have it illumined for us.

Inspiration

Let us pray more and more that the Kingdom of God may spread everywhere in the hearts of all. The harvest is great but there are no laborers. Let us work at becoming good laborers! (St. Julie Billiart)

Challenge

Step outside your comfort zone. Spend some time today talking with and listening to someone you typically avoid. Look for the interests that unite rather than separate you. Is there a joint passion for ministry the two of you could mine?

Waltrude

Died circa 688

Sainthood turned out to be a family affair for Waltrude. Not only were her parents and sister canonized, but her four children and her husband, Vincent Madelgarius, also became saints. Life changed for the family when Vincent decided to enter a monastery he had founded. Two years later, Waltrude embraced a solitary life herself and then later established a convent.

Waltrude's family wasn't perfect any more than ours are. Since they were human, it's a given they argued and fought at times. But they also had a strong shared faith that helped them get through the hard times. In the same way, a faith lived openly and jointly in our homes can help us get over the rough patches in life.

Inspiration

Again, truly I tell you, if two of you agree on earth about anything you ask, it will be done for you by my Father in heaven. For where two or three are gathered in my name, I am there among them. (Matthew 18:19–20)

Challenge

How long has it been since you said grace or shared other prayer time with your family? Find a few minutes to do it today. You may find some saints in the making.

Casilda

Died circa 1050

Casilda, the daughter of a Muslim emir, was sick, and none of the doctors she knew could help her. Eventually, some Christian friends recommended she visit the waters of Lake Saint Vincent. While her father was intolerant of Christians (Casilda, meanwhile, surreptitiously was bringing them food and medicine), he agreed to let her try this possible remedy. Casilda was cured. She chose to convert and spent the rest of her life in a hermitage near the lake.

As Catholics, we experience continual conversion. Our faith life deepens each day, each week, each month, each year. We so desire that others come to know Jesus, and the best way to do this is to share our faith in words and actions with those who do not.

✒ Inspiration

First of all you must understand this, that no prophecy of scripture is a matter of one's own interpretation, because no prophecy ever came by human will, but men and women moved by the Holy Spirit spoke from God. (2 Peter 1:20–21)

✒ Challenge

Invite a non-Christian to attend a liturgical event or assist you in a ministry. Be open to questions he or she has about your faith.

Gemma Galgani

March 12, 1878–April 11, 1903

Gemma was blessed at various times of her short life with states of ecstasy and signs of the stigmata. Many people, including her spiritual director, initially questioned her gifts, but the Church ultimately became convinced of her authenticity. "She bore in her flesh the wounds of Christ," said Pope Pius XI, who beatified her in 1933. (Pope Pius XII canonized her just seven years later.) However, Gemma's younger sister, Angelina, was not among those who believed her. Angelina mocked her sister and during Gemma's canonization process and tried to profit by selling her sister's effects.

For many of us, sisters and brothers are among our best friends. But some know our weak points all too well, and seek to use them to tear us down. If sibling relationships are difficult, Gemma's example reminds us to rise above earthly hurt and serve the brother we share, Christ.

Inspiration

I want to follow thee whatever the cost in suffering—to follow thee fervently. (St. Gemma Galgani)

Challenge

Write a loving note to a sibling or friend you find it difficult to accept, or who finds it difficult to accept you. Consider sharing a memory of a common happy experience.

Elena Guerra

June 23, 1835–April 11, 1914

Elena, an Italian sister, was passionate about the Holy Spirit—so passionate, in fact, that she sent twelve confidential letters in eight years to Pope Leo XIII asking that he do what he could to encourage Catholics to be more devoted to the Holy Spirit. The pope must have felt the Spirit as well, as he wrote an encyclical on the topic and directed bishops to pray the Novena for Pentecost when the new century began. The order she founded became known as the Oblate Sisters of the Holy Spirit and is now called Sisters of St. Zita.

The Holy Spirit is alive and well today! We see the Spirit in our brothers and sisters. And, surely, Elena also saw it in St. Gemma Galgani, who was one of her students at the Oblates of the Sisters of the Holy Spirit.

Inspiration

Pentecost is not over. In fact it is continually going on in every time and in every place, because the Holy Spirit desired to give himself to all men and all who want him can always receive him. (Blessed Elena Guerra)

Challenge

Come, Holy Spirit! Sing a song, light a candle, say a prayer, do a dance to invite the Spirit to burn brightly within you.

Mother Joseph of the Sacred Heart

April 16, 1823–January 19, 1902

Mother Joseph was a trailblazer. When she was in her thirties, she left her native eastern Canada behind to lead the Sisters of Providence to what was then Washington Territory. Once there, she helped open schools, hospitals, and an orphanage, at times getting involved in the construction herself! She was particularly concerned about the children of the area, which perhaps was not surprising since she had been the third of twelve children herself.

Mother Joseph threw herself into her work with gusto, whether it was playing with the children or checking the sturdiness of a building beam. In the same way, our own service is more pleasing to the Lord (and to us) if we do it with a smile and some enthusiasm.

 Inspiration

A voice cries out:

"In the wilderness prepare the way of the LORD,

make straight in the desert a highway for our God." (Isaiah 40:3)

Challenge

What household or work task do you most dread? Come up with ways you can make it more pleasurable. Perhaps listening to music or saying some Our Fathers as you go will help. Or, offer to trade the chores you find odious with your spouse or roommate for one you enjoy doing. You may be surprised; the task you hate may be something the other person actually likes to do!

Lidwina of Schiedam

March 18, 1380–April 14, 1433

It started out as any other day for Lidwina, just another day that the Dutch teenager was ice skating with a friend. Like any other skater, Lidwina had fallen any number of times in the past. But this time, she fell so hard that she broke a rib. That was the beginning of a series of incurable medical problems. Over the next thirty-plus years, Lidwina experienced visions and received the gift of prophecy.

We never know what challenges each day will bring. Lidwina's example shows us how important it is to be willing to accept whatever good or bad comes and to put our trust in God.

Inspiration

You will say in that day:
I will give thanks to you, O LORD,
   for though you were angry with me,
your anger turned away,
   and you comforted me.

Surely God is my salvation;
   I will trust, and will not be afraid,
for the LORD GOD is my strength and my might;
   he has become my salvation. (Isaiah 12:1–2)

Challenge

Where is God putting your faith to the test? Pray for the strength to trust amid tragedy, sickness, and disappointment.

Maria Romero Meneses

January 13, 1902–July 7, 1977

Even close family members probably didn't have much hope that Maria would have a productive adult life. When she was twelve, she contracted rheumatic fever and was ill for a year. In fact, for six months she was paralyzed, and permanent damage was done to her heart. However, she didn't let her delicate health condition get in the way of what she was called to do. She wasn't shy about asking the wealthy for money to help the poor and opened a school, a clinic, a recreation center, or a food distribution center in Costa Rica. The girl with the damaged heart lived to be seventy-five.

While we shouldn't be careless about our medical conditions, it's also important not to let them get in the way of serving God. No matter what our disability, God wants to use us. We just have to get out of the way and let him.

 Inspiration

Therefore I am content with weaknesses, insults, hardships, persecutions, and calamities for the sake of Christ; for whenever I am weak, then I am strong. (2 Corinthians 12:10)

Challenge

What are your physical limitations? Make a list of ways you could help others who face the same challenges. For example, if you wear hearing aids, can you advocate for a signing Mass or special auditory equipment at your parish? If you are in a wheelchair, perhaps you can contact the city about improved crossing capabilities at a busy intersection.

Bernadette Soubirous

January 7, 1844–April 16, 1879

We all know the story of how Mary appeared to Bernadette, a simple girl of thirteen, at Lourdes. But what sometimes gets lost in the story is Bernadette's strong faith. Her statements were challenged over and over again by learned Church officials and local authorities, who attempted to catch her in lies and contradictions. With unfailing simplicity and calm, Bernadette shared what had happened—nothing more and nothing less.

Who doesn't embellish a good story a little bit? Did anyone ever really walk twenty miles to school, each way, in a snowstorm? It can be tempting to do some self-aggrandizement, to inflate our own importance to the well-being of our family, our parish, or our employer. Yet, like Bernadette, we are all only vessels for God's work in the world. May we, as Bernadette did, respond to the profound gifts we are given with humility, modesty, and clarity.

Inspiration

From this moment on, anything concerning me is no longer of any interest to me. I must belong entirely to God and God alone. Never to myself. (St. Bernadette Soubirous)

Challenge

Do a good work for a family member or a friend in secret. Don't tell anyone but God.

Zdenka Cecilia Schelingova

December 24, 1916–July 31, 1955

Zdenka, a nun, paid a great physical price for attempting to help six priests and seminarians, who were prisoners, escape from a hospital. The state police in what was Czechoslovakia tortured her at the time of her arrest and during the three years she was in prison. She was released because of a tumor, and initially neither her motherhouse nor the local hospital would take her in.

Ultimately, a friend helped her find a place at a hospital in another town, where she died shortly thereafter. Fifteen years after her death, a court found that Zdenka had been falsely accused. Imagine the betrayal Zdenka must have felt when neither the hospital where she had worked nor her own motherhouse would help her in her hour of great need. People will let us down. We will let others down. We can't let those betrayals embitter us. Rather, we must look to the One who will always be there for us, and have faith he will provide.

 Inspiration

Put away from you all bitterness and wrath and anger and wrangling and slander, together with all malice, and be kind to one another, tender-hearted, forgiving one another, as God in Christ has forgiven you. (Ephesians 4:31–32)

 Challenge

Forgive someone who refused to help you when you most needed assistance. Pray that you or someone else will aid the person in a time of need.

Marie-Anne Blondin

April 18, 1809–January 2, 1890

Some might remember Marie-Anne as an educational visionary. Illiterate into her adulthood, she successfully advocated for a new congregation that would educate boys and girls together. Until that time, the genders had to be taught separately, which meant many parishes in her area of Quebec had no schools at all. However, we remember her as well for what happened next. When a new chaplain was named for the community just a few years later, she did not get along with him, and he orchestrated her removal. For her final thirty-two years, Marie-Anne worked in the laundry room and other low-level positions and accepted it with grace, despite the sisters' repeated efforts to restore her as superior.

Other than accepting her new role, Marie-Anne's only option was to leave her community, and she chose not to do that. Sometimes, staying in an unjust situation without complaint or whining is a ministry in and of itself.

🖎 Inspiration

Do not worry about anything, but in everything by prayer and supplication with thanksgiving let your requests be made known to God. And the peace of God, which surpasses all understanding, will guard your hearts and your minds in Christ Jesus. (Philippians 4:6–7)

🖎 Challenge

What in your life are you powerless to change? Ask God to help you learn to accept it—or, if the situation can be changed, that you have the fortitude to do so.

Savina Petrilli

August 29, 1851–April 18, 1923

It was perhaps natural that Savina would be attracted to the example of St. Catherine of Siena. After all, Savina grew up in Siena, and when she was young, she read a biography of the great saint. Her devotion was cemented when at the age of eighteen she met Pope Pius IX, who suggested she walk in Catherine's footsteps. Savina went on to found the Congregation of the Poor Sisters of St. Catherine of Siena, dedicated to helping the poor. The congregation today works in seven countries. At Savina's beatification in 2003, Pope John Paul II said her heritage "represents a providential 'talent' to be fruitfully expended in the Church and for the world."

God is so good. Sometimes, we don't get his desires for us the first time around. Or we're just not clear what we're to do next. As Savina found, God keeps looking for opportunities to light his path for us.

✒ Inspiration

Being Sisters of the Poor involves the commitment to never abandon those poor whom God gives us as brothers and sisters. (Blessed Savina Petrilli)

✒ Challenge

Where are you seeking clarity in your spiritual life? Consider spending time in silence listening to God's call.

Agnes of Montepulciano

1268–1317

Agnes had a special spirituality from an early age. She joined a monastery when she was nine and became an abbess when she was only fifteen. Later, she founded a larger Dominican monastery. Agnes was known as a peacemaker both within her community and in the city of Montepulciano. It's also said that in her ecstasies, she held the baby Jesus and received Holy Communion from an angel.

God touches us in different ways. For some of us, it's through visions. For others, it's through quiet contemplation. For still others, it's through our faith community. At any age, there is no one way, no single "better" way, to find Jesus.

Inspiration

Indeed, the word of God is living and active, sharper than any two-edged sword, piercing until it divides soul from spirit, joints from marrow; it is able to judge the thoughts and intentions of the heart. (Hebrews 4:12)

Challenge

How have the ways in which God reaches your soul changed since you were a teenager? In what ways is he trying to touch you today that you don't recognize? Perhaps when you were younger, you found him in action and today, he comes to you in community or contemplation. Pray for the faith to accept that touch however it is delivered.

Osanna of Cattaro (Catherine Cosie)

November 25, 1493–April 27, 1565

Before she was a teenager, Osanna, who was baptized as a Greek Orthodox, had been visited by Christ both as a baby and on the cross. She felt a tug at her soul to leave her village to go to Cattaro, and her parents eventually agreed to let her take a servant's position with a Catholic woman there. It was in Cattaro that Osanna chose to convert and, when she was twenty, became an anchoress. Osanna was gifted with more visions and also devoted herself to contemplation, to the point that she gathered enough of a following that she was considered the leader of a convent, even though she never entered it.

Osanna's story shows that we can lead from the quiet places as well as the public ones. You don't have to be prominent to affect the spiritual journey of others or to grow in your relationship with Christ.

 Inspiration

Now there was a great wind, so strong that it was splitting mountains and breaking rocks in pieces before the LORD, but the LORD was not in the wind; and after the wind an earthquake, but the LORD was not in the earthquake; and after the earthquake a fire, but the LORD was not in the fire; and after the fire a sound of sheer silence. (1 Kings 19:11–12)

Challenge

When you are tempted to speak up today, pray and listen instead. See where the discussion goes and where Christ wants to lead you.

Maria Gabriella Sagheddu

1914–April 23, 1939

Maria Gabriella wasn't much for going to church when she was growing up in Italy. When she reached the age of eighteen, however, people noticed a change in her attitudes and behaviors. She became involved with Catholic Action, a youth movement, and then entered a Trappist monastery a couple years later. There, due to the abbess's passion for Christian unity and the catechesis work Maria Gabriella had done with Catholic Action, she chose to offer her life to the cause. She died of tuberculosis less than two years later.

You have to think that there were times Maria Gabriella's family was aggravated by her lack of interest in the faith and her occasional rebelliousness. But their example helped Christ keep a place in her heart and soul that then grew larger and larger. Young people are always watching us and our actions, whether we (or they) realize it or not.

Inspiration

I feel the Lord is calling me. I feel urged, even when I don't want to think about it. (Blessed Maria Gabriella Sagheddu)

Challenge

Is there a young person in your life who you know is good at the core, but who chafes at working on his or her faith life? Think of how you can help in less invasive ways, perhaps volunteering together or watching a faith-based film together. Talk about the experience afterward.

Marie de l'Incarnation (Marie Guyart)

October 28, 1599–April 30, 1672

Parts of Marie's story are difficult. After her husband died, she had a vision that resulted in her decision several years later to become an Ursuline nun. She left her eleven-year-old son in her sister's care. Her sister tried to use the situation to keep Marie in France eight years later when she felt called to go to Canada as a missionary, but her son encouraged her to go. She spent the next thirty-nine years ministering to the indigenous people and translating Scripture, the Catholic catechism, and other works into several Native American languages. She and her son, who became a priest, had an active correspondence, but it does not appear that they saw each other again.

Jesus's directive to leave your world behind and follow him sounds good in theory—until we realize that sometimes that involves leaving behind the people we love. It is difficult to understand why Christ would call a mother to leave her only child and move thousands of miles away. But eventually, both Marie and her son came to accept her accepted call to missionary work.

Inspiration

O my great God, you can do all things and I can do nothing! If you wish to help me, I am ready. I promise to obey you! Accomplish your most adorable will in me and by me. (Blessed Marie de l'Incarnation)

Challenge

What is God asking you to do that you really, truly do not want to do? Pray for the strength to say yes.

Mary Euphrasia Pelletier

July 31, 1796–April 24, 1868

Politics can permeate even religious institutions. Mary Euphrasia, a French nun, had been with the same order for about twenty years, including time as a superior, when she took a stand to establish a more centralized system for the order to share resources and women religious. As a result of the resistance she faced, Mary Euphrasia left her order to found the Congregation of Our Lady of Charity of the Good Shepherd. Today, the Good Shepherd Sisters have a presence in more than sixty countries.

God often calls us to get out of our comfort zone, out of the same old routine. And while that can be a little disconcerting, we often see in retrospect that change, whether we embrace it or not, can improve our spiritual lives and those of others.

Inspiration

It is human to fail, but angelic to rise again. (St. Mary Euphrasia Pelletier)

Challenge

Where is God gently nudging you into a situation where you believe you will fail? Chat with your pastor or spiritual director or prayer group about your fears. Talk about the worst thing that will happen if you are correct. Will anyone's life or salvation be in danger?

Maria of St. Joseph (Laura Alvarado Cardozo)

April 25, 1875–April 2, 1967

The first Venezuelan to be beatified had a passion for service. Maria began working with children at an early age by inviting them into her home for religious instruction. She helped to found a congregation of nuns, and through that group, founded more than three dozen homes to help abandoned children and the elderly. Pope John Paul II said at Maria's beatification Mass in 1995:"The testimony of this simple woman of our time invites everyone…to live the Gospel faithfully."

Maria's example reminds us that we can't figure that other people or organizations will take care of the needs of the dispossessed and the unwanted. As Catholics, we are called to love our neighbors as ourselves, and to be part of those who help our less fortunate sisters and brothers.

Inspiration

Those rejected by everyone are ours; those who no one wants to receive are ours. (Blessed Maria of St. Joseph)

Challenge

Who are those that no one wants to receive today? Pedophiles? Rapists? Murderers? Pray for them, that they might come to terms with their actions and rediscover God's love as they do penance and work toward rehabilitation and forgiveness.

Maria Schininà

April 10, 1844–June 11, 1910

It took a while for Maria to realize her vocation. Her family was wealthy, and she enjoyed the clothes and the social whirl that went along with her position. Her father died when she was twenty-one, and she began to think less about this world and more about God and the next. Nine years later, the last of her siblings married, and Maria decided it was time to do something personally about the poor in her neighborhood. She discarded her finery and began ministering to those in need, ultimately founding the Sisters of the Sacred Heart of Jesus of Ragusa.

Sometimes we get impatient with our children, other family members, or friends. Why are they dining out at fine restaurants when there are children starving in Africa? Why are they buying another pair of black pumps when people don't have shoes in Asia? We never know how God is working in their souls. All we can do is provide a Christlike example.

Inspiration

For the love of money is a root of all kinds of evil, and in their eagerness to be rich some have wandered away from the faith and pierced themselves with many pains. (1 Timothy 6:10)

Challenge

Look at ways that you may be spending money needlessly. Is there a place in your budget to put aside a few extra dollars each month to help a worthwhile charity or someone in need?

Zita of Lucca

Circa 1218–April 27, 1272

When she was just twelve, Zita went to work as a domestic for the Fatinelli family. No matter how much the family or her fellow servants mistreated her, Zita continued to treat all those she encountered with love, courtesy, and respect. Ultimately, she became the household's head servant. Despite the opportunity for revenge that this promotion offered, she treated all as brothers and sisters of Christ.

Ah, sweet revenge. It's so tempting to show those who have been unkind to us just how it feels when we get the chance. It's tempting, but it's not Christlike. The better angels inside us would counsel us to treat everyone as Christ and Zita did, ignoring that opportunity for payback time.

Inspiration

But I say to you that listen, Love your enemies, do good to those who hate you, bless those who curse you, pray for those who abuse you. If anyone strikes you on the cheek, offer the other also; and from anyone who takes away your coat do not withhold even your shirt. (Luke 6:27–29)

Challenge

Spend the day loving God and loving those who challenge you. Don't waste a second wondering what you'll get out of it.

Gianna Beretta Molla

October 4, 1922–April 28, 1962

A pediatrician, mother of three, and wife, Gianna lived a life chock-full of service and love. Her great test came when, two months pregnant, she learned she had a uterine tumor. She chose the treatment option that offered her baby the best chance for life but posed risks to Gianna. She was only thirty-nine when she died a few days after her daughter's healthy birth.

Mothers today face all sorts of challenges, from managing finances so there's food on the table to carting children to play dates and sporting events. It seems there's just never enough time for anything, including our children's formation. Sometimes, we forget that we inform our children's faith by our actions when we do our jobs or our volunteer work or our family service, no matter how difficult, with the love of Christ in our hearts.

Inspiration

The secret of happiness is to live moment by moment and to thank God for all that he, in his goodness, sends to us day after day. (St. Gianna Beretta Molla)

Challenge

Write down the complaints you air in front of your children today. Then, pray for God's help in keeping your attitude positive going forward. If you don't have children in the house, try this practice by using the complaints you air to friends or family members.

Catherine of Siena

March 25, 1347–April 29, 1380

Catherine of Siena, a Doctor of the Church, is regarded as one of the most influential women in Catholic history. Not only was she a mystic, experiencing the stigmata and what she called a mystical marriage with Christ, but she also worked in the world, nursing the poor and the sick. Though she had no formal education, her letters to political and Church leaders were persuasive, and she was considered an outstanding philosopher and theologian. She battled and consulted with popes by turns, but Catherine always was faithful to the Church's teachings.

Catherine's example inspires us to stop saying "I can't" to ourselves. She didn't let the fact that she was a woman who lacked education or membership in a religious order (she was a Dominican tertiary) stand in the way of ministering to the needy or gaining public attention for her thoughts and opinions.

Inspiration

Start being brave about everything, driving out darkness and spreading light as well. Don't look at your weakness, but realize that in Christ crucified you can do everything. (St. Catherine of Siena)

Challenge

Consider Catherine's advice. If you can't start by being brave about everything, identify one thing. Maybe it's being a lector at Mass. Maybe it's helping out at a women's shelter. Maybe it's running for City Council. Resolve to spread the Light.

Mary Hermina of Jesus (Irma Grivot)

April 28, 1866–July 9, 1900

Mary, who had spent ten years as a teacher before beginning her pre-novitiate, dreamed of leaving France for missionary work abroad. But the leaders at the Franciscan Missionaries of Mary weren't sure, given her delicate health. Finally, she was approved and left for China with six other sisters to help the ailing poor and orphans. The Boxer Rebellion broke out a little more than a year after they arrived, and all the sisters were killed. Mary is among the Martyrs of China canonized by Pope John Paul II.

Mary fought for her dream despite the odds. She was doing what she believed she was meant to do—talk about Jesus with people who hadn't met him yet—even as her journey ended. Let us also not be afraid to push hard when well-meaning people stand in the way of what we believe God wants us to do.

Inspiration

Adoration of the Blessed Sacrament is half my life. The other half consists in loving Jesus and winning souls for him. (St. Mary Hermina of Jesus)

Challenge

What would you like to be doing when you're called to heaven? What is stopping you from doing it now?

Marie-Leonie Paradis

May 12, 1840–May 3, 1912

Marie-Leonie identified a need and met it. She entered the Holy Cross congregation in Quebec shortly before her fourteenth birthday and spent several years as a teacher in Montreal, New York, and Indiana. It was when she was sent to Memramcook, New Brunswick, to oversee the support staff at St. Joseph's College that Marie-Leonie came to see that a new order was needed to help with domestic duties for Holy Cross seminary students and priests. The Little Sisters of the Holy Family continue to supply this support today in Canada, the United States, Honduras, and Guatemala.

Some ministries are extremely visible: Marching for the unborn. Proclaiming the word at Mass. And some are more behind the scenes, though no less valuable, such as assisting priests and seminarians. We learn from Marie-Leonie's insight in determining her brothers' in Christ need for help and offering it.

Inspiration

Whatever your task, put yourselves into it, as done for the Lord and not for your masters, since you know that from the Lord you will receive the inheritance as your reward; you serve the Lord Christ. (Colossians 3:23–24)

Challenge

What unglamorous need in your neighborhood, parish, or other community is going unmet simply because it hasn't been identified as an opportunity for ministry? What can you do to help?

Wiborada

Died 926

Wiborada was the first woman to be formally canonized in 1047 by Pope Clement II. At the time, the pope commented that that God had been aware of her holiness for a hundred years before the Church acknowledged it. Initially, Wiborada worked as a bookbinder at her monastery in what is now Switzerland, then after a time of trouble within the monastery, she became an anchoress. Legend has it that she predicted an invasion of the area surrounding the church, but she chose to stay and pray. When the warriors arrived, they found Wiborada in her cell praying and struck her in the head with a hatchet.

When we are in a threatening situation, usually our first instinct is to run. Wiborada's example reminds us that we need to remember our duty to others, and trust in the Lord.

Inspiration

When reviled, we bless; when persecuted, we endure; when slandered, we speak kindly. We have become like the rubbish of the world, the dregs of all things, to this very day. (1 Corinthians 4:12–13)

Challenge

What situation are you tempted to run away from or avoid? Pray for the strength to stay and to face your perceived persecutors.

Maura of Antinoe

Died circa 286

Twenty days. That's how long Maura had been married to Timothy, a lector, when she was called by the authorities to help convince him to denounce his faith when he refused to turn over sacred books. Instead, with Timothy's encouragement, Maura professed her own belief in Christ and said to her husband, "I am prepared to die with you." Both were martyred.

Whether we have been married for days or decades, spouses can provide incomparable support on our spiritual journey. The example of Maura and Timothy is a strong testimony to the bonds created by a loving relationship.

✒ Inspiration

[Love] bears all things, believes all things, hopes all things, endures all things.

Love never ends. But as for prophecies, they will come to an end; as for tongues, they will cease; as for knowledge, it will come to an end. (1 Corinthians 13:7–8)

✒ Challenge

Think of a time when the support of your spouse or other significant person helped you to act in a Christlike manner when you were in a challenging situation. Perhaps it was the person's presence during a tense time, or perhaps it was during a time of overwhelming sadness or grief. Share your thoughts about the experience with the other person, and say thank you.

Blessed Caterina Cittadini

September 28, 1801–May 5, 1857

Caterina and her sister, Giuditta, two years younger, shared joy and sorrow on their journey together. They ended up in a convent orphanage when Caterina was seven years old, and their faith formation began thanks to the prior. They then went on to live with cousins who were priests, until the young women entered the Congregation of Ursuline Sisters, Caterina working as a teacher, Giuditta as the head of a boarding school for girls. Between 1840 and 1841, Caterina's life was rattled by her own illness and the deaths of Giuditta, one of their cousin priests, and their beloved former prior. In addition, the rules she had written for the Ursuline Institute were rejected. The revised version gained her bishop's approval seven months after she died.

Like Caterina and Giuditta, not all of us had ideal childhoods. But God has a way of putting people in our paths, be they siblings, other relatives, or trusted teachers, to help us survive the bad times and celebrate the good ones.

❧ Inspiration

Jesus said, "Let the little children come to me, and do not stop them; for it is to such as these that the kingdom of heaven belongs." (Matthew 19:14)

❧ Challenge

Write a thank-you note to the relative, friend, or teacher who was a non-parental influence in childhood. If the person has already died, spend some time in prayer thanking him or her.

Judith of Prussia (Jutta)

Died May 12, 1260

It was a good life, but something was missing. Judith married a nobleman who initially was less than pleased with her piety but who grew to value and appreciate her. He died on a Holy Land pilgrimage. Judith cared for their children until they were grown, then entered the Third Order of St. Francis. She gave up the trappings of her class, and eventually moved away and lived as a hermit, praying for others and caring for the Christians and non-Christians alike who came to see her.

While there are days all of us might like to become hermits, the option is not realistic for most of us. But are we where we're supposed to be in our daily lives? A stay-at-home mom? A busy, single, professional woman? A caregiver for our parents? Is there something more we should be doing? Judith's example inspires us to live in the present but be open to what God may have planned for our future.

☙ Inspiration

Incline your ear to me;
  rescue me speedily.
Be a rock of refuge for me,
  a strong fortress to save me.

You are indeed my rock and my fortress;
  for your name's sake lead me and guide me. (Psalm 31:2–3)

☙ Challenge

What is your secret spiritual dream? Pray for guidance on how to incorporate parts of that dream into your life, today or in the future.

Anna Rosa Gattorno

October 14, 1831–May 6, 1900

In the space of little more than six years, Rosa married, had three children, one of whom was left deaf and mute after an illness. She also suffered the loss of her husband and the death of a child. But rather than turn her face from God, she turned her life over to him, first becoming a Franciscan tertiary and then founding her own order in 1866. When she died, 3,500 sisters were serving the poor and sick through schools, nursing care, safe housing, and more.

"Where's the God in that?" some of us ask when bad things happen to us, when we or those we love experience illness or injury or disappointment. Rather than complaining, if we are brave enough to look, we are likely to find God right by our side, helping us through the suffering.

Inspiration
To live for God, to die for him, and to spend life for love. (Blessed Anna Rosa Gattorno)

Challenge
What trouble in your life presents the biggest roadblock between you and a closer relationship with Christ? Rather than asking questions and demanding answers, simply sit with the situation in prayer today. Listen to how Jesus loves you and wishes to heal you.

Rosa Venerini

February 9, 1656–May 7, 1728

Rosa entered a monastery when she was twenty, but after only a few months, she returned home to care for her father until he died. Later, she began gathering girls and women into the home to pray the rosary together. Eventually, with the support of the Church and two friends, Rose opened what would become Italy's first public school for girls and what would lead to opening more than forty facilities before her death. When Pope Clement XI visited one of her schools in 1716, he said, "Lady Rosa, you do what we cannot do, we thank you because these schools sanctify Rome."

Many women today are part of what is called the "sandwich generation"—caring for both their own parents and for their children. It can be a heavy load to bear, especially since this service can mean we must put aside our own hopes and dreams. God's grace in the form of patience, faith, and love helps us shoulder these responsibilities with a smile.

✒ Inspiration

Let each of you look not only to your own interests, but to the interests of others. (Philippians 2:4)

✒ Challenge

Offer some form of service to a parent, older relative, or friend today, whether it's writing a note, running an errand, taking time for a visit, or helping with home-based care.

Magdalene of Canossa

March 1, 1774–April 10, 1835

Until she was nearly thirty, Magdalene's life was one of fits and starts. Her father died when she was five, and her mother remarried and moved the family when Magdalene was about seven. She joined two different monasteries before she was twenty, only to return home each time. Then, when she was thirty-four, she founded a shelter for girls in the poorest district of Verona. Her community, the Congregation of the Daughters of Charity, Servants of the Poor, continues its work today.

Helping the poor and the helpless are among the greatest ways we can reflect Christ in our society. Figuring out how can be the most difficult part. Do we donate money to an advocacy group? Do we donate time helping at a homeless shelter or food pantry? Or do we donate our talent at organizing or speaking to a more public audience? As Magdalene found, sometimes we have to spend time in the desert before we discern our calling.

Inspiration

Do not be frightened at seeing the greatness of the aim proposed…those who love do not feel the burden. (St. Magdalene of Canossa)

Challenge

How can you embrace a spirit of poverty in your own life? Perhaps it's by adopting a practice of simplicity, making do with less. Consider ways this might change your life.

Ulrika Nisch (Franziska Nisch)

September 18, 1882–May 8, 1913

Ulrika was working as a nanny in Switzerland, far from her less than engaged German family, when she developed a life-threatening skin infection. It was while she was in the hospital that she first met the Sisters of the Holy Cross. Their kindness and care for her convinced her that becoming a nun was what she was meant to do. Despite her lack of a dowry, she was accepted and spent much time working in the kitchen and enduring abuse from other sisters without complaint. She is regarded as a mystic and a visionary.

Turning the other cheek is difficult in any circumstance, but it would seem to be even harder in a house of supposedly like-minded women religious. Ulrika's example inspires us not to become defensive or argumentative when met with negativity or cruelty, but instead to respond with love.

✺ Inspiration

It will be lovely one day when we have ended our suffering and are together in heaven. (Blessed Ulrika Nisch)

✺ Challenge

Identify someone who really gets under your skin—and seems to delight in doing so. The next time you encounter him or her, take a deep breath and say a brief prayer before you speak. You'll be surprised how much waiting those few seconds can change your response.

Maria Domenica Brun Barbantini

January 17, 1789–May 22, 1868

It would have been so easy for Maria to become hardened and embittered. Her husband died just six months after their marriage, leaving her to raise their son alone. As he grew, Maria also began helping the poor and with other women established the Pious Union of the Sisters of Charity. But then, when he was eight, her son became ill and died. While she grieved her losses, she realized what God's plan for her was and founded the Camillian Sisters, who continue today to minister to the sick in homes, hospitals, and elsewhere.

Maria's strength was amazing. If you've lost a child or a spouse, you know that it is a pain like no other. Her example reminds us that God can use our brokenness to do good in the world even as he helps us heal.

Inspiration

For this child I prayed; and the LORD has granted me the petition that I made to him. Therefore I have lent him to the LORD; as long as he lives, he is given to the LORD. (1 Samuel 1:27–28)

Challenge

Offer to accompany a friend to her child's, husband's, or parents' grave on the anniversary of his or her death. Listen to her stories. Look at her pictures. Pray together.

Sára Salkaházi

May 11, 1899–December 27, 1944

Sára had made hard choices before. She'd changed professions from teacher to bookbinder to writer to woman religious. She'd broken off an engagement. With the Sisters of Social Service, she had helped to save more than one thousand lives during World War II. It's no surprise, then, the choice she made on the day she died came quickly. She arrived at her hostel to find Nazis arresting people. Sára identified herself as the person in charge of the house. Hours later, she and five others were stripped and shot on the banks of the Danube River.

We seldom have our faith or ethics tested in the blink of an eye. Perhaps that's not a blessing. Perhaps living and acting in the moment and being present allows us to bring our best selves to God instead of taking the time to second-guess ourselves—and him.

Inspiration

Let your will be done in me and through me. No matter how hard it might be, I want to love your will! (Blessed Sára Salkaházi)

Challenge

Try to spend a morning or an afternoon saying "yes" to all the opportunities God presents you with. Don't think about it; just say yes. Write about how you feel at the end of the day.

Humility (Rosanna Negusanti)

Circa 1226–May 22, 1310

Humility experienced many losses in her young life. Her father died when she was fifteen; she married the following year, and in the next nine years, the couple lost two children in infancy, and her husband suffered a life-threatening illness. After contemplation and prayer, they both agreed to enter a nearby double monastery, where the woman who had been known as Rosanna took the name Humility. She went on to found two convents.

It's typical to feel anger and resentment when people we love die or become gravely ill. Eventually, however, we must trust in God and pick up our cross and take it where he leads us.

✒ Inspiration

He heals the brokenhearted,
  and binds up their wounds.
He determines the number of the stars;
  he gives to all of them their names. (Psalm 147:3–4)

✒ Challenge

Consider the virtues that most describe you, or those to which you most aspire. In the same way that Rosanna took the religious name Humility, what name would you choose for yourself? If you took a saint's name when you were confirmed, do you remember why you selected that woman? Refresh your knowledge of her virtues and struggles.

Maria Domenica Mazzarello

May 9, 1837–May 14, 1881

Maria was twenty-seven when she met John Bosco, who already was well known for his work with boys. The work Maria and a friend were already doing to teach girls about God, along with dressmaking, became the jumping-off point for the Salesian Sisters. Maria took her vows at age thirty-five, and also decided at that point that she and the other sisters in the order needed to learn to read and write.

It's never too late to learn a skill, whether it's a foreign language, using a smart phone, or public speaking. From Maria, we learn that with God's help, we can master whatever tools we need to do his work.

Inspiration

You must compare your heart to a garden. If we cultivate it well, it will yield good fruit. If we don't keep an eye on it and tend it a little every day, [our garden] will be overrun with weeds, true? Therefore, take courage. (St. Maria Domenica Mazzarello)

Challenge

Think about your favorite ministry or service. Is there a course you could take or some tutoring that would help you do it more effectively or more easily? Consider offering to trade something you do well in exchange for this learning experience.

Julian of Norwich

November 8, 1342–circa 1416

Never formally beatified in our Church, Julian still is often called blessed and is considered among the most important of the Christian mystics due to her book *Revelations of Divine Love*. It is based on a single experience she had of Christ's suffering as she was contemplating the crucifix. We know little else about Julian, other than that she was an anchoress who lived in Norwich, England.

Julian's book is remarkable for much beyond its best-known line: "All shall be well, and all shall be well, and all manner of thing shall be well." She calls God both our Father and Mother, and she says we sin not because we are evil but because we are ignorant, and that those sins bring us to self-knowledge and hence to God. Her views provide much to contemplate and meditate on nearly six hundred years after her death.

✒ Inspiration

With creation we started but the love with which he created us was in him from the very beginning, and in this love is our beginning. And all this we shall see it in God eternally. (Blessed Julian of Norwich)

✒ Challenge

What do you fear shall not be well—in your own life or in the world? God's in charge. He's all-powerful. Pray for the confidence to let him take care of things.

Dymphna of Gheel

Circa 620–640

Dymphna looked like her mother—too much like her mother, it turned out. According to the legend, when her mother died, Dymphna's father's grief overtook him and he became determined that she would be his wife. A priest went with Dymphna to Belgium, but the father and his men followed. Both were beheaded, Dymphna by her own father.

We know so little about mental illness and how it begins. However, we do know that even the seemingly most rational of people can have tunnel vision when it comes to their children and expect too much from them—perfect grades, perfect behavior, perfect love. God doesn't expect us to be perfect. How can we expect perfection from those who love us most?

Inspiration

As God's chosen ones, holy and beloved, clothe yourselves with compassion, kindness, humility, meekness, and patience. Bear with one another and, if anyone has a complaint against another, forgive each other; just as the Lord has forgiven you, so you also must forgive. (Colossians 3:12–13)

Challenge

Spend some quality time with a child. Refrain from criticism; focus on the gift that child is to your life. If he or she doesn't dance as well or read as well or swim as well as you did at that age, so what?

Marie-Céline of the Presentation (Jeanne-Germaine Castang)

May 23, 1878–May 30, 1897

Marie-Céline was left with a permanent limp after a bout with polio when she was four. She also developed tuberculosis, most likely when she was fourteen and caring for her ailing brother after her mother's death. Marie-Céline was taken in by the Sisters of Nazareth when her father and remaining siblings moved away. She had a burning desire to become a woman religious but was rejected by two orders before a community not far from where she was living agreed to accept her. Her health exhausted, Marie-Céline died less than a year later, just after her nineteenth birthday, taking her final vows on her deathbed.

Marie-Céline's life was beset with struggle. Yet she kept her focus on God and growing closer to him. May we do the same amid our day-to-day challenges and disappointments.

Inspiration

I am determined to be a violet of humility, a rose of charity, and a lily of purity for Jesus. (Blessed Marie-Céline of the Presentation)

Challenge

What do you have, or have you had, a burning desire to do in your life? Where do you see God's hand in fulfilling this desire?

Giulia Salzano

October 13, 1846–May 17, 1929

Giulia spent twenty-five years as a schoolteacher and then retired at age forty-four due to health issues. But the next stage of her life would prove to have a profound impact around the world. She focused her energies on religious education for children and, when she was almost fifty, founded the Congregation of the Catechetical Sisters of the Sacred Heart. This work, and her devotion to Mary and the Sacred Heart of Jesus, earned her the title of "prophetess of the new evangelization."

We often feel at loose ends when a particular stage of our life ends—when we finish high school or college, when our children are grown and out of the house, when our spouse leaves due to death or divorce, when we move, when our employment changes. It can feel that we've lost part of ourselves. Giulia's example shows us God's future plans for us can be even more challenging and fulfilling than our previous work.

⚘ Inspiration

While I have any life left in me, I will continue to teach the catechism. And then, I assure you, I would be very happy to die teaching the catechism. (St. Giulia Salzano)

⚘ Challenge

Is a stage of your life ending? Talk with a friend or spiritual adviser about how you can use your skills to God's glory during this period of change and transition.

Maria Crescencia Perez

August 17, 1897–May 20, 1932

Children were the focus of Maria's ministry. She took her final vows with the Daughters of Our Lady of the Orchard when she was twenty-one and went to work at a school. Later, she ministered to children hospitalized with tuberculosis. She then became ill herself. In Argentina, she is known for her simple spirit and humility, similar to that of the saint she most admired, Thérèse of Lisieux.

Our ministry doesn't have to be loud or public to be effective. Just by being herself—sweet and pleasant—Maria had a positive effect on the young people she met. We don't have to be overachievers or even be as good as other people we know. We just have to be ourselves, and God will take care of the rest.

✒ Inspiration

Do not be conformed to this world, but be transformed by the renewing of your minds, so that you may discern what is the will of God—what is good and acceptable and perfect. (Romans 12:2)

✒ Challenge

Ask three family members or friends to tell you which traits they most admire in you. Keep the list in mind the next time you feel inadequate or ill-equipped to do what God has asked of you.

Maria Bernarda (Verena Bütler)

May 28, 1848–May 19, 1924

Maria Bernarda had some false starts in her life. She fell in love and became engaged, then ended it to pursue the religious life. She entered a convent when she was eighteen, then quickly withdrew. She entered a Franciscan monastery several months later. After many years, Maria thought about establishing a missionary foundation tied to her Swiss home, but instead found herself called to the Franciscan Missionary Sisters of Mary Help of Sinners, where she faced a challenging internal political situation. Through it all, her faith sustained her.

Our plans for ourselves at times are at odds with what God has in mind. Even when we refuse to listen and proceed with unevenly yoked marriages or career or ministry plans that please us in the moment, God has a way of getting us back on the track he desires—and of comforting us in our disappointment.

✒ Inspiration

My guide, my star, is the Gospel. (St. Maria Bernarda)

✒ Challenge

Think about a time when you thought you knew better than God what you needed in your life. Write down your thoughts about how he got you back on track and how your faith grew from the experience.

Joaquina de Vedruna

April 16, 1783–August 28, 1854

It's no wonder Joaquina is a patron saint for widows. When she was thirty-three, her husband died, leaving her with nine children. She took care of raising the children (she came from a noble family) but also began working with young women and sick people. Ten years later, she and other women founded the Institute of the Carmelite sisters of Charity.

Joaquina and her husband had been married for seventeen years when he died. It is incredibly difficult to go from being "us" to being "me" when your spouse dies or there is a divorce. We learn from Joaquina of the importance of keeping ourselves occupied with God's work when the sorrow of the situation threatens to overcome us.

Inspiration

We must not give in to weariness: we must spend every minute in loving God. God alone, the maker of heaven and earth, must be our rest and our consolation. The love of God is the only thing we can possess forever: everything else will pass away. (St. Joaquina de Vedruna)

Challenge

If you are a widow or have experienced divorce, pray for the soul of the departed one. If you have a friend in that situation, say a prayer for her healing and offer a listening ear, no matter how long it has been for her.

Melangell (Monacella)

Died 590

Melangell left her Irish home at an early age to become a hermit in Wales. After years by herself, a hunting party encountered her. The hare they had been pursuing had found safety in the robes of the praying Melangell, and the hounds refused to chase their prey further. As a result, the prince in charge of the hunt gave her land for an abbey. Other women then joined her there, and Melangell became abbess of the small community. A shrine to her remains at the church on the site today, along with a retreat center.

Think of the way Melangell's heart must have been beating as the hunting party descended. Yet she remained focused on her prayer. It's a good reminder to us that when we talk with God, we can turn down the volume on the outside world and listen, no matter what is going on out there.

✒ Inspiration

So if you have been raised with Christ, seek the things that are above, where Christ is, seated at the right hand of God. (Colossians 3:1)

✒ Challenge

Are you feeling easily distracted when you pray? Try using a different room in your home, or take some time to pray at your parish or an outdoor retreat.

Rita of Cascia
1381–May 22, 1457

Rita endured eighteen years of infidelity and physical abuse with her husband, Paolo. When he was stabbed to death by the member of a rival family, her sons vowed revenge. She prayed that this might not happen, and both young men died of natural causes in the following year. While Rita's initial efforts to join an Augustinian monastery in Cascia were rejected because she was a widow, she eventually was accepted and spent more than forty years there. It is said that due to her devotion to Christ's passion, she received a mark on her head from his crown of thorns.

In today's world, we might scoff at Rita for staying with someone who was so violent and uncaring. Yet no one other than the couple ever really knows what goes on inside a marriage. Sometimes, people stay out of fear; sometimes, out of perceived obligation; sometimes, out of a sincere belief that the situation is where God wants them.

Inspiration
O loving Jesus, increase my patience according as my sufferings increase. (St. Rita of Cascia)

Challenge
Rita is the patron saint of desperate causes. Spend some time praying to her regarding a situation of your own, or of someone you're concerned about.

Jeanne-Antide Thouret

November 27, 1765–August 24, 1826

Some of our faith struggles are lived in public, and Jeanne definitely had that experience. She joined the Sisters of Charity of St. Vincent de Paul when she was twenty-two. During the French Revolution, she was told by government authorities to return to a secular life at home. When she refused, she was badly beaten. Government repression later sent her to Switzerland, then on to Germany, then back to Switzerland (where she founded the Institute of the Daughters of St. Vincent de Paul), and eventually back to France. However, internal Church affairs prevented her from being admitted to her order's motherhouse there. Jeanne moved on to Italy, where she continued to found convents.

Women tend to be averse to conflict. We want everyone to be happy, and sometimes that means we don't take a public stand, even on issues that are important to us. However, while it doesn't really matter whether we prepare our favorite dinner or that of a spouse or child, it is important that when it comes to matters of faith, we stand up for what we believe regardless of the consequences.

Inspiration

I would cross the oceans, I would go to any part of the world, if I knew this to be the will of God. (St. Jeanne-Antide Thouret)

Challenge

Examine your conscience. Where are you going along to get along instead of standing up for God? Pray for the strength to speak up.

Joanna

First century

Joanna is briefly mentioned in Luke's Gospel as the wife of Chuza, King Herod Antipas's steward, and as one of the women who found Christ's empty tomb on Easter morning, along with Mary Magdalene and Mary, the mother of James and John. Joanna is among the women who funded Jesus's ministry.

Women have been an integral part of our Church since the very beginning. We head committees, proclaim the word at Mass, serve as Extraordinary Ministers, and assist in so many other public and private ways. While Jesus didn't include any women among the Twelve, it is clear by his actions that he highly values women.

Inspiration

Strength and dignity are her clothing,
  and she laughs at the time to come.
She opens her mouth with wisdom,
  and the teaching of kindness is on her tongue.
She looks well to the ways of her household,
  and does not eat the bread of idleness. (Proverbs 31:25–27)

Challenge

What woman in your parish or your family most inspires your faith journey? Write her a note of thanks. If possible, do something nice for her, such as walking her dog or weeding her flower garden or inviting her out to a movie.

Magdalena de Pazzi

April 2, 1566–May 25, 1607

Magdalena's spiritual life was one of highs and lows, from raptures and ecstasies to time in what she called "the lion's den," a place of dryness. She is better known, however, for her writings, which followed the landmark Council of Trent by about twenty years. In her letters, she called for a renewal of the Church and of religious life.

The administration of our Church is ever changing, ever improving, and ever growing. It shapes our core beliefs, our dogma, our burning desire to live a life closer to Christ and to help others to do so. That means studying and understanding what our leaders say, and when we disagree, sharing our thoughts in a thoughtful, informed way. We are led by people, and people are imperfect, and part of our responsibility in the Body of Christ is to speak up on Church matters where appropriate.

Inspiration

Oh, grow in love a little; and come, in thirst, in zeal and in desire, so bring back these sheep (so to call them), these souls redeemed by the precious blood of the slain Lamb—and to reunite these members to their Head, Christ. (St. Magdalena de Pazzi)

Challenge

Pray for wisdom and grace for your pastor, bishop, or cardinal; consider sending him a card to let him know you are doing so.

Mariana de Jesús de Paredes

October 31, 1618–May 26, 1645

Mariana's initial intention was to enter a Dominican monastery. But as time went on, she realized that was not where God wanted her. Instead, she became a secular Franciscan and hermit at home, going out only to attend Mass or do service. It is said shortly before her death, she offered herself up as a sacrifice for the city of Quito, Ecuador, in the aftermath of earthquakes and epidemics. In his homily at her canonization, Pope Pius XII said, "May the world learn of the energies hidden in prayer and sacrifice."

Most of us today are overly busy, with our families, our jobs, our friends, our ministries. There's scarcely a moment to think. Mariana's example reminds us of the beauty of time alone with God and the importance of including that in our schedules.

Inspiration

Be still before the LORD, and wait patiently for him;
do not fret over those who prosper in their way,
over those who carry out evil devices. (Psalm 37:7)

Challenge

If possible, schedule a quiet day for yourself at a silent retreat (or create your own). If you can't get away, carve out a half hour of silence to spend listening to God.

Bona of Pisa

1156–circa 1207

When she was fourteen or so, she traveled from Pisa to the Jerusalem area, where her father was fighting in the Crusades. Bona was so devoted to Saint James the Apostle that she traveled the Santiago de Compostela nine or ten times, and she was among the official guides for the pilgrimage route. She died shortly after returning home after her last pilgrimage.

Oh, to be like Bona and to have made The Way! Think of the people she must have met and the experiences she must have had in Christ's name. Whether your travel takes you around the world or down the street to visit a neighbor, there's always an opportunity to learn and grow in faith.

Inspiration

The LORD will keep

> your going out and your coming in
>
> from this time on and forevermore. (Psalms 121:8)

Challenge

Why not be an armchair pilgrim? Read a book or go to a website or rent a movie about a pilgrimage if you can't make one yourself. Meditate on how you can put what the writer or actor learned to use in your own life. Or, if your lifestyle allows it, start planning a pilgrimage journey to Lourdes, Fatima, or another location your soul longs to see.

Ubaldesca Taccini

1136–May 28, 1206

Ubaldesca was concerned. She was baking bread when an angel appeared and said she should join the Sisters of St. John of Jerusalem convent. She protested that she had no dowry. The angel told her she had virtues, which were of greater need to the order than a dowry. And so she did as the angel asked. Later, when the nuns were in a situation where money was of concern to the order and its future, Ubaldesca began begging in Pisa on behalf of the congregation and those they served.

We can make all kinds of excuses for why we don't do as God desires, excuses far less flimsy than the lack of a dowry. Ubaldseca's example shows us that when it comes to doing God's will, there's always a way to make it happen.

Inspiration

Then he ordered the crowds to sit down on the grass. Taking the five loaves and the two fish, he looked up to heaven, and blessed and broke the loaves, and gave them to the disciples, and the disciples gave them to the crowds. (Matthew 14:19)

Challenge

Volunteer to help at a ministry table after Mass or for a community service in the coming week and ask for donations for foster parents, a sister parish, a work camp, or other programs.

Ursula Ledóchowska

April 17, 1865–May 29, 1939

Ursula had a quiet life as a teacher during her first twenty years as an Ursuline nun. Then she moved to Russia, where she and the others had to live secretly due to state sanctions against religious life. They were constantly under the surveillance by the secret police, but they still managed to work toward improved relations between Poland and Russia. She spent World War I in Scandinavia, and then after the war, she founded the Ursulines of the Agonizing Heart of Jesus (Grey Ursulines) and focused on religious education of the poor in Poland, Italy, France, and elsewhere.

Consider how difficult it would have been for a nun who had spent twenty years in her habit in public ministry to suddenly don civilian dress and continue her work subversively. We have the opportunity to emulate Ursula every day when we interact with neighbors, coworkers, and others who do not have an active faith life.

Inspiration

Holiness does not demand anything great, beyond the ability of the person. It depends on God's love; every daily act can be transformed into an act of love. (St. Ursula Ledóchowska)

Challenge

Consider your interactions today with a non-churchgoing family member, friend, or colleague. How do your actions and words reflect Christ's presence to this person?

Joan of Arc

January 6, 1412–May 30, 1431

She'd heard the voices since she was thirteen or so, first telling her to be a good girl, then telling her to save France by coming to the aid of the dauphin. Finally, when Joan was seventeen, she was allowed to lead the army that would end the siege at Orleans. Less than three months later, she was at Rheims when the dauphin was crowned King Charles VII. But then things changed. Charles didn't seem interested in her assistance anymore, and seventeen months later, Joan was an English prisoner. Charles and the French did nothing to help her, and she was burned at the stake as a heretic, sorceress, and adulteress. While a papal court found her innocent in 1456, she was not canonized until 1920.

Almost overnight, Joan went from being lauded as a national hero to being shunned. No one came to her aid—not even those whom she had helped. She remained confident, however, that the voices were saints and angels, guiding her to the end.

Inspiration

You have been with your counsel and I have been with mine. Believe me that the counsel of my Lord will be accomplished and will stand, and this counsel of yours will perish. (St. Joan of Arc)

Challenge

Pray for someone you have betrayed. Perhaps it's a former friend or coworker; perhaps it's someone with whom you volunteered. If it is possible to do so without causing still more pain for the other person, ask him or her for forgiveness.

Camilla Battista da Varano

April 9, 1458–May 31, 1524

It started with something small: when Camilla was eight or ten, she heard a priest ask that people shed a tear for Christ's passion. A princess at an Italian court, Camilla decided she would do this each Friday. Her devotion led her to join the Poor Clares when she was twenty-three. It guided her through difficult times, including the political killings of her father and brothers and her own spiritual dryness. Her writing and mysticism continue to inspire us nearly five hundred years after her death.

Preparing our children for the sacraments is an exciting, time-intensive process. Yet we shouldn't lose sight of the fact that their faith journeys, like ours, are lived in the day to day. As parents, aunts, and friends, we share in the challenging, delightful responsibility of helping young people be open to the small blessings as well as the large, visible ones. You may be surprised how a chance remark you make informs their lives for years to come.

Inspiration

Blessed is that creature who never gives up under any temptation the good she began! (St. Camilla Battista da Varano)

Challenge

Talk with your child or another young person about what he or she learned from a recent religious education class, and ask how the lesson applies to his or her life.

Mechtildis of Edelstetten

Died May 31, 1160

It wasn't the job she wanted. When she was five, Mechtildis's parents placed her in a monastery on their estate, and she went on to be a Benedictine nun and then an abbess. Then, before she was thirty, the bishop of Augsburg selected her to head and reform another convent. It wasn't easy—some of the nuns opposed her efforts to cleanse the site of gossip and intrigue—but Mechtildis prevailed.

Whether it's in the home or professional workplace, we all end up with tasks and assignments we'd just as soon hand off to someone else. It's much the same with our spiritual assignments. We may not always want to be kind to unpleasant people or drive the kids to religious education classes, but we keep on doing these tasks because they have to get done and because we know the importance of saying "yes" to God.

✒ Inspiration

Each of you must give as you have made up your mind, not reluctantly or under compulsion, for God loves a cheerful giver. (2 Corinthians 9:7)

✒ Challenge

What tasks are you doing out of obligation? Ask God to help you rediscover the joy in saying yes to the necessary work of our physical and spiritual lives.

Marta Maria Wiecka

January 12, 1874–May 30, 1904

Marta was more than a nurse to her hospital patients. She also prepared people for their sacraments and prayed with them. She was attentive no matter what the faith or ethnic background of the patient was. While she was an example of a living faith each day, never was she more so than when she offered to clean the room of a typhoid patient, taking the place of the nurse assigned to do so, a young father. She contracted the disease herself and died.

Sacrifice is easy when it's safe and doesn't threaten us in the least. Offering up ourselves without knowing precisely what the outcome will be is a sign of true faith—and of being Christlike.

Inspiration

This is my commandment, that you love one another as I have loved you. No one has greater love than this, to lay down one's life for one's friends. (John 15:12–13)

Challenge

Where can you make a sacrifice today as Jesus or Marta would, without a thought of how your life might be changed by your action? For surely, it will be changed—whether you take the risk or not.

Clotilde

Circa 474–June 3, 545

Clovis I, king of the Franks, fell in love with Clotilde. There was just one problem: she was Catholic and he was not. A struggle ensued when their first son was baptized but died very young. Still, after some pushback, Clovis agreed to have the next child baptized as well. The following year, Clovis prayed in battle that if he were victorious, he would accept Clotilde's faith. Clovis won the day, and he and Clotilde built a monastery in Paris. After Clovis's death, Clotilde spent more than thirty years in a monastery in Tours.

Do you ever feel like a broken record, talking about God to a spouse, children, friends, or others who lack a strong faith life? Clotilde's example reminds us never to give up on doing what we can to bring those souls to the kingdom, even when we feel we're making no progress in touching their souls. Remember, actions often speak louder than words.

Inspiration

So let us not grow weary in doing what is right, for we will reap at harvest time, if we do not give up. (Galatians 6:9)

Challenge

Talk with God about the best words and actions to use in your efforts to lead a loved one back to his flock.

Mary Elisabeth Hesselblad

June 4, 1870–April 24, 1957

Mary, one of thirteen children, left her native Sweden before she was twenty to find work in New York. There was something about the contact she had with people, including a Jesuit priest, that prompted her to convert to Catholicism when she was thirty-two. She went on to join the Order of the Most Holy Savior of St. Bridget, and she spent much of her life working for ecumenical understanding among Christians and non-Christians, which included assisting Jews during World War II.

While we long to see all our brothers and sisters worldwide united under "one holy, catholic, and apostolic Church," we acknowledge that mutual respect and love are the paths to that goal. Mary didn't judge; she reflected God's love, and showed others why Christ's way is both challenging and beautiful.

Inspiration

We must nourish a great love for God and our neighbors; a strong love, an ardent love, a love that burns away imperfections, a love that gently bears an act of impatience or a bitter word, a love that lets an inadvertence or act of neglect pass without comment, a love that lends itself readily to an act of charity. (Blessed Mary Elisabeth Hesselblad)

Challenge

Aid someone's continual (or, perhaps, initial) conversion today. Don't criticize him or her; instead, praise the beauty you (and Christ) see in that person.

Josepha Hendrina Stenmanns

May 28, 1852–May 20, 1903

Josepha knew all about housekeeping, as the oldest of seven children. She also cared for her siblings later when her mother was dying. When she was in her early thirties, she went to be a kitchen maid at a missionary training center for priests, simply so that she could honor God's will. Later, a branch for women was formed, and Josepha made her first vows when she was forty-two. Her experience with keeping things organized served her well as the directress of postulants.

The value of a clean, welcoming home is sometimes underestimated. As is the case with our souls, a tidy, well-kept place is inviting to God and to those in our families and community. It shows we care about them and ourselves.

Inspiration

Woe to you, scribes and Pharisees, hypocrites! For you clean the outside of the cup and of the plate, but inside they are full of greed and self-indulgence. You blind Pharisee! First clean the inside of the cup, so that the outside also may become clean. (Matthew 23:25–26)

Challenge

What parts of your home—and your soul—could use a little late-spring cleaning? Open the windows. Get out the soap and water. Scrub away the dark corners!

Bonifacia Rodriguez Castro

June 6, 1837–August 8, 1905

From an early age, Bonifacia knew the value of putting her hands to work for God and for community. By the time she was fifteen, she was a rope maker, helping her widowed mother make ends meet. When Bonifacia was in her late twenties, women were gathering in Bonifacia's home, which also served as her shop for rope making and needlework. Ultimately, she cofounded the Servants of St. Joseph, an order aimed at sheltering and educating women workers. A split within the congregation developed, however, and was not resolved until after Bonifacia's death. At her canonization in 2011, Pope Benedict XVI noted that Bonifacia accepted that disappointment "with the steadiness of hope, offering her own life for the unity of the work born of her hands."

Do you respect the skills and limitations of those with whom you work? How about those who bring different gifts to your ministries and volunteer organizations? Helping them to complete tasks with confidence and treating them as sisters and brothers of Christ can help make your own load lighter.

❧ Inspiration

We should be all for all, following Jesus. (St. Bonifacia Rodriguez Castro)

❧ Challenge

Ask a work or ministry colleague who is struggling what he or she needs to be more confident with the assigned tasks. Help where you can.

Pierina Morosini

January 7, 1931–April 6, 1957

It's said that Pierina made one big trip in her life, from her village in northern Italy to Rome when she was sixteen for Maria Goretti's beatification. Ten years later, the Catholic Action volunteer was attacked on her way home from her factory job by a man who tried to rape her, which was tragically similar to the Goretti story. Pierina died in a hospital two days after the attack.

Women are violated every day in our world. We may be treated with disrespect in our communities, at our jobs, and sometimes even within our own families. Standing up for ourselves, as Pierina and Maria did, can be dangerous. And yet, to value ourselves as God does, we must fight against the violence and cruelty and discrimination we face, knowing that God always has our back—if not in this world, then in the next.

Inspiration

When justice is done, it is a joy to the righteous,

but dismay to evildoers. (Proverbs 21:15)

Challenge

Are you or another woman you know experiencing discrimination or disrespect? Talk with a trusted female leader in your parish or community about strategies that could improve the situation.

Melania the Elder

325–410

This wealthy woman was only twenty-two when she was left with no family other than her son, Publicola. She began giving away her estate, and when her son was ten, left for the Holy Land, despite the fact that her relatives in Rome thought little of the idea. There she became known as one of the desert mothers who lived the ascetic life. Melania's accomplishments included establishing a monastery in Jerusalem.

Tragedy and upheaval can cause a rebirth in our spiritual life. We all learn, like Melania, that money and comfort and the approval of friends and family do not equal the kind of happiness that can be found in Christ.

✒ Inspiration

But I call upon God,
  and the LORD will save me.
Evening and morning and at noon
  I utter my complaint and moan,
  and he will hear my voice. (Psalm 55:16–17)

✒ Challenge

Think about a time your life was in crisis and there was no one you could turn to but God. Thank him for the comfort he provided in that situation. Perhaps it was when a relationship was ending or someone you loved was dying. Consider sharing that story with someone you know who is going through a difficult time.

Mariam Thresia Chiramel Mankidiyan

April 26, 1876–June 8, 1926

Mariam Thresia's relationship with God was mystical—and sometimes misunderstood. Some regard her as the Blessed Teresa of her day, taking her ministry to the poorest of the poor in an Indian community, scandalizing some as she and her companions did their work unaccompanied by men. She also experienced the gifts of stigmata, levitations, and ecstasies. She also suffered spiritual attacks to the point where she underwent exorcism. Eventually, she received approval to form the Congregation of the Holy Family for her and her companions to continue their work in a formal manner. The congregation today has nearly two thousand sisters.

It's somehow heartening that a blessed woman religious had struggles with demons so significant that exorcism seemed appropriate. After all, we all are challenged every day by internal or external forces that would separate us from God. Her story strengthens our resolve not to let the devil win—and to engage those who can help us in spiritual warfare.

✸ Inspiration

Resist him, steadfast in your faith, for you know that your brothers and sisters in all the world are undergoing the same kinds of suffering. (1 Peter 5:9)

✸ Challenge

Contemplate the behaviors and interactions that have most separated you from God recently. Be cleansed with the sacrament of reconciliation. Show the devil who's boss in your life.

Maria Rosa Molas y Vallvé

March 24, 1815–June 11, 1876

When Maria was assigned to be superior of a mental hospital, she had to have been shocked and overwhelmed. The institution had three hundred patients and failed to provide the basics of proper medical care and hygiene. Over the next eight years, Maria brought modern practices to bear at the hospital. She was fearless in her protection of patients. In June 1844, when a battle was waging in her Spanish town, Maria and two other sisters went to one of the generals and pleaded with him to end the fighting. "She had the charism to be an instrument of reconciliation and of spiritual development," Pope John Paul II said at her canonization in 1988. The order Maria founded, Sisters of Our Lady of Consolation, today provides services in eighteen countries on four continents.

Bringing change to an environment is hard. Too often, we hear, "But this is the way it's always been done." Maria's example reminds us we can effect positive change in the direst of situations.

Inspiration

We do not doubt the love of God. Although we are a small thing, we can be instruments of his mercy. (St. Maria Rosa Molas y Vallvé)

Challenge

What situation in your life requires physical, emotional, mental, or spiritual change? Pray for the wisdom to take appropriate actions.

Paula Frassinetti

March 3, 1809–June 11, 1882

You might say Paula was born to be a mother. Paula's own mother died when she was just nine, so Paula took on the care of her father and four brothers. When she was nineteen, she was so physically worn out that her brother Giuseppe, by then a priest, invited her to a seaside village to rest. But as the pair walked around talking about God, other young women began to join them. It was then that Paula realized her vocation as a teacher and leader. A few years later, she was named to head the Sisters of Saint Dorothy and reach out to needy young people.

Unconsciously or consciously, the way we live our lives has a great impact on our children and others around us. We can be a positive influence, reflecting Christ's love, as Paula was, or we can be a negative influence. It's up to us to decide which we will be.

Inspiration

Keep these words that I am commanding you today in your heart. Recite them to your children and talk about them when you are at home and when you are away, when you lie down and when you rise. (Deuteronomy 6:6–7)

Challenge

Write a thank you note to a woman who's like a mother to you—or a note of encouragement to one who is like your daughter.

Godeberta

Circa 640–June 11, circa 700

Oh, the plans Godeberta's parents had for her! They were part of the noble class and took her to the court of Clovis II in hopes of making a great match. However, while there, they encountered a bishop (who would later become St. Eligius) who told the girl he hoped she might think of a religious life instead. The idea spoke to Godeberta, and, impressed, Clovis II eventually gave her a small palace that became a convent for Godeberta and the young women who followed her.

Her prayer power is said to have extinguished a fire that threatened her town in northern France

You know that adage about people making plans, and God laughing? Well, it's true. We can plan all we want for our futures and the futures of our children, but in the end, God's will will be done.

✒ Inspiration

Trust in the LORD with all your heart,
  and do not rely on your own insight.
In all your ways acknowledge him,
  and he will make straight your paths. (Proverbs 3:5–6)

✒ Challenge

Clear your schedule of appointments and to-dos for a single morning or afternoon next week. Spend that free time in the Lord's presence.

Albertina Berkenbrock

April 11, 1919–June 15, 1931

Albertina's family owned a farm in Brazil. There, Albertina was known as a sweet, pious child who was kind to poorer families, including her father's employees and their children. One of those employees, Maneco, one day lured her into a secluded area and attempted to rape her. When she successfully defended herself, he slit her throat. Maneco later admitted to the crime.

Albertina's story reminds us that horrific things happen in this world. People will knowingly injure us even as we try to live a Godly life. We must prepare to have each day be our last, having walked as closely with Christ as we could.

Inspiration

As for what others do, by the word of your lips
   I have avoided the ways of the violent.
My steps have held fast to your paths;
   my feet have not slipped. (Psalm 17:4–5)

Challenge

Talk with a woman in your family or community about the dangers that exist in your community. What can the two of you do to reduce them? Lobby for additional streetlights or police patrols? Become involved in a safety advocacy group? Look for a place in your life to help with such a ministry.

Aleydis

1204–1250

Aleydis was only seven when she entered a Belgian convent for schooling, and it would turn out that she would spend the rest of her days there. She contracted leprosy, which eventually resulted in blindness and paralysis. In her suffering, Aleydis found great comfort in the Eucharist, but she became concerned about the fact that she could not drink from the chalice because of her fears of spreading her disease. She then had a vision in which God told her that a single species was sufficient.

It's a beautiful thing when God allays our worries. We can help by listening to our friends when they are fearful instead of discounting their concerns or trying to fix things for them.

✒ Inspiration

Do not lag in zeal, be ardent in spirit, serve the Lord. Rejoice in hope, be patient in suffering, persevere in prayer. (Romans 12:11–12)

✒ Challenge

Think about a friend whom you've been avoiding because she's a chronic complainer. Offer to get together to read Scripture or perhaps go to Eucharistic Adoration. Don't give her a solution for her problems—God will do that—but perhaps a listening ear will help her open up to grace.

Germaine Cousin

1579–1601

Germaine was one of society's throwaways. She was born with a paralyzed hand and what may have been a form of tuberculosis, and her mother died in childbirth or shortly thereafter. Her stepmother did her best to keep Germaine away from the rest of the family, saying she was fearful the other children would become ill. This meant Germaine spent much of her time tending the family's sheep, and she spent her nights in the stable or under the stairs. It also gave her the opportunity to experience God in nature, and to attend Mass on many days. When she was offered a better place in her home, she chose to go on as she had.

It's impossible to treat all your children or nieces and nephews exactly the same, and sometimes, there's simply a stronger bond with some of them than with others. Kids pick up on these things; they know when there's a favorite. Germaine's example shows that even when earthly parents find it difficult to treat a child with compassion and love, God can do so.

Inspiration

Then the LORD said to [Moses], "Who gives speech to mortals? Who makes them mute or deaf, seeing or blind? Is it not I, the LORD? (Exodus 4:11)

Challenge

Which of your children (or the children of friends or other family members) do you most struggle to understand? Set aside some time to spend with this young person. Ask him or her about dreams, fears, and passions. Listen carefully.

Lutgard

1182–June 16, 1246

Many saints dreamed from infancy, it seems, of donning the habit. That was not the case with Lutgard; the teenager enjoyed her life in the outside world. But when her wedding dowry became the casualty of a failed family business venture, she was sent to live at a convent. An encounter with Christ, however, caused a decided change in her attitude. After twelve years, she moved to a stricter convent, where she spent the rest of her life.

Sometimes, we think we know exactly what God has in store for us: A handsome husband. Beautiful children. A rewarding career. And yet, sometimes he places us in a situation that is nothing like we had expected. May we leave our hearts and souls open to his plans, not ours.

✿ Inspiration

You are a hiding place for me;

    you preserve me from trouble;

    you surround me with glad cries of deliverance.

Selah

I will instruct you and teach you the way you should go;

    I will counsel you with my eye upon you. (Psalm 32:7–8)

✿ Challenge

How is your life different today from the way you expected it to be five or ten years ago? Make a list of those differences, good and bad, and consider how they have strengthened your faith.

Emilie de Vialar

September 12, 1797–August 24, 1856

What would you do if you inherited a significant estate? Buy a mansion? Go on an around-the-world cruise? When Emilie found herself in this situation at the age of thirty-five, she knew exactly what she would do. She and three friends founded what would become the Sisters of St. Joseph of the Apparition. Emilie was among the sisters who journeyed to Algiers amid a cholera epidemic. Later, she fought with her local bishop in France over where the congregation could do its work; she was in essence excommunicated for a time, but ultimately she prevailed.

A financial windfall gives us the opportunity to treat ourselves. And while that may be fine within reason, it's helpful to call to mind what Jesus said about it being easier for a camel to go through a needle's eye than for a rich man to enter God's kingdom. We are called to share our wealth in ways it will do the most good for God's people.

✒ Inspiration

How fulfilling for the heart that is given to making another happy and to bringing relief to suffering humanity! (St. Emilie de Vialar)

✒ Challenge

Identify one of the frills in your life. Maybe it's a daily cup of gourmet coffee or dinner out with a friend every Monday night. This week, give what you would have spent to an overseas ministry instead.

Marianna Biernacka (one of the 108 Martyrs of Poland)
1888–July 13, 1943

Marianna's family wasn't politically active, nor was she well educated; in fact, she couldn't even write. But when her pregnant daughter-in-law was caught up in a mass Gestapo arrest, Marianna offered to take her place. The authorities accepted, and she was shot to death less than two weeks later.

Warfare—internal or external—can bring out the best or the worst in each of us. While we may not face the physical danger Marianna did, we put on our spiritual armor to fight hatred, prejudice, and indifference every day. Or, we can run away, fearful of what may happen to us. May we step forward with the same resolve and courage she did.

Inspiration

I appeal to you therefore, brothers and sisters, by the mercies of God, to present your bodies as a living sacrifice, holy and acceptable to God, which is your spiritual worship. (Romans 12:1)

Challenge

Think about a situation in which someone you love is struggling. Perhaps it's a physical illness, or a trying financial time for the person's family. What can you offer up—prayers, a listening ear, babysitting, a ride, a home-cooked meal—to carry some of his or her burden?

Elena Aiello

April 10, 1895–June 19, 1961

Elena's life was full of mystical communications. God told her she would not stay in her initial order because he had other plans for her. It is said she experienced the stigmata and the crown of thorns periodically for three years before being told by St. Rita that she would be cured. Elena also was visited by St. Thérèse of Lisieux, who provided guidance in establishing what would become the Sister Minims of the Passion of Our Lord, who minister to children. Elena also was said to be a vessel for prophecies.

Some of us embrace the mystics in our Church; others are skeptical of their charisms. The beauty is that God speaks through us all, and we all can find an example of a person we wish to emulate on our faith journeys.

Inspiration

Let the words of my mouth and the meditation of my heart
  be acceptable to you,
  O LORD, my rock and my redeemer. (Psalm 19:14)

Challenge

Mystics? Martyrs? Virgins? The incorruptible? How much do you know about saints? Is there a type of saint or blessed who resonates with you? Consider learning more about what the process of sainthood involves.

Margaret Ball (one of the Martyrs of Ireland)
1515–1584

In a gut-wrenching betrayal, it was Margaret's son Walter who was responsible for her spending the final three years of her life in the Dublin Castle dungeons. Margaret's husband had been mayor of Dublin, but the political climate had changed in the intervening years. Walter abandoned his faith due to his ambitions and turned in his mother and an archbishop. While she could have been released at any time if she had accepted the Church of England, she refused to do so.

Families become estranged for all kinds of reasons, and it's especially heartbreaking when all our efforts to mend the rift go for naught in this world. All we can do is what Margaret undoubtedly did for Walter: Pray that people's hearts might be unhardened and that they would discover the beauty of sharing Christ's love in their family.

Inspiration
The discerning person looks to wisdom,
  but the eyes of a fool to the ends of the earth.
Foolish children are a grief to their father
  and bitterness to her who bore them. (Proverbs 17:24–25)

Challenge
From whom in your family are you estranged, or who haven't you spoken to for some time? Make another attempt to reestablish contact today. And next week. And next month. And next year. Don't give up.

Anna Maria Adorni Botti

June 19, 1805–February 7, 1893

The postulator of Anna's cause of beatification said of her, "It's very original that one person can be a model for several states of life." And, indeed, she was. While she desired to become a nun, she went along with her mother's wishes and got married. She was a devoted wife, nursing her husband for several months before his death, and she was also the mother of six children, only one of whom lived into adulthood. Later she founded the Congregation of Handmaidens of Blessed Mary Immaculate of Parma, where she helped prisoners, prostitutes, orphans, and the homeless.

We needn't question God or turn away from him when life throws us a curve ball. Like Anna did, with his help, we can move on with confidence to discover what he has in store for us in our next state of life.

Inspiration

So then, whenever we have an opportunity, let us work for the good of all, and especially for those of the family of faith. (Galatians 6:10)

Challenge

Make a list of the times when your life had to take a drastic turn, due to tragedy or happy events. Where did you find God as you were adjusting to your new circumstances?

María Inés Teresa Arias Espinosa

July 7, 1904–July 22, 1981

The archbishop of Los Angeles said María Inés's story "is so beautiful because it is so ordinary." María Inés grew up in Mexico and then came to the United States when she was twenty-five to enter a convent of Poor Clares. On the day that María Inés made her temporary vows, the Blessed Virgin of Tepeyac spoke to her, pledging to be with her always. After sixteen years in a cloistered order, María Inés went on to establish the Poor Clare Missionary Sisters of the Blessed Sacrament, which shares the Word through retreats, healthcare, and missions in more than a dozen countries around the world.

We sometimes question our own abilities, our own ordinariness. María Inés's example reminds us that with God, our very ordinariness is extraordinary and can be used to carry his message to others.

Inspiration

He leads the humble in what is right,
  and teaches the humble his way.
All the paths of the LORD are steadfast love and faithfulness,
  for those who keep his covenant and his decrees. (Psalm 25:9–10)

Challenge

Identify the ordinary spots in your life. Maybe you're an average singer, but not great, or perhaps a mediocre cook, but not great. How can you use that ordinariness to share God's love with others?

Maria Raffaella Cimatti

June 6, 1861–June 23, 1945

You couldn't blame Maria for retiring as superior of her community. After all, she was nearly eighty years old and had been in the religious life for fifty years. But her service in her final years brought her back to her training as a nurse. Her care of wounded soldiers was so tender that they called her "Mamma." And, she personally interceded to keep a German general from plans to bomb the community to prevent an Allied advance.

Is eighty the new forty? You'd sure think so from the way Maria conducted herself in retirement. When God calls us, "I'm too old" or "I'm too young" or any other excuse isn't going to work. He's well aware of who we are and how he can best use us.

Inspiration

Youth is a gift from God. Like any other gift there is a need to preserve and to value it. Always be good and gentle. (Blessed Maria Raffaella Cimatti)

Challenge

There's more truth than we realize to that adage, "You're only as old as you feel." What can you do today to show your youth at any age or to value the wisdom of an older person in your life?

María Guadalupe García Zavala

April 27, 1878–June 24, 1963

The early twentieth century in Mexico saw disputes between religious authorities and politicians. María's congregation operated a hospital during this time, and at some risk, hid priests and the archbishop of Guadalajara. She also provided sustenance to those who opposed the Church, and in appreciation they eventually protected the sick in the sisters' hospital.

María was successful in keeping her hospital and the patients safe by treating all those in need compassionately. Extending the same kindnesses to our persecutors as to our own community can be a difficult thing. But it's what we're called to do.

✒ Inspiration

Pray then in this way:
Our Father in heaven,
hallowed be your name.
Your kingdom come.
Your will be done,
on earth as it is in heaven.
Give us this day our daily bread.
And forgive us our debts,
as we also have forgiven our debtors. (Matthew 6:9–12)

✒ Challenge

Is there a situation in your life where family members or office coworkers are at odds and are pushing you to take sides? Refuse to get involved; treat everyone with compassion.

Marguerite Bays

September 8, 1815–June 27, 1879

Suffering from intestinal cancer, Marguerite, a dressmaker who was active in her Swiss parish, made an offer to the Blessed Virgin: Exchange my illness for the type of pain Christ suffered in his passion. It is said that Marguerite's relief came four years later as the dogma of the Immaculate Conception was being announced. Thereafter, Marguerite experienced the passion each Friday and received the gift of stigmata, which she did her best to hide. At her beatification in 1995, Pope John Paul II said of Marguerite: "She walked humbly with God, accomplishing every act in her daily life with love."

Prayer works. We know that from Marguerite's life, other saints and blesseds, and our own experiences. Sometimes, the answer may be different from what we ask, or it may not be apparent at all. But our prayers always are heard.

Inspiration

What can we do to love God more? (Blessed Marguerite Bays)

Challenge

Consider Marguerite's question. She didn't mean, what could we do so that our prayers are answered differently or so that favors are granted, but what can we do to love him with all we have, and then some. What obstacles to greater love can you clear from your life?

Anna Maria Taigi

May 29, 1769–June 9, 1837

Some regard Anna Maria, a Roman housewife and Trinitarian tertiary, as among the most important mystics of the nineteenth century. A wife and mother, when she was barely in her twenties she received the gift of vision. For the rest of her life, Anna Maria would see a sort of sun-globe that revealed people's true natures and intents as well as future events. A cardinal who knew her well said her gift "was one of omniscience for it was the knowing of all things in God so far as the intelligence is capable of such knowledge in this life." Anna Maria was also given to ecstasies and is credited with a number of healings during her lifetime.

On the outside, Anna Maria looked like any other wife and mother. Perhaps it was not only her spirituality but also her humbleness and ordinariness that made God touch her in this special way. While we may not have the gift of insight she did, we each have something inside that makes us beloved of God.

✿ Inspiration

I embrace the cross of my Jesus. I will carry it, like him, in pain and ignominy. I await at his hands triumph and glory in the hereafter. (Blessed Anna Maria Taigi)

✿ Challenge

Where in your life are you saying "I can't" to embracing the cross? Pray for the spiritual fortitude to say yes to what Christ is asking.

Maria Pia Mastena

December 7, 1881–June 28, 1951

Maria had been a nun for about six years when she began to feel the call to the contemplative life. Nearly twenty years later, she entered a Cistercian monastery to do just that after years of service as a teacher. But after seven months, Maria discerned that was not her calling. She returned to teaching and worked to found the Sisters of the Holy Face to care for the poor and sick.

Imagine that! A nun, and one who would be beatified at that, who misunderstood God's desire for her. Or perhaps Maria understood perfectly, and she needed that time in contemplation to prepare for the next stage of our life. In any event, changing our minds about our ministry or life direction isn't anything to be ashamed of or embarrassed about, as long as we stay close to Christ.

Inspiration

For God did not give us a spirit of cowardice, but rather a spirit of power and of love and of self-discipline. (2 Timothy 1:7)

Challenge

Is there something in your life you would change if you weren't afraid of losing face in front of your family or friends? Pray for the confidence to follow God fearlessly.

Potamiana

Died circa 205

Potamiana, a beautiful young slave, knew she was going to be killed for being a follower of Christ. She'd heard the sentence that she would be boiled in pitch. But the man guarding her, Basilides, was kind and respectful. Potamiana thanked him, and promised to obtain salvation for him. It was not long after Potamiana died that Basilides professed his newfound belief in Christ and was jailed, baptized, and beheaded.

When life is going well, it's easy for us to be pleasant to others and attempt to emulate Christ. Potamiana's example reminds us we can be used as an instrument for conversion even when our own lives are in tatters.

✈ Inspiration

Whoever obeys his word, truly in this person the love of God has reached perfection. By this we may be sure that we are in him: whoever says, "I abide in him," ought to walk just as he walked. (1 John 2:5–6)

✈ Challenge

Strive today to reflect Christ's face to everyone you encounter, not just people you know and like. Say hello to people. Let them merge into traffic. Hold the elevator door for them. Laugh at their story, even though you've heard it a dozen times before.

Hemma of Gurk

980–June 27, 1045

Imagine losing your children. Then imagine losing your husband soon thereafter. This is what Hemma faced. Her two sons were killed by workers at a mine her husband owned because they were dissatisfied with working conditions. She convinced her husband, William, to conduct a careful investigation and punish only those who had killed the sons rather than all involved in the rebellion. Shortly thereafter, William made a pilgrimage to Rome and died after his return home to Austria. Rather than becoming bitter and blaming God for her losses, Hemma chose to devote herself to him. In addition to providing land for a monastery, she built churches and a convent, where she spent the final years of her life, and gave to the poor.

When tragedy strikes us, we have a choice. We can fight with God about what happened, or we can turn to him for comfort. It's up to us.

Inspiration

When the righteous cry for help, the LORD hears,
   and rescues them from all their troubles.
The LORD is near to the brokenhearted,
   and saves the crushed in spirit. (Psalm 34:17–18)

Challenge

Reach out to a family member or friend whose heart and soul have hardened after a senseless tragedy. Ask the person to speak frankly and fully about his or her anger. Offer to pray together.

Margaret Ebner

1291–July 20, 1351

Margaret, a Dominican nun who lived in Germany, spent her twenties and early thirties bedridden with a serious illness. While she experienced Christ's agony through his passion, Margaret is best known for the mystical, motherly relationship with the infant Jesus that she described in her letters to her spiritual director and in other writings. Margaret spent long periods in silence, and other periods in ecstasies in which she would involuntarily repeat Christ's name over and over. In 1979, she became the first woman beatified by Pope John Paul II.

Often, we think of Christ's final hours, or of Jesus, strong and vibrant, teaching and preaching. Margaret's writings present us with a different Jesus—a helpless infant who himself needs to be fed by us. It's an interesting perspective for those of us who rely so much on him.

Inspiration

Jesus Christ, my heartfelt Love, have mercy on me! Jesus Christ, my pure Truth, teach me truth! Jesus Christ, sweet Love, teach me love! Jesus Christ, boundless Mercy, come to help me! (Blessed Margaret Ebner)

Challenge

Consider Margaret's perspective—Jesus as a hungry, smiling baby—as you pray today. What can you do to feed him and his brothers and sisters?

Catherine Jarrige

October 4, 1754–July 4, 1836

You might call Catherine the Harriet Tubman of the French Revolution. A laywoman and Dominican tertiary with little if any education or formal authority, she set up safe houses for priests hunted by the New Republic authorities, helped them find safe passage, and provided altar wine and hosts so they could celebrate Mass for people. It's said she saved the lives of thousands of priests.

Catherine was fearless when it came to defending the faith. In a similar way, we must always be prepared to defend our own religious freedom—and that of others. While it seems unlikely we'll need to hide priests in our homes, we are seeing more government strictures on Catholic tenets. May we show the same bravery Catherine did in taking on these threats to our faith.

Inspiration

I hereby command you: Be strong and courageous; do not be frightened or dismayed, for the LORD your God is with you wherever you go. (Joshua 1:9)

Challenge

Where do you see Catholicism under attack? In government decisions on birth control or abortion funding, immigration reform, or same-sex marriage? Write a letter to the newspaper editor or your congressman. March in a protest. Make your voice heard.

Marie-Azélie Guérin Martin

December 23, 1831–August 28, 1877

Both Zélie and her husband, Louis, had hoped to enter religious life, but were unable to do so, in Zélie's case, most likely because of health issues. Disappointed, Zélie accepted the decision. She took up lace-making and began her own business, then met Louis. All five of their children who survived infancy became nuns; the most notable was, of course, St. Thérèse of Lisieux, who was only four and a half when Zélie went to heaven. In her final months, Zélie suffered severe pain that not even a family trip to Lourdes could relieve. The Martins were only the second couple in the Church's history to be beatified.

Zélie is remembered for her own strong faith amid disappointment; for her loving marriage; and for the godly way in which she and Louis raised their children. That makes for a pretty good legacy!

✒ Inspiration

If the Blessed Virgin does not cure me, it is that my time has come and that God wishes me to find my rest elsewhere than on earth. (Blessed Marie-Azélie Guérin Martin)

✒ Challenge

What would you like your legacy to be, both in your family and in your community? What next steps do you need to take to attain that?

Maria Crocifissa Curcio

January 30, 1877–July 4, 1957

Maria grew up in a time that girls didn't receive much of an education. In fact, her father didn't allow her to go to school past the sixth grade. Still she was an avid reader, and one day picked up St. Thérèse of Lisieux's *Story of a Soul.* The book set her down a path that included more than sixty years of service as a sister, including founding a congregation named in Thérèse's honor that ministers to families in Italy and Brazil.

One book sparked the fire in Maria's mind and soul that would go on to feed thousands of people. As parents, aunts, sisters, and friends of young people, it's our honor and responsibility to introduce them to spiritual works on paper, on film, or on the Internet that may light a spark in them. And who knows? Maybe this effort to help with their religious instruction will also feed our own continuous conversion.

✒ Inspiration

Love with holiness the treasures with which the Divine Goodness entrusts you; the souls of the youth, the hope of the future. (Blessed Maria Crocifissa Curcio)

✒ Challenge

Was there a particular saint whose early life resonated with you when you were a child or a teenager? Share that story, or a story of a saint who is important to you now, with a young person in your life.

Elizabeth of Portugal

1271–July 4, 1336

St. Elizabeth is known as Isabel the Peacemaker, and it's no wonder. Her intervention led to the end of a feud between her brother, the king of Aragon, and her son-in-law, the king of Castile. Elizabeth also accepted her philandering husband, King Denis of Portugal, as he was, and she raised his children born to other women. When Denis and their son Alfonso were at war with each other, she was the one who convinced them to resolve the dispute. After Denis died, Elizabeth moved to a convent she had helped found.

It's difficult not to take sides in family disputes. It also can be difficult in our heart of hearts to accept children from a spouse's prior relationships in the same way we love the ones we bear. Elizabeth's example reminds us of God's counsel to love all, and leave the judging to him.

Inspiration

God made me queen so that I may serve others. (St. Elizabeth of Portugal)

Challenge

Humble yourself. Spend a half-hour in the next week listening to a family member you find difficult to love. Perhaps the person is boastful, self-centered, arrogant, or just plain mean. Don't judge, criticize, or advise. Just listen. Your attention could provide the first step toward healing the person's soul.

Anatolia

Died 250

When Anatolia and her sister Victoria refused arranged marriages, their suitors informed the authorities that the women were Christians. We are told that a poisonous snake was placed in Anatolia's cell, but it refused to bite her. When a guard was sent in to kill her, he was attacked by the snake and Anatolia saved him. Because of what she had done, the guard became a Christian and was killed the same day as Anatolia.

Our Christian action doesn't end at home or in our parish or in the workplace. It extends to the ordinary as well as the most uncomfortable of situations—being stuck in traffic, being mocked or ridiculed, being in physical danger. Even in the worst situations, we have the opportunity to reflect Christ in a way that will open the most hardened hearts and souls to conversion.

Inspiration

My brothers and sisters, whenever you face trials of any kind, consider it nothing but joy, because you know that the testing of your faith produces endurance; and let endurance have its full effect, so that you may be mature and complete, lacking in nothing. (James 1:2–4)

Challenge

Plan ahead. What is the most challenging situation you expect to face today? How can you show Christian love in that situation?

Maria Goretti

October 16, 1890–July 6, 1902

Maria hadn't turned twelve yet when a nineteen-year-old man with whom she and her family shared a house came after her with a knife with rape on his mind. He stabbed her fourteen times. On her deathbed, Maria's words were: "Through love of Jesus, I forgive him with all my heart." Her murderer had a conversion experience in prison and upon his release spent his life as a monastery gardener.

Anyone can have a conversion experience—convicted murderers, pedophiles, corrupt politicians, gossiping neighbors, backstabbing coworkers. We're not called to be foolish and irresponsible about putting ourselves in dangerous situations. But like Maria, we must strive to forgive all, just as God does. Our actions and words, big or small, could help or hinder someone with a mustard seed's worth of faith. Which will it be?

✒ Inspiration

The Father loves the Son and shows him all that he himself is doing; and he will show him greater works than these, so that you will be astonished. (John 5:20)

✒ Challenge

Have a prayerful conversation with God about where you can sow some seeds of conversion. It may be in your own life!

Olga of Kiev

Circa 879–July 11, 969

You wouldn't have called Olga a benevolent ruler. She was only about twenty-five when her husband, Prince Igor I, was murdered, and she is said to have exacted great revenge, having his murderers scalded to death and ordering the killing of hundreds of their followers. But about twelve years later, she became the first ruler of Russian lands to convert to Christianity.

Change. It's a constant in life, and yet we all are suspicious of it in others. Are they really turning over a new leaf, or are they out to take advantage of us? Through Olga's story, we are reminded that people can change, and that God delights when they do. Therefore, so must we.

✒ Inspiration

You shall not hate in your heart anyone of your kin; you shall reprove your neighbor, or you will incur guilt yourself. You shall not take vengeance or bear a grudge against any of your people, but you shall love your neighbor as yourself: I am the LORD. (Leviticus 19:17–18)

✒ Challenge

Who in your life do you find it most difficult to love as Christ loves? Just for today, put aside your feelings about the person's past behaviors and treat him or her with kindness and generosity.

Veronica Giuliani

1660–July 9, 1727

Veronica was an interesting mix of mysticism and practicality. After she joined the Capuchin Poor Clares, she saw Christ carrying his cross and felt pain in her own heart. She also had a vision of the chalice, which she took as a sign that the divine passion would recur in her own soul. Later, she suffered the pain and wounds of the crown of thorns. But even as she communed with Christ in this way, she was a careful novice mistress for thirty-four years, refusing to allow her charges to read mystical books.

From Veronica's example, we learn the importance of accepting Christ in our lives as he presents himself and to be wary of imitating the experience of others who believe their relationship with him should be exactly like ours. Jesus will show us the way and feed our spiritual lives in the manner that best suits us.

☙ Inspiration

When I went to Holy Communion, it seemed that the door of my heart was thrown wide open, as if for the purpose of receiving a friend; and as soon as he had entered, it was closed. (St. Veronica Giuliani)

☙ Challenge

What religious practice—Eucharistic adoration, the rosary, contemplative prayer—might deepen your relationship with God? Explore how you might go about adding this practice to your life.

Paulina do Corção Agonizante de Jesus

December 16, 1865–July 9, 1942

It seemed Paulina's life course had been set. Before she was forty, she was recognized for the work the Congregation of the Little Sisters of the Immaculate Conception was doing in Brazil, and she was named superior general for life. But just six years later, the archbishop of São Paulo banned her from leadership in the congregation. More than twenty years passed before she was involved in a public way again. In the interim, she served the infirm sisters of the order. "Being for others represented the main reason of the life of Mother Paulina," Pope John Paul II said at her canonization Mass in 2002.

Sometimes, life throws us for a loop, even when we are doing our best to serve. We're demoted at work or removed from a parish or committee. Or when our time on a project ends, someone else takes over and somehow, things go on, better than ever. Paulina's example inspires us to accept the inevitability of change, confident of God's love amid it.

✸ Inspiration

Be humble. Trust always and a great deal in divine Providence; never never must you let yourselves be discouraged despite contrary winds. I say it again: trust in God and Mary Immaculate; be faithful and forge ahead! (St. Paulina do Corção Agonizante de Jesus)

✸ Challenge

Write down the slights in life that are bothering you. Pray over them. Then throw away the paper—and the spot they had been holding in your soul.

Anna Wang, one of the Martyrs of China

1886–July 22, 1900

Anna was just fourteen when she was among a group of Christians rounded up during the Boxer Rebellion and ordered to renounce her faith. She refused to follow her stepmother's example and deny God. The following day, she was given more opportunities and rejected them as well, even as she was struck, losing her right arm. She whispered Jesus's name three times, then lowered her head and was decapitated.

Consider the bravery of Anna, remaining faithful even as she watched others being executed. While few of us will ever face such a dramatic test, our faith is challenged in other ways—when people mock us for our beliefs or challenge us about some of the Church's stances on hot-button issues. Do we stand up for our faith—or let the comments go unchecked?

Inspiration

For I will give you words and a wisdom that none of your opponents will be able to withstand or contradict. (Luke 21:15)

Challenge

Think about situations in which you avoid talking about God and your faith to avoid confrontation or ridicule. Ask God for the right words to say and the strength to say them.

Agnes Le Thi Thanh

1781–July 12, 1841

Agnes, a mother of six, was the only laywoman among the Martyrs of Vietnam canonized by Pope John Paul II in 1988. Authorities discovered that secret Masses were being held in her home, and she was arrested along with a well-known Vietnamese priest. During three months in prison, she was tortured cruelly, including severe beatings with a large wooden bar and having poisonous snakes placed in her clothing. Even Agnes's husband, himself a Christian, asked her to reconsider her resolve for the sake of their children. She refused.

As much as we love our spouses and families, our first responsibility is always to God. Agnes's example reminds us that we must always be ready to defend our faith even if it places us in grave danger, confident that the Lord will care for those we leave behind.

🕊 Inspiration

I entrust the children to you, trust in God. As for me, I will trust and follow Jesus to the end. (St. Agnes Le Thi Thanh)

🕊 Challenge

Have a discussion with your family about the place of Jesus in each of your lives. Talk about why following Jesus is so important to you, and ask what that means.

Clelia Barbieri

February 13, 1847–July 13, 1870

Legend has it that at a very young age, Clelia asked her mother how she could become a saint. She certainly found out. Her first mystic experience occurred when she was eleven, the day of her First Communion. Clelia founded a faith community when she was only twenty-one, and the group, which became the Little Sisters of Our Lady of Sorrows, began referring to her as "Mother" shortly thereafter. As a result, she is referred to as the youngest founder ever of a Catholic religious community. Clelia died of tuberculosis when she was twenty-three.

What would you say if one of your children asked you how he or she could become a saint or pursue a vocation? Or perhaps your son or daughter has asked to go on a retreat or offer up a sacrifice for Lent you believe would have been too intense for them. While it can be a challenge to rear a child with a deep interior faith life, it's also a blessing. Remember, you may have a future saint in your home!

Inspiration

Train children in the right way,

and when old, they will not stray. (Proverbs 22:6)

Challenge

Is there a way for you to help your children or other young people grow in their faith? Talk with a member of your parish's religious education ministry about programs and activities in which you could assist.

Kateri Tekakwitha

1656–April 17, 1680

Kateri, called the "Lily of the Mohawks," had virtually no family support on her Christian journey. A smallpox epidemic orphaned her when she was very young, and left her partially blind and with scars on her face. Kateri was working as a servant in her uncle's home when she met the Jesuit missionaries who put her on a path to Christianity. It would be nine years before she was baptized. After being persecuted by members of her tribe when she prayed, she left for a Christian village, where she lived the remainder of her life.

No one has a perfect upbringing or is a perfect parent. In Kateri, we see the power of the unquenchable thirst for Christ, even when those around us ridicule and hurt us as we seek to quench that thirst.

Inspiration

If you belonged to the world, the world would love you as its own. Because you do not belong to the world, but I have chosen you out of the world—therefore the world hates you. Remember the word that I said to you, "Servants are not greater than their master." If they persecuted me, they will persecute you; if they kept my word, they will keep yours also. (John 15:19–20)

Challenge

Write a letter of thanks to the person—one of your parents, perhaps, or your childhood pastor or a teacher—who fed your spiritual fire while you were growing up.

Teresa de Jesús de los Andes

July 13, 1900–April 12, 1920

Chile's first saint joined the Discalced Carmelites when she was just nineteen. Within a few months, she learned she was fatally ill with typhus. Nonetheless, she continued her letter-writing ministry on spirituality and was able to profess her vows before she died. Pope John Paul II said at her beatification Mass in 1987 that Teresa knew "the grace of transformation in Christ, by the love that is patient, helpful, humble, and patient." She was canonized in 1993.

We sometimes become self-absorbed or self-pitying when we are faced with serious illnesses or other big challenges in life. Whatever we are going through is easier to bear when we find a way, large or small, to act in Christ's name to others even as we suffer.

Inspiration

Love is the fusion of two souls in one in order to bring about mutual perfection. Though I am absent from you, this changes nothing in our relationship. I am always with you, invisibly assisting you in all you do. (St. Teresa de Jesús de los Andes)

Challenge

What physical aches and pains are troubling you today? Offer them up with a smile as you share the Good News today with someone special.

Veronica

First century

It's one of the most poignant parts of Stations of the Cross: a woman steps forward to provide relief to Christ by wiping the blood and sweat his face with her veil. While we don't know for sure if this event occurred or, if it did, what happened to Veronica or the veil, the place where tradition indicates the encounter happened is marked with a plaque, and we honor this event in Stations of the Cross and by a feast day on July 12.

This story reminds us how small kindnesses—wiping a face, offering water to someone in distress, sharing some of our treasure—can mean so much to the recipient.

Inspiration

In all this I have given you an example that by such work we must support the weak, remembering the words of the Lord Jesus, for he himself said, "It is more blessed to give than to receive." (Acts 20:35)

Challenge

Do one small thing for someone in need today. Perhaps it's spending time with a friend in the hospital, or offering a neighbor a ride to the grocery store. It doesn't need to be a big deal for you, but you may be surprised what a difference it makes for him or her.

Mary Magdalen Postel

November 28, 1756–July 16, 1846

Mary Magdalen opened a school for girls after completing her own education, and likely thought this would be her destiny. Then the French Revolution began. Mary Magdalen helped keep the Church alive in the ensuing years, assisting priests who were in prison or in hiding, and sharing the Eucharist with the dying. She was among the women who founded the Poor Daughters of Mercy, a teaching and nursing ministry.

When she was young, Mary Magdalen probably didn't think her service to Christ would involve heroism and danger. And yet, when it did, she answered the call. We never know what opportunity will present itself on our faith journey. We can only pray for God's guidance and support when the time comes.

Inspiration

Pray in the Spirit at all times in every prayer and supplication. To that end keep alert and always persevere in supplication for all the saints. Pray also for me, so that when I speak, a message may be given to me to make known with boldness the mystery of the gospel, for which I am an ambassador in chains. Pray that I may declare it boldly, as I must speak. (Ephesians 6:18–20)

Challenge

Offer a rosary or other form of prayer for the people around the world who will risk their lives today in the name of Christ.

Rita Dolores Pujalte Sanchez and her companions

February 19, 1853–July 20, 1936

The sisters in Rita's order were praying the rosary in a chapel when Spanish revolutionaries barged in. Initially, the men allowed Rita, a retired superior who was eighty-three and blind, and another sister, who was ill, to leave. But it wasn't long before the men came after them again, pulled them down a staircase, drove away with them and then shot them. Seven other nuns of the same order were martyred in November.

Accounts of the time contrast the noisy revolutionaries and their supporters in the mob with the sisters' calm and serenity. Perhaps you've seen that with family members or friends or other acquaintances. There's often a peace when people let go of the struggle and accept the circumstances. Their faith in God and confidence in eternal life help in the transition.

✒ Inspiration

For the righteous will never be moved;
   they will be remembered forever.
They are not afraid of evil tidings;
   their hearts are firm, secure in the LORD. (Psalm 112:6–7)

✒ Challenge

If you knew death was at hand, what would you say to family members and friends today? Go ahead and tell them now.

Margarita María López de Maturana

July 25, 1884–July 23, 1934

Margarita had been part of the Cloistered Mercedarian Monastery of Vera Cruz for years, working at the boarding school. But she burned to take the Good News to people who hadn't had the opportunity to meet Christ. She formed a group encouraging young people to do missionary work, and the fire grew within others in the monastery. The sisters received temporary permission to change from a contemplative to an active missionary order, and they began departing for China and the South Pacific. Margarita, a year after being named superior, went on an expedition to Japan. In 1930, the order formally became a missionary institute.

Margarita's example reminds us to be open to change. We can tool along for years, content and serene. That's not necessarily bad. But when we fail to recognize opportunities God presents for growth and change, we hurt ourselves, and him.

✒ Inspiration

There are moments in life of special importance such as when the Lord shows us the way to be followed and then leaves it up to our will to respond. (Blessed Margarita María López de Maturana)

✒ Challenge

What new ways is God offering to improve your formation? Perhaps there's a course or presentation at your parish or a local college that could expand your spiritual horizons. Don't be afraid to say yes.

Justa and Rufina

Died 287

These sisters were particular about how the earthenware pottery they made could be used. When would-be customers tried to buy their wares for a pagan ceremony, Justa and Rufina refused. When all their goods were destroyed in retaliation, the sisters then smashed an image of the pagan goddess. They both were tortured and then killed.

It takes courage and faith in God to stand up to others when we're asked to do something counter to our beliefs and not just talk about doing so. It's likely Justa and Rufina found comfort in each other's presence as well as God's. You can't put a price on the support of a sister—or of God.

Inspiration

So faith by itself, if it has no works, is dead.

But someone will say, "You have faith and I have works." Show me your faith apart from your works, and I by my works will show you my faith. (James 2:17–18)

Challenge

Think of a time that a sister or friend who's like a sister supported you in actions as well as words at a difficult time. Let her know how important that was to you, and ask for her help with a challenge you're currently experiencing.

Julia of Corsica

Died circa 439

Julia was in bondage, but her master, Eusebius, had a heart. Though he was a pagan, he didn't prevent her from reading or praying in her free time. On one trip, Eusebius and everyone but Julia alighted to attend a pagan sacrifice. When the person in charge of the rite learned that Julia was still on board and was a Christian, he ordered her brought to the shore after Eusebius had fallen asleep. When she refused to participate in the sacrifice, even after she was tortured and promised freedom, she was crucified.

True freedom comes not in the ability to speak or act without fear, but in Christ. While Julia may have been a slave, she was the only one in this story who was serving the true Master. In the same way, we err when we bow down to the gods of money or power or pride.

Inspiration

My liberty is the service of Christ, whom I serve every day with a pure mind. (St. Julia of Corsica)

Challenge

What in your life is edging out Christ to be your master? Your job? Your financial situation? Your pride? Your fear? Meditate on ways you can bring things back into order.

Alphonsa of the Immaculate Conception (Anna Muttathupadathu)

August 19, 1910–July 28, 1946

The first Indian saint had a multitude of illnesses, including malaria and pneumonia, during her short life. She also had gastroenteritis and liver problems and was known to vomit up to forty times per day. Despite her physical challenges and a demanding aunt who wanted her to get married, Alphonsa reached her dream of becoming a nun and spent ten years as a Franciscan Clarist sister.

Chronic illnesses can be difficult to bear with grace. It's easy to engage in a pity party and continually ask God, "Why me?" Alphonsa inspires us to move beyond the "Why me" and find ways we can cope with our pain and suffering and still follow the path God has laid out for us.

Inspiration

I feel that the Lord has destined me to be an oblation, a sacrifice of suffering…. I consider a day in which I have not suffered as a day lost to me. (St. Alphonsa of the Immaculate Conception)

Challenge

Take five minutes before you get out of bed in the morning and before you fall asleep at night to thank God for your physical body, impaired as it may be, and for guidance in showing you how he wishes you to use it.

Mary Magdalene

First century

Forget about whether she was or wasn't a prostitute before Jesus cast those demons out of her. The thing to remember is that once that happened, she stuck by Jesus in his day-to-day ministry and at his crucifixion when so many others fled. No wonder, then, that she was the first to see him and speak with him after his resurrection.

Talk is cheap. We all think we would have stood by Jesus, but then, we know how the story ends. Mary Magdalene's example shows us the power of true adoration and love for our Lord.

Inspiration

Jesus said to her, "Woman, why are you weeping? Whom are you looking for?" Supposing him to be the gardener, she said to him, "Sir, if you have carried him away, tell me where you have laid him, and I will take him away." Jesus said to her, "Mary!" She turned and said to him in Hebrew, "Rabbouni!" (which means Teacher). (John 20:15–16)

Challenge

Where in your life are you avoiding standing up for Christ? Perhaps it's a situation where someone in your family is being dishonest, or a coworker is ridiculing those who have Bible verses posted in their cubicles. Pray for the strength and the words you need to defend your faith.

Bridget of Sweden
1303–July 23, 1373

It wasn't Bridget's dream to get married and have children; rather, she longed from an early age to become a nun. But she was obedient to her prominent family's desire that she marry a prince. Their marriage was happy and produced eight children (including one, Catherine, who would go on to be a saint herself). Bridget and her husband completed a pilgrimage on the Way of St. James together, and she went on a separate pilgrimage herself to a shrine in Norway. After her husband's death, Bridget spent four years living a quiet monastic life. Then, as a result of the revelations she experienced during that period, began speaking out about political and religious issues as she traveled through the Holy Land and elsewhere.

There are different seasons to our lives, as Bridget found—wife and mother, time at the Swedish royal court, and as a woman religious. Her example shows us that God knows what's best for each season; all we have to do is listen.

Inspiration
For everything there is a season, and a time for every matter under heaven. (Ecclesiastes 3:1)

Challenge
Journal about the past seasons of your life—childhood, your teenage years, college, marriage, jobs, motherhood, relocations, ministries—and how they inform where you are today.

Kinga of Poland

March 5, 1224–July 24, 1292

Kinga and her husband, Boleslaw, had a less than traditional marriage, as both took a vow of chastity. The pair reigned as prince and princess of Krakow until Boleslaw's death in 1279. At that time, Kinga sold everything, gave the proceeds to the poor, and joined a Poor Clares monastery.

Kinga's example shows us that there is a way to remain married even when both parties believe God is calling them to other service. As Blessed John Paul II said at Kinga's canonization, "Whatever difficulties may arise, one may not abandon the defense of this primordial love which has united two persons and which is constantly blessed by God. Marriage is the way of holiness, even when it becomes the way of the Cross."

Inspiration

Let the word of Christ dwell in you richly; teach and admonish one another in all wisdom; and with gratitude in your hearts sing psalms, hymns, and spiritual songs to God. And whatever you do, in word or deed, do everything in the name of the Lord Jesus, giving thanks to God the Father through him. (Colossians 3:16–17)

Challenge

Talk with your spouse about the ways in which your call to holiness intersects in matrimony and also the ways in which you each follow God on a different path. How can you best support each other?

Maria del Carmen (Maria Sallés y Barangueras)
April 9, 1848–July 25, 1911

In Carmen's view, people deserved a second chance. Her focus as a woman religious was on helping women who had made mistakes get the education they needed to leave lives of crime and prostitution. Carmen also got a few second chances herself; she left the Sisters Adorers of the Blessed Sacrament and then the Dominican Sisters of the Annunciata to found what is now known as Sisters of the Immaculate Conception.

All of us make mistakes. All of us hurt others, knowingly or unknowingly. Carmen's example reminds us that no matter how deep or intentional the wound, we are called to love as Christ loves. That doesn't mean enabling destructive behavior, but Christian love that helps and heals.

Inspiration

I give you a new commandment, that you love one another. Just as I have loved you, you also should love one another. By this everyone will know that you are my disciples, if you have love for one another. (John 13:34–35)

Challenge

Who has wounded you deeply in your life? Consider making notes on what this person did and how it affected you. Sit with it for a while, and then pray for the person's soul—and your own.

Anne

First century

Tradition has it that the Blessed Virgin's parents, Anne and Joachim, were married for twenty years before God answered their prayers for a child. When an angel told Anne she would conceive, she pledged to rear the child as offering to God. We often see images of Anne teaching Mary to read, a sign of the loving care and education she provided to her daughter.

A mother's life can be challenging today, just as it was two thousand years ago. It's difficult to keep tabs on school work, sports activities, religious instruction, and music lessons, let alone monitoring Internet and phone use. Yet the most challenging, eternal responsibility for any parent is to provide a faithful role model for your son or daughter amid all the comings and goings in your household.

❧ Inspiration

Recite them to your children and talk about them when you are at home and when you are away, when you lie down and when you rise. (Deuteronomy 6:7)

❧ Challenge

Make an extra effort this week to pray before each meal. During a meal shared with family or friends, discuss God moments in everyone's day. Turn off the phones and television as everyone sits down. Enjoy the gift of each other's company.

Lillian and Natalie of Cordoba

Died July 27, 852

Lillian and Natalie's story is one of finding strength in God's community despite a hostile environment. Both women were baptized Christians in Moor-occupied Spain, where everyone had to follow Muslim law. As a result, the women practiced their faith in secret, as did Natalie's husband, Aurelius. They decided to go public after Aurelius saw a Christian bearing a severe beating for professing his faith publicly. It was then that Lillian's husband, Felix, a relative of Aurelius, decided to return to Christianity. The foursome knowingly offered themselves up for martyrdom when the women appeared in public with unveiled faces.

Religious freedom is a gift that is not shared by all in the world today. Strict laws and practices control the lives of many women in countries where religion rules the government. We should be grateful for the ability to practice our faith here without the strict oversight and regulations about religious practices that others live with on a daily basis.

Inspiration

Rejoice insofar as you are sharing Christ's sufferings, so that you may also be glad and shout for joy when his glory is revealed. (1 Peter 4:13)

Challenge

Wear an outward sign of your faith in Christ today in a potentially hostile situation at work or elsewhere.

Bartolomea Capitanio

1807–July 26, 1833

More than twenty years separated Bartolomea and Caterina Gerosa (St. Vincenza Gerosa). But both were passionate about ministry, and Bartolomea's pastor encouraged the women to work together. The women founded the Sisters of Charity of Lovere when Bartolomea was only twenty-five. Before Bartolomea's death less than a year later, they established a hospital, school, and orphanage.

Shared life experiences—having heard the same music or read the same books or seen the same TV shows—can be a good start to friendship. But relying only on shared memories can be very limiting. Christ presents himself in people of all ages, genders, races, and nationalities. When we accept that, the sky's the limit when it comes to what we can do for God.

Inspiration

Likewise, tell the older women to be reverent in behavior, not to be slanderers or slaves to drink; they are to teach what is good,...to be self-controlled, chaste, good managers of the household, kind, being submissive to their husbands, so that the word of God may not be discredited. (Titus 2:3, 5)

Challenge

Get together with a friend who's at least fifteen years older or younger than you. Talk about your shared interests. If you don't have a friend who fits the bill, think of ways you can expand your circle.

Martha

First century

We often think about Martha being all about the busyness of service and perhaps lacking in worship, complaining about her sister Mary's lack of industry when Jesus came to visit and Jesus's rebuke that Mary had chosen "the better part." But Martha's faith also was strong; she acknowledged Christ as the Messiah even before he raised her brother, Lazarus, from the dead.

Keeping a clean, harmonious, and God-filled home is a tall order! Often, order in our physical houses reflects order in our spiritual houses. Just remember which one should always take precedence.

Inspiration

"Yes, Lord, I believe that you are the Messiah, the Son of God, the one coming into the world."

When she had said this, she went back and called her sister Mary, and told her privately, "The Teacher is here and is calling for you." (John 11:27–28)

Challenge

Make a list of the three most important things to do this week to get your home in order. Then do the same for your soul. Resolve to complete both sets of tasks with a smile on your face and joy in your heart. And if you don't get through the whole list, don't beat yourself up.

María de Jesús Sacramentado

September 8, 1868–July 30, 1959

Maria spent her early life as a laywoman, working at a charity hospital as a nurse and in serving in other roles. In 1905, she attended a retreat that confirmed her desire to become a woman religious and founded the Daughters of the Sacred Heart of Jesus. In that role, she kept the hospital open and operational amid violence in the Guadalajara area in the 1920s. At the 2000 canonization of Mexico's first female saint, Pope John Paul II cited Maria's devotion to the Eucharist and her care for the poor and sick, calling her "an eloquent example of total dedication to the service of God and to suffering humanity."

God's call to us—to love him and to love our neighbor as ourselves—is always the same, but the way he wants us to carry it out can change. At one time, raising children may be the most important ministry; at another, it may be caring for our parents, or volunteering at a homeless shelter, or taking a parish leadership position. It takes courage—and faith—to listen and obey.

✒ Inspiration

For surely I know the plans I have for you, says the LORD, plans for your welfare and not for harm, to give you a future with hope. (Jeremiah 29:11)

✒ Challenge

Ask God what he wants you to do today, and what he wants you to prepare to do for tomorrow. Then, no matter how challenging it seems, do it.

Glodesind

Died circa 608

Glodesind was somewhat of a political pawn in her early life. Despite her protestations that she had consecrated her life to Christ, her parents arranged for a marriage. But on the day of the wedding, her intended was called away by the king, who promptly locked him up for a year for crimes and then beheaded him. When Glodesind's father found another man for her, she refused again. Her father decided to pack her off to visit his sister. Instead, Glodesind ran to a church in Metz, where after six days of prayer, a stranger who appeared to be an angel put the holy veil of religion over her. Not even her father could challenge that, and he established a monastery for her there.

It's gone on since time immemorial. Children, even adult children, express their plans or dreams or desires, and parents pooh-pooh them. While Mom and Dad may know best, at some point, they can only make recommendations, love their children just as they did when they were babies, and turn the rest over to God.

✿ Inspiration

And, fathers, do not provoke your children to anger, but bring them up in the discipline and instruction of the Lord. (Ephesians 6:4)

✿ Challenge

Pray that your children, or other young people who are in your life, may heed God's guidance. Then ask questions about their latest dreams and ventures, but leave the judging to him.

Mother Maria Stella (Adelaide Mardosiewicz) and her ten companions

1888–August 1, 1943

Nowogródek, now part of Belarus, was a horrific place to be during World War II. The city changed hands several times, and by some estimates more than 45,000 residents died, including all but 550 of the estimated 10,000 Jews who lived there. Among the others were Blessed Mary Star and ten other women religious. Twice, the eleven women offered to exchange their lives for others arrested and scheduled to be executed. The second time, their offer was accepted. They were imprisoned, then killed and placed in a common grave.

The sisters made their offer in hopes of saving people with families. Their selfless act reminds us of how Christ suffered on our behalf, and our brothers and sisters around the world, so that those who know him may share in the kingdom of God.

Inspiration

If you are reviled for the name of Christ, you are blessed, because the spirit of glory, which is the Spirit of God, is resting on you. (1 Peter 4:14)

Challenge

Offer a prayer of thanksgiving for our Church's martyrs and their sacrifices over the centuries. Consider their bravery; how might praying with them bring you courage and confidence in your life today?

Louise of Savoy

December 28, 1461–July 24, 1503

We can only imagine the luxury to which Louise was exposed growing up. Her mother was the sister of the French king, Louis XI, and her father, who was beatified himself, also was a ruler. Yet beneath her fine gowns, Louise wore a haircloth. She and her husband both were given to prayer and contemplation, and encouraged those at court to conduct themselves in a more respectful manner. After she was left a childless widow before she was thirty, Louise entered a Poor Clares convent, where she spent the rest of her days.

In Louise we have a wise reminder of the trappings of the world. While we may need to dress the part of a businesswoman or socialite, we must remember that underneath it all, it's what our soul looks like that matters.

Inspiration

For what will it profit them if they gain the whole world but forfeit their life? Or what will they give in return for their life? (Matthew 16:26)

Challenge

What could you wear for a day as a reminder of the importance of your soul? A scapular, perhaps, or a holy medal? Select something that reminds you to keep your life as simple as possible.

Lydia

First century

She was going about her business in Philippi, selling purple cloth or dye. It's believed Lydia had thought about taking on the Jewish faith, but hadn't taken the final steps. Then she heard Paul talk about Jesus, and became his very first convert in Europe. Lydia fell so in love with the Word that she and her entire household were baptized—and then, she persuaded the disciples to stay with her.

Lydia may have been one of those people who claim to be spiritual but not religious, someone who had come to believe in the concept of one God, but who hadn't taken it further. Then something in her soul was stirred by what Paul had to say. In the same way, our wise, inspired evangelization today can help set lukewarm souls on fire.

Inspiration

The Lord opened her heart to listen eagerly to what was said by Paul. When she and her household were baptized, she urged us, saying, "If you have judged me to be faithful to the Lord, come and stay at my home." And she prevailed upon us. (Acts 16:14–15)

Challenge

How can you share your faith with those who claim to be spiritual but not religious? By offering to pray for them? By sharing parts of your faith journey? By listening to their challenges? No one way will be right to reach everyone; listen to your heart in your efforts to talk to others about your faith.

Carmelite Martyrs of Compiègne

Died July 31, 1794

Eleven Discalced Carmelite nuns, three lay sisters, and their two servants were guillotined in Paris as enemies of the French Revolution after they declined to swear their allegiance to the new government's constitution. The women went to their deaths showing true devotion to God, re-professing their baptismal and religious vows and singing the "Veni Creator," which is used at solemn Church occasions. One of the sisters told those gathered, "I forgive you as heartily as I wish God to forgive me." The Reign of Terror ended less than two weeks after the women's martyrdom.

The women showed breathtaking faith and courage, and were blessed to have each other nearby as they prepared to meet their ends. In the same way, we can surround ourselves with people who help us maintain spiritual confidence in spite of what the world brings our way.

Inspiration

Whenever you stand praying, forgive, if you have anything against anyone; so that your Father in heaven may also forgive you your trespasses. (Mark 11:25)

Challenge

What would you do if you knew you were going to die tomorrow? Who would you see? Who would you forgive? Do it today, for another day on this earth is never guaranteed.

Nonna of Nazianzus

Died circa 374

Imagine growing up in this family! Nonna converted her husband, Gregory of Nazianzus the Elder, to Christianity. (He later became a bishop.) Like Nonna, he was named a saint—as were all three of their children, Gregory (a monk and bishop), Caesarius (a doctor), and Gorgonia (wife and mother). Gregory wrote that his mother "excelled in both the thrifty management of her household and in the pursuit of godliness" and learned to trust in God completely.

While it's breathtaking and, let's be honest, a little overwhelming, to think about an entire family becoming saints in our Church, there is something to consider here. Families learn from each other. Whether we learn love, compassion, and faith, or bitterness, anger, and fear, the tone is usually set by the parents. Setting a Christlike example helps our children learn to navigate the world in a grace-filled manner.

❧ Inspiration

Now if you are unwilling to serve the LORD, choose this day whom you will serve, whether the gods your ancestors served in the region beyond the River or the gods of the Amorites in whose land you are living; but as for me and my household, we will serve the LORD. (Joshua 24:15)

❧ Challenge

Put away the cell phones, earphones, and television for the coming week at dinnertime. Talk to your family or other dinnermates about what has happened in your day, or reflect quietly on its events.

Imelda Lambertini
1322–May 12, 1333

Imelda longed to receive the Eucharist. She entered a Dominican convent at her own request when she was nine, but in that day, the minimum age to receive Holy Communion was twelve. Then, one day in the chapel, Imelda entered an ecstasy and what appeared to be a host could be seen over her head. A priest was called, and he felt under the circumstances he had to go ahead with Imelda's First Communion. She died moments thereafter.

How blessed we are as Catholics to receive the Body of Christ! His True Presence is the ultimate nourishment for our spiritual journey. We sometimes take for granted this great gift we can receive each time we go to Mass. May we all remember to stop and bow before receiving the host, and offer up our prayer of gratitude.

Inspiration
Tell me, can anyone receive Jesus into his heart and not die? (Blessed Imelda Lambertini)

Challenge
Contemplate Imelda's question. How do you die in receiving Jesus—death of pride, of fear, of anger? Journal about the ways this sacrament feeds you. Recall how you felt on the day of your First Communion, when you first experienced this moving sacrament of union with Christ.

Margaret Pole

August 14, 1473–May 28, 1541

The saga of England's King Henry VIII and his six wives may be the stuff of movies and romance to us, but it was deadly serious for Margaret. Henry named Margaret, a Plantagenet, countess of Salisbury and governess for his oldest daughter, Mary. However, the Pole family fell out of favor when they opposed Henry's marriage to Anne Boleyn and the establishment of the Church of England. After two years in the Tower of London, Margaret was beheaded.

Margaret's story reminds us to pray for the families of those whose behavior we find offensive, that they may come to find peace and consolation with their situation.

Inspiration

Hide me from the secret plots of the wicked,
    from the scheming of evildoers,
who whet their tongues like swords,
    who aim bitter words like arrows,
shooting from ambush at the blameless;
    they shoot suddenly and without fear. (Psalms 64:2–4)

Challenge

Look at the front page of your hometown newspaper, online or in paper. Make a list of the mothers, fathers, sisters, brothers, children, and neighbors who are hurting as the result of the behavior of those making news. Pray for them.

Mary of the Cross MacKillop

January 15, 1842–August 8, 1909

What was Mary's reward for spreading God's word by building schools and refuges for women in poverty-stricken areas of Australia? Excommunication by her bishop, who said she was ambitious and obstinate. A commission investigated the sisters, and recommended giving local priests authority over the convents of the Order of the Sisters of St. Joseph. It took a year before she was reinstated as superior of the order, which ultimately grew to more than one hundred convents. Mary is Australia's first saint.

Constructive criticism helps us to learn better behaviors and practices. Learning how to deal with criticism that's less than constructive can be hard. It's easy to simply give up or to become defensive or argumentative. Mary's example shows us the importance of standing by our faith-directed principles, even when those in positions of authority seek to undermine us.

✒ Inspiration

Could not pray or say my ordinary rosaries, only offered my weary heart's trials to my God with the wish that he would do his will and make of me what he pleased. (St. Mary of the Cross MacKillop)

✒ Challenge

Is someone trying to dislodge one of your moral or spiritual principles? Ask your spiritual director, pastor, or a trusted family member or friend to help you develop a plan for gently confronting that person.

Teresa Benedicta of the Cross (Edith Stein)

October 12, 1891–August 9, 1942

Teresa Benedicta of the Cross may be one of the best known Catholic converts of our time. She was born on Yom Kippur and was raised Jewish, but she abandoned a faith life at an early age. Her life's love became the study of philosophy. Then, in the summer before she turned thirty, she read St. Teresa of Avila's autobiography and chose to convert. She entered a Carmelite monastery in 1933, where she continued her philosophical writings. She and her sister, who had also converted, were arrested and sent to Auschwitz, where it is believed they were gassed.

People come to Christ in different ways and at different times. For some like Teresa, conversion is the result of intellectual pursuits. For others, it's an outstretched hand in a time of trouble. Remember that we always represent the face of Christ to non-believers. Make sure the face you show is full of love and compassion.

✒ Inspiration

When you seek truth you seek God whether you know it or not. (St. Teresa Benedicta of the Cross)

✒ Challenge

Invite a non-Christian or non-practicing Catholic friend or acquaintance to volunteer with you at a homeless shelter or food pantry, or attend a lecture or event together at your parish.

Clare of Assisi

July 16, 1194–August 11, 1253

That we still hunger to learn about Clare more than seven hundred years after her death is a testimony to both her boldness and her piety. Inspired by listening to Francis of Assisi, she in essence ran away from home in her Palm Sunday finery when she was eighteen to become one of his first followers. Soon other young women, including her sister Agnes, joined her. Francis made Clare superior of what would later become the Poor Clares. The nuns did not own property and lived an austere life, not wearing shoes, refraining from meat, and observing silence most of the time. Clare remained as abbess for forty years, and was canonized a scant two years after her death.

It's fitting that this saint's first name is Clare, for the moment of clarity she gained while listening to St. Francis set her life on a totally different course. We admire her for her recognition of that God moment, and for her fortitude in staying the course the rest of her life.

Inspiration

Place your mind before the mirror of eternity! Place your soul in the brilliance of glory! Place your heart in the figure of the divine substance! And transform your entire being into the image of the Godhead itself through contemplation. (St. Clare of Assisi)

Challenge

Can you identify defining moments on your faith journey? Journal about them and how they continue to inform your development today.

Mariam Baouardy

January 5, 1846–August 26, 1878

Mariam, known as the Lily of Palestine, was estranged from her family when she refused to take part in an arranged marriage. She struck up a friendship with a young man who recommended conversion to Islam as a remedy for her problems. When she firmly rejected this option, he slashed her throat and left her for dead. A nun dressed in blue cared for her in a grotto, and later disappeared. Later in life, Mariam was visited by an angel and by St. Joseph, and she received the gift of ecstasies and stigmata. She spent most of her life as a Carmelite nun.

While we seek always to let God effect the conversion of others through our actions and words, the decision ultimately rests with God and the other people. If they say, "No," we need to remember it may be "No, not now" and redouble our efforts to reflect Christ in all we do. Conversion will happen when the person is ready. We are responsible only for planting seeds.

Inspiration

Holy Spirit, inspire me. Love of God, consume me. Along the true road, lead me. (Blessed Mariam Baouardy)

Challenge

Resolve to remain loving and Christlike, not accusatory and judgmental, in your interactions with everyone you encounter today.

Jane Frances de Chantal

January 28, 1572–December 13, 1641

Jane's world had been turned upside down. She was just twenty-eight when her husband was killed in a hunting accident, leaving her with four children. She'd been further challenged in joining the difficult household of her father-in-law. Then, three years after her husband died, she heard St. Francis de Sales preach. He became her spiritual director, and ultimately, with Francis's support, she founded what is today the Sisters of the Visitation.

Just as he did with Jane and Francis, God sends important people into our lives all the time. Being open to what they say and do will help us grow spiritually. Then we must be brave enough to learn from their example and take the next steps on our faith journey.

Inspiration

If we follow his plans for us, though heaven and earth should be overturned, in truth it does not matter whether we suffer or enjoy, so long as the Divine Will be accomplished. (St. Jane Frances de Chantal)

Challenge

Write a letter of thanks to the person who has had the most profound effect on your faith journey. If that person has died, offer up a rosary or prayer of thanksgiving in his or her memory.

Radegund

Circa 520–August 13, 587

Radegund's early life was filled with violence. Her uncle murdered her father, and then chose to raise her. A few years later, another ruler killed her uncle, and that ruler's brother, Clotaire I, married Radegund. It was an unhappy union with much infidelity. Finally, when Clotaire also killed Radegund's brother, she fled and took up sanctuary in a church. Eventually, she founded a cloistered convent of the Holy Cross at Poitiers, France, where it was required that the sisters be literate and study Scripture. Perhaps as a result of the violence she had seen, Radegund also developed a reputation as a peacemaker.

Imagine the pain in Radegund's heart, to have lost her father and then her brother. At times, it seems life brings us more sorrow than we can bear. While we may never understand why this world's tragedies occur, the one lasting place we may find comfort if not resolution is in God.

Inspiration

Do not fear, for I am with you,
do not be afraid, for I am your God;
I will strengthen you, I will help you,
I will uphold you with my victorious right hand. (Isaiah 41:10)

Challenge

What sorrow are you holding in your heart? Talk about it with Jesus and ask him to lighten your load, remembering his words, "For my yoke is easy, and my burden is light." (Matthew 11:30)

Maria Caridad Brader

August 14, 1860–February 27, 1943

Maria's intelligence was obvious from an early age, and she was a standout in the classroom. Perhaps not surprisingly, her mother initially opposed her only child's decision to enter a Franciscan convent. Maria moved even further from what some might have considered her life plan six years later when she was among a group of sisters who became missionaries in Ecuador. The congregation she founded focused on educating and catechizing children and the poor. She also emphasized to her sisters the importance of their own education and prayer life.

We can't teach something we don't know. Whether you are carrying God's word to your children, your coworkers, or the disenfranchised, you must first understand and write it on your own heart and soul. To put it in popular vernacular, you must not just talk the talk, but also walk the walk.

✒ Inspiration

Do not forget that the better educated, the greater the skills the educator possesses, the more she will be able to do for our holy religion and the glory of God, especially when virtue is the vanguard of her knowledge. (Blessed Maria Caridad Brader)

✒ Challenge

Increase your religious intelligence. Join a prayer group, sign up for a retreat, set aside time for Scripture or other faith-based reading. Stick to it.

Victoire Rasoamanarivo

1848–August 21, 1894

Victoire was born into a ruling-class family in Madagascar and was sent to a Catholic school. It was there she found her strong faith, despite the family's later efforts to convert her to Protestantism. At sixteen, she entered into an arranged marriage with a cousin, a marriage that had challenges given her husband's dissolute behavior and Victoire's devotion. When foreign missionaries were expelled, Victoire was among those who kept the Catholic faith alive, ignoring orders to renounce her beliefs. Two years after the missionaries were allowed to return, Victoire's husband died, but not before he was baptized on his deathbed.

So many times in history, being a faithful Catholic has presented challenges, sometimes deadly challenges. Just as was the case in Victoire's time, we are called to keep the Spirit alive and burning.

❧ Inspiration

But the LORD is with me like a dread warrior;
> therefore my persecutors will stumble,
> and they will not prevail.
They will be greatly shamed,
> or they will not succeed.
Their eternal dishonor
> will never be forgotten. (Jeremiah 20:11)

❧ Challenge

Write or e-mail a letter to your congressional representative about your belief in religious freedom for all, including Catholics.

Jeanne Delanoue

June 18, 1666–August 17, 1736

Jeanne was what we'd call a successful businesswoman—so successful, in fact, that her shop stayed open on Sundays and holy days. Then, when she was twenty-seven, a woman entered the store and suggested Jeanne help the poor. Jeanne found herself spending more and more time in ministry and less and less time on her business. Other women saw the work she was doing and joined her, and in 1709, the Sisters of St. Anne of Providence was formally established.

Whether you're a senior executive or an hourly fast-food worker, your job becomes part of your life. And while it's important to be present at work, that doesn't mean you have to check your faith values at the door. If your job is getting in the way of your faith, it's time to examine your priorities—and to remember we can also be the face of Christ in the workplace.

✒ Inspiration

Obey your earthly masters with fear and trembling, in singleness of heart, as you obey Christ; not only while being watched, and in order to please them, but as slaves of Christ, doing the will of God from the heart. (Ephesians 6:5–6)

✒ Challenge

If you work outside the home, write down the ways you are less than Christlike while you are there: Do you gossip? Play politics? Find ways to get others to take on your responsibilities? Make a list of ways you can better align your faith with your professional life.

Clare of Montefalco

Circa 1268–August 18, 1308

You might think that a woman's spirituality would increase upon entering a convent, but that was not the case for Clare. In her first eleven years as an Augustinian nun, she felt abandoned by God. Yet, she stayed the course. Eventually, Clare had a spiritual awakening that led to her devotion to Christ's passion, specifically to the cross of Jesus.

Times of spiritual drought hit everyone—remember Blessed Teresa's feeling for decades that she could no longer connect with God? It's in these times more than any other that we must be confident that God is working in our lives and our hearts and souls in ways we can't understand, and continue to conduct ourselves in ways that are pleasing to him.

Inspiration

Draw near to God, and he will draw near to you. Cleanse your hands, you sinners, and purify your hearts, you double-minded…. Humble yourselves before the Lord, and he will exalt you. (James 4:8, 10)

Challenge

In what way do you feel estranged from God today, or have you felt estranged in the past? Journal about those feelings, and don't worry about being nice—God can take it. Put the notes in your Bible or another spiritual resource, and go back to them in a few months or a year. You'll see he was there all along.

Helena

Circa 250–330

We often hear of parents kindling or rekindling a love of Christ in their children. In the case of Constantine and Helena, it was just the opposite. Helena became a Christian after her son's famous conversion, and proceeded to develop a deep and intense faith. Constantine opened his coffers for her to travel to the sites where Jesus walked. There, Helena discovered what she believed to be the True Cross and its nails, among other treasures.

We come to God in different ways—through our children, through our parents, through our own study. And once we have declared our faith, there are different ways in which we feed it. For many people, the ability to touch relics such as those retrieved by Helena generates a powerful feeling of connection with our Lord. For others, it may be reading Scripture or working with the poor. The important thing is to keep that fire burning once it is ignited.

✽ Inspiration

They said to each other, "Were not our hearts burning within us while he was talking to us on the road, while he was opening the scriptures to us?" (Luke 24:32)

✽ Challenge

Consider approaching Christ in a different way. For example, if you are a rosary devotee, you might try volunteering at a soup kitchen. If your primary ministry is in teaching or public speaking, consider trying an hour of adoration. You may be surprised at how this experiment feeds your faith life.

Sancja Szymkowiak

July 11, 1910–August 29, 1942

To some, Sancja likely had a bright future as a teacher. She studied languages and literature at the University of Poznan, and she studied pharmacology after she had entered the Congregation of the Daughters of Our Lady of Sorrows. However, teaching was not her heart's desire; her vocation was. When the sisters were put under house arrest and forced to care for soldiers and prisoners of war, she was given permission to return to her family, but she chose to stay. She ministered to the men with love and gentleness, but her health was deteriorating. She died of tuberculosis less than two months after professing her final vows.

We wonder sometimes about people's life choices. Imagine, a young woman so intelligent and who loved learning so much, sacrificing a potential career for life as a nun. Imagine, a young woman who was given the opportunity to leave house arrest and go home, instead staying where she was. The wise among us grow where we are planted, regardless of what other people think.

Inspiration

God is everything. I am nothing. (Blessed Sancja Szymkowiak)

Challenge

Where have you sat in judgment on a friend's choice, perhaps to take a lower-paying job or to attend a less prestigious college or to date a man you regard as beneath her? Pray for the wisdom to accept and love her as she is, not as you wish she would be.

Maria De Mattias

February 4, 1805–August 20, 1866

Maria was born into a wealthy family in the small town of Vallecorsa, Italy. The area was experiencing strife during her childhood and adolescence, and as a result Maria spent much time alone. The shy child focused on her looks. Then, in her late teens, she discovered her vocation. She went on to found about seventy religious communities, mostly in rural areas, and spoke tirelessly about Christ and the Catholic faith.

Hair, makeup, clothes, and shoes—most young women go through a period when their exterior appearance seems to be all they care about. Our culture highly prizes that kind of beauty. St. Maria Mattias's example reminds us that being on fire for the Lord and spreading the flames are the ultimate beauty.

Inspiration

Do not adorn yourselves outwardly by braiding your hair, and by wearing gold ornaments or fine clothing; rather, let your adornment be the inner self with the lasting beauty of a gentle and quiet spirit, which is very precious in God's sight. (1 Peter 3:3–4)

Challenge

Spend time with a young woman who seems focused on her looks. Talk with her about what's inside her heart and soul, and validate how gorgeous she is.

Maria del Pilar Izquierdo Albero

July 27, 1906–August 27, 1945

Some people would say Maria was born under a dark cloud. She experienced physical disabilities off and on all of her short life. Gossip and intrigue was so bad within her order that she left on the advice of her confessor. Yet even on her deathbed, she prayed for those who had hurt her.

Sometimes, our lives seem to go from bad to worse with no letup. We wonder where God is in all the pain, physical and emotional, that we experience. At some level, we need to remember that what happens to us here is temporary, and to offer up our suffering for God and for our brothers and sisters in Christ.

✺ Inspiration

In this suffering I find a love so great toward our Jesus, that I at once die and do not die...because that love is that which makes me live. (Blessed Maria del Pilar Izquierdo Albero)

✺ Challenge

What is your greatest pain today? Perhaps it's a chronic physical condition, or heartache from the end of a marriage, or heartburn from rumors begun by someone you once considered a friend. Pray for God to provide some healing balm, and the strength for you to face another day renewed in his love.

Ebbe the Elder

Died August 25, 683

The early Middle Ages were sometimes challenging for those in religious life. Wealthy people who entered monasteries often went on living life the way they had before, drinking, partying, taking lovers. Ebbe, however, didn't fit into that mold. When she became abbess at the Coldingham double monastery, she worked to return it to the original principles, and had some success before her death.

Texting at meals or while we're driving. Talking over or interrupting people. Too many glasses of wine at night. We're all guilty of bad behavior that perhaps started with a single incident and then became routine. Ebbe's story reminds us to think about how our behavior aligns or doesn't with Scripture and Church teachings.

🐟 Inspiration

Now the works of the flesh are obvious: fornication, impurity, licentiousness, idolatry, sorcery, enmities, strife, jealousy, anger, quarrels, dissensions, factions, envy, drunkenness, carousing, and things like these….

By contrast, the fruit of the Spirit is love, joy, peace, patience, kindness, generosity, faithfulness, gentleness, and self-control. (Galatians 5:19–21, 22–23)

🐟 Challenge

Where has your personal behavior become lax? Perhaps it's what you wear to Church or the way you talk to your spouse, your children, or your friends. Ask a trusted person to be your Ebbe and lovingly advise you when you're out of line.

Rose of Lima

April 20, 1586–August 24, 1617

Rose was a beautiful young woman, but she found that beauty to be a distraction and trial. She tried to destroy the temptation she felt she presented by rubbing her face with pepper and her hands with lime, and trying other behaviors we might consider self-abuse. Despite this, she continued to do fine needlework to support her family and set up an infirmary for the elderly and children in her parents' home. In 1671, Rose became the first Latin American to be canonized.

We all have dark nights of the soul, places where we feel confused and unworthy and vulnerable. Rose shows us what can happen when we open ourselves up to God and his work as we are, with physical and psychological and emotional frailties.

Inspiration

If human beings knew what it is to live in grace, no suffering would frighten them and they would gladly suffer any hardship, for grace is the fruit of patience. (St. Rose of Lima)

Challenge

What fear or concern keeps you awake at night and away from doing what that quiet voice tells you God desires? Converse with our Lord or St. Rose of Lima about this in prayer. Ask for help in overcoming that fear.

Maria Micaela of the Blessed Sacrament

January 1, 1809–August 25, 1865

It was a good life. Maria Micaela was raised in the Spanish aristocracy, and she spent time at the royal palaces where her brother was the ambassador. But then, when she was thirty-five, she had her first exposure to women who were seriously less privileged, the prostitutes of Madrid. She devoted the rest of her life to helping prostitutes and other women at risk through the congregation she and her friends formed, Sisters Adorers, Handmaids of the Blessed Sacrament and of Charity.

Some ministries are more socially attractive—and accepted—than others. For example, who can resist the idea of helping an innocent child? As Maria Micaela experienced, helping prostitutes (or drug addicts, or those who have AIDS) can result in ridicule and threats. Nonetheless, we are all loved by God and worthy of redemption.

Inspiration

And the king will answer them, "Truly I tell you, just as you did it to one of the least of these who are members of my family, you did it to me." (Matthew 25:40)

Challenge

Do you consciously or unconsciously rate the ministries of your friends or others in your parish as to which are worthy and which are not? Ask a friend whose ministry leaves you cold or a bit befuddled to talk about the people he or she serves.

Teresa de Jesús Jornet e Ibars

January 9, 1843–August 26, 1897

Teresa experienced an early setback in her faith journey. She wanted a life with the Poor Clares and either was not able to join, or joined and had to leave because of health issues. After a time of indecision, she encountered a priest who encouraged her to work with him in service to the poverty-stricken elderly. Teresa became the first superior of the Little Sisters of the Abandoned Poor. In his homily at her canonization, Pope Paul VI spoke of the serenity and joy her order has returned to the lives of the aged.

Maybe sixty is the new forty and seventy is the new fifty for those of us with the means to get regular healthcare, eat well, and exercise. But Teresa's example and ministry remind us that not all the elderly have our advantages. We must never forget the earlier generations who today are living on society's margins.

Inspiration

Do not cast me off in the time of old age;

> do not forsake me when my strength is spent. (Psalm 71:9)

Challenge

Check with your parish or diocese about programs that specifically serve the elderly. Consider volunteering to drive someone to a medical appointment or the grocery store, to play music at an assisted living facility, or to visit with the residents and listen to their stories.

Jeanne-Elisabeth Bichier des Ages

July 5, 1773–August 26, 1838

The French Revolution made Elisabeth grow up fast. She was sixteen when the conflict erupted, and her father died shortly thereafter. The revolutionaries seized the family estate, and it took all the intellectual strength she and the family's attorneys could muster to regain what they could. When Elisabeth was twenty-six, she and her mother moved to a rural area, where Elisabeth met the priest who would assist her in founding the Daughters of the Cross, Sisters of St. Andrew, to help poor young women and the ill.

When did you know you weren't a child anymore? Perhaps it was when your parents died or when you began college or married or had a child of your own. Women often need to be strong for others. With God, however, we can always let down our guard and become a trusting child again.

✺ Inspiration

At that time the disciples came to Jesus and asked, "Who is the greatest in the kingdom of heaven?" He called a child, whom he put among them, and said, "Truly I tell you, unless you change and become like children, you will never enter the kingdom of heaven." (Matthew 18:1–3)

✺ Challenge

Skip down the street, sing a silly song, jump rope, or do something else that reminds you of when you were a carefree child. Just for a few minutes, turn your worries over to the Lord.

Monica

Circa 331–May 4, 387

Monica was so in love with God that she couldn't stay quiet about it. She converted her husband and mother-in-law to Christianity. Her son Augustine proved to be far more resistant, living a wild life and joining a faith that was at odds with his mother's beliefs. But Monica didn't let that stop her. She stormed the heavens with prayers for her son. A few months before she died, she had the joy of seeing Augustine baptized after he became a Christian and adopted celibacy, sending his lover and their son back to her homeland.

Maybe it's your daughter, or your daughter-in-law. Or maybe it's your grandson or your husband. We all have someone who holds a special place in our prayers, someone who has drifted away from our faith. Monica's determination inspires us to keep praying—and nudging.

Inspiration

Bury my body wherever you will; let not care of it cause you any concern. One thing only I ask you, that you remember me at the altar of the Lord wherever you may be. (St. Monica)

Challenge

Say an extra prayer today for those you know who have fallen away from their faith and who would benefit from a renewed relationship with God. Ask that their hearts be converted.

Margaret the Barefooted
1325–1395

Margaret knew what her ministry was: to help the beggars in her community. To do that, she went barefoot herself to seek alms on their behalf, even though her husband verbally abused her for this behavior.

What do you do when you see someone asking for money? Do you back away, cross the street, or do anything else you can to avoid looking the person in the face? We learn from Margaret the importance of putting ourselves in someone else's situation, and at least offering a smile and perhaps a friendly word.

✒ Inspiration

May the God of steadfastness and encouragement grant you to live in harmony with one another, in accordance with Christ Jesus, so that together you may with one voice glorify the God and Father of our Lord Jesus Christ.

Welcome one another, therefore, just as Christ has welcomed you, for the glory of God. (Romans 15:5–7)

✒ Challenge

Think about the person you find the most difficult to love. This may be someone in your family or someone you pass each day on the way to work or doing errands. Think about his or her life and what situations may have led to the behavior or appearance you find difficult. Keep these thoughts in mind the next time you interact with the person.

Margaret Ward

Died August 30, 1588

It was a dangerous thing to be a Catholic in Elizabethan England. Margaret smuggled in a rope to help an imprisoned priest escape. The escape was successful, but Margaret was arrested as she had been the priest's only visitor. After days of torture, she was told she'd be pardoned if she went to a Protestant church service, but she declined. She is among the Forty Martyrs of England and Wales.

It's relatively risk-free to volunteer at a soup kitchen or homeless shelter, but would you put your life on the line for Christ as Margaret did? We never know how our faith may be tested.

☙ Inspiration

Do not fear what you are about to suffer. Beware, the devil is about to throw some of you into prison so that you may be tested, and for ten days you will have affliction. Be faithful until death, and I will give you the crown of life. (Revelation 2:10)

☙ Challenge

Discuss with a family member or friend what each of you would do if you were in Margaret's situation. What would it take for you to act as bravely as she did?

Mary of the Cross (Jeanne Jugan)

October 25, 1792–August 29, 1879

This nun had done it all by the time she was fifty-one: founded the Little Sisters of the Poor. Begged in the streets for the poor. Bought a home, even though she had no money, that would house forty elderly people. And yet, when she was re-elected superior in 1843, the priest who oversaw the congregation superseded the sisters' vote and named a twenty-one-year-old to serve. For nine years, Mary served selflessly under others; then the same priest ordered her back to the motherhouse for what would be twenty-seven years of retirement. When she died, the order included 2,400 sisters in 177 homes on three continents.

Sometimes, we think of ourselves as indispensable—to our spouses, our children, our friends, our parishes, our employers. And yet, if we truly serve God in our work, we plan for future success and for the day that we are no longer there to serve.

✒ Inspiration

Love God very much; he is so good. Let us entrust ourselves to him. (St. Mary of the Cross)

✒ Challenge

Where do you view yourself as indispensable? Talk with God about developing a succession plan, for surely one will be needed in heaven one day.

Narcisa de Jesús Martillo y Morán

October 29, 1832–December 8, 1869

Narcisa learned her faith at home. Her father in particular was devoted to Marianna of Jesus, who would go on to be the first saint from the family's home country of Ecuador. Narcisa was devoted to prayer and penance, and spent the last year and a half or so of her life as a lay member of a Dominican convent in Peru.

While it's easy to talk about the importance of going to Mass and reading Scripture, it's harder to set a Christlike example for our children and others in the way we live. Does your family pray together outside meals? Do you study the readings together? Does your free time include working as a group to help those less fortunate?

Inspiration

But as for you, continue in what you have learned and firmly believed, knowing from whom you learned it, and how from childhood you have known the sacred writings that are able to instruct you for salvation through faith in Christ Jesus. (2 Timothy 3:14–15)

Challenge

Talk with your children or other young people about a saint who inspires you, and how his or her example affects your life. Offer a few examples of saints who might speak to them as well.

Beatrice da Silva Meneses

1424–September 1, 1490

Beatrice was a beautiful woman—so beautiful, in fact, that it caused her trouble. When Princess Elizabeth of Portugal married the king of Castile, Beatrice accompanied the princess to court. It was there the princess became jealous of Beatrice, who managed to disengage herself and seek refuge at a Dominican convent for the next forty years. She later founded the Congregation of the Immaculate Conception of Our Lady. At her canonization in 1976, Pope John Paul II noted that Beatrice's devotion to the Blessed Virgin preceded Church dogma on Mary by centuries and said: "The saints are always a challenge to the conformity of our habits.... The radicalism of their testimony is meant to be a shock to our laziness."

Jealousy is a powerful emotion. We envy people their looks, their intelligence, their connections, their possessions—the list goes on and on. May we remember that God gives us what we need, and there's always plenty of him for everyone.

Inspiration

Do not let your heart envy sinners,

but always continue in the fear of the LORD. (Proverbs 23:17)

Challenge

Who in your life do you envy and why? Remember that this person undoubtedly does not have as perfect an existence as you think. Pray for God's love to envelop him or her today, and for the wisdom to understand the great gifts that have been bestowed on you.

Anna the Prophetess

First century

Anna was there at the Temple in Jerusalem at the time of Jesus's presentation, just as she was there every day and every night, fasting and praying. Luke tells us that she was an old widow who spoke about Jesus to all who were waiting for Jerusalem's redemption. In art, she often is shown handing a scroll to the child or raising her hands to him.

Imagine the joy in Anna's heart when she beheld the Messiah! Even though she could not fully grasp everything that was to come, it must have been something akin to when a child we know is welcomed into our Church through baptism.

Inspiration

At that moment she came, and began to praise God and to speak about the child to all who were looking for the redemption of Jerusalem. (Luke 2:38)

Challenge

Write a note of thanksgiving and praise for a child to be born or baptized in the coming months, or an adult who will be coming into the Church. Tell the person of God's great love for him or her, and that he or she will be in your prayers.

Phoebe

First century

Phoebe was among the women involved in the early Church, and she may have delivered Paul's epistle to the Romans. She's the only woman Paul mentioned in the address of his letters. While she is described as a deaconess, her actual ministerial role is unknown.

Phoebe reminds us of the critical role women played in the life of the early Church, as they do today. We are all called to do Christ's work, whether it's in our home, at our jobs, within our parish, at our children's school, in a ministry position, or as a woman religious.

Inspiration

I commend to you our sister Phoebe, a deacon of the church at Cenchreae, so that you may welcome her in the Lord as is fitting for the saints, and help her in whatever she may require from you, for she has been a benefactor of many and of myself as well. (Romans 16:1–2)

Challenge

Think about a woman in your parish, on staff or a volunteer, who seems to do tireless ministry. It's a safe bet that even she from time to time feels worn out and underappreciated. Send her an e-mail or note thanking her for her service, or bring her lunch one day.

Rose of Viterbo

Circa 1235–March 6, 1252

Rose was young, on fire for God, and fearless. German Emperor Frederick II had taken over her town and was at odds with the pope. Inspired by the Blessed Virgin, Rose spent about two years preaching in the streets, advising that people should be true to the pope. Eventually, her family was expelled from Viterbo until the year before she died, when papal power was restored. It is said she accurately foretold Frederick's death. Rose had attempted to enter the Poor Clares about this time, but she was rejected because she didn't have a dowry. As she predicted, her remains ultimately were moved to the convent.

Rose didn't much care what anyone other than God thought about her. She didn't care if she annoyed or angered people; she just wanted them to hear his message. May we find the courage and confidence to do the same.

Inspiration

I die with joy, for I desire to be united to my God. Live so as not to fear death. For those who live well in the world, death is not frightening, but sweet and precious. (St. Rose of Viterbo)

Challenge

Be politically incorrect today. Talk with someone about what Catholics believe and why. Bring along the *Catechism of the Catholic Church* for reference.

Teresa of Calcutta

August 26, 1910–September 5, 1997

Teresa left her comfortable Albanian home when she was eighteen to join the Sisters of Loreto in Ireland. She was sent to India in 1929. It was there, seventeen years later, while she was on train headed for her annual retreat, that God spoke to her about a "call within a call within a call." This call would lead her to found the Missionaries of Charity. Despite a long personal spiritual drought, Teresa and her order would go on to found hundreds of missions throughout the world, ministering to the poorest of the poor. She frequently was among the world's most admired people, and she was a winner of the Nobel Peace Prize.

Spiritual drought or no spiritual drought, public acclaim or no public acclaim, Teresa kept on showing up every day and doing God's work. That's all he asks of any of us.

Inspiration

By blood, I am Albanian. By citizenship, an Indian. By faith, I am a Catholic nun. As to my calling, I belong to the world. As to my heart, I belong entirely to the Heart of Jesus. (Blessed Teresa of Calcutta)

Challenge

Who are you? Contemplate Teresa's message about where she fit into the world. What are your answers?

Ida of Herzfeld

Circa 770–September 825

Ida, who may have been related to Charlemagne, devoted herself to helping the poor after her husband died and her family was grown. We're told that each day, she would fill a coffin with food and distribute it, both to help those in need and to remind her of the temporary nature of this life.

Racking up honors and accolades from others can feed our egos, but we must remember that our primary audience is God. Pleasing him is what's important, even if those here on earth don't understand or disapprove of what we do, even if they don't reward us with plaques, trophies, and certificates.

Inspiration

More than that, I regard everything as loss because of the surpassing value of knowing Christ Jesus my Lord. For his sake I have suffered the loss of all things, and I regard them as rubbish, in order that I may gain Christ. (Philippians 3:8)

Challenge

Examine your service, in your home, at work and in your parish. Are you doing it because of God's call, or because you get compliments and atta-girls from your family, friends, and colleagues? Reconsider your priorities.

Eugenia Picco

November 8, 1867–September 7, 1921

It was far from the typical saint's or blessed's upbringing. Eugenia spent her early years with her grandparents because her father was a well-known musician and her mother lived on the road with him. However, then her mother left her father for another man, and Eugenia never saw her father again. Eugenia lived with the couple, who did not marry, and went to a nearby basilica each day to pray and think. She joined a religious order when she was twenty.

Do you worry sometimes about how your children's friends or perhaps even your own nieces and nephews are being brought up? Eugenia's story reminds us that the sins of the parents do not have to be visited on the children. We can serve as role models and reflections of Christ.

Inspiration

Take care that you do not despise one of these little ones; for, I tell you, in heaven their angels continually see the face of my Father in heaven. (Matthew 18:10)

Challenge

Have a conversation with a child you believe may be at risk due to his or her family situation. Don't judge or preach; just ask the child about school, hobbies, passions. You may be the only adult who provides a smile today.

Angela Salawa

September 9, 1881–March 12, 1922

Angela provided charity to others, then found herself relying on others for it. Her health prevented her from joining a convent, so instead she became a Franciscan tertiary and a nurse at a Polish hospital. It is said she used any money she had or could beg to provide food for the soldiers. Out of money and out of health, the final five years of her life were spent in the care of the St. Zita Association.

Angela was a selfless person. Her example reminds us of the value of a community safety net, and to give without an expectation of a return from anyone other than God.

✺ Inspiration

Love your enemies, do good, and lend, expecting nothing in return. Your reward will be great, and you will be children of the Most High; for he is kind to the ungrateful and the wicked. Be merciful, just as your Father is merciful. (Luke 6:35–36)

✺ Challenge

Smile and say hello today to everyone—stranger, friend, enemy—you encounter. Don't stop if someone looks grumpy or says something mean back to you. Your friendly gesture can open the door to a sliver of love for them.

Maria Euthymia (Emma Üffing)

April 8, 1914–September 9, 1955

During World War II, Maria Euthymia worked tirelessly with sick prisoners of war and workers from abroad. A priest who was among the prisoners called her "a canticle of hope in the midst of war." But after the war, her motherhouse reassigned her to running laundry rooms, far from the daily interaction with the world. She accepted the new assignment with grace and did it for close to a decade before she died of cancer.

Sometimes, the ministries for which we believe we are ideally suited—motherhood, teaching, nursing, writing, singing—are snatched away from us. We may look back later and believe we understand why we were nudged in a different direction; other times, we will never be able to understand the reason. All we can do is accept, and trust in God's love and wisdom.

Inspiration

The Lord can use me like a ray of sun to brighten the day. (Blessed Maria Euthymia)

Challenge

Think of an activity you once were able to do well that is no longer open to you. What joy did that activity bring, and how can you find that joy in another way, or share your experience with people currently engaged in that service?

Pulcheria

Circa 399–453

Pulcheria's life took as many twists and turns as a Hollywood movie. She grew up as the daughter of a Byzantine emperor and empress, and then she was regent briefly for her younger brother. When the brother grew up and married, trouble ensued, and Pulcheria was exiled. Eventually, her sister-in-law was banished and Pulcheria returned, and then became empress after her brother's death. Pulcheria also was known for her successful battle against those who contended Mary should not have the title Mother of God, and built three churches in honor of the Blessed Virgin. She also endowed other churches.

Where will this life lead you? Certainly, Pulcheria must have wondered when she was banished from the court. Yet she ultimately returned to rule the empire and to do God's work in the defense of Mary. The setbacks we experience often are temporary, and always temporal. God is our constant.

Inspiration

For by grace you have been saved through faith, and this is not your own doing; it is the gift of God…. For we are what he has made us, created in Christ Jesus for good works, which God prepared beforehand to be our way of life. (Ephesians 2:8, 10)

Challenge

What turns has your life taken in the past ten years, turns that seemed permanent and unbearable at the time? Thank God for helping you through those situations.

Maria Pierina

September 11, 1890–July 26, 1945

From a very young age, Maria felt herself drawn to the image of Christ's face and found herself in conversation with our Lord. After she joined the Daughters of the Immaculate Conception, Mary and Jesus both appeared to her and asked for devotion to the Holy Face of Jesus. It was through her efforts that the Holy Face Medal was struck. "The Lord endowed her with an extraordinary devotion to his Holy Face, which always sustained her in trials and illness," Pope Benedict XVI said on the day of her beatification in 2010.

Christ comes to us in different ways. For some, he's in the laughter of an infant; for others, in our own physical or mental suffering. Our Church's mystics encounter Jesus in ways most of us never will, and they serve as conduits so that we may better understand his will.

❧ Inspiration

I felt a deep longing to live always united with Jesus; to love him intensely because my death can only be a transport of love with my spouse, Jesus. (Blessed Maria Pierina)

❧ Challenge

Consider what image of Christ draws you nearest to him. Spend some time today with that medal, scapular, picture, crucifix, or other tangible form. Listen to him. Tell him you love him.

Liduina Meneguzzi

September 12, 1901–December 2, 1941

Liduina is known as the "ecumenical flame" because of her missionary work in Dire Dawa, Ethiopia's second largest city, as a member of the Sisters Congregation of Saint Francis of Sales. She worked at a military hospital from 1937 until her death, due to complications from surgery. Many of the people she encountered were Muslim, and her peaceful, helpful nature resulted in many conversions. The Congregation for the Causes of Saints' decree on Liduina praised her for bringing a message of hope and love to the Church and the world.

We don't have to move thousands of miles away to encounter non-Christians today. Evangelizing doesn't always mean quoting Scripture and the *Catechism*. Conversion more often begins when people see us attempting to live a good, service-centered life, as Liduina did.

✒ Inspiration

Everything that the Father gives me will come to me, and anyone who comes to me I will never drive away; for I have come down from heaven, not to do my own will, but the will of him who sent me. (John 6:37–38)

✒ Challenge

Ask a non-Christian friend about his or her faith traditions. Discuss your similarities. Or, ask a Protestant friend to go to Mass with you and talk afterwards about the similarities with services at his or her church.

Marie of Sainte Cecile of Rome (Dina Bélanger)

April 30, 1897–September 4, 1929

Dina's mystical relationship with Christ began when she was very young, with dreams of Jesus offering her a picture of himself and then, the year after she made her First Communion, he spoke to her soul in what she called "a soft, melodious voice." Melody was something dear to Dina's heart; she went on to study to become a concert pianist before joining the Congregation of Jesus and Mary. Even as she suffered periods of spiritual dryness, illness, and doubt, her intense love for Christ fed her and helped her diminish her personal concerns.

God appears to us in different forms. May we keep our minds, hearts, and souls open so that we might appreciate his constant presence and get ourselves out of the way.

Inspiration

As this divine fire consumed me, it seemed to me that my being shuddered, moaned, and finally, it appeared to be dead.... In the center, there remained some ashes. Jesus drew near, breathed on them and reduced them to nothing. Finally, there was nothing left of me. (Blessed Marie of Sainte Cecile of Rome)

Challenge

Ask God to light a fire in your soul that will burn out everything but him.

Notburga

Circa 1265–September 16, 1313

Notburga didn't have much herself when she was hired out as cook. But she knew she had more than some other people, and would provide what the family didn't eat to the poor. She lost her job when it was discovered that while she was giving the leftovers to the pigs as ordered, she was sharing her own food with the needy. Notburga went to work for another family, but her original employer reconsidered and urged her to come back, saying she would be welcome to share what she wanted. Notburga spent the rest of her life in service to the family—and the poor.

When we know we are doing God's work, as Notburga was, we must not let people get in our way. When we act out of love and service, we inform the journeys of others.

Inspiration

Come, eat of my bread
  and drink of the wine I have mixed.
Lay aside immaturity, and live,
  and walk in the way of insight. (Proverbs 9:5–6)

Challenge

What is God calling you to do to help the poor and needy? What obstacles will you encounter in fulfilling this call? Pray for the strength to rise above them.

Catherine of Genoa

Circa 1447–September 15, 1510

For ten years, Catherine barely tolerated her husband's philandering and wasteful spending. It was so hard that at one point, she prayed to become bedridden. But her prayers were answered in a different way. God's love was made so evident to her in a mystical experience that she stopped focusing on what was wrong in her life and began caring for lepers and other patients regarded as undesirable. Ultimately, her husband had a conversion experience and joined her in her hospital ministry. After her husband died, Catherine wrote about her experiences, including her intimate prayer life with God.

Not all marriages are able to recover from major problems like adultery and bankruptcy. However, problems in our marriages and other relationships always can be improved if we stop judging others and focus on our own journey with Christ.

Inspiration

Since I began to love, love has never forsaken me. It has ever grown to its own fullness within my innermost heart. (St. Catherine of Genoa)

Challenge

Just for today, focus on why God loves your spouse or another important person in your life, instead of focusing on the aspects about him or her that annoy you. Identify places where you can forgive—and love better.

Ludmila

Circa 860–September 15, 921

Ludmila had a special relationship with her grandson Wenceslaus, so special that her son asked her to raise the boy and to attend to his spiritual education. Ludmila and her husband both had been converts, and her daughter-in-law favored paganism. But then Ludmila's son died when Wenceslaus was just eight years old. The daughter-in-law resented Ludmila's influence over him, and five years later, she arranged for Ludmila to be strangled. Her effort was for naught, however; Wenceslaus took power the year after Ludmila's death and reigned in a way that would have pleased his grandmother.

Ludmila's story illustrates the important role grandparents and godparents can play in children's spiritual development. While religious education is primarily the responsibility of the parents, when they don't step up, other adults have the gift and duty to talk about God to the little ones.

Inspiration

Grandchildren are the crown of the aged,

and the glory of children is their parents. (Proverbs 17:6)

Challenge

Talk with your grandchildren, young or grown, or other children in your life, about Jesus and what he means to you. Ask about their favorite part of religious education class. (Be sure to let their parents know you're going to do this first.)

Hildegard of Bingen

1098–September 17, 1179

You surely have heard of Hildegard, the medieval mystic, composer, author, poet, and playwright who, in October 2012, became the thirty-fifth Doctor of the Church—and the fourth female Doctor. You may not know, however, that she was involved in controversy in the year she died. A young man who had been excommunicated had received the last rites and been buried at the cemetery next to her convent. Local church authorities ordered Hildegard to have the body removed; she refused, saying he had been reconciled. The convent for a time was barred from all religious activities, but ultimately, Hildegard prevailed.

Knee-jerk challenges to authority benefit no one. But as Catholics, we are called to study our dogma and doctrine. It is our duty to share our thoughts and discernments on issues and situations that are open to discussion and interpretation, and to provide a thoughtful alternative view where appropriate.

✿ Inspiration

The Word is living, being, spirit, all verdant greening, all creativity. This Word manifests itself in every creature. (St. Hildegard of Bingen)

✿ Challenge

Spend some time with the *Catechism of the Catholic Church*, or talk with a priest or spiritual adviser to better understand the basis for Church teachings that trouble you. You may be surprised to find your understanding of the Church's position is more nuanced than you thought.

Giuseppina Gabriella Bonino

September 5, 1843–February 8, 1906

Giuseppina always had a strong faith life, going to Catholic school and working in her parish and related organizations. A serious spine problem developed when she was in her mid-thirties, and it was corrected by surgery. She and her mother went to Lourdes to offer thanks for the healing, and it was then that Giuseppina realized that she was being called to join a religious order and help the poor. She helped found the Sisters of the Holy Family and served as superior for her remaining years.

The more we open ourselves up to God, the more of him we find in ourselves. Giuseppina's gratitude for her successful surgery led her down a road she might never have taken otherwise, and benefited thousands who were physically and emotionally hungry.

✣ Inspiration

Enter his gates with thanksgiving,

and his courts with praise.

Give thanks to him, bless his name.

For the LORD is good;

his steadfast love endures forever,

and his faithfulness to all generations. (Psalm 100:4–5)

✣ Challenge

Thank God today for favors granted, large and small—then ask what's next. Listen. You may be surprised by the answer.

Emilie de Rodat

September 6, 1787–September 19, 1852

Some people have the gift of fitting in wherever they go. Emilie was not one of those people. She tried and left three different religious congregations, but she still felt she had a vocation. Ultimately, Emilie began teaching children in her own home, and this ministry grew into the Sisters of the Holy Family of Villefranche. It was then, when she was thirty-three, that Emilie took her final vows. The order's mission expanded to caring for the elderly and other disenfranchised people.

We all have situations in which we feel like the outsider, as if we don't belong. From Emilie, we learn the importance of persevering and enduring that discomfort when doing God's work is involved.

✥ Inspiration

At my first defense no one came to my support, but all deserted me. May it not be counted against them! But the Lord stood by me and gave me strength, so that through me the message might be fully proclaimed and all the Gentiles might hear it. So I was rescued from the lion's mouth. (2 Timothy 4:16–17)

✥ Challenge

What are you avoiding because the situation or activity makes you feel like an outcast or a stranger? Pray for the grace to do it anyway.

Anna Pak Agi, one of the Martyrs of Korea

1783–May 24, 1839

Anna was not a wise woman in terms of formal education or intellectual insight. Still, she and her husband raised their children as Catholics, which was not allowed in Korea. When she, her husband, and their oldest son were all arrested, the men eventually denied Christ and were released. Anna refused, and was tortured. She died after three months in prison. In speaking about the martyrs in 1984, Pope John Paul II said, "There are surprising similarities between what we see in many of the Martyrs of Korea and the personality of [St. Paul]: total dedication to the cause of Christ; unbreakable courage…and an unshakable desire to share the interior joy of one's own Christian experience with the greatest number of souls possible."

Studying Scripture and other religious works helps to inform our Catholic journeys. Yet it's a mistake to discount the "holiness" of those who don't have the same educational advantages many of us do. Loving Christ deeply and profoundly doesn't require any classroom time.

✿ Inspiration

I don't know anything but Jesus and Mary. (St. Anna Pak Agi)

✿ Challenge

Pray the prayers you learned in childhood—the Our Father and Hail Mary, the Creed, and the Glory Be, for example. Take the time to think or say them slowly, focusing on the meaning of the simple yet soul-stirring words.

Mary of the Apostles (Therese von Wüllenweber)

February 19, 1833–December 25, 1907

Therese was restless. She was helping orphans and older women, but despite repeated efforts, she had not been able to find a congregation to which she could commit. During this time, she became increasingly concerned about children who were, in essence, forced to go to work to help their families and were lacking in religious education. Then, shortly after her forty-ninth birthday, she saw an ad for the Apostolic Teaching Society. She responded, and several years later she took her final vows. Ultimately, Mary became superior general of the Congregation of the Sisters of the Divine Savior, or Salvatorian Sisters, which today has a presence in forty countries around the world.

There's something very current about finding one's vocation through an ad. Just think, there are women today doing Internet searches to find the right order or congregation for them. It just goes to show that God will use anyone or anything to reach us and set us on fire for him.

✒ Inspiration

Everything as the Divine Savior wills it! (Blessed Mary of the Apostles)

✒ Challenge

Where does your spiritual life seem lacking today? Take note of all the opportunities—friends, reading materials, e-mails, television, everything—where God may be providing direction, while you're rushing past.

Margaret of Castello

1287–April 13, 1320

Margaret was an embarrassment for her wealthy family. She suffered from dwarfism. She couldn't see. She didn't walk well, due to curvature of the spine. First, she was kept in a small room that was part of a rural church. Then, after a visit to a shrine failed to cure her, the family abandoned her. Eventually, she became a Dominican tertiary and spent the remainder of her life as a teacher helping the poor and in prayer.

It's easy to judge people on their physical appearance and to discount their value if they suffer from any sort of disability. Margaret's story reminds us that we are all precious in God's eyes—and should be in each other's eyes, as well.

Inspiration

His disciples asked him, "Rabbi, who sinned, this man or his parents, that he was born blind?" Jesus answered, "Neither this man nor his parents sinned; he was born blind so that God's works might be revealed in him." (John 9:2–3)

Challenge

Read about the appropriate way to interact with people who have a disability, such as those who lack sight or hearing or use a wheelchair or cane. Do you look past the disability to see what God sees?

Émilie Tavernier Gamelin

February 19, 1800–September 23, 1851

It took a long time for Émilie to formalize her vocation, but that didn't mean she wasn't doing God's work. At loose ends after her husband and three sons had all died, she turned her attention to bringing sick elderly women into her Montreal home. Eventually, the project outgrew that space, and she opened a shelter, which continued to expand. Finally, in 1843, fourteen years after she took the first women into her home, she became a novice in what would become the Sisters of Providence. Their ministry today is worldwide.

"Her attention to persons and to situations led her to invent new forms of charity," Pope John Paul II said at Émilie's beatification. Her example reminds us to keep our eyes and hearts open for new service opportunities, not to simply stay in familiar patterns.

✸ Inspiration

She opens her hand to the poor,
   and reaches out her hands to the needy. (Proverbs 31:20)

✸ Challenge

As you go about your life today, look for new ways to be generous with your time. They don't have to be as ambitious as Émilie's; maybe it's something as simple as looking in on older neighbors a couple times a week, or helping a young family with childcare.

Anne of St. Bartholomew

October 1, 1549–June 7, 1626

You can't blame Anne for feeling a little less than self-confident. She started out life as a shepherdess whose brothers were opposed to her becoming a woman religious. When she persevered and became a Discalced Carmelite, the great Teresa of Avila chose her to be her secretary and confidante. They were so close that Teresa died in Anne's arms in 1572. Later, she was assigned to be the superior for a new Carmelite convent in Paris and explained to Christ she did not believe someone like her was qualified to do the job. The Lord's response? "With straws I light my fire."

If you're used to being in the background, it's difficult to be the one in the spotlight. If you're used to being told you're not good enough to do something, you start to believe it. Anne's story reminds us that with God, we can do anything.

Inspiration

So we can say with confidence,

> "The Lord is my helper;
> I will not be afraid.
> What can anyone do to me?" (Hebrews 13:6)

Challenge

Ask a friend who appears self-confident and outgoing and who shares our faith about how she prepares for challenging situations. Ask her to pray for you, that you may grow in trust.

Eurosia Fabris

September 27, 1866–January 8, 1932

They called her "Mama Rosa," and with good reason. Eurosia was already a mother figure for two girls whose mother had died before she married Carlo Barban, then the two of them went on to have nine children of their own. She was devoted to Carlo and to Christ, becoming a secular Franciscan after his death. Three of their sons became priests. "Mother Rosa represents a model of sanctity accessible to everyone," a bishop at her beatification said.

Eurosia managed the family budget in a way that still allowed sharing with the poor. She managed her time with her family so that she was still able to help care for the sick. With her example, who among us can say we're too busy to get involved in ministry outside our families?

Inspiration

But when the chief priests and the scribes saw the amazing things that he did, and heard the children crying out in the temple, "Hosanna to the Son of David," they became angry and said to him, "Do you hear what these are saying?" (Matthew 21:15–16)

Challenge

Maybe your mom was a religious education instructor, or a room mother at your school, or a Girl Scout leader. Thank her, or a woman who's been like a mother to you, for the faithful example of service she provided for you.

Thérèse Couderc

February 1, 1805–September 26, 1885

It had to be a disappointment for Thérèse. She'd had years of experience as a superior, first for the Daughters of St. Regis and then for the Sisters of the Cenacle, which she cofounded. But the Cenacle congregation had run into financial problems under her watch, so she resigned. A series of new superiors failed to improve the situation, yet the Cenacle survived. Thérèse spent the next fifty years as part of the community, doing manual labor without complaint.

Have you ever been fired or demoted, or seen your successor on a committee come up with all sorts of creative but illogical ideas? It's a humbling experience, and it can be difficult to simply stay silent and let matters unfold. Thérèse's example reminds us to offer up to God our disappointments and injured feelings.

Inspiration

The surrendered soul has found paradise on earth, since she enjoys that sweet peace which is part of the happiness of the elect. (St. Thérèse Couderc)

Challenge

Write down all your disappointments from yesterday. Then set the paper on fire, and ask God to let your hurts disappear amid the ashes. Clear your mind by writing down all the blessings you received yesterday, and keep that list in your pocket.

Lioba of Bischoffsheim

710–September 28, 782

Lioba had the respect of both female and male religious. While she was born in England, St. Boniface, a relative, enlisted her to help him spread Christianity in the northern part of continental Europe. She helped found a number of convents and participated in consultations about monastic rule for monks. She was known for her wisdom and intelligence, and she was buried near Boniface.

Even though we are living in the twenty-first century, it's still not easy being a woman. Between Church, family, friends, jobs, and ministries, attaining a balance is difficult. While no one can have it all, Lioba's example reminds us that if we are passionate about what we do and treat people with respect and love, we are being faithful to what God asks of us.

✒ Inspiration

Therefore I tell you, do not worry about your life, what you will eat or what you will drink, or about your body, what you will wear. Is not life more than food, and the body more than clothing? (Matthew 6:25)

✒ Challenge

Is there a situation where you feel unheard or unappreciated due to your gender, age, marital status, physical appearance, or something else? Pray for guidance on what you can do to have your voice heard.

Magdalene of Nagasaki

1611–October 16, 1634

Magdalene knew the price she might be asked to pay as a follower of Christ. Both her parents were martyred before she was ten. But that didn't stop her from pursuing life as an Augustinian tertiary (due to religious persecution in Japan, she could not become a nun). When her spiritual director was arrested, she told the guards that she too was a Christian. She died after thirteen days of torture that included being hanged upside down on a gibbet. Magdalene is among the Martyrs of Japan.

The example of her parents must have been an inspiration to Magdalene, especially in her final days. In the same way, we are surrounded by family members, friends, and others in our community who have made sacrifices for their faith, whether it's passing up a promotion because it would have meant too much time away from family, or passing up time with friends to help on religious education projects. Our parents often are among our strongest faith examples.

✒ Inspiration

Hear, my child, your father's instruction,
   and do not reject your mother's teaching;
for they are a fair garland for your head,
   and pendants for your neck. (Proverbs 1:8–9)

✒ Challenge

Think about your own parents' spiritual journey. What about the way they lived out their faith inspires you today? Discuss it with them, your children, or your grandchildren.

Marina of Omura

Circa 1609–November 11, 1634

Marina was among the sixteen martyrs of Japan who died between 1633 and 1637. Marina and her father had welcomed missionaries to their home, and Marina had become a Dominican tertiary. She was slowly burned to death. "May the example and intercession of the new saints help to extend Christian truth and love through the length and breadth" of Asia, Pope John Paul II said at the martyr's canonization in 1987.

We never know all the good we do in this world. How many Japanese people are Christians today because of the work of these and other martyrs in that country? But we don't have to die for Christ to influence the lives of others. We only have to reflect him in our words and in our actions.

✺ Inspiration

My enemies trample on me all day long,
    for many fight against me.
O Most High, when I am afraid,
    I put my trust in you.
In God, whose word I praise,
    in God I trust; I am not afraid;
    what can flesh do to me? (Psalm 56:2–4)

✺ Challenge

Do one thing today in Christ's name that scares you. Perhaps it's starting to change a destructive habit, or volunteering at a soup kitchen, or making amends with a friend or relative.

Rafaela Ybarra Arambarri de Villalonga

January 16, 1843–February 23, 1900

Rafaela always had a place in her heart for children. Not did only she and her husband raise their own five children (two others had died young), but they also raised five of her nephews after Rafaela's sister died. But Rafaela didn't feel that was enough, and her husband agreed. She began engaging her friends and others in efforts to establish homes and training for at-risk girls and young women. Before her death, Rafaela helped to found what would become the Institute of the Sisters of the Guardian Angels. At her beatification in 1984, Pope John Paul II called Rafaela "an excellent example for our society today and for those who want to live for God, and to continue building the kingdom of Christ."

The love we have based in faith grows the more we share it with others. We can see this in Rafaela's tireless example of raising children, as many as her family could manage. Christian charity often begins at home.

✒ Inspiration

Never tire of doing good. (Blessed Rafaela Ybarra Arambarri de Villalonga)

✒ Challenge

We all lead busy, overbooked lives. Examine your routine and determine if all those activities truly serve God. And if they don't, consider cutting back a little so that you can expand your service outside your home. Or, consider an activity you and your family could do together.

Thérèse of Lisieux

January 2, 1873–September 30, 1897

When we think of Thérèse, we think of her "Little Way," the practice of offering up even the most commonplace tasks to God's glory. But Therese wasn't afraid to stand up for herself when she needed to do so to accomplish God's will. When she was just fourteen, she felt local church authorities were taking too long to make a decision about her request to join the Carmelite Order. So, when a pilgrimage from her diocese met with Pope Leo XIII in Rome, Thérèse departed from the prescribed "kneel and kiss of the ring and feet" ritual to ask him for permission to join the Order. While the pope didn't grant her request immediately, she found out soon thereafter that she would be allowed to enter the convent the following Easter.

Thérèse was wise beyond her years in knowing when it was appropriate to adapt her behavior to serve God's will, whether it was being brave enough to approach the pope or humble enough to do despised chores without complaint. Often, we simply brush off spiritual growth opportunities by saying, "That's just not who I am." The better approach is, "Who does God want me to be in this situation?"

Inspiration

Jesus, help me to simplify my life by learning what you want me to be and becoming that person. (St. Thérèse of Lisieux)

Challenge

Ask God who he wants you to be today. Then be it.

Catherine Yi and Magdalene Cho

Died 1839

Catherine and her adult daughter Magdalene were among the 103 Korean Martyrs who died between 1839 and 1867 and were canonized in 1984. Catherine had been raised Catholic and successfully converted her pagan husband; she and Magdalene had clashed when Magdalene decided not to marry and instead to live as a virgin. They had mended their relationship and moved to Seoul in hopes of encountering less persecution than in the country. However, their hope turned to ashes. They heard that the local bishop was being sought by authorities, and the mother and daughter were among five Catholics arrested about a month later. Despite torture and beatings, both refused to deny Christ and died in prison from illnesses.

Catherine and Magdalene must have been comforted and strengthened by each other's presence and belief in Christ. In the same way, we are fed by the religious instruction we give our children, and the ways in which our parents showed their spirituality.

❧ Inspiration

Her children rise up and call her happy;

   her husband too, and he praises her:

"Many women have done excellently,

   but you surpass them all." (Proverbs 31:28–29)

❧ Challenge

Talk with your children or your parents today about the way they have deepened your faith.

Théodore Guérin

October 2, 1798–May 14, 1856

She left her home in France for Indiana before it was even a state, and a year later founded the oldest U.S. Catholic women's college, St. Mary-of-the-Woods Academy. But Théodore's life as a woman religious was not without its conflicts. After the Sisters of Providence arrived in New York, they had to travel by stagecoach, steamboat, canal boat, and train before they reached the small farmhouse in the middle of a forest that would be their first home. Later, Théodore would become engaged in a struggle with the local bishop, who went so far as to dismiss her from her congregation, tell her to get out of the diocese, and threaten her with excommunication. Ultimately, the bishop resigned and Théodore's service continued.

Taking an unpopular but prayerful stand is a hard thing to do today, too. Yet God calls us to carry his message always, even in the face of disagreement and controversy.

Inspiration

We must possess all the virtues before we attempt to teach them to others. (St. Théodore Guérin)

Challenge

Write a letter to your pastor, bishop, or cardinal about your thoughts on a controversial topic within your parish or diocese. Be true to your beliefs while seeking to unite rather than divide further.

Anna Schäffer

February 18, 1882–October 5, 1925

Anna was less than a month from her nineteenth birthday, working hard to earn money for her family and for her dream of becoming a missionary sister. That dream ended when she fell into a vat of boiling lye. After more than a year of treatment, she was released from medical care, never again to leave her sickbed. Understandably, she was disappointed and angry for quite a while. But after eight years, things changed. She saw visions and began to understand that her mission was right there in her bed—praying for people and writing about her life. She experienced the stigmata as well as illnesses including intestinal cancer and spastic paralysis.

It's easy to get angry with God when our dreams of service are smashed. Perhaps Prince Charming never appears or he dies or he finds a younger Cinderella. Perhaps it turns out we can't get pregnant. Perhaps we don't get that dream job. Figuring out why things happen as they do is beyond our human power. In such tests of faith, we can only believe in God's love for us and the strength to carry on.

Inspiration

The most important thing for me is to pray and suffer for the holy Church and her pastors. (St. Anna Schäffer)

Challenge

Are you harboring any resentment against God? Pray for the faith to accept the pain and disappointment and the wisdom to put that acceptance to work to help others.

Mary Faustina Kowalska

August 25, 1905–October 5, 1938

Nothing about Faustina's early life indicated how significant her thirty years on earth would be. She was the third of ten children born to peasants. She had only three years of schooling, and then worked as a housekeeper before joining the Congregation of the Sisters of Our Lady of Mercy the day before her twentieth birthday. In the next thirteen years, she would be blessed with revelations, visions, prophecies and other gifts that would lead to development of the Chaplet of the Divine Mercy devotion.

Appearances can be deceiving. God had a special plan for Mary Faustina, just as he has a special plan for each of us. Discounting another person because he or she doesn't display the trappings of success or intelligence leaves us the poorer.

Inspiration

Neither graces, nor revelations, nor raptures, nor gifts granted to a soul make it perfect, but rather the intimate union of the soul with God. These gifts are merely ornaments of the soul, but constitute neither its essence nor its perfection. My sanctity and perfection consist in the close union of my will with the will of God. (St. Mary Faustina Kowalska)

Challenge

Pray the Divine Mercy Chaplet or another prayer to Mary. If you are not familiar with the Divine Mercy Chaplet, you can find out more at http://thedivinemercy.org.

Mary Frances of the Five Wounds of Jesus

March 25, 1715–October 6, 1791

When she joined the Third Order of St. Francis, Mary Frances chose this name to show her devotion to Christ's passion, St. Francis of Assisi, and the Blessed Mother. She experienced stigmata, particularly during the Fridays of Lent, and she often was met with skepticism from her family and others. As a result, Mary Frances withdrew from public attention as much as she could, and spent most of the last half of her life as a priest's housekeeper.

We can be very quick to be dismissive of people whose charisms or gifts are different from ours, and the Church quite rightly is very careful about validating reports of stigmata or visions of the Blessed Virgin, Jesus, and the saints. Yet Mary Frances's experience reminds us to be open to all the ways our Lord may choose to appear to us or to others.

❧ Inspiration

It is not I whom you have offended—it is God whom you have offended, and at his feet you must bewail your sins. (St. Mary Frances of the Five Wounds of Jesus)

❧ Challenge

Pray for forgiveness for the times you have rushed to judge people who experience God in a way that makes you uncomfortable.

Marie-Rose Durocher (Eulalie Durocher)

October 6, 1811–October 6, 1849

Marie-Rose had tried to join the same religious congregation as her sister, but her health forced her to return home. A few years later, her brother, who had become a pastor, convinced her to come and work as his housekeeper and secretary. During that twelve-year period, she realized that there was a serious lack of schools for Quebec's young people, particularly those who lived in rural areas. Shortly thereafter, Marie-Rose and two friends formed what would become the Sisters of the Holy Names of Jesus and Mary, whose members today serve as teachers in six countries.

If Marie-Rose hadn't been doing office work for her brother, she might not have discovered her true ministry. Even when we are performing routine chores or duties, God may open our eyes to new opportunities we would have never otherwise considered.

❧ Inspiration

I came to bring fire to the earth, and how I wish it were already kindled! (Luke 12:49)

❧ Challenge

Don't just go through the motions today. Whether it's at work or at home, be present to your tasks and responsibilities, and see if fresh thinking about them might lead you in a new spiritual direction.

Angela Truszkowska

May 16, 1825–October 10, 1899

Angela faced a difficult choice. She had founded what is now known as the Felician Sisters to help the elderly and poor in Warsaw, and the effort was growing. Angela was in the prime of her life—her mid-forties. But her health was deteriorating, including a hearing loss that would lead to profound deafness. She chose to step aside as superior and allow others to lead, while she spent much of the next thirty years in adoration despite suffering a dark night of the soul during this time.

Angela put her pride and ego aside and did what was best for the sisters and their work. May we all be insightful enough to know when it's time to turn our work and our ministry over to others.

Inspiration

He who has the bride is the bridegroom. The friend of the bridegroom, who stands and hears him, rejoices greatly at the bridegroom's voice. For this reason my joy has been fulfilled. He must increase, but I must decrease. (John 3:29–30)

Challenge

Would the company where you work, your parish committee, or an area of service fall apart if you weren't there anymore? Meditate on ways to help others prepare to take your place. Only God is indispensable.

Publia

Died circa 362

Publia was a bold woman. As the emperor Julian was going by her community of virgins, she and the other women began chanting psalms that denounced false idols. They refused the emperor's order to stop, and Publia endured a beating. While Julian planned to have the community wiped out, he died in battle shortly thereafter, so the women were left in peace.

Consider the bravery and trust Publia and her community exhibited in publicly calling out the emperor for his pagan practices. Sometimes, in our politically correct world, we hold back and lack the courage to call tyrants and dictators what they are. While we pray for God to change their hearts and souls, we also must advocate for the people they brutalize.

✒ Inspiration

Their idols are silver and gold,
  the work of human hands.
They have mouths, but do not speak;
  eyes, but do not see. (Psalm 115:4–5)

✒ Challenge

Write a letter to support an organization that engages in Christian service abroad. You might want to focus on a group that works in a country from which your ancestors came or in an area of the world that is in the news today.

Maria Catalina Irigoyen Echegaray

November 25, 1848–October 10, 1918

Maria Catalina was fearless in her ministry to the sick of Madrid. It didn't matter whether it was smallpox, cholera, or some other dangerous contagious disease; the sister could be counted on to care for people, even when members of their own families had left them behind. She also established a facility where clothing was sewn for the needy. As a sister of the Servants of Mary, Ministers to the Sick, Maria Catalina ministered in this manner for more than twenty years, until deafness forced her to give it up.

The cardinal who presided at Maria Catalina's beatification Mass in 2011 said she "saw in the ill and needy the face of the suffering Christ." How often in our busy lives do we pass the faces of the ill and needy—some we know, some we don't—on our way to meetings, appointments, and the like. Her example reminds us of the importance of slowing down and being present.

Inspiration

All I can do is serve. (Blessed Maria Catalina Irigoyen Echegaray)

Challenge

When you ask people today how it's going or how they are, stop and find out the real answer rather than the perfunctory one. Offer to pray for their concerns.

Maria Soledad Torres Acosta

December 2, 1826–October 11, 1887

For five years, Maria had been part of the Servants of Mary, Ministers to the Sick. In fact, she was among the founding members. Then Father Michael Martinez y Sanz announced he would be taking half the congregation to West Africa to found a new mission. While staying behind as superior general was challenging for Maria—she was even removed for a brief time—she served for the next thirty-five years. Today, more than sixteen hundred sisters minister to the sick in twenty-two countries.

Maria wasn't sure she could keep things going without Father Michael, just as she wasn't sure she wanted to give up her earlier dream of the contemplative life in favor of serving the sick. But when God knocks on our hearts and souls to take on difficult situations, we must have the faith to answer, "Here I am, Lord."

Inspiration

Have faith. God will not allow more than we can endure. (St. Maria Soledad Torres Acosta)

Challenge

What is God asking you to do that seems too challenging, too difficult? Ask him to grant you the faith to say yes—and don't be afraid to let him know you need some help.

Maria Teresa Fasce (Maria Joanna Fasce)

December 27, 1881–January 18, 1947

Maria thought she knew just what it would be like to be a nun. She greatly admired St. Rita of Cascia, who was canonized when Maria was eighteen. It was just a few years later that Maria took her initial vows and headed for life at her saint's monastery. But she found more a nightmare than a dream. The sisters didn't get along, the environment was less than spiritual, and almost no one went to the chapel where St. Rita's body was housed. Maria needed a break! She returned after a few months, and spent thirty years in leadership positions, through which she was able to bring attention to St. Rita and her works.

So often, the way we imagine things just isn't the way they turn out. A new baby, a new home, a new job: like the monastery Maria had idealized, they all bring unexpected challenges. In the end, we accept the imperfect in the situation, and do what we can to improve it in Christ's name.

✿ Inspiration

Do all things without murmuring and arguing, so that you may be blameless and innocent, children of God without blemish in the midst of a crooked and perverse generation, in which you shine like stars in the world. (Philippians 2:14–15)

✿ Challenge

When were you most disappointed in a relationship, a home, a job, a trip, or a gift? What joy did you ultimately find? Thank God for the growth place you found.

Alexandrina Maria da Costa

March 30, 1904–October 13, 1955

Alexandrina was bedridden for about thirty years, the result of a leap she took from a window to avoid a sexual assault. While she originally prayed to the Blessed Virgin for a miracle to heal her, eventually Alexandrina came to realize that was not to be. Instead, she accepted that her mission in life was to be a faithful victim of Christ, and was pleasant and joyful to those who visited her, despite her physical pain and interior struggles. Her suffering included spasms and other movements each Friday as she lived Christ's passion.

Some of us wear our hearts on our sleeves; that is, everyone knows if we are unhappy or struggling. While being disingenuous or inauthentic is not a good thing, accepting our situation as it is and taking our woes to God can inspire others, and provide healing balm for ourselves.

❧ Inspiration

Our Lady has given me an even greater grace: First, abandonment; then, complete conformity to God's will; finally, the thirst for suffering. (Blessed Alexandrina Maria da Costa)

❧ Challenge

Just for today, take your complaints and pains to God only. To everyone else, present a joyful face. At the end of the day, consider how you feel compared to the day before.

Hedwig of Silesia

1174–October 15, 1243

Hedwig was only twelve when she and Henry I of Silesia married, but it proved to be a good match for both of them. They were generous with their wealth, founding numerous monasteries, hospitals, and convents in their domain. In fact, at Hedwig's request, Henry built the first monastery for women in their area. They had seven children, and were saddened by a territorial battle between two of their sons. In one dispute over territory, Hedwig went to her husband's defense against his captor, and prompted his release. After Henry's death in 1238, Hedwig gave the remainder of her estate to the Church and entered as an oblate a monastery led by one of their daughters.

Successful marriages take work. That work is so much more joyful when works and faith are intertwined. We can accomplish so much for God when we are evenly yoked.

Inspiration

Do not be mismatched with unbelievers. For what partnership is there between righteousness and lawlessness? Or what fellowship is there between light and darkness? (2 Corinthians 6:14)

Challenge

Work goes easier and faster when it is done in tandem. Talk with your spouse or a close friend about service you can do together, either on an ongoing basis or one time.

Teresa of Avila

March 28, 1515–October 4, 1582

She was forty years old. Flirtatious and beautiful in her youth, she became a nun when she was twenty-one. But her relationship with God had been lukewarm at best, with a certain amount of going through the motions amid dealing with serious health issues. Then one day as she went to pray, she passed a painting of Christ in extreme pain. That encounter changed Teresa of Avila's life forever, and put her on a path that would include her being named a Doctor of the Church for her writings on prayer.

Who hasn't had an arid spell with God? There are definitely times when he doesn't seem to listen or provide us with what we need—or at least what we think we need. Teresa of Avila's example reminds us that God is here with us always, even when we find it difficult to see his presence.

Inspiration

I was like a person who has fallen into a river: whatever the direction she takes, she is afraid the danger will be greater and yet she is almost drowning. (St. Teresa of Avila)

Challenge

Consider adding a book by or about Teresa of Avila to your reading list. Say this little prayer attributed to Teresa: "Let nothing disturb you, Let nothing frighten you, All things are passing away: God never changes."

Marguerite d'Youville

October 15, 1701–December 23, 1771

Canada's first native-born saint was a widow before she was thirty. She'd also lost four of her six children. Marguerite persevered and several years later founded the Sisters of Charity of Montreal. Her struggles didn't end there; the order's work with the poor resulted in ridicule, and reportedly the sisters were sometimes denied the Eucharist because it was believed Marguerite was still engaged in her deceased husband's liquor-running business. Her home was destroyed by fire, as was the hospital where she was director.

When we are having struggles of our own, it's tempting to focus on resolving our problems rather than continuing to reach out to those most in need of our assistance. The example Marguerite set prompted Pope John XXIII to call her the "Mother of Universal Charity" when she was beatified.

Inspiration

We had been a little too comfortable...henceforth, we shall live with everything in common. (St. Marguerite d'Youville)

Challenge

Put aside the worries and mournings in your own life for an hour today and do something to help someone you know, or someone you don't, who is less fortune. Consider writing an encouraging note or performing volunteer service with your parish or diocese.

Marguerite Marie Alacoque

July 22, 1647–October 17, 1690

Marguerite Marie had a special relationship with Christ. He appeared to her and asked for special devotions, including the revealing of his Sacred Heart to show his love for all of us and the establishment of the Holy Hour. People inside and outside her convent were skeptical of the visions, but she persisted. The Feast of the Sacred Heart of Jesus was established more than 150 years after her death.

How do we pray? In the way that works for us. For some of us, an hour of adoration of the Blessed Sacrament flies; for others, it's impossible to focus even half that long. Some of us are comfortable with the concept of visions; others are not. Some prefer standard prayer forms to spontaneous talks with God. Which is the best way? The one that lets you have an open, continuing connection to God—and him to you.

Inspiration

I need nothing but God, and to lose myself in the heart of God. (St. Marguerite Marie Alacoque)

Challenge

Spend time with our Lord today in the form of prayer that draws you closest to him. Maybe it's a walk outside to enjoy fall's splendor; maybe it's time in an adoration chapel; maybe it's saying the rosary with your prayer group. There's no wrong way.

Euphrasia of the Sacred Heart of Jesus (Rose Eluvathingal)
October 17, 1877–August 29, 1952

Euphrasia, the sixth to be named blessed in the nation of India, loved to hear her mother's stories of faith, in particular those of St. Rose of Lima, for whom she had been named. She learned to pray the rosary at an early age and was only nine when the Blessed Virgin appeared to her. She joined the Sisters of the Mother of Carmel, and came to be called the "Praying Mother" because of the time she spent each day before the Blessed Sacrament and in devotion to Mary. In addition to the ordained and those with vocations, she prayed for those separated from the Church.

Have you ever noticed that the times you feel furthest from God are the same times your prayer life is least active? It can be difficult to keep that door open to God when you feel he's throwing more at you than you can handle. And yet, setting aside time each day to pray, even if our prayer is "I'm mad at you," gives us the strength to keep going.

❧ Inspiration
My joy is to live a hidden life unknown to all. (Blessed Euphrasia of the Sacred Heart of Jesus)

❧ Challenge
What about your life, large or small, are you annoyed with or angry about? Pray about this obstacle and the way you are reacting to it.

Marie de Jésus (Marie Deluil-Martiny)

May 28, 1841–February 27, 1884

Marie, considered the first apostle of the Sacred Heart devotion, understood the value of community from an early age. When she was just eleven, she and some of her friends at a Catholic boarding school established their own rule and other organizational documents. Of course, the sisters required them to dissolve the community, but it would not be Marie's last. Later, she founded the Society of the Daughters of the Heart of Jesus. They offer themselves up for priests, much as the Blessed Mother did for Jesus with her presence at the crucifixion. When Marie was just forty-three, a disturbed convent gardener shot her to death. In her final words, she said she was dying for the priests.

Like some of the apostles at Jesus's passion, we sometimes flee out of fear, or because we reason it's better to survive and live to fight another day. Marie's story reminds us that our ministry may demand sacrifice, even the ultimate sacrifice, and we need to be prepared to offer it.

☞ Inspiration

The church is on Calvary; now is the time to rally around the Heart of Jesus wounded on the cross! (Blessed Marie de Jesus)

☞ Challenge

Are you so passionate and so spiritually confident of your relationship with Christ that you would offer whatever he asks in terms of time, talent, and treasure? If not, begin a dialogue with him to strengthen that relationship.

Maria Bertilla Boscardin

October 6, 1888–October 20, 1922

The local clergy in Brendola, Italy, called Maria a "goose," and she was generally viewed as not very bright. Still, the Teachers of St. Dorothy, Daughters of the Sacred Heart, accepted her as a member when Maria was sixteen or so, and she trained as a nurse. Her care of children with diphtheria and of patients during the air raids that rattled the town were appreciated by some, but not by her superior, who temporarily assigned her to the laundry. She was returned to caring for children shortly before she died during an operation for a chronic condition. "The Lord was always with her, directing and illuminating…[and] continues spilling the benefits of holiness in a growing field of souls to win today," Pope John XXIII said at Maria's canonization in 1961.

If we continually hear that we're too stupid, too fat, too uncoordinated, too *something* to be of much use in this world, we begin to believe it. The thing about God, however, is that he can use us in any form, just the way we are.

Inspiration

I can't do anything. I'm a poor thing, a goose. Teach me. I want to become a saint. (St. Maria Bertilla Boscardin)

Challenge

Keep a journal for a few days, noting the number of times you berate yourself and your abilities. Then read John 3:16 or 1 John 4:16.

Laura Montoya Upegui

May 26, 1874–October 21, 1949

Some called the native people living in Colombia "wild beasts." But not Laura. After all, she had been called ignorant herself as she grew up in poverty and lacked much of a formal education. Laura founded the Missionaries of Mary Immaculate and Saint Catherine of Siena, and with four other women left their homes to serve as missionaries. They lived among the people in Colombia's poorest regions, bringing them spiritual instruction and education, and advocating for their rights. In 2004, Laura became the first Colombian woman to be beatified.

We're called to love all, not just people who look like us or move in our social circles or are in the same economic class. Laura's example reminds us that even people whose lives are foreign to us are loved by Christ in the same way he loves us.

Inspiration

There's a need for intrepid women, valiant and on fire with the love of God, who would be able to unite their lives with those of the poor inhabitants of the jungle, to lift them toward God. (Blessed Laura Montoya Upegui)

Challenge

Where is your personal bias? Does it involve people from a different country, a different faith, perhaps a different age group? Investigate resources that will help you better understand their history and worldview.

Alodia and Nunilo

Died circa 851

The sisters' mother was a Christian; their father was Muslim. When he died and the mother remarried, again to a Muslim, the new husband was less than tolerant of their Christian faith. Alodia and Nunilo were arrested as part of a persecution in Spain, and both were beheaded after they refused to deny their faith.

We desire that all have an opportunity to know Christ. Yet as Catholics we also believe in religious freedom. The story of Alodia and Nunilo shows that marriages from different faith traditions can work, as was the case with their mother's first marriage, and can also go horribly astray, as was the case with her second. The support of a faith community in your own tradition is critical, especially when children are involved.

Inspiration

You yourselves know that it is unlawful for a Jew to associate with or to visit a Gentile; but God has shown me that I should not call anyone profane or unclean. (Acts 10:28)

Challenge

Perhaps you're married to a non-Catholic, or perhaps you know someone who is in such a marriage. Spend some time learning more about the other faith tradition from a reputable source. You may be surprised at how much unites you. Offer to pray together.

Josephine Leroux

1747–1794

Josephine and the other sisters had to be so excited to be back in Valenciennes, after having to flee to Belgium due to the French Revolution. Within a year after their return, however, the city was retaken. Josephine didn't challenge the authorities when they came to arrest her for treason. It is said when Josephine approached the guillotine, she kissed the executioner's hand, and informed those gathered she forgave them. Five companions died the same day.

There comes a point in our lives where we stop fighting and surrender the future to God. Sometimes, that's on our deathbed or when we face a crisis for which we can see no solution. Josephine's example shows us that our struggles can be lessened if we have already turned over our spiritual lives and placed ourselves in God's hands.

Inspiration

Could anyone fear to leave this place of exile when he reflects on the beauty of Paradise? (Blessed Josephine Leroux)

Challenge

Are you afraid of physical death? If so, why? What would it take to get to a place that you could be somewhat indifferent to the prospect? Consider asking your spiritual director or pastor for some resources, such as a course or reading materials, that might help you face your fears.

Maria Ludovica De Angelis
October 24, 1880–February 25, 1962

Maria was a hard worker, beginning back in the days she spent in the fields in her Italian homeland as the oldest of eight children. She entered the Institute of the Daughters of Our Lady of Mercy when she was twenty-four, and three years later was sent to the congregation's Buenos Aires convent to serve as a cook in a children's hospital. While Maria lacked a formal education, her drive and her belief in God and the projects he sent her provided everything she needed. She was successful in raising the money the sisters needed to expand the hospital and other facilities, and she ultimately became the convent's superior. "All this was accomplished by this simple woman who was driven by love and complete dedication," Pope John Paul II said in his homily at her beatification.

Sometimes, we make life too hard. We overthink the options available and overanalyze the possible outcomes. Maria's example reminds us that when it comes to what God desires, we need to just do it.

Inspiration
Do good to all, no matter who it may be. (Blessed Maria Ludovica De Angelis)

Challenge
What decision are you worrying about obsessively, like a dog with a bone? Pray for God to grant you clarity.

Anne Line

1567–February 27, 1601

Anne felt the call to Catholicism when she was a teenager and converted along with her brother. Since she was from a strong Calvinist family, she was quickly disinherited. Shortly after her marriage, her brother and her husband, also a convert, were arrested and had to go into exile. That only served to strengthen Anne's resolve; she oversaw safe houses for priests and was arrested at one of those houses. When she told the court her only regret was that she hadn't protected a thousand more priests, she was sentenced to hang.

From her disinheritance to the banishment of her husband, Anne knew what her support of her faith could cost her. Yet, her faith was so important to her that she continued to risk her life. It makes you wonder about the times you think you're too busy to go to Mass on a holy day of obligation, or you think you are already overbooked when you're asked to sit at a ministry table or usher, doesn't it?

Inspiration

I am sentenced to die for harboring a Catholic priest, and so far I am from repenting for having so done, that I wish, with all my soul, that where I have entertained one, I could have entertained a thousand. (St. Anne Line)

Challenge

Imagine a world where you could be arrested for attending Mass. How far would you be willing to go to do so?

Celine Borzęcka

October 29, 1833–October 26, 1913

Celine went along with her parents' desires and married when she was twenty. She and Joseph had a good marriage with two daughters who survived to adulthood. Celine provided loving care for her husband when he became paralyzed for the five years before his death. Then, at age forty, she and her daughters left their home in Vienna to visit Rome. Both Celine and her daughter Hedwig discerned that they were being called to form a community and became cofoundresses of Sisters of the Resurrection. The first house opened in Poland, and the order grew to Bulgaria and the United States. Celine suffered a blow when Hedwig died suddenly in 1906, but she continued to lead the congregation.

Even when we believe we are following God's will, we experience sadness and heartache, as Celine did with the death of her husband and daughter. Trusting in God's love and concern gets us through the bad times, and helps us to flower in the good.

✒ Inspiration

In God there is happiness forever. (Blessed Celine Borzęcka)

✒ Challenge

Think of a time when life events hurt you deeply and God provided healing balm. What can you share about that experience with a friend who is suffering today?

Teresa Eustochio Verzeri

July 31, 1801–March 3, 1852

Teresa was blessed in her early educational experiences. She studied at home and was encouraged to discern and seek God's grace. Her spiritual adviser was the vicar general of her diocese. After leaving in a monastery for a time, she and her spiritual adviser founded the Congregation of the Daughters of the Sacred Heart of Jesus, which had as one of its key missions the education of at-risk girls. Teresa believed young people should have an individualized learning experience that best suited their capabilities and temperament.

Do you expect your daughter or goddaughter or niece or another young girl in your life to hate science because you did or love English because you did? Help the young people you love learn the discipline they need to advance in their studies, but remember their passions may not be the same as yours.

Inspiration

Cultivate and attentively guard the mind and heart of your little girls while they are still young, to prevent as far as possible any entrance of evil, it being better to avert a fall with your warnings and admonitions than to have to lift them up again with correction. (St. Teresa Eustochio Verzeri)

Challenge

Call or spend time in person with a girl in your life. Ask her about her favorite class or activity, and listen without saying a single time, "When I was your age…"

Maria-Theresa Scherer

October 31, 1825–June 16, 1888

Maria-Theresa didn't think it was a good idea when the priest who cofounded her order bought a bankrupt Bohemian textile factory. But after some prayer, she agreed to send some sisters to help there. However, within five years, the priest had died and his affairs were a mess, with huge debts related to the bad investment. Maria-Theresa and her community chose to take on the financial responsibility and worked together to repay the creditors. The sisters later also made restitution to the priest's nephew, even though a court had ruled they didn't have to.

Maria-Theresa and the others repaid the priest's debts not because they were required to, but because they felt it was the right thing to do. Her example shows us that while as citizens we must abide by court rulings, as Christians we may have a greater responsibility.

Inspiration

The good Lord will help us if we remain united and if we have no other aim than his glory and the good of man. But we must also work very hard. (Blessed Maria-Theresa Scherer)

Challenge

Go beyond the letter of the law in your dealings with people today. Think about what Jesus would do in the situation. Then do it.

Chiara Badano

October 29, 1971–October 7, 1990

Chiara was just sixteen, beautiful and very active in the Focolare international brotherhood movement, when she first felt the pain in her shoulder. It turned out to be a rare form of bone cancer. In the next two years, Chiara showed people how to die, comforted other patients as well as her friends and family, and prayed. Even the doctors commented on her smile in the darkest times. She died just before her nineteenth birthday. Pope Benedict told those gathered at World Youth Day 2012 about Chiara, who was beatified two years earlier: "The key to her peace and her joy was complete trust in the Lord, and also the acceptance of the disease as a mysterious expression of his will."

Death seems especially cruel when it comes to someone as young and vibrant as Chiara. But her brave example inspires us to bear our everyday aches and pains as well as more serious illnesses with grace and trust in God.

Inspiration

For you, Jesus. (Blessed Chiara Badano)

Challenge

Give an extra hug today to everyone in your life, for we never know when or how our time will come. Offer thanks for the treasures they bring to you.

Maria Teresa of St. Joseph (Anna Maria Tauscher van den Bosch)

June 19, 1855–September 20, 1938

She was a preacher's kid—a Lutheran preacher's kid, to be precise. But in her teens and early twenties, Maria Teresa began studying other religions and became more and more drawn to Catholicism. Eventually, she took a job at a mental institution staffed primarily by Catholics and decided to convert. This cost her the position because her father and the institution director, who was not Catholic, opposed her decision. She was offered refuge at a convent and chose to become a nun. She continued her work with the elderly, the poor, and children until she died.

Many of us were born into Catholic families and began our journey with the support of loving parents, siblings, friends and others. Changing your faith as an adult means breaking with traditions and sometimes relationships, but the change can mean a fuller, deeper relationship with Christ.

✺ Inspiration

O, Lord, send me wherever you will to work for the salvation of souls. (Blessed Maria Teresa of St. Joseph)

✺ Challenge

Consider volunteering to sponsor an adult in your parish's RCIA program or to help out with religious education for the children in your parish. You'll be surprised how much you'll learn.

María de la Purisima de la Cruz

February 20, 1926–October 31, 1998

María's beatification was among the fastest to date. Many in Seville still remember her work as superior-general of the Sisters of the Company of the Cross. At her beatification, a story was told of María and a younger woman going to care for a woman in a rodent-infested home. Even though mice terrified her, María asked the younger woman to leave while she tended to the sick woman and cleaned the house.

Our lives can get caught up in fear and avoiding the things we find distasteful or frightening. María's story reminds us that with God's help, we can put aside our personal concerns and prejudices, and focus on doing the work he desires.

✒ Inspiration

For who is greater, the one who is at the table or the one who serves? Is it not the one at the table? But I am among you as one who serves. (Luke 22:27)

✒ Challenge

What task at home, in your job, or in your ministry do you find most odious or demeaning? Pray for the strength to overcome your distaste and follow through on the work.

Maria Repetto

November 1, 1807–January 5, 1890

When she joined the Daughters of Our Lady of Refuge, Maria had one request: that her chores and duties be confined to the convent. For many years, she worked as a seamstress and embroiderer, but then was named portress when her vision began to decline. She found a whole new ministry, comforting the poor who approached the convent door, praying for them, and providing them with holy cards, medals, food, money, and clothes. At one point, she was removed from this duty due to concerns about how much she was giving away. She later was returned to her post.

It's all about timing. Sometimes, the ministry to which we are perfectly suited at one time in our lives is totally different from the one to which we are called later. Maria's example reminds us to be open to where God wants to lead us.

❧ Inspiration

For as in one body we have many members, and not all the members have the same function, so we, who are many, are one body in Christ, and individually we are members one of another. (Romans 12:4–5)

❧ Challenge

What limitations have you put on what you'll do for your community or for God? Consider whether it's time to free up those constraints.

Antonia of Florence

1401–February 18, 1472

Antonia made the transition to Franciscan tertiary after being widowed twice before she was thirty. She spent more than a dozen years with the Franciscans, but then felt she wanted to offer up more for Christ. With the help of her spiritual director, she decided to join a new convent of the Poor Clares. Even though she was the superior, she took the most difficult tasks for herself. Word spread, and the rigor Antonia set forth drew hundreds of young women.

Like Antonia, we grow in faith and love. The ministry that presented us with an opportunity for growth five years ago may be too comfortable today. We continually need to look inside ourselves and ask if it's time to try something new.

Inspiration

Like obedient children, do not be conformed to the desires that you formerly had in ignorance. Instead, as he who called you is holy, be holy yourselves in all your conduct. (1 Peter 1:14–15)

Challenge

Are you looking for a bigger challenge in your faith life? Discuss with your spiritual director or the staff at your parish some opportunities for new, different service, or perhaps some spiritual reading that goes in a different direction than your usual list.

Silvia of Rome

Circa 515–circa 592

Silvia and her husband, St. Gordion, had two sons, one of whom went on to become Pope Gregory the Great, whom some call a father of the modern Catholic Church. It is said that Silvia was responsible for the excellent education the sons received. God became Silva's singular focus after her husband's death in about 573; she spent her remaining years in a small cell, similar to that of an anchoress.

We have seasons to our lives: as giggly teenagers; as studious college students; as loving spouses, friends, and mothers; as dependable workers; as gentle caregivers; as affectionate grandmothers; as caring friends. The common thread throughout it all is God, and we must live the years in a grateful, giving way.

✒ Inspiration

A time to be born, and a time to die;

a time to plant, and a time to pluck up what is planted;

…

a time to weep, and a time to laugh;

a time to mourn, and a time to dance. (Ecclesiastes 3:2, 4)

✒ Challenge

Think about the seasons of your life. Where has God led you up to this time, and where is he nudging you for the future? What spiritual practices can you use to prepare for what's ahead?

Teresa Manganiello

January 1, 1849–November 3, 1876

Teresa was extraordinary in her ordinariness. She never went to school yet felt a yearning to become a woman religious. She was considered wise and spiritually profound. When she was twenty-one, she became a Franciscan tertiary and had plans with her parish priest to begin a congregation, a plan for which Teresa gained papal support during a visit to Rome. But the following year, Teresa died of tuberculosis. Plans went forward for the Franciscan Immaculatine Sisters, which continues ministry today in six countries. "She wasn't naïve; she was innocent," the postulator of her cause said. "She had a spirit of meditation and contemplation and when she met people she was simple and profound and amazed learned persons."

What could an uneducated girl teach any of us about spirituality? Plenty, it turns out. Through Teresa, we are reminded that God appears in our lives in all sorts of vessels, and invites us to drink.

Inspiration

I can do nothing on my own. As I hear, I judge; and my judgment is just, because I seek to do not my own will but the will of him who sent me. (John 5:30)

Challenge

Think of a person whose abilities you discount based on his or her schooling, age, position, neighborhood, or physical appearance. Resolve to talk with this person soon, listening closely so that you can hear Christ.

Elizabeth

First century

The time for a baby had long passed. Elizabeth and Zachariah were in the latter stages of their lives. Then the angel Gabriel appeared and told Zachariah they would have a son and name him John. Because he doubted Gabriel, Zachariah was left without speech until his son was born. Elizabeth, on the other hand, took this startling sequence of events in stride and warmly welcomed her relative Mary when she arrived with news of her own pregnancy.

It's good to be skeptical when an e-mail or phone call promises us something for nothing. However, too often we are also suspicious of God's grace. How can it be that we can be washed clean of our sins? How can it be that God wants a relationship with us? Elizabeth's example reminds us to accept God's guidance with open arms and joyful hearts.

✒ Inspiration

[Elizabeth] exclaimed with a loud cry, "Blessed are you among women, and blessed is the fruit of your womb. And why has this happened to me, that the mother of my Lord comes to me?" (Luke 1:42–43)

✒ Challenge

What gift is God offering you that you find difficult to receive? Pray for the confidence to say yes.

Maria Crocifissa di Rosa

November 6, 1813–December 15, 1855

Maria threw herself into whatever ministry she was presented. All her siblings and her mother had died by the time she was a teenager, so she was responsible for housekeeping and caring for her father in addition to helping the young women she managed at a spinning mill. When a cholera epidemic hit her hometown, Maria became a nurse. She also established schools for people who were deaf and mute. Ultimately, she founded the Handmaids of Charity of Brescia, who continue to do work today in Africa, South America, and Europe.

God doesn't call us to be lukewarm participants in life. He asks that we be passionate about serving him and our brothers and sisters. Maria's example encourages us to reach out and be of assistance in any way we can, whether it's in our own small town or parish, or on a larger stage.

✒ Inspiration

I can't go to bed with a quiet conscience if during the day I've missed any chance, however slight, of preventing wrongdoing or of helping to bring about some good. (St. Maria Crocifissa di Rosa)

✒ Challenge

Where are you loving or serving in a halfhearted way? Pray to God to help you rekindle the fire where you are or by lighting your path to a new ministry.

Anne-Marie Javouhey

November 10, 1779–July 15, 1851

Anne-Marie was in a bit of despair after a failed effort at convent life. But then she had a vision of Teresa of Avila and children of all races. "These are the children God has given you," the saint said. Within seven years, Anne-Marie founded the Sisters of St. Joseph of Cluny, a missionary order. She and the sisters traveled to Africa and the Caribbean and provided care to enslaved people. Anne-Marie's confidence that she was doing what God wanted sustained her through difficult church political circumstances, including a two-year excommunication due to disputes with a local bishop.

Anne-Marie's dream was for dignity for all, the relief of pain and hunger, and, as she put it "winning a few souls for religion." She could have done that in her hometown. Instead, God used her bold trust to take her thousands of miles from her home. May we all show the same trust when God puts on our hearts what he wants us to do.

✷ Inspiration

Be happy since you are doing God's Holy Will. He will not abandon you in the midst of any troubles or difficulties that you may meet with. (Blessed Anne-Marie Javouhey)

✷ Challenge

Where are you thinking too small in your ministry? Perhaps you're not called to be a missionary. But who among your family or friends or fellow parishioners have you forgotten or neglected? How can you help God win a few souls?

Elizabeth of the Trinity

July 18, 1880–November 9, 1906

Elizabeth struggled. As a child, she was stubborn and threw fits of rage when she didn't get her way. As a Carmelite nun, she suffered periods of spiritual dryness, and wasn't even sure as a novice she should proceed to take her final vows. But amid all her inner turmoil, she knew she had God with her at all times. We remember her for her letters and retreat guides and her devotion to the Holy Trinity.

There is no such thing as a perfect Catholic. No matter how much we strive to live in a Christlike manner, it's not going to happen all the time. Elizabeth's story reminds us that our imperfections need not keep us away from service—or God's love.

☞ Inspiration

O my God, Trinity whom I adore; help me to forget myself entirely that I may be established in you as still and as peaceful as if my soul were already in eternity.… Bury yourself in me that I may bury myself in you until I depart to contemplate in your light the abyss of your greatness. (Blessed Elizabeth of the Trinity)

☞ Challenge

Turn off your inner critic today. When you start to put yourself down, stop and instead offer up Elizabeth's Holy Trinity prayer.

Maria del Carmen of the Child Jesus (Maria Carmela Gonzalez Ramos Garcia Prieto)

June 30, 1834–November 9, 1899

Carmen's life was divided into thirds. The first third, she spent at home with her family, the sixth of nine children and a girl known for her devotion to Mary and the Blessed Sacrament. The next third, she spent as a wife, married to a man who was difficult but who asked her pardon and lived in a Christlike fashion in the four years before his death. It was after his death that Carmen, who had no children of her own, began to reach out to young people, setting up a school in her home. The final third, she spent as a woman religious, founding the Franciscan Sisters of the Sacred Hearts, which ministers to the sick and elderly.

Time passes. Seasons change. Our life's purpose can take on a different direction or texture. God, however, always remains the same.

✺ Inspiration

Teach souls to know and love God. (Blessed Maria del Carmen of the Child Jesus)

✺ Challenge

What eternal truths have transcended the stages of your life? Make a list of the ways in which you've served God during each stage, and of ideas for what could be ahead. How can what you have learned be used to follow Carmen's directive?

Rose Philippine Duchesne

August 29, 1769–November 18, 1852

When she was young, Rose felt a call as a missionary. However, she spent the early years of her adult life at a series of convents in France. Finally, when she was nearly fifty, she was sent to the United States by the Society of the Sacred Heart of Jesus congregation, settling near St. Louis. Later, when she was seventy-two, Rose spent a year with a Potawatomi tribe in Kansas, where she was named "Woman Who Prays Always." She burned to go work with students in the Rocky Mountains after that, but her health required that she spend the remainder of her life in the St. Louis area.

God's timing reigns supreme. We can never be stuck in our own belief that time may have passed us by for some form of service. When God asks, we say yes, and wait for him to determine when and where to use us.

Inspiration

We cultivate a very small field for Christ, but we love it, knowing that God does not require great achievements but a heart that holds back nothing for self....The truest crosses are those we do not choose ourselves.... He who has Jesus has everything. (St. Rose Philippine Duchesne)

Challenge

How does the person you were ten or fifteen years ago inform your faith journey today? Consider journaling about the lessons you have learned.

Maria Domenica Mantovani

November 12, 1862–February 2, 1934

Maria Domenica was blessed to have the same spiritual director for forty-five years. Father Giuseppe Nascimbeni came to her parish as curate when she was fifteen, and encouraged her to minister to the sick and to assist in teaching catechism. Together, they founded the Congregation of the Little Sisters of the Holy Family with Maria as superior general. She continued to consult with Father Nascimbeni until his death in 1922. In her beatification homily, Pope John Paul II called Maria "extraordinarily faithful, in all circumstances and to her last breath, to the will of God, by whom she felt loved and called."

Spiritual directors, formal or informal, are a critical part of our faith journey. They know when to challenge us, and when to comfort us. They know the words to say to help us determine where God is leading us, and how to follow. They illumine our path.

Inspiration

Are not all angels spirits in the divine service, sent to serve for the sake of those who are to inherit salvation? (Hebrews 1:14)

Challenge

If you have a spiritual director, talk with him or her about the guidance that has been provided to date. If you don't have one, check in with your pastor or a trusted friend to discuss finding one.

Agostina Livia Pietrantoni

March 27, 1864–November 13, 1894

Agostina went to work at the tender age of seven, hauling stones and sand for road construction. A few years later, she helped harvest olives. She went from the Italian countryside to Rome with an uncle in hopes of finding an appropriate congregation, but she returned home disappointed. Then, shortly before her twenty-second birthday, she was accepted by the Sisters of Charity of St. Jeanne-Antide Thouret, and after taking her final vows, she went to work at a hospital that was very opposed to religion. It was there that Agostina met Joseph Romanelli, a tuberculosis patient who repeatedly threatened her and ultimately stabbed her to death. She died while saying prayers of forgiveness for him.

Following our call to be servants of God doesn't always have a happy ending here on earth. But as daughters of Christ, we go where we are sent to do God's will. May we have the strength to persevere, confident in God's power, when we are placed in dangerous situations.

Inspiration

We will lie down for such a long time after death that it is worthwhile to keep standing while we are alive. (St. Agostina Livia Pietrantoni)

Challenge

Pray today for forgiveness and healing for someone who has hurt you.

Frances Xavier Cabrini

July 15, 1850–December 22, 1917

Frances thought she knew where she was called: to China. She and six other women had founded the Missionary Sisters of the Sacred Heart of Jesus, and she was now ready to take the Lord's word East. But her local bishop and then Pope Leo XIII advised her that she was instead needed in the United States to help Italian immigrants. To this day, the schools, orphanages, and hospitals she founded have assisted millions of people in the United States, Europe, and South America.

Have you ever been rock-solid, 100-percent certain of God's plan for you—only to find out you were wrong? God does seem to have a gentle sense of humor sometimes. Mother Cabrini's willingness to listen to her bishop and pope instead of insisting on doing things her way reminds us that God can speak to us through the advice of others.

Inspiration

I have started houses with no more than the price of a loaf of bread and prayers, for with him who comforts me, I can do anything. (St. Frances Xavier Cabrini)

Challenge

Spend some time reflecting on where God wants you to use the gifts he has given you.

Maria Teresa of Jesus (Maria Scrilli)

May 15, 1825–November 14, 1889

Maria Teresa knew what it was like to be different. When she was born, her mother was disappointed she wasn't a boy. An illness left Maria Teresa bedridden for two years when she was young. She briefly joined a cloistered order, but lasted only two months. When she returned home, Maria Teresa opened a small school for girls, which grew into the Institute of Sisters of Our Lady of Mount Carmel. Politics required the closing of the school for more than a decade. The sisters' projects ran into trouble after Maria Teresa's death, but were eventually revitalized. The institute now has a presence in eight countries.

Disappointment can breed despair, or it can breed determination and caring. In Maria Teresa's case, it was the latter. She took her love of Christ and put it to work with her sisters and with the girls who came to her school.

Inspiration

I compared myself, given to God, to gold in the hand of the goldsmith, to the candle in the hand of the craftsman molding it, ready to take any shape that pleased him. (Blessed Maria Teresa of Jesus)

Challenge

What early-life disappointment or struggle made you stronger? Talk about this with a friend who is going through something similar today. Discuss how your life changed because of this experience.

Agnes of Assisi

Circa 1197–November 16, 1253

Agnes (born Caterina) might have been Clare's younger sister, but she lacked nothing in determination. Less than a month after Clare had left home to found the Poor Clares, Agnes was on her heels. It didn't matter that their father and other family members didn't like the idea at all and tried to forcibly bring her home. Agnes was selected to found her own community before she was twenty-five, but is best known for the support she gave Clare, including being with her when she died. Agnes followed her to heaven three months later.

The bond between siblings is like no other. Even when we fight and argue, we know that these people know us better than anyone else on earth. When we acknowledge others as brothers and sisters of Christ, we begin to establish relationships that are somewhat similar, that no matter how we or they might falter, we know we all love and are loved.

✿ Inspiration

There is very great tribulation and immense sorrow in my flesh and spirit, and beyond manner heavier and more tortured I can scarcely speak, because I am separated in body from you and my other sisters with whom I believed I would live and die in this world. (St. Agnes of Assisi)

✿ Challenge

Call or spend time with your brother or sister today, or a friend who is like a sibling, laughing about the old days and remembering the support you offered each other in times of need.

Margaret of Scotland

Circa 1045–November 16, 1093

Margaret's husband, Malcolm III, involved her heavily in matters of state as well as in running the royal household. They ruled with compassion, and integrated Margaret's Catholic tradition into court life. Specifically, a synod was called that resulted in rules regarding the Lenten fast and Easter communion. The couple also founded a number of churches, including the Abbey of Dunfermline, where they are both buried. Margaret died just days after Malcolm and their oldest son were killed in battle.

Malcolm and Margaret probably looked like an odd couple in the early days of their marriage, she an educated, accomplished beauty with a strong dedication to God, he a rough and tumble warrior and widower nearly twenty years her senior. Yet, they proved to be evenly yoked, bringing important reforms to Scotland.

Inspiration

A capable wife who can find?
  She is far more precious than jewels.
The heart of her husband trusts in her,
  and he will have no lack of gain.
She does him good, and not harm,
  all the days of her life. (Proverbs 31:10–12)

Challenge

Talk with your husband or a close friend about your seeming differences and the similarities that lie underneath. Pray together about ways your strengths can be united to serve God.

Elizabeth of Hungary

July 7, 1207–November 17, 1231

Arranged marriages don't always work out, but the match between Elizabeth and Ludwig certainly did. Both were dedicated to helping the poor in their area, in particular during a time of flood, famine, and plague in 1226. The following year, Ludwig died, leaving Elizabeth distraught. She ultimately rededicated herself to those in need, opening a hospital and working there. In 2010, Pope Benedict XVI called Elizabeth "a true example for everyone who holds positions of leadership."

Even the idea of widowhood can take the breath away of a happily married woman. And yet, as much as we love our spouses, we must be prepared to go on in Christ's name should we lose them.

❧ Inspiration

I want to adorn myself, not out of worldly pride, but for the love of God alone—in a fitting manner, however, so as to give my husband no cause to sin, if something about me were to displease him. Only let him love me in the Lord, with a chaste, marital affection, so that we, in the same way, might hope for the reward of eternal life from him who has sanctified the law of marriage. (St. Elizabeth of Hungary)

❧ Challenge

Schedule some time in ministry with your spouse or other loved one. Afterward, talk about how this helps you both feel closer to Christ.

Karolina Kózka

August 2, 1898–November 18, 1914

Karolina is called "the Maria Goretti of Poland," though her story is somewhat different. In the early months of World War I, a Russian soldier took Karolina and her father out of their home, and then told her father to go back. The soldier attempted to rape Karolina, but she fought so hard that the man killed her with his bayonet. About two weeks passed before her body was discovered.

Our Church places a very high value on a woman's right not to have her body violated and used for criminal purposes. The stories of Karolina and other virgin martyrs remind us of the importance of creating a safe environment for women around the world as they go about their lives.

Inspiration

Guard me, O LORD, from the hands of the wicked;

> protect me from the violent
> who have planned my downfall.

The arrogant have hidden a trap for me,

> and with cords they have spread a net,
> along the road they have set snares for me. (Psalm 140:4–5)

Challenge

Talk with your daughter or a twenty-something neighbor or friend about the value the Church places on women—not only on their virginity, but also on their dignity.

Hilda of Whitby

614–November 17, 680

You might call Hilda a truth-seeker. She converted to Christianity when she was thirteen. It wasn't until she was thirty-three that she joined a monastery. Then, nine years later, she built Whitby, a monastery for both monks and nuns, and served over abbess of all. The site hosted a synod to determine the dating of Easter; when the system Hilda supported failed, she embraced fully the synod decision, which aided its success.

Some people criticize our Church for its slowness to change, but when things do change, it often moves quickly. Think about the upheaval that resulted from Vatican II, revisions in the feast day calendar, and the debate around formal decisions against birth control, women priests, and the like. Change comes in our Church in a deliberate, thoughtful, Spirit-filled manner. And if that change is not to our liking, may we emulate Hilda in embracing it nonetheless.

✿ Inspiration

Have evangelical peace among yourselves. (St. Hilda of Whitby)

✿ Challenge

Consider the Church doctrine with which you have the most trouble. Look up some of the history behind that doctrine, or talk with your pastor, spiritual director, or another learned person to better understand the reasons behind the rule or position.

Marie-Alphonsine Danil Ghattas

October 4, 1843–March 27, 1927

Marie-Alphonsine, born in Jerusalem, had been a nun for about twelve years when the Blessed Virgin came to her with a message: I want you to form a new congregation, devoted to the rosary. It took another ten years or so, but Marie-Alphonsine was successful in founding the first congregation to be based in the Holy Land. The sisters, who number about three hundred today, minister to Arab girls throughout the region. It is said that when she died, she was praying the rosary with one of her sisters.

Leaving one community and founding another wasn't easy for Marie-Alphonsine, and yet she honored Mary's request. We can only imagine the difficulty in establishing a Catholic congregation in an area where Christians are the minority. Like Marie-Alphonsine, when we're called to service, our answer should be yes, no matter how difficult the circumstances may be.

✒ Inspiration

Like good stewards of the manifold grace of God, serve one another with whatever gift each of you has received. (1 Peter 4:10)

✒ Challenge

Put yourself in a situation in which you are the only Catholic. It might be chatting with other women volunteers at a homeless shelter, or perhaps a Protestant friend will allow you to come to her Bible study group one night. Reflect on the feelings that result when you are in the spiritual minority and how your faith gives you strength.

Mary of the Passion (Hélène Marie Philippine de Chappotin de Neuville)

May 21, 1839–November 15, 1904

Life was a struggle for Hélène. She entered the Poor Clares but had to leave after she became ill. When she recovered, her confessor recommended she try the Sisters of Mary Reparatrix. There, she spent time as a missionary in India, and more tumult resulted. Mary as the superior left India with some of the other sisters and went to Rome, where they received permission to form what would become the Franciscan Missionaries of Mary. She was deposed, then reinstated as superior.

Hélène certainly chose the right religious name, for the disputes within her orders served as a form for her of Christ's passion. It's difficult when we do the best we can, only to find that's not good enough in the eyes of others. Like her, we can only continue to be ourselves and do what the quiet still voice inside requests.

🖎 Inspiration

Sometimes it seemed to me that God would judge me without even listening to me, and would condemn me for no reason. (Blessed Mary of the Passion)

🖎 Challenge

Do you feel at times that God is pulling away from you even though you're doing your best to draw closer? Consider seeking guidance from your pastor or spiritual adviser. If that is not possible, give yourself the gift of a silent hour of prayer. Explain to our Lord how very much you need him to show himself to you.

Cecilia of Rome

Second century

Cecilia's faith must have been rock-solid. Her wealthy family arranged a marriage for her to a pagan, despite her protestations that she had taken a vow of chastity. When she explained this to her husband, we are told that he asked to see the angel she said would protect her. He agreed to be baptized, saw the angel, and became a true believer. Cecilia also was responsible for the conversion of her brother-in-law. The brothers were martyred along with a third man they had converted, a Roman official; Cecilia was arrested after burying them. Tradition tells us that the attempt to behead her was so mangled that she lived on for three days.

Conversion doesn't have to be loud or threatening. Every day, people who have been away from the faith come back by the living example of people just like you and me.

Inspiration

O Lord, I beseech thee that mine heart and body may be undefouled so that I be not confounded. (St. Cecilia of Rome)

Challenge

Take some time to talk with a non-practicing or non-Catholic friend about why your faith is important to you and how it comforts and challenges you. Answer his or her questions in a non-defensive way. If you don't know the answers, find them out together.

Enrica Alfieri

February 23, 1891–November 23, 1951

Enrica was known as the angel of San Vittore, the Milan prison where she ministered for nearly thirty years. Ironically, near the end of World War II, the Sisters of Charity of St. Jeanne Antide Thouret were housed briefly in the same prison when she was accused of helping those who opposed the Nazis and Fascists. Enrica later returned to her ministry at San Vittore.

Prison ministry is among the most challenging work God calls us to do. We may be tempted to judge those who are incarcerated or be dismissive of their protestations of innocence. But all of us make mistakes, and with that in mind—and remembering that God makes the sun to shine on both those who do good and those who do not—we can be compassionate toward the men and women caught up in the cycle of misdeeds.

✺ Inspiration

Charity is a fire which likes to expand while it burns; I will suffer, work, and pray in order to attract souls to Jesus. (Blessed Enrica Alfieri)

✺ Challenge

If your parish has a prison ministry, considering baking a dozen cookies for the next prisoner retreat. Alternatively, pray that those behind bars at a particular institution may find their hearts open to Christ.

Maria Beltrame Quattrocchi

June 24, 1884–August 26, 1965

Maria and her husband, Luigi, were the first couple to be beatified together. Faith was at the center of their lives and the lives of their four children. One of the daughters became a nun; both sons became priests, and the fourth daughter cared for her parents and then for one of her brothers. The Quattrochis received the Eucharist daily and prayed the rosary as a family every evening. The family also housed refugees during World War II. As if that all weren't enough, Maria also was an author, professor, catechist and a popular speaker for women's groups.

In his homily at the Quattrocchis' beatification, Pope John Paul II said they "lived an ordinary life in an extraordinary way" and cited their "extraordinarily rich spiritual life." Maria's life is an excellent reminder that some women are called to serve in ministries beyond being a mother and wife or the member of a religious order.

☙Inspiration

We brought them up in the faith, so that they might know and love God. (Blessed Maria Beltrame Quattrocchi)

☙Challenge

Most of us live ordinary lives. Consider what readings or activities could assist you in developing an extraordinarily rich spiritual life for yourself or for your family.

Catherine of Alexandria

Circa 282–305

Catherine would have made a great preacher. According to the legends that are told about her, she converted to Christianity as a teenager. She protested Emperor Maxentius's demands for sacrifices to his gods, and he sent philosophers to disprove her arguments. They all converted. The emperor put Catherine in prison and sent more than a hundred more people, including his wife, to see her. All converted and were martyred. He then offered to marry Catherine; she refused. Ultimately, she was beheaded.

The details of our faith can be difficult to explain to non-Catholics. Catherine's example shows us the value of grounding ourselves in Church teachings so that we can explain our positions and defend the faith to others.

✣ Inspiration

Go therefore and make disciples of all nations, baptizing them in the name of the Father and of the Son and of the Holy Spirit, and teaching them to obey everything that I have commanded you. And remember, I am with you always, to the end of the age. (Matthew 28:19–20)

✣ Challenge

Take some time to read about a few of the Church's teachings. Find a book in your local library or parish resource center, or go to the website of the United States Conference of Catholic Bishops (www.usccb.org) to find an online version of the *Catechism of the Catholic Church* as well as other important Church documents.

Gaetana Sterni

June 26, 1827–November 26, 1889

From an early age, Gaetana was a caregiver. She was married at sixteen to a widower who had three children. She loved them as her own and was pregnant when her husband died. Unfortunately, the child died a few days after birth, and there were disputes with her husband's family over her involvement in his children's lives. She entered a convent, and then left to care for her younger brothers after her mother died. Then, when she was twenty-six, she began the work she would do for the rest of her life: working in hospice care for the poor. The house she founded is called Daughters of the Divine Will.

Caregiving—as a mother, a nurse, a doctor, or a friend—is central to our Christian lives. We must do what we can to ease the physical as well as the spiritual or emotional suffering of our brothers and sisters.

✒ Inspiration

For you were called to freedom, brothers and sisters; only do not use your freedom as an opportunity for self-indulgence, but through love become slaves to one another. (Galatians 5:13)

✒ Challenge

If you have an ailing friend or neighbor, offer to coordinate meal delivery or medical visit rides either through a website or via phone tree. Or, consider taking dinner to someone who is healthy but who you know is stressed out.

Maria Helena Stollenwerk

November 28, 1852–February 3, 1900

As a youngster in Germany, Maria Helena devoured the stories that appeared in Church publications about children in other lands. She longed to be a missionary in China. Maria Helena looked without success for a German convent that had a mission in China. Eventually, when she was thirty, she found Father Arnold Janssen, who was contemplating founding a missionary congregation, and she agreed to take a job as a maid in the mission house kitchen. Maria Helena went on to cofound with Father Arnold what is now called the Servants of the Holy Spirit. Sisters were sent out to places such as Argentina and Togo, but Maria Helena remained in Europe. Late in life, she transferred to the Servants' cloistered adoration branch.

Pope John Paul II called Maria Helena "a remarkably gifted woman whose obedience to the Holy Spirit and devotion to the Eucharist provided the inspiration she needed for the work to which God called her." Sometimes, our plans for ourselves don't align perfectly with God's. That's why we must sometimes set aside our dreams, and trust in his plan.

Inspiration

To God the honor, to my neighbor the benefit, and to myself the burden. (Blessed Maria Helena Stollenwerk)

Challenge

Where are your dreams and God's nudging not intersecting? What can you let go of so that his will may be done?

Catherine Laboure

May 2, 1806–December 31, 1876

Catherine was in her early twenties when she first saw the Blessed Virgin. Mary asked that Catherine have a medal created that reflected what she saw; thus, the Miraculous Medal, with Mary standing on a globe, light streaming from her hands, foot crushing a serpent's head, was created. Not long after the first Miraculous Medal was issued in 1832, Catherine went to work at a hospice for aged men. She didn't talk of her charism again until just before her death forty-eight years later.

Shortly after the medal was struck, millions were wearing it, and millions more wear it today. Catherine could have been a celebrity as the woman who had made it all happen, the woman to whom the Mary had made her request. And yet, she chose not to do that. In the same way, it's important for us to remember that the gifts we are provided are on loan from God, not something we create ourselves, and to remain grateful and humble.

Inspiration

I knew nothing; I was nothing. For this reason God picked me out. (St. Catherine Laboure)

Challenge

Ask a trusted friend what gifts you seem prideful about—or that you are failing to use as God intended. Work on becoming more humble, giving credit where credit is due.

Elizabeth Canori Mora

November 21, 1774–February 5, 1825

Everyone, including her confessor, counseled Elizabeth to leave her husband. He had taken on a mistress and squandered their money. Yet Elizabeth chose to stay, praying for her husband and his salvation. Along the way, she experienced mystical interactions with Christ, God, and angels who provided her with revelations, and she became a Trinitarian tertiary. Elizabeth reached out to families in need despite her own financial problems. After her death, her husband confessed his sins and spent more than ten years as a Franciscan brother and priest.

Listening to other people's advice isn't always a wise thing when it comes to love. No one other than the two people involved and God really know what's at the heart of the relationship. May we remember this, and not judge others' marriages or listen when others judge ours.

Inspiration

No one can be saved all alone, and God has entrusted to everyone the responsibility of the salvation of others to carry out his project of love. (Blessed Elizabeth Canori Mora)

Challenge

Is a friend or relative constantly fretting about her marriage or another important relationship in his or her life? Rather than try to fix it, recommend that she seek professional counseling—and pray for both people involved.

Lucy of Narni

December 13, 1476–November 15, 1544

For a brief period, Lucy was the mega-celebrity of her time. Her marriage fell apart after just a few years when her husband couldn't understand her interactions with saints that led her away from home and into other unusual situations. When it became known that she experienced the stigmata and other spiritual gifts, people fought over where Lucy would live. Young women vied to be part of her community. The circus ended after about eight years when her prioress put Lucy on probation. She spent the last thirty-nine years of her life in silence, talking with no one other than her confessor.

How quickly public celebrity fades! Whether we're president of the United States or the pastoral council, captain of an Olympic team or the neighborhood watch organization, it all passes. Only God remains.

✒ Inspiration

Keep your lives free from the love of money, and be content with what you have; for he has said, "I will never leave you or forsake you." (Hebrews 13:5)

✒ Challenge

Think about a time when you had public recognition in your life, today or in the past. How did you feel when you were in demand? Did it bring you closer to God or did it crowd him out?

Maria Rosa of Jesus (Bruna Pellesi)

November 11, 1917–December 1, 1972

The cross Maria Rosa bore was a heavy one. She joined the Franciscan Missionary Sisters of Christ when she was twenty-two, and spent the three years after her first vows working at schools. Then, Maria Rosa learned she had tuberculosis, and she spent the rest of her life in sanatoriums, except her several pilgrimages to Lourdes. It is said she never complained about her condition, including the need to remove liquid from her lungs several times each day after a needle splintered and remained inside her.

Physical problems can take a heavy toll on our lives—and our souls. When we don't feel well enough to go out and be part of the world, depression and bitterness often result. From Maria Rosa, we learn that disappointment doesn't have to separate us from God; indeed, he can be the catalyst to bring us true comfort in the hard times.

Inspiration

I say this now, all that matters is loving the Lord. (Blessed Maria Rosa of Jesus)

Challenge

Think about your aches and pains and other limitations. Are you constantly complaining about them, or do you simply accept them as part of being human? Consider how a change in attitude could make your life just that much better.

Marie-Clémentine Anuarite Nengapeta

December 29, 1939–December 1, 1964

Marie-Clémentine, born in the Democratic Republic of Congo, had been a nun for five years when armed conflict broke out in her country. The sisters in her order were moved from their house, and various soldiers jousted over seducing her. Marie-Clémentine remained strong. Ultimately, a colonel shot her, but not before she told him she forgave him. There is a story that, years later, this colonel came to the sisters and asked for food, and they forgave him and helped him. At Marie-Clémentine's beatification, Pope John Paul II publicly forgave the man on behalf of the Church.

Forgiving someone you know and love, someone who just had a bad day or made a mistake, is easy. Forgiving someone who shows no indication of wanting to be forgiven, that's something else. But it's what Christ did, and it's what he asks us to do.

✎ Inspiration

Then Peter came and said to him, "Lord, if another member of the church sins against me, how often should I forgive? As many as seven times?" Jesus said to him, "Not seven times, but, I tell you, seventy-seven times." (Matthew 18:21–22)

✎ Challenge

Free yourself. Give up a grudge. Write a letter of forgiveness to the person in life who has injured you the most. Mail it if you like.

Marie Clare of the Child Jesus (Libania do Carmo Galvão Meixa de Moura Telles e Albuquerque)

June 15, 1843–December 1, 1899

"Nothing happens in the world without divine permission" was Marie Clare's motto in life, and it proved to sustain her through challenging times. She lost both her parents within months when she was in her early teens. The congregation of which she was superior often had little food in the cupboards, and then it would be blessed by unexpected gifts of sustenance. She experienced challenges to her authority. Still, Marie Clare kept her focus on service and made her order the first in Portugal to send women religious abroad as missionaries. Today, the Congregation of the Franciscan Hospitaller Sisters of the Immaculate Conception works in fifteen countries on four continents.

Control is a difficult thing to give up; Marie Clare learned that early. It's not up to us how long we have our loved ones. We also can't make the world run on our timetable. Accepting that God has a plan is difficult initially, but results in long-term inner peace.

✿ Inspiration

In spite of the most cruel bitterness, trials, and dislikes, I see a providential glance of God watching over us. (Blessed Marie Clare of the Child Jesus)

✿ Challenge

What is the greatest source of stress in your life right now? Write yourself a note about what you could do to improve the situation. Then talk about it with God, and listen to what he wants you to do.

Annunciata Cocchetti

May 9, 1800–March 23, 1882

Annunciata was orphaned at seven, and as a result was raised primarily by her grandmother. Her desire to educate young women showed itself at an early age, and by the time she was seventeen, she had opened a school and had begun to contemplate joining the Canossian Daughters of Charity. At that point, however, her grandmother died, and her uncle and guardian demanded she join him in Milan before making such a decision. After six years there, Annunciata agreed to oversee a school in a rural area of Italy. She chose to put aside her plans to join the Canossians and became a cofounder of the Sisters of St. Dorothy of Cemmo. In addition to classroom work, the sisters offer retreats and continue to be involved with the Annunciata Cocchetti Foundation, a non-profit organization that focuses on the culture, education, and history of Italy's Lombardy region.

Annunciata had a life plan—joining the Canossians. However, she was wise enough to see that God was leading her in a different direction to accomplish her passion of educating girls. We learn from her to wait for God to make our path clear.

Inspiration

Be holy, this is my greatest desire for you. Then you will do the most good for the girls entrusted to you. (Blessed Annunciata Cocchetti)

Challenge

What deadlines are you placing in your life? Stop. Wait. Listen to God. Breathe.

Christina of Markyate

Circa 1096–1160

All Christina wanted to do was fulfill her vow of chastity. But her parents were having none of that. They conspired with an immoral bishop who wanted to be with Christina, but she rejected him. The bishop and her parents then married her off to a younger man, but he left when he determined she was serious about her vow. Then another church official was bribed into ordering her return to her husband. Christina ran away into hiding with a network of hermits and eventually led her to a Benedictine convent.

Christina's parents put their own egos and potential political and personal gain ahead of what should have been their top priority: what was best for her. It's a good reminder that we need to check our own bias when it comes to our adult children's lives. We can provide counsel when asked, but the most important thing we can do is love them even when we don't agree with their choices.

Inspiration

If my father and mother forsake me,
   the LORD will take me up. (Psalm 27:10)

Challenge

Reflect on your last conversation with one of your children, no matter what the age, or with a subordinate at work. Did you play God and offer solutions where none were sought?

Maria Angela Astorch

September 1, 1592–December 2, 1665

Maria Angela entered a monastery when she was orphaned as a child, and took her final vows with the Capuchin Poor Clares in Barcelona at age seventeen. She is known as the breviary mystic, because her experiential connection with Christ came through the liturgy. In addition, Maria Angela is known for her writing, including a description of when her guardian angel presented itself to her.

How beautiful to focus on the words of the liturgy, rather than going through the motions or thinking of your grocery list. And how marvelous to encounter one's guardian angel, whom Pope Benedict XVI in 2011 referred to as "ministers of the divine care for every human being."

Inspiration

As soon as I perceived its presence, such a change in my spirit came upon me that one could say that I lived within and outside my body at the very same time. Infused with great nobility in my perceptions, my heart filled with a sweet sensation of comfort and with minuscule operation it fortified my whole spirit. (Blessed Maria Angela Astorch)

Challenge

When was the last time you encountered your guardian angel? Did you find your whole spirit fortified, as Maria Angela described? Write about the experience; work on being more aware of your guardian angel's presence.

Mary Joseph Rossello

May 27, 1811–December 7, 1880

Mary Joseph always remembered her early years. She wanted to enter a convent, but had no dowry. As a result, she spent several years as the nurse for an invalid man. After his death, she was among those who founded what would become the Institute of the Daughters of Mercy and which always accepted women into the community whether or not they had a dowry. Mary Joseph was the congregation's superior for the final forty years of her life.

Whether we come from a poor background or a wealthy one, we had challenges of some sort in our teens and twenties. Maybe it was saving for college, or being worried about peer pressure, or maybe it was despairing of ever finding "the one." Mary Joseph's example inspires us to remember those times when we deal with young people, and do what we can to ease the burdens of their lives.

✒ Inspiration

Cling to Jesus. There are God, the soul, eternity; the rest is nothing. (St. Mary Joseph Rossello)

✒ Challenge

Do something for someone who is struggling with an issue you had at the same age. For example, if your children are grown, you might offer to babysit for neighbors so they can attend a couple's retreat; if a loved one went through cancer treatments, take a friend's mother to her chemotherapy appointment.

Candida Maria de Jesus

May 31, 1845–August 9, 1912

Candida Maria's early years were difficult. She grew up in a family of poor Basque weavers, and she had to move away and go to work at a young age. She surely brought this experience to bear when, at twenty-six, she and five others founded the Spanish Congregation of the Daughters of Jesus on December 8, 1871. Candida Maria served as the first superior general. The order's focus is on saving the souls of children and youth, especially girls, through education and instruction. At her canonization in 2010, Pope Benedict XVI said of Candida Maria: "She lived for God and for what he most wanted: to reach everyone, to bring to everyone the hope that does not waver, especially to those who most need it."

Many of us experienced some type of poverty as we grew up—not enough food on the table, not enough parental love and support, not enough spiritual direction. As followers of Christ, we remember the hard times and use them to inform our ministries today.

✍ Inspiration

Where there is not a place for the poor, there is no place for me. (St. Candida Maria de Jesus)

✍ Challenge

Think about what your poverty place was as a child or is today. How can you reach out to provide nourishment to others in a similar place?

Anne-Marie Rivier

December 19, 1768–February 3, 1838

We all had falls and spills as toddlers. But in Anne-Marie's case, a tumble she took when she was sixteen months old left her barely able to stand without assistance. For four years, her mother took her every day to a chapel and prayed for healing. She was in fact healed at that point, but the damage had been done, and even as an adult, she did not stand much taller than four feet. Turned away from a convent because of her health, Marie and other women began outreach at home, caring for the poor and educating children. Amid the challenges of the French Revolution, they founded the Sisters of the Presentation of Mary (White Ladies), which today has a presence in seventeen countries. The little girl who was so damaged lived to be sixty-nine.

Anne-Marie's example reminds us to never, ever to give up on God, who has a plan for us no matter what our limitations or state in life may be.

Inspiration

You shall not revile the deaf or put a stumbling block before the blind; you shall fear your God: I am the LORD. (Leviticus 19:14)

Challenge

Where have you given up asking for God's assistance, considering the situation to be hopeless? Begin praying for the wisdom to understand God's will.

Marija of Jesus Crucified Petković

December 10, 1892–July 9, 1966

Marija was born into a wealthy Croatian family, but she still understood the value of money. She also understood what money could do to make this life more bearable for the poor. Even before she took her vows, she was involved in a lay group, the Daughters of Mary Association, which aided children in their spiritual instruction and helped those who were sick and hungry before and during World War I. In 1920, Marija became foundress of the Congregation of the Daughters of Mercy, and during her time as leader of the Daughters established nearly fifty communities that provide social services support in Europe and Latin America.

Scripture doesn't tell us that money is evil but rather, the love of it. With wise stewardship, the financial treasure that comes into our lives can provide untold spiritual and physical enrichment to those who have little of either.

Inspiration

If I had money, I would trust in money, but (without it) I trust only in God. (Blessed Marija of Jesus Crucified Petković)

Challenge

Consider what you plan to spend on Christmas presents for family and friends. Can you reduce the total by five percent and put it toward your parish's Giving Tree or another project to make Christmas merrier for families in need?

María Maravillas de Jesús

November 4, 1891–December 11, 1974

Influenced by the writings of St. John of the Cross and St. Teresa of Avila, María became a Discalced Carmelite. She had little concern for her surroundings—some criticized the poverty of her convents, and during the Spanish Civil War, she and the others in her community spent fourteen months under house arrest in a small apartment, and they eventually returned to find their building destroyed. María's response? Rebuild and continue growing.

We face destruction in many ways during our lives—physical or emotional loss of family and friends, natural disasters, financial problems, health issues. And while it's important to go through the grieving process, it's critical to recognize that our time on earth is fleeting. Like María Maravillas, we turn to God to support us through the times our lives appear to be in ruins, and show us how to rebuild and continue growing.

✒ Inspiration

Therefore do not worry, saying, "What will we eat?" or "What will we drink?" or "What will we wear?"… But strive first for the kingdom of God and his righteousness, and all these things will be given to you as well. (Matthew 6:31, 33)

✒ Challenge

What earthly loss or destruction are you holding in your heart and soul? Talk with Christ about your sadness and frustration, and how accepting this loss might help you grow in faith.

Madeleine Sophie Barat
December 12, 1779–May 25, 1865

Madeleine had a very special godfather—her brother Louis, who was eleven when she was born. He certainly lived up to those responsibilities; when Madeleine was eleven, Louis was serving as a professor at a nearby seminary and taught her Latin, Greek, history, and other topics. Louis also introduced her to the priest who helped Madeleine with her transition to a woman religious and the founder of what would become the Society of the Sacred Heart.

Being a godparent isn't a one-time event at the person's baptism. It's a commitment to assist your godchild with his or her spiritual development throughout his or her life. Birthday and Christmas gifts are nice, but it's really about the gift of a shared spirituality.

Inspiration

You shall put these words of mine in your heart and soul, and you shall bind them as a sign on your hand, and fix them as an emblem on your forehead. Teach them to your children, talking about them when you are at home and when you are away, when you lie down and when you rise. (Deuteronomy 11:18–19)

Challenge

Arrange to spend some time, in person or on the phone, with a godchild or your own godparents. Ask about their faith journey, letting them know you're prepared to support them in any way you can.

Lucy of Syracuse

283–303

Legends have grown up around Lucy, legends that may or may not be true and can't be verified today. We don't know if she actually tore out her own eyes or if they were torn out in torture. We don't know if she was sent to a brothel. We do know, however, she was an early Christian martyr and that stories that surround her have inspired Catholics for centuries. They have spawned a number of traditions and practices on her feast day, especially in Italy and in Scandinavia.

Lucy's example reminds us how much a moving story can fire our faith. However she lived and died, we admire what we do know for sure about her—she lived and died for Christ instead of turning away from him.

Inspiration

Everyone who commits sin is a child of the devil; for the devil has been sinning from the beginning. The Son of God was revealed for this purpose, to destroy the works of the devil. Those who have been born of God do not sin, because God's seed abides in them; they cannot sin, because they have been born of God. (1 John 3:8–9)

Challenge

Who in your life today inspires you by the way he or she has persevered in a struggle? Write this person a note of thanks. Ask for the wisdom to deal with a challenge you currently face.

Odile of Alsace

660–720

Odile was born blind. This did not sit well with her nobleman father, who wanted her put to death. However, her mother persuaded him that they should instead give their daughter to peasants to rear. When Odile was baptized at the age of twelve, she received the gift of sight. Her brother brought Odile back home, but her father became so enraged that he killed the son. Later, the father relented and allowed her to turn one of his residences into a convent.

You might say we are all born blind and receive the gift of Christian vision at baptism. That gift and our other sacraments provide us with visible signs of the grace God confers on us.

Inspiration

Jesus answered them, "Go and tell John what you hear and see: the blind receive their sight, the lame walk, the lepers are cleansed, the deaf hear, the dead are raised, and the poor have good news brought to them. And blessed is anyone who takes no offense at me." (Matthew 11:4–6)

Challenge

If there is a baptism at your parish this week, try to attend whether or not you know the parents and the child. Reflect on what your own baptism has meant in your life and the ways in which the sacrament continues to open your spiritual eyes.

Virginia Centurione Bracelli

April 2, 1587–December 15, 1651

Virginia was only twenty when her husband died, leaving her with two daughters. The marriage had not been an easy one, yet she lived with her mother-in-law after rejecting her father's plans for a second marriage for her. She gave away much of her wealth in the following years and then, once her daughters were grown, focused her life on helping at-risk people, from the aged and sick to abandoned children.

Empty-nest syndrome was not a problem for Virginia. She had plans to do God's work in the world in the years after her daughters became adults. In his homily at her canonization, Pope John Paul II cited Virginia's "unconditional adherence to God's will, which was nourished by ceaseless contemplation of, and obedient listening to, the word of the Lord."

❧ Inspiration

When God is the only goal, all disagreements are smoothed out, all difficulties overcome. (St. Virginia Centurione Bracelli)

❧ Challenge

Write down three ways in which you could begin helping less fortunate people today, whether your children are still at home or not, and whether you are working outside the home or not. Time has a way of expanding when you're doing God's work.

Matilde of the Sacred Heart Téllez Robles

May 30, 1841–December 17, 1902

There were nine of them—Matilde and eight members of the Daughters of Mary—who had pledged to begin a religious institute dedicated to helping the poor and to Eucharistic adoration. There was just one problem: On the day the group was to begin, only Matilde and one other woman, Maria Briz, were there. That did not prevent the two women from getting started. They helped orphans and the sick, and opened a school. When they weren't working, they were at home in silent prayer. Slowly, others started joining what would become Daughters of Mary, Mother of the Church. When Matilde's friend and right hand person, Maria Briz, died of cholera in 1884, Matilde soldiered on.

Imagine how the two young women felt when they found no one else was joining them. That's the great thing about friendship—one plus one equals more than two. It makes us stronger and capable of doing more than we could do on our own. It's another way Christ shows his love for us.

⚶ Inspiration

Love one another with mutual affection; outdo one another in showing honor. (Romans 12:10)

⚶ Challenge

Think of a time when a single friend stood by you and helped you through a challenging time, when many others abandoned you. Call her or mail her a thank you note, even if this happened years ago.

Olympias

Circa 368–July 25, 408

Olympias was the type of friend we'd all want—and we would all like to be. She came from a very wealthy family and inherited a fortune when she was young. After her brief marriage ended with her husband's death, she decided to focus on God's work. She was already a deaconess when St. John Chrysostom became patriarch of Constantinople and served as her spiritual adviser. Even when John ran into political trouble and was banished, she stood by him. The result was that her own convent was dissolved and she was exiled as well. The two died less than a year apart.

Sometimes, our friendships are situational—based on where we live or worship or work. But every once in a while, a special friendship comes along. The example of Olympias and John inspires us to cultivate and nurture those deep friendships, regardless of how our economic or social positions—or those of our friends—might change.

✒ Inspiration

Do to others as you would have them do to you. (Luke 6:31)

✒ Challenge

Which of your friendships are silver and which are gold? Reach out to a couple of the gold ones this week. Talk about the challenges as well as the joys you're both experiencing at this point in your lives.

Giulia Nemesia Valle

June 26, 1847–December 18, 1916

Through many life struggles, Nemesia kept her kind, pleasant nature. Her mother died when she was four, and she was sent away to school. When she returned after five years, her father had remarried and there were family problems. Eventually, she joined an institute and was a beloved teacher. She ran into trouble again, however, when she served as the novice mistress at her monastery for thirteen years, as her superior regarded her as too gentle and patient. She remained true to herself and the path she believed Christ had put her on.

Nemesia knew from personal experience how unfamiliar circumstances and loneliness can disorient us, and chose to be understanding and kind to those in the same circumstance. Her gentleness inspires us to think about what may be prompting the behavior of those we find difficult, and helps us resolve to accept and love them as they are.

Inspiration

Jesus, empty me of myself, let me be clothed in you. (Blessed Giulia Nemesia Valle)

Challenge

Select an hour today in which you will lovingly accept people as they are, not fire back nasty e-mails or engage in arguments or get defensive when you are attacked. Think later about how it felt to accept instead of engage.

Agnes Phila, one of the Martyrs of Thailand

1909–December 26, 1940

To say Agnes, a sister with the Lovers of the Holy Cross Congregation, was confident in her faith would be an understatement. She and another sister kept teaching after the parish's leading layman was killed by police, and then the authorities came and told the sisters to stop or they would meet the same fate. Agnes coolly asked if the police had enough bullets and advised them to polish their gun barrels. She then sent authorities a letter asking them to carry out their order, identifying those at the convent, and saying the women would pray for their persecutors. They were killed the day after Christmas. A total of seven Catholics were martyred that December in northeastern Thailand, and they were beatified in 1989.

How brave and accepting Agnes and her companions were! May we be as strong in our faith and as forgiving in our souls to those who would do us wrong.

🐾 Inspiration

You can kill us, but not the Church and God. (Blessed Agnes Phila)

🐾 Challenge

The Church is beset by threats to freedom in the United States and around the world. Do something public—with prayer, with the example of service, by wearing a medal or scapular—in your little corner of it today.

Eugenia Ravasco

January 4, 1845–December 30, 1900

Maybe it was because Eugenia's oldest brother got caught up in the anticlericalism that was pervading Italy at the time. Maybe it was a priest's call for someone to "dedicate themselves to doing good for the love of the heart of Jesus." Maybe it was the streetwise attitude of the girls to whom she taught catechism. Maybe it was all of these and more. But in any event, Eugenia heard the call to found what today is known as the Ravasco Institute, which ministers in particular to women, young people, and the needy in more than a dozen countries.

It's not always the pretty, joyous things in life that call us to ministry. Sometimes, it's situations and people who are off-putting—and whom we can't forget. We may not be able to save all of them, but we can spread the Good News to as many as possible.

Inspiration

Live in abandonment to God and in the hands of Mary Immaculate. (Blessed Eugenia Ravasco)

Challenge

At Christmastime, we all encounter family members, friends, and acquaintances who consider themselves lapsed Catholics. Invite one of those people to Christmas Mass with you. Whether the answer is yes or no, pray for the person.

María Dolores Rodríguez Sopeña

December 30, 1848–January 10, 1918

Dolores made it just ten days in a Salesian convent in Spain. During those ten days, she came to understand that the community assistance she had been providing with her Centers of Instruction were her vocation. She went on to establish what would become a family of lay movements in Europe and Latin and South America to help the poor. Her Vatican biography describes her life as a "'constant doing' but a doing with a clear conscience of being an instrument in God's hands."

Some women are called to religious orders. Others are called to lay ministry, speaking up for the underprivileged and disenfranchised in our world. Our service in God's name is valuable whether we are a layperson or professed religious. Each of us contributes to the kingdom of God when we act out of the vocation we have been called to.

✒ Inspiration

However that may be, let each of you lead the life that the Lord has assigned, to which God called you. This is my rule in all the churches. (1 Corinthians 7:17)

✒ Challenge

Spend some time today thinking about whether you have a vocation with a religious order—whether vowed or as an oblate—if not now, then sometime in the future. And if not, what are you called to do for God? Are you doing it?

Elia of St. Clement (Theodora Fracasso)

January 17, 1901–December 25, 1927

Elia's short life ended with much pain. First, there was emotional pain in her convent in 1923, where she was removed after two years of being in charge of the embroidery machine in the attached girls' boarding school. Then there was the physical pain—influenza and then severe headaches—that she began suffering in January 1927. When fevers were added to her woes in mid-December, doctors were called in and pronounced her situation to be meningitis or encephalitis. She died on Christmas Day.

Coping with physical pain can be so difficult, especially when the ailment is a headache or pain that isn't readily visible to others. They may think we're trying to get out of work, or are exaggerating the gravity of our situation. Some pain can be cured with medicine; some cannot. In either case, we give our suffering to God, the ultimate healer in this world and the next.

Inspiration

When we suffer with Jesus, the suffering is delightful; I long to suffer with all my heart, beyond this I no longer want anything. (Blessed Elia of St. Clement)

Challenge

While the sick ultimately find comfort in Jesus, we can help. Offer to take a friend or an acquaintance to a doctor's appointment, or surprise him or her with a casserole dinner so no cooking is required after a session or treatment.

Giuseppina Nicoli

November 18, 1863–December 31, 1924

Things did not always go well for Giuseppina. She was only thirty when she contracted tuberculosis. She was named to direct the novices among the Daughters of Charity in the Turin area only to have to be reassigned after nine months because of her health. She returned to Sassari, where she had run an orphanage for about ten years. The environment was much changed, so back she went to her initial location at Calgari after just a year. This turmoil, however, did not prevent her from service. In Calgari, she founded the first young Catholic women's group and laid the groundwork for Women's Catholic Action. Giuseppina also assisted in the opening of a medical facility for children.

God never promised us life would be easy. He did promise us he would be there with us, lifting us up and supporting us through the good times and the hard times. When people and circumstances make serving God difficult, we must lean on him for the strength to forge on.

☞ Inspiration

I want to serve you faithfully, practicing poverty, chastity, and obedience, and for love of you to serve the poor. (Blessed Giuseppina Nicoli)

☞ Challenge

Who or what is making your efforts at ministry difficult? Would a change to a different ministry alleviate the challenge, or is there a larger issue you need to face? Pray for wisdom and guidance.

Paola Elisabetta (Costanza Cerioli)

January 28, 1816—December 24, 1865

Christmas in 1854 was bitter for Paola Elisabetta. Her husband died on that day and her only surviving child, Carlo, had died in January at the age of sixteen. Eventually, she thought of Carlo's words before his death, that God would give her other children. Three years later, she founded the Institute of the Sisters of the Holy Family to minister to children without parents, especially poor children.

The loss of a child is one of the most difficult burdens a woman can be forced to bear. St. Paola Elisabetta's example inspires us to reach out through our pain and use it to help others.

✒ Inspiration

Rachel is weeping for her children;
>she refuses to be comforted for her children,
>>because they are no more.

Thus says the LORD:
Keep your voice from weeping,
>and your eyes from tears;
for there is a reward for your work,
>>>>says the LORD:
>they shall come back from the land of the enemy. (Jeremiah 31:15–16)

✒ Challenge

If you know someone who lost a child, whether it happened recently or years ago, reach out today and offer to pray together. Help her to feel less abandoned at this time of family and joy.

Anastasia

Died circa 304

Myths have grown up around Anastasia, but the facts are few. We do know she was martyred in the early fourth century in what today is Serbia. We do know that she is commemorated by name in the Canon of the Mass and that today's Mass originally was celebrated for her, not Christ's birth. And we do know that her name means "resurrection" or "she who shall rise again."

It's appropriate that our Church would link this early martyr and the birth of Jesus, for it is through him, his life and teachings, and his death and resurrection that we received the hope for a life with God forever.

✒ Inspiration

But the angel said to them, "Do not be afraid; for see—I am bringing you good news of great joy for all the people: to you is born this day in the city of David a Savior, who is the Messiah, the Lord." (Luke 2:10–11)

✒ Challenge

As you enjoy the day with family and friends, consider what the gift of God becoming human has meant in your life. What gift can you bring to Jesus this year?

Fabiola

Died 399

Parts of Fabiola's story may resonate with you. A Roman noblewoman, she married a man who proved to be abusive and vicious. While she got a civil divorce, the Church did not sanction the breakup. She then proceeded to remarry. But upon the second husband's death, Fabiola reconsidered her actions. She put on penitential clothes and did public penance outside the Lateran Basilica. Restored to the Church, she went on to build the West's first Christian hospital and to personally serve as a nurse. Fabiola was a restless sort; she visited St. Jerome in Bethlehem, but later returned to Rome where she established a lodging place for pilgrims.

The rules of our Church can seem unfair and limiting, especially when marriage and divorce are involved. But the rules are rooted in the teachings of the Church and in God's great love for us and his desire to protect us from harm.

Inspiration

And this is love, that we walk according to his commandments; this is the commandment just as you have heard it from the beginning—you must walk in it. (2 John 1:6)

Challenge

If you or someone you love has gone through a civil divorce and desires to remarry in the Catholic Church, reach out to a priest for guidance on how to navigate the annulment process.

Jeanne de Lestonnac

December 27, 1556–February 2, 1640

The second act of Jeanne's life was impressive. She was forty-one when her husband of more than two decades died. Six years later, she went back to her earlier dream of a religious vocation. Despite health issues that required her to leave the monastery she joined initially, she went on to establish the Order of the Sisters of the Company of Mary Our Lady. The sisters today have a presence in more than twenty-five countries, educating women and young people and assisting the poor.

Sometimes, we think we're too old (or too young) to try something new or to pursue a dream from long ago. With God's help, we can embark on any journey that would honor him. It doesn't mean we'll be successful in the way we expect, but we will have his support, and that's more important than wins or losses.

❧ Inspiration

Even to your old age I am he,
    even when you turn gray I will carry you.
I have made, and I will bear;
    I will carry and will save. (Isaiah 46:4)

❧ Challenge

Make a list of five things you once wanted to do, but put aside because you thought you were too old or too young. Pray for guidance as you choose one to pursue.

Caterina Volpicelli

January 21, 1839–December 28, 1894

In her early teens, Caterina's focus was on worldly pleasures, especially attending ballet and theater performances. She came from an upper middle-class family with many connections in society. At fifteen, she met Blessed Ludovico da Casoria, who advised her to use those connections to serve Christ, and her life took a turn. Caterina went on to found the Servants of the Sacred Heart, known for nursing cholera victims in 1884, as well as an orphanage, a lending library, and other institutions to do God's work.

Do you ever worry about your daughter or son's interest in the latest social media or fashion trends? Peer pressure can be difficult to deal with at any age. St. Caterina's example reminds us of the role a respected adult can play in keeping young people on the right path.

 Inspiration

No testing has overtaken you that is not common to everyone. God is faithful, and he will not let you be tested beyond your strength, but with the testing he will also provide the way out so that you may be able to endure it. (1 Corinthians 10:13)

Challenge

Talk with a teenager about the people who he or she respects. Are they people who can help the teen's faith life flower? If not, prayerfully consider introducing him or her to people who can.

Vincenza María López y Vicuña

March 24, 1847–December 26, 1890

Vincenza grew up in a comfortable home; her father was an attorney. Her early spiritual influences included an uncle who was a priest, and an aunt who was a nun active in ministry to young female servants. It was with the help of her aunt that she rejected her parents' plans for an arranged marriage. Vincenza then became a nun, and established the Daughters of Mary Immaculate for Domestic Service, which assists young working women.

Extended family members can sometimes provide support and encouragement where parents can't or won't. Aunts, uncles, and cousins may see us as we are, rather than as our parents desire us to be, and be more attuned to the secret longings of our soul.

✒ Inspiration

Then you, together with the Levites and the aliens who reside among you, shall celebrate with all the bounty that the LORD your God has given to you and to your house. (Deuteronomy 26:11)

✒ Challenge

If you're an aunt, spend some time on the phone or in person with a niece or nephew this week. Or, call an aunt or special relative in the earlier generation and thank her or him for the times the person provided guidance and may not have even realized it.

Martyrs of Drina

Died December 15 and December 23, 1941

It was December 11, cold and snowy, when Serbian fighters took the five nuns ranging in age from thirty-four to seventy-six hostage. They were marched for miles, then the oldest, Sister Berchmana, was separated from the group. The other four—Sisters Jula, Krizina, Antonija, and Bernadeta—marched for four more days, covering more than forty miles before they were herded into a building. The fighters then threatened them and began ripping off their clothes. The sisters leaped out a window to escape; on the ground, the soldiers stabbed them and left them for dead. The following day, an undertaker was told to push the bodies into the Drina River. After Sister Berchmana recovered, she was killed as well.

Think about how exhausted and scared the sisters must have been. Some might say it would have been easier to have given into the attack. Yet they stood by their morals and their faith in a horrific situation. Can we do any less in our day to day life?

Inspiration

Indeed, all who want to live a godly life in Christ Jesus will be persecuted. But wicked people and impostors will go from bad to worse, deceiving others and being deceived. (2 Timothy 3:12–13)

Challenge

Pray for people in bondage around the world, that they might find the strength and faith to rise up against their persecutors.

Melania the Younger

Circa 383–December 31, 439

Melania appeared destined for the religious life. While she was growing up, her grandmother, Melania the Elder, already was in the Holy Land and Africa with the likes of Sts. Paula, Jerome, Rufinus, and Augustine. Melania the Younger was still in Rome, having married at a young age and then suffered the loss of two children. She and her husband eventually chose to follow a monastic life and reached Africa in 410. Melania joined a Jerusalem hermitage near the Mount of Olives and, after her husband's death, built a cloister for men.

Losing a child—to death or to a life-change—changes a marriage. In the case of Melania, she and her husband chose to move into a celibate existence. The emotional and spiritual relationship can change as well. It takes work and prayer to redefine the marriage.

Inspiration

Do not let your hearts be troubled. Believe in God, believe also in me. In my Father's house there are many dwelling places. If it were not so, would I have told you that I go to prepare a place for you? (John 14:1–2)

Challenge

Have you lost a child? Or, have you had a child go away to college or move to another part of the country? Pray with your spouse about your feelings of anger or abandonment. How can you use those feelings in your ministry to help others?

BIBLIOGRAPHY

This book does not pretend to be an exhaustive source for information on the saints and blesseds included. To learn more about these amazing women, I recommend you consult these books. I also referred extensively to the Vatican website (www.vatican.va) to verify birth and death dates, read the women's stories, and learn what our popes and cardinals said at beatification and canonization Masses and related observances. For those who lived before the twentieth century, I found the *Catholic Encyclopedia* (www.newadvent.org/cathen/) to be extremely valuable. I also reviewed innumerable sites for the women's orders and writings.

Adels, Jill Haak. *The Wisdom of the Saints: An Anthology.* Oxford: Oxford University Press, 1989.

Bangley, Bernard, ed. *Butler's Lives of the Saints: Concise, Modernized Edition.* Brewster, MA: Paraclete, 2005.

Bentley, James. *A Calendar of Saints: The Lives of the Principal Saints of the Calendar Year.* New York: Little, Brown, 2000.

Catherine of Siena. *The Dialogue of St. Catherine of Siena: A Conversation with God on Living Your Spiritual Life to the Fullest.* Charlotte, NC: Tan Classics, 2010.

Chervin, Ronda De Sola. *Quotable Saints*. Oak Lawn, IL: CMJ Marian, 1992.

Compton, Madonna. *Women Saints: 365 Daily Readings*. New York: Crossroads, 2006.

Delaney, John J. *Dictionary of Saints*, 2nd ed. New York: Image, 2005.

Farmer, David Hugh. *Oxford Dictionary of Saints*, 5th ed. rev. Oxford: Oxford University Press, 2004.

Gallick, Sarah. *The Big Book of Woman Saints*. New York: HarperOne, 2007.

Hendey, Lisa M. *A Book of Saints for Catholic Moms: 52 Companions for Your Heart, Mind, Body, and Soul*. Notre Dame, IN: Ave Maria, 2011.

Hildegard of Bingen. *Selected Writings*. Mark Atherton, trans. London: Penguin, 2001.

Hoagland, Victor. *The Book of Saints*. New York: Regina, 2010.

Kelly, Sean, and Rosemary Rogers. *The Birthday Book of Saints: Your Powerful Personal Patrons for Every Blessed Day of the Year*. New York: Villard, 2001.

Lester, Meera. *Saints Blessings: Wisdom and Guidance Inspired by the World's Most Beloved Saints*. Gloucester, MA: Fairwinds, 2004.

Loehr, Gina. *Real Women, Real Saints: Friends for Your Spiritual Journey*. Cincinnati: Servant, 2008.

McBrien, Richard P. *Lives of the Saints: From Mary and St. Francis of Assisi to John XXIII and Mother Teresa*. New York: HarperOne, 2006.

Morgan, Tom. *Saints: A Visual Almanac of the Virtuous, Pure, Praiseworthy, and Good*. San Francisco: Chronicle, 1994.

O' Neel, Brian. *39 New Saints You Should Know*. Cincinnati: Servant, 2010.

One Hundred Saints: Their Lives and Likenesses. New York: Bulfinch, 2002.

Peers, E. Allison, ed. *Interior Castle: St. Teresa of Avila*. Mineola, NY: Dover, 2007.

Sandoval, Annette. *The Directory of Saints: A Concise Guide to Patron Saints*. New York: Signet, 1996.

Scaperlanda, María Ruiz. *Edith Stein: St. Teresa Benedicta of the Cross*. Huntington, IN: Our Sunday Visitor, 2001.

Stone, Elaine. *Saints of the Americas*. New York: Regina, 2005.

Thérèse of Lisieux. *The Story of a Soul: The Autobiography of St. Thérèse of Lisieux*. Charlotte, NC: Tan Classics, 2010.

Thigpen, Paul. *A Dictionary of Quotes from the Saints*. Ann Arbor, MI: Servant, 2001.

About the Author

Melanie Rigney is the coauthor of *When They Come Home: Ways to Welcome Returning Catholics*, a contributor to *Living Faith* magazine, and a weekly contributor to the Catholic blog Your Daily Tripod.

By Shirley Conran

CRIMSON

DOWN WITH SUPERWOMAN

SAVAGES

LACE 2

LACE

SUPERWOMAN

Shirley
Conran

CRIMSON

LONDON NEW YORK SYDNEY TORONTO

This edition published 1992
by BCA
by arrangement with Sidgwick & Jackson Ltd

© Shirley Conran 1991

CN 3883

Third reprint 1992

Designed by Laurie Jewell

Printed and bound in Germany
by Graphischer Großbetrieb Pößneck GmbH
A member of the Mohndruck printing group

For my very dear friend
Jennifer d'Abo

What women want in life is love and what
men want is power—and men want power
as much as women want love:
women think that they don't understand what
power is, but in the nursery, power is
called getting your own way.

From *A Burning Heart* by Elinor Dove

BOOK·1

Chapter · 1

Within the Château de Saracen, cream blinds had been lowered in the main bedroom, but the glare of the July sun reflected from the Mediterranean Sea below could still be felt by the gaunt, white-clad nurse as she rustled from the bathroom with a small tray. She had a sallow face; beneath her sunken eyes were dark, liverish pouches.

As the church clock struck the noon hour, the nurse checked her watch; with an angular, careful walk on legs as thin as breadsticks, she approached the bed. The magnificent eight-foot-wide four-poster had once been the property of a Spanish princess; the high canopy was surmounted by ostrich feathers made of beaten silver; the hangings were stiff with cream brocade; and the interior of the curtains was heavily embroidered in gold, with a design of lilies. This ornate silver pile only escaped vulgarity because the other furniture in the room was simple and sparse.

They'll probably be squabbling over that bed by tomorrow, thought the nurse, although it's beginning to look as if the old girl might last another few days. So far, her three granddaughters had only been anxious and concerned about her, but once they knew that she was going, then the fun would start! Confusion always built up as the end approached. The crosscurrents of emotion and the momentary paralysis of shock were followed by the whispered anxieties and accusations; then came the little plots; and after that, the squabbles and the mighty, roaring rows.

Yes, thought the nurse, when it came to money, blood was thinner than water. Her experience had been that every family was a seething caldron of violent feelings: beneath the surface of the stew simmered expectations and demands, disappointment and suspicion, evasion of responsibility, greed and fear. And a deathbed was frequently the setting in which this stew of potential violence came to an explosive boil.

An unusual amount of money, such as this old girl clearly had, was especially tempting—and therefore especially destructive in its volatile ability to draw bad or weak family characteristics to the surface.

The nurse carefully placed her tray on the bedside table and picked up the syringe. As always, she wondered what people might be tempted to do for a fortune. *Anything,* provided they weren't discovered, she decided as she flicked the syringe to expel air, preparatory to injecting the medicine into the thin arm of the feeble figure that lay in the bed.

The nurse spoke a little English but could not follow these foreigners when they talked among themselves. She didn't need to, however; she knew with certainty what had drawn them here: they had sniffed money and followed the scent of the sous here to her part of France. Now that they *were* here, she knew they would return. For once they have heard it, the siren call of the south of France will always beckon visitors back to the timeless, sensuous landscape; back to the sun, to the sharp, exhilarating intensity of the light; to the sea and the pine-scented air; to the delicious food, the delicate, seductive wine.

Luckily, the foreign tourists of July and August were usually seen only in the well-publicized resorts and rarely found the tiny, quiet villages along that sun-drenched coastal strip known as the Côte d'Azur. Saracen was exactly such a place: built on a hilltop that plunged three hundred feet to the sea on the southern side, the medieval, tan-roofed village was dominated by this eleventh-century stone chateau, firmly perched on its truncated summit.

The nurse picked up her tray and returned it to the bathroom. She lingered at the window, looking out at the spectacular view. On both sides of Saracen, cedar- and pine-covered mountains descended directly to the deep aquamarine sea. As she leaned out, the nurse could also see behind the village, to the north, the perpetually green forest of the hinterland, which still provided shelter for wild boar, rabbits, and birds.

Down below the castle, the stone arches and narrow roads shimmered in the heat; leaves drooped from plane trees and dogs panted beneath them. Windows were shuttered against the burning glare of the midday sun, which sapped all energy from the day and everyone in it. Not a single villager would be visible until four o'clock. The voluptuous summer heat of the Riviera was enjoyable only if you did not need to work in it, so by tradition, nobody did.

The nurse yawned, and wished that she, too, could take a siesta. She knew that during this long, somnolent afternoon, most inhabitants of Saracen would stay indoors in shuttered shade to doze, to make love, or simply to enjoy their temporary, midday withdrawal from real life. It was a tempting prospect. Then, when the church clock chimed four, the villagers would open their shutters, stretch their arms, call greetings to one another from their black, curlicued wrought-iron balconies, and generally behave as if, like Sleeping Beauty, they had just awakened from a slumber that had lasted one hundred years.

The nurse yawned again. Unfortunately, she could not sleep now. She had to sit with the old woman; that was what she was paid to do. She walked toward the still figure in the ornate bed.

Abruptly the nurse stopped, startled, as her patient stirred slightly, then moaned.

Lying in her silver bed, Elinor O'Dare surged in and out of consciousness, suspended in a sea of incoherence.

For what seemed a long time, a black void of fear and pain had been Elinor's only reality. Disoriented, she no longer knew in which direction the sky lay. She now felt sick and giddy, as if she were seasick, as if she were being tossed around by a monstrous wave. Elinor sensed that should she move, the steel band around her head would tighten like a tourniquet, increasing the ruthless pain.

Long ago, during the First World War, when Elinor had nursed dying men, she had at first been terrified by the noise of their pain, by the ululating groans and sharp screams that rose from their blood-soaked stretchers and their sweat-drenched beds. Even now she could recall the sweet, putrid smell of death; she also remembered the fear that had blanketed those wards, and now felt it herself, as pain wrapped her body in a formless black haze.

Was she dying? The thought was light as an autumn leaf, floating in her mind. Vaguely Elinor reasoned that if that were so, then the pain would cease and nothing else really mattered. Gradually, however, the waves of pain seemed to lessen, to lose their anger. She sensed a coming calm. Dare she hope that the pain was receding, or would that tempt the dark gods to increase it? No, there was no longer any doubt. The pain was slowly but definitely withdrawing from her body.

Eventually Elinor knew the almost forgotten luxury of *no pain*. Little by little her body relaxed, but still she dared not move, for fear of again inviting those searing stabs of agony. Elinor, who felt as if she had been holding her breath for hours, tentatively tried to take a deep breath.

Immediately a thousand needles jabbed her ribs. Her instinct was to scream, but she was unable to make even a sound. Something hard and smooth was clamped over her face, she realized with a shock, and her head was constricted by a contraption she could not see.

Though Elinor did not yet try to move, she could listen and she could smell. Concentrating, she could make out the faint, steady lapping of the sea against the rocks below her window; intuitively she sensed the sun's warmth and smelled the Provençal scent of summer.

Suddenly she knew where she was!

She was in her own bed at Saracen, on a warm summer's day. She could smell the soft breeze that blew off the hinterland, wafting rosemary, thyme, and the hot-baked-earth smell of the mountains.

Lying in her bed, Elinor decided that she must have had a nightmare, one of those terrible visions with the lingering power to convince, even after she had awakened. Better open her eyes *now* and ring for breakfast, she thought. Her bowl of milky coffee, her croissants and fruit, with the morning papers and mail would put her world in order again.

At first her eyelids seemed too heavy to lift; but slowly and with great effort, Elinor opened them a little, gradually registering the soft golden glow of filtered sunlight.

Yes. Everything was as usual. Before her, above the fireplace, hung a large, elaborately framed picture, which had been painted eight years ago, in 1957. In the life-size portrait, three girls dressed in white ball gowns sat on a misty blue brocade sofa in a shadowy drawing room. You did not have to be told that these girls were sisters: they shared a happy complicity, and although their coloring differed, they all had the same small, neat nose and large, slanting aquamarine eyes.

From the left, eighteen-year-old Clare, dark and tiny, leaned forward with a serious expression, offering a rose to tawny-haired Annabel, unquestionably the family beauty. Miranda (sixteen, skinny, still at school) perched like a bird on the back of the sofa; her face was pale and she hadn't yet dyed her beige hair that odd marmalade color. She appeared slightly withdrawn but as charming as the other two, and as heedlessly ready to fly into life.

Only Annabel could be called a beauty, for Clare's expression was too anxious and Miranda's features were a little too sharp. All three, however, reflected the charisma of breeding and privilege. More significant in Elinor's eyes, all three reminded her of her dear Billy.

The portrait always comforted Elinor. She remembered satisfying moments when the girls were small and she had taken a day off work and was about to take them out to tea or on a shopping trip: all three children would be clean and neat—socks still pulled up, hair ribbons tied—and almost quivering with eager anticipation.

Such moments of true happiness had been rare in Elinor's life and they had never come when expected but blossomed quickly, at surprising moments. She had long ago decided that you couldn't plan happiness, but you *could* plan achievement; and she had planned well, for she had succeeded beyond all reasonable expectations. In spite of all the early setbacks, the treachery, disappointments, and sheer drudgery, her success had been considerable: her twenty-two novels had been published in some forty countries; her fan mail arrived weekly by the sackful; and she received from everyone the respect that was her due. The legendary Elinor O'Dare was famous, successful, and very, very rich.

The legendary Elinor winced abruptly. The burning pain had started again, and it was *within her body*. Lying inert in the heat of her shaded bedroom, she realized that she could not move her limbs. There seemed to be no strength in her arms or legs: she willed her arms to lift, and they did not do so. She was paralyzed. She was *not* dreaming. *She could not move!*

She tried to speak, then to scream—but she couldn't. Nor could she open her mouth. Her head felt woolly and muddled. The thought slowly registered—she must have had a stroke. No! It couldn't be! She didn't want it! She hadn't yet finished living!

The effort of her anguished thinking exhausted her. Her eyelids fluttered shut, and black oblivion slowly drew over her. She willed her mind to go blank, yet somewhere outside her mental enclosure, she heard a sound. It was the well-remembered rustle of a nurse's starched apron. She smelled the hospital smell of ether and the sour whiff of medicine.

"Am I dying?" Elinor whispered in French, finally willing her frozen mouth to move awkwardly.

"No. Do not upset yourself." The nurse's voice was calm, flat, and disinterested. Elinor knew she was lying. Her first reaction was one of indignation. She was used to being in command of her life, used to writing the plot herself—as she did those of her best-selling novels. But now she was rendered impotent by her helplessness—at the mercy of this mean-voiced nurse. An invisible, inexorable pen was scribbling "The End" before Elinor had finished her story—and this time there would be no happy ending.

For years Elinor had successfully avoided thinking about death. Like many strong-minded and successful people, she had not wanted to face the fact that, one day, she would die. She had not bothered to make a will, for that would mean having to make unpleasant decisions, decisions dealing with her own mortality. So she had put it off, resisting her lawyer's gentle, persistent urging, preferring to ignore the subject, to think of herself only as enduring, invincible.

But today, lying in this shuttered room, she knew that the invincible had met the inevitable. She could only hope that she might have some time to get things in order. And she had better make her decisions quickly—or she might lose the chance to do so.

Elinor felt the uncomfortable contraption being tugged from her face. She felt too tired to move, to think, or to complain; she felt helpless and at the mercy of this impersonal stranger. Obviously, death was going to be a humiliating business, and she knew that helplessness was only the start.

Hearing the sharp, efficient moves of the nurse around her bed, Elinor fleetingly remembered daydreams from many years ago—from 1917, after she had left the small family farm near Excelsior, Minnesota, to train as an auxiliary nursing aide. She was only seventeen, still idealistic and romantic enough to envision herself as a calm, reassuring angel of mercy. World War I had inspired many young women to volunteer for auxiliary service of some kind; for most, it was a first step away from home. For most, it was also an abrupt end to innocence.

Elinor remembered her own reaction when she first arrived at the casualty clearing station in northern France to which she had been posted. She had expected the quiet orderly calm of the wards at her training hospital, not that shocking, awful noise in Ward C: the animal-like whimpers, sobs, sharp shrieks of agony, men crying in loose-mouthed delirium, while a phonograph played a Bing Boys' tune to comfort those who knew they were about to die.

Now, almost half a century later, realizing what little time remained to her, Elinor's patience vanished as instantaneously as had her innocence. Lying there, trapped in her bed, she found to her surprise, however, that it wasn't the physical act of dying that she minded, or leaving what she had fought so hard to achieve. But the girls still needed her; they needed her strength, her advice, her emotional and moral support: despite the fact that two of them were married women and the third had already established a thriving business, Elinor was convinced that the girls could not yet survive without her. Her fortune, of course, would ensure their comfort and their social prestige, but who would be there to advise and protect them?

Elinor had been able to give her granddaughters what she had not had, and what she had been unable to give her only son, Edward: a life virtually free from care; a life in which there was the time and opportunity to look for happiness and, should they find it, simply to enjoy it; a life untroubled by the financial anxiety with which Elinor had lived for the first forty-five years of her life. It was an anxiety that had faded only when—thanks to her darling Billy—she had been able to grasp success and to savor its rewards.

At the thought of Billy, Elinor's eyelids slowly lifted. In the dim light, she could just make out the small group of silver-framed photographs on her bedside table. Once again Elinor gazed into the smiling, confident eyes of the fair-haired young man she had loved so much. There he stood, flying goggles pushed back on his head, hands thrust in the bottom pockets of a battered tunic; his plane, a primitive machine made of canvas and struts, was behind him.

Billy O'Dare had been one of the few men to survive Ward C. His navigator had pulled him, unconscious, from his shot-down plane before it burst into flames. Billy had suffered a concussion, a slight cut on his head, and a bullet through his left foot that fractured the calcaneum.

Nearly fifty years later, Elinor still happily remembered the evening she fell in love with Billy O'Dare. The ward was relatively quiet when, shortly after midnight, she heard choking cries from bed 17. Grabbing the lantern, she hurried to find out what was wrong. Gently she shook the young man awake—he'd had a bad dream, that was all. Flight Commander O'Dare continued to sob, however, now clinging to Elinor's hand. His face was partly covered by a turbanlike bandage, but her lantern shone into his eyes, reducing the pupils to pinpoints of black against irises of an unusual, dazzling shade of aquamarine. Elinor thought she had never seen anything so beautiful.

"Sorry to make such an ass of myself," he mumbled.

"Don't worry. Plenty of patients have nightmares," Elinor comforted, trying to ease her hand away. She could smell, against the harsh wool of his blanket and the antiseptic whiff of bandages, the pungent male perfume of his body. He was no longer sobbing now, and she knew she should move away. Still, she could not stop staring into his eyes.

Patient 17 raised Elinor's hand to his lips and she felt the tickle of his blond mustache against her thumb. For a moment, she thought he was going to kiss her hand, but instead, he turned it over and pressed her palm to his mouth. As Elinor felt the caress of his warm breath, Billy O'Dare gently licked her hand. She felt his moist tongue run slowly over her flesh and knew again that she should move away; her feet, however, seemed glued to the floorboards. She felt a blush rise from her breast and held her breath as he continued to stroke her hand with his warm, catlike tongue. Her trancelike state was broken only when another patient suddenly screamed.

By morning, Nurse Elinor Dove knew patient 17's medical notes by heart. She also knew that Flight Commander William Montmorency O'Dare of the British Royal Air Force was twenty-five years old.

By some odd form of osmosis, the entire ward seemed to know immediately that Nurse Dove had tumbled in love with O'Dare. Beneath Elinor's nunlike white headdress, her grape-green eyes glistened, and her cheeks were even pinker than usual. There was a lively spring in her step, and Sister had to admonish her for singing to herself.

On a visit to Ward C, Billy's former navigator, Joe Grant, immediately spotted the romance. He told Billy he was a lucky dog, that Nurse Dove was special, different from the rest. When Billy repeated this observation to Elinor, she sniffed, "That's what you men say to *all* us girls. What's so different about *me?*"

Billy looked at her thoughtfully, then said, "The girls at home are pale imitations of life compared to you. You have such vitality, such get-up-and-go! You have energy. It's positively infectious!" He hesitated. "It is so American, it seems. I've seen these qualities in your soldiers as well; it's something you don't see in the Frenchies or Tommies. Whatever it is, you really *are* very special."

Looking up from his pillow, Billy O'Dare hunched his right shoulder and slightly bent his bandaged head toward it as he smiled gently at Nurse Dove. From that moment on, she was forever in his control. Long after they were married, when Elinor knew fully the true cost of love, the slow grin that so clearly showed Billy's impudent Irish charm—that complex combination of innocence and artfulness—would always wipe away her anger in an instant.

All these years after their meeting, Elinor recalled that irresistible grin; it was how she liked to remember Billy. In fact, it had become the only way she allowed herself to remember Billy—as the smiling, dashing young war hero who became her romantic bridegroom. Any subsequent unpleasant memories had been hidden in some dusty corner of her mind.

It was a pity that color photography hadn't been invented then, she thought as she stared at the silver-framed, sepia photograph. All three sisters had inherited Billy's aquamarine eyes, although only Miranda had inherited the beguiling grin. From Elinor they had inherited . . .

Elinor was suddenly reminded again that she hadn't made a will. Their inheritance: yes, there was that to deal with. She closed her eyes, then, with an effort of will, opened them again. Slowly the room settled into focus.

The nurse leaned over her patient. "Can you open your mouth, madame? . . . A little more . . ." From a spouted cup, she dribbled a few drops of water into Elinor's mouth; then she carefully rubbed ointment over the dry lips.

Painfully, Elinor whispered, "Where . . . are . . . my granddaughters?" She couldn't move the right side of her face, so she spoke slowly and awkwardly, slurring her words as if tipsy. She could move her right fingers and toes, but she could not feel those on her left side.

Feeling panic start to rise, Elinor remembered that when she was very young and woke at night, she used to clutch her rosary to keep the devil at bay; now she groped for something similarly comforting to reassure her. More urgently she croaked, *"Where are my granddaughters?"*

"I believe the ladies are on the terrace. I will call them."

The nurse went to the window and pulled back the shutters. Yes, there they were, typically heedless of the afternoon sun. She called down.

From her bed, Elinor could hear excited voices, then the sound of metal chairs scraping against earthenware tiles. Tremulously she smiled, struggling to adjust her eyes to the sudden infusion of light.

A few minutes later, her bedroom door was flung open. Elinor first saw Clare's animated, pale face, framed by long, straight dark hair.

"Darling, we've been so worried." Clare's voice was high and soft. She rushed to the bedside, knelt down and kissed her grandmother's face, then the thin, blue-veined hands.

"Don't overexcite her," warned the nurse.

"My turn," said Annabel, whose long, honey-colored hair was wet and tangled after swimming. For the past seven years, Annabel's lovely face had gazed, wide-eyed, from every Avanti cosmetics advertisement around the world. When Elinor looked at her, she thought of white Persian kittens, feather beds and pale pink peonies: Annabel was soft, voluptuous, and feminine. Gently Annabel stroked her grandmother's long, fair hair, now white at the roots, as it spread, fanlike, upon the pillow. She kissed the sunken cheeks and whispered, "Oh, Gran, we thought we'd lost you."

Both sisters were close to tears as they gazed lovingly at their grandmother. Only Clare had even the slightest memory of their parents, (killed in 1941 in a German bombing raid on London) and Elinor had always been the center of their world. They couldn't imagine life without her. She had always seemed a combination of Isadora Duncan and Elinor Glyn—a bold, dramatic, and immortal figure.

"Where's Miranda?" Elinor whispered.

"She had to return to London for the day—a business meeting," Clare said softly. "We've all been here for the last two weeks. Annabel flew from New York as soon as we heard you were ill, but it took me a bit longer to get organized in Los Angeles. Miranda's flying back tonight, by helicopter."

"And where is Buzz?" Buzz was Elinor's lifelong friend, now her secretary.

"Gone to Nice to get your medicine. After that, she's calling at the airport, to see if Annabel's luggage has turned up. Buzz never gives up hope!"

"We don't want to overexcite Madame before the doctor sees her." The nurse firmly held open the bedroom door. "You must go now, and I will call him."

Annabel turned rebelliously toward the nurse, clearly prepared to ignore the edict.

Clare, however, immediately became the anxious and responsible elder sister. "Don't be difficult, Frog," she coaxed, using the childhood nickname that referred to Annabel's large and sensuous mouth. "We'll be back as soon as they let us."

Clare gently pushed her sister out of the bedroom. Elinor turned imploring eyes toward the nurse. Silently they said, *Please get a move on. I have so much to do.* Elinor's indomitable spirit was reasserting itself.

Clare, wearing a white bikini, lay on a beach mattress by the pool. She was small and skinny, but managed to look slim and fragile; she had a fey, elusive charm: you felt that she might slip between your fingers, like clear water from a mountain stream.

Lying on the next beach mattress, Annabel wore a claret-colored silk dressing gown that belonged to her husband. She always carried this item and a set of spare underwear in her hand luggage, for the rest of her baggage seemed invariably to travel on without her. This trip had proved no exception.

When the poolside telephone rang, Annabel grabbed the ivory receiver. "Maybe it's about my luggage. If it's gone on a trip to eternity, the airway will have to pay for all those new clothes." She looked at the buttons on the telephone, which also served as an intercom, and frowned. "I'll never get the hang of this thing." She pressed a button. The line went dead. "Hell, I'm hopeless with machinery." Annabel noticed that Clare looked anxious. "Sorry, Clare. Are you expecting a call?"

"Not really. Well, perhaps . . . I thought that . . ." Clare pushed dark strands of hair from her forehead. She suddenly burst into tears, covering her face with her hands.

Annabel scrambled from her mattress and ran to her sister, embracing her, pulling her close. "What's up, darling? I *knew* something was wrong! Otherwise you wouldn't have lugged Josh and his nanny all the way from California. Tell me. Why hasn't he telephoned?"

Gradually Clare's sobbing subsided. In a tone filled with angry indignation, unlike her normal soft voice, she told Annabel of the row. Clare had gone to the beach for the day, accompanied by Josh and his nanny. She returned early because of period cramps, and in her bedroom, she found a thin, tanned woman lying naked beside her husband. A bitter scene ensued. Clare stormed to her dressing room and started to pack. She heard his car spray gravel outside her window as it took off, too fast. Kneeling by her suitcase, Clare wept until another car arrived and Josh and his nanny clattered, laughing, into the house. At that moment, Annabel had telephoned from New York.

"Then you told me about Gran's stroke," snuffled Clare.

"Poor darling," Annabel murmured, stroking Clare's long, dark hair.

"He's so clever at sidetracking. He makes *me* look like an over-emotional idiot, when all the time *he's* in the wrong." With the back of her hand, Clare wiped tears away. She had always told herself that despite his casual promiscuity, her husband loved her in a *special* way, that he would never abandon their *real* love or jeopardize their son's happiness. She told herself he was only asserting his male prowess with those other women, and he wouldn't *ever* take one of them seriously. But then, that day, Clare had suddenly found that she could bear no more humiliation. So she had left him.

In the late-afternoon Provençal sunshine, Annabel silently hugged Clare and waited.

Eventually Clare continued, "I didn't want the usual reconciliation scene, the usual flowers, the usual promises—and then the usual pain next time. Suddenly I simply didn't care what happened to him." She hugged her sister. "Oh Annabel, you won't tell anyone, will you?"

"Have I ever told your secrets? But if you've really walked out for good, everyone will have to know *sometime*. Are you sure you're going to . . ."

"Get a divorce? Yes. Absolutely. I don't want Josh growing up to be like his father."

"Well, don't let Gran know, at least not yet. You know it'll upset her. In fact, don't tell *anyone* until you're sure you're sure."

As Annabel comforted her sister, a maid approached. Speaking in French, she said, "The pool telephone malfunctions. New York awaits Miss Annabel."

"I'll take it in my bedroom," Annabel said, jumping up with almost childish enthusiasm. She ran upstairs to her pale pink apartment, which overlooked the cobbled entrance courtyard and the church beyond it.

"Darling? At last! What's your news?" Annabel could hear background sounds from the New York TV station for which her husband was a news anchorman. He was one of eleven reporters, only three of whom appeared as on-air newscasters.

"Local or national, angel? It's eleven in the morning and sticky hot in New York. Yesterday Martin Luther King called for an end to the Vietnam War, but it looks as if Johnson will order more troops in. My lead story for this evening? Kennedy's original view of Vietnam as a quick in-and-out operation might end in world war." Annabel could imagine his teasing smile. "I hope your news is less alarming."

Annabel told her husband about Elinor's return to consciousness.

"That's wonderful, angel. When are you coming back?"

"I don't know. When Gran's better. Does it matter?"

Her husband hesitated. "Sidney wants to talk to us."

"Why?" Sidney was their accountant, and the sound of his name instantly set off alarm bells.

"I've decided to go after a better job."

Annabel could hear the lack of self-confidence in her husband's voice. She said, "But you love your—"

"It's a little earlier than I planned to make my move, but that's not so terrible. We're sinking deeper into debt each day, and we have to find some way to shore up our finances."

Annabel said miserably, "Oh darling, I'm *so* sorry. *I* was the one who insisted on the new duplex. It never crossed my mind that Avanti might not renew my contract." She gave a shaky laugh. "I know I'm twenty-five, but that's not *old*. Not in the normal world. Only for a model."

"Avanti still might renew your contract. We don't know."

"I wish they'd make their damned minds up," Annabel said. "I could *kick* myself for buying that apartment! I can't *think* why I was so extravagant."

"You bought it to give me the right background. You said, 'A good picture needs a good frame,' " he reminded her. "You said in order to get into the Mike Wallace league, I have to look as if I am already in it."

"Absolutely. And you will be." Annabel cheered up. Her husband had the same quick, hard intelligence as Mike Wallace: he could be just as probing and provoking when interviewing. He could also produce the sort of insistent question that turned a news interview into a psycho-drama. *And* he had the voice.

"Darling," she went on, "you're one of the best newsmen on television. And remember, you're only twenty-nine years old. Mike Wallace was thirty-eight before he got his break on *Night Beat*. Plus I love you."

"And I love you. In the meantime, angel, don't take all the blame for the apartment. Remember, New York is a town about showing you can make it, making it, and then showing you've made it. Who knows, the apartment *may* help land my new job."

Annabel laughed. "Well, if you don't get your job and I don't get mine, we'll just have to sell the place and rent, like the rest of New York. It really doesn't matter where we live. We'll still have each other."

Strapped into the noisy helicopter, Miranda tucked an unruly strand of marmalade-colored hair behind her intercom headset as she looked out at the sullen, gray English Channel below. "We left London at two-thirty, so we'll get to Saracen by seven—in good time for dinner." Miranda kept her voice as low as possible, her tone steady and deliberate; she spoke that way because she found that it commanded attention. She pressed her face against the tough plastic bubble that enveloped them. "I do *so* wish that Gran would let me learn to fly. Couldn't you persuade her?"

Miranda then remembered that this might not be necessary. It was so hard to reconcile herself to the reality of her grandmother's illness. She bit her lip and willed the tears away.

Sitting next to her, Adam Grant shook his head. He was tall, dark, and brown-eyed, with firm-hewn features and a cynical air of assurance. Miranda thought he looked like one of those almost perfect men drawn in magazine advertisements for cashmere sweaters, or that he might have fallen from the pages of one of Gran's romantic novels.

Adam's father, Joe Grant, had been Elinor's longtime legal adviser and close friend. After his death, five years before, Elinor's business affairs had gradually been passed to Adam, who also worked for the family legal firm of Swithin, Timmins and Grant.

Adam had asked Miranda for a lift in the Bell because this was one of the rare occasions when all three sisters would be at Saracen. Having them together like this would provide him with the opportunity to discuss, gently but firmly and as unemotionally as possible, what would happen should Elinor die intestate. Despite her dual U.S. and British citizenship, Elinor was resident in France, and the French tax authorities considered theirs to be the controlling law for her entire estate. Once again Adam regretted that he had been unable to persuade Elinor to make a will, because there were always complications when anyone died intestate. Perhaps he should have been more insistent, but Adam valued their long-standing relationship, and he had not wanted to upset Elinor, who clearly hated the thought of discussing her own death.

It was Elinor who had asked Adam to guide Miranda's steps into the business world, and in the three years since Miranda had opened her first small makeup shop, her business had spread—albeit sparsely—all over Britain. Last year, Adam, her unofficial adviser, had become a part-time director. He had just restructured the balance sheet for their next leap ahead.

"You know I wouldn't persuade Elinor to do anything she didn't want to do," Adam said gently. He found it interesting that this twenty-four-year-old red-haired baby tycoon who wanted to fly should still submit to Elinor's wishes. Generally Miranda made her own rules and ignored what other people thought of her.

Looking at Miranda, Adam once again found himself thinking that if all women were basically beautiful, their bodies would probably resemble Miranda's. Her slim figure wasn't voluptuous, but it was perfect: her breasts were small, high, and rounded; her waist was neat, her stomach flat. And when she walked, her long, slim legs moved in a graceful stalk. In addition, Miranda was always appropriately dressed for the occasion: that gray silk suit, simple but feminine, had been perfect for this morning's monthly office meeting.

Miranda shrugged her shoulders and decided to change the subject. She switched off the intercom to the pilot so that he couldn't hear what she was saying. "Adam, I'm not entirely happy about Ned Sinclair."

"I think he's settled down very fast." Adam had poached their new financial director from a rival cosmetics manufacturer.

"He asked me one or two unnecessary questions about our future plans. It bothers me, although perhaps I've become oversensitive since Mary Quant started her beauty business."

"Quant doesn't own a chain of retail shops." Adam's hand flipped his hair back as if to brush away an irritation. His dark hair was still cut as it had been when he was at school; parted on the right, it flopped over his left temple and gave his face an endearing, seemingly innocent charm.

"She's my direct competition because we think along similar lines. I bet she'll be international before I am. I shouldn't be surprised to hear that Ned has approached her."

Once again it occurred to Adam that Miranda had inherited many of Elinor's characteristics: her intuition and the ability to act on it, her stubborn determination, and her guts.

He smiled. "I'll run a check on Ned. *You* could be international—if only you would agree to franchise."

"I won't franchise because I don't want to lose control of my business! However tight the contracts are, you lose control once you do. Others might not want to work as hard as we do, and they may not have such high standards of presentation. So please forget it."

"If you won't franchise, then you'll have to put up with being short of money," Adam said firmly, looking at her from large-lidded dark eyes. "What *would* you do for a lot of money, Miranda?"

"What *wouldn't* I do for a lot of money!" Miranda laughed.

"I wonder," Adam said thoughtfully.

"Oh, you're so resolute, so determined." Miranda smiled. "I can't think *why* we seem to be on an endless financial tightrope."

"Because you want to expand faster than we can afford." Adam spoke laconically. He shrugged his shoulders. "But who knows what lies ahead . . ."

How *dare* he! "I *know* what you're thinking. You're thinking that if Gran dies . . ." Miranda burst into tears.

Adam was astonished, partly because she had correctly guessed his thoughts. Also he had never before seen Miranda cry. She rarely showed her emotions.

He pulled a Paisley silk handkerchief from his navy blazer and silently handed it to her.

"Damn, I've lost a contact lens," Miranda gulped. "Can you see it on my skirt? Or has it fallen to the floor?"

"Keep still. I can see it on your lap."

As Adam leaned over her, Miranda inhaled his faint musky scent. Adam moved in a miasma of sexuality, which he seemed not to notice although it was as definite as warm breath. She thought he smelled a bit like a well-groomed horse. Close up, his odor reminded her of expensive leather. This subtle erotic scent contradicted Adam's careful lawyer's demeanor, his understated Savile Row suits and shirts, his horn-rimmed glasses.

Miranda knew that Adam had a devastating effect on women. She had first observed it on a shared family holiday in St.-Tropez, twelve years ago. Miranda, only twelve at the time, had noticed that even the grumpy old French housekeeper happily danced attendance on twenty-three-year-old Adam.

Miranda knew why Adam had never made a serious pass at her or her sisters. To have done so would have been unprofessional and might have adversely affected his job. Additionally, all three sisters, while acknowledging his attractiveness, had grown up thinking of Adam as a young uncle. He in turn had always regarded them as children, much to their indignation at the time.

Now, as Adam carefully placed the contact lens in the palm of Miranda's hand, she reminded herself that he was *not* her uncle. Then she pushed this thought to the back of her head and told herself jokingly to keep her hands off the staff. Turning away from Adam to reinsert her lens, Miranda also reminded herself that at the moment, she hadn't time for a lover. In this respect she was unusual; the Pill was now readily available and every liberated girl was on it, whether or not her mother knew. Increasingly a woman was expected to jump into bed after the first date—something that didn't suit Miranda, who felt only anxiety when in bed with a man whom she didn't know well and therefore didn't trust. At this point in her young life, there had been only one man who made her feel secure.

Adam said, "Even if it distresses you, there's something I feel we should discuss before reaching Saracen; it's your grandmother's will. She hasn't yet made one, but we have discussed the matter."

Clearly worried, Adam was silent for a moment, then continued in a low voice: "For me, this is a difficult dilemma: Do I stick to my standards of professional discretion, or do I break my client's confidence in order to do what's best for her and those she loves? Does the end justify the means? Would Elinor—my client, my friend and benefactor—allow it? That's what I can't decide. Because I know that Elinor would want whatever is most advantageous to all her granddaughters."

"I'd advise you not to break your client's confidence," Miranda said, "but be sensible and tell me what the hell this is about."

"Without breaking Elinor's confidence, I can tell you that although she intends to leave the bulk of her fortune to you three sisters, various methods of controlling the money have been considered."

"What do you mean, Adam, *controlling the money?*" Whenever it came to finances, Miranda was instinctively suspicious.

"She's anxious that the money not be . . . frittered away. There are various possible ways of protecting it. She doesn't like the French legal requirement to share the property equally among all descendants. As you know, Elinor lost touch with her family many years ago, and she doesn't want her brother's children—if he ever had any—to suddenly appear, claim money, make trouble. But as Elinor is a resident of France, this *will* happen unless she makes . . . alternative arrangements."

"What sort of arrangements?" Miranda demanded.

"She's had a few rather . . . dramatic ideas, as you would expect. She doesn't like the British system, where the eldest inherits everything on the understanding that the inheritor cares for the rest of the family."

"I should think not!" Miranda was the youngest of the three sisters. For her, primogeniture would be disastrous. "Gran saw what happened to her own husband!"

Billy's grandmother, a considerable heiress, had left all her money to her elder son, an impulsive weakling, who lost nearly all of it in an Edwardian stock exchange swindle. When he died, Billy's elder brother inherited what was left of the family estate; Billy inherited nothing.

"Elinor seems to think the Greek system is the most sensible," Adam said.

"What's that?"

"A wealthy Greek father often leaves all the family money to the child most capable of looking after it, on the understanding that the inheritor looks after the immediate family."

"The most financially capable sister is me," Miranda stated.

"In financial matters, certainly. But Clare has always been very conscientious and responsible; she was like a mother hen toward you and Annabel when you were little girls."

Miranda sat up sharply. "All my life I've had Clare shoved down my throat!" Clare was the eldest, the responsible sister, whose duty it was to look after the little ones. She could be relied upon because she was steady and practical. Conscientious Clare would never tell a lie—not even a white one—and could be relied upon always to be fair, as Clare herself never stopped reminding people.

It was Clare's much vaunted sense of justice that made her feel responsible for the whole damn world, particularly every underprivileged person in it, Miranda knew. If Clare grabbed the purse strings, then they would not be opened for Miranda, who was not Clare's idea of a needy person. Miranda would be pushed back to the position of baby sister.

"Unfortunately, Elinor thinks you . . . Would *you* say you were steadier than Clare?" Adam asked.

"You mean Gran thinks I'm too . . . rash?"

"I wouldn't say that, *exactly*," Adam said reflectively, "although perhaps Elinor does think you take too many risks. She sees you as the daring young girl on the flying trapeze of business. But of course, Elinor doesn't understand that in business, it's necessary to take risks. *I* see your adventurous streak as a business asset."

"It's not *fair!*" Miranda retorted bitterly, remembering how often she had said that as a child.

Eventually she asked, "What will happen if Gran dies without making a will?"

"There may be a nasty legal mess that might take years to disentangle," Adam said. "And that's something I don't intend to allow. As soon as Elinor is well enough to do so, I will insist she make her decisions." He paused, then added: "There *is* an alternative to the Greek system that would safeguard the money and yet be fair."

"What's that?" Miranda quickly looked at Adam.

"It would mean that you would be certain to get your fair share."

"*What is it, Adam?*"

"I wondered whether Elinor would respond favorably to the idea of setting up a family trust," Adam mused. "What do you think? If you think not, then I don't want to distract her by the idea." Adam knew that, as the shrewdest and most forceful of the sisters, Miranda would be a formidable opponent should she object to his suggestion.

"What would be the point of setting up a trust?" Miranda asked cautiously.

"Making a trust is a bit like making a will, except that you put it into practice before you die," Adam explained. "If Elinor were to set up a trust, naming her granddaughters and their descendants as beneficiaries, then the money would be protected as Elinor wishes, because there's no risk that one heir can squander it all. The trustees wouldn't allow it: their job is to guard the trust, not slavishly obey the whims of the beneficiaries."

Miranda ran her hand through wild red hair. "You mean Clare couldn't sit on the money and refuse to share it, and she couldn't give it away to charity? And Annabel couldn't buy a couple of yachts?"

"Exactly. The advantage of a trust is that there would be a permanent cautionary control over the capital," Adam said. "I suspect that *you* would have nothing to lose, Miranda, were a trust to be established—and you might possibly have a great deal to gain. Trustees do not like frivolous expenditure; they might, shall we say, guard your sisters from themselves."

Miranda said firmly, "Then I vote for a trust."

"And what do you think Annabel will want?" Adam asked. "Perhaps it would be best if *you* discussed this with her, rather than me." Such a matter was always difficult to bring up with a close relative at such a time: that was why he had discussed it with Miranda before their arrival at Saracen. Adam added apologetically, "You know better than I do how to handle Annabel so that such a discussion won't upset her. I'm afraid she'd turn on me, perhaps think I'm being cold-blooded."

"I don't see why she should," Miranda said. "But I think *you* should talk to her because you can answer her questions, if she has any; I know nothing about the legal ramifications. Don't worry, Adam. Of course, Annabel *is* ridiculously sentimental, but after all, *you* have nothing to gain—you're only trying to prevent trouble for us. Basically, I'm confident that Annabel won't want Clare holding the purse strings, back in a position to boss us around. Stress *that* to Annabel and she won't be sentimental."

The apricot flush of the evening sky paled beyond the balustrade of the terrace, and the quivering reflections of the sea faded on Elinor's bedroom ceiling. She had been drifting in and out of sleep; the churning noise of the helicopter rotors finally awakened her. After the noise ceased, Elinor heard shrieked greetings and laughter from the far terrace. Only a few moments later, her bedroom door burst open.

"Darling Gran, this is wonderful!" Miranda ran to the bedside and kissed her grandmother. "Welcome back!"

Outside on the terrace, while Clare put two-year-old Josh to bed, Adam sipped champagne and chatted with Annabel. As he had done to Miranda, he mentioned the possibility of a trust as an alternative to Clare's being left in charge of the family fortune.

Annabel reacted with surprise, followed by irritation. "I had quite enough of being pushed about by Clare when we were children. Tell me more about this trust idea."

•   •   •

After dinner, Adam suggested to Clare that they take a walk. He wanted to be sure there would be no time-wasting opposition or bickering among the sisters when Elinor had so little strength left.

"Do we really have to talk about this now, Adam?" Clare was in no mood for financial discussion as they sauntered downhill, through winding narrow streets lined by bougainvillea and dimly lit by old-fashioned lampposts.

"I hoped that I could rely on you to be sensible, not sentimental," Adam said firmly. He added, "I'm only trying to arrange what Elinor would want and what is best for all of you. That's my duty as Elinor's adviser."

Clare thought how pompous Adam sounded. Why did Gran always have to have some man around to tell her what to do? When Daddy Billy was alive, his word had always been final. Then Gran's lawyer—Joe Grant—had become the great male authority figure in their lives, and now his son, Adam, had inherited the mantle of wisdom.

"I don't see what's wrong with just sharing it out," Clare said. "In case you haven't noticed, old friend, we aren't babies any longer. I'm a grown-up married woman."

Hesitantly Adam said, "Miranda and Annabel like the concept of a trust."

Clare spoke tartly. "Of course Annabel will agree—without thinking—to whatever Miranda suggests, because that's what she's always done. But *I* don't see why a trust is necessary. In fact, it seems an unnecessarily complicated idea."

She was as stubborn as her grandmother, Adam thought regretfully as he tried a new tack.

Clare listened, then shook her head lightly and said, "It won't work anymore with me, Adam. I've heard it too often."

"Heard what?"

"The adult equivalent of 'Daddy knows best.' "

Chapter · 2

Dr. Montand stepped from the glare of the morning sun into the chateau's shaded interior. The entrance hall was scented by roses in a blue jug on a dark antique chest. He was greeted in atrocious French by an angular woman with carelessly dyed jet-black hair; as they walked to the elevator, the doctor spoke in fluent English; so many Riviera residents spoke only English that an ambitious practitioner needed to be bilingual.

The woman was Buzz, Elinor's oldest friend. In 1947, after Billy's death, Buzz had traveled to Elinor's house in the Wiltshire countryside and had simply never left it; she saw that the house ran smoothly, supervised the three little girls and their nanny, paid the bills, did the bookkeeping, and relieved Elinor of all small distracting tasks, so that she could concentrate on writing novels.

Buzz came from a working-class background and had a harsh South London accent; her frequent cockney modification of the Queen's English made it easier for the Riviera natives to understand her French than her English. Because her manner was blunt and matter-of-fact, outsiders tended to underestimate Buzz, even to ignore her. She simply ignored them in return. She watched and listened and made up her own mind about everything. But no matter what, Buzz always protected her friend Elinor—sometimes from herself.

The elevator jerked to a halt at the bedroom floor, where a maid folded sheets into a cherrywood armoire: each pile of antique, lace-trimmed linen was tied with butter-colored silk ribbon.

The family bedrooms led off this hall. On the floor above were six suites for guests, each with its own bedroom, bathroom, and small kitchen. The entire chateau had been planned so that, should Elinor ever again find herself short of cash—an unlikely event but her constant back-of-the-mind anxiety—she could easily turn the Château de Saracen into a luxury hotel. The owners of the two hotels in the village, uneasily aware of this, were almost as delighted as Elinor when each of her romantic novels leapt straight onto the world's best-seller lists.

Before opening Elinor's door, Buzz turned abruptly to the doctor and said, "You'll tell *me* the truth, won't you? I can take it, but them girls can't."

"I have told you all I know," said Dr. Montand, "Madame O'Dare has had a partial stroke—a cerebral vascular accident, as we call it." The doctor patiently repeated what he had said the previous evening. "Her left arm and leg are paralyzed and so is the left side of her face. Later, she will need further investigation: an arterial brain scan, X rays, and electroencephalography. At the moment, there's no point in taking her to a hospital in Nice: anything that can be done there can be done with nursing help here, in her home."

Buzz nodded. "A better idea. No risk of cross-infection. Hits one in four patients in Western hospitals."

"I see that you keep up to date," the doctor said, assuming that this tall, graceless woman in the unfashionable navy dress had once been a nurse. He sensed that unspoken complicity between nurses and doctors, an absence of the frightened trust that most relatives exhibited.

Buzz's shrewd eyes had asked the question before her mouth: "Will she make a complete recovery?"

Dr. Montand shrugged. "She's not overweight. You say she doesn't smoke or drink heavily. She isn't diabetic, and her blood pressure is almost normal for her age." The patient was sixty-five years old, and no civilized doctor would suggest that she go on a diet, cut out drink entirely, or take up exercise. He would counsel them to let her enjoy her remaining life—should she recover.

Buzz pushed an unnaturally black wisp of hair behind her ear. "You ain't answered my question."

"It's too early to tell," the doctor said. "It takes time to recover. A patient often has impaired mentality—but not always. I really cannot say. Now you should get some rest, madame, after sitting up with her all night." She hadn't said so, but this woman was the sort that didn't trust a night nurse.

After the doctor had finished his daily poking and probing of Elinor, Buzz returned to the bedside. Elinor lay in a cream lace nightdress against silk pillows.

"He says you'll soon be as fit as a fiddle," Buzz said. "I'm getting a physiotherapist so you'll get proper exercise."

"But I'm too weak. And I can't move or talk properly," Elinor protested, her voice still slurred.

"A physio will soon get you on your feet, Nell . . ."

"But will I ever talk properly again? My left cheek feels frozen, as if I've had a dentist's injection."

"You'll talk properly soon enough—then the Lord help us."

Elinor's anxiety dissolved, and she relaxed. Buzz was so reassuring, so comforting. The two women had shared some tough times when they were young. Buzz knew Elinor's faults and didn't care; Buzz would never reveal her secrets.

"What exactly does Buzz *do?*" people sometimes asked. Supposedly a secretary, Buzz never typed if she could avoid it, and whatever shorthand she may have known was long forgotten.

"She protects me," Elinor would say with a little laugh.

"But why do you let a secretary speak to you in that offhand way? Why do you let her criticize you? Why do you put up with her?"

Elinor would firmly close the subject by answering, "We've been together a long time. You wouldn't understand."

Although outsiders never understood their relationship, it was clear enough to the two women: Elinor was Buzz's friend and her boss; Buzz was Elinor's secretary but not her slave. Elinor was glad to have forgotten what life was like without Buzz, this odd woman who had become a vital part of her existence.

They had met long ago, during the First World War, on a drizzling autumn day in 1918. That day was to have terrible consequences for Buzz, although to eighteen-year-old Elinor it had been just another of those endless, stinking, exhausting everyday scenes in a casualty clearing station near the front line.

On that November evening, an ambulance convoy had just arrived at casualty reception. Gray-blanketed stretchers were everywhere, many on the floor. The filthy, exhausted men on the stretchers wore muddy, torn khaki; their bandages were dirty and bloodstained.

"Hey, Nurse!" Hearing the high-pitched nasal voice, Elinor turned. She realized, to her surprise, that the lanky ambulance driver with dark cropped hair was a woman.

"I've just driven in a diphtheria case," the driver said. "He's in a bad way. Should be seen immediately. He's also got a smashed left patella and a fracture of the left tibia. Get a surgeon, will you?"

A tired young surgeon took one look at the ginger-haired soldier struggling to breathe and said, "Tracheotomy. Get him on the table fast, Nurse. No time to scrub up." He gestured to the small side room, which contained an emergency operating table.

Lying on the table, the young patient gasped for breath as the membrane in his throat started to strangle him.

The surgeon nodded at Elinor. "You—take his head!" Then he

turned to the ambulance driver. "Do you think you can hold him down?"

She nodded.

As Elinor held the injured man's head firmly to the sandbag pillow, the weary surgeon lifted a sharp scalpel from the tray on the trolley. Elinor saw his hand shake.

The surgeon glanced at Elinor and hesitated. If he accidentally slit the jugular vein, the patient would die.

Elinor prayed silently. "Please God, let him get it right."

The doctor still hesitated, his shaking right hand revealing his exhaustion.

The patient's gasps changed to a gurgle. Elinor thought, If he doesn't cut now, this lad is going to die anyway.

The surgeon leaned over the ginger head and with the scalpel made a swift incision.

Immediately a crimson stream flowed from the patient's neck.

Elinor kept her eyes on the dying man because she did not want to look at the surgeon. Wearily he said, "Clean up, Nurse, and move him out of here. I'd better get back."

After the surgeon had left, Elinor looked at the lanky girl; her face was white as her dark eyes stared down at the young man who had just died.

"Did you know him?" Elinor asked gently.

Slowly, with chattering teeth, the girl said, "We was going to be married, Ginger and me."

Later, in Elinor's Nissen hut, the women shared a tin mug of milkless cocoa. Elinor knew that the white-faced girl, who had not yet shed a tear, must be suffering from shock: she was moving in a daze but chattering as though nothing out of the ordinary had happened.

"Poor Ginger was one of my stretcher-bearers. They'll let his mother think he died a hero's death for King and country, not that he tripped over someone's boot in a trench, fell off the duckboard, was accidentally shot in the knee by some trigger-happy idiot, then left out in the open too long, and afterward killed by a mistake."

"The surgeon's only human. We all make mistakes," Elinor said wearily. "I know I do."

The girl sighed. "This whole ruddy war's a mistake."

"What's your name?" Elinor asked.

"Buzz Mann."

"That sounds more American than English."

"You're right. I was christened Doris. Some doughboys gave me the nickname 'cause I always seem to be the first one in the know. Simply a matter of keeping your ears open and talking to the walking wounded before they're handed over to you nurses to sort out the mess. Cor, what a rotten job you nurses have!"

"Your job doesn't look so hot to me."

"I was ruddy lucky to get accepted as an ambulance driver," Buzz said. "Generally, the War Office don't take working-class girls from Tooting; they take nice gels with private means, because we're all volunteers and practically unpaid."

"Then how did you wangle it?" Elinor asked.

"I was working as a housemaid in Wimbledon—nice family, indoor staff of nine—and our Miss Ruth was determined to volunteer. So the mistress made me go along as well. I was supposed to look after Miss Ruth. There wasn't half a bit of string-pulling, I can tell you! Of course, I had to say I was twenty-three, not eighteen. Miss Ruth wasn't a bad sort but she wasn't used to this sort of life. Before we'd been here three weeks, she got pneumonia with complications, nearly died, and had to be sent back to Blighty. The commandant puts up with my lack of breeding—as I heard her call it—because I understand how an engine works, and there ain't many ladies as does."

After that, the two young women met often in Elinor's hut. Elinor was intrigued by Buzz's brusque attitude, her lack of concern over what other people thought of her, her contempt for anyone in command—and her carefully hidden warmth and kindness.

Just as she had comforted Buzz when Ginger died, Elinor was comforted, two months later, by Buzz, who found her crying quietly on her narrow, hard bed in the Nissen hut.

"What's up?" Buzz asked.

Without a word, Elinor handed her the letter.

"Dear Nell," Buzz read. "This is a hard thing to tell you but your dear mother passed away. She been ill six month with tubercerloosis but would not let me write you. Last Sunday about five she quietly slipt away and we buried her Wensday. I nursed her well as I could. She had Doc Mackenzie and drugs but it was too late. On Saturday she says to me, Listen Marius, I feel better. It does not matter I am thin. You can fatten me like a Christmas goose now I am healthy again. She had a decent buriel, with Casket, Hurse and Grave at St Mary to the far left of the porch. My poor girl was in her wedding dress she was all skin and bone. She was very dear to me although I did not tell her often. Your grieving father Marius F Dove."

Eventually Elinor gulped, "At least this means I'll never have to see *him* again."

•   •   •

Buzz and Elinor had now been close friends for forty-seven years, and so far as Elinor was concerned, Buzz had only one failing: she had never liked Billy.

Once again Elinor turned her head to look at the photograph of Billy beside her bed. She thought back to the humiliation she had suffered from his relatives' disdain, though in the end it had been she who restored the fortune of Billy's family. Elinor was now the *star*— more socially acceptable than they had ever been. And she certainly wouldn't make the same financial mistake that *they* had.

Now, in the warmth of the Riviera, within the splendor of her castle, Elinor looked up at Buzz and said in a faint but determined voice, "I *must* be sure that those girls are safe for life. . . . I want them to have a happy life, with no burdens. . . . I want them to have what you and I missed: more time—time to enjoy life, time to think. More time for their children than I had for Edward."

Buzz said soothingly, "You did the best you could at the time, Nell, and that's as much as any person can be expected to do. Maybe it was lucky you only had one kid." Buzz knew better than to express her opinion on why this was so.

Elinor whispered, "I want to see Adam *now.*"

"I'll not have you talk business when you're barely able to talk at all," Buzz said. "We'll wait till you beat me at Scrabble." Before Elinor's stroke, they had played one game a day, always at five o'clock. At the end of the previous year, the score had been Elinor 36 games, Buzz 329.

"Buzz, this is urgent. I haven't made a will."

Buzz turned to the bed. "That's not *urgent*, you old fool. Important, but not urgent. You'll just have to wait! I'm not letting that Adam in before the doctor okays it, and that's flat! I'm off to make you a dish of mashed bananas and cream. You can eat it with a teaspoon. *I* know what you like, Nell."

Elinor smiled. She had spent her life looking after other people and now it felt strange, but pleasant, to lie with her eyes closed while other people glided around her, murmuring and making the decisions for her.

MONDAY, 19 JULY 1965

Two weeks later, seated on one of the silver-gray sofas in front of Elinor's bedroom fireplace, Adam quickly sorted out his papers, then placed them on the low table before him. Buzz had warned him that he had only a few minutes.

Elinor's voice was still weak and she remained able to talk only out of the right side of her mouth. "I'm sorry I didn't do this earlier, Adam," she said.

"There's no hurry." The lawyer had been well briefed by Buzz. "We might as well settle it now, though, if you feel up to it."

With difficulty, Elinor lifted her head. "Put those papers down, Adam. Come and sit by me."

As Adam moved to the bedside, he glanced toward the photographs clustered on Elinor's table. One was a group photo of World War I pilots, their faces flushed with victory. He found it sad that one of those jaunty, carefree young men had turned into his careful, punctual father—a pillar of the local community, respected in the legal world; a man who had never been allowed by his wife to forget that he had married the boss's daughter and had better live up to it. He had done so, concealing his feelings, hiding them behind a carefully organized life in a comfortable country mansion not far from London.

The sight of frail Elinor, so recently close to death, nearly caused Adam to momentarily lose his composure. Her fragility, her pale face, the smell of the sick room, stirred his sense of loss. His father had died, very slowly, from lung cancer. What Adam most regretted losing was what he had never had: the father-and-son companionship that other chaps casually enjoyed. Of course, there had been little chance of spending time with his old man when Adam was a child and confined to the nursery by a mother who had preferred bridge to motherhood. Adam also wished that when he was growing up, he'd been more understanding of his father's behavior. The old man hadn't really been as harsh and demanding as he seemed. Adam grew to understand that he'd only wanted his elder son to get the best out of life. And when Adam was articled to the family law firm, he knew, Dad had been careful to have nothing to do with him in the office because he hadn't wanted to appear to favor him over the other clerks. Adam had always known that was the reason, but it had hurt at the time.

Elinor noticed Adam's glance at the photograph and whispered, "I still miss your dear father. Joe looked after my affairs so well, especially after Billy died."

Adam smiled reassuringly. "I'm here to help you, just as Father would have done. Simply tell me what you want and I'll arrange it. I have a list of your assets here. Perhaps you would like to tell me which people you might . . . want to have something . . . at some time in the future, and then I'll draw up a . . . document for you to consider."

Noting Elinor's silence, Adam wondered if her mind worked more slowly now. He said, "Do you want to leave any money to your family in America?"

She reflected briefly on her brother, and again considered whether he might still be alive, with children of his own. She remembered the jealousy she had felt at her father's obvious love for Paul, and her pain because of his lack of interest in her. She had always felt guilty for being a girl and therefore not strong enough to carry out the perennial chores on the farm in Minnesota. Her childhood had been spent in terror of her father's rages and his ability to reduce her to a cowering, bewildered creature. How she had dreaded his anger, which always seemed to be directed at her. How she had hoped for—just once—some sign that he loved her; instead, the only love she ever felt came from her mother, a sad, broken creature. Elinor remembered her relief at finally breaking away from her family and their hold on her.

She shook her head slowly. "No. They never did anything for me. And I haven't heard from them since 1932, when my brother had to sell the farm. I inherited nothing and I owe him nothing. So I think the simplest thing would be to divide everything between the three girls and Buzz . . ."

Adam looked worried. "The simplest thing is not always the wisest," he said gently. "The girls must be protected from possible exploitation, embezzlement, and theft. You've always protected those three lucky sisters from harsh reality, from the jungle of life." He hesitated. "Perhaps they should now also be protected from . . . themselves . . . unless you truly believe that they will always look after the money carefully and prudently, taking no risks and resisting the temptation of extravagance."

Elinor considered Adam's words of caution. She didn't care to think of her girls as wasteful, but there were warning signs. Fleetingly she thought back to Annabel's eighteenth birthday, when, exuberantly, the girl had jumped into the terrace fountain and ruined her pink Hartnell ball gown. Miranda clearly took dangerous risks in an already high-risk business, and she seemed to think nothing of hiring a helicopter, at heaven knows what cost, simply to travel to London for a few hours. Why did Miranda waste money in this way?

Adam said, "Of course I know that Clare, as the eldest, has always been very responsible, but I am concerned lest she be persuaded to be, shall we say, overcharitable? Clare seems to think that it's her responsibility to look after the entire world."

Elinor understood that Adam was warning her that her hard-earned fortune might well go down the drain with amazing speed.

"The girls must be prepared," Adam went on, "to spend a considerable amount of time doing their financial homework and discussing their business affairs with stockbrokers, accountants, lawyers, and other professional advisers."

Elinor considered what he had said. "Well, you already look after Miranda's affairs, don't you, Adam? And the other two have husbands to handle that sort of thing."

Adam looked slightly embarrassed. "I feel I should perhaps play devil's advocate and point out—do forgive me—that Clare's husband is a film producer: some of his films have been successful—but not all of them. I'm sure that, should he persuade Clare to invest your money in his movies, he would *expect* them to be successful . . . but such risky investment can be hugely expensive, as well as dangerous."

Inwardly Elinor shuddered though her rigid body stayed still.

Adam continued, "And there is one other thing: the divorce rate is rapidly increasing. There now is one divorce to every three marriages in Britain, and I believe the rate is even higher in America. Of course, we all hope that they will both stay happily married, but Clare's husband has been married twice before, and as a lawyer, I can tell you that it is a rare husband who will put his wife's financial interests before his own in the event of . . . such a sad event." He paused briefly to let Elinor consider.

"Clare and Annabel are both charming and delightful young women, but are you completely confident that they have the financial acumen to handle a fortune—especially as they have no training or experience in such matters? In particular, do you think that Annabel would be willing . . . or capable?" Annabel was everybody's favorite sister, but she was also known as the family scatter-brain—a not-too-bright beauty with a sunny temperament.

After a few moments of silence, Adam added, "And I can't help wondering, should Annabel ever be on her own, whether she would not be easy prey for fraudsters or . . . the sort of men who, frankly, *stalk* women with money."

Elinor spoke in a whisper. "Please tell me what to do, Adam. You always know best."

So Adam explained the advantages of setting up a family trust, concluding, "Of course, a main advantage would be that the trustees—men of impeccable reputation—would relieve the girls of all responsibility, make all business decisions, and operate the trust smoothly, to your satisfaction, before . . . during your lifetime."

After a thoughtful silence, Elinor whispered, "A *very* sensible idea. The Dove Trust. Why didn't you suggest it before now, Adam?"

"You preferred me not to discuss your . . . these matters," Adam reminded her.

"Whom would you appoint as trustees?" Elinor asked.

Briskly Adam replied, "I do *not* advise a bank, no matter how respectable. They are in business to make money for themselves." He knew that the aim of a bank would be to get as much money as was possible and legal out of the trust account. This might well erode the money—a small percentage here, another there—by as much as five percent a year; if so, within twenty years, Elinor's fortune would belong to the bank. Adam cautioned especially against Swiss banks. "They are the best publicists and the worst extortionists. That's why they put up such an impressive facade of you-can-trust-us reassurance, with expensive writing paper and old-fashioned business offices meant to look as if they have been doing respectable and reliable business for hundreds of years."

"Then whom *do* you advise?"

"You need reliable, responsible professionals whom you can confidently expect to keep a careful eye on all the affairs of the Dove Trust. The trust will hold all your major assets, although, of course, you will also need to make a will for minor things, such as the disposal of personal effects.

"The trust will then administer the estate," Adam went on, "and annually consider whether to apportion any of the trust income to the beneficiaries named by you, and if so, how much."

"How much does a trust cost to run?" Elinor whispered. Adam's well-intentioned warnings had enervated her.

"The cost of setting it up would be about a thousand pounds, perhaps a little more, if property, such as the chateau, is involved. The yearly charge might be half a percent of the trust value. The trustees could continue to work with your present bank, stockbroker, and other advisers."

"Would STG continue to be my lawyers?"

"Of course. In fact, should you wish, our firm could act as trustees."

Buzz's head appeared around the door. "Two minutes more, Adam." Then she saw Elinor's pale face and said, "No, you'd better leave *now.*"

"Two more minutes." Adam smiled gravely at Buzz, who hesitated, nodded, then shut the door.

Adam looked at Elinor thoughtfully over the top of his horn-rimmed spectacles. "That reminds me. In my judgment, it would be best not to include Buzz in the trust. She can be looked after by them—exactly as you wish, in the same way as the girls—but for many reasons, in our experience—the experience of Swithin, Timmins and Grant—it is simplest to confine a family trust to family members only. And there are other legal reasons that I won't bother you with."

"Are you *sure* Buzz will be properly looked after?" Elinor inquired anxiously.

"I'm absolutely certain of that." Adam shuffled his papers into order and stood up.

"How long does it take to set up?"

Immediately Adam understood the implications of Elinor's question. He said reassuringly, "It could be done in two weeks, but in an emergency—overnight."

"Better do it as fast as possible," Elinor murmured, adding, "I'd like you to explain everything to Buzz and the girls as soon as possible."

"I'm here to do whatever you wish," Adam reassured her. "I'm happy to explain your wishes to Buzz and the girls . . . but only when your doctor allows such a meeting. We mustn't tire you, Elinor."

That afternoon, all of them sitting on prim Directoire chairs arranged around Elinor's sumptuous bed, Adam could see that the girls felt uneasy, as if they had suddenly realized that this was a formal occasion; something important was about to happen.

Buzz clucked a bit to ease the atmosphere. "Them shorts you're wearing don't leave much to the imagination," she said to Clare, who wore white tennis clothes. "Why didn't you put on something pretty for your gran, like Annabel?" Annabel had changed from her swimsuit into a bluebell silk dress.

"Don't nag, Buzz." Miranda, in pink slacks and matching blouse, knew that she had passed the decency test. "Let's start this meeting, Adam."

Gravely Adam said, "Your grandmother has decided to establish a family trust, for the benefit of you, her granddaughters." In a carefully neutral voice, he then explained Elinor's plan and stated the amount of money involved.

"Just under nine million pounds!" Miranda gasped.

Annabel's mouth stayed half open. "Heavens, that's . . . that's about twenty-seven million dollars!"

Clare spoke hesitantly. "That's much too much money for just one person . . . or one family." Detecting a certain frostiness from her grandmother's direction, she added, "I mean *nobody* should have such a huge sum when half the world is starving."

Adam saw that Clare was behaving exactly as he had expected: ever the romantic idealist and liberal. Priding herself on her honesty, she would end up a loser. Starting now.

"How does a trust work?" Buzz asked warily.

"It's a bit like setting up a company, but one run by trustees instead of directors," Adam explained. "To check that the trustees do their job properly, a trust protector is appointed, to act as a sort of policeman. The trust is funded by the person who sets it up—in this case,

Elinor—and will be run for the benefit of the beneficiaries named by Elinor—in this case, her descendants. In case," Adam added, "at some future point, there should be no descendants, a final beneficiary should be named, although that might not be relevant for a couple of hundred years."

Elinor liked the idea of her trust continuing for hundreds of years, producing yearly dividends.

"But if Elinor isn't a beneficiary, will she have any future control over the trust possessions?" Clare asked.

"What about Buzz? *She* isn't a descendant of Elinor O'Dare," Annabel said.

Adam ignored that for the moment and said, "The trust will always consider Elinor's wishes in every respect. She can put *all* her requests in writing to the trust."

"And must the trustees obey her?" Miranda asked.

"The trustees use their own judgment, as do a board of directors, and should always act in the best interest of the beneficiaries."

"Sounds a bit complicated—a bit unusual—ain't it?" Buzz said suspiciously.

"A trust situation is not unusual among the wealthy," Adam explained. "To avoid death duties and bad money management, Lord X makes over his fortune to his children, on the understanding that they will provide for him until he dies."

"What if the kids don't see it that way?" Buzz asked. "What if the kids change their minds, after Lord X has signed over all his worldly wealth?"

"If the children aren't trustworthy, then of course you wouldn't consider such a trust." Adam's voice was carefully civil.

Buzz said, "If Elinor gives everything she owns to this here trust, then what does *she* live on?"

"The trust can provide Elinor with a salary for the work she does, which will provide ample money, after tax, for her to live on."

Miranda concealed her exasperation. Couldn't Buzz see that the reason for a trust was that Elinor was almost certainly dying?

"And who will these all-powerful trustees be?" Clare asked.

"Elinor's lawyers have been asked to provide trustees," Adam said. "Elinor knows that STG are capable and reliable, and she doesn't want to deal with people she doesn't know. So I propose to ask our Bermuda office to set it up. Offshore trusts are not liable to alteration by changing laws."

"You mentioned a protector. Who will that be?" Miranda inquired.

"Probably Paul Littlejohn, who now works in our Bermuda office. He is familiar with Elinor's affairs."

Buzz frowned, looked at Elinor's white face, bit her lip, started to speak, then clearly thought better of it and stayed silent.

Relieved that the meeting seemed to be finished, Elinor asked in a shaky voice, "So it's settled then?"

Clare said uncertainly, "Can we talk a little more? Because I don't *like* this idea. If Gran wants to leave us some money, why can't she just do that? Why complicate the situation?"

"Adam knows best," Elinor told her firmly. "Don't be difficult, Clare."

"I think I'm old enough to be in charge of my own financial affairs," Clare protested.

"There's no proof of that," Miranda said sharply. "You've never had *any* business experience."

"I'm confident that I can manage my own." Clare was indignant now. "I'm a married woman with a child. Surely that's proof of my responsibility. Why do I need to be nannied by lawyers?"

Elinor said faintly, "Adam has gone to a great deal of trouble to organize this, and Adam knows what's best for us, darling."

"*Why* does Adam know what's best for me?" Clare asked in an exasperated tone.

"Because Adam's a professional man," Elinor whispered. "He's a qualified lawyer with years of legal experience. That's why."

"Gran, all my life you've told me that some man in a dark suit knows best," Clare said. "It started when we were little girls, with Daddy Billy. 'Daddy knows best' was what you always said. But we all knew—even then—that he didn't. I don't want to find myself in *another* nursery situation, being told that Daddy knows best—only this time Daddy is some lawyer that I've never met, some faceless man who's sitting in the middle of the Atlantic."

"Now, Clare, no criticism of Daddy Billy," Buzz warned. She hated this name Billy O'Dare had given himself, she suspected because he couldn't bear to think of himself as old enough to be a grandfather.

"Sorry. I didn't mean to criticize Daddy Billy," Clare said quickly, but she knew that this was an important conversation with her grandmother, so she leaned toward Elinor and said, "I'm only trying to be truthful, Gran. *I don't like this idea!*"

"Adam's gone to all this trouble . . ." Elinor repeated faintly.

"But why didn't you discuss the idea with us beforehand, if we're to be the beneficiaries?" Clare protested.

"I told you. Because Adam knows best, dear. He's an expert. I pay him to think about these things carefully and decide, and it would be foolish not to take his advice."

"Miranda doesn't treat Adam with such deference," Clare pointed out. She couldn't understand why her grandmother had never had confidence in her own decision making, had never trusted her own instincts and judgment.

"Clare," Elinor said, "please show a little more respect for Adam! I am *so* sorry, Adam."

"I wish you'd stop treating us like children," Clare cried. "You sound just like you did when we were little. Whenever we questioned some decision, you always said, 'Because Daddy knows best'! It wasn't a logical answer then, and it still isn't. Can't you see that, Gran? *Why* do you always say, 'Because Adam knows best'?"

"Because he does," Elinor said firmly.

"You've always taken some man's advice, and you've always managed to produce some good reason for doing so." Clare wondered whether this was her grandmother's way of trying to avoid final responsibility for her actions.

"Now, now, Clare," Buzz said reprovingly. "You ain't writing *Wuthering Heights.*" This was a gentle family joke, used when Elinor became overdramatic.

Equally anxious to defuse the situation, Annabel—the family peacemaker—spoke up. "I'd also like to ask a question. Could this trust set up awards, bursaries, things like that?" Annabel, who remembered Elinor's beaming pride when the University of Minneapolis asked her to donate her manuscripts to their library, continued. "For instance, could the trust use some of this money to set up an annual Elinor Dove prize—a literary award on a popular level—a really big award that couldn't be ignored by reviewers who sneer at popular fiction? And how about an Elinor Dove traveling scholarship for the most promising first novel of the year, and a few more similar things that would impress the literary world?"

Clare burst out, "You *can't* be serious, Annabel! Anything like that would make the literary world see Gran as an even bigger—"

Buzz stood up. "That's enough, Clare! If you can't behave, you'd better leave."

"Am I being told to leave the room like a disobedient child?" Clare retorted.

"That's about it," Buzz said levelly. Clare's the one that's most like Elinor, she thought to herself. Got that same passionate, extra stubborn, extra strong, and willful nature.

Nobody spoke. Everyone watched Elinor.

In the stormy silence, Elinor croaked, "If you are so dismissive of my work, my money, my advisers and their plan for the future, then perhaps you would prefer not to participate in it, Clare. You need not be named as a trust beneficiary."

"That's okay by me!" Clare's lips trembled. She was damned if she was going to be manipulated like this. And she certainly wasn't going to cry in front of Adam.

Adam said reprovingly, "I think you had better apologize to your grandmother, Clare."

Clare stood up and silently left the room.

Adam coughed. "Elinor, do you wish Clare included in the trust?"

"Of course," both sisters said in unison.

Elinor said crossly, "*I* don't want Clare put in the trust as a beneficiary until she has apologized to me." Her voice was clear and firm.

"You *can't* leave Clare out!" Annabel protested.

"You *must* put her in!" insisted Miranda.

Adam looked embarrassed. "I suppose, formally, I . . . er . . . ought to protest on my client's behalf at this attempt at coercion," he said lamely.

"Oh, shut up, Adam," Buzz said.

Everyone present knew that Elinor was generous and indulgent, except when she thought she was being taken for granted or taken for a ride. Then she could be as tough as nails. At that point, if criticized or made in any way to feel guilty or vulnerable, Elinor became incredibly stubborn.

Buzz said, "Elinor, I'm sure it bothers you that Clare would prefer you wrote that kitchen sink stuff about poor people with miserable lives. I know she criticized your books. But you don't want to hurt Clare in this way." Buzz's last sentence was almost an order.

"Clare hurt *me*," Elinor responded stubbornly, a theatrical note in her shaky voice. Another page from *Wuthering Heights*, they all noticed.

Sourly Buzz said, "I suppose you'd like the butler to hand Clare a tourist-class ticket back to Los Angeles."

"That's enough, Buzz." Elinor leaned back limply against the pile of pillows.

"Elinor, you're just being stubborn." Buzz spoke crossly now. "What you don't like in Clare is what she's inherited from you!" The kitchen timer in Buzz's pocket blared, and she stood up. "Time's up," she said. "Outside, the lot of you! In double-quick time!"

"I have just one further thing to say, to Adam—alone." Elinor's voice was faint.

After the door closed and Adam and Elinor were alone, she said slowly, "You'd better get this trust set up as fast as possible, dear boy. A little later, we can add Clare's name to the beneficiaries."

"No," Adam said, "the trust would be irrevocable in that respect."

"Well, go down to the pool and ask Clare to apologize." Elinor's voice trembled with exhaustion now. "Ask her nicely. Come straight back and tell me what she says. I hope I've already made it clear that I won't be intimidated and I won't be bullied. I'm sure she'll be a sensible girl. And then everything will be neatly settled." She gave a deep sigh of relief. "Hurry," she whispered.

Adam sauntered to the swimming pool and squatted on his haunches by the pool. "Your grandmother wants an unconditional apology from you for what you said about her books, her money, and her advisers. She wants it immediately, and I think you should know that she intends to punish you severely should you not do this."

Clare looked up, astonished. She stood in the water and smoothed back her wet hair. "I'm a married woman, Adam, not a child who can be stood in the corner until it gives in. I won't respond to threats. I believe that what I said was true and I see no reason to retract any of it."

"So you won't apologize?"

"Certainly not."

Elinor looked up, cheerfully expectant, as Adam entered her bedroom. Her expression changed when she saw his perplexed face.

"I'm sorry," Adam said, "but Clare refuses to apologize. I put the matter to her fairly forcibly, knowing . . . the possible consequences."

Elinor sighed. "What exactly did Clare say?"

"She said, 'Certainly not.' "

Adam broke the silence that had fallen between them. "Do you wish Clare to . . . er . . . be included in the trust?"

Elinor's voice sounded very weary. "Of *course* I want Clare included in the trust. But please don't tell her—not until she has come around. You would think she could put aside her stubbornness at a time like this."

Adam glanced warily at Elinor and said nothing.

Through the window of her ground-floor office, Buzz could clearly hear angry voices at the swimming pool, where Miranda and Annabel had joined their sister.

Sadly Buzz thought, Hardly a cross word among them since they were children—and now listen! And when their grandmother is on her deathbed! She knew that because the sisters were so close, they knew exactly where to jab at each other's sensitive spots. They're exactly the same as they were eighteen years ago, she thought, when she first went to live with Elinor. But now, instead of cheerfully bickering over hair ribbons or stolen pencils, they were quarreling over a fortune.

At the side of the pool, Clare said crossly, "Of all the unctuous, hypocritical little creeps, you two are the worst! I never *realized* that your devotion to literature was so great, Annabel. Scholarships, prizes, and bursaries to perpetuate her life's work, indeed!"

"Well, why not!" Annabel cried. "It's *her* money! I wanted to cheer her up, after you'd been such a bitch."

"Well, why *not?*" Clare yelled. "Because Gran's life's work has probably done more damage than she will *ever* realize!"

Her sisters groaned theatrically: together, they mimicked Clare's high, soft voice: "Those sentimental novels give women readers a romantic, unrealistic, and dangerous view of life."

"Well, they do," Clare said defensively. "All those women readers have been taught to believe in happy endings. If they're going through a tough period of life, they simply tell themselves that they're in the middle of chapter five, but the hero will be waiting, to put things right, in chapter seven. They've been indoctrinated to be passive, to put up with their lives, not to try and change them."

"What's so terrible about escapist literature?" Annabel demanded. "Most women read it—and why not? *I* do."

"Gran's books sell by the million," Miranda said, "so obviously a great many people enjoy them."

"Clare, why not check out your own reality," Annabel suggested, "and stop yelling at *us* because of *your* domestic problems."

"That's probably why she's in such a foul mood," Miranda continued. "I bet they've had a falling out, and she's temporarily disenchanted. No longer believes in romance or true love."

"True love died out with pterodactyls," Clare said curtly.

"No it didn't. But I'd like to know where to find it," Miranda mused.

"That wonderful vibration between the two of you," Annabel said dreamily. "That stars-in-your-heart feeling, when you don't need words to communicate . . ."

"I've never met a man who knew what I was thinking," said Miranda, "and if there's no need to communicate, how come you telephone New York so often? At Gran's expense."

Exasperated, Clare said, "I really don't understand how you two can chat so flippantly about any form of love or communication after that hypocritical scene you just played. I was disgusted by your calculating flattery!"

"And I was disgusted by your squeaky self-righteousness!" Miranda snapped.

"At least I didn't suddenly turn into a lover of literature, like Annabel!"

"I simply wanted to make her *happy!*" Annabel shouted. "After *you* had upset her."

"You know I can't stand her Daddy-knows-best line," Clare said.

"Who cares what *you* think, when she's dying, you self-righteous little prig!" Miranda said angrily.

Clare burst into tears and ran indoors. Stumbling to her bedroom, she wondered, as she had so many times, how Miranda could, with so few words, goad her to feel such violence and passion. Once again Miranda had reduced her to a point where she felt as though she were naked and vulnerable, being mercilessly poked by an electric cattle prod.

The pool area was silent.

Buzz sighed. She left her office and returned to Elinor's bedroom: Buzz liked to appear there unexpectedly, to make sure that when her back was turned, the nurse wasn't slack.

White and exhausted, Elinor lay against the pillows; one thin hand upon the sheet clutched the silver-framed photograph of Billy as a young flier. She looked up at Buzz, and her face was frightened as she whispered, "I'll soon see him again."

"Rubbish. I'll have you back on your feet in no time," Buzz said firmly.

"You don't understand about Billy, Buzz. You never understood."

"I understand that Billy owed everything to you."

"Oh no, Buzz, I owed everything to Billy," Elinor whispered dreamily. "He was the only man for me—right from the beginning . . ."

Chapter · 3

On night duty in the casualty clearing station at La Chapelle in northern France, eighteen-year-old Nurse Elinor Dove was in love and that, for the moment, was all that truly mattered. It was the first time she had experienced the intoxicating effect.

After that first night, when Billy had kissed her hand, Elinor blushed whenever she had to go near bed 17; if he called for her, she tried to avoid touching him. Her nervousness seemed to amuse him, and the rest of the ward.

One morning, just before she went off duty, Nurse Dove, exhausted, was wearily scrubbing up the carnage from the previous day's many operations. Alone in the sink room, she suddenly heard a tapping sound approaching from behind. She turned to see Flight Commander O'Dare, on rubber-tipped crutches, swing himself through the door. Under his aquamarine gaze, Elinor felt an all-too-familiar blush. Why didn't this fellow get back into his bed if he felt ill? Why did he look at her so steadily, with that hint of a smile? Why did he make her feel so warm and embarrassed and vulnerable? And why did she feel guilty?

He *knew* he was making her blush.

"Why are you out of bed?" she asked, feigning irritation.

He grinned. "You know I might be transferred soon," he said as he moved toward her. Suddenly one of his crutches slipped on the wet tiles and he lost his balance, crashing to the floor.

Nurse Dove dashed to her patient. "*Don't move!* Let me help you!"

Carefully she turned him on his back, then gently felt his neck. "Can you move your head to the left? . . . Now to the right . . . That's fine."

Billy O'Dare opened his aquamarine eyes, and in them, Nurse Dove saw not pain but determination. Without speaking, he gripped her upper arms, pulling her down on his chest. For a moment, he stared into her eyes, mesmerizing her. Then silently he pulled her closer and fastened his warm mouth upon hers. Once again she was overwhelmed by the seductive, forbidden smell of him.

Lying on top of him, feeling his body beneath her, Elinor started to tremble: an odd, compulsively strong urge seemed to knock all the sense from her head. Her eyes were closed. She felt as if she were pleasantly drowning in warm water. Then she felt the tip of his tongue part her lips and gently explore her unresisting mouth as his hand reached beneath her nurse's headdress to the thick fair hair coiled in a bun at the nape of her neck. Billy gently stroked the back of her neck, and every time he did so, a shiver ran down her spine. Through her navy serge uniform, she felt his knowing hand on her breast, his gentle touch warming her heart.

Elinor was oblivious of the ward noises around her. As if of its own volition, her body arched against Billy O'Dare. His arms enfolded and imprisoned her. He kissed her harshly, bruising her lips against his. His hand slid downward to press her buttocks against him, and she felt his hard body against hers.

She stiffened in alarm.

Between kisses, Billy murmured soothing words: ". . . lovely creature . . . wanted you the moment I saw you . . . lovely eyes . . . love . . . love . . . *love.*" As he kissed her, one calculating hand slowly raised her skirt and groped beneath it.

Nurse Dove sharply returned to reality. Frantically she fought against his insistent strong hands. All the sensuous excitement evaporated, turned off as if by a switch. She knew what happened to girls who let a fellow go too far, and it wasn't going to happen to her.

Billy lay on the floor looking up at her, his eyes imploring. "I'm sorry! But you're so lovely, so special," he whispered.

Elinor scowled at him again, her pale green eyes flashing with indignation.

"You don't understand how a fellow feels," Billy said reproachfully. "Besides, Nurse Dove, I really *do* love you."

Two weeks later, somewhat to his surprise, Flight Commander William O'Dare asked Nurse Elinor Dove to marry him.

To Elinor's dismay, Buzz did not share her joy at Billy's proposal.

Sitting on Elinor's bed in the Nissen hut, Buzz eventually said, "*You* know the dangers of wartime marriages, Nell. There are so few women out here . . . their attractions are magnified . . . and all the men fall for them. Even my boot-faced commandant has a string of beaux. Things get out of perspective—on both sides." She inhaled cigarette smoke. "I admit Billy's a good looker. Them blue eyes and that tangle of fair hair. I agree he's got plenty of lanky, twinkle-eyed Irish charm. But what do you *know* about him, Nell? You know nothing, except he's six foot tall, good-looking and could charm the bloomers off practically anyone. Why get married so fast? They say the war's nearly over, so Billy's unlikely to get killed. There's no hurry—or so you tell me!"

"What a wet blanket *you* are!" Elinor said crossly.

"What a romantic, headstrong idiot *you* are," Buzz retorted. "You know *nothing* about his family. What's Billy going to do in peacetime? What will you live on? Suppose he turns out to be a lazy layabout or a rotter? What if he turns out to be tricking you?"

"Tricking me?" Elinor exclaimed indignantly. "Why would Billy want to trick me? I haven't got a bean!"

"I don't *know*," Buzz worried. "I just think he's too good to be true. If he's such a good bet, then why not wait until you've met his family?"

"I've had enough of death and depression, and so has he! I want some *life,* and he's offering it to me."

Eighteen-year-old Elinor and her twenty-five-year-old bridegroom were married by a French Catholic priest in a church (most of which was still standing) five miles from the hospital at La Chapelle. Elinor wore her best cream silk blouse and a borrowed burgundy wool skirt. The marriage witnesses were Billy's observer, Joe Grant, and Buzz, who wore a pink blouse and an air of suspicion.

The newlyweds were given official permission to spend three nights in the *estaminet* at La Chapelle. After a wedding meal of red wine, rabbit casserole, and a blackberry tart that cost Billy a fortune in cigarettes, he led Elinor upstairs.

The bedroom, papered in bronze chrysanthemums, contained only a few sticks of furniture; by the light of a flickering candle, Elinor saw a large feather bed. She looked away from it, partly out of embarrassment, partly out of fear, and stood in the middle of the room, still, stiff, and silent.

Billy grinned at his bride, opened a second bottle of wine, and unbuttoned his tunic.

Elinor was hypnotically aware of Billy's musky smell and the light blue flash of his eyes as he lifted her in his arms. Without speaking, he carried her to the bed and laid her on the quilt. He pushed her skirts up, then slowly slipped off her shoes. Next he removed her blue satin garters and peeled silk stockings from her pale legs.

He kissed her bare feet, sliding his tongue between her toes, and licked them. His kisses crept up her plump thighs.

Elinor lay rigid with embarrassment.

Billy untied the drawstring of her bloomers and felt below; softly he stroked her navel, then moved downward. Slowly he pulled down the bloomers, until Elinor's white belly and blond hair were revealed to him.

Impeded above her waist by a wrinkled mess of clothing, Elinor felt trapped and alarmed. She clamped her eyes shut as her entire body blushed with shame. Even though Billy was moving slowly, it all seemed to be happening so fast.

Carefully, caressingly, Billy unbuttoned her blouse, then unbuckled the belt from her narrow waist and removed her skirt. He pulled the string of her underskirt and lifted off her chemise. When, finally she was completely undressed. Billy paused to touch her breasts and lightly pinch her nipples, just enough to excite her.

Still Elinor kept her eyes shut. Had they been open, she would have seen Billy undress like an eight-armed Indian god, hurling his clothes to the floor.

Billy was fascinated by the whiteness of Elinor's skin as she lay naked in the soft, golden candlelight. He was enchanted by her heavy, beige-tipped breasts and the slender waist below it, which then swelled again to a rounded belly, above pale thighs.

In the quiet candlelit room, there was no sound, not even of breathing. Elinor was so tense she could not draw a breath.

Billy laughed and whispered, "You are a beautiful and voluptuous woman. I'm going to make you realize that—and enjoy it—before the night is over."

Again he began to caress her slowly, his eyes open to watch her reactions: the soft, fleshy mysteries of a woman's sensuality were no secret to Billy.

Elinor shrank from her bridegroom, squirming slightly beneath his touch. Her head tried to pretend that it didn't know what was happening to her body.

He tickled her stomach with his mustache and slipped his tongue into her navel and then licked upward until she felt his breath—scented by her own body—against her lips; to her, it tasted scandalous.

Gently he breathed into her ears and her mouth. His lips sucked at her eyelids, her cheeks, her chin, and her lips; his tongue tickled her white throat. Softly he bit at her breasts, then her buttocks. Inch by inch, his hands and his mouth discovered her body, leaving no secret place unfound. Subordinating his pleasure to hers, Billy slowly led her into a new and thrilling but frightening world.

She felt his fingers traveling delicately over all of her body . . . touching, probing, sliding into every shadowed crevice, until his hand finally moved toward the division of her thighs. At the bottom of her triangle of blond hair, his index finger located the little bump no bigger than a pea and he started, gently and rhythmically, to rub it.

Slowly Elinor relaxed. Her body surrendered to the pleasure of Billy's touch; it seemed to melt, no longer controlled by her, and then it lifted, taut as a bow beneath his fingers, and her spirit soared.

Panting, bewildered, she opened her eyes. Above her, in the candlelight, she saw Billy's smiling, triumphant face.

"That's only the beginning," he promised. "Now let's have a look at you." He bent his head toward her belly, and his fingers slipped between her legs.

"Open your legs," he whispered.

Elinor stiffened at this command, so totally contrary to her strict upbringing.

"Please," Billy insisted.

His strength demanded her submission. She must surrender this, and with it her moral responsibility. Had she not just promised to love, honor, and *obey* him?

Quivering as she moved her legs slightly apart, Elinor felt timid and guilty; her heart pounded with anxiety. She felt unbearably vulnerable.

Slowly she parted her legs.

Billy's interest seemed curiously objective, and his eyes narrowed at the corners, as if he were a connoisseur examining a hothouse orchid, an exotic flower surrounded by pale pink, fleshy leaves and nestled in a soft blond bird's nest.

Carefully he pushed her lips apart and continued his clinical exploration. He lowered his head and licked her, until once again Elinor's body ignored her mind and ecstasy triumphed over shame.

Billy raised his head and looked up at her. "Now admit that it isn't so bad," he muttered as he slipped his hand between her thighs.

By the time his hand reached its goal, Elinor was once more quivering with fear. Billy's fingers softly probed her moist warmth until his middle finger met less resistance. Insistent, he pushed. Eventually his finger found the small opening and worked its way inside, enlarging it, with minimal pain to his bride. Elinor whimpered as he won his gentle battle.

At first she felt panic as he entered her. With his body stretched upon her, Billy lay still and reassured her with gentle kisses until she relaxed.

"Like this," he whispered, and his hands twisted her hips in a circular motion.

Slowly her body took up the motion.

In silence, Billy controlled each movement, each twist. Limbs entangled, they writhed in a leisurely, horizontal dance as they explored each other. Through the night, they slid from one side of the feather bed to the other, sometimes moving slowly, sometimes lunging swiftly, as their hunger for each other mounted and then was satisfied, only to grow again.

At times, he crouched above her like some great triumphant beast, looking down on his conquest spread out below him.

She felt that the entire world existed only as a vague two-dimensional blur. Only their crumpled nest of pillows and sheets, and the pungent male body on top of her—sliding, slipping, thrusting inside her—were sharply in focus, three-dimensional, and real. She could not think beyond this erotic joining of their flesh in the dimly shadowed, voluptuous bed, perfumed by their bodies.

Sometimes he lay beneath her, cradling her breasts in his hands, feeling her soft flesh quiver against his lips, and she sat panting upon his stomach as his strong hands held and rotated her hips. He gripped her to control her movements, so she could not move as she wished, could not move except as *he* wished.

At first she had demurely crossed her arms to hide her breasts, but eventually, flinging her arms high in abandon, she rode him like a plunging dolphin, until she fell forward, exhausted, and her breasts rubbed against the damp hair of his chest.

By morning, her flesh was bruised in places, like an overripe pear, and these pale contusions marked her as the property of Billy as surely as a cattle brand.

She was besotted, enchanted, in love, completely in Billy's thrall. Like lightning, he excited, frightened, and fascinated her.

That morning, momentarily disoriented, Elinor sleepily lifted her head from the pillow. Then she remembered the night, and she buried her face in the bedclothes. Her face grew hot as she recalled how Billy had manipulated her senses and rendered her boneless and helpless beneath his touch.

Then she realized that, in the billowing warmth of the feather bed, she could feel no body next to hers.

She sat up.

Billy—*her husband*—was leaning out of the open window. He was stark naked. For a moment, Elinor looked through lowered eyelashes at his cropped fair hair, his strong neck, his long back; she gazed admiringly at his long, lean legs—the left foot still bandaged—and his muscular buttocks, so different from her soft, pliable flesh. Throughout her life, this private peek at Billy's body was frozen in her mind, and at the memory, Elinor would melt, and forgive him anything.

• • •

During the first weeks of her marriage, Elinor slid slowly, agreeably, voluptuously into sensuality.

What had originally attracted Billy to Elinor as much as her beauty and exuberant energy was the innocence that she had protected so firmly, and to which Billy had responded with classic male determination.

Having destroyed that innocence, Billy now sought to artificially rebuild it, for the pleasure of again breaching it. At first Elinor refused to reenact her timid virginity so that Billy could then pretend to break her in as he had on their wedding night.

"Why can't we undress before we go to bed, as usual? I don't understand why you want me to playact," she protested. But then she grew to enjoy his little fantasy.

Dexterously, swiftly, Billy turned his bride into a slave of her own eroticism. She could think about nothing else. She was still at heart a farm girl, and in bed, Billy encouraged her impudent flirtatiousness, her adolescent awkwardness, clumsiness, blushing and innocent corruptibility. To Billy's young and unsophisticated bride, this physical passion—her adoring proof of love and devotion to her husband—came as an undreamed-of surprise. In bed with Billy, Elinor shook and trembled and sobbed until she was exhausted, until she felt overwhelmed and ecstatically weary.

Every time Billy touched her, Elinor felt herself fall, spinning dizzily into a void. When he raised his eyelids and the intense blue light of his eyes flashed straight at her, Elinor always caught her breath. When Billy spoke to her as a prelude to love, his voice would deepen, holding a silken note of promise—and of threat. His voice alone could make Elinor's legs tremble. And when, in this voice that reminded her of dark honey, he called her name, she felt his mouth caress her without touching her. So vivid was the sensation that she was astonished that other people in the room did not notice it, especially when the newlyweds visited his family.

Without being told, Elinor knew that, for her, sex alone could never be fulfilling. The abandonment of her body had to be combined with the passion in her heart and the devotion in her soul. For her, such a feeling of complete, abandoned love was possible with no man except Billy. Only he knew when to coax, when to tempt, when to insist. He was the only man to whom she could trust her body. She knew instinctively that there would never be another man for her.

After being shown by a maid to an impressively large bedroom, Elinor turned, grinning, to her husband and asked, "Why didn't you *tell* me?"

Billy took her into his arms, tilted her chin up, and kissed her tenderly. "It would only have made you nervous. Better you see for yourself what my family are like."

"But why didn't you *say* your folks were rich?" Elinor asked.

"Because they aren't!" Billy laughed. "Look how threadbare this carpet is. See how shabby the curtains are. You'll soon feel the darns in the sheets. And wait until you taste the sherry!"

"Then how come they live as if they are rich? And what about the silver and the servants?"

"My father lost most of his inheritance through unwise investments, the silver's only plate, and there aren't really as many servants as there used to be; the ones that remain aren't paid much and they eat food grown here on the estate."

Elinor shook her head. She was truly in a foreign land. It defied all logic. Here was a penniless family, living in a house stuffed with servants, in which elaborate meals were served and all the women wore pearl necklaces. Yet, as Billy explained, it was impossible to find a stamp, or anything else that had to be paid for with cash.

"And why did the man in black call your mother 'milady'?" Elinor asked.

"Because my father is a baronet."

"You mean he's a *lord?*"

"Nothing so grand. I'll explain the English class system to you someday when I have the strength and the time. Believe me, it truly isn't important to us. For now, let's forget it. Besides, we mustn't be late for dinner. It's the one thing my mother never forgives."

That night, after dinner, a maid helped the embarrassed Elinor to undress. Lying in a four-poster bed with blue brocade curtains, Elinor watched her bedside candle's hypnotic flicker. As she waited for Billy to appear, she mentally reviewed the events of the long day.

As nervous as any bride about to meet her mother-in-law for the first time, Elinor had been tense with apprehension as the pony and trap trotted from the station through a marzipan-colored, curving land of brown and green. Suddenly, across open parkland, she had seen what looked like a gray Greek temple nestled in trees, and Billy had said in an offhand voice, "That's Larkwood." Already overawed, Elinor had followed the butler into the drawing room, where a group of tweed-suited, staring people were gathered around a fireplace at the far end of the dark room. Even at a distance, Elinor realized that she was about to undergo some sort of test; she was so nervous that she was unable to link names with relationships until much later—except for Billy's mother, a faded version of Billy, who brushed Elinor's cheek with a hint of a kiss.

Later at dinner, there was a lot of political talk that Elinor didn't understand. She sat next to Billy's father, and followed his example when picking up the silver cutlery that surrounded her plate; it was the first time she had eaten a pear with a knife and fork.

Now, lying in bed, Elinor longed for Billy to appear and reassure her of his love, because clearly his family felt none for her.

Where was Billy?

Elinor slipped from her bed and quietly opened the door. Then she froze as she heard her name.

Outside, on the landing, she heard Billy's mother speak angrily of her new daughter-in-law with words that hurt and angered Elinor.

"It's perfectly clear why you married her, darling. She is a *very* good-looking girl, and luckily, she has that charming American accent. But perhaps you might tell her—in the most *tactful* way, of course—that she really cannot sit at my dinner table and say nothing: she must learn to talk, to listen, to *sparkle*."

"She sparkles enough when she's feeling confident," Billy said. "I think you might *all* be a little more patient and generous-spirited. Whether you like it or not, Elinor is now part of this family."

"Ah! That's the *point*. This is some sort of punishment for me, isn't it? Heaven knows what I have done to deserve it—except not give birth to you first! Don't you think it's a *little* unkind to have married someone out of your own class, Billy?"

"I'm penniless, I have no prospects, I'm slightly disabled, and I can't get a job, Mother. What sort of class does that put me in?"

"You know you can always live here."

"And watch Marjorie count each mouthful of her husband's inheritance that we consume? No thank you!"

With that, Billy turned and entered the bedroom. He found Elinor staring tearfully at her reflection in the cheval mirror.

"Oh, Billy, I feel so sad. . . . I so much wanted your family to like me."

"Don't be silly. The family thinks you're a corker." He stood behind her and pulled her body against him, his arms encircling her, his hands caressing the thin fabric that covered her breasts.

Elinor knew, however, that she had not misinterpreted what she overheard. She felt hurt, inadequate, and inferior in this nest of effortless superiority. And for the first time in a very long while, Elinor was aware of just how far away from home she was.

Billy slipped her nightgown from her shoulders, but for once Elinor did not immediately respond to his lovemaking. She was overcome by indignation. She was an American who had just survived a war, and she had earned her place in the world. She was not about to be put down by these out-of-date, supercilious, upper-class Britishers of unearned privilege. They regarded her as inferior because she came of humble folk who worked with their hands. Well, she would show them.

But Elinor was unaware of the degree to which her bullying father had conditioned her, and how this would adversely affect her future, and her ability to show them.

Even after they were comfortably settled in their own flat, Billy visited his home as often as possible. For him, it was a place of security, a refuge from a world that made demands he was not yet ready to face. Nonetheless, he obviously felt himself to be anybody's equal; Elinor wished she could be as comfortable and secure as he seemed, in the presence of the O'Dare family.

"I feel I'm not as good as them," she confided to Billy as, on a subsequent visit to Larkwood, they lay in bed, "and sometimes I suspect they *want* me to feel like this."

"They don't mean to embarrass you, old girl," Billy comforted her as he stroked her body. "You just aren't used to our offhand English ways."

"But I only feel this way with them," Elinor puzzled. "I feel comfortable and equal to anyone at school." Elinor now attended evening classes at the Polytechnic, hoping that an improved education would enable her to hold her own more easily against Billy's standoffish family.

"And so you are," Billy murmured, caressing her pale flesh.

"You don't understand," Elinor sighed. "Because *you* can hold your own anywhere."

But Elinor was wrong. True, Billy was an educated, well-mannered gentleman, handsome, sensual, and possessed of animal grace. He had experienced life's abundance and assumed it would continue, for he knew that he was intelligent and clever. What he did not know, or could never admit, was how very lazy he was.

Indeed, to all appearances, Billy was a sophisticated man-about-town who knew the ways of the world. Before the war, he had already made an impression in the drawing rooms and ballrooms of London as a charming young fellow and a polished conversationalist.

In the masculine world of London's clubs, however, Billy had projected a different image. There it was recognized that the sexes had clearly defined and different purposes: Men shared sport and danger; they gambled and provided each other with companionship and conversation. Women provided sexual pleasure, children, and home comfort. In these clubs, Billy had not been considered the equal of his respected father and elder brother; rather, he was rumored to be unreliable and unscrupulous—dangerously close to a cad—with perhaps too practiced an eye for a pretty ankle. Jealous men referred to him as a "ladies' man."

For his part, Billy remained impervious to their remarks; he seemed to feel it was his duty in life to charm *all* women, debutantes and married women alike. His self-confidence appeared unassailable.

In prewar London's plush bordellos, Billy's careless generosity, his atypical concern for the sexual fulfillment of his partner, his voluptuous exploits, and his sometimes delicate, sometimes harsh exploration of human flesh had also made him a favorite of expensive whores. For Billy, sexual pleasure consisted not only of lust but of frivolity, licentious play, and a perverse, detached curiosity. He was as inventive and imaginative as he was unscrupulous, as adventurous as he was amoral. He was almost irresistible in bed.

Postwar London, however, was different, especially for a penniless married man.

At first Billy had no anxiety about his future. His wonderful, get-rich-quick schemes were put to Elinor with such confidence that, for a short time, she believed in them. Gradually, though, she realized that the mercurial Billy—incautious and impractical, feckless and immature—was not the stuff from which successful self-employed businessmen were fashioned. Finally he tried to find a job, but could not get one.

Still, they had to have a home, and in Earls Court Square, Billy found a cheap, shabby two-room apartment with one communal bathroom. "It will do for a few weeks," he said. Elinor, with a newlywed's enthusiasm, tried to make the depressing flat into a comfortable home. She seemed to be able to do little, however, to improve the increasingly depressed spirits of her husband or to shore up his rapidly eroding self-confidence.

One morning, six months after the war had ended, Elinor, still in her teens and now pregnant, lay in bed and watched as Billy shaved. She was bewildered and distressed by the transformation of the assertive, devil-may-care air ace she had married into a man who grew more and more bitter and morose, who seemed mired in apathy, frozen in a state of anxious despair. She wanted to reach out and comfort him, to try to reassure him, but she knew she dared not.

"You might stop looking at me so reproachfully!" Billy said, catching Elinor's eye in his shaving mirror.

"Honey, I'm only a little concerned. You seem so tired." Already she had learned not to say more.

What Elinor wanted to say to Billy was, "We are alive, aren't we? We aren't about to be blown to bits at any moment. And we surely won't starve so long as there's food to feed the family servants at Larkwood!" And they had each other, didn't they? Surely she and Billy could enjoy being together, able to comfort each other and cheer each other's spirits when life was tough. Wasn't that the whole point of being married—being loving and protective and struggling together through the hard times? That was a lot more important than sailing through the sunny days.

Elinor still failed to understand that Billy, the golden boy, so brave and dauntless as a sky fighter, was uniquely unprepared for life's real and continuing battles. There he proved himself to be not only a dispirited and disheartened combatant but a bad loser as well.

Billy looked into his own eyes, reflected in the shaving mirror. In that same mirror, he had watched his face develop from a handsome lad's into that of a self-confident man. Gradually, however, since the war, since he had married Elinor, that splendid male arrogance had been replaced by anxiety, soon followed by desperation, as Billy searched unsuccessfully for his place in the postwar world. His failure left him feeling ashamed, emasculated, bereft of self-respect. What had gone wrong? He really had been a golden boy, and he still couldn't quite believe that he had been abandoned by the gods. They had smiled upon him so indulgently for the early part of his life, given him his privileged background, his good looks and fine body. Surely they had guided and protected him as an air ace? He had not only survived, he had been called a hero.

But now the gods seemed indifferent, abandoning him to this postwar purgatory, where heroes were two a penny and there were no jobs.

Billy had originally tried to get a job that involved airplanes—but so had every other ex-flier, and many did not have the disadvantage of an injury. It was ironic that so few flying jobs should be available, when Billy was certain that aviation—to carry mail and even, perhaps, passengers—was one of the few industries that could be expected to expand rapidly.

But there were just no jobs for him, and Billy found it humiliating. How was it that he couldn't manage what was surely the basic requirement of a man—to care for his wife and family?

Observing the frustration reflected in Billy's face, Elinor considered how fortunate it was that she knew one surefire way to bolster his self-confidence.

In bed, Billy was in charge of their world. There, he regained, if only fleetingly, a sense of potency—something that seemed to be inexorably dissolving from the rest of his life. Making love, he felt the power that he knew was his due.

As Billy stropped his razor, Elinor lay back in the bed and stretched languorously. She smiled at her husband. "I've never seen anyone with eyes like yours; they're the color of sea water over white sand; they shine with secrets. No wonder all the nurses fell for you. But I was the lucky one."

In the shaving mirror, his eyes met Elinor's and he smiled. Billy recognized her invitation. He wiped the lather from his cheeks and turned toward the bed.

With each month of Elinor's pregnancy, Billy's disposition worsened. She, of course, worried that her husband's changed attitude was due to her increasing inability to provide the full sexual involvement he needed. In truth, Elinor could never provide what Billy needed, which was self-respect.

At first Billy seemed merely sullen. Gradually he became volatile, short-tempered, sarcastic, and deliberately unkind. Elinor became more and more disconcerted, eventually immobilized by her own confusion. What had become of the man who had made love so real, indeed almost tangible? The loss of his affection so depressed her that it became an effort to do anything. A year earlier, she would not have put up with such behavior, but rebellion was now the last thing on her mind because, quite simply, Billy and pregnancy had knocked it out of her. Little by little, Elinor's vivacity, bounce, and drive were submerged, buried in despair.

Almost childlike in his determined self-absorption, Billy became Elinor's master. If he wanted her to do something, she knew she was expected to drop whatever she was doing and turn her attention to him; otherwise he sulked. Billy also attempted to overcome his insecurity by subtly reminding Elinor that *he* had the education, the worldly experience and knowledge that she, as a woman, lacked. He attacked her humble background, and once introduced her to a male friend as his "American bumpkin." Billy enjoyed her helplessness and her inability to stand up to his glib, facile verbal cruelty.

Elinor watched Billy struggle with his demons as, bewildered and frustrated, he increasingly sought oblivion in drink. And whenever he drank, the dashing, popular charmer became aggressive and maudlin, occasionally even abusing her verbally. On the day after a drinking bout, however, Billy would always be childlike in his remorse, relentless in his contrition, and he was always both hurt and astonished if Elinor did not forgive him immediately.

By being wistfully contrite and then making her laugh, Billy could coax and wheedle his wife into doing anything he wanted. On the rare occasion when that ploy didn't work, Billy would withdraw in sullen temper: immediately anxious, Elinor always crumpled before his projected disapproval. Sometimes Billy would become exasperated by her timidity; sometimes he found it erotic. Invariably these episodes ended the same way, for he was always forgiven in bed.

But in the long run, nothing really worked because nothing fully erased Billy's sense of failure and of despair.

Feeling powerless outside his home, Billy compensated by being dictatorial within it. Like the chairman who snarls at his secretary, like the secretary who snaps at the office boy, who then kicks the cat, Billy externalized his anxiety upon the only person willing to put up with his bullying—his wife. He was contemptuous of her meek acceptance of his bad behavior.

But Elinor had learned from her mother, who had humbly accepted her husband's tyranny, that authority was a masculine concept. Vaguely she understood that a bearded God possessed ultimate power in the universe, before which everyone bowed down; the equivalent domestic power was a husband. From her mother, Elinor had learned that every woman needed a man and a shouting bully was better than no man at all. At least, Elinor comforted herself, Billy never walloped her, as her father had done; at least life could never be as terrifying as it had been when she was young.

Then one Sunday, Billy didn't turn up for the major meal of the week until midafternoon—after the pubs had closed. Elinor took the dried-out leg of lamb from the oven and placed it on the table. *"That's not fit to eat,"* Billy said. He grabbed the joint of meat and threw it at the wall.

As Elinor stared at the greasy, dark stains and the gravy dripping down, she remembered another time. She had been helping her ma to prepare their Thanksgiving dinner. Eleven-year-old Nell had slapped her small brother's fingers away from the cranberry sauce and Paul had yelled in protest as their father came in from the barn.

Seeing his son's tears, Marius jumped forward and boxed young Elinor's ears. As he turned to comfort Paul, Nell crept toward the door. Marius yanked her back. "And where do you think *you're* going?" he roared, then pulled off his leather belt, sat down, shoved Nell over his knee, and roughly pulled down her drawers.

"It wasn't Nell's fault! Don't spoil our Thanksgiving!" her ma cried, but he took no notice. As always when he strapped her, Nell howled with pain. Her ma burst into tears and ran from the kitchen.

"There, see what you've done!" Marius shouted at Nell. "Now you've spoiled our Thanksgiving!" From the kitchen table, he picked up the platter of turkey and hurled it at the dresser. Quivering with fear, Nell watched the grease and gravy drip down and form a puddle on the floor. . . .

Now, Elinor found herself quivering with the same fear as she watched the gravy dribbling down the wall. In silent apprehension, she heard Billy slam the front door. She refused to admit to herself that she had chained herself to another bully, but Billy's behavior made Elinor feel as hopeless and inadequate as her father's had when she was a girl. Increasingly she dreaded Billy's disapproval, his growing coldness and contempt, and his lacerating sarcasm. And her dread merely seemed to make him feel the more superior.

So Elinor remembered how to be stoical. When nervous and timid, she reapplied her childhood techniques of willing herself to be inconspicuous, fading into the background; anesthetizing her mind to the brutality of her father; her anxious passivity made her an easy victim.

Gradually all Elinor's frightened responses resurfaced, having lain dormant during the war, when courage and determination had overridden her other characteristics.

Just as Elinor's father had dominated her childhood with his violent and unquestioned parental authority, so when Billy demanded obedience, she almost always did as he told her without resistance.

Billy especially enjoyed his ability to dominate Elinor sexually. He used sex to thrill, to control, and to comfort her—although never to reassure her, because Billy knew that an uncertain woman is always obedient, whereas a self-confident woman might want her own way. After their son was born, Billy expanded his powers of sexual mastery: he enjoyed seeing how quickly—or how excruciatingly slowly—he could produce her climax. His rampant masculinity was reinforced by the knowledge that whenever he pleased, he could, sometimes with careful cruelty or unexpected kindness, reduce Elinor to a trembling, acquiescent creature at the mercy of her own flesh.

Although she did not realize it, Elinor enjoyed this abnegation of all responsibility, sexual and otherwise, to her domineering, overpowering, excitingly threatening husband. For her, Billy held the dangerous, sensual excitement of a wild animal that had been domesticated yet never tamed. There was a threat in everything he did, and she never sensed it more than when they made love. Even when their financial situation began to improve, his sexual hold on her did not change.

Eventually, in 1921, through the influence of a family friend, Billy was hired as a society gossip writer on the *Daily Globe,* a London newspaper. It was a job that suited him perfectly, for Billy's Irish gift of gab meant that he could talk to anyone about anything; his outward cheerful ebullience put everyone at ease, and his charm and sympathetic demeanor—those journalist's weapons—lowered all social drawbridges. But, although Billy attended all the smart parties, he knew (as did the other guests) that between him and them lay a line which could not be crossed, for Billy was present as a paid servant, a hired hack.

Elinor, of course, never accompanied Billy to these functions, and in truth, she did not want to: that was his world, not hers. To her, the only real drawback to Billy's new job was that he was never at home in the evenings, except on Sunday. Also, one of the side effects of his employment seemed to be a permanent hangover, but nevertheless, Elinor was certain this situation had to be a better one for Billy; she did not realize the sense of humiliation he felt at being an outsider in the world to which he had been born. She only sensed the relief that he was now working, and that it was no longer necessary to borrow money from his old friend, Joe Grant, now an articled clerk to a firm of London solicitors.

Elinor suspected that Billy—who never wrote anything longer than a frivolous paragraph if he could avoid it—actually could write serious articles if he wanted to do so. One of his colleagues also told her that Billy had the makings of a good theater critic, but he did not care to subject himself to the concentration necessary to write the review in his head as he watched a play. Billy, who did not like hard work, preferred to amuse himself at the theater, and afterward in restaurants, at fashionable dinner parties, or at the daring new nightclubs.

Once, Billy had been a man with high expectations and high ambition, known by everyone; now, although he *knew* everyone, he seemed to be nobody's friend. It was clear to him that he was going nowhere. As a result, his smiles and his charm were reserved almost exclusively for the people he saw when he was on the town. At home, he wore his depression like a cloak and only rarely allowed any warmth or humor to show through.

In spite of all this, Elinor managed to be happy. She loved living in a big city with all of its conveniences. She cleaned and cooked, she cuddled her baby son, Edward, and she borrowed romantic novels from the local penny library: these books (in which the heroines never wore secondhand clothes, and the heroes were as considerate as they were handsome) had provided her with precious hours of escape from the anxieties of life she had known when pregnant, with Billy out of work. Now Elinor read romantic fiction while waiting for Billy to come home, because she could never get to sleep until he lay safe beside her.

On one occasion, when he slammed the door of their bedroom at four o'clock in the morning, Elinor whispered, "Don't make a noise! You'll wake the baby! Where have you been?"

"Stop nagging," Billy yawned as he removed the studs from his evening shirt.

"What do you mean, nagging?" Elinor whispered indignantly.

"I mean your constant criticism, your silent hurt looks of reproach, your unreasonable demands," Billy said, pulling off his socks. "This sock needs mending." He peered at it somewhat drunkenly.

For once, Elinor decided to give full vent to her true feelings. She hopped out of bed and stood angrily in front of Billy, her legs apart, her hands on her hips, her body hardly hidden by a flimsy peach-colored nightgown and robe.

"How can you be so unfair?" she asked in a low voice. "Wouldn't *you* want to know where *I* had been if I went out and left you at home every night?"

Billy turned slowly and looked intently at his wife. He stared at her shadowed breasts, glanced at his watch, grinned, and moved toward her.

As his right hand slid beneath the peach chiffon, Elinor felt her nipples harden; immediately her body betrayed her and her anger melted away. As his lips caressed her ear, her neck, her senses swirled; their argument was forgotten.

Billy murmured, "Have you got it in?" Shortly after Edward's birth, he had sent Elinor to the shop in Holloway where Dr. Marie Stopes gave free advice and cheap contraception to women.

"Yes." Now he'd know that she had been hoping.

With one hand, Billy pushed his discarded clothes from the bed and with the other, he pulled Elinor's body to his. Her kimono fell from her shoulders to the floor, and she felt his warmth and strength against her.

As he lowered her to the bed, she pushed down the thin straps of her nightgown. "No, don't take it off," he murmured, and touched her breasts with the tip of his tongue.

His right hand stroked her thighs, then felt beneath the taut peach gauze . . . Where *was* the damn thing? He located her tiny clitoris, felt it harden beneath his thumb.

"Lie on top of me," he ordered. "Now spread your legs, wide." That way she climaxed so much quicker.

Elinor could not bear her husband's displeasure. One Sunday evening, after Billy had complained that she didn't iron his shirts well enough, she cooked his favorite dish for dinner. Afterward, her finger traced his cheek, her usual delicate signal to him.

Billy frowned slightly and jerked his head away. At first, instinctively, Elinor wondered what she had done wrong. Then she wondered why she should feel guilty. There were, of course, no answers. Whatever the cause, his rejection of her timid sexual advance made her feel ashamed of being so forward.

Billy grinned to himself. His disapproval always bewildered Elinor—and always brought her quickly to heel.

Some days later, when Elinor had had time to reflect on the incident, she decided to try the same thing with him. When Billy touched her breast, she flinched slightly; she wanted to see if his reactions were the same as hers.

Billy laughed at her refusal. He lifted her into his arms and carried her to the bed. Silently and deliberately he undressed her, button by button.

Resolutely determined to resist him, Elinor would not be wooed. When he laid her on the sheet, she did not move, willing herself to lie passively still.

Kneeling, Billy slowly pushed his knee between her legs and forced them apart. He felt her, quivering and moist, beneath him.

"You see, it's no use," he said. "I *know* when you want me."

He took her especially harshly that time, and when she whimpered, the face above her smiled.

"You've got to learn who's boss," Billy said softly, pinching her nipples a little too hard.

Although their erotic life was still one of intense passion, some of Billy's requirements puzzled Elinor. In bed, Billy preferred a half-dressed woman to a naked one, and he liked her to wear thick black stockings—like those of a schoolgirl—rather than her best silk pair.

One summer evening, Billy returned home with a gift box for Elinor. Inside, she found a white smock and a plain pinafore.

"Oh, Billy!" she cried in confused disappointment. "Surely you don't expect *me* to wear this! It's the sort of thing I wore when I was a little girl and wore my hair in braids."

"Then braid your hair," Billy said evenly.

"But—"

"*That's enough!* If you want to please me—braid your hair."

"No, I *won't*."

"Then I shall go to someone who will." Billy left the room, whistling.

He returned at six o'clock the next morning, his step unsteady, his speech slurred, his clothes reeking of the sour, sharp smell of whiskey and stale tobacco. On his skin, Elinor detected the strong scent of perfume. Her eyes registered a look of hurt and bewilderment.

Billy laughed. "Well, *you* didn't want me."

All day, Elinor hugged her baby to her and wept with shame and grief.

Billy did not touch her for a month.

During that month, Elinor's nipples ached to feel him; her belly longed to feel his fingernails scrape lightly across it, before his hand slipped knowingly between her thighs. Alone, restless, and unable to sleep, she tossed in their big brass marital bed; she banged pillows into shape, tortured by mental pictures of Billy doing all those private things to someone else.

On the fourth Sunday evening of her enforced celibacy, Elinor timidly entered the living room and stood before Billy. She was dressed in the white smock, the pinafore, and the thick black stockings; her hair was in braids.

"Do you like it?" she asked him shyly.

Later, she remembered her surprise at the passion unleashed by that pinafore as, on their bed, his hand groped beneath the tangle of her childish clothes.

This seduction of innocence—or the pretense of it—seemed to be the core of Billy's sexual pleasure, providing the energy that fired his loins with greatest power. Gradually their relationship grew from that of a man and a woman to that of a calculating seducer with a trusting child, for Elinor was now also expected to behave like a submissive child bride outside the bedroom. In public, Billy now liked her to appear submissive and deferential; dutifully passive, with head bowed, she looked meek and acquiescent, but both she and Billy knew the secret passion that lay behind her lowered eyes.

Only once more did Elinor protest at being dressed as a child. Standing ready for bed, wearing only a white frilled pinafore and long black stockings, she said hesitantly, "Billy, I don't mind dressing like this *sometimes*, but must I do it always? We never seem to do anything else!"

"And why not?" Billy lay on his back, both arms behind his head. Elinor looked at the blond hair glinting in his pale armpits and on his upper chest; below the nipples, his body was hidden by rumpled sheets.

"Because . . . because . . . I feel you're behaving like a strict father with his little daughter . . . and that would be wrong, wouldn't it Billy?"

"It would certainly be incestuous." Billy stretched his arms in a yawn. "But what does a little more corruption matter?"

"*Corruption?*" Elinor stared.

"Certainly," Billy said. "The delights of the flesh to which you are so addicted are viewed by the world as corrupt behavior. Ask any decent woman."

"*What* do you mean? Surely what we do is normal between a man and his wife?"

"*Normal?* You know perfectly well, Elinor, that *ladies* find the sexual act distasteful. The things that you and I get up to are considered unspeakably degrading, and would shock any decent woman." He laughed. "No respectable woman enjoys the sexual act—only whores."

"But . . . but . . . *you* showed me all those things."

"Because you clearly enjoyed them, my dear. You *always* wanted what I offered. I did *nothing* against your will. You clearly have the heart of a whore. You enjoyed every perversion that I offered you. You positively shook every time I touched you. You *love* it all."

"But . . . what *are* these perversions?"

Slowly and deliberately Billy listed the acts of eroticism in which he had encouraged his wife to participate, clearly enjoying her confusion.

He smiled again. "Don't worry, Elinor. *I* enjoy your depravity. But we'd better keep it a secret, hadn't we?"

"Depravity?" Elinor stammered.

He laughed. "I think you're more depraved than I am, darling. But if you don't agree, then why don't we ask other people for their opinions."

Her frightened expression aroused him so much that he carefully repeated his accusation. Observing Elinor's guilty, crimson face, Billy suspected that in the future, he would be able to manipulate his wife in any way he wished, and get her to agree to do anything he requested, simply by hurling this suggestion at her.

Elinor was simply unable to resist the temptations offered by Billy. And of course, she did not dare resist, although she now felt bitterly ashamed of the physical desires of her body and her willing capitulation to Billy's domination. With some success, she made excuses to herself: I didn't want to do it, but Billy *made* me do it, and he's my husband, and I *must obey him.*

Torn between her pleasure and the resultant shame, Elinor felt her guilt steadily grow. And increasingly Billy manipulated, dominated, and exploited her.

Hidden beneath his apparent sophistication lurked the little boy who enjoyed pulling the wings from moths. At bottom, Billy was still a bully who found pleasure in domination.

Sometimes in the street Billy asked Elinor if she had noticed some young girl's fine eyes or long legs. Aloud he wondered what it would be like to caress her. He enjoyed seeing Elinor's jealousy, which she thought she hid so well, as he developed these erotic daydreams.

What he said he would like to do to the girl, Billy later did to Elinor, whispering further erotic details as he touched her. He told Elinor that both men and women fantasized in this way. "Stop being a stupid farm girl, and acquire a little more sophistication in these matters," he ordered.

And Elinor acquiesced. Against her will, she became fascinated by his erotic fantasies, and eventually she willingly collaborated in this sensual playacting. Then she looked forward to it, as an alcoholic looks forward to feeling his senses swim when his brain abdicates after the first few drinks.

Billy continued to be openly flirtatious and did little to conceal his occasional infidelities from Elinor; the worse he behaved, the more submissive she became, for she was now so completely insecure that she was terrified of losing him. Whatever was wrong was her fault; whatever was wrong she must make right. Obsessed by Billy, she had become addicted to his love.

Also obsessed by jealousy, Elinor wanted to know nothing of Billy's amorous sorties, and yet perversely she longed to know every detail of them. She knew that Billy would obligingly provide these details, that he would both torture her and satisfy her craving—but he always made her ask for them. Always, in the end, she did.

It became a game—a game that Billy obviously enjoyed. He would ask her what she thought had taken place between himself and the lady in question. He would have Elinor state her anxieties in specific detail, occasionally interrupting her jealous visions by murmuring remarks such as "You mean you suspect I did this to her." And then he would touch Elinor's body in the way she had described.

Eventually the game itself became a passion for Elinor, the passion an obsession. There lurked behind the game, however, the secret fear that—one day—one of Billy's street girls, or one of the schoolgirls, or one of the society beauties he met, would unexpectedly gain as slavish a hold over him as he had over Elinor.

In fact, Billy's passing physical thirsts were quickly slaked and as quickly forgotten, but he took care that Elinor should not realize this. Slowly she built up in her imagination the figure of her husband as an irresistibly attractive, potent, and all-powerful man.

Billy would now rarely tell Elinor that he loved her. He liked to keep her in a permanent state of anxiety and jealousy, so that he could make her do anything he wished. Elinor longed for the words that she now seldom heard. It was essential that Billy love her. And of course, it was essential that she love Billy, because this assuaged her feelings of guilt about enjoying sex.

Elinor was also terrified of losing Billy because, like so many women of her generation, she felt inadequate, unable to face life without a man, no matter how badly he behaved. She had no money of her own and would be unlikely to get even domestic work, accompanied by a small baby. Like most other women, she was totally dependent upon her man, and so never allowed herself the luxury of reacting with anger to his bad behavior.

But one morning, as Elinor did the dishes after breakfast, she suddenly found herself shaking Billy's breakfast mug in a fury. The previous night, Billy had stumbled home, late and drunk. While undressing, he had knocked a photograph frame to the floor and then accidentally stood upon it; this had smashed the glass and torn the only picture of her mother that Elinor possessed.

As, enraged, Elinor shook the mug, she suddenly realized, with cold horror, that Billy could make her feel as anxious and muddled, as miserable and worthless as she used to feel after a strapping from her father.

But Billy was not the inescapable tyrant of her childhood! Billy was Elinor's husband, chosen by her. He was her beloved . . . wasn't he?

Bewildered by the sudden violence of her emotion, Elinor made herself a cup of tea and sat at the kitchen table. For almost an hour, she stayed there without moving as the cup of tea cooled before her. For once, she considered Billy's behavior toward her without rationalizing it. She did not mentally suppress his cat-and-mouse cruelty and remember only the charm he had shown during courtship. Instead, she asked herself why both Billy and her father could make her feel the same dragging unhappiness.

Suddenly Elinor could no longer refuse to admit that she had indeed chained herself to another bully—one who would darken the rest of her life. Her savior had become her tormentor. And with that realization came tears that burned with pain. Elinor put her head on the scrubbed wooden table and sobbed until she was breathless and her eyes were so swollen that she could hardly see.

Lifting her head, she pulled herself together. Billy was her husband, and Edward was her son, and this was her life. She had no choice but to go on.

She turned her face away from the reality that she couldn't bear to the romantic vision of Billy with which she had fallen in love. Last night's drunken oaf was not the man she had married. The *real* Billy was the handsome, charming hero in the photograph at her bedside. He was having a difficult time at the moment because he had been forced to take a job that wasn't good enough for him. Of course he had reason to be upset. She would push all unpleasant thoughts out of her mind and focus only on helping Billy. Surely, in time, things would get better, life would improve. Of course it would.

Chapter · 4

❈

The next ten years were difficult for Elinor, as she saw less and less of "the real Billy," and her husband's drinking increased.

More and more, she found it necessary to justify and to compromise. Bewildered, she found it hard to understand what was happening to her life. She wondered miserably whether she was doing all she might to help Billy, because everything would be all right and their life would be happy—if only Billy didn't drink.

Sometimes Elinor also wondered whether, as Billy often said, his drinking was in any way her fault. If so, how had she disappointed him, as he repeatedly accused her of doing? And she wondered too why she could never stick to her ultimatums. Why did she always believe that Billy would change simply because he always promised to do so? He never did.

Elinor never knew when he would be home for meals, or whether he would be home at all. Eventually she learned not to count on Billy for anything, neither his presence nor his absence. If, thinking Billy safely out of the way, she invited a friend from her Polytechnic class to her home, Billy invariably staggered in and insulted the friend. Elinor, who didn't like to embarrass people, gradually stopped inviting anyone home, except Buzz, who was impervious to Billy's bad behavior. On the few occasions when Billy not only was sober but did not have a hangover, he was so defensive that Elinor was rarely able to discuss his drinking.

Edward, a pale, quiet child, kept out of his father's way as much as possible. He was a self-contained boy, who seemed able to communicate almost wordlessly with his mother, much to the irritation of his father. He had a gentle and sensitive nature, although he had inherited his father's impressive, wide-shouldered physique and was clearly going to be tall and strong. He also had his father's untidy strawlike hair and neat features, though after Edward's nose was broken in a football game,

Billy wouldn't allow the boy to have it reset, because it made him look tougher: Billy was exasperated by his son's lack of obvious manly qualities and his preference for nature study to sports.

Some aspects of their life together remained normal. Billy still saw Joe Grant, who had married his boss's daughter early in 1929. Elinor still saw Buzz regularly. Buzz never said, "I told you so."

But one summer Sunday evening, after Billy had been particularly abusive to Elinor in front of Buzz, the two women went to the cinema. As they reached the Kensington Odeon, Buzz quietly asked, "How much longer are you going to put up with Billy's rotten behavior? For the rest of your life?"

"Don't tell me I ought to leave him. It'll spoil our outing."

"But why? You've got the guts and the gumption—we all saw that in the war—but where's your backbone gone? I've *never* understood why you don't just get up and leave Billy."

"It's not that simple." Elinor shook her head.

"Don't say that! Why don't you stop inventing obstacles? Why don't you decide that next time he's a bastard, you'll just walk out of that front door! Nell, you ain't got a hero to save you. No woman has. *You got to save yourself.*"

"I know you mean well," Elinor said as they entered the Egyptian magnificence of the theater foyer. The fantastic architecture reminded her of her childhood daydreams of being a changeling, when she hoped that one day she would be swept off to become an adored princess. Now her forlorn hope was that one day her fairy prince would turn back into a fairy prince, that one day Billy would see how destructive his behavior was; this pathetic hope enabled her to live with him, as did her equally pathetic insistence on seeing Billy through rose-colored glasses.

As they entered the darkness of the auditorium, Buzz added, "You used to have a mind of your own before you married Billy, but now you can't seem to make any decision for yourself."

"Do we have to discuss that again?"

"At least you used to know when Billy treated you like a doormat. Now when he treads on you—you don't even *notice!* You almost apologized to *him* this afternoon when he'd finished criticizing the meal."

"Be fair, Buzz. Billy isn't violent; plenty of husbands are; but Billy's never lifted a finger against me . . ."

"No, only his tongue: he's beaten you black and blue with that."

Elinor said, "I know I'm short on self-confidence, but Billy means well."

"*I* don't think Billy means well," Buzz said. "I've watched him *smash* your self-confidence. That's not a well-meaning thing to do."

"Billy only criticizes me to be helpful. He means to be kind."

"There ain't no such thing as being cruel to be kind! People like Billy are cruel to be cruel! Don't mistake *that* for loving kindness." Buzz lit a cigarette. "I can't think why you don't leave him."

"Because he loves me—he does really!"

Buzz snorted. "A funny sort of love! I can see that you love *him*—you make endless sacrifices for that rotter. And like all doormats, you do it because you secretly wish that's what he'd do for you! Nell, I know you fell in love with Billy. I was there, remember? He was a charmer—a girl would've had to be made of stone not to take a shine to him. We all watched him when he turned his charms on you, and we was all a little jealous. So I know, Nell. I know why you fell for him, and I know how. What I don't know, and what I don't understand, is why you can't see that the Billy O'Dare we met and fancied then is not the same man you've got to go home to tonight."

"But Buzz, he loves me. I know he does."

Buzz paused. "Maybe he does, Nell, I can't speak for him," she said slowly. "But I can say that his love ain't enough anymore. Not the way he treats you. And don't you deny it. Yes, maybe in his own twisted way he does love you, but again, Nell, *it ain't enough!* What's gone, and what you'll never get back, is the romance he used to win you over, and that's what a woman needs. It's an important part of a woman's life, and men just don't understand it, or respect it, for that matter. They think it's silly. But it ain't, and when it's gone, it leaves a void. I know."

Buzz realized suddenly that she'd allowed her voice to rise enough to attract the attention of others in the cinema. Besides, they were still standing in the darkened aisle, both a little startled by the passion in Buzz's plea.

Self-consciously they sat in the nearest empty seats. Mellifluous, soothing music rose from the cinema organ, a warning that the movie would soon be starting. Struggling to lean forward from the depths of the crimson plush seat, Buzz couldn't resist raising one other important point. "And just how long do you think you can stand Billy's boozing?"

"I can't stop him. I can't do anything about it," Elinor said miserably. "But Billy's always sorry in the morning. He always promises he'll change. I'm sure that one day he'll really mean it." Often a repentant or badly frightened Billy had promised that he would stop drinking. The sad thing was that several times he *had* seriously tried to stop.

"One day pigs'll fly," retorted Buzz, who knew that hope can be destructive where, in reality, there is no hope.

"You know I couldn't leave him! Where would I go? And what would Edward and I live on?"

"You *could* leave him," Buzz said quietly. "You could get some sort of a job; you could be a waitress or a shop assistant. After all, Edward isn't a baby now—he's nine years old, and at school all day. You could both sleep in our front parlor until you got yourself sorted out. Ma wouldn't mind."

Elinor shook her head. "No, I could never leave Billy. He needs me." She could not imagine life without him. "Look, this is my night out. Please don't let's talk about this anymore."

It was still light when Elinor hurried home. As she put her key in the front door, she hesitated. It sounded as if Billy had company.

In the living room, she found nine-year-old Edward, naked and with his head hidden under a black top hat, sitting on a table. He was gurgling with laughter. In his hand, he held a tumbler containing an inch of green liquid.

His father was sprawled in the chintz armchair, a drink in his hand, a bleary smile on his face.

Elinor dashed forward. In one movement, she swept the hat from Edward's head and grabbed his tumbler. She sniffed it: crème de menthe.

Edward gave his mother a slack, happy smile. He swayed and nearly fell from the table.

Elinor caught him. Her son's body was cold. She tried to control her voice. "Time for bed, Edward."

A silly smile spread over Billy's face. "It's a father's job to teach a chap to drink," he said.

White-faced, Elinor snapped, "How dare you!"

She dressed the swaying Edward, then went to the kitchen. From her best teapot, she took the two bank notes that she kept hidden for emergencies. Without saying a word, she took Edward and left the apartment.

On the following day, Buzz visited some friends, two doors down, who were looking for a lodger. For an extra ten shillings a week, they were persuaded to take both mother and son.

On Monday, at midday, when Elinor knew that Billy would be at work, she returned to Earls Court Square to pack.

As she entered the dark entrance hall, a woman looked out of the ground-floor flat. "I thought it was you, Mrs. O'Dare," she said lugubriously. "I knew someone would have told you about the accident. The police want to see you, dear."

Forty-five minutes later, Elinor was sitting beside Billy's hospital bed. His bandaged leg was raised in traction, and one arm was in a plaster cast. His head was also bandaged, and the left side of his face was badly grazed.

"I ran after you." Billy sounded sheepish. "But the curb seemed to move, and a lorry got me from behind. Bloody stupid thing to do."

"Poor, poor Billy!" Elinor said as she tenderly kissed him. "Don't you worry about a thing, darling." For only a fleeting moment, she feared the wrath of Buzz.

But it was Edward who objected. Still suffering from a hangover, he looked at his mother and said in a voice of hopeless misery, "I didn't think you'd make me go back. Oh, *why* can't you leave him, Mummy?"

"Things are going to be different," Elinor promised, but as she saw disbelief in Edward's face, she suddenly wondered how *she* could have stubbornly held on to that belief for so long. She remembered hoping that things would change when her baby was born. As long ago as that! Then she hoped that things would change when the baby stopped crying, then when the baby stopped teething. She had always managed to find an excuse for Billy's bad behavior; she had always managed to produce an apparently rational reason—however tortured her rationalization— for his hurtful words and actions.

"Darling," Elinor said sadly, "what would Daddy do without me? And what would everyone say?"

"It won't matter what people say—we won't be there to hear them. And what happens to Daddy will be *his* problem, not ours." Edward grasped her hands and pleaded. "You know as well as I do that Daddy's a drunk and a bully and a rotter. *Please* let's not go back."

"Oh Edward, you don't understand," Elinor said miserably. "You see, I love him."

Elinor could not explain—because she did not herself understand— her love for Billy. She simply knew in her heart that Billy was her man, and she would love him to distraction and destruction until death parted them. Elinor longed for and believed in hope and in love, with the firm confidence of one who never dared to doubt it for a moment.

Edward said, "Mummy, you don't understand how *different* you are when Daddy isn't around. When you're with Daddy, you let him kick you around. I hate to see it."

Elinor remembered that Buzz had accused her of being a doormat. Sadly she said, "I can't help it, Edward. That's the way I was brought up. We're going home now."

FRIDAY, 7 AUGUST 1936

Every month or so, Billy took his family to Larkwood, which continued to crumble into decay. His parents were now quite frail and seemed to spend their time huddled like sparrows in bad weather on either side of the drawing room fire. Elinor occasionally wondered why she had been frightened of them.

Elinor spent her visits to Larkwood either going for long vigorous walks in the park or reading in the library, a dark room that smelled sourly of old books and ghostly cigar smoke; it contained no books of value but the complete works of many popular nineteenth-century novelists, outdated atlases, musty reference books, and many boxes of family papers.

One threatening afternoon in early August, when the sky was slate purple and the air ominously still, Elinor opened a dusty box of old household books: the earliest account book was dated 1712. The weekly household accounts had been analyzed in thirteen columns, and so had annual general expenditure. The menu books—written in careful copperplate—showed exactly what had been ordered from the cook on each day. The wages book recorded amounts paid long ago to staff, under the headings "House," "Laundry," "Stables," "Kennels," "Game-keepers," and "Gardeners." The cellar book noted what wines had been bought and when they were drunk. Fascinated, Elinor started to read.

Later, she looked up as her mother-in-law entered the library. "Look what I've found!" Elinor held up a small chunky book bound in green leather so dark it was almost black, except on the corners, which had worn away.

"Oh, that's Rachel O'Dare's diary. One of our family treasures. She lived in the reign of Queen Elizabeth. There are some interesting recipes in it—you purchased one recipe at a time in those days, and they were expensive. I seem to remember that Rachel paid a guinea for a dish of peas with bacon and chopped onion. Of course, she also had her own family recipe book: they were copied out by a clerk for each daughter, upon her marriage."

Elinor leafed through the thin, brittle pages. "Here's a recipe for candied flowers!"

"We still use that for crystallizing violets, primroses, and rose petals. Rachel also had some pretty ideas for using flowers in salads."

Elinor said, "I think I'd like to try some of these. Could I take the book to my room and copy some of the recipes?"

"By all means."

More than three hundred years after they happened, Elinor shared Lady Rachel's adventures. In the blue bedroom, as Elinor carefully turned the pages, she learned about Rachel's life. In her diary, Rachel had recorded every detail of her country day, every domestic squabble and reconciliation, every wager her husband lost, every gown he bought her, every game she played with her children, every problem she had with her servants, every time she felt depressed and was "loste yn melencholy." Rachel noted in detail what happened at the local fairs, on the holy days, on Christmas and other feast days. Once, she was presented to the Queen, when Her Majesty paid a visit to a neighbor, the cost of which nearly bankrupted him.

Before dressing for dinner, Elinor started to decipher the crabbed hand and odd spelling of Rachel O'Dare's candied flower recipe.

"Thinking of starting a sweetshop, Elinor?" Billy was looking over her shoulder.

"No. I'm copying a recipe from an old diary."

Billy's arm reached around and slowly turned the pages of the worn green book.

Busy scribbling, Elinor murmured, "She has such a wry sense of humor. I feel I know her. In fact, that diary seems like reading a letter from an old friend. I know all Rachel's friends. I know she didn't like her father-in-law."

"He wasn't a very likable man." Billy yawned. "He had to get out of the west of Ireland pretty quickly, after leaking information to the English. He was a sort of collaborator—a fearful swine, by all accounts." Again he peered over Elinor's shoulder at the little diary. "It's damned difficult to read, isn't it! Spidery handwriting and crazy spelling."

"You need patience." Elinor slowly read: " 'Today I walked the orchard with Parson, and we did talk upon Joanna's wedding, which now grows near. As we did turn beneath green leaves, Parson did eye the fat, black cherries, until I promise him a basket. He spoke then of the feasting here. Again I see his eye right hungry, when I do promise 'twill be mighty. "What manner of dishes?" asks he. "Five spits of roasting meat are set up in the kitchen," say I. "We also shall feast on roasted swan, boiled fowls, and many little birds. Also much pike and salmon, with mighty, hot meat pies, and a cold one with live larks—to set the ladies skipping and shrieking." ' "

Billy said, "Don't stop." He was listening carefully.

"I'm glad you like it too. I'll go on with the greedy parson." Elinor read, absorbed: " ' "And sweetmeats?" asked Parson. "Such as never have here been tasted," promised I, "following my mother's receipt book for creams and syllabubs, jellies and puddings. Also my own spiced fruit cake." "And drink?" asks Parson, so I poured for him from my mouth a stream of claret wines from France, with sack, mead, cordials, and liquors, such as is meet for this marriage feast. Then doth he lick his lips, whether at the sound of this banquet or thinking upon the swiving that would follow, I know not.' "

"What does 'swiving' mean?" Billy asked.

"Making love, I guess."

"*Don't* say 'I guess.' "

"Sorry, Billy," Elinor responded mechanically. Although she didn't attempt to alter her midwestern accent, she tried not to use American expressions, because Billy didn't like her to and the British didn't understand them.

"Better stop that and dress for dinner. You know how testy Mother gets if we aren't down before the gong stops ringing."

TUESDAY, 11 AUGUST 1936

When they returned to Earls Court from Larkwood, Billy was in a bad temper. A visit to his family home always reminded him that his elder brother would inherit the estate in its entirety. Edward, now sixteen, disappeared to the bedroom they rented for him on the floor above their apartment.

Elinor opened the sitting room window and leaned on the sill, looking down on the square. The soft summer breeze smelled of dust, roses, warm grass, and horses' droppings.

Billy poured himself half a tumbler of whiskey, sat down in the sagging chintz armchair, and said wearily, "I suppose I'll have to tell you sometime. I've been fired." His nonchalant air did not disguise his pain.

Elinor turned from the window. "Billy! *Why?*"

"First thing a journalist must remember when he's fired is that the reason probably hasn't a bloody thing to do with his work. The *Globe*'s getting a new editor, and he wants to bring in his own gang." Billy added casually, "I don't think I'll look for another newspaper job."

Elinor realized that he meant no other newspaper wanted to hire him.

The following morning at seven o'clock, Elinor carried a cup of tea to Billy. Sitting on the edge of his bed, she said, "Why don't you see what other sort of work is available? Perhaps you could apply for this job?" She handed him the newspaper: she had ringed one entry in red pencil.

Reacting slowly and reluctantly, Billy read, " 'Needed at once, for large manufacturing chemists, live-wire men qualified to call upon doctors and chemists. Splendid prospects for sound men.' " He looked up at Elinor. " 'Sound men.' That means no war veterans need apply."

"I know that your limp is painful, Billy, but a limp doesn't make people feel uneasy—like a missing arm or leg," Elinor said persuasively.

"You needn't think I'm going to turn into a commercial traveler," Billy snarled.

"What *are* you going to turn into, Billy?" Her clear green eyes carefully studied him. Although he took little exercise, Billy's body was still tall, lean, and firm. But today he had a hangdog air and his shoulders sagged—familiar signs of a hangover. Elinor looked at the leathery pouches under his eyes and his gray cheeks covered by silver stubble.

She could not think why she loved him.

Billy gave her a sly smile. "It so happens I have a better idea for making money."

He threw back the bedclothes and walked naked to the chest of drawers. He pulled open a top drawer, then turned to face her. In his hand he held a small dark green leather object.

"Why, that's Rachel O'Dare's diary! Does your mother know you have it?"

"No, she doesn't. She'll never notice it's gone. Don't worry, I'm not going to sell it. I've only borrowed it, and I'll return it."

"*When* are you going to return it?" Elinor was shocked that he had so casually removed something valuable.

"When you've written a book called *Diary of an Elizabethan Housewife,*" Billy said triumphantly. "I know just the right publisher for it!"

For a moment, Elinor wondered if he was still drunk after his bout of the previous evening. She studied Billy's face: if he was drunk, his facial muscles slackened, giving him a vacant look. But that telltale sign wasn't there this morning.

Quietly she said, "Billy, I'm not a professional writer. I love scribbling letters and I once won an essay prize in school, but I don't know how to *begin* to write a book."

"You've got the beginning here." Billy waved the little green diary at her. "Simply translate it into modern English. Add explanatory paragraphs, where necessary, to expand what Rachel is saying, or what's going on in the rest of the sixteenth-century world—print those bits in bold type instead of footnotes: you don't want the thing to look scholarly."

"Where would *I* find out what was going on in the rest of the sixteenth-century world?"

"What's the British Museum for? Ask the librarian to guide your research."

"But I don't know *how* to do research!"

"Ask Edward to show you." Edward was studying history, hoping for a scholarship to Oxford. Billy added with airy truth, "Research just means finding out things."

Elinor and Billy planned the book together; he advised her to stick as closely as possible to the original text, as that would be the easiest way to operate. Billy drew up a list of work deadlines for each item so that he would know immediately if Elinor was falling behind schedule. Edward showed his mother how to handle her research in an orderly way: plywood orange boxes were piled against one wall of the living room, and at Christmas, Billy gave Elinor a second-hand filing cabinet.

By the end of March 1937, Elinor had finished *Diary of an Elizabethan Housewife*. The book was to be published in November by Stansfield and Hart.

Just before publication, Billy hurled himself into a flurry of activity. He wrote press releases; he persuaded every suede-shod gossip writer he knew to mention the book, in return for various favors. Billy also carefully chose Elinor's outfit for the book launch party, to be held at the Russell Hotel in Bloomsbury.

Elinor did not care for his choice. Standing in a changing room at Fortnum and Mason, she exclaimed, "What's gotten into you, Billy? I can't wear a bright pink moiré cocktail frock at three o'clock in the afternoon! Your mother would say it was dead common. And we can't afford it!"

"Joe Grant's paying for it," Billy said, and turned to the sales-woman. "The hat will be very important for the photographs. Let's try that white silk turban with the pink ostrich feathers."

"*What* photographs?" Elinor asked, bewildered.

Billy looked carefully at his wife; she was nearly thirty-seven now. Elinor's face was thinner, but her pink, white, and golden coloring was still striking. "Pity they won't be in color," Billy said. "I've booked a sitting after lunch with Angus McBean—he's the best theatrical pho-tographer. You're going to be launched like a leading lady!"

And Billy saw to it that everything went according to his plan. He supervised the press coverage, the interviews on the wireless, and the trips to bookshops for autograph sessions, to which Elinor traveled, at Billy's insistence, in a hired white Rolls-Royce—paid for by Elinor's astonished publishers, who had never before done anything to attract publicity beyond sending review copies to a few literary editors.

To the surprise of everyone except Billy, *Diary of an Elizabethan Housewife* by Elinor Dove was an immediate success. The illustrations were copious and charming; the book was historically correct yet didn't read like a dull history book, for Elinor had re-created Lady Rachel's life so vividly that readers felt they could lean out and touch her. As Billy kept telling the press, almost anyone would find the book an acceptable Christmas gift, and many did.

Edward, who had won a senior exhibition and was now reading history at Merton, was as delighted by his mother's success as he was by his new freedom. He loved Oxford—all the more so as he had just acquired his first girlfriend. Her name was Jane, and she, too, was a first-year history student.

SATURDAY, 1 JANUARY 1938

Elinor leaned back against her pillows and stretched luxuriously in the weak warmth of the winter sun, marveling at how her life had recently improved. This was the first time since she'd known him that Billy hadn't had a hangover on New Year's Day! He had started to cut back his drinking after a painful illness, when his doctor warned that his body wouldn't stand up to such punishment. He hadn't minced words, and Billy had been frightened by the verbal sketch of cirrhosis of the liver.

Lying naked beside her, Billy yawned and stroked his mustache. "I've got a present for you, darling. A new contract for the next book."

"Oh, good. The Elizabethan cookery book?"

"Not exactly," Billy said. "They want a novel."

In the crimson and gilt splendor of the Café Royal, Billy had lunched with the publisher and his senior editor. They both thought that Elinor had a natural talent for writing. Her work showed a rare observance, fresh directness, and an eye for the unexpected. Her characters were not two-dimensional stereotypes but real people who leapt right off the page, prepared to talk or argue with the reader.

Billy had sat back, immediately thinking: international best-seller ... first novel ... Margaret Mitchell ... *Gone with the Wind* ... Hollywood ... movie rights. He said, "I have to tell you that we have already been approached by Billy Collins ..."

The advance was agreed by the end of the meal.

Billy now saw a new life stretching before him, and it was very like his old life before the war. It was clearly in his interest to develop Elinor's ability as a novelist because if Elinor could earn good money, then Billy—as her manager—would never need another job.

As he sketched Elinor's new career to her, she sat up in bed and blinked. "But, Billy, I've never written a novel!" She was bewildered. "I couldn't do it—I wouldn't know how to start!"

"I'll teach you. It's simple."

Elinor knew immediately that Billy was serious, and that it would be useless to argue. She realized that her day would be wasted trying to change his mind. "I'll get breakfast," she said, shifting to get out of bed.

"No," Billy said, restraining her, "I'll get breakfast."

Ten minutes later, Elinor stared at a worn, flower-patterned tray upon which stood a jug of milk, an apple, several slices of buttered bread, and a red exercise book.

Billy said, "That's all you're getting until you fill ten pages—to my satisfaction."

"But what shall I write about? What do *I* know about? Life on a farm? The horror of a French hospital in the war? Trying to survive after it? People don't want to read depressing stuff like that—they know too much about it!"

"Write what other people don't know about," Billy suggested. "Then they can't check on you. Write a historical novel. Start with a rape."

"But I've never . . . I don't know what—"

"Then I'll show you." As Billy hurled himself upon her, the milk jug crashed to the floor.

Later, Billy murmured, "You have talent, but that is only the beginning. The first thing a writer has to learn is discipline."

To teach her this, Billy locked Elinor in the bedroom.

Her first reactions to imprisonment were defiance and revolt. She did not touch the red exercise book.

"What an ungrateful bitch you are!" growled Billy at midday, when he brought her bread and milk. "If it wasn't for me, you wouldn't have *had* this success that's so clearly gone to your head!"

Elinor, of course, knew that this was true, because Billy had said it to her so many times.

After a day of boredom, with no one to talk to and nothing to read, Elinor capitulated. At teatime, she dipped her pen into the bottle of Steven's blue-black ink and started to write.

Billy made it clear that he was not satisfied with her efforts. "You're not trying hard enough!" he exclaimed with a frown as he read what she had written.

"*You'd* think that Scott of the Antarctic wasn't trying hard enough!" Elinor said, showing a flash of her old spirit.

He gave her a slim book on punctuation. "Learn this by heart. I'll test you on a chapter every evening, before supper. If you don't know it, you get no supper."

When Elinor flubbed the third chapter, Billy locked her in the bedroom again, as if she were still a schoolgirl who hadn't learned her lesson. Then he left the flat and stayed out all night.

He returned at eight o'clock the following morning, disheveled and tired. He smiled at Elinor as he stood in the bedroom doorway. "Can you now tell me the difference between a colon and a semicolon?"

In a frenzy of jealousy, anxiety, and fear, Elinor quickly recited the carefully memorized lesson, moving all the while across the floor toward Billy.

Her heart pounded when he bent to kiss her; she lifted her face toward his, as a prisoner toward the light. She felt his hand grasp her breast with rough passion; then, without a word, he swept her into his arms and carried her to their bed.

She felt the erotic, harsh scraping of his mustache against her soft hair, and the light scratch of the stubble on his unshaven face. Her anxiety was replaced by the tension of passion.

Eventually Elinor produced a story synopsis that Billy found satisfactory. Together, they visited the London Library and left with fifteen research books.

Elinor felt a little more cheerful. "I suppose I must remember that everyone has at least *one* book in them," she said.

"That's a lie, as any publisher will tell you," Billy grunted. "Some people haven't got so much as a paragraph of a pamphlet in them."

Billy proved to be an unsympathetic, tough, but ultimately excellent critic, who repeatedly urged Elinor to concentrate on plot, pace, and action scenes. "Cut scenic descriptions to a maximum of two lines," he told her. "If your readers wanted to read about birds, trees, and sunsets, they'd buy a nature book."

Elinor wept when she didn't understand what Billy wanted her to write, or felt that she couldn't do it. "Why? *Why* do I have to rewrite it *again?*" she complained one evening. "I can't see what's *wrong* with what I've written!"

"Then listen to me more carefully," Billy said in a soft voice that raised the hairs on Elinor's spine. "As you write, you must think yourself *into* each of your characters. Be an actress! I want to know what Lydia *feels* when her sister's husband kisses her!"

"But I've told you—"

"Don't *tell* me what's happened—*show* me what's happening! I want to experience it!" Billy roared. "This dull rubbish sounds like a newspaper report. Get some life in it! Remember that you are the eyes, the ears, the nose, and the heart of your reader. Always remember that. I want to feel that I'm *there*, hidden in the cold shadow behind the hedge, as Cynthia watches her husband kiss Lydia. I want to see them embrace in the garden, and I want to shiver in the moonlight as I bite my lip to stop myself from crying or cursing at them!"

Elinor stared at Billy with surprise. He had just sketched what it felt like to experience jealousy. He must therefore understand the pain that he had made her suffer.

The following evening, she cried tearfully, "Yesterday you told me that I need more emotion in my work, that I must feel the passion that my characters feel—and today you hand me this dusty little book on grammar. How *can* I feel passion when I have to think about grammar?"

"Try," Billy advised grimly, *"and never forget that I know what's best for you."*

Often, in despair, she flung herself upon the bed and wept, but tears did no good. Paradoxically, the only thing that made her forget her helplessness, her bewilderment, her anxiety, her indignation, and her despair was scribbling in the red exercise books.

Every morning, Elinor hurriedly threw on a bathrobe and ate the meager breakfast Billy fixed for her. He then locked her in the bedroom, and did not unlock the door until she banged on it at midday and then pushed ten pages of scribbled manuscript under it. If her pages were good enough, Billy carried a tray of fruit and coffee to the little desk at the bedroom window, where Elinor worked. If the pages were not good enough, he simply tore them up and threw the pieces out of the window, to flutter slowly down to Earls Court Square.

When Elinor finished her frugal luncheon (Billy feared a large meal might make her sleepy), she hurriedly washed and dressed while mentally preparing the next ten pages. After a further ten pages (a total of five thousand words a day), she was released from the bedroom to prepare the evening meal.

While Elinor cooked supper, Billy scribbled his transitional suggestions in the margins of her work; he corrected her grammar, her punctuation, and her abysmal spelling. After supper, Elinor rewrote her work; Billy stood over her, urging her to cut this or emphasize that.

When her writing was finished to Billy's satisfaction, he would pick up Elinor in his arms and carry her to bed.

There he would caress her exhausted body until it wearily responded to his touch, with increasing willingness, and finally with a passionate abandon she had not thought possible, spent as she was from writing.

After a few weeks, Elinor no longer resented the sound of the key turning in the lock of the bedroom door after breakfast. Instead, she trembled with carefully concealed excitement as she waited for the little click of the lock, which now transported her into the mysterious and limitless world of her imagination.

But by the end of the day, Elinor was not only exhausted but anxious; she worried whether her work was good enough. Only Billy could lull this anxiety; only Billy could reassure her that her work reached his high standards; only Billy could then caressingly transport her to a world of passion in which description and narrative thread were forgotten.

In Billy's arms, Elinor felt successful, sensuous, desired, protected, happy—and safe. She did not see herself as a bird imprisoned in a cage, for no cage was needed. Elinor was bound to Billy by the invisible, secret silken cords of a voluptuousness of which she was ashamed but to which she was addicted. She was both captivated and motivated by Billy, who, having made her totally dependent upon him both mentally and physically, kept her firmly under his thumb.

Elinor was bullied, cheated, rejected, and treated with amused and open contempt, but she was Billy's victim, his invisibly-shackled slave: she was helplessly, hopelessly enthralled by him. Billy's mesmeric gaze could still make Elinor feel worthy or unworthy, anxious or confident. And sometimes he permitted her to be happy.

One of these occasions was in June 1938, when Elinor's work was interrupted by the marriage of their son, Edward, to Jane, the girl he had fallen in love with at Oxford. The ceremony took place in St. Bartholomew's, a small Norman church north of Oxford that had not been much altered in the past nine hundred years. Elinor helped with the decorations and, in the process, got to know more of her daughter-in-law, a young woman she found both intelligent and endearing. Elinor liked Jane's quiet tenacity and her earnest but forceful speech. In truth, she wished that Edward had not insisted on rushing into marriage, but if he must (and he had hinted that it was necessary), then he could not have chosen a more appropriate bride.

Eventually, after much effort, anxiety, and pain, Elinor produced a well-constructed novel with well-developed scenes and believable characters; she finished it in early January of 1939, two days before Jane produced her and Billy's first grandchild.

As she sat by Jane's hospital bedside and held baby Clare in her arms, Elinor was astonished to find herself a grandmother, for, at the age of thirty-nine, she still felt seventeen inside.

Again she examined the tiny, perfect toes as they curled and uncurled. She lightly stroked the miniature, Nefertiti-like head, marveling at the still-visible skull joins beneath the dark fuzz. With joy, she gazed into the old, wise eyes of this poised newborn baby.

"She has Edward's eyes," Jane said proudly.

"Apart from that, she's the image of you." Jane was small and thin, pale and dark.

Although they were so young, Jane seemed perfect for Edward. They lived in a big house in North Oxford with Jane's father, a widowed history professor, who didn't seem to notice. He didn't care what happened, provided nothing upset his routine.

To Billy's disappointment, Elinor's Elizabethan romance, *Rebellious Princess*, did not achieve the same level of success as the diary. No messenger appeared from Paramount or MGM, and although Billy personally delivered a copy of the book to Vivien Leigh's London home, he never received an acknowledgment.

The publishers were more pragmatic. "You can hardly expect her to pull off a winner with her first nonfiction book *and* her first novel," Mr. Stansfield said, over oysters at Wheelers. "The book is selling well for a first novel, and we're pleased with her progress." Stansfield and Hart had purchased an option on Elinor's next five novels. "I'm only sorry that your wife couldn't spare the time to have lunch, for I could then reassure her in person."

"She hates to break up the day—finds it stops her momentum," Billy murmured, having neglected to tell Elinor of the invitation. "She's already started on the next novel—kept to the same period, as you suggested, which cuts down her research. She's settling down in that period nicely. Shouldn't be surprised if she started to wear padded sleeves and a farthingale."

Billy now spent his mornings reading the newspapers, and behaved as if Mr. Chamberlain relied on his advice—which was to kick those German bastards out of Austria and back into their own country, before the British found themselves in another war. But Mr. Chamberlain didn't listen, and by September, when baby Clare was nine months old, Britain and France declared war on Germany.

Jane was again pregnant. "Just as well her mother left her a bit of money," Billy said sourly. Elinor said nothing, although she secretly agreed with him. Edward had done the right thing when Jane first became pregnant, but they should both have been more responsible and taken precautions after Clare's birth: two children were too much of a load for two kids of nineteen—especially now, when Britain was at war.

"Appeasement," Billy said, on the morning before Christmas. "We should have been tougher with the bastards earlier. We were too aggressive the first time, and not aggressive enough this time. We should have rubbed their Nazi noses in it, like puppies, when they made their first little mess and marched into Austria."

That evening, Billy returned home late, only mildly drunk and very happy because of his new job; he was to work in an administrative capacity at the War Office, liaising with the R.A.F.

As he was telling Elinor about it, the telephone on the hall table rang. Billy picked it up, listened, and said in his new, clipped voice, "Well done, m'boy. I expect you'll want to tell your mother. . . . Edward and Jeremy, that friend of his, have joined up. They've been drafted into the intelligence service."

On the afternoon of Monday, 11 March 1940, Edward telephoned his mother to tell her that Jane's second baby, Annabel, had just been born, two weeks early.

Elinor was unable to reach Billy, as he was not in his office, so she had to contain her excitement until that evening, when they had planned a rare night out to see Greta Garbo and Melvyn Douglas in *Ninotchka*.

Outside Billy's favorite pub, the Star and Garter at the top of Whitehall, people slowly groped their way through the blackout. As Elinor walked into the bar, a blast of light and noise greeted her. A piano pounding "Roll Out the Barrel" was surrounded by a singing khaki-clad crowd, their fists wrapped around tankards of beer. Elsewhere a group of sailors gathered round an accordionist were bawling, "All the nice girls love a sailor." The place smelled of stale cigarettes, stale hops, and stale sweat, but nobody cared, and the atmosphere was one of cheerful euphoria. Elinor struggled through the crowd to a small corner table where she had spotted a couple of unoccupied seats.

When Billy appeared in the doorway, she stood up and waved until he saw her, then cradled an imaginary baby and gave him the thumbs-up sign.

"Boy?" he mouthed questioningly.

Elinor shook her head.

Billy shrugged, smiled, then fought his way to the counter to buy drinks.

As he carried them from the bar, Elinor saw a young girl, hatless and slim as a bulrush in a dark brown coat, dash forward and tug at Billy's sleeve; her face was anxious as she spoke to him.

Billy looked exasperated as the girl clung to his sleeve. With a sudden movement, she laid her head against his shoulder.

Billy angrily jerked his head toward Elinor.

The girl looked her way and Elinor saw a freckled, oval face with short brown hair and large, tearful dark eyes.

Billy yanked his sleeve free, then continued to battle through the crowd toward Elinor.

"Who was that?" Elinor asked him when he reached her.

"Oh, just a girl from the newspaper office. One of the secretaries."

"What's her name?"

"I forget, actually."

"If you don't tell me, I'm going to ask her."

"For Christ's sake, Elinor, can't we *just once* have a night out without your jealous imagination taking off like a Spitfire? I think she's called Pat Kettle."

"Why is she crying? And why did she ask you to help her?" That had been obvious.

"Some trouble at the office. Some documents are missing. She's under suspicion. *I* can't do anything about it, as I told her."

"She's in love with you—I can see it."

Standing by the bar, the girl still gazed sadly at Billy; she wore an expression that Elinor knew well, the expression of a puppy that has just been kicked by its master.

"I can't help that," Billy said tersely. "Drink up, or we'll be late."

"For heaven's sake, Billy, she's only a child," Elinor said angrily. "Couldn't you have left her alone?" She watched as Miss Kettle turned despondently away, toward the door, and disappeared in the crowd.

"Be reasonable, old girl. Can I help it if some woman takes a shine to me?"

"Yes, you *can* help it," Elinor replied bitterly. She put her untouched drink on the table. "We've been married for twenty-two years and you're nearly fifty, for heaven's sake. How old is she? Nineteen? A young girl doesn't fall for a man of your age unless she's pursued and courted. I can just about remember your romantic approach, Billy. It was very effective."

Billy laughed this off. "No, darling—*you* were always the romantic. Now tell me about my new granddaughter. And drink up. We're already late for the cinema."

Chapter · 5

Almost three years after they were married, Edward and Jane were celebrating Jane's birthday at the Café de Paris in London, when two fifty-kilo German bombs fell down an air shaft of the nightclub, straight onto the dance floor. Edward and Jane were killed instantly, their bodies charred almost beyond recognition.

Billy, silent and regretful, was kinder to Elinor than he had been since their marriage. Elinor, in a state of shock from which she felt she would never recover, took charge of the orphaned children and had to adapt quickly to the demands of a young family.

A few months after this tragedy, at closing time at the Star and Garter, Billy fell in the blackout, with a resultant compound fracture of his left fibula, which was slow to heal. He now found it difficult to walk and was unable to continue with his job. Eventually he joined Elinor in the country with the three little girls; everybody said how sad it was that Miranda had been born only a month before Jane and Edward were killed. The near-derelict cottage was on the Larkwood estate; there was no space at the big house, which now served as an officers' convalescent home.

Their new circumstances required new literary discipline. Billy now made Elinor get up in the dark, at five a.m., to write until nine a.m., seven days a week. But those few hours a day belonged only to Elinor, and during that time, she forgot the cold, discomfort, and deprivation of war; she even forgot the loss of Edward, which otherwise was constantly present in her waking time, sapping the strength and hope from her body. As her pen detailed the rich clothes, splendid jewelry, and sybaritic banquets of delicious food with delicate wine, Elinor escaped back to the leisurely, bountiful, lyrical life of Elizabethan England.

The rest of her day was spent looking after the three baby girls, struggling to shop and cook for all of them, and coping with life without electricity, running water, or inside sanitation: there was a wooden shed at the end of the garden, and water was pumped from a well in the courtyard. Elinor ignored this lack of comfort. She was determined to see only the romantic charm of the cottage, which stood on the southern slope of a wooded hill, with a view of undulating fields beyond the small garden where Billy raised neat rows of vegetables. Elinor enjoyed the peace of the country, especially in winter on cold, clear snowy days, and in summer when the wind rippled through the field of ripe wheat; then, she was always reminded of her childhood, although British wheat fields were tiny compared to those of Minnesota.

And Elinor quickly became a doting grandmother. Everybody said what pretty little girls they were: all three had Billy's mesmeric aquamarine eyes, solemn and staring. Clare, the eldest, was dark and frail, a quiet child as her father had been. Annabel looked like Elinor as a child; she was a rosy-cheeked, chubby little thing, with thick fair hair and an unusually pretty face. Miranda, the youngest, had a pale, freckled face; she was skinny and small for her age.

"Yes, we're very lucky," Elinor would smile when anybody complimented her on the three sisters. But no number of adorable grandchildren could replace Edward. Like most mothers, she had thought of her own child as still flesh of her flesh and blood of her blood, still a part of her own body, joined by an invisible umbilical cord that could never be cut; and so now she felt bereft, as if a part of her had been amputated.

Every time Elinor saw aquamarine eyes staring up at her, in her mind's eye again she saw Edward as a child and felt poignant, wistful regret. She wished that she had not been so careless of those ordinary hours when he had been in the room while she ironed, or darned, or listened to the radio. Every time she remembered her beloved only son, Elinor's heart seemed to shrivel and she felt a physical pain in her breast. Rather than give in and break down in tears before the frightened little girls, she would make an effort of will and turn her mind to her plot problems with her book, a diversion that was always successful.

SUNDAY, 5 AUGUST 1945

Nearly two years after starting it, Elinor finished her fourth novel. She had enjoyed almost every moment of it; she had even persuaded herself that getting up in the dark was exciting, although the past winter had been so cold that she wore her coat at her desk, draped blankets around her legs, and propped her feet on a hot-water bottle.

Elinor worked all day on the novel. Billy, knowing that the rhythm and crescendo of the ending should be uninterrupted, saw that she was undisturbed. He brought fresh cups of tea and soup to her desk and took away the cold, untouched ones as she scribbled, oblivious to his presence.

Just after eleven o'clock that night, Elinor put down her pen, removed her spectacles, rubbed her eyes, stretched, and like any novelist, started to have doubts.

Perhaps it should not be called *Deadly Fortune* but *Fatal Fortune*. Elinor didn't want it to sound like a detective story, although that was exactly what the novel was—a series of murders in one Elizabethan family, in order to gain control of an estate.

Elinor stretched again. She felt as if she needed a walk. She felt as if she wanted a drink. She felt hungry. She felt wide awake. She felt light-headed.

A bottle of cider stood on the kitchen dresser, a lamb chop lay in the metal-mesh meat safe that hung outside the kitchen door; she cooked the chop and drank the cider. For the moment, she felt completely alone in the world, and comfortable. She picked up the *Daily Telegraph* from the kitchen table, folded it at the crossword, then decided not to do it, because she could never finish the thing and it made her feel inadequate. She looked at the headlines once again: nothing much was happening.

Far away on the other side of the world, where it was early morning, a small parachute was floating down from a B-29 bomber. At 8:15 a.m., a nuclear chain reaction in the bomb built up a temperature of several million degrees centigrade, which created a fireball that seemed brighter than the sun. This fireball expanded to measure two hundred and fifty yards in diameter. One second after it had been detonated over Hiroshima, the world's first atomic bomb signaled the end of the war.

TUESDAY, 9 JULY 1946

Joe Grant's office in Carey Street, immediately behind the assizes court, was almost a replica of his study in the country, with its dark green leather appointments. Joe looked older than fifty-one, Elinor thought as she sat in a wing chair by the side of the empty fireplace. She suspected that he carefully cultivated his Pickwickian traditional-lawyer look.

Joe smiled and said, "You haven't changed at all, Elinor. A touch older, as we all are, but you haven't changed." He basked in her wide, delighted smile.

"What flattery," said Elinor, now forty-six. "How's your family, Joe?"

"Ethel has a touch of arthritis, but the boys are fine. Michael has finally settled down at Eton—it helps if your elder brother is already there."

Elinor briefly reflected that, while Joe's children had benefited from their mother's money, she was glad Edward had not been brought up as strictly as Adam and Michael Grant. Their mother—five years older than Joe—had been forty years old in 1930, when Adam was born. After the difficult birth, she had suffered badly from what was not then recognized as postpartum depression, and seemed never to have forgiven Adam for her misery; Ethel was more lenient with Michael, who was born two years later, although she had not welcomed either pregnancy. Elinor had never seen Ethel Grant kiss her children; even at bedtime, she merely offered a cool cheek to be kissed by them. They had been restricted to the nursery by a severe and strict nanny and had been expected to behave as little adults rather than as children. At least in Edward's too short life, he had known the warmth of a mother's love.

Joe looked over his neat desk. "Why did you want to see me, Elinor?" Billy made all her business arrangements and had signed all the contracts prepared by Joe for the thirty-seven publishers around the world who had purchased *Deadly Fortune*.

When Paramount Pictures bought the film rights to *Deadly Fortune*, which had been an instant best-seller, and Vivien Leigh agreed to star in it, Billy had bought a vintage Lagonda, and Elinor had once again made a secret visit to an empty house about twenty miles distant from the cottage, a dilapidated estate called Starlings. The house was too big to run comfortably in wartime but not big enough to be useful to the forces, so shortly after war was declared, the entire estate had been turned into carrot fields; after the war, when the boisterous land girls and Italian prisoners of war who raised the carrots happily abandoned them, the land was left neglected. Now the place had fallen into disrepair, its earth knee high in coarse grass.

In Joe's dark office, Elinor outlined her plan with barely contained excitement. She wanted to surprise Billy by buying him his own country place!

"It's not as grand as Larkwood, but it's just as pretty!" Elinor said. "It's outside a little village called Maiden Bradley, near Warminster. I'd like you to handle the purchase, Joe." The folder she gave him included snapshots of a decrepit but beautiful small stone Elizabethan manor house, with a cherry orchard to one side of it. "Don't you think, Joe, that if Billy lived in the way he was brought up, he would . . . settle down, and relax, and be happy?"

Poor Elinor was still hoping that she could tame the old rascal, Joe thought. Aloud he said, "It's beautiful, Elinor, but . . . how can you afford this house?"

"It's a bargain—five thousand pounds!" Elinor exclaimed. "Paramount paid forty thousand dollars for *Deadly Fortune*. There *must* be enough money somewhere, even after tax."

Joe said uncomfortably, "All the money was paid to Billy, as your manager." There was a note of sorrow in his voice.

Elinor looked sharply at him. Slowly she said, "You mean . . . he's spent it *all?*"

Joe hesitated. "I believe that Billy may have made some unwise investments on the stock exchange." He realized that Elinor, who could rationalize and excuse her husband's drunken bullying and lechery, was now faced with undodgeable evidence that Billy was a liar, a cheat, and—some might say—a thief. Joe added, "To be fair, Elinor, Billy insisted on repaying every penny I've ever lent him."

Elinor's eyes filled with tears. *Nothing* in her hand, for all that work.

Up to now Elinor had willingly believed Billy's plausible explanations of his lying, cheating, and other petty dishonesty: he had done it to help someone out; he hadn't realized what he was getting into; he had been lied to; he had been let down. But nothing could explain away this betrayal.

"I might be able to raise a loan for you," Joe said, "or a further book option—of course, I couldn't go directly to your publisher behind Billy's back . . ."

Which meant that he would, Elinor reckoned.

"I'm confident," he went on, "that Stansfield and Hart would be open to some agreement so that you could purchase this house. After all, you will probably be happier and write better in more congenial surroundings."

Fighting back tears, Elinor said, "Please speak to Mr. Stansfield as soon as possible." She looked hard at Joe, who knew that she was also saying, *I'm trusting you to do this in some way that won't humiliate Billy, because otherwise my life will be intolerable, and I shall have to live with the real Billy instead of my romantic view of him, which is the only thing that makes the reality bearable for me.*

Mentally replacing her rose-colored spectacles, Elinor said firmly, "Without Billy to make me work, and to sell my work, I would have achieved *nothing*. So I suppose it *is* really his money. . . . Because truly I owe my career to Billy." She had once argued that the talent was hers, but Billy had quickly pointed out that the talent had been trained and disciplined by him, and so her success was due to him. Billy repeatedly told her, "You owe *everything* to me. Without me, you would be *nothing!* Without me, you would never be able to write. And without me, you would *certainly* never be published. *I* am the one who persuaded publishers to risk their money on your work."

Elinor had to admit there was some truth in what he said. Before Billy's schooling, she had known nothing of the craft of writing, and she had had no idea how to discipline herself.

Joe looked at Elinor. There were things he would have liked to say to her, but it wouldn't be correct to do so. Besides, Billy was indisputably the man in Elinor's life, and Joe did not intend to interfere in their marriage.

SUNDAY, 13 JULY 1947

One year later, after her brisk midday walk, Elinor strolled up the winding drive of her new home, between rhododendron bushes that formed great banks of shiny, dark leaves splashed with mauve and white blossoms. This floral guard of honor meandered half a mile, from the house to the hedged boundaries of nineteen acres of garden and parkland.

After she rounded the final bend and could see Starlings in front of her, Elinor paused to admire it once again. The long, low, beautifully proportioned Elizabethan house, with its front of mellow brick, stone mullions, and tall chimneys, now looked as well kept as it probably had been four hundred years earlier.

Briefly Elinor remembered their Earls Court home: the entire apartment would have fitted into the oak-paneled entrance hall of Starlings. Edward had been raised in that cramped flat in sooty London, but his daughters were now able to enjoy a gracious life in the country, thanks to their gran's busy brain and ever-scribbling right hand.

As she inhaled the honey-tinged air, Elinor wished that her mother could know about her success, could see her lovely house, as romantic as if it had sprung up from a child's book. How strange it was, she thought, that her mother's idea of bettering herself had been to get away from the grinding, incessant toil of life on the land. But now that Elinor could do as she pleased—after midday—what she most loved was to work in the soil. Gardening gave her great satisfaction; it also gave her time to think of new plots for books, to dream up new schemes, imagine new characters.

Sometimes, of course, her mind wandered to real matters, some of them quite disturbing. One memory she couldn't seem to escape was the day they had moved into Starlings, when she had accidentally uncovered a batch of battered photographs in Billy's den. They were black-and-white studio pictures of what looked like a ten-year-old girl, shot from the waist downward. Her slim, coltish legs were sprawled across a bed; Elinor recognized the dragon-patterned blue bedspread that she had scrapped when they left Earls Court. The child wore short white socks and black, Shirley Temple, ankle-strap shoes, and that was all. In some pictures, she lay on her back; in some, she was on her stomach, one leg languidly kicking back, bent at the knee.

When, with shaking hands, Elinor showed these pictures to Billy, he shrugged his shoulders and agreed that the photographs were obscene. He said he thought he had destroyed them: they had been taken years ago by a photographer who had been bombed out of his studio, when Billy had put him up for a few days. Elinor had been in the country, preparing the cottage for their occupation.

Elinor wanted to believe him.

With stubborn determination, she focused on the many pleasant things in her life and shut her eyes to Billy's increasingly unpleasant behavior which was, Elinor told herself, only due to the fact that once again he was drinking far more than was good for him.

Billy's three granddaughters, now six, seven, and eight years old, were embarrassed and bewildered when "Daddy Billy smelled funny," which invariably meant he would "act funny" as well, frequently teasing them in a rough way, sometimes even scaring them.

Annabel and Miranda ran off and hid whenever they heard the front door slam followed by Billy's heavy, uncertain tread upon the stairs. But Clare reacted differently. Perhaps it was because he was irritated by Clare's anxiously self-righteous air—the air of an elder sister who felt she was supposed to look after the little ones—that Billy picked on Clare more than on the other two.

But of course, Billy treated Clare with cruelty only when there was nobody around to see him do it: when Elinor was visiting her publisher in London, or when it was the nanny's day off. Clare, whose instinct was to smooth, not ruffle troubled waters, never mentioned her grandfather's harsh treatment, and indeed she would have found it difficult to describe what she was complaining about. Few children feel that they have the power to complain about an adult; and every child in Clare's class at school talked of being slapped occasionally, or beaten if the crime was serious.

As a result of his mistreatment of her, Clare avoided Billy whenever possible. When she returned from school, she always asked, "Is Daddy

Billy at home?" And if the answer was yes, no matter how cold the weather, Clare would immediately ask if she could play in the garden or go for a walk in the woods.

Poor Clare. As the eldest, she was the only sister with vague memories of her dead parents, and she had a forlorn air, as if she were a lost child, forgotten on some railway station platform. She survived Billy's cruel attacks in the only ways that a vulnerable young child could: by mentally withdrawing from any painful scene and by hopefully using magical means. Hidden behind the rhododendron bushes, she would mix potions of berries and grass and daydream, as she willed Daddy Billy to die.

Other minor superstitions also helped Clare: *if* she could count up to seventy-five while holding her breath; *if* she put her knickers on in the morning, left foot first; *if* there was an even number of letters in the advertisement on the side of the school bus—then *he* wouldn't be at home when she returned from school. Sometimes these spells worked.

As Clare grew more apprehensive and frightened (reported as "highly strung" by her school), Elinor saw that, like her father, she was developing into a quiet, nervous child. Elinor tried to blank out these comparisons because they conjured up guilt when she recalled unpleasant memories of Edward's childhood: his father's bewildering behavior and humiliating, drunken cruelty had wrecked Edward's self-confidence—until he grew bigger and stronger than his father; then, when Edward was at home, Billy curbed his bullying.

Instead, Elinor reminded herself how well Billy treated Annabel. Golden-haired and pretty, she was Billy's favorite grandchild; she would jump on his knee, put her little arms around him, and lean her silken head against his shirt. Billy was flattered by her flirtatious manipulation and responded with generosity. When Annabel had made Billy smile, she would quickly ask him for what she wanted.

Shrewd little Annabel.

Billy couldn't be bothered to torment Miranda. "Dull little thing," he said. "Nothing to say for herself. No fun."

Clever little Miranda.

Unfortunately, Billy's increasingly bad behavior no longer caused only local scandal. He had given several regrettable interviews to London newspapers; Elinor's publisher had pointed out to her the folly of such actions. Her public wished to think of her as a romantic creature draped upon a chaise lounge in a negligee, who wrote with quill pen on crackling parchment to a background accompaniment of gentle Scarlatti. They should not hear that Elinor was a half-witted puppet who could not have written her books without her husband's Svengali-like direction and inspiration. There had also been strong rumors (also, unfortunately, started by Billy) that he had actually *written* Elinor's books.

"But surely nobody believes that?" Elinor had protested. "*You* have all my manuscripts, written in longhand, in my handwriting."

"Plenty of hacks will print a malicious story without bothering to check that it's true," Mr. Stansfield had said. "Malicious gossip sells newspapers, which makes money for newspaper proprietors."

"Why tell *me*? Why don't you talk to Billy?" the wretched Elinor asked.

"I *have* talked to your husband, but unfortunately, it hasn't stopped him. I hope you can make him see how damaging such publicity is—for all of us."

As Elinor stared now at her beautiful house, she couldn't help recalling that depressing luncheon with her publisher. She felt vexed with herself. Why did such unpleasant thoughts not stay hidden at the back of her mind? Particularly today, when she should be looking forward to her hour of triumph in her new home. She should be checking that the Georgian mahogany table had been properly laid and the wine decanted, and that the food preparation was proceeding smoothly for her luncheon party. Because, for the first time, Elinor was about to meet her sister-in-law as an equal.

Behind her, a horn hooted. She turned to see Marjorie waving from a battered prewar Armstrong Siddley. Drat! They had arrived early. Elinor steeled herself to assume her normal air of optimistic happiness as she prepared to show her romantic home to her sister-in-law.

Marjorie's admiration for Starlings somehow left Elinor feeling depressed. "*Such* a lovely old house—have you had it checked for woodworm?" Marjorie trilled as she ate her rabbit pie. "And subsidence? The Crawleys lived in a house *very* similar to this. Had to be pulled down before it fell on them. . . . *Delicious* carrots, although I find a knob of butter helps the flavor. . . . What an original idea to spread a *lace* tablecloth on a luncheon table . . ."

After their guests had departed, Billy returned to the dining room to help himself to another glass of port. "You'll never get it right, old girl," he grinned at Elinor. "Marjorie will *never* let you forget that, to her, you're a jumped-up farm laborer, and whatever you do, she's never going to change her view. I can't understand why you bother with the old bitch, but then whatever you hold against me, no one can say I'm a snob."

"No, you're not a snob," Elinor said, trembling with fury, "but you do love using me to tease your family. You were teasing them when you first took me to Larkwood. You were showing your brother, who was going to inherit all the family wealth and power, that you had it in your power to humble your family by introducing me into it." She paused as an idea struck her. "No, it's not teasing—what you really enjoy, Billy, is *tormenting* people! I bet that when you were little, you pulled wings off butterflies, and legs off wasps, and . . . and . . ."

"Steady on, old girl. Save the drama for your plots." Billy refilled his glass.

Elinor stormed out. In the entrance hall, Betty, the nanny, stood at the bottom of the stairs. "Might I have a word with you, madam?" she asked. Betty's normally plum-colored cheeks had flushed almost to purple.

"Certainly, Betty. What's upset you? Has one of the girls been naughty?"

"It's not the little girls, madam," Betty said hesitantly. "Perhaps you'd best come to the nursery and see for yourself, madam. Now that they dress themselves, I wouldn't have noticed until bathtime tonight, but Miranda pushed Clare in the lily pond, so I had to change her clothes."

In the sunny day nursery, Betty exhibited eight-year-old Clare, wearing white vest and navy knickers; Elinor could see the bruises on her upper arms.

"Maybe you could have a word with him. He doesn't know his own strength, madam," Betty said coldly. She pulled Clare's hands forward; the nails were bitten to the quick, and the surrounding skin was ragged from nervous picking.

The befuddled Billy had rarely seen Elinor so angry as when she confronted him in his study about Clare's bruises.

Elinor concluded, "If it happens *once more,* then you leave this house! You are never again to hurt *any* of them! *I won't have it.*"

Billy, for once, was horrified by what he had done: "I'd no idea that I was holding Clare so hard. I'd had a few and didn't realize . . ."

"What do you think Edward would do to you if he could see Clare's arms?" Elinor cried. "You couldn't bully *him* after he was big enough to lick you!"

"Elinor, I'm truly sorry. What can I do to convince you? How do you suppose *I* feel?" Billy pleaded.

"I don't *care* how you feel! Just make sure I never see a bruise on that child again!"

For once, Billy could not coax Elinor into forgiveness.

On the following morning, after a sleepless night, Elinor almost canceled her business trip to London, but she knew that her publisher had taken a great deal of trouble to arrange two press interviews and lunch at the Savoy with the W. H. Smith fiction buyer.

As Elinor was driven to the station, she waved to the three little girls, but they did not notice. They sat in a circle under a magnolia tree: they had removed their sandals and socks, and each child was bending her head down to her foot. Elinor smiled. It was their latest craze, a competition to see who could first get her toe in her mouth. Elinor found this sight reassuring.

Elinor caught the last train from London and returned home at about ten o'clock. She found the house in darkness except for the lights in the hall. Her depression returned as she slowly mounted the polished stairs to her bedroom, where she quickly undressed and washed, wearily pulled on a peach chiffon nightgown, and fell into her bed.

At seven o'clock the next morning, Mabel burst into Elinor's bedroom. "Oh madam, something awful . . ."

Elinor sat up abruptly. "What's happened?"

"He's in the hall, madam. . . . He's . . . lying there!"

Elinor jumped out of bed and ran down the stairs. On the Oriental carpet at the foot of the stairs, Billy, fully dressed, lay in a pool of vomit. An empty bottle of brandy lay near him. Billy's eyes were open; they stared at the ceiling, the aquamarine now faded, the whites yellowing, bloodshot, and glazed.

Elinor knelt by Billy and felt his cheek, which was cold. There was dried blood on his left temple. He smelled of stale drink.

"Telephone the doctor," Elinor told the maid. "And keep the children upstairs."

Kneeling by her husband, she grasped his hand and stroked it. She remembered his face as she had first seen it. How she had loved that smiling young man she had met so long ago. But where had he gone?

Softly she began to cry, her body racked with pain for Billy, for herself, for what might have been.

BOOK·2

Chapter · 6

"Who do them scissors belong to?" Buzz asked, producing them from her pocket at the breakfast table. "Come on! Own up!"

Annabel and Miranda looked at each other and kept silent.

Ten-year-old Clare, spooning yogurt, casually said, "They're from the nursery sewing box."

"Colonel Bromley found them scissors in his greenhouse," Buzz said tartly. "He said someone—someone not very tall—had stolen his grapes."

"*Sneak!*" Annabel spat at Clare.

"Shut *up*, Annabel," hissed Miranda, too late.

Buzz knew that further questioning was pointless because freckle-faced Miranda would never sneak on her sister, the two were inseparable, but although Miranda was the younger, it was always she who thought up the devilry and led the way, while Annabel trotted after her. Buzz said firmly, "You two young'uns go round and apologize to Colonel Bromley, and ask if you can do any odd jobs in his garden this morning."

"Sneak," Annabel hissed again at Clare.

Buzz looked crossly at Clare. "You should have stopped them."

Clare ran a hand through her short, dark hair. "But I didn't know . . ." As the eldest, Clare was often unfairly blamed for their naughtiness.

"That's what you always say," Buzz scolded. "If you didn't, you should'a done, so you must share their punishment."

"It's not fair!" howled Clare. "They're *always* getting me into trouble! And Annabel *always* gets off lightest!"

Buzz knew that this was true and she knew why. Buzz, an inconspicuous and plain child, had seen early in life that pretty, self-confident little girls like Annabel, with charming, flirty ways, could wriggle their way out of trouble.

"Life is unfair, Clare," Buzz said, "and the sooner you find out, the better."

Clare scowled. Buzz had lived with them long enough for Clare to know that she never changed her mind or relented, as Gran did.

After Billy's death two years earlier, Buzz had immediately gone down to Starlings, intending to stay with Elinor for a week. She never returned to her hated stenographic job in the City of London. Buzz now handled Elinor's secretarial work, ran the household, and organized the details of Elinor's life for a considerably larger salary than she had been paid by the grocery-chain head office. Furthermore, she was no longer lonely, no longer hungry for affection.

Buzz was meticulously efficient and irritatingly critical, and a constant but amicable battle was waged between Elinor and Buzz, the only person who dared criticize Elinor, and who wasn't particularly tactful about doing so. To each of the women, these minor arguments were proof of affection. Their friendship could withstand the squalls.

Buzz protected Elinor from outsiders with common sense and bulldog ferocity. Immediately after Billy's death, such protection had been necessary to deal with the bureaucratic requirements; the extravagantly vulpine suggestions of the undertaker, who naturally wanted as expensive a funeral as possible; and the crowd of reporters that had appeared.

In due course, the coroner concluded that, while intoxicated, Mr. William O'Dare had fractured his neck in a fall from a staircase, vomited while unconscious, and been asphyxiated by his vomit. The verdict was death by misadventure.

Elinor had appeared to be dazed after Billy's death. In public, she did not shed one tear: she stared into space and asked to be left alone. Buzz knew why; she had seen mortally wounded men, fresh from the battlefield, who could not feel pain because they had been anesthetized by shock. The young local doctor had confirmed Buzz's diagnosis to her as she showed him to the front door.

"It's often the case with widows," he said. "They literally *cannot* feel anything until they can accept the death, which may be long after the loss of the husband."

"I'd have called it good riddance," Buzz muttered.

The doctor decided to ignore this. "You can expect Mrs. O'Dare to be totally unlike her normal self: she may be bewildered, disoriented, and frightened by her own feelings. If she had recently quarreled with her husband, she might even feel guilty, because now they can never kiss and make up."

Looking at Buzz's face and remembering stories he had heard about Billy, the doctor added, "Especially if she ... er ... felt resentment toward Mr. O'Dare or had ... hmm ... sometimes wished him dead. . . . I hear he was a difficult man." He paused. "On the other hand, don't be surprised if Mrs. O'Dare's mind now blanks out all bad memories of her husband, exaggerates the good ones, and starts to view him as a wonderful person, in which case it is kindest not to contradict her."

"She's been doing *that* for years," Buzz said sourly.

In the days that followed the funeral, Elinor felt numb and cold, permanently weary: her movements slowed down, as if she were sleepwalking, and any movement seemed to take a lot of effort. She felt wizened, as if the juice had been squeezed from her body. For the first time in her life, she felt old.

After a few such days, Buzz shooed Elinor to her desk. Thanks to this, and to her own imagination, Elinor was able to escape from her misery: it was difficult to think about anything else when writing the first draft of a novel.

Elinor's romances were never out-and-out bodice rippers: each sexual chase was described in detail, but once the heroine was in the hero's arms, only a row of dots followed. Although breasts heaved frequently and there was a great deal of panting, the heroine always—even if only by a hairbreadth—went a virgin to the marriage bed (never described) that she was about to share with the dark, winged-eyebrowed, aristocratic gentleman on the book jacket, who was called Peregrine or Torquil and lived on some vast country estate: Elinor's heroines never married mechanics.

Now Elinor chose Paris as the glamorous setting for her next novel—Paris in the year 1870, when the city was besieged by the German army. Happily she turned to planning the romantic situation, the problems that would confront the lovers, and the solutions. Always, in Elinor's novels, it appeared that the heroine would be forced to choose between two ghastly alternatives; always the plot twisted ingeniously at this point, to provide the heroine with a third alternative and eventual, eternal happiness. In Paris with her heroine, Elinor would once again forget the misery of reality.

Immediately after their grandfather's death, the three small sisters howled for days. Clare wept from guilt as much as sorrow, blaming herself for her grandfather's death. It must have been that last spell—the mixture of primrose, violet roots, and sheep droppings. She must have wished too hard.

Miranda bellowed in sympathy, and then asked for the recipe.

Long after her sisters had dried their tears, Annabel continued to sob; she was afraid to go to bed in the dark and woke screaming every night.

"She's the softy of those three," Nanny explained to Buzz.

Buzz knew that Annabel wasn't the only inhabitant of Starlings who had a soft heart. The former ambulance driver did not find it difficult to be firm: she dealt briskly with truculent plumbers, lazy domestic staff, and insolent girls behind shop counters—who never ignored her. Buzz dealt with life's small exasperations as she dealt with buzzing gnats: she swatted at them, then dismissed them.

But after Billy died, like a punch-drunk boxer, Elinor found it difficult to stand up for herself. Her timid and unaggressive behavior and her obvious wish to avoid an argument (let alone a row) left her vulnerable.

"Nell, you shouldn't let people walk all over you," Buzz scolded one morning as they stood in the hall. "You're a ruddy sight too generous and helpful." She gazed through the window at a purple figure disappearing down the drive. "You've just given your new coat to Doreen, haven't you?"

"I know she stole the spoons, but she said she was sorry," Elinor said defensively. "And it's such a cold morning for July. She was wearing only a flimsy cardigan."

"She's ruddy lucky not to be in prison. And she could have worn the green coat you gave her last year. You're a mug, Nell."

Elinor scowled; she preferred to see herself as warmhearted.

"And while we're on the subject, why the hell did you bail out Stinker Baldwin?" Buzz asked, referring to the village drunk.

"His wife came to see me, with three of the children. She said it was his birthday next week."

Buzz threw her a look of scorn. "A ruddy good reason for getting drunk and beating her up again. Stinker should *always* be in prison on his birthday. Did you give her money?"

Elinor hesitated. "Just a little."

"There you go again! And I'll bet you thought of some *good* reason to do such a daft thing."

"Is it so wrong to give the poor woman a little money?"

"Yes. Because she'll drink it—just like Stinker! You'd have done better to give her food in a basket."

"It would have humiliated her," Elinor said, rationalizing her impulsive action.

"Rubbish! She'll soon be back for more cash!" Buzz knew how easily Elinor was able to identify with the wretched, and how quickly the wretched realized it.

"Well, I can afford to give it," Elinor said.

"Not at the rate you're going, my girl! I've just balanced your checkbook! We send a check off to every blinking begging letter that drops on the mat! You haven't enough money—or time—to solve all the problems of the world—and it ain't your job."

"I only try to help people."

"Charity begins at home, Lady Bountiful. You're a soft touch, Nell. The girls can twist you round their little finger. I punish 'em for stealing grapes, so they run off to you and you dry their tears, cancel the punishment, and give 'em chocolates. You're far too lenient with 'em, Nell—they're getting spoilt rotten."

"You see, I can't help remembering . . . that the poor little things have no parents."

"Poor they ain't!" Buzz scoffed. "You should put a stop to their weaknesses, not encourage 'em."

The following morning, Buzz came into the breakfast room, shuffling envelopes. "Only one for you today, Nell. And I've had a long letter from Bertha Higby." Buzz still corresponded with the mother of her dead fiancé, Ginger Higby; in 1922, the family had emigrated to Cleveland, Ohio, where eventually Mr. Higby opened a hardware store.

Reading excerpts from Bertha Higby's letter, Buzz did not notice Elinor's face until the door burst open and the three girls bounced into the breakfast room.

"Look what we've got for you!" Miranda thrust a wilting bunch of wildflowers into her grandmother's hands.

"What's wrong?" Clare asked, looking at her grandmother's face, at her untouched breakfast, and at the crumpled handkerchief in her hand.

"It's nothing . . ."

"Yes it is—we can see you've been crying," Annabel said.

"Well, that was silly of me. I thought I might win a prize—the International Romance Writers Award, but they gave it to Daphne Du Maurier."

"Well, *they're* silly!" Miranda shouted. The three girls flung themselves upon their grandmother and hugged her.

"We think *you're* the best at *everything*," Annabel said loyally.

"We'll make you your favorite chocolate cake," Miranda promised, "and we'll write 'Number One Gran Award' on top."

Smiling at this display of loyalty, Buzz knew that Elinor would forget her disappointment by teatime. Elinor had long ago acquired the knack of instantly dismissing or forgetting anything that made her unhappy. Buzz supposed that this was how she had managed to survive life with Billy. For a moment, Buzz remembered Billy's drunken, angry, bloodshot, half-closed eyes, yet she knew Nell remembered only the clear, sea-blue flashes that had originally entranced her. Over and over Nell astounded her as she told some journalist that the reason she had not remarried was that she knew she'd *never* find anyone to replace her darling husband.

Whether or not Nell had brainwashed herself into believing that, Buzz knew the truth of the matter. Elinor, now freed to fly high in the sky, was afraid of finding herself chained to another bully.

SATURDAY, 24 MARCH 1951

"What's that noise?" Twelve-year-old Clare, in a ginger tweed coat and black gum boots, ran to the bottom of the orchard, followed by her sisters. Beyond the boundary hedge was a rough meadow above which rooks swirled in a light blue sky. Elinor's overgrown woods lay to the left. From the hill on the right came the faint sound of horses' hooves.

Again the melancholy sound of a horn hung mournfully in the air.

"It's the hunt!" Clare climbed the five-barred wooden gate and sat upon it. Her sisters joined her, and they watched a wisp of russet streak down the hill to their right.

Hard-hatted black heads appeared above the hill, followed by shoulders of scarlet or black; then the heads of horses, followed by their graceful bodies and long, delicate legs: the hunt looked an unstoppable mass as it rushed toward the hedgerow at the base of the hill, and even from a distance, the girls could sense the exuberance of the Warmingford Hunt in full cry on a fresh, damp day.

The hounds were gaining on the exhausted fox: streaks of black and tan, they bayed with the excitement of the chase.

Some four hundred yards behind the hounds, a bunch of about thirty horses and ponies now thundered down the hill. Straggling behind were a group of children from the Pony Club mounted on shaggy, dark ponies; their hooves threw up clods of earth as they leapt the hedge in pursuit of the fox.

The desperate vixen was clever: several times she had thrown the hunt off the scent by running through streams, past manure heaps, and once through a flock of sheep. But after being hunted for four hours, she was bedraggled and exhausted.

"It's the vixen who lives in our woods!" Annabel exclaimed. Only the previous week, the vixen had broken into the O'Dares' chicken house again, gnawing through the planking to steal a couple of birds. "Can't we hide her? She's *our* fox; she lives in *our* woods." Annabel jumped down on the far side of the gate and started running toward the frightened animal.

"Come back! The hounds'll knock you down!" Clare shouted after her sister, jumping down to run after her, followed closely by Miranda.

The fox was a pathetic sight; her eyes were glazed, her tongue hung out of her mouth as she panted, and her breath came in heavy gasps. She slowed her pace, then staggered and swayed, unable to go farther.

When Annabel was about ten yards away, the hounds caught up with the vixen, who had no chance. Weakly she turned her head and bared her teeth at her tormentors; then the leading hounds flung themselves at the fox's body, each seizing whatever part of her flesh it could reach. The rest of the pack piled on top of the exhausted animal, like a rugger scrum upon the ball.

As the hunt cantered down the hill toward the kill, Clare recognized a couple of local farmers, the vet, and Colonel Bromley on a well-groomed bay.

"You girls! Keep out of the way!" shouted the Master of the Hunt. Mounted on a gray, he was a splendid sight in scarlet coat, white breeches, and black boots with tanned tops.

"You damn, damn, damn bastards!" screamed Miranda, using forbidden swear words.

"You damn, damn murderers!" yelled Annabel.

Colonel Bromley, in black bowler and beige raincoat, moved toward the girls. "Don't be sentimental," he said. "Foxes kill my lambs, my pheasants, and your chickens. You mustn't cry over a fox. Hunting keeps the foxes down, and it isn't as cruel as other killing methods."

Clare sobbed, "Why can't you kill the foxes some other way? With traps or with poison?"

"Farmers can't put down poison, in case their working dogs eat it. And if an animal is trapped, it might be held in fearful pain for days."

"Well, shoot them! That's fast and not so cruel," Annabel shouted.

"Farmers can't sit up all night waiting to shoot foxes."

"I'm glad I'm not the sort of person who hounds an animal to death for fun," Annabel shrieked, "and then watches while other animals tear it to pieces!"

"Keep your voice down," Colonel Bromley said. "Your grandmother will not be pleased if you upset the Master."

"We don't *care*, you bloodthirsty old pig!" Annabel shouted.

Colonel Bromley looked at them in silence, and kept his horse between the girls and the rest of the hunt until it had moved off.

Two hours later, when Elinor and Buzz returned from a shopping trip, the sisters were in the orchard burying what was left of the fox.

Having heard the car come up the drive, the girls hurled themselves at the returning travelers before they had time to unbutton their coats.

When Elinor disentangled their story, she said indignantly, "I'd like to see the Master after *he'd* been hunted for four hours by huge bloodthirsty, baying creatures—I bet that'd change his point of view! Expensive dressing up can't disguise barbarity."

Later, Elinor skimmed the hand-delivered letter from Colonel Bromley: ". . . undisciplined . . . worse than hooligans . . . no more disturbance . . . police . . . their headmistress . . ."

"Around here you can't upset the hunt without running into trouble," Buzz said. "And the Master of the Hunt has complained to the police. You'd better lay on the charm, old girl."

Elinor looked worried. She had now been accepted by local society, but she knew that, should she argue against the hunt, she would be . . . well, not exactly ostracized but . . .

"The girls were absolutely right to behave as they did," Elinor said firmly.

Nevertheless, hoping to circumvent any further complaint from the Master of the Hunt, Elinor saw Sergeant Brown, who was well aware of her generous annual check for the police widows and orphans fund. Elinor also visited the headmistress of the local school.

"Frankly, I'm not surprised to hear of this behavior from Annabel," said Miss Pryor. "She behaves as if she were an only child." Spoiled, selfish, imperious, was what she didn't say.

"Annabel is overshadowed by her sisters," Elinor rationalized, "because Clare is clever and Miranda has a very strong character."

"Annabel is certainly *jealous* of her sisters," Miss Pryor said firmly. Overprivileged little tyrant, she thought. "Had you considered sending them to boarding school? Not Benenden or Heathfield—somewhere where they'd learn to fend for themselves."

After a long pause, Elinor said, "I'll think about it."

She went home and telephoned Joe Grant.

TUESDAY, 27 MARCH 1951

On the back lawn, swaying golden stretches of daffodils bent before a wind that swept scudding clouds from the sky; they looked like fat cupids being shooed off to bed by Nanny, Elinor thought. She pulled her coat collar up and turned to Joe. After a delicious meal of grouse and an excellent claret, he was dutifully admiring the daffodils: they ran down to a stream that wandered along the back of the garden, under pale green fronds of weeping willows.

Elinor laughed with excitement as the trees rustled before the frisky

March wind. Her blond hair whipped around her cheeks. "I feel as if my face has been dipped in a snowdrift, Joe. Isn't it *exhilarating?*"

"It's damned cold." Joe left *his* garden to the gardener and only enjoyed looking at it from behind snugly closed, draft-proofed windows. "I don't know why you want my advice," he added. "You're perfectly capable of making up your own mind."

"A woman needs a man to guide her." Elinor smiled at him. "I know how lucky I am to be guided by you. Thank you for that income forecast, by the way."

"You could do that sort of forecast much more cheaply from *here* if you had a bookkeeper in once a month."

Elinor looked up at Joe with gratitude. "You see? Bookkeeping is the sort of thing that I simply don't know about—so it would never have occurred to me to do that forecast. Remember that the girls of my generation had *no* business training."

"Business training is useful but not all-important," Joe said. "Common sense and hard work are just as important. What a business boils down to is having a product, or a service, and selling it, and that applies whether your product is a book or a bulldozer. You increase your income in two ways: by decreasing costs and by increasing prices, or production."

"But that doesn't apply to an author."

"Oh yes it does. I think you should try to dictate your books. You'd double your output. Incidentally, I've arranged for that history professor to correct your manuscript; he'll pass it on to an English professor, to check the grammar and spelling."

"Of course I learned Yankee spelling," Elinor said, "but then I ended up over here, and now I can't spell in either language. But I didn't ask you here today to talk business."

In answer to Joe's raised eyebrows, she added, "I want you to advise me about the girls."

Joe laughed. "You've always said that Ethel and I are too harsh with our boys. But boys need discipline—and so do girls. I've always told you that you should send those girls to boarding school when they're old enough. It's not fair to keep them at the village school so you can have them at home with you. They'll suffer for it later. Quite frankly, it's your duty to send them somewhere where they'll get an excellent education and be among the sort of girls that they'll mix with socially when they grow up."

"I want . . ." Elinor paused. "I never want them to feel the sort of amused and supercilious contempt that I ran up against when I met Billy's family. I don't want them ever to know that sort of anxiety and humiliation. I want those girls to be the social equal of *anybody.*"

"You are the equal of anyone," Joe said angrily, "and you always were! Billy was lucky to have you." He remembered Elinor's vitality, her cheerfulness and popularity in that Frenchie hospital where he had visited Billy so long ago. He remembered her wedding day, when Elinor carried a bouquet of white chrysanthemums, which Joe personally had liberated from what was left of somebody's garden.

"We were all a bit in love with you, Elinor—with your vitality and warmth—but Billy made sure that nobody else got a chance to get near you." Fiercely Joe added, "Billy married you because you were the prettiest girl he'd ever seen, and he wasn't the only one who thought *that!*" He smiled at her. "And now you're a beautiful woman. But I don't suppose I'm the only man to tell you so."

Elinor looked delighted. "Nobody's told me for a long time, Joe."

Joe glanced lovingly at her. "The only possible reason is that you don't allow a man to get close enough to say so. But you need a man in your life, Elinor. You're still young enough to enjoy . . . male companionship."

"Men want more than companionship. I don't want to lead a man on and then refuse him," Elinor said. "Because I shall never remarry. Nobody could ever replace Billy in . . . in certain ways." She looked Joe straight in the eye and softly added, "And as I'm sure you realize, I would never have an affair, Joe."

Well, Joe thought, he'd hinted and she'd given him her reply. He smiled again and put his arm affectionately around Elinor's shoulder.

"About the girls," she said. "As you know, I want them to have the best I can give them, Joe. A proper society debut. And I want you to tell me how to arrange it."

Joe understood at once what she meant. He had come a long way himself and knew that Elinor wanted her family to go a lot farther. He looked at the little girls playing on the front lawn. "If that's what you want, I can certainly help you," he said. "But remember that too much privilege can be a disaster." Briefly he thought of one or two of Adam's arrogant friends at Eton.

Elinor nodded. "That's what I want."

Joe said, "You start by getting a better car."

"But it's almost impossible to get *any* car! The dealers' waiting lists are *years* long!"

"I think I could get you a prewar white Rolls. Chap I know wants to get rid of his."

"But *I* can't drive a Rolls-Royce! It's far too heavy."

"No," Joe agreed, "you'll need a chauffeur. And the first place he should drive you to is Norman Hartnell."

"*I* can't afford the Queen's dressmaker!"

"Hartnell is the best designer of appearance clothes, and that's why the Queen goes to him. And you *can* afford it if you produce more books. You must dress the part before you play the part." He added, "As you no doubt know, you can only be presented at Court by a lady who has herself been presented. I'll arrange for someone to present you next year and give you a season in London. I happen to know that Sonia Rushleigh came out of her divorce badly, and she needs money."

"But how can I spare the time for a London season, Joe, if I'm writing books to pay for it?"

"Get up earlier."

"That's what Billy always told me."

Hastily Joe said, "About the girls. Finishing school in Switzerland or Paris, where they'll acquire all the social graces. They must all be able to—"

"Sparkle?" Elinor suggested, tongue in cheek. When Joe nodded, she said, "They *already* sparkle. What else do they need to know?"

"Only seven things." Joe ticked them off on brown-leather-gloved fingers. "*One*, never criticize the royal family, blood sports, or newspaper owners, because they gang up to protect each other. *Two*, don't get any publicity in the cheaper papers during the Season. *Three*, pick a newsworthy charity to support, preferably connected with dogs or children. *Four*, support your local community and make sure you're seen doing it. Open the vicarage fete, and when you do it, publicly present a check for the church roof—that sort of thing." As they drew near the front door, he shivered. "Dear Elinor, I think I've had enough nature for one day. Can we please, please get back to that log fire in your study?"

Elinor laughed. "Not 'til you've finished."

Joe wrapped his arms across his chest to keep warm. "*Five*, show an interest in one of the arts, but nothing too avant-garde—ballet or the opera is fine." He quickened his step as they arrived at the front door. "*Six*, buy some place that people long to be invited to—somewhere like Somerset Maugham's villa on Cap Ferrat. There's a place called St.-Tropez that's getting popular."

"And the seventh commandment?" Elinor asked.

"Always write thank-you letters immediately and post them within three days." Joe grinned.

Elinor looked guilty. She hated writing letters, especially letters of thanks; instead of dashing them off while she still felt grateful, she delayed until the last minute before she risked offending people. At that point, she would contritely write several pages, invent some reason to explain why she hadn't written before, feel guilty about her lie, and send flowers.

Elinor pushed open the ancient oak front door. "But all that you've just suggested will cost a fortune!"

"Then make one, Elinor."

Buzz looked dubious when she heard about Elinor's plans for the girls' future, starting with boarding school. "Don't you think you're being a bit old-fashioned, Nell?" she said. "I know you want them girls to have what you didn't, but you ain't realized that by protecting a woman, you leave her unprotected if she's ever left on her own."

Fleetingly Buzz remembered what it had felt like, after her home had been bombed in the Second World War, suddenly to be without a family, without anyone.

When Miranda heard that her two sisters were going to be sent away to school in the autumn but that she wasn't old enough, she raged, proclaiming she was *sick* of being the littlest, because she was always left out. Eventually Elinor yielded; Miranda could accompany her sisters.

SATURDAY, 29 SEPTEMBER 1951

Hazlehurst Park Manor School was only thirty miles away from Warminster—a minor reason for Elinor's choice. It was a nineteenth-century reconstruction of an eighteenth-century reconstruction of a Gothic priory. All the teachers were clearly ladies who had known better times in better years; they seemed amiable and well-meaning, but were by no means intellectuals.

On their first Saturday afternoon away from home, the three sisters—who were not allowed in each other's dormitories—felt lonely and homesick. Together, they walked down the school's drive, heading for the nearest sweet shop.

"I can't think why Gran sent us to this *prison!*" Annabel grumbled.

"Because she wants us to be ladies," Clare said gloomily.

Miranda added, "Because she was put through hell by all the ladies when she was a young bride."

"They don't like us here." Annabel kicked at the bracken by the side of the road.

"They don't know us yet," Clare pointed out.

"How will we know when they like us?" Miranda asked, darting forward to pick up a spiked greenish ball that enclosed a shining conker.

"When they share their secrets with us," Clare said.

Soon, of course, secrets were exchanged. All three girls quickly learned that the period after lights-out was a time when the girls of Hazlehurst Park, amid steady giggles, shared their common fascination with boys and sex.

These inaccurate accounts of the strange things that adults did to each other in bed in order to achieve ecstasy, combined with the behavior of the demurely romantic but firmly virginal heroines of Elinor's novels, gave the sisters an odd picture of adult coupling: This involved a wildly romantic waltz into the future, wearing a low-necked dress as if you didn't realize that your top was showing. After your wedding, you had to allow your husband to see you naked without being embarrassed, and let him kiss you hard, an action which fused true twin souls together, to think as one, after which no verbal communication was needed. Your true love, now your husband, would read your thoughts, enjoy everything you liked to do, and give you everything you wanted, including spotless babies; that was his function in life.

A few months into the girls' first term, in February—Joe said it was the best time to buy and the worst time to sell property in Europe—Elinor and Buzz flew to France for a week, during which Elinor purchased a small but pretty villa on the outskirts of St.-Tropez; the sea could be seen beyond the pink oleander bushes at the end of the small garden. Sufficient funds for the purchase were obtained by Joe Grant, who had Elinor's French publisher make the financial arrangements.

MONDAY, 6 JULY 1953

By early July of the following year, Elinor's villa had been redecorated, furnished with simple Provençal furniture, and curtained with intricately patterned, bright traditional country fabrics. She invited Joe Grant and his family to be her first guests. It was arranged that his son Adam should fly to Nice in advance of the rest of the family, who were to drive through France.

Before the visit, the two Grant sons were much discussed by the O'Dare sisters, who had not seen the boys for several years. On the day of Adam's arrival, the girls took three hours to dress in cinch-waisted, flowery dresses that were both too tight for the temperature and too elaborate for the occasion; they then sat on the patio for nearly two hours, none admitting that she was waiting for Adam.

At last, as late-afternoon shadows crept across the patio, Adam, in naval blazer and open-necked white shirt, sauntered through the living room. As he did so, he again wondered whether his father was having—or had ever had—an affair with Elinor O'Dare. They seemed unusually close for friends of the opposite sex, and Adam had noticed his mother's almost imperceptible withdrawal when in the same room as Elinor: it was something that Adam had noticed in rival cats.

Adam, now twenty-three years old, had spent his two years of national service in the navy, where he obtained a commission; he had decided to be a lawyer, and in due course became articled to the family firm of Swithin, Timmins and Grant, this being the simplest way to obtain his legal qualifications.

When he wasn't studying, Adam acted as his father's assistant and was also loaned to any of the firm's other lawyers who needed a spare pair of hands to prepare a case: while the senior lawyer conducted the main interviews, Adam ran around, acquiring the evidence and bringing it into the office, where he checked it and then sorted it into appropriate files. He now looked forward to a luxurious holiday in the sun, during which he would not be treated like the messenger boy.

On the wide steps that led from Elinor's living room down to the patio, Adam paused, grinned, and said, "Why, it's the three Graces!"

This was the first time that the sisters heard the tag line destined to be pinned on them; they were flattered and dazzled by a compliment from this tall, tanned young man with dark hair and big brown eyes. All three immediately fell in love with him.

That evening, before going down to dinner, fourteen-year-old Clare stuffed socks in the sides of her bra, which pushed her small breasts together. She had heard about this trick at Hazlehurst, though it didn't quite accomplish the look she was striving for.

Annabel sneaked Gran's new camera and flash so that she could take photographs of everyone, and made sure that she took more of Adam than anyone else.

That night, Miranda hugged her pillow and daydreamed about being with Adam in his private plane: "Oh my God, Miranda, I feel a touch of my old malaria coming on . . . Do you think you can manage to land her?" Wearing a glamorous white flying suit and leather helmet, Miranda said, "Of course, Adam, simply tell me what to do." Adam gasped out the instructions before losing consciousness. . . .

When the girls came down for breakfast the following morning, they found that Adam had already left to charter a speedboat. He did not return for lunch.

That afternoon, Clare was lying on the beach, sleepy as a cat in the sun, when she felt a shadow fall across her face. She opened her eyes and knew instantly that the young man standing before her in scarlet swim trunks was Adam's brother; they had the same flyaway dark eyebrows that almost met in the middle. But Adam's face was leaner, his mouth tauter, his eyebrows drawn closer to each other. Adam's finely cut features looked—Clare now had to admit—just a little bit twitchy, like Gregory Peck when worried about what the villain was going to do next.

The young man stared at her navy-blue school swimsuit. "Are you

Clare? I'm Mike." Mike's clear gray eyes, set wide apart, gave him an air of transparent honesty that he found very useful in getting out of trouble at school. He added, "I've been sent to find you. Adam hired a motorboat and we're taking it to the islands. Like to come along?"

Mike looked less cynically amused and more approachable than Adam, although there was something violent about his stillness, as if his body wanted to leap forward. Mike had even longer legs and wider shoulders than Adam; dark hair curled crisply on his chest and descended in a faint line to below his navel.

Clare almost fell out of love with Adam.

Later, as the motorboat cleaved the water, trailing churning foam in its wake, each sister felt similar turmoil beneath her breastbone. They all returned to the villa dazed by a love far more exhausting than that which Clare had felt for the tow-haired games mistress, Annabel for Robin, her pony, and Miranda for the milkman.

The next day, the five of them drove to the long sandy crescent of Tahiti Beach; here each sister, for the first time, felt the painful and humiliating sorrow of rejection.

Adam and Michael took one look at the lithe, suntanned young Frenchmen flirting with feline French girls in sexy bikinis and made no attempt to hide the fact that this was their idea of paradise. The two Englishmen immediately lost interest in the three young sisters.

That evening, none of the sisters came down to supper. Buzz found them, still wearing swimsuits, in Clare's bedroom. Clare was crying, facedown on the bed. Also sobbing, Annabel was spread-eagled, facedown, on the floor. A scowling Miranda leaned against the wall with legs crossed and arms folded.

"What are you all moaning about?"

"Go away, Buzz—it's none of your business," Clare hiccuped.

"I'll never, never love anyone again," Annabel sobbed.

"They're both *beasts*," growled Miranda. "And we must all buy bikinis as fast as possible."

"Don't be silly little geese," Buzz chided. "Adam's twenty-three years old and Mike's twenty-one! Of *course* they like the look of them curvy, pretty French ladies!"

"But Mike was *charming* to Clare before he saw those girls on the beach," Annabel gulped.

"Adam showed Miranda how to water-ski before he saw those old bags, but after that, he *ignored* her!" cried Clare.

"Frog is just as pretty as those beastly tarts on the sand," Miranda said, scowling again.

"Don't use that nasty word, or I'll give you what for," Buzz corrected automatically. "Of course the lads were polite to you—

because they're nice lads." She hesitated and then said firmly, "To them lads, you're still only kiddies. Now have a wash and come downstairs—there's chocolate meringues for supper. And no more of this nonsense about bikinis. What would Annabel and Miranda put in the top bit—tennis balls?"

Chapter · 7

At the crossroads, Adam pulled the wheel of the family Humber to the left: in the moonlight, the silver road ahead disappeared between dark conifers.

"Hey, Adam, you've gone the wrong way," Michael said, waking from his reverie. "You've taken the road to Nice."

Adam turned left again onto the coast road; below them lay the dark glitter of the sea. "We're not going to Nice, we're going to Cannes—to the casino."

Mike laughed. "I suppose that's why you offered to drive old Maclean back to his villa." Mike knew that his brother was an opportunist.

"*And* why I asked you to come along. It was pretty early for old Maclean to leave Elinor's dinner party, pleading a headache. I reckon he's jumping into bed with something juicy at this very moment."

"Dad'll kill us if he finds out we've been gambling," Mike said.

Adam laughed and pressed the accelerator. "Dad's determined that we're not going to take after *his* dad." Joe Grant's father had been a racecourse bookie, a fact that his wife tried to hide.

"Granddad Grant *never* gambled—he took the money *from* gamblers. He always said that gambling was a mug's game."

"Look, Mike, do you want a night out or not? If so, stop being so bloody pious." Adam's persuasive nature and elder brother's self-assurance overshadowed his brother, who quickly gave up arguing.

"Sorry. It's a great idea," Mike said hastily. "After all, we can't gamble at home." Gambling was illegal in Britain, supposedly because of its bad effect on public morality. "But what'll we do for money?"

"I've got four weeks' wages," Adam said. Through the open car windows, he could now feel salt air on his face and smell the beguiling aroma of pine.

"Surely forty quid won't get us far in the Cannes casino?"

"It'll get us *in*. We have a drink at the bar, we look at the glitterati, we have a mild flutter. That's all. Easy."

But Mike knew that behind Adam's supercilious sophistication and condescending facade, his brother was unsure of himself. Talking down to Mike always subdued Adam's own anxiety. Mike made Adam feel equal to anything or anyone, because Mike always assumed that his elder brother would be successful in everything he did, and Adam assumed that Mike would always fetch and carry, jump to obey him, and protect his secrets.

Adam could confide anything to Mike and Mike wouldn't raise an eyebrow—or tell anyone: Mike had worshiped Adam through their lonely childhood, in which neither brother had ever felt close to their rather cold parents who seemed to love neither their children nor each other. The boys had spent their early years with a rota of swiftly changing nannies, who never seemed able to reach Mrs. Grant's imperiously high standards. Adam and Mike had shared an expensively efficient, forlorn, and loveless life in the nursery, devoid of any tenderness except that which they had shown to each other. Now each knew that he could depend on the other, and neither really trusted anyone else.

As Adam drove the Humber a little too fast toward the casino, Mike sighed. It was such a beautiful night. Perfect for a bike ride. Wistfully he remembered his first night rides on the Norton Dominator with the feather-bed frame—his first brand-new bike. Motorbikes were Mike's passion. When he was fourteen, he had acquired his first bike, a secondhand army surplus BSA M20; it was a messenger bike with a bouncy saddle and no suspension. Mike had concealed the bike in an unused potting shed, where it was later joined by an equally ancient Triumph Speed Twin 500, which had a lot of poke for its size. None of his subsequent smarter bikes had given him as much pleasure as those two.

At the Palm Beach Casino—considered more chic than the Casino Municipal—the brothers produced their passports and purchased chips with which to gamble: to avoid theft, cash bets weren't allowed at the table.

Waiters glided around the gaming room; cigarette girls proffered their tray. A couple of security men in dark uniforms stood, immobile, although their eyes never stopped moving.

"They're shills," Adam murmured as he stared at the glamorously dressed women who sat on revolving stools before the long bar, their sophisticated faces reflected in the mirrored rear wall. "Their job is to get the punters to play the tables."

At the bar, Adam and Mike ordered whiskey sodas, sniffing the agreeable odor of good food and expensive perfume; they swiveled their stools around to watch the gambling.

An effervescent excitement hovered above the sixteen tables. People stood around them, the men in dinner jackets and the women wearing long strapless dresses cut to display décolletage. A few elderly ladies sat, firmly clutching their purses, their wrinkled bosoms bulging over strapless net bodices. The gamblers seemed to be mostly French, German, or Greek, although Mike heard a couple of Englishmen playing at a nearby table while their noisily disapproving wives worried about British currency restrictions.

"Well, how do we start?" Michael asked. "You'd better tell me what the form is. I was never asked to any of the smart games at Eton." The Grant brothers were not nearly so rich or aristocratic as most of their schoolfellows.

"I haven't the slightest idea," Adam was obliged to admit.

"I'll show you if you like," offered a pale, angular Englishman who sat next to Adam. "The name's Giles Milroy-Browne. You should start on roulette—most beginners do, because you need no knowledge to start playing."

The three men drifted to the nearest roulette table and stood behind the players. Here the atmosphere was tense, the anxiety level high, and the action very fast. The three croupiers—handsome, clean-cut young men in immaculate dinner jackets—moved with great speed as they called out the winning numbers or paid winnings.

"The easiest way to bet is simply to gamble that the ball will fall in a red or a black slot," Mr. Milroy-Browne explained to Adam. "There are thirty-six slots and the odds are even, which means that if you put two thousand francs on, you win two thousand. If you 'play the dozens,' you gamble on which of three sequences of twelve numbers the ball will fall in—and that pays two to one. But the most exciting and dangerous way to play is to bet the numbers. Actually pick one number because the casino pays out thirty-five to one. So, if you put a thousand francs down, you get thirty-five thousand back."

Carefully Adam bet, on red, a chip that cost the equivalent of one pound. He felt a rush of anxiety as the ball clattered around the wheel, slower . . . and slower . . . It settled in a red slot, number 3. Adam had won!

He lost his winnings on the next throw, but told himself that it didn't matter because, overall, he'd lost nothing. Still, he trembled as he laid the equivalent of ten pounds—a week's pay—on red. But suddenly Adam no longer felt self-conscious and anxious; he felt sophisticated and excited. And although determined to play modestly with small stakes, he nevertheless felt a weird new impulse: a need to challenge fate.

Again red won! Adam felt his fingers and toes tingle. Then, as if it didn't belong to him, he watched his right hand carefully place twenty pounds on red. It would hurt if he lost, but the pain would feel exquisite. . . . Again the ball fell into a red slot! Clearly, he had been right to bet on red. It was as though he were guided in his choice by some invisible, benevolent force. He felt as if he were breathing rare air, and a tremendous sense of well-being flooded his body.

Adam did not always win, but he lost very little.

Playing roulette seemed a beguilingly easy way of getting rich in a couple of hours, without doing any work. It was as if money grew on trees and Adam merely had to stretch out his hand to pluck bank notes. Each time he won, he felt release, and relief, as with a sexual encounter. Winning made him feel more manly, more virile. It also made him feel different from the other people gathered around the table: Adam had the golden touch; he was favored by the gods.

Two hours later, when Adam had won a total of one hundred pounds—the equivalent of ten weeks' salary—Michael whispered in his ear, "Stop now, Adam, while you're ahead, you silly ass. You *know* it's a mug's game. You *know* that the only people who win are the organizers, the casinos, the bookies."

"Shut up and let me concentrate." Adam shook off the restraining arm, but he knew that Michael was right. Adam looked at his pile of winnings; he should take them *now* and leave. Leave! *Leave!*

But he couldn't.

Just one more bet—then he would go.

But Adam could no more stop himself than an alcoholic could stop himself from picking up an open bottle of whiskey.

His earlier tentativeness had vanished and he now looked around the table with increasing confidence; no longer was he merely a junior articled clerk. As he had always subconsciously suspected, Adam was one of God's chosen. He began to experience a feeling of power: if he concentrated, then that little white ball would obediently fall where he wished it to.

The exhilaration of winning made Adam feel a little high and a lot larger than life. His heart pounded, adrenaline coursing through his blood. He was almost ill with excitement, this dark joy that spread throughout his body, making him feel aglow, as if his veins were red neon tubes.

Michael, who had not bet at all, returned to Adam's side at two o'clock in the morning and suggested once again that they leave.

"No, not yet." Adam looked at his pile of winnings, which totaled a hundred and eighty pounds. "Okay," he relented. "Just let me have one more bet." Half expecting to lose, he put his original ten-pound stake on a number—36.

The ball rolled into slot 36.

Adam had just won thirty-five times his stake! The croupier paid him three hundred and fifty pounds—almost a year's pay!

Inside his head, Adam shrieked with joy, for he knew that his winnings were not due to blind chance. He felt as if he were smelling the hair of the most beautiful woman on earth and inhaling the perfume of her skin: Lady Luck was at his side.

After that first casino visit, Mike refused to accompany his brother. Their father, who believed that Adam had found a girlfriend, winked as, each night, he handed over the car keys.

Sometimes Adam won and sometimes he lost. After ten days, he had won a total of more than two years' salary, and in a manner far more exciting than doing the donkey work for some lawyer.

On the tenth evening, Adam started to lose steadily. At first he didn't worry because he knew he'd win it all back on the next throw.

But by two o'clock in the morning, when Adam usually left the casino, he had lost over six hundred pounds and could hardly believe it. He felt the desolate despair of a man who discovers his loved one in bed with somebody else. He felt guilty and ashamed. How *could* he stupidly have lost so much money so fast? It had taken him two weeks to win six hundred pounds—and then he had lost it in less than an hour. *Why* hadn't he stuck to his system?

Adam had abandoned the system he had decided upon, because at times, in order to follow it, he had to stop gambling—and he was now unable to do this: he felt *so strongly* that his luck would return on the next throw . . . in a few minutes . . . within an hour . . .

Adam slowly left the casino and, in a daze, drove home. His clothes felt crumpled and grubby, and as he slumped in the driving seat, he felt depressed, as if he were about to catch influenza.

"Adam seems down in the dumps," Mrs. Grant said to her husband the next day at sundown, as she tucked the Ambre Solaire bottle into her beach bag. "He turned down that invitation to visit the Boccasso yacht, and he's spoken to nobody all day. He ignored that nice girl he water-skied with yesterday."

Adam's father could not keep back a grin. "I think he's got a woman tucked away," he said in a man-of-the-world voice. "He's clearly had a row with her."

"But why hasn't he brought her to the beach?" A new thought struck Mrs. Grant. "Joe, do you think she's a . . . shopgirl type?"

"She's more likely to be one of the married women on the beach with young children. Nothing to do after the little 'uns have been put to bed . . . husband slaving away somewhere . . . No, Ethel, you're to say *nothing* to Adam. He's twenty-three, he's spent two years in the navy, and he won't thank a mother who tries to interfere in his love life."

On the following day, Adam found it hard to get out of bed. He only did so eventually because he knew that if he didn't, his mother would call a doctor, and then maybe he wouldn't be able to get to the casino that evening.

All day, Adam baked his body on the beach as feelings of apathy and lethargy swaddled him like a wet, dark fog. He couldn't eat or drink. He could only wonder if his luck would turn tonight at the casino.

One of the great failings of gamblers is to follow their losses. Adam did this, returning each evening to lose. He kept hoping that the next throw would cancel out those losses. It never did.

He borrowed thirty pounds from Giles Milroy-Browne (who by now knew quite a lot about Adam's background), but he didn't win it back.

Two days before he was due to return to London, Adam sold his gold wristwatch (a twenty-first birthday present) but when he attempted to repay his borrowing, Milroy-Browne refused to accept the money, saying that the debt could wait.

By midnight, Adam had lost the proceeds from the sale of his watch. Giles lent him a further fifty pounds, which Adam also lost.

Adam left the south of France deeply grateful—and three hundred pounds in debt—to the obliging Mr. Milroy-Browne, who said there was no hurry, Adam could repay it when convenient. Adam agreed to pay one percent interest per month on this debt.

Adam was not unduly worried. When he returned to London, where gambling was illegal, he'd go to a private gambling party and make it back.

He was simply, temporarily, on a losing streak.

Chapter·8

"Do you think it will stop snowing before lunch? It's so boring indoors, with nothing to do." Kneeling on a window seat, sixteen-year-old Annabel twisted her blond ponytail with one finger as she pressed her nose to the diamond-leaded panes of the drawing room window. Seen through flickering snowflakes, the garden that encircled Starlings was a lumpy white blanket; beyond it, the bony branches of the orchard were weighed down by snow.

Annabel turned to look at her two sisters: Miranda was waltzing around the piano, tartan skirt aswirl. Clare, in a black batwing sweater and black stretch pants, lay on the carpet in front of the fire, reading a book.

Two years before, Clare had left her smart boarding school for an equally smart finishing school in Lausanne. No dreary secretarial school threatened the three sisters; neither Elinor nor Buzz considered it necessary: of course, the girls were destined for marriage.

At the finishing school, Clare had not learned to speak French, cook, sew, or write business letters; she had learned to jitterbug, to apply makeup, and not much else, except to glide downstairs gracefully.

By the time Clare returned from her year in Switzerland, Elinor had planned her eldest granddaughter's social debut with the painstaking thoroughness that she reserved for her book launches. So Clare was photographed regularly at chic events for the newspaper gossip columns or for *Tatler,* high society's picture magazine. Lady Rushleigh presented her to the Queen at Buckingham Palace. Clare wore a slim, white satin dress that looked like an upended arum lily; she hated it because it was so different from the white net crinolines of the other debutantes, which is why Elinor had chosen it.

Clare then devoted herself to the exhausting life of pleasure that constituted a London season, during which a girl was introduced, at great expense, to society. Clare, like all the other girls, was conscious of the unspoken hope that she might "meet someone nice"—by which all the mothers of the debutantes meant someone wellborn and rich.

She went to debutante lunches, at which girls became acquainted, and then she was made to rest at home during the afternoon, in order to save her strength for the cocktail parties, dinners, dances, or balls of the evening. She cheered loudly at the Oxford and Cambridge boat race, clapped sedately during cricket at Lord's, clamped binoculars to her eyes at Ascot, ate strawberries and cream between tennis matches at Wimbledon, held her breath with excitement at the clash of polo sticks at Cowdray Park and Cirencester, appreciatively sniffed the Chelsea Flower Show, and admired the mediocre pictures at the Royal Academy summer opening: at the previous year's exhibition, Pietro Annigoni's romantic portrait of the Queen (looking remarkably like Ingrid Bergman) had drawn unprecedented crowds, but this year there was no showstopper.

Finally, having sent thick, properly engraved invitation cards from Smythsons, Clare appeared at her own coming-out ball, which was held at the Orangery in Holland Park. A new young designer, David Hicks, had turned the place into a white net, candlelit fairyland.

During Clare's debut, inevitably Elinor also attracted a lot of publicity. By now Elinor Dove had become a legendary figure, beloved by thousands of hopeful girls and women whose dreams were disappointed but not yet dashed. Briskly recirculated stories of the former farm girl's struggles against adversity, her growing fortune, and what she spent it on were tangible proof to Elinor's readers that fairy stories *could* come true. As charmingly professional to photographers as H.M. the Queen Mother, Elinor was constantly photographed: descending from her white Rolls-Royce in glittering ball gowns, beaming in white fox furs, cuddling photogenic white Pekingese, or smiling from beneath one of her elaborate apricot hats—she had decided that apricot was "her color."

Two steps behind her, Clare sometimes felt as if she were one of her grandmother's accessories—something more important than Elinor's handbag but less important than her five-strand pearl necklace: merely a part of the glamorous picture that she so carefully presented to her public.

By the end of the season, Clare felt that she never wanted to shake another hand or clap her white gloves just hard enough to sound enthusiastic but softly enough to be polite. She had acquired a lot of dancing partners, about five regular escorts, and plenty of girlfriends with whom to giggle about them. Clare knew that she was a lucky, lucky girl, and she hoped that she would never have to make the debutante round again: a life of pleasure left her feeling exhausted and curiously empty.

Although she dared not say so, Clare thought she had wasted the year. She tried to explain this to Annabel, who would shortly be exposed to the same blaze of pleasure and publicity, but Annabel did not understand her sister's warning. Annabel, after her first term at a Swiss finishing school, *longed* for the boys, the balls, and the ball gowns; she longed to be photographed for society magazines and couldn't wait to dance until dawn in the arms of a man—preferably an older one.

But that was later. Right now Annabel was stuck with her sisters, snowbound at Starlings, which was not her idea of fun. She jumped down from the drawing room window seat. "Clare, let's have another bridge lesson."

Clare looked up and yawned. "Not enough time before lunch."

When the telephone rang, like a black cat Clare flung herself toward it. "Hello?" she cried hopefully, then, disappointment in her voice, said, "Sorry, Buzz, but I'm expecting an important call." She crashed the phone back on its cradle.

"I bet it's Henry," teased Miranda.

"It can't be Henry." Annabel returned to the window seat. "Henry's regiment's just been posted to Suez."

"Shut up, both of you!" Clare snapped.

Again the telephone rang. Clare leapt from the sofa, but Miranda had snatched up the receiver. "Who's speaking? . . . C.N.D.? What's that? The Campaign for Nuclear Disarmament . . . I think you have the wrong number."

"It's for me!" Clare blushed violently, grabbed the telephone, made an appointment to meet someone in London, and replaced the receiver.

"Who was *that?*" Annabel asked.

"What was that *about?*" Miranda chimed in.

"None of your business," growled Clare.

"Gran won't like any ban-the-Bomb movement," Miranda said. "She'll say the atom bomb won the war for us in ten minutes. . . . The Prime Minister doesn't need to be told how to run the country by ignorant ungrateful rabble-rousers. . . . *You* know what Gran will say, Clare."

"C.N.D. is perfectly respectable," Clare said defensively. "Bertrand Russell and six other Nobel Prize winners support banning the atomic bomb, and Albert Einstein did too. In any future war, nuclear weapons might wipe out this whole planet."

"Gran still won't like it," Miranda warned.

• • •

"I cannot stand deceit!" Elinor croaked as she waved a letter at Clare the following morning; she lay in the sunny opulence of her bedroom, nursing an attack of bronchitis.

To avoid her grandmother's eye, Clare looked around the pretty room. The walls were cream, the curtains buttercup, to match the brocade hangings of the four-poster bed. Upon the faded yellows of the Bessarabian rug stood a Regency sofa with tiger-skin cushions. Piles of books and fragrant pots of narcissi filled the room.

"Kindly look at me, Clare." Elinor sneezed. "I'm waiting to hear what you have to say for yourself," she added crossly as she gazed at Clare, who stood before her in a pink sweater and tweed skirt, a furtive expression on her face.

Again Elinor wondered anxiously whether Clare had a lover: this was what all the mothers worried about, although none of the debutantes (more innocent than their mothers realized) ever knew it. She wondered if the man was married, if he made some business excuse to his wife on Tuesday and Thursday evenings, when Clare was clearly not doing what she said she was doing.

I'll have to lie again, Clare thought miserably. She remembered being puzzled as a child because grown-ups taught children not to lie, but then they looked you in the eye and lied about where babies came from. So from adults, Clare learned to tell "fibs" to avoid hurting people's feelings, to protect somebody else, or to avoid adult wrath.

"I'm waiting," wheezed Elinor, furious. She sneezed again, and one of her letters slid to the floor. Clare could see the Swithin, Timmins and Grant address flowing across the top of the page.

Looking away again, Clare said without thinking, "I was with Adam Grant."

"Twice a week? And always home by ten? Exactly *what* were you doing with Adam?"

"He was teaching me to play bridge. I want to be really good."

"Well, that's easy enough to check." Elinor reached for the cream telephone.

Clare, never a facile liar, felt helpless.

"Good morning, Adam? Have you seen Clare recently?"

Clare's heart sank. She had hoped that Adam might not be in his office.

"I fail to understand why you can't give me a straight answer," Elinor said, "but you may talk to her if you wish." She motioned to Clare to pick up the telephone.

Adam's voice in Clare's ear said: "Listen, Clare, I can't lie to my client. If you're in trouble, I'll try to help you, but tell me the truth or I can't help. . . . Are you seeing some man secretly? . . . No? Good! Are you doing anything illegal? . . . No? *Then tell Elinor where you've been!* Tell her straightaway. Whatever you've been concealing from her can't be nearly as bad as her fears, so you *may* be forgiven immediately. And next week, I *will* take you out to dinner—so that will be something to look forward to."

Clare replaced the receiver and, in a low voice, said to Elinor, "I go to night school."

"*Night school!* But that's for people who haven't . . ." Elinor, remembering the impoverished students at her Polytechnic classes, was puzzled. She said, "You've had a *good* education, Clare."

"I don't think so. I didn't learn much at Hazlehurst Park. I only got two O levels before you whisked me off to that stupid finishing school."

"What ingratitude! No man wants a bluestocking for a wife—a man wants someone who will grace his drawing room, in a ladylike manner."

"I don't intend to sit in a drawing room for the rest of my life! We're living in the twentieth century, not in the old days at Larkwood!" All three sisters knew that Elinor still smarted from the hurt feelings of inferiority inflicted upon her by Billy's family. Clare added, "I want to do something useful with my life!"

"Aren't wives useful? Aren't mothers useful?"

"There can be more to life than being a wife and mother!"

"Well, what exactly are you studying to make you more useful?"

"Sociology," Clare said defiantly.

Elinor looked astonished and alarmed. "My dear child, surely you're not going to be a *social worker?*"

"I don't see why I shouldn't be," Clare replied defensively. "It's a very useful job."

"Of course it is. That's all very well for other people. But not *you*, Clare. Not traipsing around slums."

"*Why not?* Gran, what have you got *against* sociology?"

Elinor sighed. "What exactly *is* sociology?"

"It tells you how society developed and how it functions—or doesn't function sometimes," Clare said.

"But, darling, your studies at school never reached the level required for these subjects, so . . ."

"*Exactly!* I'll also be studying anthropology, psychology, and philosophy."

"Surely not in only two evenings a week?"

"Since you now know about it, I'd like to be a full-time student. If I have enough basic qualifications. And if not, I'd like to get them."

"To what *purpose,* dear child? Nice men don't want to marry a sociologist or a philosopher. Why can't you study something less highbrow and a bit more useful? How about a cookery course at the Cordon Bleu school? It's always an asset to know how to plan menus."

"Gran, can't you understand that I'm interested in the world beyond my kitchen?" Clare spluttered angrily.

"Of course you are. You're an intelligent young woman and you must follow what the men are talking about."

"*I* want the men to follow what *I'm* talking about—which will *never again* be cocktail party chitchat!" Clare shouted.

"*How can you say that to me?*"

"Gran, I don't understand why I *can't!* Why do I have to be furtive? Why don't you understand what I want to do, and why?"

"But sociology . . . how will that help you?"

"Gran, I'm interested in helping other people. Everywhere I look, I see inequality."

"But philosophy . . . isn't that flying a bit high? And what has philosophy got to do with slum children?"

"Philosophy is concerned with ideas, and ideas are what democracy is based on," Clare said, exasperated. "I don't understand how the world got into this state, but I'm going to try to find out—and then do something about it."

"One young woman can't do anything to right the wrongs of the world," Elinor said, equally exasperated.

"I'll never do anything if I don't try." Clare was wearing her stubborn look.

"Why can't you leave such things to politicians, who've been trained to do their job?" Elinor cried.

"Your generation is going to be the last one to have blind faith in politicians!"

"My generation seemed to manage without *your* intellectual pretensions," Elinor said acidly.

"*Your* generation was the one that got us into the Second World War!"

TUESDAY, 18 DECEMBER 1956

As she handed her green satin cloak to the butler, Clare once again felt the butterflies rise in her stomach—the wish-I-could-turn-around-and-run-out-of-here feeling that she always experienced when she arrived at a party. Everyone else seemed so self-assured. When she knew nobody, Clare liked to slink to the cloakroom as fast as possible and stay there as long as possible, before facing a throng of people who all seemed to know each other.

Tonight Clare felt doubly nervous, because Adam had taken her, for the first time, to one of the illegal gambling games that were fast becoming fashionable in London. These parties were always held after dinner, from ten o'clock to dawn; no charge was made for the abundant and delicious food and drink, or the traditional English breakfast of bacon and eggs, sausages, kidneys, and kedgeree that was served from two a.m.

Clare knew that tonight's party had been organized by Michael Grant. Good-looking, presentable, an old Etonian and ex–Guards officer (although only national service), he was the perfect sort of person to organize a chic but illegal game.

All invitations were issued on the telephone—nothing was ever put on paper—to people who had plenty of money and enjoyed a little naughty excitement and glamour. It was reminiscent of Americans during Prohibition.

Merely to know the venue meant one was chic; no one considered the danger. Michael Grant's guests had been brought up to consider the police as people who got you out of trouble, not into trouble. Besides, the possibility of a police raid added to the thrill, and to be caught on such a raid was considered proof of sophistication and daring.

For the fashionable young people who flocked to the gambling parties, there was also the added thrill of rubbing shoulders with genuine criminals, whom they were unlikely to encounter in any other way. Tough bouncers were hired to protect the organizer; they saw that no drunk tore the place apart, and that losers paid up promptly. The protective services were paid for with a cut of the house take, and one of the mob was always present in order to check on it. Thus, rich young society gamblers were now on first-name terms with some of the toughest hoods in London's East End; this, too, was considered chic.

As Clare and Adam walked into a well-furnished Belgravia drawing room, Michael Grant stepped forward. "Here you are at last! We've got an interesting crowd tonight—nearly all the Eton gambling mafia's here. . . ." Michael looked at Clare as her eyes played around the roomful of people in evening dress talking quietly over drinks. "*This* is Clare O'Dare?"

It had been almost four years since their holiday in St.-Tropez. No longer small and skinny, Clare was now gracefully slim, pale, and elusive, with the flashing blue-eyed stare and enigmatic allure of a mermaid. Tonight her fey quality was emphasized by a blue-green chiffon gown.

Clare said shyly, "You look exactly the same, Mike—but you seem somehow . . . different." She sensed recklessness in this wide-shouldered, well-groomed man in the beautifully cut dinner jacket; and Mike's slow smile did not contradict a feeling of menace. Clare felt uneasy with him, whereas she felt completely safe with Adam.

Adam murmured something to his brother that Clare couldn't hear; they seemed to be very close, she thought as they laughed together. Adam looked around the room and laughed again. "It looks as if you've lived here for years, Mike!"

In order to avoid the police, these illegal games took place at a different address each night. Mike persuaded socially acceptable people, for a huge fee, to rent out their London home for twenty-four hours; sometimes this was done by a son or daughter while the unknowing parents were abroad or in the country. On the morning following a party, the furniture removal van that Mike kept permanently employed would arrive to shift the furniture, china, linen, and cutlery to the next house. Mike always used the same firm of first-class, professional caterers, the normal servants of the house not being considered trustworthy on these occasions.

"Let's get some champagne and go into the back rooms, where they're playing roulette and chemmy," suggested Adam, not present for pleasure only.

Mike had asked Adam to look around, because Mike's game was straight and he wanted to keep it so. A few games had been quietly taken over by their "protectors," after which the games were crooked. East End thugs were astonished at the idea of running a straight game. Of course you let the punter win a bit at first, in order to encourage him, but after that—naturally, the house won. You were in business to make money. And if, by chance, a punter had a big win, he was generally relieved of his winnings on the way to his car, and nobody could prove that the mugging was connected. However, this was rarely necessary, since the punter usually lost—it was the law of nature.

Mike reckoned that, should anyone try to put pressure on him, Adam would know someone to apply a little firm counterpressure.

Adam now worked full-time for the family firm; he had taken his solicitors' finals the previous year and was now fully conversant with trust accounts and bookkeeping, papers and property law, conveyancing and the law of contracts. At night, whenever possible, he gambled.

By one o'clock in the morning, Clare was tired and ready to go home but Adam was still playing roulette. Again he offered Clare fifty pounds with which to gamble but she shook her head. "Take money from a man? Gran would throw me into the snow and cut me off without a shilling."

"Rubbish. She's mad about all of you. *You'll* never be cut off without a shilling. She may lose her temper from time to time, but Elinor's bark is far worse than her bite. Look how your row ended—she's agreed that you can go to a crammer and study."

"I won't be able to study anything tomorrow unless you get me home soon."

"Just one more throw," Adam promised.

Clare yawned as she watched Adam swiftly place his stake. She felt too tired and shy to speak to anyone else, and anyway, the people in this quiet room were intent only on gambling.

Above the rattling clunk of the ball, Clare heard a faint commotion from the hall.

Adam's head jerked up. Ignoring his winnings, he took Clare by the arm in a grip that was hard enough to bruise. "That sounds like a police raid. Follow me quickly."

"But, Adam . . . my cloak . . ."

Adam had hustled Clare out the rear door while other guests were still looking puzzled.

"Ow, Adam, you're hurting me," Clare cried, but Adam took no notice. He opened a door at the back of the hall and pushed her down the stone stairs to the basement. She nearly collided with a waiter, who was carrying champagne up from the kitchen below.

Once at the bottom of the stairs, Clare could hear hammering against the front basement door, around which scared kitchen staff had gathered.

"Better let 'em in, Ernie," she heard someone say as Adam dragged her out the back door and into the dark garden.

"There should be a ladder to your right," Adam whispered. "Get up it and wait on top of the garden wall."

"But I can't . . . my *dress!*"

In the dark, Adam grabbed Clare's chiffon skirts, pulled them up to her waist, and threw them over her shoulders. "The ladder's right in front of you, Clare! *Climb it!*"

Clare pulled off her silver slipper—she'd lost the other on the stairs—and slowly climbed the workman's ladder, which wobbled each time she cautiously moved her foot up a rung into the darkness.

"Get a move on!" Adam whispered urgently. "I can hear the police in the kitchen!"

Tentatively Clare groped with her left hand, feeling for the wall, but pawed only air.

"*Hurry!*"

She moved up two more rungs and again stretched her hand

upward, but still felt nothing. This wall was as high as the Great Wall of China!

Again Clare reached out her hand, and this time touched the damp, uneven, unyielding bricks. Below her, she felt the ladder tremble as Adam started to climb. Clare thought she preferred to be caught by the police, rather than break her neck falling from a ladder in the dark.

After she climbed the next rung, Clare's hands groped forward, but she grasped empty air. Clearly she was now at the top of the wall and would have to get off the ladder.

As she crouched atop the wall, she heard windows thrown open with a crash. Someone shouted, "Send two men into the garden!"

Adam nimbly scrambled up beside her.

No time to pull the ladder up so we can climb down the other side, Adam thought, and pushed the ladder backward. Before it hit the ground, he had jumped into the dark safety of the neighboring garden.

"I'm in a flower bed," he whispered up to Clare. "You'll have to risk it. I can't see to catch you. For God's sake *jump!*"

Clare clung to the top of the wall, too frightened to jump.

"What about Mike?" she whispered anxiously.

Adam hesitated a moment, as he thought of the many occasions when Mike had loyally shouldered the blame for his adored elder brother. Adam fleetingly remembered the bi-weekly ceremony of stealing chocolate from the local sweetshop counter, where, eventually, the police had been brought in by the irate shopkeeper and were waiting for the two schoolboy thieves; Mike confessed (although Adam had been the ringleader) and Mike refused to name the other schoolboy conspirator, for which bravery he was soundly whipped by his father. Adam also remembered the ringing-doorbells-and-running-away episodes when Adam, the ringleader and the faster runner, had always managed to hide in someone's garden or up an alley, where he listened—heart pounding—to Mike's capture, knowing that a thundering row with their father would follow, and that Mike, after loyally swearing that Adam had nothing to do with it, would be beaten and punished.

Through childhood and adolescence, there had been many similar instances and never once had Adam confessed to having taken part in them. He had become used to this useful, fraternal hero worship. So now, in the earthy, damp darkness, he shrugged his shoulders and whispered to Clare, "Mike won't mind, he never does. Now, for God's sake—jump!"

The back door behind Clare opened with a crash.

She jumped downward, into the dark, into Adam's arms.

Before she had caught her breath, he grabbed her right wrist. "Let's get to the back door. It should be open."

As quickly as he could, Adam groped his way along the garden wall toward the silent house, shoving shrubs aside as he did so.

Eventually the garden wall ended and his fingertips moved to the left: they touched . . . a window . . . more brick wall . . . and then a paneled door. He felt for the handle, gently turned it to the left, and pushed.

The door opened.

Adam yanked Clare into the house; then slowly and very quietly he shut the door. His fingertips found the key in the lock, and he turned it carefully to the right. Swiftly he pushed upward, until he found the bolt and rammed it home.

"Adam, we've just broken into someone's house!" Clare whispered.

"Mike always plans an escape route for himself."

"But you pushed the ladder away, so Mike couldn't use it!"

"Your grandmother wouldn't like anything to happen to you."

"What do we do now?"

"We sit here until morning. Then we'll borrow a couple of coats and simply walk out of the front door—and pass the police."

Adam draped his jacket around Clare's shoulders. They both sat on the stone-paved floor of what seemed to be an old scullery, leading off a kitchen.

In the dark, Clare shivered as much from excitement as from cold. The voluptuous gambling party represented the kind of decadence that she had always considered waste, but it had been exciting to feel decadent, and wickedly sophisticated, just for a few hours.

After that evening, Clare always felt protected when she was with Adam. It never occurred to her that, had Adam not taken her to an illegal game, there would have been no need to rescue her from it.

Chapter · 9

"I don't suppose you deserve breakfast in bed," Buzz said as she carried a tray into Annabel's frilled pink bedroom. "How many hearts did you break last night?"

"Ow! Buzz, darling Buzz, please don't pull back the curtains. Ow! That sunshine is *blinding*."

"It's nearly midday." Buzz cruelly drew the curtains farther apart, and looked down to see Elinor picking anemones beneath the white and pink blossoming trees of the orchard.

Eighteen-year-old Annabel sat up and stretched. She looked older than her age, Buzz thought. Beneath that tangle of tawny hair, Annabel was the sister who most resembled the young Elinor; she had the same steady gaze and full, moist mouth with a natural curve, so that she seemed always to be smiling slightly, even when asleep.

The difference between Annabel's debut and Clare's had been that Annabel loved every minute of it. Lady Rushleigh had again been very helpful, and Elinor not only had paid her expenses for the London season but also had given her a sunburst diamond brooch she had admired when Elinor wore it.

Lady Rushleigh's protégée had met with great success. Beautiful, indolent Annabel was always surrounded by men; flirtation seemed natural to her, and she was as gently provocative to the postman and the butcher's boy on his bicycle as she was to the more eligible young men with whom she danced. Lighthearted, gay, and frivolous, Annabel did not restrict her encounters with these gentlemen to the dance floor: there had been much furtive groping on ballroom balconies, in taxis, and, early in the morning, in the cold and darkened drawing room of Elinor's London flat.

Annabel was wildly excited by the eroticism of the forbidden as well as by the turbulent hormones that coursed through her body. No matter how tired she felt when she left a party, she was always reenergized by the feel of a man's arm around her waist, a man's hard, warm palm on her naked shoulder as he pushed straps aside and explored the soft flesh of her breasts: Annabel felt a swooning, delirious tug from the bottom of her stomach as she murmured, "You mustn't . . . you really *mustn't . . .*"

Trembling from these touches, Annabel would sometimes allow what, earlier in the evening, she had decided on no account to permit; and a man's hand would slide beneath the net or taffeta skirt to her smooth, nylon-covered knee, eventually to move stealthily over the stocking top, over a taut satin suspender, and slip inward over Annabel's soft, quivering thigh. The young man was then pushed off into the night, tumescent, throbbing, painfully frustrated.

"Time you was up and packing," Buzz said, turning again to the window.

Elinor, in the orchard, looked up, saw Buzz at Annabel's window, and waved. In her gardening clothes, she did not look the glittering, glamorous legend that she had become since Billy's death. Buzz had been astonished by the change in her personality: Nell had blossomed; she had clearly become a person in her own right as well as a soaring success in the world.

Her American publisher now wished her to meet her readers on the other side of the Atlantic, so Elinor, accompanied by Annabel, was about to fly to New York, the first city on her U.S. tour.

Annabel yawned. "Buzz, has anyone taken breakfast to Harry?"

Buzz sniffed, placed the tray before Annabel, and chopped off the top of Annabel's boiled egg with an unnecessary violence that clearly showed her opinion of Harry.

"You don't want to bother too much about *him,*" Buzz said. "There'll be tears before bedtime over that young masher."

"I don't understand why you dislike him, Buzz. You've hardly met him," Annabel protested. Buzz had lectured her incessantly about the pitfalls of love.

Buzz poured herself a cup of coffee and sat on the end of the bed. "Seen his type before: Don Juan." Buzz pronounced the *j,* as in *jab.* "Harry don't love you, my girl—Harry don't love *anyone.* Pays the girls a lot of attention, o'course, but so does a hunter stalking deer. I bet Harry rushes from one girl to the next, just to show himself he can." She wrinkled her forehead. "I ain't never fathomed why a man who gets through a lot of women is reckoned to be some sort of hero, while a woman who has a lot of fellas is called a nympho maniac."

Annabel said, "And how do *you* know so much about men, Buzz?"

Buzz hesitated. She still felt mild astonishment that Ginger Higby had, long ago, so clearly preferred her to all other women. She still kept all his letters, and his mother—showing great kindness—had given her two photographs of Ginger as a child. Buzz was comforted by the big buff envelope that contained these remnants of all the sexual love she would ever know.

The feelings that Ginger's body had aroused in her had, after his death, led Buzz to touch herself experimentally, hoping to remember those past moments of thwarted passion. To her astonishment, she discovered the erotic climax, which should have been the culmination of her always abruptly severed lovemaking with Ginger. Because she alone was responsible for her pleasure, Buzz felt guilty, felt disloyal to Ginger. She knew instinctively that this was a forbidden game. But why, she asked herself defensively, should she not experience those physical feelings she had been denied by some unknown soldier who would never know—if he still existed—that an accidental squeeze of his finger had caused an eternal void in Buzz's life, which had not seemed empty before she met Ginger.

Looking at beautiful Annabel, able to have any fellow she fancied, Buzz sighed and said, "I know about rascals like Harry because I've got eyes, miss, and I've been using them for years. The Harrys don't bother about an old stick like me—they don't notice I'm watching 'em." Harry reminded Buzz of Billy.

The door was flung open and seventeen-year-old Miranda made her entrance; she wore Stuart tartan slacks and a black sweater; her thick, shoulder-length hair was the brilliant orange of marmalade.

"Like it?" As Miranda twisted her head from side to side, the flaming hair swung outward. "John French. Cost a fortune—four guineas."

Annabel was impressed. "Gran'll *kill* you."

"Theatrical," Buzz sniffed. "You'd better wash it off before she sees you."

"Can't. It's dyed." Miranda was triumphant.

"She'll definitely kill you," Annabel said respectfully. "Dyed hair is unladylike."

Miranda was defiant. "Gran's fifty-eight years old, hasn't got a single gray hair, and is as blond as Marilyn Monroe. Gran goes to John French."

Clare pushed open the door. "So this is where everyone is. What are you talking about?"

"Love." Annabel stretched happily. "Love that makes you feel as if you're high in the clouds, with masses of energy and no need for sleep."

Remembering, Buzz nodded. "No wonder women long for it. Gives 'em something exciting to think about while they're doing the dull things that women do—which is where your gran comes in."

"Gran!" Annabel exclaimed through a mouthful of buttered toast. "How?"

"When a woman reads about some exciting man in a novel, she forgets she ain't got a man, or she ain't got the right sort of man. She falls a little bit in love with the hero, and although he don't exist, her feelings about him exist, all right. She *really* feels a bit excited."

"That's the whole point of escapist literature," Clare said tartly. "You can pretend you're really living it."

Buzz nodded again. "Some women get hooked, like a drug, on romance and they'd rather have it out of a book than not at all . . . the sort of woman that feels hopeful before a party, wonders if her Prince Charming will appear, is disappointed when he don't, and goes home feeling a failure."

"I don't want to marry Prince Charming," Clare said firmly. "Just an honest . . . trustworthy . . . supportive . . . sensitive . . . man."

"That doesn't sound very exciting." Annabel licked her buttery fingers. "I want one that's strong . . . fascinating . . . dynamic and a bit mysterious."

"I want a man of action," Miranda said. "A romantic-looking leader of men, like Rupert of the Rhine."

"Titled? Rich? Powerful?" Buzz queried. "Good-looking, tall, blue-eyed?"

"Blue eyes aren't absolutely necessary," Annabel conceded.

Buzz said sourly, "And this almost perfect man that you all want—*if* he exists—what exactly are you each offering him? Similar perfection?"

"Oh Buzz, we were having a nice sexy talk and you've turned it into a lecture again." Annabel yawned.

"I'm trying to knock a bit of sense into your head before exciting Mr. Heartbreaker Harry wakes up." Buzz reached for the tray. "There ain't no perfect men, and exciting men make women miserable." Again she thought of Billy.

MONDAY, 21 APRIL 1958

In spite of the air freshener, the windowless greenroom of the New York TV news station still smelled of dead cigarettes and stale coffee.

A girl dressed casually with an oversized man's shirt over her skirt opened the door and beckoned to Elinor, who stood up feeling terrified but looking calm and self-possessed. She wore a Christian Dior apricot silk dress and duster coat, suitable for any formal day or evening occasion that didn't call for an ankle-length dress. Her blond hair was in a chignon. Careful dieting had kept her weight what it had been when she was seventeen; neat cosmetic surgery around her eyelids and chin had left only a few, faint lines at the sides of her mouth to indicate her age.

"Good luck," whispered the publisher's press agent.

"Knock 'em dead," encouraged Annabel, who wore heavy makeup and a silver, sleeveless sheath from Bazaar.

In the studio, the charismatic fair-haired young interviewer introduced Elinor as this year's winner of the International Romance Writers Award and then, predictably, asked the secret of her success.

Elinor beamed. "The secret of writing good romantic fiction is to *feel* romantic, *look* romantic, and *be* romantic."

"Some people describe your books as trash. What do you feel about that?"

The publisher's press agent had warned Elinor that Scott Svenson would listen to her every word, remember her every word, and not hesitate to use it against her; he never gave anyone an easy ride, but he was the station's best interviewer. Elinor continued to beam. "Millions of my readers wouldn't agree. Today's classics were sometimes described in the past as trash—Charles Dickens's books were serialized in popular magazines, and Thomas Hardy's work was called pulp fiction. Even Shakespeare—a very commercial writer—was accused by his contemporaries of writing potboilers."

"And what is *your* formula for a potboiler?"

"The ingredients of a good novel are as basic and simple as the ingredients of a soufflé," Elinor said with a smile. "Good characterization, a believable, well-constructed plot, detailed research, and dialogue that's easy to read. I keep to the point, write short paragraphs, ration my adjectives, and try never to use superfluous words."

"Your sex scenes have been described as 'limp.' Would you agree?"

"My books contain love scenes, but *never* a sex scene. I see no need to follow my heroines to the marriage bed: we all know what happens there."

"You have been accused of lack of realism in this respect."

"Realism is the last thing my readers want: they get enough of that at home. My books provide a holiday from reality. . . ."

She was a tough old bird, Scott thought. How could he shake that smile? He tried again. "Although you live in a world of romance, you have never remarried. Why is there no man in your life?"

Elinor still smiled. "There will be a man in my life when I choose to have a man in my life," she said, "just as the heroine of my new novel, *Heartbreak in Jamaica* . . ." After all, the point of being on this show was to publicize her book.

• • •

Annabel and her grandmother came out of the greenroom just as the interviewer was exiting the stage door.

Scott stopped. "Hi." He threw them the careless, boyish smile that made thousands of women stop their husband from switching channels.

"I'd like to say how great you were, Miss Dove," Scott said respectfully. "Is this your daughter?" Maybe he was piling it on too thick? "I wondered if . . . The Plaza's just around the corner, if you'd care for a drink?"

"Thank you, but we are tired after our trip." Elinor swept out. She had felt under slight but unyielding pressure during the entire interview.

Annabel lingered, unwilling to be dragged to bed on her first night in New York. "Why don't you come to our suite for a drink?" she suggested. They were, in fact, staying at the Plaza.

By the time they reached her hotel suite, Elinor had heard that she possessed a natural screen presence, although Scott would like to suggest one or two little professional tricks. He added, "As a matter of fact, I could tell you were from the Midwest. It wasn't only your accent, it was your forthright, no-nonsense attitude."

Elinor gave a genuine smile. "I could tell straightaway that *you* were. I knew I couldn't pull the wool over your eyes."

By the time the champagne bottle was empty, Elinor had thoroughly interviewed Scott, to his amusement.

Scott came from Cleveland, Ohio, where he'd started to write for his high school paper in his senior year, then studied communications at college. He worked as a junior assistant on a local Cleveland paper—no, unfortunately, not the *Plain Dealer*—and eventually slid into the foreign editor's office as a free-lance researcher. At that point, a locally owned and operated TV station wanted a cheap, fast, noncomplaining researcher-writer, and as the job paid twice as much as the newspaper, Scott took it. Gradually he was allowed to cover minor stories.

Scott did not mention that his boyish good looks and engaging smile had earned him the malicious nickname of "Pretty Boy."

He had been lucky that he first appeared on the box when stations were out to woo the youth audience and all newscasters over the age of thirty-five were secretly having their eye bags removed. With just enough training and experience, Scott had turned up at the right time, but not quite in the right place. A year later, he applied for the job of news reporter on a local TV station in New York City. Once hired, he surprised the director of news by his hard-nosed, carefully researched stories and hard-hitting interviews: recently he had been allowed to appear as a relief newscaster and interviewer.

By midnight, Elinor was asleep in her bed, but Scott and Annabel (having promised not to return too late) were drinking more champagne at "21."

An hour later, they creaked around Central Park in one of the romantic horse-drawn black cabs that wait dolefully outside the Plaza. Scott gently kissed Annabel's nose and tried to think of ways to keep her in New York.

Then the obvious idea hit him. "Why don't you try modeling?" he murmured in her ear. "I can fix you an interview with the best agent in town."

"*All* the girls I know want to be air hostesses or models," Annabel said. "But I'm not sure Gran would let me."

"Then don't ask her."

On the following morning, Annabel sat opposite a well-groomed blonde, aged forty plus, in a beige gabardine suit. The wall behind her desk was covered by citations. Scott had briefed her on Bates Model Agency—run by a husband-and-wife team, Moses and Jenny Bates. Ten years before, they had borrowed a thousand dollars to set up their company; within three years, they had a stable of thirty-nine models and total billings of $300,000. Mrs. Bates chose and supervised the models; her husband was responsible for their bookings. They discovered that marketing the most beautiful women in the world was not very difficult, but finding them was a problem.

Each year, the Bateses saw and rejected about five thousand applicants; they held talent contests all over America and also overseas— for blond models were the most popular, and the best were to be found in Germany and Scandinavia. The cosmetics industry was especially willing to pay very high fees for an exquisite new face; while complaining about the Bateses' high charges, cosmetics companies continued to pay them because there was no cheaper way to find girls of the high standard of beauty, charm, grooming, and professional behavior (punctuality, patience, and amiability) so carefully set by the Bateses.

"Don't pluck her eyebrows yet, just tidy them up—we'll see how they photograph," ordered Mrs. Bates. She tapped her pencil against her teeth and scrutinized Annabel's face once more. "Go and wash your face in the dressing room. I need to see you without makeup."

When Annabel returned, Mrs. Bates squinted at her, then nodded briefly. "We'll fix a few test shots. Janey here will arrange them for this afternoon."

When she saw Annabel's test shots, Mrs. Bates smiled and called her for a second interview.

• • •

Jenny Bates leaned forward across her white desk. "Don't think a model's job is easy or glamorous. Less than one percent of beginner models are immediately successful, and when they are, it's rarely because of their beauty but because—for some odd reason—they catch the eye of an advertising agency as being 'different' and 'right for now.' " As with newscasters, a girl who was the toast of the town for one period would—automatically—not look right for the next.

"And if she's to stand out from the rest," Mrs. Bates added, "a girl needs some extra, unique quality that the other models don't possess." The model's face also needed enough sensual appeal to attract a man, but not so much that it would make a woman feel threatened.

"Have you heard of Suzy Parker?" Mrs. Bates asked.

Annabel nodded. Who had not? Redheaded Suzy Parker and her brunette sister, Dorian Leigh, had been the top models of the fifties: they both possessed classic beauty, an exquisite sophistication, and dazzling "glamour"—the cosmetics industry's euphemism for sex appeal. Now they were past their professional peak; in a blaze of publicity, Dorian had opened a model agency in Paris and Suzy had signed a film contract. The top seats were vacant.

Jenny Bates, looking over the flowers on her desk, wondered whether Annabel might fill that vacancy. She had beauty, feminine charm, and that unmistakable, uncopyable old-money look; her sleepy aquamarine eyes were most unusual, as was the large mouth that should have looked too big for her tiny face but didn't. While kitten faces were currently fashionable (Leslie Caron, Audrey Hepburn, Brigitte Bardot), Annabel's face was more like that of a wild mountain cat.

"Stand up once more, and walk to the door, please," ordered Mrs. Bates. She watched Annabel closely. This girl was not glamorous, groomed, or sophisticated; she didn't even shave her legs. She must be tidied up immediately, but without losing that just-tumbled-out-of-bed look.

And then she *might* prove right for Avanti. Avanti was looking for a face to work exclusively for them; they were also willing to pay the face to do nothing when they didn't need her, rather than be used by a rival. Avanti had asked for a classic Scandinavian blonde because all cosmetics companies believed that a blonde could sell anything to anyone. Annabel was not such a blonde, but golden highlights would probably do the trick.

Avanti had pulled itself into a position where it almost rivaled Revlon: they hoped that their next, ambitious promotion would rival Revlon's "Fire and Ice" campaign of 1952, regarded by the trade as unbeatable. Featuring Dorian Leigh in a tight-fitting sheath of silver sequins and a flowing crimson cape, it had combined elegance, class, and sensuality; it suggested that beneath the ordinary woman lay another woman—a smoldering temptress.

Avanti's shorthand specification for the girl they were seeking to rival the Fire and Ice girl was "a class act and a tiger in the sack." The creative director had specified: "young—but not too young, a graceful and sophisticated international woman," lively but not noisy, glamorous but approachable, sporty but not sweaty, and equally at home in town and country.

And the final requisite would be no problem, for Annabel clearly came from a respectable background: The morality clause included in her contract would stipulate that, should she be (or have been) involved in a scandal, which might adversely affect the Avanti promotion, the contract would immediately be terminated.

Annabel had better spend tomorrow at the hairdresser, Mrs. Bates decided, first for highlights, then to try different hairstyles. For her interviews, Annabel would need more sophisticated clothes than this butter-colored shirtwaister. After the hairdresser, she'd better take her to Bergdorf.

Jenny Bates, wondering whether, at last, she had found a contender for the number one slot, said, "Do you really have to leave for Chicago tomorrow?"

WEDNESDAY, 23 APRIL 1958

"It must have been something I ate last night—maybe those oysters," groaned Annabel, who had carefully chosen oysters. She knew that only a supervised and not-too-serious illness would persuade Elinor, who could not easily cancel her tour, to leave her granddaughter alone in New York.

The hotel doctor was puzzled. "I can't find anything wrong with her, but you say she vomited and suffered from diarrhea during the night, so she's clearly not well," he said. "She shouldn't travel yet. Better leave her here under observation—she'll be perfectly safe at the Plaza. I'll visit her every day and keep you informed of her condition."

The publisher's press agent shot him a look of gratitude and relief. She didn't want Elinor to miss the Chicago plane.

"But I can't leave a child alone in New York!" Elinor said, "*especially* if she's ill." Nevertheless, she hesitated, knowing how carefully her publisher had planned this expensive tour, and how long it had taken to organize.

"There's clearly nothing seriously wrong with your granddaughter," the hotel doctor reassured her. "It'll probably clear up in a couple of days."

"No, I can't leave Annabel alone," Elinor decided.

"But all the dinners, and the signings . . . You can't disappoint all those people who are looking forward to meeting you," the publisher's agent pleaded.

Elinor shook her head. "I'm sorry."

"Couldn't you ask Buzz to fly over?" Annabel asked. "Although I'll probably have joined you in Chicago by the time she arrives."

Elinor considered. "That *might* be the answer. . . ." She went to the phone.

A startled Buzz agreed to get to New York as fast as possible, and then insisted on speaking to Annabel about her symptoms. "A touch of colic," she decided. "Now you be a good girl and stay in bed with a hot-water bottle until I get there."

"Oh, I will," Annabel promised, feeling increasingly guilty.

Annabel stayed in bed until after the plane's departure. Then she threw back her bedclothes, tore off her nightgown, and danced like a whirling dervish in the middle of the room. She was free! She was alone in New York! Alone at the Plaza!

She rushed to the window and looked down on the green treetops of Central Park; to her right, beyond the line of listless horse cabs, a fountain sparkled in the sun. Behind it lay the excitement of Fifth Avenue, and somewhere behind that was the Bates Model Agency, where her future—her life perhaps—would be decided. . . .

Jenny Bates had no idea that Annabel had faked illness to stay in New York. She knew that Annabel had no cash, although she could order anything she wanted at the Plaza; it was the same with all the British, who had to budget on a ludicrously low, government-regulated travel allowance and rely on friends to finance them.

Later that morning, Mrs. Bates took Annabel across the street from the Plaza to Bergdorf Goodman: Bates Model Agency paid for her new clothes, in advance of fees due.

At lunchtime, Annabel telephoned Buzz, hoping it wasn't too late to tell her not to buy her ticket to New York yet: Annabel's "colic" was much better and tomorrow she might be well enough to join Elinor in Chicago.

"Thank heaven for that," said Buzz. "You haven't *half* given us a fright. I wasn't able to get a seat until the morning. . . . Keep well wrapped up, and do as the doctor tells you."

"I will," Annabel promised her, and skipped off to Saks.

On the following morning, after another glorious shopping spree, Annabel walked in spring sunshine down Fifth Avenue to the crimson door of Elizabeth Arden, where a grooming session had been booked for her. Five hours later, a perfectly groomed Annabel emerged with a personalized makeup chart, false eyelashes, and false nails. Her hair had been trimmed, streaked blond, and restyled. Roberto had designed a wig and two hairpieces for her (one a chignon), but these would take three weeks to complete.

She rushed back to the Plaza to telephone Buzz before her bedtime, and reported that she now felt fit enough to join Elinor.

"That's good news," said Buzz. "Wish I could speak to Nell myself, but it takes hours to get through. The Warminster telephone operator makes enough fuss about booking a call to London, let alone New York!"

"I'll give Gran your love," Annabel told her, and dashed off to Bloomingdale's.

That evening, Annabel also used maybe-tomorrow tactics when Elinor telephoned. Considering that mothers have been daughters, Annabel thought as she waited for Scott to finish his broadcast, it's surprisingly easy for a young girl to deceive them.

Early the next day, Annabel returned to Elizabeth Arden's pink gymnasium for a personal head-to-toe reshaping course, during which her exercise expert found body exercises for muscles that Annabel never knew she had. She also had her posture corrected; she was taught to lift her rib cage and "box" her stomach and rear with her hands, as ballet dancers do before dancing, and also to walk as if she were lightly holding a coin between her buttocks.

"I never realized that being beautiful is a full-time business," Annabel told Scott that evening as they sipped martinis in the Plaza bar.

Scott looked at her with bemused surprise: in four days, Annabel seemed to have changed into a taller, paradoxically wilder but sleeker version of herself. She now projected a feline delicacy, a demure but concentrated look, as if deciding whether to pounce.

This air of being totally in command of herself was what Jenny Bates hoped Annabel would project on film; this was the quality that distinguished her from the other models in the Bates stable. It was, Mrs. Bates hoped, the look that matched the female mood of the moment— the look of the approaching sixties.

Mrs. Bates decided that before she was presented to Avanti, Annabel needed to lose her self-consciousness and gain modeling experience before the camera, or she would photograph at only twenty percent of her potential. As she was inspecting Annabel's composite sheet of photographs, a frantic photographer telephoned the agency. A model had been taken ill at his studio and he needed an immediate replacement; the client had specified a blonde.

"Would you try a very promising beginner?" Mrs. Bates asked.

"Send her around fast."

· · ·

On her first assignment, Annabel was stiff and nervous. She felt like an artist's lay figure: it seemed to take a conscious effort to move her limbs.

"You need to, like, loosen up," said the photographer, who had been suggesting this for thirty years. "Forget everything except the camera. Ignore everyone else in the studio. Look, talk, smile to the camera, as if you were in love with it." He knew he was lucky to save his session, but he also knew that the shots wouldn't be very good. Beginners had a lot to learn.

Beginner models were easy to exploit too, as Scott told Annabel that evening, over fettuccine Alfredo at the Café des Artistes. "Young models are notorious prey for lecherous photographers," he warned, "especially the older ones. Don't be fooled by their masterful act; don't let them mesmerize you with their charisma of authority or their Daddy-will-look-after-you pitch. These guys like to be seen all over town with the face of the moment; they're often domineering and frequently abusive, to keep the girls under their control."

"Then you'd better keep an eye on me," Annabel said.

"I'm going to be guiding you every step of the way," Scott assured her.

"Lucky me," Annabel breathed demurely, batting her eyelashes and ignoring Scott's warning. *She* had never had any trouble with older men. She could twist them around her little finger as easily as she could younger men; what intrigued her about Scott was his refusal to be thus manipulated. He was also refreshingly nonjudgmental, the first man she could talk to as openly as to her sisters, and the two of them laughed a lot. Besides, Scott was even better-looking in real life than he was on a TV screen.

On her way to appointments, Annabel would peer from yellow cabs at the city. Her favorite sight was the silver, spiked top of the Chrysler Building, which might have been built by the Wizard of Oz; that apart, clearly the only bit of Manhattan featured in movies was the relatively small area of glittering glass and steel skyscrapers around Central Park South. Although other parts of the city were endearingly eccentric—apartment buildings were topped by ancient Egyptian temples, Gothic towers, or Moorish arches—most of Manhattan was unglamorous, noisy, crowded, and dirty. But Annabel gazed with excitement at the hectic, nonstop life of the street, where fire sirens wailed constantly and steam mysteriously billowed up from manholes, as if direct from hell. The polyglot mix of nationalities, colors and religions seemed to tolerate any behavior: it was clear that you could do exactly as you pleased in New York City.

· · ·

After his fifth "house" call, the weasel-sized hotel doctor looked over his spectacles at Annabel and said rather coldly that in spite of her symptoms, he could find nothing medically wrong with her and would inform her grandmother accordingly.

"You'll have difficulty getting in touch with her," Annabel warned. "Gran is in Chicago; then she's going to Los Angeles. All day she gives lectures and autographs books, and then in the evening she has literary dinners; she says she's kept very busy." On her telephone calls to Annabel, Elinor had sounded weary, and her American accent had become more pronounced, as always happened when she was tired.

When Elinor next called, Annabel announced her recovery and said she'd really like to stay in New York. There was so much to do there; the Metropolitan was about to start a series of lectures on the Impressionists, and at tea in the Palm Court, she'd met a nice girl who was studying history at Sarah Lawrence. Couldn't Elinor ask her publisher to introduce Annabel to one or two more nice girls?

After a certain amount of argument, Elinor admitted, "I'm certainly not having much fun—it's all too tiring."

"So you see, Gran, why drag me along?"

"Perhaps it's best that you're in New York. . . . I'm glad you aren't lonely, darling. Incidentally, have you heard from that charming TV interviewer?"

"Had lunch with him yesterday," Annabel said as nonchalantly as possible. "He showed me around the TV station."

"You sound a little feverish," Elinor said anxiously. "Are you *sure* you've recovered?"

"Oh yes," Annabel said. "I've started to go on long walks. Get plenty of exercise. There's a lot to see." Now *shut up*, she told herself. Miranda said that she always knew when Annabel was fibbing, because she said too much, too fast.

In fact, Annabel wasn't seeing as much of Scott as she had hoped. He seemed to work nonstop from ten in the morning until eleven o'clock at night, when the news broadcast ended. During these hours, their meetings were brief, but after the broadcast, Scott took Annabel to dark bars where tinkling pianos played brittle 1930s Gershwin, or to dimly lit, smoke-filled jazz clubs, or to parties given by avant-garde painters in the lofts or converted warehouses of SoHo. Scott seemed to find it amusing that bohemian artists now lived where once the city's vegetables had been stored.

By the beginning of her second week in Manhattan, Annabel had learned to relax in front of the camera. She preferred studio shots to location shots, where there always seemed to be lighting problems and something vital was always forgotten.

To Annabel's surprise, she found that it was very exhausting work to dress and undress all day long. And at the end of the day, when everyone was exhausted, she must not let tiredness show on her face; grimly she learned to dredge up vitality on demand.

Annabel also found it surprising that the models were treated as if they were wooden cigar store Indians, with no brains or feelings; nobody paid the slightest attention to them—they were the meat—until the girl was needed before the camera ... when she was cooed at, encouraged, and flattered.

By her third week, Annabel's feet ached permanently, but now, immaculately groomed, she felt her self-confidence increase with each assignment and harden with each rejection. No matter how experienced or famous, a model always had to audition for the next job, and if ten girls were interviewed, then nine were rejected. Often this was not because of any lack of beauty but because one was too tall, one was too short, another was in some other way not "right" for what the creative director had in mind. Young models were philosophical about this, but tension and anxiety were visible on the faces of those who were approaching their twenty-fifth birthday: after that day, the skin started to lose its bloom.

SATURDAY, 10 MAY 1958

On the day before Elinor was due to return to New York, Annabel was called for her preliminary audition for Avanti.

In a big attic studio on Forty-sixth and Fifth, colored background papers fell from overhead rollers, lights stood in groups, and black cables snaked on the black linoleum floor, a hazard even when you knew they were there. A group of horn-rimmed male executives from the cosmetics firm and BBSQ, the advertising agency, were seated in a corner on dark slab chairs; this part of the room was dimly lit.

The batteries of harsh lights in the studio were focused on a black backdrop, in front of which each model had to walk, stand, turn, and hold her smile.

The door of the models' dressing room opened. "Annabel O'Dare," an assistant's voice called.

Annabel, who had refused a seat in order to avoid crumpling her white piqué dress, stepped out and into a blaze of light.

· · ·

Late that evening, in a dimly lit nightclub, Scott murmured, "Of course you'll get the job." He eased Annabel's collar away from the back of her neck and blew gently down her dress. She quivered as she felt his warm breath lift the hairs of her spine: she could not have stood up at that moment. A hopeful trance of lust enveloped her body, but Scott made no further move. He guessed that a gaggle of lovelorn young men danced attendance on Annabel, so he had decided not to pounce until a disappointed Annabel was wondering why he hadn't. He knew that she saw other men during the day, but as she had a standing date with Scott at eleven p.m., he also knew that these men were not a serious threat to his intention, which was that Annabel should fall in love with him so thoroughly that *she* would pursue *him*.

Again Scott breathed lightly down the back of her dress.

"Where do you learn these things?" Annabel whispered.

"In the brothels of Hong Kong," Scott breathed.

"I don't believe you."

"It's true. I managed to wangle my way out there for a couple of months, when I was working for the foreign desk in Cleveland."

"You . . . er . . . actually met Chinese prostitutes?" Annabel was both intrigued and repelled.

"I did indeed. I learned a lot."

Annabel longed to know what but didn't like to ask.

In her private sitting room at the Plaza the next day, Elinor stared again at Annabel. Not only did she look completely different—and about ten years older—but she behaved with a new self-assurance. How could her darling have changed so in three weeks?

"What do you *mean* you aren't going back to England with me, Annabel? *Of course* you're leaving with me tomorrow, and I don't want to discuss this again."

"I know you're tired, Gran, but if I don't tell you now, you'll say I've been deceitful. I'm staying in Manhattan."

"*No you are not!* Anyway, you only have a four-week visitor's visa! You'll be *forced* to leave!" Elinor's brain tried to grapple with Annabel's defiance. Had Miranda behaved like this, she would not have been surprised. But Annabel was so gentle and easygoing.

Suddenly Elinor realized. "It's that young man, isn't it? The TV interviewer." She did a double take. "*What did you mean when you said that if you don't tell me now, I'll say you've been deceitful?* Have you been . . . Have you let him . . ." Blushing, Elinor said, "I mean . . . *Have you been to bed with this young man?*"

"No, Gran," said Annabel, truthfully. It had happened not on the bed but on a rug in Scott's apartment.

"Then *why* do you want to stay here?"

"Gran, I have a chance at a big modeling job."

"If you want to be a model, you can be one in London, where you won't be lonely and don't need a permit. I can keep an eye on you in London. Manhattan is no place for a young girl!"

"Gran, Mrs. Bates's lawyer says that there will be no problem about the work permit . . ."

"*Who* is Mrs. Bates, pray?"

"You'd better meet her."

Over lunch, Elinor was slowly reassured. Mrs. Bates was elegant, well-spoken, and well-mannered. Mr. Bates, a Harvard man, projected authority and reliability; he made it clear that he understood and shared Elinor's concern for Annabel's safety.

"We pride ourselves on looking after our models as if they were our daughters," Mr. Bates promised her, "and every one of those girls understands that *her* reputation is *our* reputation."

Elinor looked at Annabel's imploring face, then back to the reassuring bulk of Mr. Bates. "Very well," she said reluctantly. "Annabel can stay for another month, provided she stays in this residential hotel for young women that you recommend."

TUESDAY, 13 MAY 1958

When Elinor returned to Starlings, Buzz—forewarned by telephone—looked at her exhausted, miserable face and said, "No need to look so low—Annabel ain't *dead*. You can call New York any time you please. It only takes an hour or two to get through."

Slowly Elinor removed her coat. "Where are Clare and Miranda?"

"Shopping in Warminster. We wasn't expecting you for another couple of hours. What you need, Nell, is a nice hot bath."

Elinor had a long soak and wondered whether her aching bones were due to old age or that bumpy twelve-hour flight on the Britannia. She then put on her garden coat and gum boots and stumped out for a comforting chat with Mr. Jeffreys, the head gardener, who was planting sweet corn and French beans. After that, she wandered around the garden, hungry to see what had happened in her absence. As she admired the wisteria that fell from the wall above the kitchen, Buzz joined her. They walked in silence, enjoying the weak spring sunshine.

"You can't keep 'em with you forever," Buzz said eventually.

Elinor said sadly, "I never realized until now that, one day, all three of them will leave, with never a backward glance or thought for us."

"It's only natural. You wouldn't want it any other way."

Elinor was not consoled. Of course she wanted her girls to marry and have children, and obviously, in order to do that, they had to leave home. But Annabel hadn't left home with a husband, she had left to get a *job*—although heaven knew why the child should want one.

As they scrunched along the gravel drive back toward the house, Buzz said, "Clare's got another bit of news for you. It ain't exactly bad, but you ain't going to like it. No, it's her business to tell you. I'm just warning you—so you don't get in a temper and say something you'll later regret. Remember that Clare can be as stubborn as you are." Buzz dug in her pocket. "I almost forgot! I've got a letter here that might cheer you up. The rest of your post can wait till tomorrow."

Elinor held out her hand for the opened cream envelope with the O'Dare crest on the flap. Quickly she read the short letter from Marjorie, her sister-in-law. ". . . Since John's death . . . Of course, my daughter-in-law is very capable . . . To be blunt, I feel unwanted here . . . hope you will let bygones be bygones . . . would like to come and stay with you . . . seems such a long time . . . frankly lonely . . ."

Elinor stared at the letter. For years, she had suffered Marjorie's spiteful arrows. Now it looked as if the time had come for retaliation. Perhaps she should invite Marjorie to Starlings to subtly hurl her success in her face. Or write back a barbed letter, reminding Marjorie of the many occasions on which she had been willfully cruel to Elinor.

She reread the letter which in the past would have brought her such reassurance. Now that revenge was within her grasp, Elinor found it worthless, pointless, demeaning.

Slowly she tore the letter into small pieces. "No reply," she said, and tossed the pieces to the breeze.

From her bedroom, Elinor heard Clare's Triumph two-seater slide on the gravel. She heard shrieks of laughter, the barking of the Labradors, the bang of the front door.

Clare, in dark gray sweater and slacks, and seventeen-year-old Miranda, in her lumpy green school uniform, tumbled through the bedroom door and flung themselves upon Elinor.

"Darling Gran, we've missed you so."

After Elinor had presented the girls with gifts (suits and shoulder bags from Bloomingdale's), and had filled them in on the news of Annabel's stab at modeling and her American boyfriend, she said half playfully, "What's this nasty surprise you have for me, Clare?"

Clare was standing in front of the mirror, holding her raspberry linen suit before her. She took a deep breath and said, "I've started to do voluntary work in London."

"But I think that's a very *good* idea. The Red Cross?"

"No," Clare said. "C.N.D. Ban the Bomb. When you thought I was staying with the Bedfords last month, I was actually on the Aldermaston protest march, with twelve thousand other people." Clare looked pleadingly at Elinor. "Oh Gran, if you could have seen all those people—especially the mothers with young children, who don't want them blown to bits. . . . Anyway, while you were away, I agreed to work in their London office."

"And what about your sociology course?" Elinor asked.

"That can wait. This can't. No use having a sociology degree if the world is blown to bits."

Elinor was grateful for Buzz's warning. She had just said goodbye to one granddaughter; she didn't want to drive another one away. Biting back her consternation, she said, "I'm proud of you, Clare. I want to hear *all* about it—and I'd like to help. Now, where have I put my checkbook?"

SATURDAY, 24 MAY 1958

Scott's studio apartment on East Eleventh Street seemed simultaneously bare and covered by paper: newspapers, letters, and files were heaped on tables, chairs, and the floor.

The afternoon was an advance warning of the muggy heat of summer, and Scott wore only blue jeans. He leaned back in a big black leather swivel chair, took a sip of white wine, switched on the record player, and said, "Okay, I'm ready."

A sensual rhythm with a steady tempo started.

Annabel slid out of the kitchen, wearing her severe, sophisticated black linen suit from Bergdorf. She looked self-conscious and very embarrassed.

"Not too many clothes with not too many buttons, or I'll go to sleep," Scott warned.

Annabel untwisted her golden chignon and hair fell upon her shoulders. Moving slowly and stiffly to the rhythm of the music, she unzipped her skirt and stepped out of it, which left her wearing a waisted jacket, black French knickers, garter-belt stockings, and four-inch heels with ankle straps.

"Even slower," Scott said, "and look proud. This is a therapeutic exercise to overcome your physical shyness, so that I can turn a light on now and again."

"This jacket has only two buttons and I've still not taken it off. Can't be much slower than that."

"Don't take your shoes off," Scott reminded.

"How can I take my stockings off if I don't take my shoes off?"

As Annabel spoke, the telephone rang. She froze, her eyes fixed upon it.

"Should have left it off the hook," Scott said. "Ignore it."

"Darling, I can't. I gave the agency your number. They said they might know early this evening." Annabel flung herself at the telephone. "Hi! Yes. . . . I *have?* Oh, that's wonderful news!" She turned from the telephone. *"I got it, Scott!"*

"Congratulations," Scott said in a voice that didn't sound very enthusiastic. He knew that from now on, Annabel would be a pampered, glamorous figure constantly in the limelight. By later this evening, she would be the talk of New York, and a clutch of handsome young men on the make would telephone her, send her flowers, and ask her out to dinner.

Annabel whirled around excitedly with her arms in the air. "How shall we celebrate, Scott?"

Scott said firmly, "Let's get married."

Astonished, Annabel stopped dancing. "You really mean it?"

"Let me prove it."

Some time later, Scott's tousled head looked up from the crumpled sheets. He said, "I cannot go to the altar with a lie upon my lips."

"What do you mean?"

"I've never been to Hong Kong."

"You *invented* that sexy rubbish?"

"Not quite. . . . Ow! Ow! My brother works for a toy importer and they sent him to Hong Kong for six months. He came back with these strange stories. Ow!"

Chapter·10

Clare, who had always longed to see how a movie was made, wangled an invitation to the set of *Grain Race* from a quiet, stout young man with black curls, tight as a sheep's. She had met him on the Aldermaston march; Steve, a graphic designer, was working on the titles sequence for the movie, which was based on a nineteenth-century seafaring story.

Clare shivered on Cargill's Wharf, a disused area of the London docks just below Tower Bridge on the river Thames; it was a cold, bright day—more like March than May, Clare thought, wishing she'd worn a scarf. Wearing a Burberry mackintosh over her green tweed suit, she had been introduced as a free-lance journalist and was doing her best to make herself invisible on the set, standing in front of a pile of barrels, well back from the scene, at the rear of the cobbled wharf, where actors in nineteenth-century clothes were waiting to be shot as extras.

During the previous week, the interior scenes had been finished at Pinewood Studios, and now they were shooting the final exterior shots. Some of these were supposedly set in the Port of Liverpool, but the old Liverpool docks were silted up and couldn't be used, so the scenes were being shot at Cargill's Wharf, away from the portion of the dock still in use.

Grain Race was the story of two competing brothers: the elder one was an adventurous buccaneer, the younger a charming, deceptively mild, devious man. After inheriting a three-masted trading schooner, the brothers, with a combination of ruthlessness and good luck, built a shipping empire, from which the younger gradually ousted the elder. Their final confrontation came when each brother, in a different ship of their fleet, competed in a grain race around Cape Horn; they also competed for the wife of the skipper of a third ship.

The actors, wearing seafaring clothes, sat talking with the director, a lean and anguished-looking man who wore expensive jeans. Clare could just hear William Holden, who was playing the elder brother. Justin Watton, a thin, supple man with red-gold hair who was only just getting good parts, played the less important part of the younger brother. Simone Signoret also sat with them; she played the third skipper's wife.

Holden was arguing over the emotions in one scene. "*Anyone* who spots the way Simone looks at me would know she's crazy about me."

Heedless of the cold, Clare watched in fascination as the three actors walked through the scene, rehearsed it twice, and made minor adjustments.

The director opened his mouth to say "Action!" Then he paused. "I want more barrels—a bigger stack. I can see a modern window in that far building. We need to block it out."

A group of assistants moved toward Clare, who was still standing in front of the stacked-up spare barrels. She dodged out of the way, then crept back to her previous position.

The clapper board, now reading "Take 2," was held in front of the camera. The director called "Action!"

Clare screamed.

From behind, a man had pushed her, which sent her flying violently forward. She landed on her face with a strange, heavy body on top of her, pinning her to the ground. Barrels bounced around them, rolling over the cobblestones.

"What the hell do you think you're doing?" the deep voice above Clare roared. "Those barrels weren't properly stacked. If I hadn't pushed this girl out of the way, they would have fallen on her—she might have been injured."

The man scrambled off Clare's back and helped her to her feet. He was built like a bear, with a well-worn, tanned face, merry black eyes, and abundant black hair: his wrists were hairy, and so was the top of his chest, which showed above his unbuttoned collar. He looked carefully at Clare's skinned hands, her dirty face and clothes. "Come to the dressing rooms and we'll call a doctor." His accent was clearly American.

"Oh, don't bother with a doctor. I just need cleaning up."

"Call a doctor!" the man ordered. He wanted to establish that there was no serious injury, in case of a phony insurance claim later. When he smiled at her, Clare noticed he had slightly crooked teeth—obviously because he couldn't be bothered to get them fixed: all the other Americans on the set had expensively perfect, gleaming choppers.

An hour later, Clare was back on the set—but this time she was sitting on a canvas director's chair. The bearlike man—the producer, Sam Shapiro—was sitting beside her. In contrast to the somewhat tense atmosphere on the set, he projected a careless bonhomie that was very appealing. Clare, who decided he must be around forty years old, noticed how he dominated the set, with both his big physical presence and his strong animal vigor.

"Lucky I came along today," Sam said. "I'm not usually on the set during productions."

"Then how do you know what's happening?"

"I see the dailies every evening, when we pick out the best shots."

"Then why were you here today?" Clare asked.

The man shrugged. "Shooting's always a tense time, but especially in the last week, so the director likes a little backup when everyone's exhausted. Tempers explode, tears flow. My role tends to change from producer to diplomat. I keep everybody off each other's throats. It's a tough time for everyone because any extra shots have to be squeezed into the schedule, which drives everyone crazy. In fact, we're doing a couple of scenes here tonight after dark. I have to see a guy for dinner, then I'll be back. D'you feel like dinner?"

"I'm not dressed for dinner."

"Who cares? I promise they won't throw you out."

During the lunch break, when the cast and crew ate in the private room of a nearby pub, Sam Shapiro solved everyone's problems with his cheerful bonhomie. He clearly loved action, excitement, and to be surrounded by people, all working on his project. Clare noticed that he was warm and generous with praise; his laughter was a roar; his ebullient, quicksilver charm was hard to resist. Behind this front of camaraderie, Sam Shapiro was shrewdly persuasive; he marshaled his arguments logically, presented them skillfully, and seemed able to rationalize any situation to suit himself, while persuading everyone else that he was acting for the general good. Clare had never met anyone with such vitality and authority.

In spite of his agreeable persuasiveness, Clare could see that Sam had an explosive temper. When the second male lead complained of a headache and asked if he might have the afternoon off, Sam's tightly controlled patience suddenly evaporated. He thumped the cherry plastic tabletop with his hairy fist and growled, "*No.* I'm not going to pay for your hangovers, Justin." The chilling tone of voice revealed the potential violence behind Sam's affability, which was clearly what helped to preserve discipline on the set.

Clare managed to rush back to Elinor's flat in Chester Terrace, where she dived into her best Belinda Belville black taffeta and telephoned the C.N.D. office to say that she couldn't manage this evening.

Instead, she dined with Sam Shapiro in the crimson plush and gilt splendor of Les Ambassadeurs Club. Clare, who had never been asked out by an older man, and who barely remembered her father, was fascinated by the strength and power that Sam projected. She felt safe and protected. As he entered the restaurant, people sat up and whispered to each other.

Clare sat on the plush banquette next to Sam's other dinner companion—a small, weary-looking, neat-mustached banker, whose business proposals were constantly interrupted by people who came to say hello to Sam Shapiro.

Sam whispered to Clare, "I've known this guy for years; he represents Paramount. I work pretty closely with their business and creative staff—been under contract for the past ten years, on a per-picture basis."

"How many films do you make a year?" Clare asked.

"One picture every two years. That's fairly slow, but I'm a working producer. I tend to get obsessively involved in every detail. It isn't the most productive way to work, but it's the only way for me."

"Are you only in England for this film?"

Sam shook his head. "Last year I moved my base to London. Right now, Europe—especially Italy and England—are the cheapest, most efficient places to make movies."

"Say! Sam Shapiro!" Another beaming dinner jacket thumped Sam on the back and looked down at the empty gilt chair. "May I?"

Paramount's banker sighed, reached across the table, and returned the sheet of figures to Sam. "I think we'd better discuss this some other time." He smiled at Clare, to whom he had hardly spoken. He could see what Sam Shapiro liked about her: the pastel, ladylike look, her evanescent charm—a class act, very different from what was available in L.A.

As Sam's navy Rolls-Royce stopped at Cargill's Wharf, the director jumped inside. "That bastard Justin's drunk again."

"He clearly had a hell of a hangover at midday," Sam growled. "I thought you'd have had the sense to stick close until we're through with him."

"I'm not his fucking nursemaid, Sam. I've been going over a scene with Bill and Simone—I'd like you to see it, by the way. Next thing, Justin's lying in his dressing room surrounded by empty vodka bottles, dead to the world."

"Has he been stomach-pumped?"

"Of course. The doctor's still with him, but he's not fit to work."

"Get his agent. Check his contract. First thing tomorrow, I want details of the time he's cost us." Sam jumped out of the Rolls and walked fast toward the trailer dressing rooms.

Just before he reached Justin Watton's trailer, the door was flung open: silhouetted against a yellow rectangle of light was the thin figure of the actor. He saw Sam and staggered toward him. "Fucking big shot! Fucking stupid script! Fucking lousy money. Fucking waste of my time."

Sam did not move out of his way. "You're the one who's wasting time, you stupid bastard."

Justin pulled back his right fist and punched at Sam. For a heavy man, Sam dodged nimbly. He grabbed the actor by the collar and called to the director, "For Chrissake, don't let anyone hit him! If his face is marked, it'll cost us more lost time. Get the handcuffs and hose him down until he's fit to work."

"Okay, okay."

"No, wait!" Sam shouted. "I've got a better idea!" With one swift move, he pinned the drunken actor's arms behind his back, then frog-marched him to the edge of the wharf and shoved him into the cold black water.

Then Sam said, "Someone dive in and haul him out. If he drowns, we'll be even more over budget."

By one o'clock in the morning, the scheduled scenes were, miraculously, in the can, and Sam remembered Clare. He walked over to the edge of the set, where she sat, wrapped in a topaz velvet cloak.

"I'm sorry. This wasn't the sort of evening I had in mind, Clare. But we're finished here now, so what would you like to do? Dancing? The Orchid Room? The Four Hundred?"

Clare, who wanted to seem like a sophisticated woman of twenty-six, said, "How about a gambling game?"

"Whatever you want. Where?"

Clare swiftly telephoned the only other older man she knew: Adam agreed to take Clare and her chap to Mike's gambling game, one of the most popular in London. It had been over a year since a court had ruled in favor of a man who had been charged for keeping a common gambling house at a London flat. Since then, the police had turned a blind eye to smart gambling parties, which, it was thought, would shortly be legalized.

Sam, who enjoyed an occasional gamble, took some time to lose a hundred pounds at chemin de fer, at which point he stopped playing. He and Clare wandered to the roulette table.

Adam looked up. "I don't know what's got into this wheel tonight. I've lost a packet. I'd better see Mike."

Mike reluctantly agreed to a further loan. "But watch it, Adam," he warned. "You're near your credit limit and they won't extend it."

"Rubbish! They know I bring well-heeled punters to their parties. And they're making a fortune from me!" As Adam lost larger sums, the interest on the money he borrowed had been increased to one percent a week.

Mike didn't hide his worried look. "Don't say I didn't warn you."

"I hear you've been to see Dad," Adam said.

Mike followed his train of thought. "Yes, yesterday. But he's not going to kick the bucket yet." The previous month, Joe Grant, now over sixty, had fractured his breastbone when his Mercedes rammed a bus. The fracture was relatively unimportant, but, beneath it, the damage to heart and lungs was serious.

"I'm going home again this weekend. Like to come?" Mike offered. "I'm trying out a new bike." Mike still kept every bike he had ever owned. No longer housed in a potting shed, the elderly bikes were sumptuously stabled in an immaculate garage at the end of Eaton Terrace, alongside Mike's Manx Norton single-cylinder racer; his Norton Inter, with its high-torque overhead cam engine; and the quick but noisy BSA Gold Star, Mike's cross-country bike, used for weekend scrambling with the boys.

"You and your bikes," Adam said, half indulgent, half contemptuous. He was more impressed by Mike's success than he cared to admit. Adam felt astonished, irritated, and humiliated by his younger brother's prosperity and his house in Eaton Terrace. At the age of twenty-eight, Adam still earned a pittance as a lawyer's clerk in a dark and stuffy office, where he was only just being trusted to handle important clients. In contrast, Mike effortlessly earned a fortune, and seemed to live at a permanent luxurious party, surrounded by beautiful people.

"How was Mother when you were home?" Adam changed the subject.

"She hasn't missed one bridge game since Dad's accident," Mike said. "She's reached the Surrey County semifinal."

Sam and Clare approached to say goodnight. After they left, Mike commented, "He seems a bit old for Clare."

"She's unlikely to meet a teenage film producer," Adam said. "Shapiro produced *Windjammer* and *Whaler*."

"Those Humphrey Bogart films?" Mike was intrigued.

Sam was not so intrigued by the two brothers.

Clare was disappointed. "I could see you didn't like them. But why not?" she asked, settling into the soft pigskin comfort of the Rolls.

"Adam seems too terribly, terribly British to be true," Sam said.

Clare laughed. "You mean too handsome!" Men were frequently jealous of Adam's lean good looks, his big dark eyes and almost blue-black hair that still flopped boyishly over his forehead.

Sam shook his head. "Good-looking guys are a dime a dozen in

L.A.," he said. "There's something odd about Adam. And his brother. Mike's the type who gets a charge from taking risks." In the shadowy privacy of the limousine, he put his arm firmly around Clare's topaz velvet shoulders.

"No, it's Adam who takes risks. Mike never gambles," Clare said.

"I didn't mean that sort of risk." Gently he tilted Clare's chin up toward his mouth.

FRIDAY, 30 MAY 1958

"I'd like to come home for tea—just once—and not find the house full of strangers!" Miranda fumed, after the departure of Elinor's last guest.

"I only have tea parties on weekdays."

"Gran, you have tea parties *every* weekday!"

Elinor shut the heavy front door and turned to look at Miranda, who stood, scowling, beneath the portrait of the three sisters painted the year before by Pietro Annigoni. Elinor wished that Miranda more resembled her demure painted likeness.

Elinor turned away from the triple portrait and smiled at Miranda. "Surely I can invite my friends to my own home? Be reasonable. They only come for an hour or two."

"Friends? Publishers, journalists, fans, strangers!" Miranda said crossly. "Sometimes I can't decide whether I'm living in *my* home or *your* publicity center."

"My visitors sell and buy my books, so they help pay for *your* home," Elinor reproved. "And it doesn't take up much time."

Elinor entertained from four o'clock to half past five: this did not interfere with her writing and was a relatively inexpensive way to play hostess to many people every year.

Delighted visitors were met at the station by a chauffeur in a claret-colored uniform at the wheel of her white Rolls. Over tea (served in the old-fashioned way, on a big mahogany table in the dining room), Elinor effortlessly kept in touch with her publishers, most of whom were now accustomed to making this pilgrimage to Wiltshire whenever business took them to Britain. She listened carefully to their opinions because she knew that to achieve the star status of a best-seller writer, it took the right book published by the right publisher, at the right price, at the right time—and the right, expensive promotion: Elinor's contractual conditions had taken years to establish, and now before she signed their contracts, her publishers were requested to outline their promotional plans over the tea table.

Elinor's tea parties also provided her with useful feedback. She particularly liked to check the response of her visitors to the jacket design of her next book. Elinor had spent a lot of time observing bookshop customers, trying to learn what attracted them to a book—and the jacket was crucial.

So, no matter how it bothered Miranda, Elinor couldn't give up her tea parties. Looking at her granddaughter now, she said without conviction, "You *know* you love parties, Miranda. All girls do!"

"Not me!" Miranda shook her head. "You'd like to think that, Gran, but I *hate* your literary tea parties almost as much as I *hate* the smart London ones. As a matter of fact, I *hate* being a deb!"

"How can you say that, you ungrateful child? The Season's only just started!"

"I've had enough of it to know that I'm bored by an endless round of parties at which the same people say the same things."

"Most girls—" Elinor began.

"Would give the eyes out of their head for a chance to be a debutante! I know, I know! But not me!" Miranda preferred to sneak off to the jazz club at 100 Oxford Street, or the socially unacceptable and totally forbidden Hammersmith Palais, where she could dance to rock and roll.

"After all the trouble I've taken . . ." Elinor fumed.

"And all the money you've spent!" Miranda nodded. "I don't want you to waste any *more* time or money on me, Gran."

"You haven't been a debutante long enough to decide whether you like it or not! Once you get to know the people better . . ."

"I'll be yawning more!" Miranda said firmly. "If I asked one of those deb's delights what he thought of Harold Pinter's dialogue, or how much MJQ was influenced by Bach, he'd look at me as if I'd tried to bite him!"

Equally firmly Elinor said, "You've got to learn the social graces, and I don't want to hear another word about it, Miranda! You can't always do as you please."

"I've been doing what pleases *you* for seventeen years!" Miranda retorted. "Why can't I stay in London? Why do *I* have to come down here for weekends? You let *Clare* stay in London by herself."

"Clare has work to do. You're not old enough to stay alone in London without a chaperon, and that's final!"

Glaring, Miranda stormed off to her bedroom. She knew why Clare stayed in London at the weekend, and it wasn't extra work for C.N.D., as Elinor thought: Clare was—at last—in love with an older man who was—what sophistication!—*divorced*. Miranda, of course, could be relied upon to tell nobody, and Clare had decided that, for the time being, it was prudent to keep this a secret. In Britain in 1958, the subject of divorce was for other people's families perhaps but not for one's own, never mind allowing such a person into the family. Clare did not want to risk upsetting her grandmother unnecessarily, should her romance not end in marriage.

Just then Buzz bounced into the hall from the kitchen. "All the guests gone?"

"Did you hear what Miranda said?" Elinor exclaimed. She knew Buzz had been listening.

"A bit of it," Buzz admitted.

"And that girl has had *all* the advantages we never had!"

"She's at the rebellious age," Buzz reminded Elinor. "She's a teenager." The teenager was a recent phenomenon: For the first time in British history, young people were earning good money, so after years spent obeying their parents, they could now do as they pleased. They spent their paychecks on clothes and cosmetics, music and dancing. "Wasting it," their fathers grumbled, but their mothers, who knew what lay ahead for them in life, said, "They're only young once."

Christened "the Youthquake," this new market force had invaded the media, music, fashion, and photography; the boys modeled themselves on James Dean; the girls wore black jeans and sweaters, long shaggy hair, and no makeup except for their Cleopatra eyes.

Buzz knew that, by nature, Miranda did not feel at home in the soft, predictable world of the debutante. With her marmalade ponytail and pale pink lipstick, Miranda, a natural rebel, belonged with the Youthquake.

Elinor gazed up at the triple portrait. "None of those girls have any respect or gratitude! Sometimes I feel as if my heart is broken."

Firmly Buzz said, "Save that overdramatic, sentimental rubbish for your next novel! *The girls are growing up!* You should stop thinking of them as children and treat them as young women. Remember what we was doing at their age—fighting a war! *You've got to let them go,* Nell! Then they'll come back to you. But if you try to stop 'em, they'll only resent you: then a visit to you will be a duty and they'll only come when they can't put it off any longer."

Elinor glared at Buzz. Eventually she said, "Of course, you're right, as usual. But I *do* remember the tough times we had. I want to protect them from that . . . from danger and poverty, give them all the things that poor Billy tried so hard to provide for Edward . . ."

"Hey, wait a minute, Nell. This is Buzz you're talking to . . . remember? We've been through this before, and I ain't buying it. Usually I'd hold me tongue, but you'd better remember that the real Billy isn't the Prince Charming you talk about at tea parties. It's about time, Nell, that you started to live life as it really is."

Chapter·11

On the Tuesday following Clare's first meeting with Sam, *Grain Race* finished shooting. Clare attended the wrap party, at which almost everybody quickly became drunk, due to the release of so much nervous tension. The film crew was friendly but cautious and overpolite to Clare: they had known before she did that Sam Shapiro had his eye on her.

After the party, Sam fished a black bow tie from his pocket and took Clare to the Four Hundred. Women in frivolous cocktail hats and taffeta dresses energetically danced the samba under the benign eye and baton of Edmundo Ross. Sam suddenly felt very tired.

"Let's get the hell out of here, Clare," he said. "I want to talk to you."

During the limousine's short journey to Sam's flat in Hill Street, he sat with his eyes shut, his head thrown back. Clare, sensing his weariness, said nothing.

Once, Sam turned his head to look at Clare, pretty in lime taffeta. He patted her hand.

Later, in his comfortably impersonal beige sitting room, Sam put his arm around Clare in a paternal rather than loverlike gesture and said, "There's no nice way of saying this, but I think we should stop seeing each other."

Clare felt as if her stomach had gone into free-fall. "Why? What have I done wrong?" She was hurt, astonished.

"There's only one reason, but it's insurmountable. I'm twenty years older than you."

"That's not a good reason to stop seeing me!" Clare said fiercely. With sudden insight, she realized that Sam's suggestion must mean that his feelings were engaged, that he cared for her, that he preferred *her* to those confident, beautifully groomed actresses who had tonight changed from their drab nineteenth-century outdoor costumes into clinging silks and satins.

Sam looked down at Clare. "I'm too fond of you to hurt you." He had reluctantly decided that she was too young to bed without a lot of postcoital trouble.

Clare twisted away from him. She couldn't think properly—couldn't think at all—with Sam holding her gingerly, the way some uncle might do. She threw herself into one of the elephantine leather armchairs. Sam had practically said that he loved her. There was no reason why he shouldn't have an affair with a much younger girl . . . unless he cared a lot for her . . . enough to marry.

Like a candle, hope lit Clare's small, pale face; she glowed with radiance and sat up. She wanted to rush back into Sam's muscular arms, smell his curly hair, feel his bristly square jaw against her own. But not in the frustrating grab-and-tussle embraces they had shared before.

She said, as seriously as she could, "I think your age is irrelevant. I love you. I want to marry you."

Sam had heard many a veiled proposal—usually from beneath tousled sheets—but never had he had such a direct one. He felt spellbound by Clare's aquamarine eyes. "What will your folks say?"

"I don't care what they say!" Clare rushed into Sam's arms, and he wrapped his hard body around her until she felt that her legs could no longer support her. *"Do it,"* Clare said.

Sam picked Clare up and, still kissing her, carried his lime-taffeta bundle toward the bedroom door. Moonlight fell through the ugly steel-framed windows. Without speaking, he laid her upon his bed, and gently slipped her lime satin shoes from her feet, as if even her feet were precious to him. Then slowly he undid the long row of tiny taffeta buttons that reached from her breasts to her knees. He gazed at her body with anticipation and frustration: a white lace, boned corselette stretched impenetrably from bosom to midthigh.

Clare trembled with passion and fear, eyes shut, waiting. She knew that this was *the moment*. She was glad that it was about to happen with someone mature, experienced—not with a fumbling, clumsy youth.

Sam slid off her pale stockings, stroking her thighs, then felt the dark, damp area that lay between them. Smoothly he unhooked her lace corselette, with nimble expertise.

Clare, who neither moved nor spoke, felt eroticism surround her like a cloud. She thought that she would swoon from pleasure. As Sam started to caress her breasts, her excitation built gradually toward its peak. He felt for her hymen with his middle finger, which he gently and slowly inserted into her delicate little body. It hurt her, a bit.

Without speaking, Sam stood up and stripped, fast as a Buster Keaton sequence.

Clare was glad that he hadn't switched on the light, so she didn't have to look. But she felt it, firm against her thighs, before Sam gently pried them apart and slid into her. She felt his body on hers, and smelled his odor: his scent reminded her of a sweaty horse, tired after a good gallop; she loved it. She felt his heavy masculine body ride her. Sam grabbed her buttocks with both hands and pulled them up to meet his thrusts: as the tempo of his drive speeded up, he gasped faster and faster.

Suddenly his body shot forward, then relaxed upon her, as if boneless.

Sometime later, Sam murmured sleepily, "Darling, you were wonderful."

Clare did not dare move. She felt sticky liquid trickle down her inner thighs, then a sticky tongue of flesh fall between them.

Sam shifted his body and lay beside Clare. He put his hand on her breast and whispered, "Happy, baby?" In a moment, he was asleep.

Clare lay rigid in the moonlight. She felt breathless, as if she needed more oxygen in her lungs. There was a turgid ache in her lower back. She wished Sam would wake up and kiss her; she longed to feel again his mouth tugging at her nipples.

An hour later, Clare still lay wide awake. She felt unhappy, disappointed, and resentful—not of Sam but of something. She didn't know what.

Perhaps love was addictive, like caviar; perhaps you had to practice it and get used to it. Clare wished she could talk to Annabel, in case she was doing something wrong.

Two hours later, Clare wriggled away from Sam, moving one limb at a time in order not to awaken him. She groped her way to the bathroom. Closing the door slowly to avoid any noise, she groped around the unfamiliar space until she found a light. She allowed herself only a glimpse of the disheveled person she saw in the mirror, quickly turning on the basin tap to disguise the tinkling sound as she peed. She then washed her hands—something she normally never bothered to do, except in a cloakroom where someone was watching her. Subconsciously Clare hoped that the righteous and justifiable noise of the tap would wake Sam up, but it didn't.

Toward dawn, Clare cried quietly into her hands, then fell asleep.

Shortly after sunrise, Sam woke and again made love to Clare. Afterward, he felt refreshed and vigorous: he whistled in the shower.

At eleven o'clock, breakfast for two was sent up from the restaurant on the ground floor. A subdued Clare ordered only hot milk and toast; Sam ordered a full English breakfast.

As they ate breakfast in the beige satin bed, leaning against the art deco headboard, Clare felt an urgent need to know further details of Sam's divorce. Feeling immodest because she was bare-breasted while eating marmalade and toast, she wondered how to tactfully approach the subject.

He had already told her about his parents, Russian immigrants who had lived in New York and worked on Seventh Avenue: his father had been a tailor, his mother a presser. Sam was their only son.

"I suppose everyone asks how you got into show business?" Clare ventured.

"No. Nobody except you has shown a burning desire to know anything about me. It was through my first wife." Sam poured his second cup of coffee.

"*First* wife!"

"We met when I was on leave." Clare knew he had been a naval supply officer during the war. "I would go to L.A.," Sam said. San Diego was a staid, naval town: the women were in Los Angeles. "After I left the navy, we got married. It was 1945. The only job I could get was in a supermarket. Sheila was assistant to a story editor at MGM. I read for her when she had too many scripts. She said I summarized well: the navy taught me that."

Timidly Clare asked, "When did you break up?"

"We only lived together for a few months. Then she ran off to Toronto with another guy, but found she was three months pregnant by me, after which the other guy ran off. I haven't seen her since she left me. The baby died at birth."

"I'm sorry." But Clare felt relieved. No threat, no passion, no rivalry there. "So how did you become a producer?"

Sam said, "I went to night school to study screenwriting, then took a folder of my MGM summaries to the chief story editor at Paramount. Some months later, there was a vacancy. I was taken on as the story editor's assistant." No need to tell Clare of his passionate affair with Rhona, the chief story editor.

"And then?" Clare prompted.

"In 1948, I gave an NDG assessment to a sea story script called *A Life on the Ocean Wave*."

"NDG?"

"No Damn Good. After we turned it down, I met the screenwriter." Sam had telephoned him, pitching himself as an independent producer with special naval history expertise: they arranged to meet for dinner at Chasens. Over the meal, he persuaded the writer to agree to a contract that gave Sam exclusive rights to the rewritten script for three years and allowed him fifteen percent of the sale price, should Sam manage to sell it. The writer also agreed to equal billing. He figured, What did he have to lose? The script had been turned down all over town. Even his agent stood to gain if Sam sold the script.

Sam added, "After we'd rewritten the script for costume and called it 'Windjammer,' I persuaded a . . . friend of mine to get her boss to read it. He liked the script and wanted to buy it, but I said I wanted to produce it. The studio refused, but they'd shown the script to Bogart. He liked it, so Paramount eventually agreed to my terms, I agreed to their money, they gave me a good line producer, and *Windjammer* was a success. Then Bogey and I did *Whaler,* and after that, *they* rang *me.* Anything else?"

In a low voice, Clare asked, "Any other wives?"

Sam laughed and planted a kiss on her forehead. "So *that's* what you really wanted to know about. Yes, I've been married twice—a very low average for L.A. Louise and I split up three years ago, after five years together, no kids."

"No more?"

"No, I swear."

Clare said, "I don't know how I'll tell Gran."

"Is there any need to tell her anything yet?"

Grain Race moved into postproduction, which took over three months of barely controlled frenzy as everyone worked against the clock to release the film in time for the Christmas holiday season.

Sam flew to L.A., first to negotiate terms and play dates with release theaters and then to schedule the previews, at which he and the director sat among the audiences to check reaction: by torchlight, they scribbled notes about timing mistakes, any unscheduled mirth, or, worse, comedy that didn't make people laugh.

When Sam was in London, Clare was caught up in the excitement for *Grain Race:* she was whirled into the kaleidoscope of action and drama in which Sam seemed to move. But when he left for Los Angeles, she felt deflated: every morning, she battled against inertia in order to get out of bed. During this period, it dawned on Clare that her passion for Sam was matched by his passion for making movies: more demanding than most careers, producing dominated his life and thoughts. At times, Clare felt a little jealous.

The month before the release date, Sam flew to Los Angeles to plan the publicity campaign and link the trailer, the TV ads, the print and PR campaign. As usual Clare accompanied him to the airport. Seeing her sad little face as yet again she waved him off, Sam turned back and leaned over the barrier.

"Anything to see you smile," he said. "I'll break our news to your grandmother after the British premiere."

MONDAY, 3 NOVEMBER 1958

Like most men, Sam looked his best in a dinner jacket, so he was at his most charismatic when he arrived at Elinor's Chester Terrace flat to take the O'Dares to the Odeon, Leicester Square. Sam's blue eyes sparkled with anticipation of the movie's success: word of mouth was good, so were bookings, and the advance publicity for *Grain Race* had been a rising wave of adulation.

In her bedroom before leaving for the theater, Elinor slipped a crimson evening wrap over her black lace gown and murmured to Buzz, "Of course, he's too old for Clare, but he's *very* good-looking."

Buzz said, "I can see why Clare might like a mature man. She's never known one." Two hours earlier, Clare had confided in Buzz, who realized that twice-divorced Sam wasn't the dashing young earl for whom Elinor had hoped. Buzz had promised to soften up her old friend, but there was undoubtedly going to be a big row—because Clare was almost as stubborn as Elinor.

After the premiere, Sam was greeted by applause from the theater supper crowd as he and his large party entered the Ivy. Now he could relax. He would wait up all night to read the reviews in the morning papers, but the tense silence during *Grain Race* and the loud clapping at the end had foretold a hit.

Two hours later, Sam insisted on interrupting his party to escort Elinor and Buzz back to Chester Terrace; there he spoke alone to Elinor and told her that Clare and he were to be married.

Elinor was speechless, even though Buzz had warned her ahead of time—dating him was one thing, but marrying him quite another. "But you're too . . . But *Clare's far too young!*" she gasped.

"Clare doesn't think so," Sam said gently. "She'll be twenty soon. How old were you when you married?"

"That's got nothing to do with it," Elinor said, a hundred questions whirling through her mind. "I suppose you *can* look after Clare . . . financially?"

"Very well," Sam promised cheerfully. He was established and respected in a way that few young men could match.

"It's too late tonight for me to think clearly," Elinor said, suddenly feeling exhausted. "I'll talk to Clare in the morning."

Five minutes later, she shook Buzz awake. "You can't imagine what that man's just told me!"

Buzz mumbled, "He wants to marry Clare."

"So she told *you!*"

"Yes, because she was frightened to tell you. Don't worry too much, Elinor. We'll talk about it in the morning."

Elinor shook Buzz again. "I won't sleep a wink! I *must* talk about it now. It's so unexpected! What does she *know* about this man? Where are his family? What is she walking into?"

Buzz sat up. "I seem to remember that *I* said that to you before you married Billy. And did you take any notice? *No!* Clare's just as stubborn as you are, so you'd better not ask those questions if you don't want to see them marry. Because he's a real charmer."

"Yes," Elinor said, "but what does *he* see in Clare? She's not the glamorous type, not sophisticated. Sam clearly isn't interested in improving the world for a future generation; he isn't the bookish type, like Clare. I can't help wondering how long it will last. These Hollywood types seem to get married again and again. I don't want that for Clare."

Firmly Buzz said, "Why not try looking on the bright side, and just be glad that Clare is happy? If you object, you'll lose her even faster."

The following morning, Elinor knocked on Clare's door. As there was no reply, she entered, and saw that the bed had not been slept in.

Just before lunch, white-faced from lack of sleep, Clare quietly pushed open the front door and started to tiptoe across the hall.

"Is that you, darling?" Elinor called from her study. "Would you come here, Clare?"

Clare blushed as she entered the room; she still wore the hyacinth chiffon gown, now very crumpled, that she had worn the previous evening.

"Sit down, darling." Elinor cheerfully patted the place beside her on the sofa. "I want to tell you how much I like Sam: such drive, such force, such self-assurance and authority. I'm so glad you've chosen someone older who clearly knows his way around the world and can protect you from it."

Clare's eyes shone with astonishment and pleasure. "I'm so glad you can see why I think he's wonderful! I feel so . . . safe and happy when I'm with him."

"I hope and pray that you always will, darling. Now run along and change."

SATURDAY, 28 FEBRUARY 1959

"It's beautiful," sighed Miranda. She wore dead-white makeup, ghostly pearlized lips, black-outlined eyes; her orange hair was plaited into a coronet.

"I wish *I'd* had a proper wedding gown!" Annabel cried, having forgone a formal marriage ceremony in her rush to marry Scott.

In Clare's bedroom at the Chester Terrace apartment, the two sisters gazed at the bride: she wore a high-collared, tight-waisted, full-skirted, calf-length dress of cream satin by Norman Hartnell; her hair was dressed in a Grecian knot, cross-bound with cream satin ribbon.

"I feel wobbly," said Clare. "I think I'm going to cry . . ."

"Not on your wedding day!" Annabel pleaded. Although Clare looked lovely, she was almost outshone by Annabel, who wore a crimson silk suit and an air of triumph. Avanti's campaign "Do you dare to wear Avanti?" had not been as successful as Revlon's Fire and Ice campaign, but it had been successful enough to shoot Annabel into the headlines. American women had been surprised that an English girl (traditionally mouseburger material) should project such sensuality. Annabel seemed to epitomize the surprising emergence of London, as that once stodgy city metamorphosed into the fashion leader of pop culture.

Miranda looked at her sisters and gave a mock scowl. "How do you suppose *I* feel? You've both gone and left me without a backward look! Off you dash with your glamorous husbands—I'm the one who should be crying!" Nevertheless, it was tough to look forlorn in the pale pink satin-bound tweed coat dress by Sybil Connolly.

"Nobody's going to cry," Annabel said firmly. "We're still sisters, and when we meet, we'll still feel the same way and do the same things."

"What sort of things?" Clare's voice wobbled.

"Everything from a night at the opera to toe-in-mouth competitions," Annabel said cheerfully.

Miranda jeered, "You two old married ladies couldn't get your toes in your mouths now."

"Bet I can," said Annabel, sitting on the carpet. "Bet you two *can't*," she added as she pulled off her crimson slippers.

Miranda immediately kicked off her shoes, sat on the floor, grabbed her big toe, and guided it toward her mouth, but couldn't get it closer than six inches from her lips. She giggled. "I'm a bit stiff."

Clare started to laugh. "You both look idiotic!" Removing one slipper and carefully smoothing her dress beneath her, Clare sat on the carpet and took hold of her big toe.

"I've nearly done it!" Miranda gasped.

Annabel mumbled, *"I've done it!"*

As he opened the bedroom door, Sam said, "Honey, I know I'm not supposed to see you yet, but is there any chance of a Bloody Mary? . . . What the *hell* is going on in here?"

The three sisters collapsed on the floor, shrieking with laughter.

• • •

Before the reception at Claridge's, the small wedding group posed on the steps of Caxton Hall Registry office for photographers. Besides being twice divorced, Sam was Jewish and thus not eligible for an Anglican church wedding. The photographers were unable to persuade Clare to smile; having been very disappointed by the brisk civil ceremony, which had about as much romance as a buff envelope, she now felt even more wobbly and close to tears.

SATURDAY, 23 MAY 1959

"She won't allow me to do anything that's fun!" Miranda complained to Buzz.

"If you mean flying lessons," Buzz said, "you'll never convince her that it ain't dangerous. She'll never allow it."

"I'm sick, sick, sick of being treated like a baby! I'm more likely to hurt myself skiing than flying."

"You ain't likely to *kill* yourself skiing."

"Other grandmothers don't *hover* like she does!"

Elinor, severely depressed by the suddenness with which she had been deprived of Annabel and then Clare, now lavished affection on Miranda, to whom it was a claustrophobic burden.

"I feel guilty if I'm not with her," Miranda added, "and guilty when I am—because I long to get away. She doesn't really like the sort of things I like, she only pretends. I can tell because she gets the names wrong—Pelvis the Elvis and Buddy Holiday indeed!"

They sat in Miranda's bedroom at Starlings listening to the thumping rhythm pumped out by Miranda's new stereophonic speakers, surrounded by wall posters of rock heroes (Buddy Holly swathed in black net) and the better-looking revolutionary leaders.

Hopefully Miranda asked, "Do you think Gran might ever get married again? That would take her mind off me!"

Buzz shook her head. "She falls in love with her heroes, and they ruin ordinary men for her."

"I don't mean *that* sort of love!" Miranda said, confident that passion could not be felt by those over thirty. "I mean . . . companionship."

"A husband likes a lot of attention," Buzz said. "And when would Nell find time for that? She's writing in the morning, and still has her head in the clouds when she gardens in the afternoon. Then there are the tea parties, and if she ain't going out in the evening, she's doing research in the library or going to bed early with a pile of galleys. That's the life she likes, and what husband would put up with it?"

"Another writer?"

"He'd expect to be pampered. And what man would put up with the fuss Nell makes over you and your sisters? Annabel lifts her little finger and your gran pops across the Atlantic to visit, pretending she's off to see her American publisher. And since Clare got back from the West Indies, Nell drives to London every week to help her buy things for that little house. If she had a husband, your gran wouldn't be able to drop everything when you three call her. Men are used to ruling the roost. Nell would never knuckle under again."

In a wheedling voice, Miranda said, "Then, Buzz, darling Buzz, will you help me do something? *Just* this once?"

Buzz knew that this always meant, "Will you gently break my news to Gran, and be on my side?"

"What is it this time, Miranda?"

"I want to be trained as a beautician," Miranda said excitedly. "It's a one-year course in London, and it starts next month. I've already put my name down, but now they want a deposit. I thought of flogging my pearls, but what's the point? I'll have to tell her sometime."

"You mean a *manicurist*, a *massoower*? She ain't going to like that one bit—she likes to think of her girls being on the receiving end of all that!"

"I suppose I'll have that lady rubbish flung at me again." Miranda bit her lower lip. "I've told her I hate those parties."

"You met that nice Angus at a deb dance," Buzz reminded. "*And* he's on the List." The List was prepared by an aging, sycophantic gossip columnist and circulated among ambitious mothers with eligible daughters: it listed young men whose birth, wealth, and position made them suitable escorts or husbands.

Miranda blushed; then, from beneath heavily mascaraed eyelashes, a lopsided smile slowly spread across her face. She said, "Angus would *never* waste his time at deb dances, but he had to turn up at that one: it was his sister's coming-out ball."

She had met him shortly after Clare's wedding. Miranda, who longed to leave the overheated ballroom, had refused another dance, yawned, looked at her wristwatch, and reckoned she could leave in half an hour. *If* she stayed awake that long! She had opened the French windows and slipped onto the terrace for a little fresh air.

After the smoky fug of the ballroom, the dark night was quiet, crisp, and refreshingly cold. Before her, Miranda could dimly see the brown lace outline of the huge chestnut trees lining Rotten Row. From behind her came a scent that reminded her of Lifebuoy soap and flannel pajamas.

Miranda turned sharply. "Who are you?"

"I'm Fiona's brother, Angus."

As Miranda's eyes adjusted to the dark, she saw a large man in a dinner jacket leaning against the wall, in the shadows, smoking a cigar. He said, "I was about to leave. Got to get to work in the morning. Here, take my jacket or you'll die of pneumonia before I get a chance to know you." His laconic speech sounded like a paratroop commander sending his troops into battle.

When they went back to the ballroom, Miranda turned to look at Angus Maclayne; he returned her glance with an ice-blue stare from a face that appeared to have been rough-hewn from rock, although his hair was Viking gold and his mustache was ginger.

As soon as Fiona had recovered from her hangover, Miranda hauled her out to lunch. She discovered that Angus had been the Captain of Boats and had ended his school career as the Captain of the Oppidans. He had also edited the Eton College *Chronicle;* at Oxford, where he had been a rowing blue, he read politics, philosophy, and economics, after which he worked for two years in New York as a trainee banker. Angus had then gone to Paris for a year, as a trader on the Credit Suisse foreign exchange desk, after which he spent a year in Hong Kong, and then a further year in New York before returning to London, where he worked for Chase Manhattan. He liked salmon fishing and playing poker, and it was difficult to make him lose his temper.

"Honestly, there's nothing else to tell you," Fiona said when pressed for further information. "Nobody knows much about their own brothers. Angus is . . . all right. If you want to know him better, why not come up to Scotland for a weekend at Easter?"

"Thanks, but I can't manage it at the moment," said Miranda; she didn't want Fiona to think she was that keen on her brother; Miranda preferred to wait until the invitation came from Angus.

Angus now frequently took Miranda to an evening at the cinema or theater, after which they ate at Wiltons, Rules, or other London hotels that provided (at great expense) the food of Angus's youth: sausages and mashed potatoes, toad-in-the-hole, milk puddings, steamed puddings, treacle pudding, or jam roll.

In case something drastic happened to the dollar, Angus could never be far from a telephone until late evening, which was late-afternoon closing time for the American market. He never took Miranda to a nightclub because he was always at his desk by seven in the morning, for the Hong Kong closing prices.

Unlike other fledgling bankers Miranda knew, Angus wasn't stuffy and didn't shoot his shirt cuffs or keep tightening the knot of his tie. Although his suits fitted well around the shoulders, not even the best

Savile Row tailor could produce a suit for Angus that didn't look as if it had been made for somebody else: his craggy Scots frame looked ill at ease in anything other than a heavy jersey and kilt, or baggy trousers tucked into Wellington boots.

Because Angus was unexpectedly posted back to New York for nine months, Miranda had to wait over a year for her invitation to Scotland. As she had been forbidden by Elinor to go to New York ("Look what happened to Annabel!"), Miranda ran up enormous telephone bills, finished her beauty course, and (edged in by a friend of Elinor's) started work behind Elizabeth Arden's crimson-doored salon in Bond Street as a trainee beautician.

SATURDAY, 6 AUGUST 1960

Just before the shooting season started, Miranda took the overnight train to Inverness to join Angus, on holiday with his family at Maclayne. The sleeping-car attendant locked her into a single compartment, which contained a let-down bed and a piece of linen called a drugget, upon which to stand while she undressed. She had difficulty in locating the sanitary arrangements, but eventually discovered a cracked white chamber pot concealed in a cupboard beneath the washbasin.

Maclayne Castle was a large, ugly, late-nineteenth-century building with fairytale turrets. Along its long, dark corridors dashed what seemed like many children in well-darned blue jerseys and tartan kilts; these clothes were also worn by the adults of the family and all their friends. Even in August, howling winds blew along the corridors, the longest of which was from kitchen to dining room: this had been deliberately planned, in order to prevent the odor of food from permeating the place. Unfortunately, it meant the meals were always lukewarm when served.

The castle walls were hung indiscriminately with paintings: on one side of a Lawrence portrait was a watercolor of Venice done by some Maclayne great-aunt, while on the other side hung photographs of long-dead hunting dogs. Also suspended upon the walls were many ancient relics of the British empire: assegais from Boer War campaigns, ceremonial flyswatters from the Sudan, moth-eaten stuffed heads of dead animals, and the occasional oar, lettered to indicate in which university boat race it had been pulled.

Miranda decided that the castle sanitary arrangements were little better than those provided by the railway: raised bathtubs with ineradicable greenish-brown marks on their enamel, caused by years of leaking taps; lavatories, encased in mahogany boxes, operated by stiff hanging chains.

When Angus was not out shooting or fishing, he took Miranda sightseeing, either in an estate car with a wired rear compartment to keep the dogs from licking his ears, or in an arthritic Daimler, the back seats of which were flecked by straw and smelled of chickens. Angus would stop this car at the base of some heather-clad craig, and he and Miranda would scramble to the top of it, to gaze over other heather-covered hills, all the color of Angus's ginger tweed jacket.

At the knobbly summit of one of these hills, as the sun was setting in a particularly lurid salmon-pink sky, Angus took the hand of a breathless and puffing Miranda and asked her to marry him. Miranda, who had been hoping for this for months, was taken by surprise.

After she had puffed her acceptance, Angus briskly burrowed beneath the heather and pulled out a ginger wicker basket; this contained a tartan rug, a thermos flask of ice, a bottle of Veuve Clicquot, and two glasses.

At Miranda's look of astonishment, he grinned and said, "Never accuse me of being unromantic. I heaved this up here before breakfast."

That night, Angus crept along a long, dark corridor to Miranda's room, and was allowed to enter.

Elinor, depressed at losing Miranda but delighted to lose her to the brother of an earl, was determined that one of the O'Dare girls should have a traditional white wedding: it was planned for Monday, 3 April 1961, at St. Margaret's, Westminster, the reception afterward to be held at the Savoy Hotel.

After her beauty classes, Miranda often drove her new purple, custom-painted Mini to Clare's smart little terrace house in Poulton Square. The visits continued even after she had started to work, and here in Chelsea, as autumn leaves drifted from the trees in the square, the sisters pondered over Miranda's many lists. There were lists of guests, of hoped-for presents, of seemingly endless suppliers of seemingly essential nuptial purchases: all details of these purchases were of vital importance, from the correct source of invitation envelopes (Smythsons of Bond Street) to the specific red-coated major domo who would announce the guests (Mr. Pecksniff).

MONDAY, 14 NOVEMBER 1960

"Why do I need fish forks? Why does *anyone?*" Miranda asked. Clare's pert, careless, nineteen-year-old French au pair (only two years younger than her mistress) was serving them tea from an elaborate silver tray before the fire in the drawing room.

Clare, no longer a bride but a housewife, checked that everything necessary was on the tray: tea, cake, plum jam from Starlings, and a pile of muffins to toast. Both sisters had kicked off their uncomfortable stiletto-heeled, sharp-pointed shoes. Clare wore a primrose linen suit with a short, tight skirt, Miranda a spinach-green tweed tube with an enormous black knitted collar.

"Fortnum's chocolate Sacher torte!" Miranda cried. "When I'm married, I shall have it every day!"

Clare laughed and said, "Please put towels in the pink spare bedroom, Marie-France. My sister is staying the night." Sam was away, on business.

At two o'clock in the morning, Clare was shaken awake. Alarmed, she quickly sat up and saw Miranda's face, weakly spotlit by a silver shaft of moonlight that fell over the dark trees of the square.

"Listen, Clare," Miranda whispered, "I *must* talk to you. At teatime, I was too . . . Hell, I was embarrassed." She climbed on the bottom of Clare's bed, where she sat cross-legged, her face again in the shadow.

Clare rubbed her knuckles into her eyes and reached for the bedside light. "Can't it wait until morning?"

"Don't turn the light on," Miranda urged. "It's easier to talk in the dark. I can't . . . I've never been able to talk to anyone but you and Frog about sex, and I can't discuss it over the telephone, with New York operators listening . . ."

"What's wrong, Miranda?"

"Do you know about *Lady Chatterley's Lover*?"

"Of course, everyone does," Clare said, puzzled. A few weeks before, Penguin Books had been acquitted of a charge of obscenity for publishing this book after the Public Prosecutor had asked the jury, "Is this a book you would wish your wife or servants to read?" The question had become a public joke.

"When Angus and I are in bed together," Miranda went on, "it doesn't feel for me like it did for Lady Chatterley. No peaks of ecstasy."

Silvered by moonlight, Clare pulled her knees up and clasped them. "Me neither, as a matter of fact."

Both sisters were silent, until Miranda said, "I can't understand why I find it so difficult to talk to you about sex now, when at school we used to discuss nothing else."

Clare pushed her hair behind her ears and said sadly, "Do you remember how we all used to wonder what a good lover does? And how one could be better than the other?"

Miranda nodded.

"Well, I *still* don't know," Clare said. "Sam seems to think that being a good lover is doing it in a hundred acrobatic positions. Sometimes I feel I'm back in the school gym."

"Angus seems to think it means banging away until I'm sore and exhausted and sort of embarrassed for him because I know it won't work. He doesn't seem to notice that I have a problem—since he's clearly satisfied, I expect he thinks I am, too."

"Sam says I'm frigid . . . although it often feels as if something is *about* to happen to me, but then at the last moment—it doesn't."

"I know the feeling."

Hesitantly Clare added, "Before we married, Sam said it was probably because I was afraid I'd get pregnant. He said I'd relax after we married, and then everything would be okay."

"But it wasn't?"

"No. Now after we've made love, I get back pains that last for hours, and I can't get to sleep because I feel so churned up I want to cry."

"I want to shake Angus awake and kick him *hard.*"

After another long silence, Clare said, "Who would have thought it would be so disappointing? I never expected to feel frustrated; I expected to feel a oneness with Sam that I'd never experienced before, as if we both floated on the same warm cloud. I expected ecstasy."

"That's what Gran's heroines always get," Miranda replied mournfully. "Endless bliss in his strong arms. How did Gran manage to convey the idea that a virile, masterful lover was the ideal lover—without describing what he did?"

"By endlessly repeating that he was virile and masterful, as if that was all that mattered," Clare said tartly.

"But where did she pick up that idea? I wouldn't describe Daddy Billy that way." Miranda looked thoughtful. "In fact, I can't imagine them ever doing it!"

"Those two certainly had *something* going," Clare said. "You could sense the electricity, even when Daddy Billy was quite old."

"Perfect lust and mutual climaxes like Lady Chatterley and her gamekeeper?"

"D'you suppose that's really possible?" Clare asked.

"I've no idea," Miranda said, "What *is* good sex supposed to be like?"

"I suspect that D. H. Lawrence's sex was as idealized, in a

masculine way, as Gran's romantic, no-knickers-off sex in her silly novels."

"So how can we learn what we're missing?"

"I don't know," Clare said helplessly. "I thought of talking to Annabel about it: she *said* she doesn't have a problem."

"Lucky bitch!"

After a few minutes, Clare said gloomily, "I must be doing *something* wrong."

Miranda retorted crossly, "You're taking the blame, as usual: that's the difference between you and me. I think that *Angus* is doing something wrong. Or perhaps . . . perhaps Angus is the wrong man for me. Perhaps I'm too small for him." She sighed. "If I didn't love Angus so much . . . But I'm not sure I'll be able to live like this forever . . . On the other hand, perhaps we just need more practice . . . perhaps things will improve."

"They didn't for me," Clare said morosely.

Miranda looked worried and depressed. The room darkened again as the moon disappeared behind a cloud.

THURSDAY, 17 NOVEMBER 1960

In the dimly lit living room of his chambers in Albany, Angus crumpled up another sheet of paper and hurled it into the cozy glow of the fire. At least Miranda hadn't sent him a letter to tell him. Yesterday she had told him, face-to-face, in this very room—not that this had helped Angus to understand her reasons for calling off their wedding.

Miranda had dodged the issue; she said she thought that, at nineteen, she was too young to marry, she wanted to see a bit of life before settling down, she hoped to have her own business one day and she'd never get around to it if she was married. She swore there wasn't another man, which was the first thing that had occurred to Angus.

Too young? Angus pointed out that Miranda's mother had already given birth to two children by the time she was nineteen.

Miranda burst into tears.

Okay, so he was tactless, but Angus had merely meant to point out that life might be short, and it was crazy to put happiness on hold if it wasn't necessary.

After she stopped crying, he had pointed out that, as the wife of an international banker, Miranda could expect to travel a lot and so see plenty of life *after* settling down; he added that he was happy to set her up in a little business, should she want some distraction from domestic life.

Miranda had abruptly stopped looking evasive and apologetic; instead, Vesuvian rage erupted as she repeatedly accused him of masculine complacence. After she stamped out, banging the mahogany door behind her, Angus immediately telephoned Elinor, who already knew.

"Perhaps the best course of action would be to ignore her for a few days," Elinor suggested. "Give her a little time to calm down; the poor darling is clearly experiencing wedding nerves *well* in advance of the ceremony, instead of the night before it."

"What was odd," Angus said, "was that Miranda wouldn't say that she didn't love me. I kept asking her, but I couldn't pin her down." He added sadly, "But neither would she say she loved me."

"Do you love *her*, Angus?" Elinor asked. She seemed a trifle nervous.

"Good Lord, *yes!* I've never before asked anybody to marry me. Of *course* I love Miranda!"

He agreed with Elinor that the best plan was to keep calm, do nothing, and give Miranda a chance. She was certain to reconsider her hasty action.

However, the following morning, Angus opened the *Times* to read that the wedding of the Hon. Angus Maclayne to Miss Miranda Patricia O'Dare would not take place. Only Miranda could have inserted the announcement.

After the sixth call of commiseration, Angus angrily took his telephone off the hook.

Now he started another letter to Miranda, but again threw it in the dying embers of the fire. He could not put what he felt into words. His instinct told him that he hadn't heard all of Miranda's story; he felt also he would have a better chance of getting what he wanted if he kept quiet, refused to discuss the matter, and let everyone think it was over between them. Angus was determined to marry Miranda.

Chapter·12

The week before Christmas, Adam drove to Starlings in a maroon Rolls-Royce Phantom V: this Christmas present to himself had just cost him nearly nine thousand pounds. He whistled cheerfully as he turned off the main road down the bumpy country lane that led to Elinor's home.

On a winning streak, Adam had recently paid off all his debts. Strangely, this did not bring him relief but a feeling of unease. He worried that if he wasn't using all his available credit, then he wasn't deploying all his available assets. And if he didn't use all his assets, he would never be able to afford a house like Mike's in Eaton Terrace. And Adam was determined that when he could afford it, he would purchase an even grander house than his brother's: a reassuring facade was just as important to his business as it was to a bank.

If he didn't make the money by gambling, he might well do so from insurance, for Adam had just become an external member of two insurance syndicates at Lloyds of London. Each big risk at Lloyds was generally shared among a number of syndicates, in order to reduce any individual loss. It was a pity that Adam could afford to belong to only two, because the risk would have been better spread had he belonged to, say, twenty of the four hundred syndicates.

Each syndicate member of Lloyds had to meet the necessary financial requirements, which included showing assets of £75,000, part of which had to be kept in interest-bearing deposit at Lloyds. Although Adam did not possess £75,000, he had enough cash to lodge the deposit, and he had been able to borrow the remainder, temporarily, in order to pull the wool over the eyes of the council of Lloyds, which regulated the business ethics and standards of its market and everyone in it.

Beside Adam, on the seat of the maroon Rolls, lay his briefcase containing a Lloyds prospectus and also a list of Elinor's investments, together with their total current worth and reasoned suggestions as to which should be sold. The briefcase also contained several contracts that required Elinor's signature. After his father's death the previous January, Adam had checked years of back correspondence to familiarize himself with Elinor's business affairs, and now she gratefully turned to him to advise her on all decisions; in fact, Adam had almost reached the point where he would describe himself as her business manager as well as her lawyer.

As the butler took Adam's coat, they both heard angry voices coming from behind the door of Elinor's study.

"Perhaps you would care to wait in the drawing room, sir?" said the butler, serene as a Buddha. "Shall I bring you sherry or tea, sir?"

"No, I'll wait here in the hall. Whiskey and soda, please." Adam sat on a sofa, vexed that Miranda clearly hadn't informed Elinor on the day before his appointment, as he'd asked her to do.

As he sipped his drink, he could clearly hear what was being said next door.

In the oak-paneled study, Elinor, in electric blue, faced a scowling Miranda.

"I don't understand what's gotten into you this year," stormed Elinor. "First, you broke your engagement . . ."

"Angus and I would never have lasted," Miranda said firmly, not liking to acknowledge to herself that she still missed their comfortable intimacy. "He'll be much happier with a traditional Kensington deb. He's the only twenty-nine-year-old man I know who wants to get married and settle down."

"That's not something to hold against him!" Elinor said vehemently. "Then you badgered me for dangerous flying lessons—and now you want to open a shop! My granddaughter is *not* going to be a shopgirl!" Biting her lip to stop tears of anger and disappointment, Elinor turned away from Miranda and looked out past the garden, now having its winter rest; the two flame-shaped holly trees on either side of the gate to the orchard never failed to provide red berries for Christmas.

"And you know *nothing* about commerce!" Elinor added.

"Neither did you when you started work." Miranda, in a purple jumpsuit, stood her ground, arms akimbo, before the slowly burning applewood fire.

"You would be fighting against huge competition. Arden, Rubenstein, Revlon . . ."

"Gran, I work at Elizabeth Arden. I know what kind of fortune a woman spends on her face once she walks through that red door."

"Exactly! You wouldn't stand a chance!" Elinor turned, triumphant, to face Miranda.

"*Yes I would!* Because Arden isn't interested in someone with only a few shillings to spend! *But I am!* Think of the millions of Youthquake girls who can only buy old-fashioned, masklike, heavy makeup in middle-aged colors. . . . Sure, they can go to Woolworth's—but is Woolworth's trendy?"

"*You* know how much money the big firms spend on development. Miranda, if there were a gap in the market, as you claim, they would have spotted it!"

"There *is* a gap!" Miranda insisted. "And they aren't interested in spotting it. That sort of firm simply doesn't understand what young girls want, and they don't understand what a lot of money these girls can collectively spend." Her voice rose in exasperation. "I want to sell to the other girls I see dancing at Humph's—we're forced to paint our faces from a child's paint box. Ask Annabel about it. She knows I'm right."

From Annabel, Miranda had learned the makeup techniques used by American models. Annabel had ransacked Concorde, the dimly lit chemist on Madison Avenue that seemed to contain every cosmetic in the world, to send samples to her sister.

"*Why* must you be so difficult, Miranda?"

"*Why* must you be so unhelpful? Didn't anyone help *you* get started when you were young?"

"No!"

"All the more reason why you should help me," Miranda retorted.

"I'm not going to throw thousands of pounds away on a risky, foolish venture that has little chance of success . . ."

"Although you were willing to spend thousands of pounds on my wedding, which I think had *no* chance of success."

"Let's not harp back to *that* again! That poor young man!"

Miranda changed her tactics. She jumped to the fire, took up the poker, and prodded the smoldering wood until it flared. Then she lowered her voice and spoke winningly. "Gran, I can *prove* that you wouldn't be throwing money away—if only you'd pay for a bit of research. Cosmetic profit margins are huge! Sixty percent of the retail price goes to the manufacturer, and only *eight percent* of that is spent on raw materials."

"I don't want to hear any more of this nonsense! It costs *millions* to launch a cosmetics company—"

"Rubbish!" Miranda leapt to the sofa table, thumbed through a copy of *Vogue*, and stabbed her finger at it. "There! You only have to look at the small ads in the glossies to see that there are plenty of small companies—but those ads have no style. *I have!*"

"You're too young, Miranda, and that's final!"

"Annabel says there's a girl in New Jersey—Adrien Arpel—who

started in 1959, when she was only eighteen. Her *father* gave her four hundred dollars to start, and now she's thriving! What would *my* father want you to do?"

Elinor had been halted.

After a few moments, she said in a quieter voice, "As a matter of fact, my mind is not as closed as you think, Miranda. I spoke to my stockbroker. He said that getting a line of cosmetic products into the stores against the competition of the big companies is *almost impossible.*"

"A fat lot that bald old Billy Bunter knows about it! There's still room for starting up in your own salon!" Miranda cried. "And what does *he* know about the sort of lipsticks girls want? Look at my face!"

Elinor looked, and managed not to shudder.

"You can't get *any* of these colors in London," Miranda rushed on. "And Annabel says you can't get them in New York either! To get a light, shiny pink lipstick, I have to use theatrical whitener under light pink Caran d'Ache crayons, then top it with Vaseline. *I want to do it all with one product!* And I'm sure there are *plenty* of girls like me! And I can sell to them from my own little shops, instead of going the expensive route in the big stores: I'm *never* going to waste time flattering the buyers, or jostling for cover space, or waiting months for late payment that'll upset my cash flow!" Miranda continued, seeming not to pause for breath. "Oh Gran, won't you even let me have a market survey done—to prove what I say? Annie Trehearne says—"

"Your new friend, Miss Trehearne, is a fashion editor, not a fortune-teller!" Ebullient, blond Annie Trehearne was known for her outrageous ideas and her uncannily accurate fashion predictions.

"Exactly! She's fashion editor of *Queen.* Her business is spotting trends. *That's* why she understands what I want to do! *She* can see the gap! The young want something different, and Annie senses that!"

"A pity you didn't just quietly paint her nails. Do you tell *all* your customers of your hare-brained schemes?"

"Gran darling, Annie *specializes* in hare-brained schemes! Come off it—you know you like her, really." Miranda added, "And Annie's wheedled an advertising agency into doing a cut-price market survey. She told them she wants it for a story, and she's offered to splash me when I launch. And Adam has got a financial projection."

"How *dare* you go behind my back to my lawyer!"

"Gran, I've known Adam since I was a little girl," Miranda pleaded. "He's *my* friend as well as *your* lawyer. And he didn't have to pay for the financial projection. The merchant bank prepared it."

"*What merchant bank?*"

Miranda moved to the mantelpiece, picked up a little globe, and started to spin it as she spoke. "When I go into business, Gran, I'm going to need a merchant bank, aren't I? Won't you *please* look at Adam's figures? . . . I have them here."

Elinor looked less sure of herself. "Why didn't you say that you had consulted Adam? If Adam thinks there's a possibility . . . I suppose there's no harm in looking at the figures."

In the hall, Adam stood, picked up his briefcase, and knocked on the door of the study.

Three hours later, Elinor had agreed that for Miranda's twenty-first birthday present, she would buy her a little beauty shop and provide enough money for a secretary and two shop assistants for three years, plus sufficient working capital to cover other overheads and products to stock the shop.

Adam was to be Miranda's business adviser, and Miranda had agreed that for the first three years, she would not take any action that was contrary to his advice.

In return for all this, Miranda agreed not to take flying lessons. Adam noticed that Miranda did not say that she would *never* take flying lessons.

Miranda decided to call her business KITS. She spent the spring of 1961 in a whirl of work, not all of which she enjoyed.

Rather than sell the overpriced, branded products produced by other firms, Miranda wanted to package and retail her own cosmetics; then, she knew, she would have direct control over quality, packaging, and pricing, which would also help to sharpen the identity of KITS.

She knew exactly what this all-important image of KITS should be: bold and young, visually sophisticated but inexpensive. It would project excitement, and it would also be practical. In the KITS store, a customer could buy a set of empty bottles and boxes and then select her colors to fill them: this meant that instead of a collection of gaudy, ill-matched bottles and boxes in her bathroom, she would have only one well-designed, matching set—stamped with the KITS logo, of course.

Miranda also knew that, where two products were indistinguishable, a shopper tended to buy the one with the clearer public image; dull packaging, and subsequent lack of image, was the reason for the failure of many private-label, inexpensive cosmetics. And she knew that inexpensive cosmetics need not mean inferior ones; the same products from one factory were frequently sold at different prices: a face cream might cost a pound in one pack but five pounds in another pack with a more expensive name.

Having targeted her market, Miranda now had to locate suppliers, choose or design her makeup and her skin-care range, write her sales literature, acquire a shop, and hire staff.

After deciding on a final list of basic cosmetics, Miranda developed them in Elinor's kitchen at Chester Terrace, much to the indignation of the housekeeper, who hated the pungent smells. Miranda was less confident about her skin-care products: although she had learned basic formulas during her training, she planned to discuss this line with a qualified cosmetics chemist. So Miranda telephoned four cosmetics manufacturers: Three refused to see her, brusquely explaining that her order would be too small to bother about. The fourth was Ladyface.

FRIDAY, 31 MARCH 1961

Sitting in the Ladyface reception area, Miranda fidgeted; her appointment had been for eleven o'clock—it was now forty minutes past. Was this an example of Ladyface reliability?

"Hello, I'm Cherry Dawson, the publicity officer." A charming blonde in her late twenties stood smiling in the flimsy doorway. Her job was to deal with timewasters like Miranda and save her charm to entertain the press and the groups of American executives who flew in regularly from the New York office. Miss Dawson smiled regretfully. "I'm afraid we have no vacancies of any sort at the moment."

"I don't want a job, I'm a potential customer," Miranda said firmly.

When Miranda proved persistent, Miss Dawson (growing less charming by the minute) said that clients were not her department and escorted her to the office of Miss Scotson, a brand manager known for her ability to get rid of anyone, with speed. While Miranda was describing her plans to Miss Scotson—a suspicious and dismissive woman in her mid-thirties—the brand manager was abruptly summoned by her boss.

Waiting yet again, Miranda looked gloomily around Miss Scotson's office, a tidy white shoe box covered with notice boards. She wondered how it was possible to become so deeply depressed in only twenty minutes. She stood up, stretched, and examined the schedules on the notice boards, none of which she understood. She then glanced at the pile of letters on the manager's desk: the topmost letter was headed "Arthur Bell Cosmetic Products Ltd., Birmingham." The letter started: "We much regret the late delivery of the EPO2 range for Nigeria . . ."

Miss Scotson suddenly materialized. "So good of you to let me know your plans, but we can't help you, especially in view of your . . . unusual . . . testing requirements." Miranda wanted no animal testing involved in her product development.

"Perhaps I can help *you*," Miranda said pleasantly. She pointed to a dummy advertisement pinned on the wall. It read, "Let your skin feel Ladyface sink into it . . ."

"The skin is an excretory organ," Miranda said. "You can't shove things into it, any more than you can into any of your other excretory organs, and any cosmetic claims to do so are ludicrous."

She stalked out.

The following Monday, Miranda's taxi drew into a grimy, dark red brick Birmingham back street, at the end of which "Arthur Bell Cosmetic Products Ltd." was painted on a large pair of gray gates.

Kenneth Bell, a cadaverous-faced man with a sallow complexion and wearing a brown leather jacket, treated Miranda as a lark, an unexpectedly interesting happening in the dull routine of his life. He asked Miranda out to her first business luncheon: they sat on cane furniture in Birmingham's first and only coffee bar, among a jungle of rubber plants, listening to the squawks of an indignant caged macaw.

"You can get all the cosmetics you want from us, except the lipsticks,' Ken said, spooning up runny chili con carne. "For them, you want to visit Shama Cosmetics—in Manchester, they are."

"Can you help me with the skin-care products, Ken? I won't feel confident unless they've been properly tested."

"Can do, Miranda, can do." Ken blew the froth from his cappuccino. "A pal of mine's a dispensing chemist in Wimpole Street—he'll work on the formulas with you. He works for them smart dermatologists in Harley Street; you'll be safe with him."

From that day, Ken Bell acted as Miranda's supplier, industrial spy, and adviser, and he oversaw her ambitious efforts with fatherly concern and pride.

WEDNESDAY, 7 FEBRUARY 1962

Another important factor in Miranda's business had been choosing the right property, for she would at first rely on sales from passing trade. Looking for the best and busiest street location that she could afford, she searched for a property as near as possible to an underground railway station, a main bus stop, or a street crossing. Eventually she chose a small shop and overhead flat on the corner of Oxford Street and Tottenham Court Road.

Once Miranda had signed her expensive lease, she had to move fast because from that point, she was spending money: rent, local taxes, utilities, insurance, lighting, heating, and refurbishment all had to be paid, yet the shop would generate no income until KITS opened its door.

Before sunrise on her twenty-first birthday, Miranda was ensconced in her own shop window, watching the half-awake working crowd shuffle past her store.

For her opening party that evening, Miranda needed a striking window display. She had sprayed a window dresser's model with silver paint and dressed her in a wild silver wig with a few wisps of pale gray net. The model stood with her legs apart, toes turning in, and arms outspread, seemingly to catch a shower of crimson KITS boxes and containers, suspended from the ceiling by invisible nylon cord. Miranda had chosen white and crimson as her house colors, when she hired a designer to project the KITS image: she had noticed that at Christmas, people always opened the red packages first.

Miranda couldn't afford a publicist, but not to worry, said her friend Annie Trehearne. Annie advised her to promote herself. After all, Miranda had seen her grandmother entertain journalists, keeping them informed about her books, so why shouldn't Miranda do the same thing to publicize her makeup?

Just before the opening of the shop, leaflets and price lists were printed entitling customers to a "buy one, get one free" makeup sample. Miranda and her new assistant, Linda Grey, spent the morning distributing these leaflets to the many nearby university and college buildings. This saved further money on publicity.

On the afternoon of the KITS opening, Elinor appeared in the shop to find chaos: carpenters hammered, electricians swore, and painters dripped silver paint.

Miranda, in jeans, stood in the middle of the confusion. "Put those boxes on the upper shelves, please.... Careful, Jim, I don't want another spot of paint on the floor tiles.... Did you get those blue spotlights? ... Gran, darling! What a surprise!"

"I can see that you're busy, dear girl," Elinor said. "I just thought I'd call to wish you good luck and to say ... to say that I'm sorry I doubted your business ability, but I'm right behind you now. Whatever happens, you can depend on me."

"Whatever happens?" Miranda grinned.

"Until the right man comes along, of course."

At six o'clock, Miranda opened her door to the public for the first time.

KITS looked vaguely like a smart photographer's studio: it had black floor tiles and matte black walls; chrome theatrical spotlights shone on the merchandise. The sales staff wore crimson jumpsuits. From the moment the door opened, KITS was jammed by students, passersby, journalists, and many friends of Elinor's: she had sent a crimson invitation to every person in her address book, and had also insisted that

Miranda invite Angus. Miranda, who had already invited Angus, crossly told her grandmother to stop hoping.

Miranda was vexed with Elinor because she didn't like to admit to herself that she still missed Angus far more than she'd ever thought possible. But she couldn't again risk making fools of both of them by suggesting a replay. And she certainly wasn't going to be miserable in bed for the rest of her life. She had suspended her search for a suitably sized Prince Charming until she was less busy at the office; at any rate, that was her excuse. It was a pity that Angus had this one great drawback, because he was so perfect in every other way, which was why she missed him so much—more than he missed her, Miranda suspected. Because Angus now made it clear that he thought of her only as a friend—although, of course, they weren't yet comfortably friendly: maybe later, she wouldn't feel so stiff and uncomfortable whenever she saw him.

In the excited atmosphere of the crowded shop, Elinor waved as she saw Angus trying to push through the crowd toward the corner she shared with Buzz.

"Angus is the only man here who doesn't look as if he's escaped from the zoo," Elinor said approvingly to Buzz. "I'm so glad he's turned up. *I* know that Angus won't take no for an answer, not with that square jaw: the dear boy is just biding his time. Miranda is riding on the crest of a wave at the moment, but the time will come when there are difficulties, and then she'll need a strong man. *That's* when Angus will make his move."

"Romantic codswallop, Nell," Buzz growled, then added, "Funny sort of cigarettes they're smoking. No wonder you're coughing, Nell. We don't want another bronchitis attack. You've only been out of bed for a week!" She fanned her invitation. "Cor! What a noise! And what a crowd! And what *weird* clothes!"

But the headiest substance to get high on was not the pot, it was the optimism and euphoria that hung above the chic crowd, which so clearly demonstrated that fashion was no longer reserved for the daughters, wives, and mistresses of the rich. Annie Trehearne had persuaded all the big names to turn up. Models talked to photographers and trendy hairdressers; pretty girls talked to advertising men in dark glasses; debs chatted to Bow Group young Tories; truculent left-wing journalists argued with art directors in black turtleneck sweaters. Cockney and Liverpudlian accents mingled with upper class accents: "Isn't it groovy?" . . . "So switched on" . . . "super birds" . . . "fab shop" . . . "smashing" . . . "totally with it." The evening was clearly a right rave-up.

"Annabel's late again!" Elinor worried to Buzz.

But Annabel wasn't late; she was peering at the party through the two-way mirror that Miranda had installed behind the back wall to watch KITS customers and see which items they first picked up.

Miranda had insisted that Annabel (who had flown over from New York especially for the opening) should not appear until the party had been running for two hours; both sisters feared that Annabel's now famous face would steal Miranda's limelight. So Annabel would not enter until all the photographers had left. Until then, she contented herself with her surreptitious view, and wished that Miranda would fall for one of those very attractive men at the party instead of talking to Angus.

Finally Miranda flung open the door. "Okay, Annabel, you're allowed in now. Everyone please meet my beautiful sister!"

Ten minutes after Annabel joined the party, she felt a tug at her shoulder. It was Clare, who looked white and ill. She said, "Please get me out of here fast, darling. I think I'm going to faint. Don't spoil Gran's fun. Just get me home."

Annabel drove Clare's little scarlet car back to Poulton Square, where she helped her sister up the stairs, tucked her into bed, and brought her a glass of brandy.

"No, darling, I don't want a drink." Leaning back against her pillows, Clare still looked haggard. "Don't look so worried, Annabel, it's not serious. I've had tests, and I'm not pregnant—although my gyno took me off the Pill a couple of months ago, to make sure that wasn't the cause of my problem: so I'm back with the messy Dutch cap—whenever Sam gives me time to get it in."

"But what's *wrong,* darling?"

"Awful back pains. I feel as if I have a permanent, bad period."

"Where's Sam?"

"He left for Paris at dawn this morning. He'll be back tomorrow evening," Clare said shortly.

Annabel asked tentatively, "Are things okay between you and Sam?"

"Yes, of course," Clare said. She burst into tears.

Annabel hugged her sister, reached for the box of tissues, silently handed it to Clare, and waited until her snuffling stopped.

"Now tell me what's happened," Annabel said gently.

Clare started to speak, stopped, stuttered, stopped again, then burst out, "My gyno thinks my backache is because I get physically excited when we're making love but I don't climax—so there's no relief. He said a man feels the same way if he doesn't climax after having an erection." After renewed sobs, Clare wailed, "But Sam thinks I'm frigid."

"Can you masturbate?" Annabel asked.

Speechless, Clare blushed and nodded.

Annabel said briskly, "If you can masturbate to orgasm, then you *aren't* frigid and you *are* orgasmic. There's no great mystery about it."

"Then why does Sam think I'm frigid?"

" 'Frigid' is a man's word for a woman who can't have an orgasm in two minutes with the kind of stimulation that works for him."

Clare laughed bitterly.

Annabel said, "Why don't you . . . do it yourself if your back pains are so bad?"

"What's the point of being married unless we do it with each other?" Clare added resentfully, "If Sam really loves me, he should know what I need in bed."

"How? By divine guidance? ESP?" Annabel asked. "Sam isn't a mind reader: you have to *tell* him what you like—or take him by the hand and *show* him. Of *course* Sam loves you, or he wouldn't have married you, but when you're making love, you mustn't be shy about telling him what turns you on. Simply establish two things: what you like and what he likes."

"You make it sound so *easy*."

"So it should be. But there's only one person who can teach a woman to be a good lover, and that's her man. And there's only one person who can teach a man to be a good lover, and that's his woman."

"What did you tell Scott?"

"That I like to be on top, then I can control the rhythm and pressure. We . . . sort of rub rather than bounce . . . as in rock and roll."

Clare said, "Sam doesn't like to talk when he's making love. Suppose he won't listen?"

Annabel shrugged. "You can tell some men something until you're blue in the face, but if they don't want to hear it—you might as well save your breath. In that case, maybe you should go with Sam to a marriage counselor."

"I keep hoping things will get better . . ."

"You've been married three years! How much longer are you going to wait?"

"Don't rush me," Clare said crossly. "And how come *you're* such an expert, Annabel?"

"Scott taught me. And sex is practically the *only* thing that models talk about in the changing rooms. In New York, everyone talks openly about things that the British would blush to even think about: they're accustomed to discussing these things with their psychiatrists."

Clare gave a wobbly laugh. "If you told a man from Mars that the sex act was a human being's ultimate pleasure and then described it, he'd laugh until he burst into green fragments."

In the end, Clare found that the best way to talk to Sam was simply, casually, to repeat her conversation with Annabel.

Sam said, "Why the fuck do you have to discuss our private life with your sister? Don't worry. Lots of women can't climax."

"But I can when I . . . when I . . . do it myself."

"Look, Clare, nobody ever complained to me before. Everything is functioning perfectly, thank you." He lay back, bare-chested against blue-striped pillows, and clasped his hands behind his head. "Come here and I'll prove it."

Before entering Clare, Sam thrust two fingers up her; he twisted his wrist and wriggled his fingers around, harder and harder. Having entered her, he thrust longer and harder than usual, as if trying to reach some not-quite-attainable spot, like a plumber desperately trying to reach whatever is blocking the sink.

From underneath, Clare tried to do the rock-and-roll wriggle, but Sam's hands reached down and guided her hips to his movement.

Afterward, Clare, who had not climaxed, sensed Sam's silent exasperation. Eventually he gingerly felt for her clitoris. Four minutes later, she climaxed.

A few weeks later, Clare reported progress to Annabel, now back in New York.

"So everything's fine now?" Annabel asked.

Clare hesitated. "Not altogether. I can sense . . . there's still something wrong. . . . Sam's trying very hard," she said. "In every possible position. But it . . . doesn't feel loving or caring. Now I feel as if we're a couple of acrobats, performing."

"To be blunt," Annabel said, "efficient fucking isn't necessarily an act of love."

"The most depressing thing is . . . Sam won't acknowledge that the way my body works is *normal,* so that makes me resentful, when Sam clearly thinks I should be grateful."

After a long silence, Annabel said, "Maybe you should lighten things up a little. You might try a little playful fantasy."

"What *do* you mean?"

"Erotic fantasy. Next time you're in bed with Sam, use your fantasies. Say, 'A picture just came into my mind of you unhooking my black satin corselette . . .' "

Clare looked doubtful.

FRIDAY, 2 MARCH 1962

Nevertheless, the next day, Clare told the au pair that she would be out all day, then took a taxi to the Matelot restaurant, where she was to meet Lizzie Bromley for lunch. There the headwaiter handed her a note saying that Lizzie couldn't make it because she had a toothache. As Clare didn't feel hungry, she took another taxi to Fenwick's.

An hour later, clutching two large green boxes of frivolous underwear, Clare returned home, planning to spend the afternoon trying out a few fantasies. She ran upstairs to her bedroom, opened the door . . . and froze.

She stared at Sam's bum moving up and down, and beyond it, the startled face of Marie-France.

Clare's first sensations were of pain and rage, followed almost immediately by sexual self-doubt: Just what did that French au pair have that she didn't? It wasn't *fair!* She was making such an effort to improve things, and had just spent a fortune at Fenwick's!

When she could speak, Clare yelled, "Get out of my bed and out of this house. *Now!*"

She dumped the green boxes on the floor, tore one of them open, dipped into it, and started to pelt the speechless Sam with black lace garter belts, fishnet stockings, half-cut satin bras, black chiffon French camiknickers, a pair of long black satin gloves trimmed with ostrich feathers, and a pair of ridiculously high-heeled scarlet patent ankle-strap shoes.

Leaving the front door open, she then ran out of the house, toward the Kings Road, where she hailed a cab and directed it to Elinor's flat.

Elinor had decided to sell the flat, for it seemed silly to keep it for just the occasional use of one person. She rarely stayed overnight in London and could stay at Claridge's if she did.

When Clare banged on the door, Elinor and Buzz were there, making lists of furniture: what to send to Starlings, what to store, what to sell, and what to give to Oxfam.

"My dear child, what *has* happened?" Elinor held out her arms, and Clare flew into them.

"I've come home," Clare snuffled against the shoulder of Elinor's gray flannel Digby Morton suit. "I never want to see him again! I fu-fu-fu-fu found him in bu-bu-bu bed with the au pair!"

Elinor tried to soothe and comfort her: "Oh my dear, you mustn't take these things so much to heart. I know you haven't been married that long, but men are all the same: they have . . . lusty appetites. You must learn when to turn a blind eye."

"Your generation might have settled for that, but *I* won't put up with it! I'm never going back to Sam!"

While soothing and sympathizing with Clare, over her head Elinor mouthed to Buzz, "Cancel the estate agent."

Sam didn't think it mattered if he cheated on his wife, provided she never found out: he'd been unlucky. Okay, he was sorry. He grew increasingly irritated as he realized how stubborn Clare could be; no persuasion would mollify her fury.

For over three months, Sam tried to persuade Clare to return.

Eventually his barrage of telephone calls slowed down, then stopped. He figured Clare would either return or not. Time would tell.

In mid-June, three prisoners, using teaspoons, gouged an escape route from Alcatraz. Reading about this in Elinor's *Daily Telegraph*, Clare felt similarly trapped, but without a teaspoon. She had just received the results of her test. She was pregnant. Abortions were illegal. No escape for Clare. Back to Sam.

TUESDAY, 18 DECEMBER 1962

Shortly before Christmas, Adam and Mike escorted Elinor and Buzz to the theater. The two ladies, so handsomely escorted, felt as glamorous as Adam intended they should. Heads turned toward them as they took their places in the royal box, to watch Peter Brook's production of *King Lear* for the Royal Shakespeare Company.

Afterward, over supper at the Savoy, Adam said, "I didn't much care for that. It was too bleak and contemporary for me." Again he wondered whether he should have taken the two old dears to see Agatha Christie's *The Mousetrap*.

"Paul Scofield acted very well as Lear," Elinor pointed out, careful to be positive about an evening that somebody else was paying for. "But anyone could have told the conceited old idiot what would happen."

Buzz said, "It ain't always easy to see what's happening, while it's happening to you."

"Very true," Elinor said.

"Take that bookkeeper we just fired," Buzz went on. "Fancy having to go to court for a minor gas bill!"

"An unwise choice. I should never have trusted somebody else's judgment," Adam said, annoyed by Buzz's tactlessness. The incompetent bookkeeper had led to nonpayment by Elinor of a heap of small bills, which in turn led to a bunch of complicated small lawsuits, which need never have taken place.

"Paul Littlejohn handled the lawsuit very well," Elinor said hastily, referring to a junior partner at STG.

Buzz had complained several times that there were never any problems when Joe Grant handled Elinor's legal business; he had simplified her affairs and Buzz had always understood them, whereas in less than a year, Adam seemed to have made things more difficult.

Elinor reproved Buzz and reminded her that her writing business had become more complicated since Adam restructured it into a group of companies.

Buzz retorted that she didn't understand the reasons for the restructuring, any more than Elinor did. "But you never question Adam's decisions. You just do as he says, and in my opinion, a lot of what he says is what the army calls—"

"That's quite enough," Elinor had said crisply, unwilling to consider that Adam was unreliable. What other man could she turn to? What other man could advise her what to do? Adam was understanding and sympathetic; he lifted all the cares from her shoulders, which enabled her to get on with her work: she would be lost without him.

As Adam consulted the Savoy wine list, a waiter approached the table with a silver salver upon which lay a note for Mike.

Mike quickly read it, then twisted around in his chair; he nodded briefly and respectfully toward a group of men in dinner jackets dining at the best table in the room.

After the meal, when Elinor and Buzz had retired to "powder their noses," Adam asked Mike, "What was that note about?"

Mike looked at his brother with a mixture of affection, exasperation, anxiety, and pity. "I wasn't going to tell you until tomorrow. I'd no idea that the brothers would be here tonight. I'm sorry, but they won't give you another extension. You've got to pay them back within ten days."

"Have I *ever* not paid my gambling debts?" Adam demanded angrily.

"No, but they can't afford to let other people see that you don't pay when you're supposed to pay. Suppose all their debtors behaved like you do?"

"All debtors don't provide them with the legal services that I do. I've managed to ease them out of some pretty unpleasant situations."

"Then do the same for yourself." Mike called for the bill.

Elinor and Buzz returned to the flat in Chester Terrace to find a message from Sam pinned beneath the door knocker: upon a hastily torn-out page of his diary, he had written, "Clare's gone into labor early. I've taken her to hospital."

Thirty-two hours later, after a difficult labor, Clare gave birth to an eight-pound boy.

As Elinor reverently held Joshua, not yet an hour old, in her arms, she could see the almost imperceptible ridge of his skull join from ear to ear and the slight dip of the fontanelle on top of his downy head. Eyes shut and sleepy, he looked small and fragile, quiet and long-suffering.

Gently Elinor pried open one tiny fist and put her forefinger into it. The sleeping baby grasped it firmly. She marveled at the tiny fingers and fingernails.

"I hope he'll wake up soon," Elinor whispered from beneath her face mask to Buzz. "In the first couple of days, before the face has fattened, you can see what the baby will look like when he's grown up."

Suddenly the baby opened his eyes and seemed to look up at Elinor.

She almost gasped, for the eyes that looked straight up at her were the aquamarine eyes of Billy.

Elinor was not to enjoy her first great-grandson for long. On New Year's Day, Sam broke the news to Clare that he wanted to return to live in Los Angeles.

Sam hadn't had a hit since *Grain Race,* released three years earlier. He didn't think he'd lost his touch, but he had realized that being out of the movie mainstream was being *out.* Working for the motion picture market requires the producer's presence in the marketplace, in the town where the movie action is; the town where each inhabitant, even a waitress or gas pump attendant, has an agent and at least one lawyer; the town where everyone lives, breathes, eats, talks, and definitely sleeps movies: Los Angeles.

Sam was to find that it was easier to leave than to return.

Chapter·13

After four days in Los Angeles, Clare still felt euphoric, as if she'd stepped off the plane and traded her brain in for a driver's license. Nobody could get around L.A. without a car—in some places there weren't even any sidewalks. But she loved wearing shorts in January and sauntering by the ocean in midwinter. She also loved listening to the way everyone talked; she was fascinated by the quick, flip repartee of Sam's friends, the languid, spaced-out chat in the restaurants near the beach, the omnivorous movie gossip: by the end of her first week, she was reading the trades over breakfast.

Clare quickly found and furnished a sprawling, split-level, glass-and-timber ranch house, with pool and patio, in Brentwood. Accustomed to pleasant surroundings, she was determined to make their home a comfortable, quiet retreat from the dazzling, dizzy, absurd, totally unpredictable, and delightfully startling life of Southern California, which fascinated her but also left her breathless.

Josh was far more tiring than L.A. Clare had no idea that one small baby could be so exhausting; he was noisy, restless, demanding—and seemed to sleep only three minutes a night.

The day he found her sunburned after she fell asleep by the pool, Sam took pity on her. Putting his arm around Clare's blistered shoulders he said, "Get a nanny. No more argument about it."

To Sam's surprise and the astonishment of his friends, he doted on the baby. When Josh was one month old, Sam was certain that the baby could focus clearly on him, although Clare told him that it wasn't possible. At two months, Sam knew that those were real smiles, not wind. At three months, there was real laughing and excited waving of fists whenever Sam appeared, and Josh clearly recognized his father.

Sam's problems always vanished when he lowered the naked, wriggling Josh into his bath, or made silly goo-goo noises at the pram, or crawled on the terrace like a bear, or tried unsuccessfully to coax the four-month-old Josh to say "Dad."

Elinor hired a young English nanny who reminded Clare of a small, bright-eyed blackbird. In the way that people tend to gravitate toward each other when feeling slightly homesick, they quickly became friends, and from the day Kathy arrived in L.A., Josh metamorphosed into a quiet baby; he lay in his pram or crib or rug, blew bubbles, gurgled, burped upon demand, and gave no trouble: Clare thought it most unfair but was delighted, and so was Sam.

After Kathy's arrival, Clare started to entertain. In L.A., this was serious business, nothing like having your friends over for supper. Sam needed backup, and Clare was determined to help her husband as much as she could: she remembered the success of Elinor's daily tea parties, and methodically applied her considerable organizational ability to throwing lavish soirées. Clare was not needed at Sam's business breakfasts in the El Padrino Room of the Beverly Wilshire or lunches at the Brown Derby or Scandia on Sunset Boulevard, but she presided over all evening entertaining, whether at home, in the leafy courtyard of the Bel Air Hotel, or at Romanoff's. Sam's oldest friends were particularly impressed by his classy English wife, granddaughter of an internationally famous, best-selling author; not only was she pretty and young, Clare was an effortless and charming hostess—which is more than anyone could say for either of Sam's previous wives.

Sam had to work hard to reinstate himself, and the first order of business was to locate the right script. He spent his time searching for material, while trying to ignore the cold claw that gripped his stomach— and pocketbook—as he realized the world's indifference to Sam Shapiro. Sam had reached the time of life when it wasn't so easy anymore: he was still in the game—but only by the skin of his teeth, and he knew it. So did everyone of consequence in L.A., except Clare. Sam was still welcomed with a flourish by the maître d's. Cary Grant and Frank Sinatra still nodded to him. But there were little things, like being demoted from Swifty Lazar's "A" list to the agent's "B" list: these things reminded everyone that Sam hadn't had a hit since *Grain Race*.

Clare had known before she came to L.A. that being married to a movie producer wasn't as glamorous as she (and her envious and astonished girlfriends in England) had once thought. She learned quickly that the annual seasons were no longer spring, summer, autumn, winter, but research and development, preproduction, production, postproduction and marketing. But Clare did not know that Sam's money was running out: the income from the big hits had gone in taxes, alimony, and surprisingly high overhead.

Not realizing that Sam couldn't afford it, Clare continued to entertain lavishly. One evening in late April, she telephoned Annabel in New York and reported, "We're having seventy-five to supper this evening. I've had such a pretty, yellow-striped marquee set up beyond the pool."

"I don't get time to entertain formally at home," said Annabel. "So if it's business, we take them to '21,' and if it's friends, I invite them for brunch on Sunday."

Clare giggled. "That wouldn't do in L.A. Sunday brunches are considered tacky. So are beach picnics or any casual get-together. Here the entertaining is rather old-fashioned and formal. I give big parties and dinners for up to sixteen at home—the caterers are wonderful, by the way—and anything in between takes place in some smart hotel."

"And are these parties filled with beautiful actresses and sexy starlets?"

Clare giggled again. "Never. The important people are family men, so there are never any beautiful starlets at the best parties, in case they make the wives feel insecure. A lot of sensational-looking women wander in and out of the hotels and restaurants—but you'll never find them at the best parties. And you never invite unimportant actors, in case they might pester someone for a part. No, the whole point of these parties is to do deals, to put all the right people together so that the next picture gets made."

None of Clare's entertaining showed the returns for which Sam hoped, however.

Because of his anxiety over his career and his failure to reinstate himself, Sam had neither surplus energy nor libido. He and Clare made love regularly, and Sam dutifully gave orgasms to Clare, who (although she didn't say so) still felt that something was missing. There was no spontaneous excitement, no loving warmth; she was not swept to the stars in his arms. Crossly Clare told herself that her expectations had been as stupidly unrealistic as one of her grandmother's breathlessly ecstatic heroines.

One afternoon, when Annabel phoned, Clare found herself asking, "How's your love life, darling?"

After a pause, Annabel said, "Mechanical."

"Yours too?"

"I always know when Scott's got something big going on at the station, because his head is someplace else when he's with me."

"I don't believe it! After you had me believing that Scott was God's gift to women?"

"He seems to be taking a sabbatical," Annabel said curtly, and changed the subject.

Clare had noticed that Sam's libido perked up when young actresses clustered around him at poolside bars and in smart hotel lounges; for them, a producer was a producer, and Sam still had his reputation. Sam clearly felt soothed by this flattering attention, but Clare felt sad, and a little jealous. She wished she had what those women obviously thought she had, which was what she herself had expected: a powerful, all-protecting, sexy husband. Perhaps if the two of them could get away alone to some perfect place . . .

When Sam asked Clare the day after her big party if she'd like to accompany him to the Cannes International Film Festival, he was surprised that she decided to leave Josh alone with Kathy for ten days: but Clare looked forward to a carefree second honeymoon.

Unfortunately, at the last minute, Sam—unaware of Clare's romantic plans—invited Elinor, who was recovering from another bad bout of bronchitis; he thought she would be company for Clare, who would then not mope around alone all day while he—he hoped—put deals together. Sam decided to stay at the Carlton rather than Elinor's villa in St.-Tropez, which was too small and too far from the action.

MONDAY, 6 MAY 1963

One week later, Clare, Sam, Elinor, and Buzz sat on the terrace of the Carlton Hotel under a dazzling sun. White yachts flitted across the bay; crowds on the beach peered at starlets; photographers snapped girls in spangled bikinis, mink bikinis, and flower-covered bikinis. Clare could spot no stars: Sam said they generally stayed in the hills behind Cannes in luxurious rented villas, descending only for their own screenings when the publicity machine had been organized to receive them.

Clare and Sam smiled at each other across the table. She was happy to be here watching the cinematic rites of spring.

Elinor noticed the exchange and felt relieved. A baby often reunited a couple who had been having problems. She hoped that little episode was behind them.

One week later, cigar smoke wafted from the windows of the Carlton and the Negresco as negotiations became serious and deals firmed up, but Sam seemed to have no part in them. Clare learned not to ask, "But was anything *definite* agreed?" after he returned weary but still hopeful from lunch with some big player at the Hotel du Cap or the Eden Roc at Antibes. Sam's wonderful aura of assurance, which had originally captured Clare's heart, was visibly wilting.

Then one evening, Sam and Clare dined at the Majestic with a distributor who had clinched deals in seven major territories, was clear to closing another nine, was working at his negotiating strategy for the remaining twenty-one major territories, and just hoped he could pack it all into the remaining week of the festival. Watching Sam's face, Clare wondered if her husband's desperation was as clear to other people as it was to her.

After dinner, she suggested a stroll along La Croisette, the palm-tree-lined promenade: she hoped that the two of them might walk in the dark beneath the stars and forget the feverish atmosphere of the festival.

On the darkened beach, small groups of young people drank, smoked, talked, laughed.

"Who are they all?" Clare asked.

"Young movie hopefuls and out-of-work actors—you've already seen most of them; they prowl around in hotel and restaurant lobbies, deeply disappointed to find they're talking to each other and not Dino De Laurentiis or Franco Zeffirelli," Sam said. "They're all impoverished dreamers, would-be screenwriters, directors, and producers. They turn up from all over the world, carrying cans of film, files of projects, ideas, treatments, scripts . . . Most of them will have sold nothing by the time they fly back to reality."

"But what are they all doing on the beach?"

"If they can't find a cheap pension outside town, they sleep here."

Clare could not feel sorry for these healthy young hopefuls necking in the moonlight on a Riviera beach. But she felt increasingly sorry for Sam. Lack of success seemed to make it necessary for him to talk a little louder, tip a little too much, flirt a little more with would-be starlets, who didn't realize they were wasting their time.

As they reached the deserted end of the beach, Clare nudged Sam. "Let's go down on the sand," she suggested, taking his hand.

Where the sand ran into the dark sea, Clare kicked her shoes off, turned to Sam, and put her arms around his neck. "Let's forget everything for a few minutes," she whispered. "Let's forget movies and money and deals and doubts. Let's enjoy the soft sound of the sea on the sand. Let's enjoy each other."

Sam pulled her close and said helplessly, "I can't figure out what I'm doing wrong . . . I'm sorry, Clare."

"It doesn't matter. Forget it for a few minutes." She took his face in her hands and kissed his mouth hard. "Nobody can see us."

They kissed with passion, holding each other tightly. For once, Sam allowed Clare to share his human vulnerability. For the first time, he felt her strength and reassurance. For the first time, he shared, in whispers, his doubts, fears, regrets.

Clare pulled his head down and kissed away his words. "It doesn't matter, Sam. I swear it doesn't matter. Forget all that. Just remember that we're together—*and I love you.*"

Sam crushed her against him, and Clare could feel his need for her. And there on the damp, cold sand, Clare finally felt what she had always yearned for, the release she had searched for: to her surprise, she recognized Elinor's ecstatic descriptions of twin souls uniting. Finally Clare's hoped-for moment came, as she and Sam shared joy.

TUESDAY, 14 MAY 1963

On the eighth morning of the festival, Elinor gazed around the lobby of the Carlton, lined with film posters for *Cleopatra* and *Tom Jones*.

Beside her, Buzz sniffed, "Bloody circus. Crowds everywhere. Waiters rushed off their feet. Can't get a decent cup of tea."

Behind her, Elinor heard drifts of conversation.

"When does your plane leave?"

"Why, whenever I'm ready, of course."

". . . I can't get decent vegetable gardeners."

"I have a couple of Filipinos. Costs forty dollars a carrot, of course, but at least I know they're fresh . . ."

"Richard Burton isn't going to buy that chateau at Saracen after all. Sounds like alimony . . ."

"Did you hear that, Buzz?" Elinor said. "Do you suppose that chateau really is for sale? Why don't we drive there and see?" She knew that Saracen, one of the few unspoiled medieval French villages, had been deemed a national treasure: no new building was allowed.

Buzz grunted, "Anything to get away from this lot."

So they picked their way past the Afghan hounds, disdainful borzois, and exquisitely groomed Pekingese, whose owners sat in the sun drinking champagne or expensive bottled water. Elinor obliged two Scandinavian backpackers, who asked for her autograph. Eventually they found Sam's air-conditioned limousine and drove east.

In contrast to the noise, heat, and dust of Cannes, the surrounding countryside looked eager, freshly washed, and pretty as a girl before a dance. To their right was the sparkling azure sea; to their left were lavender fields and dark green forests, behind which mountains rose, to fade in soft lines of mauve back to the white horizon.

None of Saracen's labyrinth of winding streets were wide enough for a car, so the air of the village was fresh and clear. Some of the streets opened into small, unexpected squares, each shaded by lime trees around an old stone fountain. The narrow houses had mysterious porches and bridges that crossed from one building to another; on many a worn wooden door hung the iron hand of Fatima, to ward off evil spirits.

The high ironwork gate of the chateau creaked open at Elinor's tentative touch. She and Buzz walked into a cobbled courtyard choked by weeds. Against the castle walls grew white oleander and rosemary bushes, and trees that drooped beneath strange pale yellow blossoms: the branches were so low that the two women had to stoop beneath a ragged arch of green and yellow to reach the front door—an ancient slab of oak studded with ironwork of different periods.

They rang the bell and waited. Elinor looked up to see, high above her, a row of narrow slits. She imagined the castle defenders hiding behind, shooting arrows at invaders.

Just as Elinor decided that the building was deserted, the front door was slowly opened by an unsmiling gray-haired woman who wore a cotton overall and a pair of sneakers, cut to allow her bunions to protrude. This caretaker confirmed that the chateau was for sale, but she knew nothing of price or availability; it was for the agent to occupy himself with such matters.

Eventually Elinor persuaded this harpy to telephone for the agent, a thin, dismissive young man who clearly didn't take these English-women seriously. Everyone knew that the English no longer had money. At breakneck speed, he showed them around the chateau.

The building was not in a good state of repair: The interior was damp, and the plaster was peeling. Some of the shutters were hanging off the windows, some were missing, and none had been painted for years. The two upper floors were a dusty, shuttered warren of bedrooms. The only bathroom had been installed before the First World War, and there was no central heating or air-conditioning. The agent assured the women, somewhat unconvincingly, that the chateau was kept warm in winter and cool in summer by the six-foot-thick walls. Their tour ended where it had started, on the south terrace overlooking the sea.

Elinor sauntered to the ivy-covered balustrade. To her right, in the distance, the Bay of Nice curved like a Dufy painting, edged with tall palm trees and pretty villas. Below her, rough-hewn gray rock fell abruptly to a sandy crescent of beach, where the sea was aquamarine shot with silver; beyond the bay, the water spread, deep blue, to the horizon; the color changed to indigo as it met an azure sky, across which clouds sailed, fat as cupids, in the brilliant, dazzling, inimitable light of the French Riviera.

"And the price?" Elinor slowly turned to the dismissive agent.

Buzz suddenly realized that this was no casual spring afternoon excursion. "What would *we* do with a place this size? Just look at the mess it's in! Ain't been cleaned since it was built, if you ask me." She snorted. "You're a romantic idiot, Nell!"

Both women knew that Elinor would buy the chateau.

• • •

Later, as they walked downhill in silence, Elinor noticed that a surprising number of trees grew in the narrow streets and little squares: weeping willows, olive and apricot trees. They drank coffee at the only café, in a street studded by tubs of pink geraniums; pigeons swooped to pick up the cake crumbs that Buzz threw. Then they wandered past the dark green, studded door of the *syndicat d'initiative* and the lavender shutters of the local cooperative to the pale-blue-painted *mairie* that stood next to the blue and green pharmacy. Opposite the ancient Church of St. Peter was the village shop; in the window, plastic champagne glasses stood next to a jumble of red flyswatters, bottling jars, dusty casseroles, insecticides, local eau de cologne, honey, and herbs.

"It's almost too charming," said Elinor. These quiet sunny streets had altered little over seven hundred years. She and Buzz had driven only a short distance, but they might have been a thousand kilometers from the hustling streets of Cannes.

"It's a rash, impulsive move," Buzz grumbled on the return journey.

Elinor laughed. Having unexpectedly and romantically been tempted by fate to leave Britain, she could see only the advantages: no more fog, no more bronchitis. Instead, sunshine, warm sea, delicious food and wine.

"Won't you miss Starlings?" Buzz couldn't believe that Elinor would leave her beloved garden.

Elinor suddenly became serious, "Starlings isn't the same since the girls left." The silent void that Starlings had become made Elinor miserably conscious that the girls no longer lived there. Everywhere she looked, something reminded her of them and made her long to relive the past. In her own home, Elinor felt homesick. Perhaps at Saracen, she would find a new way of life; perhaps there she could again look forward, instead of being constantly and painfully tugged back by memories.

On the following morning, Paul Littlejohn, now a junior partner of Swithin, Timmins and Grant, flew from London to Nice. Funded by money earned outside Britain and not subject to exchange controls, Elinor eventually found herself mistress of the ancient French chateau. Although this was a relatively simple arrangement, Paul Littlejohn managed to make it sound as complicated as the division of Berlin between the Allies, and charged accordingly.

Buzz urged Elinor to query the bill. Elinor said that she had Adam's assurance that the charge was normal for such a transaction.

"It ain't *normal* to buy an eleventh-century castle," Buzz retorted.

"And why does that Mr. Littlejohn always write 'done under request' in his letters to you?"

"I request it and he's confirming it. What's wrong with that?" Elinor asked irritably. "I expect the wording covers some legal point, or has something to do with exchange regulations. Besides, it's not something for us to worry about. Adam and Mr. Littlejohn know what's best for me, and I trust them. Now where *is* that decorator?"

Chapter · 14

Adam sauntered up the marble steps of the Clanrickard Club. Two years before, the law had been changed to allow gambling in Britain; since then London had become one of the world's gambling centers. The grandest London clubs were Crockfords in Carlton House Terrace; John Aspinall's Clermont Club in Berkeley Square, which attracted the richest and most daring gamblers; Les Ambassadeurs, where you dined, danced, and then went upstairs to play chemmy; and the Clanrickard Club, run by Mike Grant.

As Adam reached the door, the owner, Toby Sutch, hurried out. Adam hadn't expected him to be there so early in the evening.

Toby Sutch paused. "I expect you've come to settle your account, Grant, without any trouble."

"That's what I'm seeing Mike about," Adam parried, realizing what Toby meant by "trouble." An immaculately dressed Old Harrovian, Toby Sutch was a tough bully, accustomed to being obeyed. His powerful self-confidence attracted people who couldn't control their gambling, and who often became dependent upon him. He introduced such people to moneylenders who provided six-month loans for four percent monthly interest. Should there be a repayment problem, toughs visited the borrowers and persuaded them to pay up.

Adam entered Mike's office without knocking. "You're late again, Adam," Mike said from behind his rosewood desk. "You'd better make this quick, because I'm meeting Miranda to show her a shop I've found in Pimlico."

"Miranda can wait." Adam sat in a leather chair and propped his feet up on the desk. "I want a whiskey and soda and a quick word with you, about Miranda's business."

"She's expanding at the speed of light," Mike said. Miranda had acquired seven shops in eighteen months, two of which had been found by Mike, who had property connections, a good nose for a bargain, and plenty of free time during the day.

Using her first shop as collateral, Miranda had borrowed from the bank to buy the lease of a second shop, near Holborn. Using the second lease as collateral, she had then similarly purchased the lease of a third shop. As she had launched her business just before a small London property boom, Miranda found that her collateral value seemed to increase weekly with no effort on her part: the steadily rising KITS profit figures reassured the bank of her ability to leverage property in this way.

Adam said, "She's spending too much of her time on property deals when she should be running the business. She's got an eye for good property, but she's not adept at dealing with the people who sell it: estate agents have little respect for a woman, particularly, it seems, if she's young and pretty. But *you*, little brother, have a flair for real estate, *and* you know how to handle the agents: you can wine and dine them here, introduce them to some nice girls, drop the occasional envelope of cash, and learn to lose at golf. Then you'll get first pick of properties for sale. It won't take up much of your time. You'll get two percent commission."

As he poured Adam's drink, Mike's clear gray eyes looked worried. He knew the hidden drawback to this reasonable-sounding deal: if he accepted it from Adam, Mike would be expected to persuade Toby Sutch to extend Adam's credit. But Mike did not want to ask any favors, especially not from Toby.

"Two percent," Adam said firmly.

Reluctantly Mike nodded.

Adam stood up. "What Miranda needs is to get her operation under one roof. So look for a large industrial building, somewhere outside London, in central England where rents are lower. That way we can locate the factory, warehouse, garages, and offices in the same place."

"Why not build?" Mike suggested.

"No time." Adam downed his drink and left.

FRIDAY, 24 APRIL 1964

"I love it, Buzz," Elinor said as she waited on the south terrace for her guests to arrive: the traditional finishing feast for the builders was about to start. Saracen would be ready just in time for the film festival. This year, Sam would have one of the most impressive backgrounds on the Riviera to conduct his business.

The stonemasons' wives had baked pizzas and prepared huge bowls of chopped tomatoes, olives, and onion, marinated cucumber, walnuts, and lamb's-foot lettuce—all tossed in the local salad dressing that used sesame oil instead of olive. Champagne and Provençal *vin rosé* had been opened, and the homemade lemonade was pressed from local lemons.

Elinor had enjoyed every minute of the restoration. Her French architect had strengthened the structure and roof beams, then renewed the tiles on roof and terrace. He tore out the foul-smelling bathroom and the kitchen, which consisted only of a sink with a cold tap, and installed a new kitchen and many bathrooms. All peeling wallpaper was scraped off, and the walls and ceilings were plastered creamy-white magnolia. Windows were replaced, woodwork painted, and floors polished. The new electrical system provided indirect lighting, so the walls and ceilings glowed.

While this work was in progress, Elinor and Buzz visited the auction houses of Nice, Toulon, and Draguignan. They also frequented antique shops off the beaten track, in the hills, where they purchased splendid beds, fruitwood tables, armoires, and charming antique chairs; modern sofas were ordered from Nice. The village dressmaker, Madame Annette, sewed all the curtains, made of cream linen, after Elinor purchased four bales at a Toulon auction.

During the restoration work, Elinor and Buzz stayed alternately at the Hotel de Provence and the Fountain Hotel; fierce rivals, they faced each other across the Place de la République. The Provence was run by a matriarch of ninety-three, Madame Sartour, and her enormous family. The Fountain was run by a male couple, Americans, known as *les pédés*. When the Fountain hired a chic Paris decorator to install soft lighting and cover the walls in *toiles de Jouy,* the Provence didn't bother to change its unflattering fluorescent lighting but installed a swimming pool. The Fountain retaliated by moving four-poster beds into all the best suites, whereupon the Provence announced Saturday evening barbecues . . .

Now, content with the results of her building upheaval, Elinor leaned against the terrace balustrade and looked up at the chateau. The newly painted white shutters were faintly tinged with pink, a blush applied by the still-golden evening sky.

Seeing her pleased expression, Buzz asked, "What do you like best about it, Nell?"

To Buzz's surprise, Elinor did not pick the spectacular view, or the silver four-poster bed that had once belonged to a Spanish princess, or the elevator that plunged three hundred feet down to the beach.

Elinor slowly smiled. "I like to think that Billy would be proud of me."

Buzz stared at Elinor; she knew that look on her friend's face. Elinor was playing one of her own heroines. This place was like one of the stately homes in her novels; here in Saracen, Elinor could live in the sort of imaginary world she created for her readers—a world she had actually come to believe in, where she no longer separated reality from fantasy, fact from fiction. Part of Elinor's fantasy was the myth of Billy O'Dare, the perfect romantic lover; in her mind, she had re-created him as a strong, dependable hero, forgetting his weaknesses, his excesses, and his ill-treatment of her.

Buzz turned for a moment and looked at her friend. They had known each other so long, and still Elinor amazed her. Billy! How she clung to his memory, reinventing him still, after all these years. Buzz knew there was no point in once again trying to remind Nell of the true nature behind Billy O'Dare's easy and intoxicating charm. He had been the one man she truly loved, and there would never be another.

"I wonder . . . I wonder what he would say if he knew I had bought a castle for myself," Elinor said.

Buzz suspected that Billy would laugh and say, "You could buy Buckingham Palace, old girl, but you won't change Marjorie's opinion of you."

Buzz said, "I'm sure Billy would be proud of you, Nell."

MONDAY, 12 OCTOBER 1964

Miranda, her long flaming hair pulled behind a navy Alice band, wore a navy dress with a white organdy Pierrot collar for the first executive meeting in her new sales office—a converted warehouse off Oxford Street, found by Mike. Sitting at the head of her egg-shaped, white plastic boardroom table, she was surrounded by her male executives. Adam sat on Miranda's right; she had recently persuaded him to join her board as a part-time director.

Adam had appeared reluctant to accept this appointment and had pleaded other commitments, but he had finally capitulated after Miranda agreed that, should KITS ever go public, she would sell Adam fifteen percent of the total issued shares, at a nominal sale price of £15,000. Miranda considered this share option a minor concession compared to the advantage of having the experienced Adam on a board composed of people who were young, enthusiastic, and talented but had never before been directors of a company. Adam made Miranda feel safe.

For a brief moment, Miranda wished that her two sisters could see her, sitting at the head of her boardroom table while everyone listened to her and took notes of what she said. No longer was she the littlest sister, to whom no one paid any attention. She was an emerging star of the business world.

Miranda said, "The first item on our agenda is the acquisition of

Framwells." This was an ailing chain of small London tobacconist shops, which had not yet been put on the market. KITS financial resources, already stretched to their limit, would be subjected to even greater strain should KITS acquire Framwells. But they could not risk this unique chain falling into the hands of a rival. So the board voted to buy Framwells. It would be expensive, but worth it.

All further items on the agenda were briskly agreed upon, until the final item, a hosiery manufacturer's offer of a licensing deal, which caused argument.

Adam spoke persuasively in favor of the deal. "We would get an assured income for lending the KITS name and logo and publicly endorsing the product. All *you* have to do, Miranda, is make a few public appearances wearing their tights: *they* then have a public image, while *we* have a decent profit margin without working for it."

Linda Grey nodded; she was no longer Miranda's assisstant, but publicity manager. "We've built up a very clear image of a young, smart, intelligent woman who wants sophisticated merchandise at reasonable prices, and we project that image through Miranda herself. Customers buy her products because they see her on TV and read about her in the papers. They see Miranda as glamorous, fashionable, and giving good value. We have a high-profile managing director who projects a household name."

"Yes, that's our asset, and we're not fully exploiting it," Adam said.

Miranda wrinkled her forehead. "You said the same sort of thing about franchising. I know this *sounds* like money for nothing, but that's what's worrying me."

Linda said, "If anything's wrong with the product, the manufacturer won't get blamed by the customer—KITS will."

"And that dissatisfied customer won't only stop buying the tights— she'll also stop buying KITS cosmetics," Miranda said. She added, firmly, "We can *never* be sure that goods sold under our name are up to standard if they're manufactured by somebody else—because we don't control the quality."

Adam smiled. "Would you agree, theoretically, that it *is* a good idea to use our name to sell other goods if we *can* control the quality of those goods?"

Looking puzzled, Miranda nodded.

"We employ full-time marketing experts because that's cheaper than using consultants, and it gives us more control," Adam said. "So we have a first-class, underemployed marketing division."

"That's unavoidable, until we can afford to expand," Miranda said defensively.

Adam smiled again. "Then why don't we set up an acquisitions office, to buy old-fashioned firms that are solidly established but getting nowhere because they have no clear marketing image, so nobody wants to buy their products? Instead of licensing tights, why don't we buy some ailing stocking firm—such as Daintyfeet—and put our name on them?"

The financial director, Ned Sinclair, threw up his thin hands in protest. "You're suggesting that we turn KITS into a holding company!"

"Why not?" Adam said.

"We'd be running before we can walk!" Ned objected.

"But it's boom time," Linda said slowly. "And very few manufacturers understand what's happening in fashion right now."

Adam nodded. "Exactly. The Youthquake."

Everyone started to talk at once.

Two weeks later, the board of KITS decided that the holding company project would be pursued, provided adequate financing could be arranged. The new company would be called SUPPLYKITS, to avoid confusion with KITS.

Adam's responsibility as commercial director would be the development of SUPPLYKITS. He would seek small companies with a weak image, which needed design, publicity, and marketing services but had good management staff. There was one essential ingredient to every potential company: it had to generate cash, in order to provide SUPPLYKITS with a steady income, with which to repay the bank loan necessary for its acquisition.

"Adam, d'you think you'll be able to do all this while working part-time?" Miranda asked worriedly as the two of them sat in the boardroom after the office had closed.

"I don't see why not," Adam said, pouring Dom Perignon for both of them. "Mike finds the companies and Ned produces the figures I need from their own accounts."

"Mike's last bill was pretty high."

"The contract I drew up specifies that Mike gets two percent, but it doesn't specify *when*."

"You mean . . ."

"Legally, we could wait a thousand years before paying it."

Miranda said sharply, "If I buy somebody's services, I want to pay for them."

"Business is business," Adam said. "My little brother should have checked out his contract with a lawyer." He topped up her glass. "Relax, Miranda. Business isn't a life-or-death matter—it's a sort of game, a huge gamble; it's exciting, and that's something you seem to have forgotten lately."

"I worry that the stakes are getting so high, so fast."

"That's what's exciting!" Adam said, his eyes shining.

"Perhaps it's getting *too* exciting for me," Miranda suggested. She noticed that Adam had relaxed the careful reserve with which he normally treated her.

"There's no such thing as too much excitement." Adam grinned. "Especially not when you're around, Miranda. You create it, you know."

Surprised, Miranda looked at Adam's handsome face. Was he really flirting with her? Was she reading an invitation in those dancing brown eyes? Did she want to?

Miranda remembered the painful calf love she had felt for Adam long ago in St.-Tropez, when she was a vulnerable, flat-chested school-girl. She remembered Adam's perfunctory politeness, and her misery.

"You didn't always think that," she said.

"I do now." Adam leaned toward her.

Swiftly Miranda told herself that she couldn't afford to get emotionally involved with Adam: he was too important to her business. Suppose they had an affair and then broke up—perhaps he would want to leave the business. She couldn't yet manage without Adam's calm reassurance, Adam's authoritative decisions, his brushing aside of anxiety, his strength of purpose. She could only just manage *with* him.

Miranda stood up. She wasn't going to mess up her new career.

FRIDAY, 25 DECEMBER 1964

By Christmas, Elinor and Buzz had settled down in Saracen. The only major change in Elinor's work routine had been that she now flew to London to do her research instead of traveling by train from Wiltshire. Buzz supervised three bilingual secretaries, who came daily from Nice to deal with correspondence, clean-type Elinor's manuscripts, send them to relevant experts for checking, then dispatch them to the dynamic American agent who had sold Elinor's work around the world since Joe Grant's death.

Early on Christmas morning, Elinor's bedroom door burst open. As always, Elinor's heart looped the loop as two-year-old Josh appeared in Donald Duck pajamas. The child's eager blue eyes reminded her so of Billy.

Frantic with excitement, Josh showed Elinor the contents of the knobbly red stocking that he dragged behind him.

Sitting up in bed, wearing a purple paper crown and pulling a cracker with Josh, Elinor felt happy and replete. She wanted nothing more from life: all the people she loved were gathered today under this ancient roof. Sam, Clare, and Josh had flown from California, Annabel and Scott from New York, Miranda and the Grant boys from London.

Later, wearing dressing gowns, everyone ate a champagne breakfast in the cream-tented pavilion by the swimming pool, which was used as an outdoor dining room. Josh ate seven tangerines and raced around the terraces on his new French tricycle—a present from Father Christmas.

Sam gave Clare a gold neck chain; she gave him a primitive Greek painting of a fishing boat. Annabel gave Scott a set of Mark Cross luggage; he gave her a green leather Gucci jewel case. Miranda watched her two sisters hug their husbands and suddenly wished again that she hadn't broken up with Angus. But it wouldn't have worked.

Elinor murmured to Buzz, "It's wonderful to see the girls together again, so loving, so loyal, so happy and secure!"

Buzz smiled. "They're making as much noise as ever they did. You'd think they was teenagers again." Since the arrival of the sisters, their conversation, which consisted of half-sentences and puzzling allusions, had been constantly interrupted by giggles and shrieks of laughter.

"And the men seem to like each other." Elinor nodded with satisfaction. "*Everything* is going well!"

Standing beside Miranda at the buffet table, Adam whispered, "Annabel's put on weight, hasn't she?"

"I always thought she was too thin," Miranda said without conviction.

"Well, she isn't now."

Annabel, who was sitting with Clare by the pool, was aware of her weight problem. When her bookings started to slide, Mrs. Bates had crisply told her to lose twenty pounds and given her the telephone number of New York's smartest slimming doctor. With great effort, Annabel had shed three pounds.

"I love your jewel box," Clare said cheerfully.

"I chose it myself. If I hadn't, Scott would have sent a secretary out to buy something for me."

Surprised, Clare said, "Scott must be . . . very busy."

"Nobody need be too busy to buy his wife a Christmas present. Scott isn't interested in me anymore."

"Don't be silly, Annabel. He's here with you, isn't he?" Clare laughed. "After six years, you can't expect the same nonstop attention that you had as a bride—even though you're supposed to be one of the world's most beautiful women."

"I get *no* attention!"

"Rubbish. Men fall at your feet and you flirt with everyone in sight—even Adam."

"I mean that Scott ignores me—not here, of course, in front of you all. If I flirt, it's only to reassure myself that *other* men still find me attractive."

"Cool it," Clare said curtly. "Remember, it's Christmas." She didn't want to think about marital flirtation. Sam had resumed his disguise of masculine invulnerability as soon as they returned to L.A. two summers ago, and Clare never again penetrated his armor or shared the loving warmth they had experienced when their minds, as well as their bodies, were joined on the darkened sands of Cannes.

Clare had started to suspect that Sam was a compulsive womanizer; she noticed the too-casual way certain women spoke to him at parties and the way his black eyes twinkled when they did so. She told herself that Sam's affairs were probably not much more than one-night stands, and that adultery was almost unavoidable in his business, but such rationalization did not assuage her sadness.

Beyond the pool, Mike strolled to the terrace balustrade, against which Adam leaned to watch a speedboat skip across the blue water. "Shall we take a boat out after lunch? Just you and me? Get away from Elinor's family set piece?"

Adam said cheerfully, "If you've got a message for me, Mike, tell me now. No need to go miles out to sea for privacy."

Mike hesitated. "You're in trouble if you can't pay back your debts by the end of the year." He paused again. "You know what I mean by trouble. This time I can't do anything."

"You can make sure Miranda doesn't hear about it," Adam said crisply. "And don't worry. I'll fix it. I always do, don't I?"

"They all say that. Until the day they *can't* fix it."

"Ease up, Mike. Remember, we're here to have fun. Okay, this afternoon we'll sneak away on the speedboat, escape from Elinor's brood."

"Nothing wrong with the O'Dares," Mike said, "except they pick god-awful men."

Adam nodded. "I don't mind Sam, but Scott is unbelievably vapid—only interested in his job." Scott seemed incapable even of playing Monopoly without being interrupted by calls from his New York office.

Mike said, "I prefer Scott to Mr. High-Powered Hollywood. Can't think what Clare sees in him."

"Maybe the father she never had. She fell for his air of assurance," Adam said.

Standing together at the far side of the pool, Scott and Sam, both in bathing shorts, watched the Grant brothers.

Scott said, "I can't think what these women see in that insufferable couple of snobs. And they both talk like faggots."

"Nah, they're just British," Sam said. "Stand up when a woman walks in, leap around to pull chairs out—they all behave like footmen in a costume picture. I don't mind Mike, but Adam's a royal pain, and he behaves as if he owns everything in sight."

Later, as they dressed for lunch in their bedroom, Sam looked at the maroon Cartier traveling clock that Adam had given Clare for Christmas and said, "Why's he so generous to you?"

Clare laughed. "Surely you're not jealous of Adam? Can you hook my back up, please?"

"Of course I'm not jealous of that pompous legal asshole. But I can't think why Elinor invited him for Christmas."

"Because Adam is almost family, and his parents are both dead. And Gran would be lost without Adam—she's got into the habit of relying on him."

Sam shrugged his shoulders. "Some lawyers can be a very expensive habit."

In the late afternoon, after a traditional English Christmas dinner had been served in the dining room, Elinor listened happily to the shrieks of laughter around the table. She gazed with satisfaction across the oak refectory table to Buzz, with whom she had shared so many Christmases; what a pity it was that Joe couldn't see his sons, so handsome in their light suits and Christmas-gift ties. How wonderful it was to see them and her girls together again—still happy, still friends after all these years, and all reunited under one roof.

She was pleased that the girls had bothered to dress up, although their clothes were a little startling. Miranda wore a cream lace trouser suit over a nude body stocking; Annabel wore a white minidress and a bonnet of daisies tied with satin ribbons beneath her chin; Clare wore a sleeveless jumpsuit of scarlet linen edged with mustard. Buzz wore a Pucci blouse-and-pants outfit in turquoise silk, which is what she had worn every Christmas Day for the past seven years, after inheriting it from Elinor, for whom the outfit had been a little too tight.

How lucky she was, Elinor thought, gazing around at all the

beloved faces. Her heart felt settled when they were all together, in a way that it had not done since her last granddaughter left home. She decided to make a little speech and tapped the table. Slowly the happy chatter subsided.

Elinor lifted her glass of champagne, but found herself unable to speak as happiness welled up from her heart. She smiled and said, "To our happy family."

Her words were echoed around the table as everyone raised a glass.

BOOK·3

Chapter · 15

MONDAY, 19 JULY 1965

From her office window, in the west corner of the chateau, Buzz could see what was happening anywhere on the two main terraces. Now, she stared out only at empty space shadowed by the late afternoon sun. Soon, thank God, things would return to normal. Elinor would be sitting out there again, and they'd be having their usual glass of champagne before lunch. The days of anxiety and concern were almost over; Elinor's recovery would, of course, be slow, but that didn't matter. Buzz had warned Clare that there were to be no more arguments, and now all Elinor had to do was get well.

Buzz's office was briskly efficient; she did not care to spend one second more than necessary in it, and nothing was superfluous in the sparsely furnished room. It held filing cabinets, bookshelves, and a desk upon which an unused I.B.M. typewriter crouched like a gray electronic cat. Behind the desk stood a sturdy swivel chair. In front of it were two nineteenth-century metal conservatory chairs for visitors; they were not very comfortable: Buzz didn't like people to stay too long.

Buzz looked at her watch. If Adam didn't arrive soon, he'd be late for the telephone calls he had booked. She opened the door and gazed down a splendid vista of reception rooms that opened out one into the next, which Buzz had learned was typical of grand French houses. Adam appeared in the distance; he hurried through the bar, the summer salon, and the television room before he finally reached the privacy of Buzz's office, which contained the only telephone that did not have extensions all over the chateau. Buzz left the room.

An aggressive French operator informed Adam that his first call had been delayed; as he waited impatiently, he glanced at the bookcases, which held first editions of all Elinor's books. Adam swiftly read the titles, most of which contained romantic words like "love," "heart," "arrow," "passionate," "fire," "dream," "kiss," and "enchanted."

Dream of the Heart, Passionate Fire, and *Fire of the Heart* in particular caught his eye.

Unlike many men, Adam did not regard Elinor's books as a subject for jokes. He remembered a conversation he'd once had with his brother, who had teased him about his interest in the works of Elinor Dove. With an earnestness that had surprised Mike, Adam had responded forcefully. "You're wrong Mike. Leave it to the intellectuals to deride romance novels. Men like you and I can learn from them. They are our guidebooks to what women want. Often a woman reads them because they supply what's lacking in her relationship; she doesn't yearn just for sex, or even for love—she also needs romance. And so does a man, or at least he does when he first falls in love, when he's too caught up to pay any attention to what other fellows think. Then gradually, when reality starts to intrude again, he gets embarrassed about the sensitivity he's shown, and so he gradually pushes it away, to deny it's even part of his nature. It's a trap we all fall into, something I don't see changing soon. And until it does, Mike, until men and women are equal partners in romance, men who understand how women—particularly married women—feel about romance will always be able to twist them around their little fingers."

Adam could truthfully tell Elinor that he read every word she wrote and found her books absorbing. This was because he used them as guidebooks. He coldly worked out what each of his women wanted, and then coldly gave it to her. And it worked. Given this level of knowledge, almost any man could become successful at seduction.

Adam answered the telephone on the first ring. "Mike? Great to hear from you. How's the new bike? . . . How do I know? Because you *always* have a new bike."

In London, Mike laughed. "It's a rather nifty Ducati. Three fifty with single, overhead cam. Handles very well, but a bit unreliable. I've had trouble twice and she's only three weeks old." His voice became serious. "How's Elinor?"

"Much better. No more talk about scattering her ashes over the Mediterranean by moonlight. She'll soon be well enough to make her will."

"Does that matter now?"

"Not now, but it will someday, and I'm not risking this scene again."

"I'm so glad she's better," Mike said. "D'you remember how great she was to us when we were kids? She lent me the money to get my second bike—that Triumph Speed Twin: it had a lot of poke for the size. When I went to repay Elinor, she wouldn't accept the money."

"Is that why you wanted to speak to me urgently? To discuss Elinor's health?"

"Unfortunately not," Mike said. "I called to tell you that you have to pay Toby Sutch, and fast."

After a pause, Adam said, "I'll talk to Giles."

"*He* can't lend you money. As of last Wednesday, Giles Milroy-Browne is doing seven years in an open prison, for embezzlement."

"Toby's waited longer than this before."

"Exactly. He's running short of patience. I can't fix it, Adam. Remember, Toby has already paid your *French* gambling debts." Mike wished to God that when Adam went to the south of France, he would stay on the beach like everyone else.

"I don't know what I'd do without you, Mike," Adam said winningly. "Just keep Toby off my back for a few more days. Let him think that Elinor may go at any minute. Imply that I might soon have funds."

"I can't do that. . . . I don't know how you're going to get it, but you know how deep the shit will be if you don't produce at least a hundred thousand pounds . . ."

After replacing the receiver, Adam stared through the French windows to the terrace, drumming his fingers on the desk. He tugged his hair over his left eye, then jerked his head to flip it back: a gesture that revealed his anxiety. He smoked a cigarette, sucking hard at it. Finally he called Johnny Briar, a member of his insurance syndicate at Lloyds.

"What's the news? It can't get much worse, old boy," Johnny said. "We've had unbelievable bad luck. We seem to be the only syndicate that's involved in all three natural disasters. American Insurance Services have just released final estimates on the Chile earthquake. Of course, we reinsured for a cut of the premiums, but we'll still stand to lose well over sixteen million dollars. No final figures yet on the American tornado."

"And the tidal wave in Pakistan?"

"They reckon it killed sixteen thousand people."

Eventually Adam asked, "How soon will we know our final losses?"

"It looks like an open year. No money will be paid to members for three years," Johnny said, "and probably a further call after that. Frankly, this'll clean me out. I'll have to sell the house."

Adam cursed. The famous Lloyds unlimited liability probably meant that Adam would also be declared bankrupt. "How long will they wait for payment?"

"You know Lloyds don't wait, old boy. It's cash on the nail as soon as the arbitrators reach a settlement—the Lloyds reputation stands on that." Johnny added, "It's not worth messing with Lloyds, Adam, you know it isn't: no one would ever touch you again—Lloyds would see to that."

Adam's next call was to Ned Sinclair, financial director of SUP-PLYKITS. With an effort, Adam steadied his voice. "Ned? I want you to take another look at that new Carefree proposal—the duty-free airport shops. I know they're asking more than we want to pay, but if we can assemble a package of cash, stock options, and newly issued shares as a good inducement, I think we'll convince the key manager and he'll persuade the others to sell. So talk to him, see what he wants, then stitch something together for next week."

"I'm already working on it," Sinclair said cheerfully.

Adam sighed as he replaced the telephone receiver. Again he ran his left hand through his hair, but this time he felt a tingle of anticipation. There *was* always something around the corner if you didn't lose your head. He had a definite feeling of success about the Carefree deal. And there were plenty more deals.

And perhaps it was time to play the trump card up his sleeve. He'd never be in a better position to do it. Perhaps it was time for a little more reinsurance.

Annabel's call from Scott came through to Saracen just as dinner was announced. She raced upstairs to her apartment and threw herself on the bedcover, a Welsh patchwork quilt in a soft pattern of cream and pink.

Waiting for Scott to pick up the telephone, Annabel could visualize the scene at the TV station. She could clearly remember the first day that Scott had shown her around, could remember being impressed by the overwhelming glamour of it all. From that day, Annabel had worshiped him. She sometimes felt that were Scott not sitting at the studio news desk, face made up and hair sprayed, ready to roll and clearly in control—why, then the news might never happen.

Eventually Scott's voice came through faintly on the line. "Angel, you aren't going to like this one bit, but you asked the agency to call me as soon as Avanti decided. They don't want to renew your contract."

Annabel suddenly felt that her mind was spiraling out of control. Her forehead felt clammy and her hands began to shake. She found it difficult to swallow. Her heart was thumping so loudly that she wondered for a fleeting second whether Scott could hear it. Her rib cage seemed too small and she panted for air. She also felt a sudden, massive drop in the pit of her stomach, the place where her self-confidence dwelled.

"Annabel? Are you still there?" Thousands of miles away, Scott heard a gulp. He said reassuringly, "Angel, it isn't the end of the world."

"It is for me," Annabel said.

• • •

Exhausted by anxiety and emotion, Clare had decided to go to bed early. In the thirty-foot-long, dark-paneled bedroom, she lay upon the Jacobean four-poster bed and gazed up at the crimson brocade canopy. Stripped down to her petticoat, she felt too tired to undress further. She wished that someone would invent a button that you pressed, and *shazam!*—you were tucked in bed, washed and with your teeth brushed. Languidly she turned her head to the west-facing windows, staring out at the neighboring mountain high above the hill upon which Saracen was built.

Again Clare wondered if she had gone a bit too far, speaking so negatively about Gran's novels, and being so emphatically against the trust.

Hearing a knock, she called, "Come in."

Slowly the door opened.

In the doorway was the craggy outline of her husband. Sam looked sheepish and apologetic.

For one glad moment, Clare wanted to rush to him, put her head against his big chest, feel his strong hands stroking her back, and let Sam do all the worrying for her. But she remembered the sight of him in bed with that would-be starlet and fought the impulse, staring angrily at him instead. "What are *you* doing here?"

"I came as soon as I heard that Elinor was . . . ill. It was in the *Tribune* a couple of days ago. I came to see if you needed me. And if Elinor is going, I want to say goodbye."

"Very touching, but Gran is getting better. You needn't have come."

"I know. Adam already told me. He was about as welcoming as you are. Why's he here if she's recovering?"

"Adam has every right to be here," Clare said pointedly. "He's been our family lawyer for years."

"I'm not the only one who doesn't trust the devious bastard. Buzz doesn't like him," Sam said, "and she is a lady with a very reliable built-in shit detector."

"Adam isn't Gran's only lawyer," Clare retorted. "There's another chap, Paul Littlejohn."

"From the same firm? Then he's probably under Adam's thumb."

Suddenly Clare realized why Sam had come, and cried scornfully, "*You* can't criticize Adam for being devious! I suppose *you* are straightforward? You've just hurtled halfway round the world *only* to say goodbye to your estranged wife's grandmother! How touching!"

Sam nodded. "Of course, I'd also like to see Josh."

"Not now. He's asleep!"

"I know. I was told by a French sourpuss nurse in the hall; she's clearly had charisma bypass surgery."

"You should see the day nurses!" Then Clare was vexed that he'd almost made her laugh. She stiffened as Sam shut the door and took two steps toward her.

Hopefully Sam said, "I also want to see *you.*" He advanced, a dark, disturbing masculine presence. Each time Sam took a step forward, Clare took a step backward, toward the windows.

"You're seeing me now!" she said. "I haven't changed much in four weeks."

"I have." Sam took another step.

"That contrite line won't work anymore, Sam." Clare's voice was cold. Retreating until she bumped into a Spanish walnut table that stood before a window, she put her arms back to lean on the table, then decided that her position might look inviting, folded her arms, and scowled at Sam. "I have enough to worry about," she said crossly. "Please *leave,* Sam! You can come back and see Josh in the morning—but don't think you can march in here and wheedle your way back into my heart in half an hour—not this time!"

"Of course I know I can't change things in half an hour. I've had four weeks to realize what a stupid bastard I've been," Sam said.

Clare cried, "You don't want a real relationship, you only want ego-boosting, pseudo relationships!"

"I admit that's what it has been like in the past."

"I've had *enough!*" Clare stormed. "*You* think that if I don't know about your affairs, it can't disturb our relationship. That it doesn't matter if you cheat on your wife, so long as she doesn't find out. But it *does* matter because our relationship becomes dishonest. Even if *I* don't know it, *you* do, and that changes *your* attitude to me."

"What the hell do you mean by that?" Sam seemed genuinely perplexed.

"You invent, or goad me into, some failing to give *you* cause for complaint, so that you can then screw around with a clear conscience. Well, I've had enough of being the wife who doesn't understand you! Now I *do* understand you. And I can't stand your treachery and deceit! I can't stand that parody of a happy life in that parody of a place."

"No more affairs, I promise."

"*It's no use,* Sam. We both know that history will only repeat itself. You want to nibble every biscuit in the tin, and nothing will ever change you! I'm *never* going to forget what I saw—or stop wondering whether it's happening again."

Sam's mind quickly returned to the last time he had seen Clare, when she had returned early from the beach to find Sam in their bed, and not alone. Clare had recognized the girl—the would-be actress daughter of a neighbor who had been kind to Clare when the Shapiros first moved in.

Under Clare's glare, the frightened girl had shrunk against the headboard, her knees drawn up to hide her slim, naked body. Clare continued to stare until the girl scuttled from the bedroom to the patio; there, she hesitated, remembering her nakedness. Desperate, she cast one backward glance at Clare, then fled.

Hairy and naked, Sam had crouched on the bed feeling exposed and helpless. Then Sam had thrown her a pleading look, like a naughty little boy caught with his finger in the jam pot.

Finally Clare had screamed, "I've had enough of these scenes." Without being told, Sam knew at that moment that Clare would leave him. This time she would fling no bitter accusations or black lingerie at him. As he stared at the torment, fury, and despair in her face, he knew that Clare would not forgive him. He also knew that this disastrous episode was entirely his own fault and could easily have been avoided. After all, he could have taken the girl someplace else.

Now Sam looked at his wife as she stood at the end of the long, dark paneled bedroom, her back to the window, beyond which olive trees rustled in a hot breeze. Leaning against the walnut table, Clare felt her face tighten as she, too, relived that painful scene. Slowly she said, "I hate to admit this, but what hurt as much as the treachery was the humiliation. My self-esteem disappeared and I felt worthless, although I told myself that I was still an attractive woman, that there was no need to feel sexually inadequate."

"So it's the sex thing again!" Sam said with exasperation. "I thought we'd settled that!"

"It's not sex that's the problem, it's what you demonstrate during sex!" Clare's cry was from the heart. "A sexual relationship isn't separated from the rest of reality, Sam. It never once occurred to you that *you* might be an ignorant, selfish, lousy lover. It was arrogant of you to assume that *I* was inadequate! Deep down, you *still* don't think I'm a normal woman! You're *still* afraid of any attack on your divine male right to know everything there is to know about sex."

Sam realized that, for the first time, Clare was yelling at him instead of building up a silent volcano of resentment. He wasn't sure what to do: He didn't want to go over all that again. On the other hand, Clare was finally able to express her anger clearly to the person who had caused it.

Sam knew better than to interrupt her flow.

". . . And while we're talking about the man's divine right to know, little babies are *born* knowing all they need to know about love: they're unself-conscious, they can communicate, and their first experience—

sucking—is a sensual one! But by the time a baby boy grows up, his head has been stuffed with myths and taboos, and the idea that in sexual matters, *the man always knows best!*"

Sam looked suitably unsure.

Clare paused, then shook her head wearily. "There's no point in this, Sam. You've never listened to the things I say, and even when something is an obvious fact, you never quite seem to believe me, or to trust me. You're too trapped in your own ego to be able to hear or to understand."

"They should teach a guy these things at school," Sam said lamely, as he was clearly expected to make some response. "Please believe me, Clare, I'll do anything to get you back."

"Exactly *what* do you want to get back?" Clare asked.

"My wife and my son," Sam said firmly.

"And of course, your career?"

"Yes." Sam's last movie, *Mainsail*, had performed unimpressively.

"So at *last* we have the truth!" Clare shouted. "You turned up here because you thought I was about to inherit enough money to stage your movie comeback!"

"That isn't fair, Clare. Sure, I could use any investment that's floating around. Who can't? I've got an option on a terrific screenplay. It's called 'Voyage to the Moon.' It's about—"

"Get out!"

Sam did not retreat. "You say that you want total honesty from me, and then you throw me out when you get it! You know movies always came first in my life until I met you. Now they come second, but I'll admit it's a close second."

Clare wondered why she felt so hurt, when she'd always known the truth. Sam was a movie creature, first and foremost. He might say now that he put his wife and child first; he might even think it. But the fact was that ninety-nine percent of his energy, his concentration, his time, and his money was devoted to his business. His family got what was left.

Sam looked again at the dark smudges of exhaustion under Clare's eyes. He saw how thin she'd become in only four weeks. He longed to take her in his arms, but she swiftly dodged around the table to the window so that the Spanish table was a barrier between them.

"Get out," Clare said again.

The next morning, Buzz sat on a pale blue chair before the window in Elinor's bedroom. "Only one visitor at a time, the doctor said," Buzz reminded her firmly. "And keep it short. Remember, you didn't feel too good yesterday. Ten minutes each girl and not a second more! You'll see Miranda first, then Annabel."

"And Clare?" Elinor asked.

"Clare's seeing Sam and Josh off for a day on the speedboat. She'll be along later."

The day nurse pulled down the cream window blinds against the morning sun as Miranda entered.

Elinor smiled as she said, "Hello, darling." She had trouble pronouncing the words. She asked anxiously, "Can you hear me properly, Miranda?"

"Of course she can," Buzz said. "You sound as if you've got a bit of a toothache, that's all."

After ten minutes of understandably strained, cheerful chat, Buzz jerked her head toward the door and Miranda quietly disappeared. She was replaced by Annabel, who had clearly been crying.

As she talked, Annabel picked up a little box from the bedside table; it was an antique ebony snuffbox, the lid inlaid with a geometric pattern of tortoiseshell and ivory.

"That was the first antique I ever bought," Elinor said. "Cost tuppence from a junk barrow in Earls Court Road. Take it now, dear child, as a gift."

Buzz said sharply, "Annabel! Put that back! You ain't dying, Nell, and I won't have you behaving as if you was."

Annabel jumped and replaced the little box. "Sorry. I was only fiddling with it." She had wanted to disguise her trembling hands: she was not about to explain to her sick grandmother the reason for her fright, for the panic that rose within her chest.

After Annabel left, Elinor whispered to Buzz, "I want to see Clare *alone*."

"Not on your life," said Buzz. "I'm sticking to you, close as a limpet. You ain't going to overdo it today, my girl. *Nobody* is going to see you alone."

"Please, Buzz," Elinor pleaded. "I want to ask her to go back to Sam."

Buzz hesitated, knowing that Clare would never discuss this in her presence. Reluctantly she nodded. "Don't forget, I'll be sitting next door in the library with my stopwatch."

She marched past Elinor's bed into the library; in front of the large window that overlooked the sea was the wooden kitchen table upon which Elinor had written *Deadly Fortune* and her every book since.

From the window, Buzz could see Clare sunning herself on the terrace below. "Okay, Clare, you can come up now," she yelled.

Two minutes later, Clare stood at her grandmother's bedside; after a sleepless night, she looked almost as pale and exhausted as Elinor.

Elinor said, "I saw Sam for a few minutes, darling. He told me you'd had a serious tiff, but he hopes to persuade you to return to L.A."

Clare looked carefully at Elinor. "Sam only tells people what suits him, Gran."

"He's apparently just flown halfway round the world to tell you he loves you."

"Sam can certainly *act* the devoted husband," Clare said sourly. "But if he's flown halfway round the world to tell me he loves me, then why *didn't* he tell me he loves me?"

"Any Don Juan can *say* he loves you." Elinor attempted a smile as she quoted what Buzz had so often told the girls in years past. "You have to watch what Sam does, not what he says. If he gets up in the middle of the night to fetch you a glass of water, then he loves you."

"A Busby Berkeley lineup in front of his bed couldn't wake Sam in the middle of the night," Clare said. "Gran, I didn't want to tell you, especially now, but you must understand. He . . . was with somebody else. That's why I left."

"She probably threw herself at him. A little tart. Dearest girl, I've told you before, you mustn't let a little bit of fluff spoil your marriage."

"You know, she was only *one* of them," Clare said, vexed. It was typical of Sam's chutzpah to get his story in first, to gain sympathy and support, to get Gran on his team.

Reluctantly Elinor said, "I had the same problem with Daddy Billy, but in my day, wives had to put up with that sort of thing. Please be patient, darling, for Josh's sake as well as your own. Don't throw away your marriage because Sam is giving you trouble. *All* men give trouble."

Clare said indignantly, "I really don't want to discuss it, Gran, but I don't see why I should put up with my husband's adulteries just because you did—so please don't try to force me!"

"After six years of marriage, Clare, you can't expect the same relationship as on your wedding day."

"Of course I don't expect the same relationship!" Clare exclaimed. What she *had* expected was a loving and trusting relationship based on a realistic assessment of each other's virtues and faults.

"Being in love . . ." Elinor dreamily remembered what it was like to feel that your lover possessed all the wonderful qualities you wanted, before you realized that he didn't possess them, and that perhaps you had forced those qualities on him in the first place. She shook her head sadly. "Being in love isn't being married."

"Is that why you never write about marriage?" Clare inquired bitterly. "Only being in love?"

"There's no need for that tone of voice," Elinor said, clearly hurt.

"Being in love isn't a solution to every female problem!" Clare

cried. "I've never seen *that* spelled out in a women's magazine story, or a film, or . . . a novel."

Clare was prepared to do without the ups of being in love in return for never experiencing the downs. She never again wanted to experience the feeling of being out of control and dependent on someone else's approval, at someone else's mercy. She never again wanted to feel that someone else could send her to heaven or to hell. She never again wanted to experience that feeling which led women to do too much for, and demand too much from, a partner.

"Understandably, you're feeling cynical because of Sam's naughtiness. . . ."

"Gran, he's not some mischievous schoolboy." Last night, Sam had tried to manipulate Clare, and now her grandmother was trying to do the same thing on his behalf.

For the second time in twenty-four hours, Clare's indignation overcame her caution. Having come to terms with the failure of her marriage, she was trying to pick up the broken bits of her pride, glue them together, and get on with her life. She wished that people would not interfere, would leave her alone, especially people who didn't know all the facts.

"Why not try to look upon whatever happened as a little misdemeanor," Elinor persisted, "Sam *loves* you. You know he does. And love is important because you can't live without it, dear child: without love, you only exist."

"I'm not sure that *I* love Sam. And I *can* live without love! Lots of people do—nuns and lighthousemen, for a start," Clare raged. "*You* taught me that without a man, a woman's life is bleak, empty, and dangerous; *you* taught me that a woman isn't complete without a man. But I wonder if that's so. *I* felt inadequate *because* I was living with a man."

Elinor whispered, "Don't throw away your marriage, Clare. No woman wants to live without love and romance—that's what makes a woman feel transformed . . . excited . . . attractive . . . alive. That's what I've always tried to convey in my writing."

"Romance has a bad influence on reality," Clare said. "You encourage your readers to believe that one day their prince will come."

"What's wrong with that?"

"*What's wrong is that he won't!* He will only ever be a paper prince on a paper page! You should have shown your readers that there *isn't* a Prince Charming, so they won't feel disappointed and cheated if their prince turns into a frog, like mine did. The story Sam tells about the frog is sad because it's *true*. . . ."

"The story about the frog?"

"It's not as silly as it sounds. A frog asked a princess to take him to bed with her so that he could turn into a fairy prince. But when she woke up in the morning, the frog was *still* a frog. He croaked, 'Sorry to disappoint you, but princesses always fall for that line.' "

Elinor was silent as she allowed herself to see, for once, the soft and gentle cobweb of romance she had carefully woven around her life with Billy. Quietly she asked, "Is it so terrible to let an unhappy or humiliated woman forget, for a few hours, the problems that she will probably have to put up with for her whole life?" Elinor believed that her novels provided her readers with excitement, helped them to escape from insecurity and anxiety, frustration and drudgery, misery and sorrow, and of course, the boring daily routine of a life in which nothing was likely to change.

Clare sighed. "You shouldn't encourage your readers to think that their lives might turn out like your novels. You encourage them to turn to romance rather than face reality. And then they're at a disadvantage when they have to deal with real life problems." Her voice rose.

"Clare, you're getting overexcited." Elinor's own voice had weakened to a whisper. Clare suddenly noticed that Elinor's hands were gripping the bedclothes, betraying the emotion hidden by her quiet words. In trying to articulate what she felt so strongly, Clare had forgotten that she was talking to a very sick woman.

"I'm sorry, Gran. I hadn't planned to talk about this today. But you know it's what I've always thought. And it doesn't mean that I don't love you."

Elinor was not mollified. She said sharply, "My romantic novels enabled you girls to have a carefree life, the sort of life I wish I'd been able to give your father." Elinor waited for the apology she felt was due from Clare. After a few moments of uncomfortable silence, she said stubbornly, "If you denigrate my life's work, you shall not profit by it—unless you apologize to me, Clare."

With an effort, Clare spoke softly. "Gran, I don't want to denigrate your life's work. And I don't want to talk about money. That's not important, Gran—"

"Are you going to apologize to me or not?" Elinor demanded in a shaking voice. She thought that Clare was being contemptuous of all she had done for her. In fact, Clare had been going to say that Elinor's health was what was important at the moment.

Buzz strode in from the library. "Your ten minutes was up half an hour ago, Clare. And if I'd known there would be raised voices, I wouldn't have let you in here." Clare's visit with Elinor was abruptly terminated.

Furious at the angry words, Clare telephoned Thomas Cook in Nice for tickets to London. She wasn't going back to L.A., and she wasn't staying *here*. She would take Josh and Kathy, go to cozy, comfortable London, where she knew so many people, and there she would sort out her life.

Miranda, wearing a green bikini, sunned herself on the south terrace. As she listened to the faint smack of the sea on the rocks below, she thought again, regretfully, of Angus. She had to face the fact that she still missed him.

Although she'd seen a couple of nice men recently, when it came to the heavy breathing, Miranda found that she didn't want to be touched intimately by anyone she didn't know well. She didn't feel comfortable and safe with anybody but Angus: *he* hadn't tried to push her into bed at the first opportunity.

Three weeks earlier, her secretary had unexpectedly announced Mr. Angus Maclayne on line three. Miranda's heart had looped the loop as she happily accepted an invitation to lunch at Rules, his favorite restaurant. She hoped Angus wanted to rekindle their love affair, as she did.

Rules was decorated like a Victorian library; it smelled of superior malt whiskeys and very old leather. Miranda and Angus sat in a velvet-lined, crimson booth that reminded her of an old-fashioned first-class railway carriage. The Dickensian waiter flapped his napkin and advised with more truth than tact, "Shouldn't have turbot today, sir, although the salmon's passable." They ordered vichyssoise, followed by sea bass with fresh peas, and iced apricot soufflé afterward.

There had been no expression of undying love on the angular face she had come to love. Instead, Angus treated Miranda with distant respect, twitching his sandy eyebrows and speaking of inconsequential things—just as though she were his aunt . . . or maybe his stockbroker.

Once during lunch, she thought for a moment her hopes would be realized. Over the sea bass, Angus leaned across the white linen tablecloth, his lips close to her ear. "Miranda, I've been thinking a lot about you."

Miranda smiled encouragingly. She longed to hear him say, "God, how I've missed you! Let's get out of here, darling! I want to be alone with you!"

Angus said, "I'm worried that you're expanding too fast. You seem to be financing yourself by borrowing against your leases—leveraging in an expanding property market while interest rates are low."

Miranda felt her heart crash to the bottom of her rib cage. "What's wrong with that?" she muttered.

Angus carefully dissected his fish. "If this property boom suddenly collapses, or if the government decides to jack up the bank rate to curb consumer spending, then you might find your loans withdrawn, in which case you'd have a serious cash-flow problem on your hands."

"I appreciate your concern," Miranda said crossly.

"Higher bank interest may also mean a property slump," Angus added. "And then you'd have another big problem: the leases that act as your collateral would sink in value, so the banks would run scared and ask for fast repayment." Angus sipped his hock reflectively. "That sort of situation has been known to end in . . . bankruptcy."

"Thanks for warning me, but I have no intention of going bankrupt," Miranda replied coldly; she was too disappointed to enjoy the apricot soufflé. For the remainder of the meal, they chatted politely about business and exchanged city gossip. Afterward, they parted awkwardly on the pavement, each refusing the other's offer of a lift. Neither suggested a further meeting.

Angus, who admired guts and gumption, had missed the adventurous and spirited Miranda even more than he expected. He asked her out to lunch because he hoped that she had missed him. He had kept a discreet close watch on Miranda, who, he knew, had not been seriously involved with any other man since she broke off their engagement. Angus reckoned that fast business expansion was absorbing all her time and energy, which was why he had decided to take things one step at a time and discuss only business over luncheon; a business chat would avoid putting either of them in a rejecting position.

Sadly, Miranda, too, had clearly wished to discuss only business.

However, Angus did not intend to give up his pursuit of her; she fascinated him as no other woman had. Sometimes she was fiery, or she could be ice cool: qualities that intrigued the male in Angus, although they disturbed the businessman.

Chapter · 16

Miranda lay half asleep on a sofa in front of her sitting room window, which looked down on the Place de la République; from there, the road led to the distant perfume factory which Miranda wanted to buy. It had been built in the depression of 1870—when most villagers were out of work—by the Countess of Saracen, whose birthday was still celebrated, and a mass said for her soul in the local Church of St. Peter.

Miranda was startled by a knock on the door. She called, *"Entrez,"* and then said, "Oh, it's you, Adam."

"May I come in?"

"Sure. I've finished my siesta." Miranda yawned, stretched, and wriggled her bare, brown toes. She was wearing an emerald silk shirt and bikini.

"I see an old friend." Adam pointed to a framed cartoon, which he had given her the previous Christmas: a startled businessman gazed at a ghost; rising from his desk drawer, it said, "I am the spirit of old notes to yourself."

"You hit home with that one." Miranda yawned again. "What do you want?" She rubbed her stiff neck. "Big mistake to go to sleep on the couch."

"I can fix a stiff neck in no time," Adam offered. "I learned massage at the gym. Lie flat on the floor."

"Okay." Another yawn. "Shirt on or off?"

"Oh, keep it on."

Miranda lay on her stomach on the kilim rug; it was patterned in ocher and the same faded blue as Adam's flared jeans and shirt.

Adam knelt behind her head and started to massage her shoulders. After ten minutes, Miranda's neckache had vanished: she lay on the rug, her eyes shut; she felt boneless and sleepy.

Adam's voice was quiet and firm. "Your body is getting lighter and lighter. . . . You feel light enough to float on a cloud. . . . When I count to ten, you will relax . . ."

Miranda thought, Why, he's hypnotizing me, and then floated to sleep.

She woke to see Adam lying with his legs up, on the sofa, reading *Paris Match*. Miranda looked at her watch. "I've been asleep almost an hour. You did a great job. I feel as boneless as a squid."

"You were very tired," Adam said, "and we've all been worried about Elinor."

"Yes." Miranda's face crumpled and she started to weep. She rubbed both eyes, then winced as, too late, she remembered her contact lenses. She edged them out and scrambled to her feet. "I can't think why I'm crying."

"A natural reaction, after this strain and anxiety," Adam said reassuringly. He watched her, his head to one side, as if undecided. He stood up. He moved toward her. "Don't worry. I'm in control of everything. You can relax now."

Miranda sniffled. She felt the flimsy cotton of Adam's shirt against her as muscular arms wrapped around her. Her body relaxed and she leaned her head against his strong chest. She felt his hand beneath her shirt; his thumb pressed along her naked backbone all the way to the nape of her neck.

Each time Adam gently pressed against a vertebra, Miranda was pushed against his body. She could feel his flat, muscular strength: she could also feel his arousal as Adam kissed her firmly on the mouth.

Long ago, Miranda had realized that sexual involvement with Adam could only complicate her life, but she had been only half awake and off guard when he made his move. Rebelliously she thought, What the hell. Why shouldn't I forget business—just for once? And why shouldn't I do as I please with my own body?

In silence, Adam lifted her into his arms and carried her (five feet nine and no lightweight) onto the bed. Miranda's hair flamed against the pillow as she lay back with her eyes closed, thinking, Too late to stop him now. And I don't want to.

Almost motionless, she lay in a trance of sensuality, Adam's mouth against the soft skin of her breasts. He whispered, "Keep your eyes closed. You're not to *move*. Here, I'm in charge."

"But don't you want me to—"

"I want you to lie still and let me . . . love you."

Miranda felt a melting and tickling inside her stomach as if someone were stroking it with a feather. Her body relaxed in Adam's strong and clearly skilled hands as he stroked her bare, smooth belly, and a warm glow spread from her navel over her entire body. His mouth warmed her as his lips traveled slowly downward from her breasts.

Some time later, Miranda said, "But *you* haven't."

"There's plenty of time," Adam said. "*I* like to do things to a woman. I get my pleasure from seeing you climax." She had thrashed around like a freshly caught trout on a grassy bank. "I told you, you're not to *move*." Adam firmly replaced her arm on the pillow.

"And what if I do?"

"I'll tie you to the bed."

Miranda opened her eyes. "Bondage? How sleazy."

"Not if it's playful," Adam promised. "I'd blindfold you with a silken scarf and tie your wrists and ankles to the bedpost with silken ribbons."

"I'd bite them off!"

"I was only joking," Adam murmured, feeling again for her breasts.

An hour later, Miranda, lying on top of Adam's suntanned, naked body, said sleepily, "That was a big surprise."

"I've been wanting to do it for years."

"Why did you wait so long?"

"The same reason as you. Prudence. But nobody could feel platonic about you, Miranda."

Miranda remembered howling as a twelve-year-old because Adam treated her as a child. Briefly she wished that child could have looked into this future. She said, "I think . . . I think I've always wanted . . . this."

"I know I have." Adam again bent his lips to her breast.

Miranda said sleepily, "I've never had an orgasm during sex like that. Sometimes I've been on the verge, but then the feeling vanished."

"I have to confess, you're not the first woman I've made love to."

Miranda inhaled the earthy smell of the bed, propped herself on one elbow, and started gently to scratch Adam's arm with her fingernails, stroking the sensitive inner flesh, from wrist to elbow.

He shivered with pleasure. "No woman has ever aroused me as you have."

"You too?"

"I've never felt like this before, Miranda. I feel that we're equals, that you'll never allow me to dominate you. I suspect you'll always keep me guessing, keep me on my toes." Roughly he pulled her to him.

His kiss was deep and passionate. Miranda fleetingly wondered how she could ever have thought that Adam had a withholding, guarded nature. And then she was drawn again into his spell and she stopped thinking altogether.

Later, Adam lazily stared past Miranda to the windows—twin

rectangles of blue sky, between which hung an old mirror in an elaborately carved mahogany frame. The silvered glass was faintly green in places and speckled black where the silver had flaked off the back. Beneath this mirror stood Miranda's surprisingly feminine dressing table, skirted in spotted white muslin frills.

Adam said, "I'm surprised to find your dressing table looks like Scarlett O'Hara's underdrawers."

"Sometimes a frill is just a frill." Miranda shrugged.

"My clever darling," Adam murmured.

Miranda stretched voluptuously. "Annabel and Clare are going to get the surprise of their lives when we tell them about *us!*"

"I'd prefer to keep our secret to ourselves for a bit," Adam said firmly. "I have to settle Elinor's affairs. I don't want anyone to suspect that I favor you over your sisters, which is something they already fear because of our business connection."

He did not mention his other reason for secrecy, although they both knew it. Everyone close to her knew that Elinor's unspoken dream was that Miranda—her only remaining unmarried granddaughter—should marry into the British aristocracy. While Elinor lived, Adam dared not risk flinging a monkey wrench into that dream.

At eleven o'clock the following morning, Buzz sat down on the blue chair by Elinor's bedroom window, pulled the kitchen timer from the pocket of her navy cotton dress, and set it to twenty minutes: the mechanism began to tick in an irritating way.

Elinor, in a cream silk bed jacket, was propped up by a stack of frilly pillows; she looked old and frail.

Elinor's cat, Fudge, now allowed back into the bedroom, padded to the gray sofa in front of the fireplace, where Adam sat, and rubbed against his jeans.

"Cats always like me." Adam leaned down and stroked the pale ginger fur; the cat curled up against his feet and went to sleep. From the briefcase that lay open at his side, Adam extracted a document. He spoke briskly. "Before I return to London, I'd like to propose a strategy, should Elinor ever again be ill, to prevent the problems that Buzz has experienced during the past few weeks." Because nobody had been empowered to sign checks on Elinor's behalf, no household bills or salaries could be paid: for three weeks, the servants' wages had been paid by Buzz from her own bank account.

"If, for any reason, Elinor can't sign checks, then I suggest I sign them for her," Adam said.

Buzz looked up sharply.

Adam continued, "But I would be empowered to draw *only* on Elinor's housekeeping account in Nice. The power of attorney would specifically state that no checks could be made out to me or the firm. We would wait for any payment until Elinor was well again."

"Why not have two signatures required?" Buzz suggested. "One of the other STG partners, perhaps?"

"Certainly." Adam nodded, then turned to Elinor. "And the STG professional insurance would automatically cover malpractice."

Elinor looked at Buzz. "That okay with you? Yes. Then please do it, Adam dear." Her voice was feeble.

After Elinor signed and the document was witnessed, Adam produced a second sheet of paper. He said, "In order to prevent literary contracts being held up, I also suggest that a general power of attorney be given to me—again only in a limited area and only to be used if Elinor is indisposed."

Buzz asked, "Is that also covered by the malpractice insurance?"

"Yes," Adam said. "Incidentally, if I deliberately breached a power of attorney and exploited it for my own benefit—although I can't think how that would be possible—I would be struck off the Roll of Solicitors by the Law Society."

"That all right with you, Buzz?" Elinor asked faintly.

"Do you have any specific objections, Buzz?" Adam inquired politely.

After a moment, Buzz shook her head. These powers of attorney were only for day-to-day transactions. If Buzz protested without cause, it might even sound fishy—as if she wanted to control Nell's money.

"Then I also agree to that," Elinor said.

WEDNESDAY, 21 JULY 1965

At five p.m., Scott finished his coverage of the anti–Vietnam War demonstrators. In the newsroom, reporters hung around drinking coffee as they read or talked. Desks were littered with yards of wire stories, celebrity bulletins, picture handouts, telephone messages, and empty coffee cups. In the background, teletype machines clacked, and a bank of television monitors showed different pictures, some of which were material being fed through to the station. Somebody wailed, "You mean after *two* lawyers passed this, I *still* can't run it?"

In the news editor's office, an assistant was reading the list of stories from her scratch pad, "Report from Washington on the senator bribe story. The mayor of New York and the antiwar demonstrations. We have the mayor bugging out on this, Scott."

A head poked around the door. "Call to Europe in your office, Scott."

"Sorry, you guys." Scott hurried to his office and carefully closed the door. "Annabel? What's happened, darling?"

"Scott . . . *I miss you!*"

"I miss you too, angel."

"*I need you here.*"

Scott was sensitive to the pressure his wife had been under for the past month. First she'd learned that her grandmother, whom she adored, was dangerously ill, and had been at her bedside ever since. Then her contract had not been renewed. This was a double-barrel blow for both of them in terms of loss of money and prestige. The humiliation was worse because it was so public, and it was a good thing that Annabel had not been in New York when the news broke, when gloating gossip writers had jammed Scott and Annabel's home phones with their venomous questions.

Scott knew that Annabel was now facing the worst moment any model can face: she was officially over the hill, gaining weight, losing her looks and on the downward path to wrinkles and sag. No reassurances from Scott had been able to lull his twenty-five-year-old wife's anxiety about her fading beauty. It was ludicrous to be so young and yet a has-been.

Scott tried to handle her diplomatically. "Angel, I wish I could be with you, but we both know I can't. We've talked about this so often: you know I want to be supportive, but I also have to do my job properly. We're short-staffed here—the summer holiday period's started and everyone's stretched. I can't just walk out. If I'd come when you first asked me, I might have been in Saracen for an entire month: I'd probably have no job to come back to." Gently he added, "And what use would I have been, angel?"

Once again Scott felt that she was asking for something unreasonable, something a child might ask of a parent. He wished Annabel were not so insecure and dependent upon him; for the past few months, as she waited for Avanti to make up its mind, she had needed constant emotional support and reassurance from Scott, who had felt her clinging to him, almost like a physical weight on his back.

"I wanted you with me," Annabel wept. She had forgotten that she telephoned to tell Scott the news of the trust.

"My job means having to give up a lot of things that everyone else takes for granted in their life, and you've always known that, Annabel," Scott again reminded her.

"Your job seems to suck up your entire life," Annabel sobbed reproachfully.

"Yes, that's why I married you. Because I love you, and I want what little private life I have to be steady and permanent," Scott said.

"You're so involved with your precious career that you put it before your private life," Annabel retorted. "You put *us* on the back burner—you'll deal with it next week, next month—you'll do that until you *retire!*"

"My career *is* precious to me—and you knew that when you married me. It's not as if I worked for a large network news show. You know that *everyone* here does the job of at least two people. How would it look if I suddenly disappeared for weeks—leaving a gap that other people would have to fill—because my wife's grandmother is ill on the other side of the world?"

"*Please* come, Scott."

"It's not necessary. I can't walk out on everyone here. Please try to understand that, angel."

"Scott, I want to hold you . . . It's been months since we were in bed together. Don't you remember how good it used to be?"

"*Nobody* gets the honeymoon treatment forever, angel. That sort of twenty-four-hours-in-bed passion changes into a different sort of comfortable, caring love."

Annabel wailed, "You mean I don't attract you anymore? You don't love me?"

Exasperated, Scott said, "You've become spoiled, neurotic, over-anxious, and self-absorbed. What's so lovable about that, Annabel?"

Scott's office door burst open. "You're wanted in the cutting room."

"Thanks, I'll be right along!" To Annabel, Scott said carefully, "You just have to tough it out, angel. These situations sometimes happen in life."

"That's not all." Annabel gulped, then managed to say, "I think I'm having a heart attack."

"*What!*"

After he calmed down, Scott reasoned that if Annabel were having a heart attack, she wouldn't be able to talk on the telephone. Cautiously he said, "Why do you think that, angel?"

"My heart is thumping! I can't breathe properly—I'm gasping for air!"

"It might be another anxiety attack," Scott suggested gently.

Annabel said in an agitated voice, "I feel as if my mind is whirling madly, like a hurricane. I can't control it. I feel taut and tense. I'm literally *shaking!*"

"Are you sweating? Are your hands clammy? Is your stomach knotted?"

"*Yes,*" Annabel wept.

It was another panic attack. Scott said, "Is Adam still around? Get him to the phone, darling."

Another head appeared around Scott's door. "They can't cut until you're on the spot, Scott."

Scott nearly said, "My wife is ill," but he had cried wolf too often: other people's wives didn't telephone the station as relentlessly as Annabel.

Eventually Scott heard Adam's faint but reassuringly calm voice. "Anything I can do to help, Scott? Annabel seems upset. We thought she'd gone to bed. It's nearly midnight here."

"Annabel thinks she's having a heart attack," Scott told him.

"I don't think so," Adam said firmly. "I'll take her to Elinor's night nurse immediately—I expect she'll give Annabel something to calm her down. The situation here has been very tense. It's understandable that Annabel is a little . . . overwrought."

Scott thought, He's telling me that she's hysterical. He said, "Tell me straight, Adam. Just answer yes or no. Does Annabel look ill to you?"

"No."

"I'm between a rock and a hard place. Of course I'll fly over straightaway if Elinor . . ."

"There is no necessity to do so." Adam spoke firmly again. "Elinor is progressing well, and I have everything under control here."

"I'm sure you have," Scott said with great relief.

WEDNESDAY, 28 JULY 1965

A week later, just before her luncheon was served, Adam took the trust documentation to Elinor's bedroom to be signed.

As he laid the twenty-four-page Declaration of Trust before her, Adam said, "There are no changes, but one alteration. As Paul is to be the protector, the STG partners think it best to have trustees outside the firm, so we'll arrange that through the group of accountants we deal with in Bermuda."

"Did you ask Clare once more?" Elinor, looking frail, was not interested in the fine points of the trust.

"Yes. I'm afraid she's still adamant."

Elinor thought for a minute. With an effort, she lifted her head. "Remember that I don't want Clare to know she's included in the trust *until she apologizes!* She is *not* to think she can get away with behaving hurtfully. Now, where do I sign this thing? You'd better call Buzz and that sour-looking nurse to witness it."

• • •

At 7:20 that same morning, Scott had been at the site of an unusual hit-and-run story: two older men had been killed and another injured by a police patrol car. At midday, Scott returned to the studio with twenty minutes of film footage, which would be edited to two minutes plus. It looked as if it would end up their lead story.

The news editor suggested, "Let's team it with this other hit-and-run story that's just come in: two black kids, in a car out of control, ran over four children, who were hurt but not badly. The black kids have been paraded in handcuffs to the press."

Scott was interested. "The cops suspected of killing the two old guys have been suspended but not arrested, even though I'm told there's a suspicion that murder is involved. But the DA's office says they can't pin it on them yet. So let's run the story 'Why the delay at the DA's office?'"

The door opened. "Call from Europe for you, Scott."

Scott said nothing. What could he say? The entire station knew about his spoiled child bride. He hurried to his office. Once again he listened calmly to her tearful pleas, and once again Scott refused to walk out on the station and join Annabel.

That evening, Scott took his place at the news desk and ran an eye over his script. Just before airtime, a story had come in on a drug bust: space was hastily made for this.

At one minute to air, Scott grinned across to the other newscaster, looked up at the control room, and nodded.

The stress level in the newsroom was high. There was no noise whatsoever. Control said, "Roll feed one ..." The floor manager pointed at camera two and counted down: "Four, three, two, one. Cue Scott." A red light flicked on camera two as the floor manager silently pointed to it.

"Good evening. I'm Scott Svenson with tonight's news."

Even while the show was going out, work continued in the newsroom. Reporters handed their just completed text to the news editor, who edited the stories and telephoned any alterations in the program to the newscaster: "Scott, kill story four from Moscow—something better's come in, so we aren't going to run it." . . . "Scott, hold item seven, medical malpractice, for later in the show. The guy's just died, so we must update it."

As the camera pulled back on the last shot and credits were shown on the screen, the tension in the studio relaxed, replaced by an exultant mood. The interrupter-feedback button in Scott's ear said, "Nice work, Scott. Now beat it to your office. Long-distance call from Europe."

Scott tore off his mike, thinking, It must be five in the morning in France.

He ran to his office and lifted the phone. "Annabel? What's happened?"

Annabel could hardly speak through her tears. "Gran had a relapse four hours ago. Adam is here to speak with you if you don't believe me. They say there's no point in moving her to a hospital. Now you've *got* to come, Scott."

Chapter·17

Ten weeks later, the ambulance team that had driven Elinor from the Nice hospital carried her into the chateau and up to her bedroom.

Elinor, her arms draped around the necks of two paramedics, said, "You can take that thing right away!" She meant the wheelchair waiting in her bedroom.

"Please," Buzz pleaded. "You gotta be careful for a bit, Elinor. You gave us such a fright. We thought you was a goner."

"Well, I feel fine now," Elinor said. "Where's that bottle of champagne you promised me?"

The specialists had said that if she was careful, she could live a long time. Her doctor had told her that she had completely recovered. He saw no reason to add that from now on, her body would break down: she would gradually become slower in her movements, she would tire more easily and lack stamina, and she would probably have another stroke in seven years' time—at the latest.

TUESDAY, 12 OCTOBER 1965

In the gray morning light, Clare, still in her nightgown, stooped to pick up the little bottle of sleeping pills from the floor. She shook it. Empty. Better get another prescription. Careful not to wake Josh in the back room, Clare pulled on her dressing gown.

Josh was still bewildered by the sudden change in living standard from California sun and the constant care of cheerful Kathy (now working for another family in nearby Markham Square) to the stuffy flat in Pimlico where his babysitter, Mrs. Gooden, a retired cook, watched over Josh and her other six little charges, one of whom always seemed to be bare-bottomed and on the potty.

Clare hurried to the kitchenette to make Josh's breakfast. Their basement apartment cost more than she could afford, but at least she felt at home in Chelsea.

Once again she wished she understood what had happened to her in the last three months. She had such a strong sense of being in the right, of having behaved in a morally correct manner. Why then had she ended up in such a mess?

After Clare's sudden departure from Saracen, Miranda had immediately located her through friends, then telephoned and urged her sister to be sensible and apologize to Elinor, "because we all know you really love Gran."

"Of course I do, Miranda," Clare had said. "But that's beside the point." She was determined to allow nobody to treat her as a child in future—not Sam, not Adam, not Elinor, not Buzz, and certainly not Miranda.

"This tiff is escalating to a ridiculous degree!" Miranda exploded. "Adam says the trust is going to be *irrevocable,* so for heaven's sake, think ahead, for when Joshua goes to Eton—"

"I don't think I'm being ridiculous. I hope Josh *never* goes to Eton, or any other privileged school where he's kept away from reality," Clare said stiffly. Correctly feeling that Miranda thought she was being tiresome, she added, "What counts in this tiff—as you call it—is the principle of the thing."

Miranda said, "People only say that when they can't think of any other reason for doing something damned stupid."

Clare was impatient to hang up. Enraged, Miranda said, "Okay, I can take a hint." She promised herself she wouldn't approach Clare again.

At first Clare kept in touch with Annabel after her sister returned to New York, but as her own life became increasingly difficult, she found herself unable to write the sort of letter that would prop up Annabel's crumbling self-esteem.

Via his lawyer, Sam refused to give Clare money because he didn't want a divorce. He wanted his wife and child back, and he reckoned he could tough it out longer than she could.

Clare's solicitor explained to her that men often forced their wives to return by refusing to grant a divorce and making it difficult for them to obtain money—even when it was awarded by a court. He said that returning to Sam might be best for her and her child. Clare wondered whose side her lawyer was on. She was clearly and legally in the right; she wasn't going to be manipulated and brought to heel by lack of funds.

"I'm damned if I'm going to let him bully me with money!" Clare cried. "I'll earn my own money!"

She soon found out how difficult this was.

Clare fell into the poverty trap experienced in the sixties by many single mothers. Because she had no man, she had no income beyond what she could earn. And because she had no training, she had no salable skills. She could only get a poorly paid job as a sales assistant in a Kings Road shoe boutique.

Because she had no man, Clare also suddenly found she had no public identity and was not likely to get asked to dinner parties, for society seemed to move only in couples. A full-time job, a small child, and no home help left her little energy for dinner parties anyway. And she was too proud to accept hospitality when she couldn't afford to return it. She, who had always helped lame dogs, now refused the many helping hands that were held out to her, because they only hauled her back, temporarily, into a life of comfort from which she would later have to return to reality. She became abrupt and ill at ease with her friends, who sensed this. Eventually they stopped trying.

Clare was surprised to find how much money it cost to lead what she considered a normal life. She earned eighteen pounds a week after tax. Her rent was ten pounds a week, and the babysitter cost a pound a day, which left three pounds to live on—just enough to pay her grocery bill. She didn't know how to budget or how to keep track of her expenditures, and she cried every time she opened her bank statement.

Apart from basic necessities, any other purchase was clearly now an extravagance for Clare. Her wages only just paid for her expenses: now a taxi was a memory.

Bewildered, Clare did not understand why she couldn't manage. What was she doing wrong? The other assistants in the shoe shop seemed to manage on their wages. Of course, none of them was supporting a child, and the male assistant got sixty percent more than the women. And she was living in an area of London that was relatively expensive, while her new peers lived in Battersea and Wandsworth.

But Clare was not yet accustomed to a life in which ice cream, sherry, and a telephone were luxuries. So she economized by drinking cheap cooking sherry. She felt humiliated by her poverty, especially when the telephone was cut off for nonpayment and she had to confess this to Gilda, the senior assistant in the shoe shop.

"Poor? *You* ain't poor, Clare," scoffed Gilda during their tea break. She lit up a Woodbine and puffed on it serenely. "Poor people don't have bank accounts and refrigerators and money for the launderette."

"I'm starting to realize that," Clare said humbly. "But I still need more money than I'm earning, to look after Josh."

Clare had not wanted to leave Josh (who would be three in December) with a babysitter, but she found that none of the local nursery schools, public or private, had an available slot.

When she tried to get Josh into a free day nursery, she discovered that the local authority did not regard her situation as difficult. "Difficult" seemed to mean that your pimp had beaten you up and thrown you out, and you had no money for a fix and couldn't stand up until you'd had one. In the Chelsea library, Clare read the 1944 Education Act, Section 8(2) (6). It said that a local education authority "shall, in particular, have regard to the need for securing that provision is made for pupils who have not attained the age of five years by the provision of nursery school."

So—where were the nursery schools? Clare felt protest rise within her. She was determined not to be bludgeoned into submission by lack of money and a system that seemed not to care for mothers and children.

On the following weekend, Clare sold all her jewelry except her engagement and wedding rings. She accepted the first price offered by the first jeweler, not realizing that she could probably have raised fifty percent more money by bargaining or trying other shops.

That night, as often when she put Josh to bed, Clare held the most precious thing in her world close to her heart and felt guilty and ashamed that she wasn't providing him with the things she thought she should. She lived with guilt even as she fiercely told herself that it wasn't fair that her life now should be so miserable and exhausting.

Josh had to be squeezed into Clare's tight weekday schedule: After taking him to the babysitter in Pimlico, she caught another bus to the shoe shop where she worked. Lunch hour meant a hurried visit to a launderette or one of the new supermarkets. At six o'clock, Clare again caught the bus to Pimlico, took Josh back to her basement, cooked his supper, cooked her supper (increasingly, the same nursery food sufficed for both), put Josh to bed, had a drink, looked over any paperwork required by her solicitor, crawled into bed with a book, fell asleep after reading a page, and woke two hours later, unable to get back to sleep. Insomnia plagued her and sapped her strength. Exhausted and without much hope for the future, she gradually slipped into a permanent state of depression, which made life even more difficult for Josh, although neither of them realized this.

Thankfully, on weekends, Clare felt almost normal again. On Saturdays, she stayed in bed late—although as Josh bounced up and down beside her, it wasn't a very restful experience. But she didn't mind as she cuddled his warm little body next to hers, played hide-and-seek under the bedclothes, or read aloud to him. Later, soaping her son's slippery body in the bath as he wriggled from her grasp and splashed water up at his mother, Clare would again feel happy.

On Saturday afternoons, Clare pushed Josh's collapsible canvas pram up Sloane Street toward Kensington Gardens, where she mixed happily with other children and working mothers. They were all sniffed at by the uniformed nannies, who wheeled old-fashioned perambulators rather than the canvas collapsibles.

On Sunday mornings, Clare and Josh went to Mrs. Gooden's. Here Clare (who could cook a hamburger but not much else) learned to prepare a traditional British lunch of roast meat and vegetables, followed by a fruit pie or tart.

"You've got light fingers," Mrs. Gooden said approvingly one Sunday as she watched Clare, with the tips of her fingers, mix flour and lard in the big yellow mixing bowl. "We'll make a baker of you yet."

Shortly after this, Clare started to swap babysitting evenings with Stephanie, a mother who also took her small son to Mrs. Gooden. This arrangement ensured that, once a week, both women had an evening and a night off, followed by a leisurely rise the next morning.

On Clare's first such evening off, she went to a dinner party given by an old school friend who persisted in keeping in touch. Clare's partner was a just-divorced man who talked endlessly about "that bitch who needn't think she has a free meal ticket for life," then took Clare to dance at Annabel's, London's most expensive new nightclub. He tore her dress on the taxi journey back to her flat, and after a tussle, finally, standing on the pavement at three a.m. he realized that she really wouldn't allow him in. The following morning, Clare arrived late for work.

When Gilda heard what happened, she said, "A man who's just staggered out of a nasty relationship wants a bloody nursemaid at first, and then he wants to play the field for a bit. But what he *really* wants is another relationship."

Clare said, "*I* don't want another relationship until I've struggled free of this one."

"Maybe you ought to play the field a bit," Gilda suggested.

"That's what my solicitor's afraid of," Clare said. "He says it would ruin my case. He'd like to shut me up in a box for the next two years. But Sam can apparently do what the hell he likes, with as many women as he pleases!"

On her next evening out, Clare remembered Gilda's advice. Feeling self-conscious at entering a pub by herself, she slunk into the Markham Arms, a glamorous tavern in the Kings Road where men-about-Chelsea relaxed in the evening.

Sitting on the next barstool was an antiques dealer called James; he discussed his feelings with Clare for the next two hours and then took her to dinner at the Ox on the Roof, where she chose the most filling dishes. Eating spaghetti, Clare began to suspect that James would rather talk about a relationship than have one; wolfing boeuf bourguignon, she wondered whether James was flaunting his insecurities in order to attract the maternal feelings he clearly believed nestled within every woman's breast—and from which Clare was trying to escape for the evening.

By the time the crème brûlée was served, she realized that James wasn't the gentle, sensitive, vulnerable charmer that she had first imagined but a crashing bore.

Nevertheless, having had far too much to drink, Clare woke up the next morning in James's bed, saw that it was nearly nine o'clock, fled to work in her crumpled clothes—but arrived late again. Gilda winked.

The following week, Clare avoided the Markham Arms and went instead to the Bunch of Grapes in Knightsbridge. There she met Ian, a fruit exporter. Ian was boyish, athletic, charming, and, Clare suspected, terrified of his fortieth birthday: there had been a bit of the Peter Pan in Sam, and Clare recognized the symptoms.

During dinner at the Pheasantry, Ian clearly expected Clare to be frivolously entertaining. He belittled any attempt at serious conversation with phrases such as, "Well, you're quite a bluestocking," or, "Actually, I didn't come out to discuss politics."

The next morning, Ian woke her up with a cup of tea, said he was sorry about last night, he'd had a bit too much to drink. Again Clare was late to work.

"Of *course* they both seemed nice guys," Gilda commiserated. "But they was fake nice guys, *pretending* to be nice guys. If you're going to get picked up in bars and hand it out free on the first date, you'd better check in regular at St. Stephen's."

"Is that a church?"

"No, the local clap clinic."

Always, when Clare's hangover subsided, she wondered why she did it. She found no sexual pleasure in going to bed with strangers, but, in contrast with the rest of her week, she was comforted by the feeling of being thought desirable, of having someone's arms around her, of warm cuddling beneath the quilt.

One morning, Clare found herself in a rumpled bed in a strange bedroom with only sixpence in her purse—not enough to get to work. If she was late for work one more time, she knew, she would be fired. Clare panicked and telephoned Miranda.

Wondering whether the prim Miss Goody-Goody of a few months ago had really metamorphosed into this forlorn and wanton creature, Miranda said, "I'll send a car for you, straightaway." She hesitated. "Couldn't we meet, Clare?... Won't you let me give you some money—just to tide you over?"

"No," Clare lied. "I have plenty of money at home."

"Gran's worried about you. We all are."

"How is she?" Clare asked wistfully. In the past, when she felt depressed, she knew that she could always rely on her grandmother to lift her spirits.

"Gran would feel a lot happier if you paid her a visit. Couldn't you fly to the south of France, just for a week?"

"No," Clare said, feeling rage rise. "I can't take time off."

"How about a better job?" Miranda suggested. "You've had experience as a shop assistant, so you could work in one of our shops. You'll probably be better paid, and have a better time of it."

"No. I want to learn to manage by myself. Don't worry. I'll survive."

"But what about Josh?"

"Josh will have to put up with the life that his mother can afford to lead."

Clare was fired for turning up late after she had to wait for a doctor because Josh had a temperature. As the shop manager pointed out, it was the third time that month she'd been late for work, and if they hadn't needed her to turn up on time, they wouldn't have hired her in the first place.

Having decided to start her own nursery playgroup, Clare sold her engagement ring, a flashy marquise diamond, in order to buy the lease of the first floor of a big Edwardian house in Pimlico: it contained a ballroom, a small rear room, and a bathroom. Clare's assistants were two other single mothers whose children were also cared for by Mrs. Gooden.

Mrs. Gooden lost three kiddies and three pounds a day but, instead, found herself cooking lunch for thirty-four, a far more lucrative occupation. At midday, Mr. Gooden cycled round to the playgroup with lunch hauled behind on a trailer. He also did Clare's bookkeeping. Clare doubled her income overnight, and felt that she was doing a useful job.

In contrast to Clare, her sister Miranda was leading the fast and frivolous life of the exciting sixties as Britain launched into the first real business boom since Hitler's war. A rush of stock exchange takeover bids coined money for shareholders, and Britain imported more French champagne than any other country, although one in three families still couldn't afford a TV.

The former aristocratic standards of who and what was acceptable were now dumped; everyone wanted to belong to the new meritocracy, based not on birth but on talent, achievement, and the resultant financial reward—the with-it people, as opposed to the dull, unwith-its.

Annabel was painted by David Hockney, and Miranda's portrait—a gloomy study in grays by Brian Kneale—was exhibited in the National Portrait Gallery. They both wished that Gran would hide her triple portrait: Annigoni was definitely *not* with it.

Fashion was madly exciting: Grannies happily wore miniskirts and platform thigh boots, while young girls wore button-up granny boots and Victorian-style, flower-printed dresses. Females under thirty tried to look like thumb-sucking little girls; with turned-in toes, they skipped around in buttock-skimming shifts over pale tights. All females in their thirties dressed like chic astronauts; all women over forty wore jaunty, flared trouser suits.

Makeup manufacturers made a fortune.

TUESDAY, 11 JANUARY 1966

Snow lay on the park outside as Miranda showed her new house in Cumberland Terrace to fashion editor Annie Trehearne. Since the heating wasn't yet working, the two young women stamped around in winter coats and boots, dodged whistling workmen, who no longer wore baggy dungarees but tight jeans as they carried planks from one room to another.

Annie looked down from the first-floor drawing room windows to the gaunt trees of Regent's Park and said, "It's simply super. Fab. Smashing. Let's face it, Miranda, not many people of your age can afford to buy a house like this. KITS must be doing frightfully well."

Miranda nodded. "But KITS has expanded so fast we're permanently short of capital. The money for this place came from a family trust."

"Everyone should have a grandmother like yours. How is she?"

"The doctors say she's responding very well to the new treatment, and *she* expects to live for another hundred years."

"Glad to hear it."

"Now, I want to know what you think of my new skin-care range," Miranda said. "It's targeted at the young twenties and I'm calling it Image. What do you think of launching it with pictures of Deneuve?"

"Pix by Bailey then. Expensive," Annie said. Photographer David

Bailey had recently married French film star Catherine Deneuve, with Mick Jagger as best man.

"Of course." Miranda nodded again.

"By the way, how's Annabel enjoying her retirement?"

"Off the record? Relieved, I think," Miranda reported. "She's neatly switched to the life of a successful New York hostess—she's on every charity committee in town."

Miranda was not going to let anyone know that Annabel's self-confidence had been shattered. It had been painful to watch her struggle for her self-respect, but she had managed to ward off the threatened nervous breakdown. Endless reassurance had been necessary—not of her beauty, for nothing could persuade Annabel that it had not vanished, but of her value to them all, and of her family's affection.

Airily Miranda continued, "Annabel's just bought a new apartment. You really ought to hop over for a weekend and see it, Annie. It's a penthouse in a high rise on the Upper East Side, with a spectacular three-sided view over the city and across the river. It's simply stunning. Someone else had practically bought the place, so Annabel was lucky to get it."

"How did she manage it?"

"Simply offered more money. Adam fixed it."

"That family trust again? What lucky girls you are! What news of Clare?"

"I don't see much of Clare these days," Miranda said. "She's very busy, now that she's running a nursery playgroup." She looked out over the smudged white landscape of Regent's Park, then peered at the road below. "Hell, I've just got another parking fine. Those stupid new meters! It's getting really difficult to drive in London."

"Or out of it," said Annie.

"Yes. I was pinched for dangerous driving last month, in a radar trap. Luckily, Adam fixed it."

WEDNESDAY, 12 JANUARY 1966

Clare still swapped one night a week off with Stephanie and reported subsequent events to Gilda, who now managed the shoe shop: occasionally she visited Clare for an evening meal.

As Clare poured sherry, Gilda asked, "So how was the BOAC pilot?"

"Tony was the worst yet." Clare never felt embarrassed discussing sex with Gilda, who could talk about little else. "He'd read all the sex manuals ever printed. Whipped a porn magazine out of his flight case after the first gin and tonic. He was coldly determined to be a good lover. For me, that was a total turnoff."

"Porn pictures are a turnoff to most women. Women like words, not pictures," Gilda said as she sipped her drink. "But I'm starting to think that everything's a turnoff for you, doll. You clearly can't have sex with fellas you ain't fond of. I expect you need a chap you know well, someone you feel comfortable with, not these one-nighters." She swallowed half the glass. "Now me, I'm the reverse. If I don't give a damn about 'em, I ain't anxious, and if I ain't anxious, then I come easy." She drained her glass.

"When Tony couldn't get me to climax, he wanted to ask another girl over," Clare said. "He automatically assumed that I was a lesbian."

"*That's* not what he meant," Gilda said. "Lots of guys find it a turn-on to watch two women making love."

"How very odd. Can you imagine a woman trying to get two men into bed so *she* could watch them?"

"Forget this guy," said Gilda. "I know what *you* need, Clare: someone you know and trust, someone who won't make you feel anxious. Then you'll relax and it'll happen—then you'll stop being one of them miserable nymphos who hop from man to man, hoping for Mr. Right, the man who can satisfy her." As Gilda held out her glass to be refilled, she added reflectively, "Although you seem more lonely than horny. Are you looking for sex, or just someone to talk to? You ain't likely to pick up Prince Charming in a bar."

Clare said, "I'm not looking for Prince Charming. I don't want the disorder, the pain, the mess, or the misery of being in love. I just want a short-term relationship, without responsibility."

Gilda laughed. "So do these fellas you pick up. But I'm not convinced that's right for you. *You* need a secure situation with someone you can trust, who you know will stick around because he loves you. I'll tell you who you ought to fall in love with, Clare."

"Who?"

"Yourself. You clearly think that you're a piece of worthless rubbish, and if *I* pick up those vibes, then so do the blokes. Why not give sex a rest for a bit, and pay a bit of attention to yourself? You never want to make a man the center of your existence. That place is for *you*, Clare."

"I am the center of my existence," Clare sang, as if chanting a psalm, pitching her voice an octave lower, as she pushed Josh to her playgroup the next morning.

A man stood on the porch, his hands in the pocket of his beige mackintosh.

"Good morning. Are you a prospective parent?" Clare asked. She felt in her pocket for the key.

"No," said the man. "I'm an inspector for the local education authority."

After examining the bathroom, the inspector pointed out that legally one toilet was required for every seven kiddies.

Clare said, "But if each child goes there every two and a half hours, one lavatory is adequate. There is a potty for emergencies. We have never had a problem."

The inspector was not listening. He was making notes on other violations.

Half an hour after the inspector left, as if to prove his point, the lavatory refused to flush.

The following morning, Clare's playgroup was ordered to close.

Two days later, Clare's mind was unexpectedly diverted from her personal problems—no job, no man—when the C.N.D. office telephoned to ask her for voluntary evening help: they were organizing another protest after a nuclear accident. Over Spain, an American B-52 bomber carrying an H-bomb had collided in midair with another aircraft. The H-bomb, with an explosive capacity of more than a million tons of TNT, had fallen into the Atlantic Ocean off southern Spain.

Clare felt cheered to be back among like-minded people, doing something worthwhile.

MONDAY, 14 FEBRUARY 1966

Valentine's Day brought two happy events. The radio reported that the missing H-bomb had been located on the Atlantic seabed. And to Clare's delight, she sold the lease of the apartment in which she ran her playgroup—for a profit of twenty-three percent.

Clare felt as if she had won a sweepstake. On the following morning, she bought a portable TV, a warm winter coat for herself, and new clothes for Josh. She didn't buy any toys for Josh because she had decided to open a toy shop.

Two weeks later, Clare bought the short lease of a small shop in the Pimlico Road, close to Mrs. Gooden's home. Though there was a lot to do, Clare, busy redecorating the shop and visiting wholesalers to buy stock, still managed to work one evening a week for the Movement.

In mid-April, just before her toy shop opened, Clare's weary, amiable National Health doctor looked up from his desk and said, "About your vaginal symptoms, Mrs. Shapiro. You'd better go to St. Stephen's for tests: they're properly equipped to handle this sort of thing." He seemed uneasy.

"What sort of thing? . . . Not . . . cancer?"

"No, gonorrhea," the doctor said apologetically.

Clare almost fainted from surprise and anxiety, horror and shame. Then she wept.

The doctor refused to give her more sleeping tablets but scribbled a prescription for tranquilizers, which were increasingly prescribed for women like Clare, with symptoms of anxiety in stressful situations such as poverty, divorce, or bereavement; women with marital problems and women who were out of work also found them helpful, although the pills did nothing to resolve the problem responsible for the initial anxiety.

Clare, who blushed with shame whenever she thought about it, waited anxiously for the result of her tests at St. Stephen's Hospital.

The tests were negative.

But within a month, she couldn't get through the day without tranquilizers; she felt less anxious, calmer.

Clare managed to open the Red Rocking Horse by mid-May. At the opening party, an excited three-and-a-half-year-old Josh rode the pretty antique red rocking horse in the shop window.

MONDAY, 15 AUGUST 1966

Standing by the swimming pool at Saracen, Miranda beckoned to Adam, who was floating on the water in a transparent blow-up plastic armchair.

In a voice of soft persuasion, she said, "Will you do something for me, Adam? I'm going to learn to fly. I want you to break the news gently to Gran."

"But you promised your grandmother *not* to learn to fly," Adam objected. "It was a condition of her gift to you—the ten thousand pounds' capital to start KITS."

"I didn't say forever. I'll pay the money back to her." Miranda was defiant. "I've always wanted to fly. I won't be held by a promise that was unfairly extracted from me before I legally became an adult. And I get bored with nothing to do on holiday but lie in the sun."

"When are you starting?" Adam asked, resigned.

"This morning, at the Cannes flying school. They have English instructors. Four hours of instruction a day for two weeks. And of course, this time of year, it's perfect flying weather!" Miranda was triumphant now. "I've already passed the two written exams. Did law and meteorology last Easter, and now I've finished navigation, radio-telephony, and technical—that was the toughest."

"So that's why you're so pale."

• • •

Three hours later, two thousand feet above the Mediterranean, Miranda, alert and exultant, sat next to her instructor at the controls of a trainer plane, an ugly little single-engine Rallye which her instructor described as efficient and forgiving: you could do something wrong in a Rallye without getting immediately punished for it.

Flying was even better than she had hoped: better than skiing, better than driving a sports car. As the Rallye droned toward the lighthouse on the tip of Cap Camerat, Miranda had felt as if she were breathing the air of the gods. Gently they swooped, turned, and climbed in the azure sky.

After they reached two thousand feet, the instructor showed her how to fly level; he then encouraged her to experiment with the stick, maneuvering the plane in every direction. Miranda felt that the aircraft was an extension of her arms and her fingertips, outspread in flight.

Heading west on the return flight path, the instructor said, "This is the first time I've flown with a pupil and haven't once needed to touch the controls."

Miranda pushed home this advantage. "Then can I land?"

The instructor hesitated, then said, "Why not?" The girl was clearly a natural flyer.

After being given clearance to land, Miranda, following her instructor's directions, started her approach; she throttled back to reduce speed and control her descent as she flew toward the threshold—the point just before she intended to touch down. The plane was now moving at not much above stalling speed. As the Rallye dropped to about thirty feet above the runway, Miranda throttled back completely and held the stick back.

The plane seemed to glide forward and land itself.

The undemonstrative Miranda flung her arms around the instructor. "Oh, thank you! Thank you! . . ."

"Quite a smooth landing," the instructor said approvingly. He hesitated, then warned, "Next time be careful not to land too fast or you'll run out of runway." This woman was adventurous and ambitious: such pilots did not live long. He added, "*Careful* pilots are the ones that survive. A good pilot never takes a risk."

"The opposite of a good businessman," Miranda said, still on a high. "A businessman has to take risks constantly—and win sixty percent of the time."

"In the air, that risk factor would kill you."

Nine hundred years earlier, the great hall had been the hub of castle life: wolfhounds ate on floors strewn with rushes; servants slept on straw pallets thrown on the floor. Then, the winter salon did not smell of lilies and expensive leather but of stale, fat, stinking human bodies and animal ordure. Elinor sometimes thought of all the love and the hatred, the treachery and the killing that this hall had undoubtedly seen, when strong men fought hand-to-hand to the death, to protect their women and children.

Now the winter salon at Saracen, where Elinor waited for Adam, was not only the coolest but the most impressive room in the chateau. High arched walls of pale, honey-colored stone were hung with bluish-green tapestries; around the big stone fireplace, where logs burned in winter, stood sofas covered in the blues and greens of the tapestries; here and there were lamps, flowers, books, and piles of parlor games.

"What's keeping Adam?" Elinor asked Buzz, who was adding up the Scrabble score.

"You said three o'clock. It's only two-thirty," Buzz said. "Ninety-three for you, two hundred and sixty-four for me. That's not a bad score for you, Nell." Buzz never cheated to let Elinor win: she knew that Elinor would immediately sense this and feel humiliated.

After an intensive rehabilitation program of physiotherapy and speech therapy, Elinor appeared to have completely recovered from her stroke, although she could no longer think of three things at once, which Buzz said was a mercy for the people who had to live with her.

Elinor was sometimes at a loss for the right word, or name, and then became impatient with herself; she was often frustrated because she couldn't move as swiftly as she did before. At times, she was downhearted and wondered whether she would ever write another book. "When you want to write, you'll write," Buzz would tell her then.

Now Buzz grunted, "Look what I tore out of the *Daily Mail*." She dug into her pocket, unfolded a bit of newspaper, and read, " 'Sportsman Jim Clark today opened a splendidly equipped physical training college at Larkwood in Wiltshire, formerly the family home of the O'Dare family. Lady O'Dare commented, "I wish them well." ' "

"I doubt that." Elinor peered at the photograph of the new owner, a motor-racing hero, standing with her sister-in-law, Marjorie.

The doorbell sounded. "I'll go," Buzz said. "It's either Adam or the postman."

Buzz returned reading a postcard. "It's for you, from Sonia Rushleigh . . . Whoops, I mean Bromley. Who'd have thought them two would marry? She says the Colonel's taken up petit point, and Miss Hawkins is teaching him. Remember her, the schoolmistress?"

"I do indeed," said Elinor. "Frumpy sourpuss! Who's the letter from?"

"Clare." Buzz held the envelope out to Elinor.

Elinor shook her head. "You open it."

"It's marked personal."

"I don't want to read it, unless she apologizes."

Buzz opened the letter and read it. She shook her head. "It's just a friendly letter, asking how you are. But reading between the lines, I think Clare needs money."

"If she took her poor child back to his father and gave her husband a second chance, she wouldn't need money."

"How about a bit of generosity?" Buzz said. "You're a silly, stubborn old woman. And Clare's just as stubborn and just as silly. It wouldn't have hurt her to say she was sorry."

Elinor looked anxious. "Do you really think she's short of money, Buzz? I wouldn't want her to have a rough time."

This remark was overheard by Adam as, in pale blue shirt and jeans, he sauntered through the door. He said, "Elinor, you allowed ample provision in the trust for helping Clare—if the trustees consider that help is needed. I'll check on Clare when I get back to London." He put a pile of papers on a side table. "There's rather a lot of paperwork here, things that you should be aware of."

"We've had more paperwork, not less, since the trust took over," Buzz said tartly. "And I tell you frankly that I can't follow it, Adam. I thought the trustees were going to manage the business. Elinor shouldn't be made to wade through pages of paragraphs with no commas in 'em."

"Of course the trustees manage the business, and they do it very well," Adam said. "And there's no reason for Elinor to see any of this if it tires her. In fact, I'm about to suggest something that would simplify matters."

"What's that?" Buzz asked.

"I'd like to substitute Paul Littlejohn for myself in the power of attorney that I hold on your behalf, Elinor. I'm trying to reduce the number of business administrators: the fewer there are, the simpler the system and the cheaper it will be."

"Does that mean that Paul will be legally responsible for Elinor's affairs instead of you, Adam?"

"Yes, but that's only a technicality. Paul will do as I say. And I'd also like you to sign this document," Adam added, "which absolves me and STG from any further responsibility once Paul Littlejohn has been substituted."

Buzz said, "But surely . . ."

Smoothly Adam explained, "The responsibility must clearly rest in only one area. It's in your interests to clarify the situation. It's customary."

"If you think that's best, Adam dear." Elinor frowned slightly at Buzz.

Adam decided to hold back Miranda's bombshell until later, after Elinor drank her evening glass of champagne.

Just before five o'clock, when the business session had ended and the afternoon was still hot, quiet, and heavy with languor, Buzz left to get some tea.

Adam escorted Elinor to the elevator; after taking her to her bedroom, he intended to go to the beach for a swim.

In the high-ceilinged kitchen, surrounded by the smells of mint and basil, Buzz whistled "Roses of Picardy" with much dramatic warbling as she prepared Elinor's tea. Leaves and yellow blossoms obscured the top of the window, while the bottom was covered by aggressive pink hollyhocks, seemingly determined to fight their way inside.

Sylvie, the cook, sat at the big kitchen table by the window, writing a list and shooing pigeons away. The bane of Sylvie's life was the pigeon droppings that littered the windowsill and had to be cleaned up daily.

With a shudder, Sylvie refused a cup of tea. Still whistling, Buzz laid the tray.

The soporific calm of the drowsy afternoon was shattered by the bell indicator above the kitchen door.

Someone was jabbing the bell—nonstop—in Elinor's bedroom.

Knowing that Adam was probably in the elevator on his way to the beach, Buzz hurled herself out of the kitchen and ran upstairs.

Frantically she tore open the door to Elinor's apartment. In the passage, she stumbled and almost fell, then flung back the door to the bedroom.

To her relief, Elinor was not slumped on the floor; deathly white, she clung for support to the silver brocade hangings of her bed. Wordlessly, she pointed above the fireplace.

Buzz turned her head to the left, where the portrait of the three sisters hung.

At first Buzz saw nothing, but then she gasped in horror.

Each of the three long, creamy necks had been cut horizontally: a small triangle of canvas hung downward from each slashed throat.

Chapter · 18

In the foyer of the Clanrickard Club, Mike Grant leaned against the wall at the bottom of a double-sided curving staircase. With his hands in the pockets of his dinner jacket, he surveyed the room. It was going to be a good night, in spite of the fact that it was August and a Wednesday. Making sure to appear casual, he carefully watched the men in dinner jackets and the women in full-length décolleté dresses move slowly over the red carpet toward the restaurant at the rear, or climb the staircase to the gaming rooms.

Mike noticed a group of heavy gamblers, most of them Greek, move toward the baccarat room, where the Sultan of Rupolei had been losing for the last hour. His attention was also caught by a woman dressed in midnight-blue satin and diamonds; the sister of a Mideastern ruler, she was known as an audacious gambler. He stiffened as he recognized a man move upstairs with a distinctive, boneless saunter: he had better send someone up to check the backgammon room. The club owners, the casinos, and the multinational bookmakers knew which professional gamblers successfully played games that contained an element of skill—such as backgammon and poker—and they preferred to have nothing to do with them; ideally, the house welcomed inexperienced, rich idiots.

"This is certainly a good night to play the odds." Mike heard a sarcastic voice from behind him.

He turned and smiled at Adam. "Come into my office for a drink. What's up?"

In Mike's office, furnished with heavily varnished Victorian club furniture, Adam shook his head curtly at the offer of a chair. "I'm not staying," he said. "I merely wanted to tell you that you've scared the hell out of everyone at Saracen—except me. So kindly curb your theatrical, James Bond streak. I knew immediately what your message meant: 'If you don't pay up, one slash is all it takes.' " He glared at his brother. "I thought you were fond of Elinor. I seem to recall that Elinor helped you to buy your first good bike. Why drag her into my problems? You might have given her another stroke."

"I don't know what the hell you're talking about, and I can't comment until I do." Mike, his face alert and wary, lit a cigarette.

Adam briefly described how the triple portrait had been slashed and added, "D'you really expect me to believe that you had nothing to do with it? *Someone* told some cat burglar where to find that picture!"

Mike stared at his brother, then slowly said, "Not me. I agree, it's clearly a warning to pay, but I swear I know nothing about it. It couldn't have been the brothers—they'd be even less subtle . . ." He inhaled deeply. "Who else do you owe money, Adam, you stupid bastard?"

"No one who'd do anything so bloody childish! How do I stop this bloody nonsense?"

"How many times must I tell you that if you let things go too far, nobody can stop what will undoubtedly happen? Adam," Mike went on quietly, "you've always taken full advantage of anyone who's fond of you. You think you can push me around because you've been doing that since we were in the nursery. You also grew up watching Grandfather's clients literally get away with murder." He sucked on his cigarette, furiously threw it into the fireplace, shoved his hands in his pockets, and glared at Adam. "Do you *want* to be found washed up on the seashore with a few vital bits missing? Are you so anxious to know what it feels like to have both eyeballs gouged out, one at a time? Do you *want* to be slowly battered to death, before dying in agony?"

"Of course not, you bastard," Adam said. "I only want to know who slashed that picture if you didn't."

"Whoever they are—and only you know that—these people are serious. Punters often try to avoid paying. Examples often have to be made. You know that." Mike started to stride up and down the room. "Take that fucking urbane look off your face and face reality, Adam. If you lose money, that's tough. But if you don't pay up, that's insanity."

"I've had enough of your melodrama," Adam snarled.

Mike glared at his brother again. "I'm not exaggerating. Remember that incident when the Sultan's sister had her Rolls stopped, at two in the morning on the Grande Corniche, after leaving the casino? They blew away the chauffeur's head with a machine gun. *She* wasn't touched. She paid all her gambling debts the very next day. And when the story was carefully leaked to the newspapers, quite a lot of other debts were suddenly settled in full."

"I'm not some goddamned sultan's sister."

"No, but you also like playing with fire. You never believe that the gods will really let it burn *you*. You think you're omnipotent—but you aren't."

"Keep your voice down," Adam growled.

"I'll do what I bloody well like in my own office," Mike said. "Don't you understand? I'm on your side, Adam. You're the only brother I have." His voice deepened. "I'm probably more worried about this than you are. If anything happened to you ... I'd be left without you. So for God's sake, pay up, you stupid shit! Don't think you can get away with it just because you've always got away with everything, since you set that nursemaid's apron alight."

"I thought you were too young to remember that," Adam said uneasily. He added, "She shouldn't have left the matches within reach of a child."

"She was in hospital for six weeks, and I was the only one who knew it wasn't an accident. I knew you wanted to see *how far you could go.*"

"Let's not argue about something that happened over thirty years ago," Adam said finally. "Can you raise money to help me fend them off? I promise you, within six months I *know* I'll have no more money problems. Never again."

"You'll have money problems as long as you gamble, Adam."

Annabel was determined to get a grip on herself and do as Scott advised: remember 1965 as the year she stopped having to go to auditions and 1966 as the year in which she blossomed into a successful young New York hostess as she met Andy Warhol, Lenny Bernstein, Baby Jane Holzer, and all the other gossip columnist fodder. By July, Annabel was a Junior Friend of the Metropolitan Museum, a Friend of the Museum of Modern Art, and a patron of the Bronx Zoo. She also allayed her insecurity with a massive spending spree: each charity dinner required a new ballgown, and each new glittering friend—contacts for Scott— required a glittering party. So the year thus far was a busy one.

FRIDAY, 19 AUGUST 1966

On the hottest morning of the year, Scott's news editor asked him to step into his office.

From behind the untidy piles on his desk, the news editor said, "Shut the door and prepare to listen to some good advice, Scott. I know you went after an anchor job last year and didn't get it. I know you're now up for another anchor job. I know you're going to be interviewed and I know which network it is, so don't deny a thing." He shoved a paper cup of lukewarm coffee across the desk to Scott. "I'd rather you went after it with my support than behind my back. At least if a guy from a local station gets a prominent network job, it reflects well on that station." He picked up his cup, took a whiff of it, and put it down again. "In order to get that job, Scott, you have to clarify one thing in your mind—a picture of what they're looking for as an anchorman."

Scott said nothing.

"Forget the crusading-journalist approach, Scott. Or the hard-nosed, insistent, tough approach. That's what *everyone* applying for that job will pitch. The network is looking for something extra. They want someone who looks as if he's been shot at, wounded, and spent the day crawling through minefields to deliver the dispatches. So don't go looking too neat. On the other hand, don't go looking *too* battered: they aren't looking for Walter Huston, they're looking for a younger, well-scrubbed, cheerfully confident Robert Mitchum."

"I don't think they're looking for a battered glamour boy," Scott said. "They're looking for a first-class professional journalist."

The news editor looked cynical. "Viewers don't switch channels for a good professional journalist; what prompts that switch is something less tangible."

"And they also want something else," Scott went on quietly. "A quality that you and I share."

"What's that?"

"Devotion. We love this business. You'd rather be doing your job than anything else in the world. You feel guilty about enjoying it so much. The real reason you often put in fourteen hours seven days a week is because you think it's important that people know what's happening in their world."

Jake laughed. "You can buy me a drink after you land the job."

One week after Scott's interview with the network, Jake arrived at his office to find a bottle of pure malt Highland whisky standing on top of the papers on his desk.

FRIDAY, 26 AUGUST 1966

The feather—an ordinary pale gray pigeon's feather—softly traced Miranda's thighs. She sighed sleepily. They'd had a wonderful afternoon.

The secret of Adam's sexual success with women was simple: he took plenty of time to stroke or massage, to make sure that his partner was completely relaxed before they made love. Then he always made sure that she climaxed before he entered her. Gradually Adam would discover where and how each woman liked to be touched, and he would change his techniques to suit her, then moving on to something that she wasn't expecting or had never experienced.

Adam blew the feather into the air and let it drift to the floor. He stretched. "Looks as if we're in for a storm."

Miranda slipped from her bed and wandered to a window; leaning out, she smelled rosemary and eucalyptus as she watched the summer storm approach from the distant cobalt-blue mountains. The bright light of Provence changed theatrically as the sky darkened to gray, then turned slate purple.

After an ominous moment of silence, when not a leaf fluttered, two incandescent white worms of lightning flashed across the sky. A mighty clash of thunder followed, after which heavy rain fell. Below Miranda, the dusty terra-cotta tiles of the medieval roofs were slicked and sharpened to glistening ocher, tangerine, and brown. Then it was as if a gray curtain fell in front of the window, blotting out all color.

Miranda frowned at the rain; her visitors would shortly be arriving at the village hotels, for she had decided to hold the KITS annual sales conference weekend at Saracen.

The sales conference, held just before the all-important Christmas run-up began, was meant to psych up the sales force for the new line. Miranda loved everything about the sales conference except making her speech. She really ought to rehearse that presentation again, she thought. She drew in her head, shut the windows, pulled the heavy cream linen curtains, and switched on the lamps; they glowed cheerfully over the primrose chair covers and the yellow silk bed quilt, upon which Adam lay naked.

"I'd better creep off," Adam said. "It's nearly five o'clock. This place will be humming with staff in a few minutes."

Miranda, sounding slightly mutinous, said, "I don't see why we can't sleep together openly."

"Because we're not married," Adam said, "because I'm not an earl."

"I don't intend to marry to please my grandmother."

"Soon," Adam said firmly, "but not yet. I'm too busy with SUPPLYKITS. But there's something else I must discuss with you before I leave."

Miranda, not wishing to quarrel with Adam, did not pursue her argument.

SUPPLYKITS was negotiating for three businesses, and Adam was handling all three deals: a direct-mail business, a premium-gift business, and a public-relations business. Should all the deals be successful, SUPPLYKITS would then own five subsidiary businesses, including KITS.

A director from each of the new companies would acquire shares and sit on the SUPPLYKITS board; as Miranda owned the entire company, these inducement shares would reduce her holding, but Adam had convinced a reluctant Miranda that by relinquishing fifteen percent of her shares, she was exchanging a hundred percent of a small orange for eighty-five percent of a crateful.

Adam turned onto his back, his hands behind his head, and looked at the ceiling. "It's about time we considered going public."

Astonished, Miranda sat down on the edge of the bed. "So soon? Why?"

"We can't do it until next March, when we'll have five years' trading figures to show," Adam said. "But such a move would provide more cash for acquisitions. We can't go on leveraging forever."

"No," said Miranda, remembering that Angus had warned her about this. "But won't it be expensive to go public?"

"Very expensive," Adam said. "But you want more outlets for KITS and you want them in the best and most expensive locations."

"So the reason to go public is to finance expansion?"

"Not only that. We'll also be more respectable and creditworthy."

"What about control?" Miranda worried. "I don't want to lose control of my business."

"You won't lose control so long as you retain over fifty percent of the shares," Adam reassured her. "But *nobody* should have all their capital invested in one sector of the market, as you have. You should sell some shares for cash and invest that money in other areas. Arrange a nice, well-spread portfolio for yourself. It's about time you saw some financial reward for your work and responsibility."

"How many SUPPLYKITS shares would I have to sell?"

"Legally, twenty-five percent of the shares have to be made available to the public. The new directors will probably be pleased to sell their incentive shares for such a quick profit, so you should only lose ten percent of your present holding. If we issue new shares, you'll end up with seventy-five percent of the business *and* a large sum of cash."

"I'd like the staff to be able to have shares," Miranda said, "to benefit from the success of the business."

"We can certainly arrange that, should SUPPLYKITS go public."

"I'll think about it."

Adam said, "It will take at least six months to organize, so think fast."

FRIDAY, 9 SEPTEMBER 1966

Four months after Clare opened her toy shop, her bank manager advised her to close it as quickly as possible, because she was losing money at a steady and frightening pace. He advised her to sell the shop and deposit the money in the bank. She had better not invest it in the stock market, because she couldn't afford to lose a penny and there was no such thing as a safe share.

Over supper at the basement flat, Clare discussed her woes with Kathy, her former nanny.

"It was apparently doomed from the start," Clare explained sadly, over the baked beans. "The sort of people who can afford handcrafted learning toys don't shop at the wrong end of the Pimlico Road." She scraped out the dish. "I concentrated on toys for preschool children because I thought I knew about them. But those children didn't want well-made, tasteful, pale wood Swedish toys. What they wanted was cheap, bright, plastic toys from Hong Kong, and I didn't stock those."

"Couldn't you sell Lego and stuff like that?"

"I had plenty of Lego, but what they really wanted were the expensive toys they saw advertised on children's TV."

"Well, couldn't you have sold a few of those?"

"By the time I realized that, I had no spare cash," Clare explained. "And that wasn't my only problem. The importers weren't reliable, and neither were the craftsmen, especially those who persuaded me to pay them in advance. Then I got in a financial muddle because I didn't keep my bookkeeping up-to-date."

"It sounds like a nightmare," Kathy said.

Clare shuddered. "The worst problem was theft." Her entire gross profit for the first four months had been negated by shoplifting tots. The first time Clare caught a little girl hiding a rag doll up her knickers, she angrily threatened to call a policeman. The child burst into tears. Clare, contrite, gave her the doll as a gift.

At the beginning of October, Kathy, who had again been invited for supper, arrived at Clare's apartment to find that nothing had been cooked. Clare, wearing a dirty dressing gown, was sitting on her unmade bed, staring into space.

"Where's Josh?" Kathy asked.

"I put him to bed early. It's good for him."

Kathy made two cups of tea and said firmly, "You aren't yourself, Clare, and you haven't been for months."

"I'm still depressed about the Red Rocking Horse," Clare replied vaguely.

"This started before that toy shop closed," Kathy said. "I think it's those pills you take. Why not stop them?"

"Don't be silly—my doctor prescribed those tranquilizers," Clare said. "He's a qualified doctor and you aren't, Kathy."

"But I *know* you better than he does! You aren't the same person since you started taking those things, Clare. You don't listen to what I'm saying. You don't play with Josh like you used to—you just sit! You've even stopped working for C.N.D."

"I could easily do without the pills," Clare said crossly. "But not just yet." She started to weep drearily. "I don't seem to be successful at *anything*. I used to be such a smug little prig. I was so sure I knew what was right, so critical of other people. Now I've found out how hopeless I am on my own. . . ."

"You'd be a lot less hopeless if you were thinking straight," Kathy advised. "Why don't you get away from Chelsea, move to the country? You're always saying you wished you still lived in the country. And you *could* live in the country on what you're wasting in rent for this dump!" She looked around the room with distaste. "Go to that place where you grew up and tell a local estate agent you want the cheapest thing he's got. Try to get it before Christmas, because I've got a bit of time off then, and I'll help you settle in."

Mrs. Gooden agreed to let Josh stay with her until Clare sorted out her problems and found somewhere to live.

The day he left, Kathy said to Clare, "I'll come round every evening and you can phone me anytime—I've asked my boss." To Clare's horror, Kathy then flushed the pills down the sink drain. "Now you know you'll have to manage without 'em," she said firmly.

During the first day without her pills, Clare grew increasingly depressed and agitated. By the evening, her mouth was dry, her hands had started to shake, and she felt dizzy. She didn't sleep at all that night. Her hands trembled too badly to cook and she sweated as if in the tropics. Frightened by these bodily reactions, she collapsed on the sofa and cried.

The following evening, when Kathy came to check on her, it was obvious that Clare blamed her for the shape she was in.

"If you go back to the doctor for another prescription," Kathy told her, "we'll only have to go through this again later. Now eat this stew I've brought."

By the fifth morning, Clare's hands no longer trembled.

On the eighth day, she felt her normal, clearheaded self again. Deeply grateful to Kathy, she said, "Tomorrow I'm going to pick up Josh, take the train to Warminster, and look for a place where we can start all over again."

Applebank Cottage, made of local soft Bath stone, was damp and cold, but as the agent pointed out, what did Clare expect for two pounds per week? All it needed was some heat.

From the garden gate to the front door, a herringbone brick path divided a neglected vegetable garden. Apple trees grew on either side of the double-sided small house, and behind it, the land rose smoothly to a small wood that followed the ridge of a hill.

Clare moved in just before Christmas, with a minimum of furniture, bought secondhand at an auction in Warminster. She hoped that Kathy was right, and that once away from the city, with enough money for her simple everyday needs, she would gradually find herself able to cope again.

SUNDAY, 25 DECEMBER 1966

Neither Annabel (the hostess at a big charity children's skating party at Rockefeller Center) nor Clare (not invited) was present at Elinor's 1966 Christmas Day luncheon at Saracen, but Miranda and Adam were there; both arriving with bulging briefcases of work papers.

After the traditional turkey and Christmas pudding (made by Buzz, for Sylvie thought the recipe ludicrous), everyone left the table for a siesta. A few minutes later, Miranda sneaked to Adam's bedroom.

After they made love, Adam lay naked on the bed, staring contentedly at the ceiling. Beside him, Miranda felt too tired to think, too tired to move. She wondered how long she would be able to continue at her present pace.

Adam picked up a yellow legal pad and scribbled on it. He murmured, "Can you manage that dinner at the Mansion House next Thursday?"

"If you insist." Miranda yawned. Miranda was the prominently displayed figurehead of the SUPPLYKITS flotation, planned for three months ahead: she had become the living corporate identity of the company; her face, clothes, and style had become the visual embodiment of her business. Miranda was publicly perceived as an intelligent, modern woman on the move—the new sixties woman, not content to sit at home and wait for things to happen to her.

Because of this, Miranda, who hated being photographed or interviewed, had been obliged to entertain important people: pension fund managers, stockbrokers, bankers, and financial journalists. These business obligations made her feel impatient and frustrated: she would have preferred to spend her time working in her cosmetics business. KITS needed much more of her attention than it had been getting recently, and was now in a disturbing financial position; it didn't look as if the company would make a profit in 1966.

Although Adam pointed out that a profit was projected for the whole group, and that the group expansion had been phenomenal,

Miranda felt a wistful longing for the old, less comfortable days—not so very long ago—when KITS had been her brilliant baby.

Now Adam interrupted Miranda's reverie by saying, "By the way, Paul Littlejohn says that the trustees regretfully must turn down your request for funds to redecorate your house. Apparently there have been big extra bills for Saracen this year; this place costs a fortune to run."

"Blast," Miranda mumbled into her pillow.

"The trustees are only doing their job," Adam soothed. "After all, you can't expect them to go on saying yes forever." He turned away from her as the telephone rang. "Hello? Mike? Had a good Christmas? So it arrived on time. . . . A Harley-Davidson Sportster was exactly what you wanted. . . . Of course I can afford it. . . . No, the panic's over. . . . Happy New Year, little brother. . . . I *know* you're thirty-four years old. . . . Then I won't in future. . . . We're coming back tomorrow, in Miranda's plane. . . . *Ciao.*"

The day after Christmas, at six a.m., when it was still dark outside, Elinor stood in the entrance hall waiting to say goodbye to Miranda and Adam. Buzz, only half awake, wore an old Jaeger dressing gown that now looked like something from a dog basket.

"Buzz, please go and hurry Miranda!" Elinor said, smiling apologetically at Adam.

"It's been a wonderful Christmas," Adam said to Elinor as soon as Buzz disappeared. "I've used this peaceful break to consider something very important to me, and last night I reached my decision. I am going to leave STG and start my own practice."

Elinor stared, astonished. "But *why,* Adam? It's your family firm . . ."

"Quite frankly, Elinor—and in confidence—STG has been handling too many criminal cases for my liking. I don't think a respectable firm should take such a direction, however lucrative. I'm certain my father would never have allowed it. I'm not letting down STG—there are now seventeen senior partners and I'm only one of them. And since my speciality is international tax law, I feel . . . somewhat regretfully . . ."

"How will your decision affect my business?" Elinor asked sharply.

"It's up to you, Elinor. You will have to choose between STG and me. . . . I shall carry the same professional insurance as STG, by the way."

"I wish we could have talked about this when we had more time, Adam." Elinor was vexed.

"Until last night, I was undecided. *You* are the first person I have told, Elinor. I only wish that my father could know that I'm at last setting up on my own. . . . If you want to stay with STG, I'll be happy to arrange to have your work handled by one of the other partners—although it may take him a little time to be able to handle your affairs completely on his own without asking you a lot of questions."

Elinor said, "I don't want to deal with some new lawyer. I'm far too old to change. I want my affairs handled properly *without* a lot of questions. And if you're setting up your own firm, I'm sure your dear father would want me to help you start. So please arrange it."

"The simplest thing would be for you to write to STG and say you no longer wish them to represent you. Ask them to submit their bill to date—I'll check it, of course—and hand all your papers to me. No need to type the letter—in fact, a handwritten note would perhaps be best." Adam's brown eyes looked sincere. "I can't tell you how much I appreciate this, Elinor. I only wish that Dad could know of your loyalty."

Chapter · 19

On the morning after Christmas, peaceful demonstrations organized by the C.N.D. took place all over Britain.

In Bath, the march started from the courtyard of Bath Abbey, which demonstrators had been forbidden to enter; the beautifully carved golden stone entrance to the abbey was protected by police horses. They stamped impatiently, legs shifting and snorting breath visible on the crisp, thin air.

Clare, wearing an old red ski suit, stood in a crowd of about three hundred people. She had left Josh with Kathy, who was spending Christmas at Applebank Cottage. Clare's banner, made from an old sheet kept taut by two broom handles, was painted with the red words BAN THE BOMB.

At eleven o'clock, the demonstrators formed a line in front of the abbey and prepared to parade slowly through the streets of the historic Georgian city. They were watched by a straggle of housewives and schoolchildren, and a photographer from the local paper.

Clare took up her position on the abbey side of the line. Just as the column began to move, a schoolgirl, pushing a baby in a pram, accidentally backed into a police horse. The horse, trained to keep calm, hardly moved, but the schoolgirl shrieked in terror and let go of her pram, which ran into the column of marchers; it hit the man standing next to Clare, who stumbled heavily against her, knocking her sideways.

As Clare staggered, her arms dropped and her banner wrapped around her head: she could not see where she was going. She tottered to her right, bumped into a police horse's hindquarters, stumbled against the horse, then screamed as she was pulled violently backward by strong arms.

Someone helped her to struggle free from her banner. Clare looked up and saw the tallest man she had ever seen; he had curly black hair and black-lashed, dark brown eyes, now filled with worry.

The man half carried, half pulled her into a nearby pub, where he propped her in a Windsor chair and went to fetch water from the bar. Clare, who felt dizzy and tearful, wondered whether she would ever again be able to move her jaw, which had received a painful blow, probably from the broomstick of her own banner. She looked across the bar to the back view of her rescuer: he wore jeans and an old maroon suede jacket buckled around lean hips; his boots were muddy.

As the man returned with a glass of water, Clare stared at his short, straight nose, above a mouth to write poems about: it was full-lipped, finely chiseled, subtly curved. Michelangelo's David come to life, Clare thought. She wished she had worn some makeup, then chastised herself for such a feeble thought.

Her rescuer said impatiently, "Sorry I took so long. It's almost impossible to get water in a bar since they don't make any money out of it." He poured water on his handkerchief, then gently dabbed at Clare's chin. "You'll have a huge bruise . . . Is there anyone with you?"

Clare shook her head.

"You shouldn't drive, or ride a bicycle, after a wallop like that. I'll take you home."

Clare mumbled with difficulty, "No, I'm okay. I'll get a lift home after the demo. I've just moved into a cottage on the edge of Warminster."

He drove her back in a battered silver sports car.

To Clare, his milky warm smell was like that of a newborn baby. She sternly reminded herself that she wasn't going to fall in love with the wrong man again just because she was sexually attracted to him, and she was *never* going to get married again. Having decided not to marry him, Clare directed her rescuer, David Arrowsmith, to Applebank Cottage.

In the kitchen, Kathy's look of incredulous congratulation was followed by concern when she noticed Clare's battered chin.

Abruptly Clare said to David, "Thank you for bringing me back. I'll be perfectly fine now. Kathy will look after me."

Clare knew that women often made up their minds very quickly, and without enough information, about other people, particularly those who were physically attractive: she had just seen Kathy do so. She also knew that, generally speaking, good, worthy men did not look flashy and glamorous, let alone theatrical; on the other hand, many rats were as good-looking as they were confident. Clare wouldn't put it past Sam to use a rat to lay a trap for her. Like many divorcées, she now viewed the man she had married as a monster of depravity, as capable as Richard III of any dirty deed. Clare's divorce petition would not be heard until July; she had been warned by her solicitor not to be seen alone with a man right now, or it might affect her petition and the custody of her son. She couldn't afford to run any risks, and there was certainly something mysterious about David Arrowsmith, something she couldn't identify for the moment: so she didn't trust him.

The following morning, after breakfast, a bruised Clare cut a photograph of herself from the local newspaper; luckily, her face was totally obscured by the banner, which had wrapped itself around her like a winding sheet. She looked like an Egyptian mummy in boots, but it was a good picture of her rescuer. She slipped the newspaper cutting into the top drawer of her bedside chest, then took the opportunity to go for a walk by herself, without Josh.

Once past her garden, Clare turned off the narrow lane onto a path hedged high with hawthorn, which led up the gently rising hill behind the cottage to the wood.

The wood was disturbingly still and silent; the twisted trunks and naked branches of the trees looked lonely and forlorn. Not a leaf moved, except for the dead leaves that Clare trod on. When she stepped on a stick and snapped it, the sudden noise caused a rook to rise from its nest with a startled beating of wings.

She looked up at the rook's nest and the gray sky beyond, then bent to pick a clump of white winter aconites to take home to Josh. As she did so, a rusty trap sprang shut, clamping her left foot.

Clare yelled in pain as she fell on scratchy, frosted bracken. Luckily, she was wearing tough boots, so the trap had not torn her leg. She felt little pain unless she moved, which she tried not to do as she struggled to pull apart the serrated jaws of the trap. It was attached to a rusty chain hidden in the bracken. Clare could see more rusty chain around the slender, peeling, silver trunk of a nearby birch tree. She would only be able to move within the circumference of that tree. She was truly trapped.

The air didn't feel sharply cold enough for snow, and Clare hoped it wouldn't rain; she peered upward at the dull, gray sky.

She wondered how long it would be before Kathy grew alarmed. If Clare wasn't home and hadn't telephoned by two o'clock—or three at the latest—she reckoned that Kathy might phone the police, who would surely find her before long.

Unfortunately, Clare lay off the path in a place where the ground dipped, so she could not be seen. With difficulty, she rolled her body into a more comfortable position, pulled up the collar of her cherry wool coat, twisted her scarf around her head, and heaped bracken to form a pillow; with her head upon it, she stared crossly at the now leaden sky overhead. She pushed her hands deeper in her pockets and wished she had worn heavier gloves. She wondered if fate had just punished her for picking wildflowers.

Just before midday, Clare heard a noise behind her. Abruptly she sat up, winced at the pain this produced, then listened as the sound grew nearer: somebody was whistling "Lillibullero" with warbles and elaborate trills, off key, but with clear enjoyment.

Clare yelled, "Help!" several times, then stopped. She could hear nothing. Again she yelled.

This time a man's voice shouted, "Keep calling."

Eventually Clare heard a distant crackle. As it grew louder, she twisted around to face the sound.

"Oh!" she said. "It's you!"

"And vice versa," said David Arrowsmith as he scrambled toward her.

He towered above Clare, his hands tucked in the front pockets of the suede jacket. "I called to see how you were. Your nanny told me you'd gone for a walk. She saw you come up here." He squatted beside her. "Hey, not much of a country girl, are you?" He examined the trap.

"As a matter of fact, I am," Clare said. "We used to live near here. But as this is hunting country, I didn't expect a trap in the woods. And Kathy isn't my nanny. I can't afford a nanny. She's been staying with us over the Christmas holiday."

David tried without success to release Clare. Eventually he said, "This is a very old, heavy trap, and I don't think I can force the thing apart. I'd better phone the police—they'll know who owns this wood, and get him to free you. Take my gloves, and try not to get into any more trouble while I'm gone." He added ruefully, "I know I should tear that trap apart with my bare hands, but I'm not as tough as I look."

An hour later, the trap was pried apart by two mechanics from the local garage using steel bars. Teeth chattering, Clare limped back to Applebank Cottage with David, telling herself not to make a fuss.

After she had a hot rum toddy in a steaming, warm tub and showed Josh the trap marks on her leg, they all sat around the wooden kitchen table to eat vegetable soup, local Stilton cheese, and a salad of walnuts and chicory, followed by gingerbread that Clare had made with Mrs. Gooden's special recipe.

Then Josh had his nap and Kathy took Clare's bicycle to explore the country.

"You must be an Escoffier when you're in full possession of your faculties," David said. "May I have another slice of that delicious gingerbread?"

"It's a bit overdone. I've only just started to cook in a convection oven," Clare said apologetically. "And it's a bit difficult to manage with no fridge—just that metal meat safe hanging outside the back door. When I get a job, I'll get a fridge."

David, who had been briefly told about the flight from Sam, joked, "You might try selling gingerbread. I'd be your first customer."

Clare laughed. "What do *you* do for a living?"

"I'm an architect. I work in Bath. Mainly house renovations. I add an extension, convert a barn, chop off a couple of wings to make a house a manageable size—that sort of work. It's always a headache, but you have to take anything you can get when you're newly qualified."

"I thought of converting the attic," Clare said. "Making a room for Josh to sleep and play in, with bunks for visiting children. This house has only two bedrooms, which isn't ideal."

"I'll have a look at the attic, if you like."

"Well . . . I can't afford anything yet."

"But you might like to know what's possible, and how much it would cost?"

"Very much."

In the attic, David said thoughtfully, "As there's a window, you only need to lead the electrical supply upstairs, lay a soundproof floor covering—cork—and insulate the roof."

"It'll have to wait until I have some money."

After Josh had gone to bed, the three adults spent the evening roasting chestnuts before the living room fire.

At ten o'clock, David said, "I must go. But I'll be back." At the front door, he kissed Clare on the tip of her nose, then left.

SATURDAY, 31 DECEMBER 1966

Just after Kathy left for London, David arrived with a bottle of champagne to spend the day and celebrate New Year's Eve. Clare wondered suspiciously why this sensationally good-looking man seemed not to have any New Year's plans.

At lunch, Josh misbehaved. He pushed his food off the table and refused to eat even the cheesecake.

Clare was mortified. She had so hoped that Josh would like David. "He's tired," she apologized, and took Josh off for his afternoon nap. He kicked and screamed, furious that his mother's attention was being distracted from himself.

Darkness fell early, and it started to snow. After tea, Clare pulled the sitting room curtains together but didn't switch on the light: she preferred to watch the firelight flick shadows over the walls. In the embers of the fire, David again roasted chestnuts for the now sunny-tempered Josh, until his bedtime.

When Clare returned from putting Josh to bed, David wordlessly took her in his arms; they sat on the floor, leaning against the broken-backed armchair, and necked like teenagers.

As David's nose nuzzled the back of her neck, Clare had an overwhelming need to be even closer to him. She felt as if she were lying naked on a hot rock, stretching languorously toward the sun.

As the light of the friendly flames played over their faces, Clare felt she was in a dream world where time was suspended. She felt a physical longing too strong to resist; she breathed fast and grew a bit light-headed; she could smell the soft, milky smell of David's body and the warm wool odor of his sweater; she felt a frenzied yearning.

At midnight, David kissed her gently and left shortly afterward, saying he hoped that snow hadn't blocked the roads.

Disappointed, Clare wondered what had gone wrong. After all, he needn't have visited her. Why hadn't he wanted to stay?

Of course, she wouldn't have let him.

WEDNESDAY, 11 JANUARY 1967

"What's so urgent and private that you couldn't discuss it over the telephone?" In his study, Adam, wearing a dinner jacket, poured whiskey into a cut-glass tumbler and confronted his brother.

Mike wore black leather biking trousers and a heavy seaman's turtleneck sweater. He said, "I've now been waiting two bloody years for my commission on the Framwell deal."

Mike's agreed commission was two percent of the purchase price of any property that Miranda acquired, either directly or indirectly, through him. The commission had been correctly paid on all the relevant purchases except that of Framwells—the chain of tobacconist shops—which was easily the biggest deal Mike had handled.

"You'll get your money," Adam said. "But Framwells was a self-financing deal. Frankly, the interest we've had to pay on the loan is very high."

"Fuck that. It isn't my problem."

"With the greatest respect"—Mike knew this phrase meant Adam was annoyed—"it *is* your problem, Mike, because no date of payment for commission was written into your contract. Legally, I could keep you waiting a hundred years for the money."

"We didn't have a contract. You wrote the arrangement on a sheet of paper over dinner, and we both signed it. Here it is!" Mike pulled a paper from his pocket and looked at it. No period of payment was mentioned.

"If you're going to be difficult," Adam said, "I suggest that either you wait for a hundred years or agree to reduce the amount payable, by half."

Mike looked at Adam in astonishment. "You're my *brother,* you bastard! Brothers aren't supposed to fuck each other over! You use me when it suits you, you get me to fix your dirty work—"

"If you didn't do it, there are plenty of others who would."

"You ruthless, evil bastard."

Mike, furious, could see that Adam clearly felt he had nothing to fear from his little brother. Adam stopped now to light a cigarette, contemptuously confident of his ability to maneuver and control.

"Kindly remember that I provide the legal know-how to protect you and your—friends," Adam said calmly. "I'll speak to Miranda about your payment. I'll see if I can hurry it."

"I'll damn well speak to Miranda myself," Mike growled.

Adam looked up sharply from his cigarette. "No. Don't do that. It isn't necessary!"

Mike suddenly realized what had happened.

"Miranda thinks she settled this bill months ago, doesn't she?" he yelled. *"What did you do?* Forge my name on the back of the check and endorse it to yourself?"

Mike saw a fleeting guilty look in Adam's eyes before his lids were lowered and his attention seemingly focused again on his gold lighter.

"No doubt you told yourself that you were only *borrowing* my money to pay your bloody gambling debts, but I call that *theft!"* Mike thundered.

Coolly Adam ground out his cigarette on the hearth.

Adam's apparent lack of concern enraged Mike, as hurt by his brother's treachery as he was by the theft. He wanted to *hurt* Adam. He wanted to feel his fist bruise flesh, smash bone, draw blood.

His fist shot out.

Adam stumbled backward, tripped over the steel fireplace screen, then lost his balance and crashed to the floor.

As Adam fell, Mike heard the sound of his head hitting the elaborate steel fender. It happened so fast that Mike was left with his arm still outstretched, toward the dinner-jacketed body of his brother.

Immediately contrite, Mike crouched by Adam and lifted his head: it lolled sideways. Mike's face was very pale.

Christ, thought Mike, I *can't* have killed him, not just with one lousy punch . . . could I? He knew that only a very good fighter—a much better fighter than he was—could knock a man unconscious with one punch to the jaw.

Hastily Mike pulled at Adam, until he lay full length on the rug. He tore Adam's tie loose, undid his shirt and collar, and stuck his finger in

Adam's mouth to check that his tongue was free. He grabbed the telephone and dialed 999. He knew that the housekeeper wasn't in, because Adam had opened the front door.

After the fourth ring, the emergency operator answered: "Police, fire or ambulance?"

"Ambulance! Fast!" After giving full address details, Mike ran to the kitchen for water and a towel. How could he have hit his brother, the only person in the world with whom he felt fully relaxed, happy, and at home?

As he swabbed his brother's temples with cold water, Mike muttered, "I'm *sorry*. I can't tell you how sorry I am, Adam. My bloody temper again! Look, forget the money. Just, for God's sake, open your eyes. *Please.*"

Adam's eyelids moved slightly. Mike carefully wiped his face.

Adam looked up and said weakly, "God, my head's splitting. What happened?" He tried to lift his head, but the room tilted. Giddy, he fell back on the rug. With eyelids still closed, he murmured anxiously, "Where's my watch?"

"It's still on your wrist, old boy," said Mike, dabbing with the towel at his brother's face. "An ambulance is on its way—should be here any minute."

Adam slowly lifted his left wrist and looked at it.

Puzzled, Mike wondered what was so special about that ordinary-looking Omega watch.

Adam said weakly, "I don't need an ambulance. . . . You hit me, that's all. You're not Superman. . . . I'll be okay in the morning."

FRIDAY, 20 JANUARY 1967

Just after six o'clock, Clare heard the squeak of the garden gate hinge. Her heart jumped. She caught her breath, dropped her oven gloves to the floor, and leapt to the window. David was walking up the garden path, half an hour earlier than expected.

As he came through the kitchen door, he said, "I'll oil that gate for you tomorrow when we clear the garden . . . Mmm, what's that delicious smell?" He took her in his arms.

"Leek-and-potato stew." Clare's newfound, short-term leisure meant that she now enjoyed cooking, instead of seeing it as an added, rushed three-times-a-day chore to fit in around earning her living. She mumbled against David's tweed jacket, "We're having chicory-and-orange salad with vinaigrette sauce, followed by mushroom crous-tade with a hazelnut topping, then Stilton and homemade oatmeal biscuits."

"Sounds delicious." He kissed the top of her head. "By the way, are you a vegetarian?"

"Only since last week. I decided I don't like eating dead bodies—not after being caught in a trap. I know most people think it's cranky."

Clare served supper early so that four-year-old Josh could stay up late and eat with them. She would have preferred a romantic candlelit dinner for two, but even more, she wanted Josh to see David as one of life's pluses and not as an interloper.

After Josh had gone to bed, they again sat on a rug before the fire with their backs to the broken-backed armchair, holding hands as they listened to a radio concert.

Clare murmured, "There's something I have to tell you."

She had carefully thought out what she was going to say, but when, in the firelight, she looked into his dark-fringed eyes, she forgot her rehearsed words. She sighed and said regretfully, "You're so good-looking."

"I know what you mean. I hate it. It's embarrassing. And believe me, it's a drawback. Women are distracted and men don't trust me because of my looks," David said. "But there's nothing I can do about it. I wear my hair long and I comb it forward to hide as much as possible of my face. I used to wear clear glass spectacles, although I didn't need them." He added, "But there is one great advantage: nobody wants to fight me. Sometimes if I'm sitting in a bar, I'm teased by strangers, who think I'm a homosexual. Then I slowly stand up, and they see the length of me and back away. They're not to know I'd never fight." He laughed apologetically. "I also have some cranky principles."

Clare didn't laugh. Instead, she said what she had to say, knowing that this was the time to get it out. "David, I find you almost unbearably attractive. I love feeling close to you. *But I don't want to go to bed with you. I want to make that clear!*"

"Why not?" David settled his arm more comfortably around her.

Clare lost her nerve. She had intended to say, "Because I went through a promiscuous period after I left Sam, and it was a hateful, shameful, humiliating time, and I'll never let it happen again." She also feared that early sexual disaster in this relationship would doom it.

But Clare forgot her lines; instead, she burst into tears. "Because my love life has been such a mess!"

"Well, that's in the past," David murmured as he cuddled her. "But what happened?"

Clare snuffled a bit. "Sex isn't what I was led to expect."

David said, "Sex without a close emotional relationship doesn't work for me either. I can't separate sex from old-fashioned feelings like love and affection."

"But that's what *women* usually say!"

"You know, Clare, what I like about you is your innocence. Maybe what I'm saying is the only sure-fire, tried and tested way to get a girl's knickers off in thirty seconds—which, by the way, it is. But what I said *is* the way I feel."

"I know why you're so easy to talk to," Clare said. "You don't bother to try and prove yourself. You really *listen* to what I say—and you respond to it. My husband didn't take me seriously."

"And you haven't had another relationship since?"

Clare hesitated, then took the plunge. "I had a ghastly series of one-nighters. Usually they hopped on and pumped away and suddenly it was over. I never climaxed and I was too shy and too timid to ask for what I wanted, so afterward I'd be resentful . . ."

"But if you never told them what turned you on, how could you expect—"

"I agree, it seems crazy. I wasn't too shy to leap into bed with them, but I was too shy to tell them what I needed."

"How you feel is how you feel and how you climax is how you climax, and so long as you let a man know those things, there shouldn't be a problem," David said. They settled down to some serious kissing.

FRIDAY, 27 JANUARY 1967

The following Friday evening, after spinach soufflé, baked potatoes with sour cream, and rather a lot of excellent claret, Clare found herself sitting naked to the waist in the firelight. "Let's go to bed," she whispered.

"Promise you won't anticipate?"

"*What?*"

"No anxious thoughts."

"Such as?"

"I hope I'm going to come. . . . I hope my body's as good as his other girls'. . . . I hope I don't take much longer. . . ."

Shyly Clare added, "I hope he isn't bored or tired. . . . he'll be disappointed if I don't come. . . ."

"Hell, it's all too much trouble. I'm not going to come. I'll fake it."

Clare nodded.

David stood up and pulled her to her feet. Hand in hand, they moved upstairs to bed.

Chapter · 20

"Oh my God, darling, I'd forgotten I ever signed that!" Miranda looked with dismay at the document that Adam had just placed on her white horseshoe-shaped desk. She suddenly felt as cold as the raw wind of March that swept the streets of London outside her office window.

Adam stared thoughtfully at Miranda; he leaned across her desk. "I've spent a long, long time thinking about this. Of course, I know you won't like giving up fifteen percent of the total equity of SUPPLYKITS—nobody would. On the other hand, it was on this condition that I joined your company: you agreed that should your business ever go public, I would have fifteen percent of the equity for the nominal sum of fifteen thousand pounds. I would like to hold you to your bargain, Miranda."

"But I thought that only referred to KITS!" Miranda said, dismayed.

"The wording of the document clearly states, 'and/or any other businesses that arise from this company.' That means fifteen percent of SUPPLYKITS, Miranda. Surely you read the document before signing it?"

"But, darling . . ." Miranda looked pleading.

Regretfully Adam shook his head. "This is not a personal matter, it's a matter that concerns your business integrity. What made me finally decide to insist on this was when I realized that had you been a man, Miranda, or had I not been personally involved with you, I wouldn't have *hesitated* to ask for these shares."

From opposite sides of the desk, they stared at each other impersonally. It was as if a glass wall had gone up between them. Miranda said quietly, "In that case, Adam, I'd like to get a second legal opinion."

"Of course. But you'd better inform Freddy Swanson immediately that there is a problem. After all, it's only two days to the flotation."

"Why the hell didn't you bring this up before now?" Miranda fumed.

"I've only just reached my decision," Adam said softly. He hadn't intended to give her time to try a countermove.

Miranda telephoned her lawyer. Having ascertained that she would, indeed, be forced to sell fifteen percent of SUPPLYKITS to Adam for a token amount, she added, "In that case, please rewrite my will and delete all reference to Adam Grant. Instead, reapportion those shares to my staff. . . . No, I've had a better idea! Add Adam Grant's bequest to that of Buzz—I mean, Miss Doris Mann."

Miranda replaced the receiver and called for her secretary. "June, please cancel all today's appointments. Ask Mr. Swanson if he would be kind enough to see me here, as soon as possible. I mean within the hour."

Miranda's ten-man board of directors had recently been expanded to include a new chairman, the Earl of Brighton, and Frederick Swanson of Seligman Swanson, the merchant bank chosen to handle the SUPPLY-KITS flotation. The bank had organized everything concerning the various consultants, the share price, and the prospectus, a forty-page, glossy volume about the company's structure, trading situation, and future plans. As was customary in Britain, existing contractual obligations had been included; as was also customary, two weeks before the flotation, the essential details of this prospectus had been published in national newspapers.

Mr. Swanson arrived at the reception area and was shown to the private lift that went straight to Miranda's office on the top floor.

When he stepped out, he was astonished by his first view of the place. The entire sixty-foot room was white, including the marble floor. The furniture was white and chrome, and even the many vases of spring flowers were white. The space looked clean, glamorous, and exciting. At the far end of the room, spotlights shone on white tables, upon which cosmetics, in various stages of testing, were spread. Overriding the scent of flowers was the faint suggestion of a peculiar smell, slightly reminiscent of a school science lab, but fruitier.

Miranda walked forward to welcome her visitor. "Good morning, Freddy."

"What's happened?" Freddy Swanson asked. He was pleased by the progress of the flotation: SUPPLYKITS was thriving; KITS had sacrificed its 1966 profit only to facilitate the other company's expansion.

Swiftly Miranda outlined her problem, grateful for once that her personal involvement with Adam was a secret.

"Why did Adam wait until so late?" Freddy thundered. "An undisclosed stock option worth three hundred thousand pounds throws

out all your figures! That means our brochure and advertisements are inaccurate."

"Originally he decided not to take up the option because he thought it would upset me," Miranda said lamely. "But Adam eventually decided that he couldn't afford such sentimental generosity."

"Which, of course, *did* upset you."

"To be frank, Freddy, he's earned it. I doubt SUPPLYKITS would be going public without him."

"Nevertheless, Adam's a qualified lawyer," Freddy said, "yet he put his name to a prospectus which says that all material information has been disclosed—but does not mention a fifteen percent stock option that I wasn't told about." He sat down on a white, tulip-shaped chair. "I'll calculate the exact figures," he murmured, "Adam has acquired one hundred and ninety-two thousand thirty-shilling shares worth two hundred and eighty-eight thousand pounds for fifteen thousand pounds, which leaves you, Miranda, holding sixty percent of the shares." Slowly he looked up from his calculations. "I suppose we can't do anything about it at this stage. All the expensive consultants' work has been done, all the donkey work is over, everyone is exhausted, and some of the public have already applied for the shares, so *very reluctantly* I will take no action. Those shares mustn't be sold to Adam until after the flotation."

Everyone in the office noticed the new, impeccably polite coldness between Miranda and Adam. Nobody guessed the reason. But Miranda felt exposed and lonely.

Early on the following Thursday morning, she grabbed the pale pink copy of the *Financial Times* from her breakfast tray. SUPPLYKITS was now on the London Stock Exchange: the share price had risen to thirty-three shillings. As Miranda poured her coffee, she realized that checking the share price would now be her first priority every morning. She was no longer the proprietor of SUPPLYKITS but the managing director and major shareholder of a public company.

For a moment, Miranda's eyes sparkled: the little sister—number three in the nursery—to whom no one had paid much attention, was now, at the age of twenty-six, clearly a number one in the business world! She was one of the few self-made women in Britain. *In the world!* She remembered her early unsuccessful struggles for equal treatment and wondered what her sisters would think of this news. To hell with equality now.

She wished she could share her glee with Adam. Miranda hated the coldness between them. Perhaps she should not have been so aggressive. After all, she *had* agreed to the option when she wanted Adam to join the company: he was only taking what he was entitled to.

Hearing a knock, Miranda turned her head to the door as the housekeeper entered; she carried a Victorian brass birdcage, in which was a dove. Attached to the ring at the top of the cage was an olive branch with silvery-gray leaves.

She tore open the card. Adam's angular black handwriting read: "Can I tell you tonight how sorry I am?"

Miranda threw back her sheets and took the cage to the window. She laughed as she watched the dove soar above the chestnut trees, which were already showing the first flecks of green.

That evening Miranda ran down the stairs to her drawing room; her heart was beating hard and she was short of breath.

Adam, in white dinner jacket, turned from the window and stared. "Darling, are you dressed or undressed? One never knows these days." Miranda wore a sheer cream chiffon Grecian gown with thonged gold sandals that crisscrossed to her knees.

"Definitely dressed. It's Zandra Rhodes."

"That dress was designed to be taken off." Adam held her by the shoulders; through the gauze, he could feel her warm flesh. As he pulled her against his body, she breathed in his body scent and felt his excitement. "How I've missed you," he murmured as his hands slowly moved down her back and then traced the swell of her buttocks.

Hungrily Miranda groped for his body; her knees shook and, together, they fell upon the thick cream carpet, where, wordlessly, they came together again.

Toward dawn, Miranda no longer knew whether or not she was dreaming, as she felt Adam's flesh against hers and inhaled the pungent almond smell of love; by the dying embers of the drawing room fire, she could just see his face.

Sleepily Adam whispered, "I find it an extraordinarily erotic idea."

"What?"

"To be in bed with a self-made millionairess."

"But we aren't in bed, darling."

"Let's get there quickly. There are things I must do to you."

SATURDAY, 19 AUGUST 1967

Outside, the sun beat down on the red baked earth of Provence, but the summer salon was cool. A Scrabble board lay on the floor, a reminder that so far this year, Buzz was beating Elinor by 147 to 17. Miranda, in black linen shorts and halter top, lay with her feet up on the terra-cotta-colored sofa, enjoying her idleness. She yawned and stretched; she wished her siesta could have lasted until the following morning—no, the following week.

The SUPPLYKITS interim dividend had been seven percent—an excellent figure—but in spite of this satisfying result, Miranda still fretted about her neglect of KITS. After the SUPPLYKITS flotation, the analysts, investors, and competitors had taken a much closer look at the company. An exhausted Miranda found that instead of having more time, she had almost a full-time job keeping present and future shareholders informed and happy: she prepared official reports, gave institutional and pension fund presentations, attended City lunches, and made time in her overfilled schedule for the financial press. Overworked and depressed, she felt as if she were being turned into a glamorous business machine.

Miranda sniffed the heavy scent of the lilies; in the flower room beyond the bar, she could hear Elinor and Buzz talking as they made their way slowly into the summer salon. A maid arrived with the tea tray as soon as they sat down.

"Cucumber sandwiches." Buzz nodded approvingly, "*And* chocolate éclairs."

Miranda yawned again. "Buzz, I can't understand how you can eat *anything* after these huge, delicious French lunches. The others are still working it off on the tennis court."

"Not me." Adam sauntered into the room.

The maid put down the tea tray and fished in the pocket of her dress. "*Une lettre par courier pour Mademoiselle Mann.*"

"For *me?*" Buzz was puzzled. "Nobody sends *me* letters by courier. An American stamp . . ." As she turned the letter over, her face became eager and younger. "It's Bertha Higby!"

Since the death of her fiancé nearly fifty years ago, Buzz had continued to correspond with his mother. Every year, Ginger's parents traveled to France to visit his grave, sometimes accompanied by Buzz. Now eighty-seven years old and recently widowed, Mrs. Higby remained in Cleveland.

Buzz read the short letter. "*Oh! . . . Oh . . . But I couldn't . . .*"

"What is it?" Elinor asked, teapot suspended.

"Eric left a bigger windfall than Bertha expected. She says at her age, she might not have long to enjoy it. She says she's spent her life living modestly, as Eric wanted, but now she wants to blow a bit of it on some fun. . . . Strewth! She wants to take a luxury winter cruise . . . next January. . . . Six weeks on the *Stella Polaris*. Round the Caribbean islands and South America, until the end of February . . . *and she wants me to be her guest!*"

"Why did she send it by courier?" Miranda asked.

"She wants a quick reply, to book our passages."

"Then why didn't she telephone?"

"Such extravagance! Eric would turn in his urn. Anyway, it's out of the question. I couldn't leave Elinor on her own."

"I don't need a chaperon, you old fool." Elinor handed Buzz a cup of strong Indian tea. "I can do without you for six weeks, Buzz. Perhaps I'll get a bit of peace, for a change."

"No. Six weeks is too long to be away," Buzz said, blowing on her tea to cool it.

Adam said, "Elinor has five servants here, three secretaries, and a doctor almost within shouting distance. Perhaps it's time you had a real rest, Buzz."

"I agree," said Miranda.

"I don't *need* a rest." Buzz was affronted.

"Of course you don't," Adam soothed. "But I expect Elinor feels that as your friend is eighty-seven, she probably shouldn't be traveling alone."

"That's for sure," Elinor said seriously. "And I *do* think you need a rest from me, Buzz. It's two years since my . . . er . . . incident and you've hardly had a day off ever since—you've fussed around me like a mother hen. How long is it since you've seen Bertha?"

"Four years," Buzz said. "They came for a weekend just before we left Starlings."

"We could easily arrange for a nurse to be here during your absence," Adam suggested.

"Fiddlesticks! I don't need a nurse!" Elinor said.

"You need *somebody,*" Buzz said firmly. "And she'll have to sleep in my bedroom because it's nearest to yours."

Elinor smiled at Adam. "Tell the trustees that Buzz must have a bonus, Adam. She'll need to keep her end up on a luxury cruise."

Adam pulled a notebook from his trouser pocket. As he scribbled, he said, "By the way, Elinor, Paul Littlejohn has decided to leave STG, Bermuda. He's setting up his own firm there."

"What a nuisance!" Elinor said. "Why does he want to do that?"

"For much the same reason as I did. I'm afraid that STG is no longer as reliable as it was in my grandfather's day. I've never regretted leaving. In fact, it was a great relief."

"But who will superintend *my* work in future?" Elinor asked.

"That *is* a problem," Adam admitted, "although, of course, we could transfer our affairs to Paul's new firm. We know that he can handle everything."

Buzz looked disapproving.

"Why not?" Adam said casually. "He could avoid mistakes and the need to brief someone else. But there's no need to make a decision yet. Paul has to give six months' notice to STG, so he won't be leaving until well after Christmas—probably in February."

"Plenty of time to think about it carefully," Elinor said. "Another cup of tea, Buzz? Tell us more about this cruise."

SATURDAY, 3 FEBRUARY 1968

A week after the affairs of the Dove Trust had been transferred to Littlejohn and Partners (Bermuda), Adam surprised Elinor with a trip to Saracen for the weekend. Every time his plane touched down at Nice airport and he saw palm trees and tanned porters in white, short-sleeved shirts, Adam enjoyed afresh the glamour of a life where one stepped onto a plane in bleak winter weather and shortly afterward stepped off in warm sunshine.

That evening, he and Elinor drank aperitifs in the summer salon.

Adam pointed to a pair of elaborately carved chairs in cinnamon-colored wood, inset with ivory. "Are those new?"

"Yes. Found them at my pet antiques dealer in Cannes. Eighteenth century, from Goa, made for some rich Portuguese trader. I also snapped up those two new chairs in the hall—the ones with angels' faces carved on the back: really too good for family use, but I couldn't resist them."

"What did they cost?"

"Too much to tell you, dear boy," said Elinor gaily.

As Adam refilled his glass, Elinor said, "I never realized how much I'd miss Buzz. How she'll crow when I tell her! She's obviously having a wonderful time. Every day, I get a postcard from some tropical place called Brown Sugar Island or Crab Cove. She says there are no men on board—the ship is full of hopeful widows—but the crew are wonderful and she's friendly with the purser, who dances a mean Charleston."

Adam sipped his drink. "As well as a winter break, there's another reason for my visit, Elinor, but I didn't want to alarm you unnecessarily by discussing it over the telephone."

Elinor sensed trouble.

"It's the new book contract," Adam went on. "The publishers would feel . . . happier . . . if they had a medical all-clear before signing. They know it's been over two years since your illness, but they'd appreciate reassurance. They're all overjoyed about it, but before they make their plans and get the sales force excited, they want to be . . . quite sure . . . that you are . . . completely fit."

"It's not as though I were writing a new book," Elinor said crossly. "The boxed set is a reissue."

"Yes, but you've agreed to promote it," Adam said patiently. "And before they spend vast sums on the publicity launch, they'd like to know that it won't be too much for you."

"I feel fit as a fiddle," Elinor protested.

"Elinor, this is a reasonable business precaution to take," Adam persisted. "Film stars, sports stars—everyone in businesses where heavy investment depends on the health of one person—know that a regular medical check is considered a reasonable—and *professional*—precaution." Adam knew that Elinor would go to great lengths to avoid being called unprofessional.

"Oh, well, if it's only a medical check, I can go to that American nursing home at Cannes."

"They'd prefer British medical reports."

"Oh dear. How long will it take?"

"Perhaps four days."

"A pity Buzz isn't here. Although she'd only fuss if she were. She doesn't like the London Clinic. Noisy place, she thinks."

"You can be there and back before Buzz returns," Adam said. "And you needn't go to the London Clinic. I'll arrange for the best possible care. As you say, you aren't ill—so your friends will be able to visit you. Life will be one long party, with a matron to shoo people away, should you get tired or bored. And the night you leave, I'll take you to the theater."

"You make it sound quite fun, dear boy. Could you see that there are a few crates of champagne—those half-bottles, so convenient for visitors."

"I'll arrange everything," Adam promised.

SATURDAY, 10 FEBRUARY 1968

One week later, as the plane took off from Nice for London airport, Adam outlined his arrangements to Elinor.

"*Eastbourne!*" she exclaimed. "Why *Eastbourne?*"

"Elinor, you sound like Dame Edith Evans saying, '*A handbag?*' in *The Importance of Being Earnest*. Eastbourne isn't the Gorbals," Adam said easily. "Eastbourne has the highest sunshine rate in Britain."

"I can get plenty of sunshine at Saracen. And I'm not on my last legs yet, *thank* you very much! Eastbourne is filled with nursing homes in Victorian mansions with names like 'The Gables.'"

"And that is why the best specialists for this sort of medical checkup are in Eastbourne," Adam said persuasively. "It's only for a few days, Elinor, and it's just an hour and a half away from London. There will be plenty of flowers and books, delicious food, TV and a telephone . . ."

Elinor pursed her lips. "You should *not* have made these arrangements without my approval, Adam!"

Adam looked contrite. He said, "I can, of course, cancel them should you wish, but Sir George is undoubtedly the best-qualified heart specialist in the country. And he *himself* told me that the Lord Willington Nursing Home is the most *professional* of the local nursing homes. Dr. Craig-Dunlop, who owns it, prides himself on having all the latest equipment."

"Oh well, I suppose it won't hurt me for a couple of days. Stop fretting, dear boy."

With the South Downs behind it and the turbulent gray English Channel in front, the Lord Willington Nursing Home looked like a country mansion. As she stepped from her Rolls, Elinor shivered in the unaccustomed raw air of February.

Inside, a faint whiff of disinfectant was almost overpowered by the heavy scent emanating from bowls of blue hyacinths. A smiling receptionist apologized for the matron's absence.

After Elinor had signed her voluntary consent form, she and Adam were taken to her suite of rooms. But for the mechanical hospital bed, she might have been in a first-class hotel: the sitting room was agreeably furnished in *eau de Nil*, the bedroom in old rose; the interconnecting rooms faced the sea over lawns and flower beds, though they were bleak at this time of the year.

Elinor read the cards from two identical large vases of lilies which took up all the space on the dressing table. She laughed. "One is from Miranda, one from Annabel. They both know I love lilies."

Adam smiled. "Miranda wanted to be with you today, but Dr. Craig-Dunlop wants you to settle in quickly, with no excitement. Your tests start tomorrow. Miranda wants to know as soon as you're allowed visitors. Annabel has already telephoned three times, but I've asked her not to call again, in case she disturbs a treatment. It's best if you call her."

Coffee was served in the sitting room right after their arrival. Then a smiling procession of medical staff presented themselves, each of whom told Elinor that if there was anything she wanted, she had only to ask. Finally she was given an enormous burgundy leatherbound folder that looked like some medieval city charter: it was the menu.

"Don't worry, dear boy," Elinor said over a glass of champagne poured from one of the little bottles. "I can see they're going to look after me really well."

"I'm sure of it." Adam smiled as he lifted his glass in a toast.

•   •   •

On the following day, Elinor's door was thrown open by a nurse who then stood to attention as, smiling benignly, Matron Ivy Braddock appeared in the doorway.

Elinor's first astonished impression was that Matron Braddock looked like a female impersonator—a sergeant major in drag: she couldn't wait to describe her to Buzz. The matron was one of the biggest women Elinor had ever seen; her neck seemed sunk between strong shoulders, and her red hands hung from beefy arms. Her face looked rough-hewn, as if carved from a cliff. Her yellow hair was cut very short, and on it, like a cake frill, perched a nurse's cap, tied beneath the square jaw. The matron moved toward Elinor's bed on legs that seemed to be joined to her feet without ankles: she did not walk so much as stomp.

"We're going to do *everything* we *can,* Mrs. O'Dare, to make you comfortable." Matron Braddock's voice was surprisingly light and pleasant.

First, blood and urine samples were taken; then Elinor was X-rayed, after which she spent the rest of the day being wired up to various machines for tests. That evening, Dr. Cyril Craig-Dunlop stopped in just to visit. He was a small, mild-mannered man with surprisingly beautiful, black-fringed gray eyes.

The next morning, the heart specialist, Sir George, was ushered into Elinor's bedroom by Matron Braddock. Elinor hated to be interrupted: she was reading Truman Capote's *In Cold Blood.*

Other specialists followed.

On the third morning, Dr. Craig-Dunlop again visited Elinor. "I've had the results of nearly all the tests," he said, "which are more or less what we expected. However, as you know, you must be very, very careful with the few years that remain to you."

In Cold Blood fell to the floor.

Elinor sat upright. "What do you mean? I have recovered completely! That's what I was told!"

Dr. Craig-Dunlop stammered, clearly confused, "I—I'm so sorry, Mrs. O'Dare. I assumed you were the type of patient who would have been told . . ."

"Told *what?*"

"The truth about your condition," Dr. Craig-Dunlop said apologetically.

"The few years that remain to me? Are you sure?" Elinor blanched, her pallor more obvious against her peach chiffon robe. "I'd like a second opinion."

Dr. Craig-Dunlop coughed. "Your three specialists are all of the same opinion."

Elinor stared bleakly out the window, beyond the sloping lawn to where the sludge-colored sea met with the gray sky. There was no sound in the room.

Eventually she said, "I don't want my granddaughters to know. They would worry, you see."

Shortly after the doctor left, a smiling nurse, smart in a lavender-and-white-striped uniform, entered; she carried two pills in a small vial.

"This will make you feel better." She watched to make sure that Elinor swallowed the medication. The nurses were well trained in dealing with rich patients who were used to doing as they pleased and often disliked accepting the discipline of routine; they knew that the very old, the alcoholics, and the more than slightly batty patients (called "eccentric") had to be carefully supervised. This old dear, who was to be kept under heavy sedation, clearly didn't know that she was a long-term patient, being treated for depression.

During the next two days, Elinor slept a lot, which Dr. Craig-Dunlop said might be because she wished to evade reality. But the reason was simply that Elinor was very sensitive to medicine; for her, a normal dose of sedative was an overdose.

In a moment of clarity, just before her eleven a.m. medication on Friday, a bewildered Elinor threatened to leave and was told by a nurse that this was not possible without the prior permission of the matron.

Elinor, used to prompt obedience to her wishes, flew into a rage, of which the nurse took not the slightest notice. An injection was swiftly administered, and Sister correctly reported that the patient had become uncontrollable and needed sedation.

"Paranoia," Dr. Craig-Dunlop said quietly to Matron upon reading this report.

Matron Braddock nodded. She knew that a classic symptom of paranoia was the suspicion that those who were caring for you were trying to harm you.

SATURDAY, 17 FEBRUARY 1968

After Elinor had spent a week in the nursing home, Annabel and Miranda were allowed to visit. On the way, sitting in the back of the Bentley that drove them from London, the two worried sisters spoke little. Finally, Miranda inquired after Scott.

Annabel snapped, "Don't ask *me* how Scott is! I hardly ever see him—I don't even suppose he's noticed that I'm not there this week!"

"What do you mean?" Miranda was surprised.

"Oh, he's too wrapped up in his work to bother about his wife. He even forgot our tenth anniversary!"

"That doesn't sound like Scott."

"Well, he *would* have forgotten," Annabel amended, "but I reminded him."

Annabel and Miranda were shocked by their grandmother's appearance: her golden hair was lifeless, her eyes were dull, her speech was thick and slurred, she seemed inert and limp. Forewarned by the matron to treat her normally and to ignore anything eccentric that she did or said, the two sisters immediately wrapped Elinor in an invisible cloud of affection.

Afterward, in the matron's office, where Adam and Dr. Craig-Dunlop were waiting for them, Annabel burst into tears. "I can't understand why *I* couldn't see that she was ill."

Miranda put her arms around her sister. "Don't cry, Frog. I had no idea either. It's lucky she's being properly looked after."

"Oh, what bad luck that Buzz was away!" Annabel sobbed. "She could have been here with Gran."

"What exactly *is* paranoia?" Miranda impatiently asked the doctor.

"We prefer to describe it as a personality disorder," he said. "A chronic, slowly progressive mental disorder. In this case, I fear that there will be delusions of persecution."

"What treatment is she having?" Miranda asked while Annabel wept.

"She is being given a drug called Mellaril. And sedatives as necessary."

"How long will she be ill?"

There was a short, ominous silence.

"How long?" Miranda repeated shrilly.

"I cannot say. Not yet. We'll have to see how she responds to treatment, but it may take quite a long time."

"How many weeks?"

"Perhaps you should think in terms of months," Dr. Craig-Dunlop said gently. He added, "But I must emphasize that at this stage, we simply cannot tell. She is an elderly lady, she has had one stroke, and she has a personality disorder. We simply cannot say what will happen."

"How *can* she have deteriorated so seriously in such a short time, when she only came here for a checkup?" Miranda persisted.

"It was *extremely fortunate* that she came here when she did," said the doctor gravely, "or her situation might have been much more serious."

Over a depressing hotel lunch of beige roast beef and sour cabbage, Miranda asked, "Why didn't you tell us, Adam?"

"I didn't want to cause you unnecessary anxiety until Dr. Craig-

Dunlop and the specialist consultants had reached a definite conclusion." In front of Annabel, Adam was careful to speak to Miranda formally and without endearment. Although many people suspected them to be lovers, Adam still insisted on secrecy.

"But we can't leave Gran in that place," Miranda said. "She must come to London—where we can get the best medical advice, and I can look after her."

"She seems to be getting very good care where she is. The sea air is bracing, and you won't find a London nursing home in acres of garden, like this one," Adam said. "But if you want further opinions, we can go to any London consultant you choose."

"Why can't Gran go back to Saracen when Buzz returns and be nursed there?" Annabel pushed aside her untouched plate. "She loves Saracen."

"That might be a bit too heavy a load for Buzz," Adam suggested. "Remember how she knocked herself out after Elinor had her stroke? Round-the-clock nursing, such as Elinor is getting here, would mean overseeing four nurses, organizing their schedules, plus providing meals, transport and the rest of it."

"We don't want Buzz ill as well," Miranda agreed.

"I've telephoned Dr. Montand at Saracen," Adam continued. "He agrees that the best place for Elinor is an English nursing home where she can get round-the-clock medical care if necessary. In any case, Dr. Craig-Dunlop is adamant that, for the moment, she must be under proper medical supervision for twenty-four hours a day, in case her condition deteriorates rapidly."

Both sisters looked alarmed at the thought of possible further deterioration. Both were glad of Adam's presence. He was always so comforting in times of trouble.

"If you're sure this is the best place . . ." Annabel said hesitantly.

Miranda said, "Firstly, I'd like to be sure that a nursing home is the best place for her, rather than a hospital. Secondly, if she's likely to . . . be like this for some time, that the Lord Whatsit is the best nursing home available."

Annabel nodded in agreement.

From his briefcase, Adam produced a sheaf of colored brochures for nursing homes. Silently he handed them to the two sisters.

Miranda looked at the imposing exteriors and the bleak interiors of the nursing and residential homes. "These reception rooms look like pub lounges. Gran wouldn't put a maid in one of these bedrooms! I'm sure they're comfortable—but they look so deeply unattractive."

Annabel read aloud, " 'Each bedroom has a fitted handbasin.' *Big deal.* No private bathrooms."

"Elinor has her own bathroom at the Lord Willington," Adam pointed out. "But these other places have a certain number of amenities—physiotherapist, chiropodist, hairdresser."

" 'Singsongs and sideshows'!" Annabel read. " 'Bingo'!"

"I brought only the most attractive brochures," Adam said.

"I hate to think what the others are like," Annabel said. "But *look* at the prices they charge!"

"Gran could practically live at the Ritz for what the Lord Whatsit is costing," Miranda pointed out.

Adam said in a stiff voice, "I went to considerable trouble to choose the best place, so naturally it isn't cheap. But you're welcome to move her if you wish."

The sisters looked at each other and shook their heads.

"It's not the nursing home we hate," Annabel acknowledged. "It's what's happened to Gran that we can't bear."

"We must find Clare and tell her straightaway." Miranda did not look forward to this.

Adam coughed. "I must warn you that any mention of Clare agitates your grandmother. I really feel that her wishes *must* be respected. Elinor *clearly* doesn't wish to see Clare."

SUNDAY, 18 FEBRUARY 1968

Standing barefoot in her pink-sprigged Laura Ashley nightgown, Clare looked from her bedroom window at the quietly falling snow. The moon dimly lit the woods, faintly etched against the hill behind Applebank Cottage.

She shivered, jumped back into bed, and snuggled lower under the patchwork quilt. In half an hour it would be time to take her loaves out of the oven: the only drawback to her new business was that it meant getting up early every single morning of the year. Because her business had long outgrown the kitchen, David had drawn plans to convert the outhouse into a proper bakery.

Clare had accidentally metamorphosed into a baker ten months before, when David took some of her homebaked bread to friends who lived nearby: they asked if they could buy bread regularly from her. Why not? she thought, and packed a sample treacle cake and some shortbread with her first order.

One month later, Clare had tacked a plastic-covered price list to her back door and another to the garden gate. She now baked rye bread, whole-grain bread, soda bread, and date bread; pasties, rich chocolate cake, rum-flavored fruitcake, brandy snaps, and shortbread. She cooked fruit flans when fruit was in season. Clare baked nothing that could be found at the local baker and charged what she considered exorbitant prices, which people seemed happy to pay in cash.

The main reason Clare did not allow credit was because it complicated her bookkeeping. Having experienced that particular chaos, she was careful to keep her books up-to-date, a simple matter of filling in two columns each day, "Purchases made" and "Total cash takings."

Under the patchwork quilt, David turned over and sleepily pulled Clare toward him. Her nightgown had ridden up around her waist, and she enjoyed feeling his hard, muscular legs entwined around hers. Still half asleep, he kissed her cheek and fumbled beneath her gown, seeking her breasts.

With a loud crash, the door burst open, and Josh, in yellow Donald Duck pajamas, leapt upon the bed. "Ith thnowing! Ith thnowing! David, can I have a thledge? I'm old enough now. *Oh, pleathe.*"

David sat up, turned on the light, yawned, and scratched his hairy chest.

"You can take a tea tray up to the wood and slide down to the back garden. But not now. It's the middle of the night. After breakfast." He turned and smiled at Clare. "*You* are going to have breakfast in bed. . . . No, not a word! Josh and I planned it yesterday evening, didn't we, Josh? After you've taken your loaves out, you're coming back to bed. Isn't she, Josh?"

Josh nodded happily.

"There must be a catch," Clare said. "You're *too* perfect!"

"Yes, there's a catch," David said quietly as he made room for Josh in the bed.

Later, David pulled on Clare's toweling bathrobe and led Josh down to the kitchen.

After twenty minutes, her breakfast tray arrived; upon it was boiling red soup, chocolate ice cream, and a fizzy orange drink.

David winked over Josh's head. "Josh chose the menu."

"Delicious," Clare said feebly as she looked into the smiling face and aquamarine eyes of her son. She looked down at the tray on her lap. "That's too much tomato soup just for me. Perhaps you could help me eat it, Josh?"

Suddenly Clare's baby was wearing jeans and a navy nylon anorak, and howling for tough boots like the village boys'. Now five years old, he went to school in Warminster and was trying hard to adopt a Dorset accent, having been teased about the snob way he talked. Josh liked reading comics, watching TV (especially *Dr. Who*), and peeing in his bath when his mother was looking the other way. He loved soccer and couldn't remember baseball; neither could he remember California, except for a vague recollection of sunshine and a white house and what seemed an enormous swimming pool, although Clare laughed and told him it had really been quite small—for L.A.

When Josh had scraped the plates and gone to "tea-tray" down the hill, David produced another tray with coffee, Clare's own homemade croissants, and strawberry jam.

After that, huddled under the patchwork quilt, they made love in a lazy, unhurried way. This morning Clare felt tender and loving; she wanted to be close to him. But sometimes after they made love, she felt wide awake and energetic, beautiful and happy, strong enough to lift the stove.

"It's a pity more men aren't like you," Clare murmured. "You're so sensual. You enjoy physical intimacy and affectionate contact as much as women do. I wish *all* men enjoyed their whole bodies, rather than just a little, wobbly bit of it."

"I've always thought the most important sex organ is between the ears," David said, kissing hers.

Chapter · 21

On the last day of February, a suntanned Buzz flew into London airport, wearing Bertha's farewell gift—a snappy white Capri pants suit. She felt energetic, almost girlish as she left the plane.

To her surprise, a ground hostess met her and took her to a VIP lounge, where Adam was waiting.

"*Something's happened to Elinor?*" Buzz turned white.

Gently Adam told her what had happened.

Buzz was out of the car almost before it rolled to a halt on the gravel forecourt. It was an unusually sunny day for the end of February, and cheerful nurses in scarlet cloaks wheeled or walked their patients slowly around the garden.

One nurse moved a wheelchair toward her, and Buzz suddenly realized with a shock that the cocooned creature within it was Elinor. She looked small, frail, and feeble; her face was dazed and vacant, as if she'd just been woken up and couldn't quite remember where she was.

Buzz said, "Hello, Nell."

Elinor did not look up.

In silence, Buzz listened to the nurse's nonstop starling twitter. "We've had a *good* morning, *haven't* we, Mrs. O'Dare? . . . We watched the birds at the birdbath and we *fed crumbs* to them, *didn't* we? . . . Lean forward a bit, dear—you've pushed your cushion down again. There, that's better, isn't it? . . . Then we had a chokky bikky and the usual little argument about our nap. Then we listened to a *nice* concert on the radio, didn't we?"

Slowly Elinor looked up and glared.

Buzz felt tremulous hope. She said, "You seem a bit under the weather, Nell. Don't worry, I'll have you out of here in no time."

In Elinor's overwarm bedroom, Buzz peered at the temperature chart and medical instructions clipped to the foot of the metal bed. She frowned when she saw five different tranquilizers and sedatives listed: no wonder Nell looked bewildered and depressed. Buzz recalled Elinor's swift rage and felt another glimmer of hope, but a thought occurred to her: If they insisted on treating Nell like a crazy person, she might actually end up like one.

Peering again at the list of medications, she started to say something to Elinor, then stopped short, remembering that Adam was in the room.

Buzz turned to him. "I've a present for Elinor in my hand luggage. It's in a red box. Would you mind getting it from the car?" She turned back to Elinor and said in the rather loud, slow, and contrived voice that people use for the deaf, "I've brought you a *surprise,* Nell."

As soon as the door closed behind Adam, she whispered, "What have they *done* to you, my girl?"

Lying back on her pillows, Elinor slowly shook her head from side to side but said nothing.

"I'll be back tomorrow," Buzz told her. "I'll just turn up, without warning. Until then—don't swallow them pills. Do you hear me, Nell?" She leaned forward and shook Elinor's shoulders. *"Don't swallow them dratted pills!* Hold 'em under your tongue and play possum. Then spit 'em into a handkerchief and hide it under the pillow."

The door opened and Adam came in. "Just straightening Nell's pillows," Buzz said airily.

As she and Adam left, Buzz turned back to see Elinor silently looking at the ceiling.

Buzz's gift, a nacre box, lay ignored upon the bedside table; but even in the dull afternoon light, the shell surface gleamed.

As their hired limousine purred back to Heathrow Airport, Buzz asked, "Why didn't you let me know she was ill? They had a radiotelephone thing on the *Stella Polaris.*"

"Had you been present, Buzz, there was nothing you could have done, so it was thought best not to disrupt your holiday," Adam explained. Buzz noticed he didn't say who had "thought it best." He added sadly, "It's not yet certain that Elinor will ever again be well enough to live without nursing support."

"Just as well I know a lot more about nursing than some of these young Australian madams," Buzz sniffed.

Then Adam quietly explained that she no longer had a job.

Tight-lipped and pale, Buzz listened in silence and near disbelief. *Nobody* had ever sacked *her!* Even after she had been caught in that ruined church with Ginger Higby, that old bitch of a commandant in the women's ambulance service hadn't wanted to lose her.

Eventually she asked, "Does Elinor know about this?"

"Of course not," Adam said. "As you saw, she's in no condition to discuss anything. But the trustees have considered the matter most carefully."

"Them trustees are sitting miles away in their offices in Bermuda!" Buzz snorted. "*I* know Nell better than they do! *And* better than *you* do, you young whippersnapper!"

"Of course you do," Adam said soothingly. "But in fact, it is Elinor's doctors and consultants who feel that she will no longer need you. I thought I had made that plain."

Shocked and incredulous, Buzz could say nothing more, but as the limousine glided on, she remembered a great deal: the teashop outings in Earls Court when Edward was little, comforting Nell, time after time, when Billy had had a few and behaved badly. She remembered the difficulties they'd had repairing Starlings after the war, when you couldn't get a brick or a plank of wood, not even if you was royalty; and she remembered comforting Nell as each granddaughter left home.

Now they were kicking her out! And the worst part was that she couldn't talk to Elinor about it.

Finally, Buzz stifled her feelings enough to ask calmly, "Do the girls know about this?"

"They asked me to tell you," Adam lied. "We all have to face the fact that Elinor's life has suddenly changed and she will probably continue to deteriorate."

"And they didn't mind me going?" Buzz asked painfully.

"Of course they mind—they're very, *very* fond of you," Adam said. As soon as he'd seen Buzz safely on the plane to Nice, he planned to drive back to London, where he would telephone Annabel in New York before seeing Miranda. The sisters would be told that Buzz had agreed it was best for her to leave.

"Of course them girls are fond of me!" Buzz bit back further words. She'd wiped their tears, she'd wiped their botties, and she'd loved them as if they were her own.

Adam shrugged his shoulders and said nothing.

Buzz growled, "Where am I supposed to go?" She refused to accept this mortifying disgrace. Who did this little twerp think he was? Too big for his boots, as she'd always said. Slowly her face reddened as she fought to control her anger and her tears. Eventually her voice grated, "*You* can't kick me out like this. Not after all these years."

"Of *course* we're not kicking you out." Adam spoke soothingly, but Buzz sensed a hint of contempt—or was it triumph?

"Then what exactly *are* you doing?"

"I am not doing anything. I have been asked to see that you are properly looked after in your retirement."

"Retirement?"

"You are eight years over the legal age of retirement," Adam reminded Buzz. "The trust has approved a generous pension; it will be paid to you monthly wherever you wish—anywhere in the world." He waved his hand expansively.

"You make it sound as if I've won a sweepstake!" she said bitterly, still fighting to control her feelings. What was that favorite saying of Elinor's? Buzz could almost hear her voice: "Stupidity is the operation of intelligence hampered by emotion."

Buzz sensed that she had to be careful, she had to box clever, she had to let Adam think she had accepted what he said and would go quietly. Seething with indignation and fury, she told herself that this was the best way to catch Adam off guard and discover what was going on.

Thoughtfully Adam said, "It was, perhaps, a pity that you were unable to stay on with your friend Mrs. Higby."

Once again Buzz noticed that Adam didn't speak like other people: he always gave himself an out. Adam couldn't say, "The cat is black." He would say, "To the best of my knowledge, the cat appears to be black."

You've got to have the sense to hold your tongue, my girl, Buzz told herself. Play along with him. Let him think that he's able to plant these ideas in your head. Let him think that he's getting away with it. She said, "I suppose I *could* always go and live with Bertha, if Nell really doesn't need me."

"Living with Mrs. Higby might be an excellent idea," Adam approved, "particularly as—eventually—it might be necessary to sell Saracen."

"Sell Saracen! Elinor would never allow it."

"Saracen now belongs to the trust," Adam said firmly. "If Elinor is unable to live in Saracen, the trustees might consider it an unjustifiable expense: apart from the income that might be generated by the capital that's tied up in the place, keeping five full-time domestic staff members and three secretaries would no longer be viable. Have you any idea of the cost of running that place, compared to the cost of a couple of rooms in a nursing home?"

"No idea," Buzz said, "but I'm sure you know what's best for Nell."

Buzz waited in the departure lounge. When the flight to Nice was called, she informed a brisk blue-uniformed redhead that she was feeling ill and thought she'd better cancel her ticket. He took her to the airport nurse, who could find nothing wrong with her but agreed that she might be suffering from jet lag and needed only to rest.

An hour later, Buzz hailed a taxi and returned to Eastbourne, where she booked into a modest residential hotel recommended by the taxi driver.

Buzz did not feel like sitting in the small lounge at the Eastbourne hotel, which contained a great many genteel, inquisitive, elderly ladies, all of whom seemed to be knitting. She would have liked to go for a long walk past the charming wedding-cake buildings that lined the promenade, but although it was only teatime, it was already too dark to see anything. Instead, she wandered into town, where she bought a bag of chips, well soused in vinegar and wrapped in newspaper; she took the bag to her room, where she sat on the edge of the single bed, slowly eating chips in the dark and thinking.

Buzz decided that her first priority was to see Elinor again. She would then telephone Miranda, the most decisive of the three sisters.

She did not blame herself for going on the cruise, although she sensed that Adam, always an opportunist, had taken advantage of her absence. Buzz had read newspaper accounts of old people who had been forcibly removed from their homes and admitted to nursing homes; such people had been robbed by the very guardians who were legally supposed to care for them.

She had also read about old people's homes that ruthlessly exploited their pensioners: unscrupulous proprietors grabbed all they could squeeze from the social services but gave little back to the residents; they cut corners on staff, food, laundry, and amenities and added to their profits by pocketing the difference between their sparse expenditures and the sums they actually received. If such moneygrubbing goings-on could happen in cheap nursing homes that were checked by the authorities, Buzz wondered what might occur in expensive ones, where there was a greater possibility for profit? The Lord Willington looked the sort of place into which dishonest rascals might put their inconvenient relations in order to get them out of the way: uncles with the D.T.'s, incontinent aunts, senile granddads, and cousins who'd been odd since they was born. Buzz remembered Nurse Evans, who'd been with Nell in Ward C at La Chapelle; after the war, Evans had worked in one of those rich bins before she'd married a Lutheran minister and gone to live in Scotland. Evans had relayed some hair-raising stories about the exploitation of her rich patients.

Because for what reason, other than profit, would a nursing home prescribe so many drugs for Nell?

Did Adam know what was going on? Buzz didn't know what was

going on, but she certainly smelled dishonesty: it probably involved fraud, and it probably involved Adam.

Having finished her bag of chips, Buzz licked her fingers, switched the light on, and prepared for bed. She had not felt this alone and lonely since she first set out for the French battlefields over fifty years ago.

On the following morning, Elinor lay with her eyes closed, apparently sleeping. For the past twenty-four hours, she had swallowed none of her medication, although she had been unable to refuse an injection. She trusted Buzz. She knew instinctively that Buzz would reappear to get her out of this place and help her to recover.

While she lay waiting, Elinor fought back the fears underscored by the hospital bed and the smell of antiseptic. Her foremost fear was that she might lose her mind, for trying to think made her feel as if her head were filled with cotton wool. She felt muddled . . . couldn't keep track of one thought for long. She wasn't ill when she came in here . . . yes, she was sure of that . . . but she was ill now. How could that have happened . . . unless they were making her ill? . . . How could they do that? . . . Easy . . . with medication. She feared that decisions were being made behind her back, and that she was not being told the truth by that apologetic mouse of a doctor. Was she really more ill than she'd been led to suppose? If so, why hadn't she felt ill? Or was she not ill at all? And if not, then why was she imprisoned here?

It was too difficult. She would wait for Buzz.

But as she lay there, demons slid possible visions of the future into her mind: Suppose she lost the use of her body? She dreaded being immobile and physically dependent, and she certainly felt as if heavy weights were attached to her feet and her legs; she felt as helpless as if she were buried to her neck in quicksand.

Another vision slid before her, of a half-wit locked in a cell. Perhaps she would never again be able to function normally. She saw herself wheeled along white corridors, wired up to huge machines that clicked, whirred, and flashed lights: this was her greatest fear, that she might be kept alive artificially by machinery, a mumbling vegetable, after her natural time to die had arrived.

She felt isolated in this comfortable place, but paradoxically, she also wished that these young women, with their bright faces and inane chatter, would go away and leave her in peace.

The next day, the taxi arrived at the nursing home as the clock above the entrance portico struck ten. Buzz carefully counted out coins for the taxi driver, who said, "That ain't much of a tip, lady."

"It's exactly ten percent," Buzz retorted. "And what have you done to deserve a tip? You didn't help me out of the cab."

"Well, it's snowing."

"Exactly."

Before entering the nursing home, Buzz stood under the imposing portico and carefully stamped the snow from her shoes. She settled the squirrel evening cape that had belonged to her mother on top of her light summer coat, then walked in and asked to see Mrs. O'Dare.

The smiling receptionist disappeared.

Smiling Matron Braddock appeared in her place. The stocky woman looked intently at Buzz with raised eyebrows. "Is Mr. Grant with you?" Her voice was light and charming, but her eyes were hard. "He usually accompanies visitors. We don't want Mrs. O'Dare disturbed by people she would rather not see."

"I came with Mr. Grant yesterday," Buzz reminded the matron. "And I'm going back to the south of France tomorrow. I wanted to see Mrs. O'Dare once more before I go."

As Buzz entered her room, Elinor's eyelids slowly opened. "Hello, Buzz," she whispered, feeling warm relief flood her body. Now she could stop worrying. Buzz would take care of everything.

Buzz settled herself on the upright chair by Elinor's bed, firmly clasping her old-fashioned handbag on her lap. The nurse left the room.

"Can you walk, Nell?" Buzz whispered back. "Do you go to the lav by yourself?"

"Yes," Elinor said weakly. "They're not going to lay me out yet, you know."

Buzz said, "Soon as my back's turned, look what happens! That stuff they're giving you would kill a dozen cats. But once you're out of here, I'll have you well in no time. And I ain't *never* going away again."

"Dear, dear Buzz. But they'll never let me leave. Not without a fuss. I signed something."

"I expect you signed in as a voluntary patient; then they're covered," Evans said. "Course they don't want you to leave. They won't get paid if you leave—I bet this costs a pretty penny." Buzz looked around the room. "But I ain't scared of that great ox of a matron, even if she does remind me of my old commandant. And I ain't scared of Adam."

Elinor's eyes filled with tears. "Do you really think that Adam . . ."

"Adam brought you here in the *first* place, my lamb."

"Why did the girls allow it?" Elinor asked sadly. She could vaguely remember Annabel and Miranda's visit, but Clare hadn't come. On the plane to London, Adam had said that Clare still refused to see her; he had hinted that she expected an apology. What sad stupidity. How silly they had both been. Of course she would apologize to Clare.

Buzz said, "The girls trust Adam, but he's getting too big for his boots—ordering everyone around. Adam even says Saracen costs too much to run. He says them trustees are going to sell it and keep you here because it'll be cheaper."

"*Sell Saracen! Never!* Why should Adam bother to do that? *He* doesn't benefit from the trust. . . . ."

"Adam's up to no good," Buzz said firmly. "But we won't worry about that now. What's important is to get you out of here. And this is how we'll do it!"

Elinor listened carefully as Buzz leaned close to her ear and outlined her plan.

"I'll go straight back to Eastbourne. I'll buy two identical coats and hats in some bright color. Tomorrow I'll turn up here again at ten and tell the taxi to wait. I'll ask him to move along a bit, so he ain't blocking the entrance. I want him waiting by this corner. Then I come in with my suitcase, and Matron thinks I'm on my way to the airport. *She's* not to know I was supposed to catch yesterday's plane."

"Thank God you didn't."

"In that suitcase, Nell, will be a coat and hat—same as mine—for you to wear. I get you dressed. I open them glass doors to the garden. You walk out *slowly,* with your head turned away from the house, to my taxi. You get in the taxi. I wait for you to do that; then I simply walk through the main hall, my empty suitcase in my hand. Then we drive hell-for-leather to the airport and catch the next plane to Nice."

"Buzz, darling Buzz, that's a brilliant escape plan." Elinor's face crumpled and she started to cry.

The door of the bedroom flew open to reveal the huge, forbidding presence of the matron. Firmly she said, "We don't want to overtire Mrs. O'Dare."

Buzz stood up. "I was about to go. I'll pop in tomorrow to say goodbye on my way to the airport." She wagged a finger at Elinor. "Now be a good girl and do as you're told."

In the cab on the way back to her Eastbourne hotel, Buzz checked her plan; she was determined to look upon this as a lark, as she and Nell had regarded some of their dangerous escapades in the Great War. Buzz spent the cab ride reminiscing about those times, some grim and some sad, but all of which made her smile.

In the darkening afternoon, the taxi pulled up to her hotel. She paid the driver, and as she turned to enter, she felt a snap. Buzz found herself lying face up in the snow, in great pain, unable to move: as helpless as a black beetle flipped onto its back.

Immediately Buzz knew she'd broken her hip. It irritated her to think that she hadn't been doing anything reckless like running to catch a bus; but she had a private theory that an old person didn't break a hip because she fell, but fell because her hip snapped, after gradual erosion.

The taxi driver jumped from his cab and hurried to her side. "Lucky thing I saw you in the rear mirror just as I was driving off!"

As he ran to the hotel for help, Buzz realized that Elinor's escape would have to be postponed. She must let Elinor know this. She would telephone Miranda.

The following day, Elinor again hid her medication under her tongue, slipped it into her handkerchief, and later flushed it down the lavatory. With carefully suppressed excitement, she waited for Buzz to arrive.

But Buzz did not come.

After a few days, having received no telephone call, letter, or message of any kind from Buzz, Elinor started to lose hope. The medical staff had realized that she wasn't swallowing her medication, and it was now dissolved before being administered. In her occasional lucid moments, Elinor again wondered if she was losing her sanity.

Chapter·22

"Mr. Grant? Tell him to come straight in." As she replaced the telephone, Miranda, prim in a high-necked gray flannel suit, checked the Cartier traveling clock on her white desk. She had to finish reading the pile of reports in front of her—and make the necessary decisions—before tomorrow's management meeting.

Adam sauntered in, his hands in the pockets of his dark city suit. He looked at Miranda's white, exhausted face and said, "I thought you might like to knock off early and go to *Hair*."

Hair, the psychedelic tribal-love-rock American musical that celebrated hippie values, free love, hash, and hatred of the Vietnam War, had opened the day after stage censorship by the lord chamberlain had been abolished.

"I'd love to, but . . ." Miranda pointed to the piles of papers. "*And* I have to find time tomorrow to visit Buzz." Buzz was still in an Eastbourne hospital.

"Forget everything else, just for one evening. We've got something to celebrate. In our first year as a public company, our pretax profits have increased by twenty percent."

"But KITS showed a loss of thirteen thousand pounds," Miranda reminded Adam.

He shrugged his shoulders. "That's understandable. KITS paid the expenses of SUPPLYKITS during its first year of trading—including those huge consultants' fees and all bank interest. It's not really a loss if you look at the overall company situation."

"It's not only the loss that's worrying me," Miranda said. "KITS now has weak middle management and poor internal communication; that's causing us big problems. And we need better distribution, but can't afford it."

"So long as you know what's wrong, you can fix it."

"Sure—if I had the time." Wearily Miranda put down her pen. "I wish I could turn the clock back two years, when my time was spent running KITS. It depresses me to waste time being photographed and hyped."

"Your real problem is that you've become very successful, very quickly, Miranda. Some people would like your problem."

"Every morning when I wake up, I ask myself, If I'm so damned successful, why do I feel tired and miserable?"

"You just need a couple of days off," Adam soothed. "Why not fly to St.-Moritz for a long, lazy weekend? Get a little snow and sunshine." Hands in pockets, he moved into the horseshoe of her desk.

Miranda swiveled her white leather chair around to face him. She laughed. "That's unlike you, Adam. What do you want?"

He leaned forward and quickly unbuttoned the top of Miranda's prim suit. "I want you," he said firmly, and slid his hand beneath the gray flannel.

Adam had never touched her in the office, and she was not expecting it. Miranda felt the immediate and powerful reaction of her body to this forbidden sensuality. Trembling, she reached backward for the telephone. "June? No more calls, please." Her voice was slightly overcontrolled.

Adam pulled her from her chair, undid two more buttons, quickly unzipped her skirt: Miranda was left standing in a daffodil-yellow camisole and black high-heeled boots. Adam gently slid the daffodil straps from her shoulders.

Miranda gasped, "We always said . . . never in the office . . ."

"I don't remember." Adam picked her up in his arms and laid her on her desk: reports slithered off it and the Cartier clock crashed to the floor.

"We'll leave the boots on," Adam said.

"Adam, I simply can't risk it. If June came in, this would be round the entire company within seconds. And I can't lock the door. Let's go back to my place and—"

What Adam said then was the last thing that Miranda expected. He looked down at her flaming hair and beige, naked body and whispered, "I love you."

That left Miranda speechless.

Adam started to stroke her body. He murmured, "I love your boobs, and I love your ass. And I love you because you're so exciting. And I love the way you love it."

"Only with you," Miranda whispered.

Adam reached to a shelf behind Miranda's desk and picked up a case of cosmetic samples. He flicked it open, picked a magenta lipstick, and scrawled across her breasts, GREAT BOOBS.

Gently he turned her body over. He picked up a pot of turquoise eyeshadow, dipped his forefinger in it, and scrawled across her buttocks, GREAT ASS.

Then he turned her once more, gently, and pried her thighs apart; in violet eyebrow pencil, he drew an arrow up each white thigh. At the head of each arrow, he scrawled further appreciation.

With a lipstick pencil, he drew bracelets of crimson hearts around her wrists; with green eyeliner, he encircled her ankles with bracelets of kisses. He covered her body with colorful graffiti.

Adam then selected a very expensive makeup brush, intended to apply blusher, and started carefully to brush Miranda's tuft in a circular motion.

Later, on their way to the theater, Miranda snuggled happily against Adam in the back of the chauffeur-driven Mercedes.

"By the way," he said, as if he had almost forgotten to mention it. "Remember you said you wanted a better distribution system for KITS?"

Miranda nodded.

"And you'd like to expand into other countries, where the KITS system is already being copied? . . ."

Miranda nodded again.

"It so happens that SUPPLYKITS also needs more cash. It looks as if we'll be able to buy the Stiebel-Stein mail-order business, so I've been working on ways to raise the money. As a matter of fact, that's what I came into your office to discuss, you gorgeous mantrap."

"Explain," Miranda said sleepily, wondering if she'd be able to stay awake until the end of the show.

"We'll have a rights issue."

Miranda sat up abruptly. She knew that if a company issued extra shares to raise more money, the value of the existing shares was diluted. "I don't like the idea of further diluting my shareholding," she said.

Adam ignored her objection. "To raise sufficient capital, we'll probably need a one-for-three issue."

"That'll mean issuing one extra share for every three existing shares. You're telling me that instead of owning all of three oranges, I'll own three quarters of four oranges."

"Exactly. You'll still be worth exactly the same amount, but the company will have more working capital."

In a worried voice, Miranda asked, "Won't a rights issue make SUPPLYKITS more vulnerable to a takeover?"

"Theoretically, yes, but that's unlikely to happen so long as the company is successful and the shareholders approve of the way it's run." Adam patted her knee. Miranda instinctively pulled away from him.

"You should remember that very few chief executives of public companies own a controlling interest in them," Adam said patiently. "There's no need for you to worry. Your shareholders have complete confidence in you. And let's not forget, you're all-important to the company in other ways: you're the chief shareholder and the public image of the firm."

Miranda sighed. "Adam, I do wish you wouldn't spring these things on me when I'm not expecting them."

"I'm sorry, darling. I thought you'd be as excited as I am by the idea." He should have stuck to his usual tactics. When Adam had a document for Miranda to sign that he thought she might argue about, he always included it in a sheaf of other papers he handed to her at the end of the day, when she was exhausted. He always said that these documents needed immediate decisions. While she examined the papers, he would distract her attention by asking questions about other matters. If she queried anything, he blasted her with expertise. Because she trusted Adam, Miranda allowed herself to be convinced.

On the following afternoon, Miranda went to Eastbourne. As always, she was depressed by the sight of her grandmother: Elinor lay inert, neatly tucked into her bed, white, frail, and exhausted.

And as always, although she clearly recognized Miranda, Elinor seemed almost too tired to speak. "How's Buzz?"

"She's fine, absolutely fine," Miranda said. She hadn't told her grandmother about Buzz's accident; she did not want to further distress Elinor.

"Then why doesn't she visit me?" Elinor asked.

"She's . . . back at Saracen," Miranda lied.

"I wish they'd let me have my telephone," Elinor whispered.

"No, darling, not while you're on medication," Miranda said sadly.

She then drove to Eastbourne General Hospital. Buzz lay on a high, black-barred hospital bed, in a pale green room as small as a shoe box. Pale green pipes writhed around the top and bottom of the walls and in a complicated pattern over the ceiling.

Buzz took off her radio earphones. "You're a good girl, coming to visit your old Buzz. I been looking forward to this all day. A pink azalea! Wicked extravagance, you naughty girl!"

"And I've brought this bed jacket from Annabel."

"Pink marabou! I'll feel like a blooming film star!"

"Can't they give you a prettier room?" Miranda asked as she

contrasted Elinor's luxury to this austere little cubicle, the best that Eastbourne General could offer.

"Now don't you make a fuss, Miranda," Buzz admonished. She added carefully, "Have you visited your gran? Why can't I phone her?"

"They still want her to rest. They took away the telephone after Gran tried to telephone Buckingham Palace to complain to the Queen."

"They're pumping so much rubbish into her! Half the time, Nell don't know what she's doing! You should take her away from that place, my girl! Get her to the London Clinic and see what another doctor says."

Miranda looked away. If she mentioned paranoia, Buzz would insist that Elinor was the victim of a lot of quacks. Buzz's views on psychiatry were well known: psychiatrists were "trick-cyclists," not to be taken seriously, people who said that grown men were in love with their mothers: disgusting.

Gently Miranda said, "I'm sure Gran's in the best place, for the time being. We mustn't interfere with her treatment."

"Treatment!" Buzz snorted. She wondered why strong-willed Miranda was going along with what Adam wanted. Because she was, Buzz couldn't confide in her. So she couldn't rescue Elinor until she left Eastbourne General. She couldn't even write to her, lest her letters be opened by that two-faced ugly bitch of a matron.

In the thirties-style luxury of the Savoy Grill, Adam chose expensive wines to accompany the meal—Colchester oysters, foie gras, and porterhouse steak—chosen by his guest, Alistair Stacey-Cripps, a former school friend, now a stockbroker.

When the wine steward left, Adam's guest continued, "At midday, the share price was forty-six shillings, which makes the value of SUPPLYKITS three million pounds."

Adam nodded. "We're offering the new one-for-threes to existing shareholders at a discount of eight percent."

"You're *sure* that Miranda won't want to take up her rights issue?"

"Positive." Recently the trust had refused Miranda's request for a new plane and an extension to her house. Thinking of that, Adam added, "In fact, she'll be delighted to sell them."

"And you're *sure* that this Bermuda company controlled by you will lend me the half-million pounds in cash to buy these shares, at no interest?"

"Absolutely certain. Later, you'll sell them to me—at sixpence profit to yourself."

"After you've notified," Alistair reminded Adam. Although not a legal obligation, the director of a public company was supposed to notify the chairman before he dealt in company shares. "I must get this absolutely clear," he went on. "Miranda currently holds sixty percent of the shares, you hold fifteen percent, and twenty-five percent are held by the public. But if we go ahead as planned, then Miranda will own forty-five percent—a minority holding—and after acquiring her shares, and taking up your rights issue, *you* will own thirty percent."

Adam tasted the wine and nodded. The waiter carefully poured the '45 Château Margaux.

Alistair said, "And then you want me quickly to buy as many publicly held shares as possible."

Adam nodded again. "Funds will be made available as you require them."

"By this same Bermuda company?" Alistair asked.

Adam nodded a third time.

"You realize, Adam, that I'm legally obliged to inform SUPPLY-KITS of my acquired shareholding?"

"If anyone asks at some later date, you can claim some oversight in your office administration. If you produce a copy letter from your files, then it will look as if you *did* inform the company. Letters are often lost in the post."

"A wonderful claret," Alistair said. He lifted his glass. "Here's to your controlling interest."

TUESDAY, 7 MAY 1968

In the library of his apartment, Adam sipped a pure Highland malt whiskey as he waited.

Eventually Alistair telephoned. "I've bought a further sixteen percent of SUPPLYKITS. So you now control forty-six percent, which is one percent more than Miranda holds. I couldn't buy more because the price is shooting up—too much buying. Closing price was sixty shillings, which values the company at five point one million pounds."

"Good. How much did the shares cost?"

"One million four hundred and sixty-one thousand one hundred and fifty pounds."

"Then you made a decent profit, Alistair," Adam reminded him.

Alistair couldn't resist asking, "Didn't Miranda smell a rat?"

"Alistair, Miranda is extremely happy: her shares have shot up in value and are now worth well over two million pounds."

In fact, that afternoon, Miranda had been worried by the swift rise in share price; she had asked Adam whether he thought anyone might be buying with a view to a takeover bid.

Adam had laughed and told her not to be dramatic. They could expect takeover bids when the company was more firmly established, but not when it was still learning to walk.

As Adam replaced the telephone, his guest was announced—a small, mild-looking, bald man who looked at least fifteen years older than his actual age of thirty-five.

"Hello, Paul," Adam said. "Have a good trip?"

"Not bad. Weak whiskey, please." Paul Littlejohn settled himself carefully onto the sofa. "How is Mrs. O'Dare?"

"I'm sorry to say she's still alive," Adam said. "But not for much longer. I've made it clear to Craig-Dunlop that the family doesn't want her life prolonged, for religious reasons. He got the message: an enormous bonus when she dies, removal to some other nursing home if she doesn't."

"Her death no longer matters. I'm virtually in control of the trust now. You're legally responsible for nothing, Adam." Littlejohn shrugged his shoulders. "And our actions can't be legally queried under Bermuda law, British law, or any other law."

Adam smiled. "What's the income situation?"

"All book royalties have been received; two percent has been deducted by my firm—the agreed management fee. The remainder was immediately sent on to the appropriate numbered Swiss account."

"And the transfer of the capital—how's that proceeding?" The capital was the bulk of the fortune.

"Ah, that has to be done more slowly, and cautiously." Paul Littlejohn sipped his whiskey. "The shares have all been sold and cash lodged in various banks, according to your instructions. However, I can't just ship it all—in one huge transfer—to Switzerland. If I did that, there would be nasty questions from the Bermuda authorities when the sisters discover that the money's gone."

"Leave the authorities to me."

Littlejohn lifted a hand of caution. "As *I'm* going to be blamed, I must be cautious."

"You're being paid a bloody fortune for being blamed. Is everything else going according to plan?"

Littlejohn nodded. "The funds are currently being invested in our bogus companies; their value will fall dramatically over the next six months."

"Good!"

"But I'm warning you, Adam, I'll have to leave something in the Dove Trust—a bit over fifteen percent—or I can't justify what I've done."

"I don't see why you can't empty the account."

"There's nothing wrong with choosing the wrong investments," said Paul Littlejohn carefully. "Nobody can see into the future, and all stock exchange investment is a gamble. But if we don't leave something in the till, it will be spotted as a cheeky scam, and bribery or not, I won't get away with it."

Adam thought briefly. "If they're going to keep fifteen percent, then I'm going to stop showering money on those bitches—in fact, I've already started to cut back. And I'll sell that bloody great chateau as fast as possible."

"Don't be too greedy," Littlejohn cautioned. "We can't afford an official inquiry during the next year. It's the only thing that worries me. During that time, we just can't risk having our moves queried. You will have to keep the sisters quiet—I don't care how you do it."

"Leave them to me too," Adam said confidently. "I'll keep them quiet. *You* move the money into those Swiss accounts—the faster, the better!"

Paul Littlejohn nodded. Without being told, he knew that as fast as the payments were made into the five Swiss bank accounts, the money was transferred into five different accounts—the numbers of which were known only to Adam.

T H U R S D A Y ,　2 3　M A Y　1 9 6 8

Adam sat at his usual lunchtime table in the Savoy Grill—the one discreetly opposite the main entrance, so that without seeming to do so, he saw everyone who entered the restaurant. Eating quail's eggs, he frowned as he reread the letter from Lloyds: it warned him of the amount that he would shortly be expected to produce in settlement.

He looked up as the lean figure of his guest approached. Then he shoved the letter in his jacket pocket and stood. "Good to see you, Scott."

Scott Svenson wore blue jeans and jacket over a navy T-shirt and a wide, striped kipper tie, which looked ridiculous. The tie had been loaned by the headwaiter; unless male guests wore a tie, they were not allowed in the Grill.

Scott sat down. "Hi, Adam!" He noticed that Adam's appearance was unchanged. While all around him, men wore their hair at shoulder length and sported gold chain necklaces, frilled pink shirts, flared-leg hipster trousers, and colored boots with platform soles, Adam had remained carefully traditional. Scott would bet that he had never worn the snakeskin overcoat Annabel had given him the Christmas before.

Spurning the menu, Scott said, "I'll eat whatever you're eating, Adam, plus a glass of milk. I've a heavy afternoon ahead, and I'm off to Paris tomorrow—by parachute if they can't get me in by any other method. I'm covering the riots."

"You lead a more exciting life than I, I'm glad to say."

"It isn't so easy." Scott's network job was taking up more time and concentration than he'd expected.

"Nothing ever is."

"I really wanted to see you on behalf of Annabel," Scott said.

"Has something come up? I saw her briefly only two weeks ago. She was on her way to visit Buzz."

Just before Buzz was due to leave the hospital, the pin in her hip had worked loose, and a total hip replacement had been necessary.

Scott's speckled green and gold eyes looked speculatively at Adam. He said, "Annabel doesn't understand why the trustees originally allowed her large sums of money but are now refusing relatively small sums."

Adam sipped his wine. "Initially the money on deposit was distributed between Annabel and Miranda. Having emptied the honeypot, I understand that the trustees are now allowing the income to build up again before further distributions." As steak-and-kidney pie was placed before them, Adam added, "In addition, the trust has to pay Elinor's very heavy medical expenses." He sniffed the dish of peas. "Good, cooked in fresh mint. As you know, Scott, I don't control the Dove Trust, but if Annabel needs extra funds, then I would be happy to suggest further payments."

"Annabel would prefer a modest regular income to occasional lump sums," Scott said. "And if you don't control the trust, Adam, then it's time we knew who does. We want to know everything about the Dove Trust and its officers. We want to understand the structure, the aims, the obligations. We want to know precisely what funds the trust handles, where those funds are, and what regular income might be expected from the capital sum."

Adam helped himself to peas. "I thought Annabel already had that information—although, of course, there's no legal reason why she should. The trust is run like any other business, with annual accounts prepared by qualified accountants—although, again, that isn't legally necessary. I understand the final accounts for 1967 were signed last week. I'll see that a copy is sent to Annabel."

"Are accounts produced only once a year?"

"That's the usual procedure." Adam decided to stall for time. He didn't want this newsman poking his nose into the trust. "If you like, Scott, I could suggest quarterly accounts, although that's an expensive business."

"That's what I intended to ask you."

"Then I shall arrange it," said Adam, who had no intention of producing quarterly accounts for this inquisitive journalist. He decided to arrange that a large monthly income be paid to Annabel until next May: that should shut her up. Similar sums would also have to be paid to Miranda, blast it, for very quickly she would learn of Annabel's new income. Still, lose a lure to catch a mackerel—or, in this case, a whale. But Scott could stir up a lot of trouble before next May. Something would have to be done about Scott.

That evening, having explained that the best place to enjoy a peach was in the bath, Adam fed one slowly to Miranda.

The mirrored walls and ceiling of her large bathroom reflected the room to infinity. In spite of a complicated lighting system, only one candle flickered in an antique silver candlestick.

In the warm water of the square, sunken marble tub, Adam lay beside Miranda; he soaped her body as though she were a royal baby. Dreamy and passive, she lay in the scented water and gave in to Adam's sensual massage. They listened to the Beatles on Miranda's new stereo; the magical mystery of "Strawberry Fields Forever" reminded her of her grandmother, so lonely, isolated, and unreachable in the prison of her own head. Sharply Miranda diverted her thoughts: she did not want to plunge again into pointless depression.

"Where did Scott take you to dinner?" Adam asked.

"That new Italian place in the King's Road," Miranda murmured. "Why is it that pansies seem to run the best restaurants?"

"The queers are all coming out of the closet after last year's legislation," Adam said. Homosexual acts between adult men were now legal in Britain. "What was the restaurant like?"

"The usual Italian thing. Vaulted ceilings, everything white, one perfect flower spotlit in the center of each table, impeccable fettuccine primavera."

"Did Scott have anything interesting to say?"

"He was a bit too earnest to be amusing." Miranda gently splashed scented water at Adam. "As a matter of fact, Scott spent most of the first course warning me against you. He wants me to visit STG and find out more about the trust."

"The trust no longer has anything to do with STG," Adam said, hiding his annoyance as he soaped Miranda's soft right underarm. "And you saw the trust accounts for last year, remember?"

Adam turned his attention to Miranda's other tender places and casually added, "Perhaps you'd better give Annabel a call, to reassure her that you're keeping a watchful eye on the accounts. Explain again that trustees are very careful with somebody else's money. . . . That reminds me, did I tell you that the trustees have turned down a request from Annabel?"

"No," Miranda said. "What for?"

"She wanted a large sum of money to fund some project at the Bronx Zoo. Unfortunately, this request didn't come within the trust beneficiary limits. I expect that's what's behind Scott's concern."

"The trust was absolutely correct to say no," Miranda agreed. Then she added, carefully casual: "What I'd really like to talk to Annabel about is *us*. I'm sure everyone in the office guesses."

"Our relationship isn't *your* secret, it's *our* secret, and I want it *kept* secret," Adam murmured, his voice smooth but determined.

"I've never understood *why* you want to keep it a secret—I wish I did," Miranda said, returning to their perennial source of disagreement. A year ago—and again at Christmas—she had proposed, playfully. On both occasions, he had laughed the idea off as a charming joke.

Miranda was puzzled and humiliated by Adam's rejection. He had now been her lover for nearly three years: the physical side of their relationship seemed to be perfect. Miranda, while not vain, did not suffer from false modesty. She knew that she was beautiful, although her looks were not as sensational as Annabel's. She was a perfect size ten: at five nine, perhaps a little too tall, but Adam was well over six feet. Rich and famous, Miranda knew she was also an interesting companion.

Besides, Adam said that he loved her.

At the back of her mind, Miranda heard the ghostly voice of Buzz say, "Any Latin lover can say 'I love you,' " but she pushed the thought away, just as she had pushed away other silly possibilities. Perhaps Adam sought a bride with better status. If so, Miranda thought sarcastically, Princess Anne would soon be old enough for him.

The only other reason Miranda could think of for her failure to get Adam to the altar was her success; she knew that while many women were attracted to a man by his status, many men saw a successful businesswoman as a direct competitor. An insecure man, she knew, might not want to be married to someone more powerful than himself.

But Adam was extremely successful in his own right. *So why wouldn't he marry her?*

Knowing that Adam always liked to keep his options open, Miranda was forced to the lonely conclusion that he didn't love her enough to commit himself to her for life. As is always the case when a person wants something and can't have it, her frustration merely increased her desire.

As he soaped Miranda's back, Adam knew perfectly well that she was about to propose to him again. But if he tied himself to Miranda, he would have less influence over Annabel, who would then have legitimate reasons to doubt his objectivity. However, Miranda, who couldn't stand indecision, wasn't the sort of woman to be fobbed off for much longer.

Until he controlled all the money, Adam couldn't risk either sister querying his moves: he needed to placate and control both of them.

So Adam intended, when Miranda asked him, to reassure her by promising to marry her *one day*. In fact, if she got too insistent, he might agree to an engagement on … say, February seventh, Miranda's twenty-eighth birthday. With any luck, the trust funds should be in his hands shortly after that date, at which point he would say goodbye to Britain forever.

Adam's wet arm lazily reached for another peach. He said, "I can tell you're thinking about something."

"You know what I'm thinking about," Miranda replied sadly.

"Well, stop it, or I'll tie you to the bedposts with silk ribbons and do wicked things to you, so you won't be able to think of anything else."

He slid his hands beneath Miranda's soapy body. As he caressed the two pale curves of flesh that rose above the water, he decided what to do about Scott.

TUESDAY, 22 AUGUST 1968

Adam drove his DB4 Aston Martin rather too fast through the peaceful country lanes of Sussex. He was taking Annabel to see the latest production of *Figaro* at the Glyndebourne Festival, both of them wearing full evening dress. Some people might consider it surreal, even ludicrous, to set off for a country outing in midafternoon in full evening dress, but this eccentricity is part of the Glyndebourne Opera tradition, which began in 1934 when John Christie gave his opera singer wife a wedding present—her own little opera house, set in the sylvan parks of a stately house in Sussex. Now few musical occasions are more beautiful, more typically British, more exquisitely performed, and more elitist than an evening at Glyndebourne.

As usual, the seats were all occupied: part of what made the little theater so special was the fact that tickets were almost impossible to obtain. The London Philharmonic started the overture, and the audience settled back to enjoy itself as the opening bars predicted the lighthearted frivolity and charm of Mozart's enchanted eighteenth-century world.

Adam, who was not musical, found it difficult to accept the elaborate plot, with its disguises and unlikely mistaken identities, its concealments in closets and too-coincidental overheard assignations, as Figaro, the valet, fought his master, the Count, for the favors of the chambermaid Susanna. But Adam had not come here for pleasure, he reminded himself as the lights went up for the intermission.

During this especially long interval, the audience either ate a three-course dinner in the manor house or took champagne picnics onto the lawns, enhanced by the Sussex Downs in the background.

"Before the war, people used to bring their own butlers to serve their picnics in those woods." Adam pointed to the spot. "Let's have our dinner there," he suggested as he helped Annabel maneuver across a grassy ditch in her silver-beaded gray chiffon Jean Muir dress. Black-faced sheep viewed their efforts with mild surprise.

Adam carried the wickerwork picnic hamper over the grass to the trees; they walked beside a chain of woodland pools which followed the course of a stream and led to a small clearing carpeted by wildflowers.

"This might have been painted by Botticelli!" Annabel kicked off her shoes and sat down on Adam's rug. Green leaves rustled slightly on the soft breeze, and she heard the faint hum of a bee.

Adam took off his jacket, spread a white linen cloth on the grass by a still, clear pool, then poured champagne into Annabel's glass, and looked in the hamper. "We have quail's eggs, chicken in curry-flavored mayonnaise, cucumber salad, and strawberries Romanoff."

In the twilight, they ate and talked, Annabel looking like a woodsprite in her will-o'-the-wisp gray chiffon. Through the trees, in the distance, they could see the manor against the sky, decked out in lights. Annabel said, "What a delightful way to end my British visit."

"I'm sorry it's been such a sad trip for you." Adam helped himself to some quail's eggs.

Annabel had arrived in England two weeks earlier, intending to take Buzz back to Saracen to complete her recovery. But when Annabel collected her, Buzz had asked to stay the night at a posh hotel in Eastbourne. Puzzled, Annabel agreed.

Shortly afterward, when Buzz was supposedly resting, she had appeared, wearing a bright mustard coat, at the Lord Willington Nursing Home, where she asked to see Elinor. As she insisted upon carrying a suitcase into Elinor's bedroom, rather than leave it at the reception desk, the receptionist feared that Buzz was perhaps smuggling alcohol to an alcoholic patient; she immediately informed the matron.

Matron Braddock hurried to the bedroom, to find a vacant-looking Elinor being helped by Buzz into an identical mustard coat.

When the furious matron asked Buzz to leave, she refused. The matron called two male nurses, who firmly escorted Buzz to her waiting taxi. Matron Braddock later telephoned Adam, and he readily agreed that Buzz should be banned.

The following day, Buzz tried to enter the nursing home by the side gate but was spotted by a gardener. The matron had threatened to call the police if she tried again.

"What was sad," Annabel said, "was seeing poor Buzz refuse to believe that Gran was . . . how she is. Poor darling, she really isn't with us anymore, but Buzz won't accept that, as we all must. She seems to think we're part of some conspiracy to imprison Elinor. She's refused to stay with Miranda, and she's very cross with me."

"It must be hard for Buzz to accept the fact that she's also . . . deteriorating," Adam said sympathetically.

"She's taken a room in a boardinghouse in Earls Court, full of noisy Australian students. She says that once Gran used to live in the next square."

"I don't want you or Miranda to worry about Buzz," Adam said firmly as he refilled Annabel's glass. "You've helped Buzz as much as she wants to be helped." He smiled at Annabel's worried face. "I'll make a few quiet investigations. The trust will pay her rent, as well as her pension, and also any special medical care she might need. I expect she'll soon calm down and see reason."

He poured more champagne for himself. "Oh, by the way—there's something I want to discuss before you leave. Scott says that you want the trustees to provide quarterly accounts, and they're a bit mystified as to why because, as you know, Miranda keeps a close eye on the accounts. The trustees wondered if there was any particular item that *you* wanted to query in the 1967 accounts."

Somewhat confused and not wishing to seem impolite, Annabel said, "Oh no . . . nothing particular." She laughed apologetically. "I know Miranda has the business brains of the family. It just seemed odd that when I asked for a relatively small sum . . ." Her voice trailed away as she carefully examined her forkful of chicken.

"My dear Annabel, the job of the trustees is to *protect the capital*," Adam said gravely. "They can't whittle away the capital without risking serious legal charges. They are legally obliged to act for the benefit of the beneficiaries, whether or not you all agree to their actions: that is the whole point of a trust." He refilled her glass again and said reassuringly, "When enough income has accumulated, then, in addition to your present allowance, you'll probably get the same large lump sum that you had last year—especially if Saracen is sold."

"Miranda told me the trust might sell Saracen. We both hate to think of it!"

"Now that de Gaulle's had his landslide victory—with the Communist seats halved—it seems a prudent time to sell. Sadly, Elinor may never leave the nursing home. Should she do so, she could no longer manage to run the chateau, and neither, I suspect, can poor old Buzz."

Annabel put down her glass and looked about to cry.

Adam leaned over and patted her hand. "You must let the trustees make these worrying decisions. That's why your grandmother set up the trust in the first place. She wanted you to have no worries."

"She's always been so caring."

"Of course." Adam patted her hand again. "If you'd like to go over all the legal paperwork with me again—in detail—I'd be happy to do it. Can you spare, say, three hours at my office tomorrow?"

Suspecting that she might be even more confused after three hours of perusing legal documents, Annabel hastily said, "It isn't really necessary. Scott's a little overprotective. I'm sure Miranda's capable of checking these things."

"Miranda's special gift is for business." Adam nodded. "Your gifts are quite different, Annabel, and . . . very rare."

"I'd like to think I've got *something* going for me. I'd like to think I was good for something other than smiling to camera."

"Of course you are, Annabel. I've just told you so."

"Now," Annabel said sadly, "when people say nice things about me, I can't believe them. When you're a model, the praise and flattery is endless and addictive. But as soon as your bookings start to slide, the flatterers just . . . melt away. That's when you know you're a has-been."

"What a sad little speech," Adam said gently. Annabel's beautiful face was not only her strength but also her weakness. She was afraid of getting ugly, fat, old. Her dreaded thirtieth birthday came nearer every day. "*I* think your looks have *improved* since you stopped modeling," he continued. "Since your face filled out, it's lost that worried, anxious look. You now have a delicious, serene quality."

"Do I *really?*"

"Yes, really," Adam said, looking into Annabel's astonishingly beautiful eyes. "You're really an old-fashioned girl, Annabel, with charming, traditional feminine qualities. You're so much softer and more gentle than . . . your sisters."

"Oh! Do you *really* think so?"

"Miranda's obviously the new sort of woman who's trying to take a man's place in a man's world, but when things get tough, she still dodges final responsibility and turns to a man—me," Adam explained. "Clare's another type of new woman: she also tries to take on a man's responsibility, but she won't do things in the traditional way. So she makes a mess of it, can't manage on her own and can't understand why—and when she's bewildered she becomes aggressive."

"She certainly does," Annabel said with feeling. "She was unspeakably rude when I telephoned."

"Your generation of women wasn't brought up to handle ultimate responsibility." To Annabel, at that moment Adam looked ready to shoulder the world. "Traditionally, men have always done that, and *they* know how tough it is." He smiled gently. "But *you*, Annabel, don't need or want to prove anything. *You're* happy to be looked after and to enjoy life! You're the only O'Dare sister who's a realist."

Even as he spoke, Adam couldn't believe that Annabel was swallowing this rubbish. But she was still an underdeveloped child, easily led, dependent, and naive. No wonder she had no children. Annabel was still a child herself. She wanted to be taken care of. She didn't want to grow up and grapple with responsibilities and problems.

Smiling, Adam offered the silver pudding dish, but Annabel shook her head. "I have to be careful."

"What rubbish!" Adam laughed, looking Annabel's figure over appreciatively. "I agree that you no longer look like a starved greyhound, but you *must* know that you are a sensuous and beautiful woman."

Annabel's basic amiability and good nature made her instinctively a flatterer: she always wanted to make people feel happy. Because of this, she did not recognize flattery when it was used as a weapon against her, to breach her defenses and melt her resistance.

Adam saw that, as with most women, praise would turn Annabel's head; careful flattery would counteract her insecurity, for which she would unknowingly feel grateful—and the rest would be easy.

He leaned toward her and stroked her pale, chiffon shoulder. "You look like a charming wood nymph in that gauze thing."

Through the flimsy material, Annabel felt the heat of Adam's palm against her skin. He was close enough for her to feel his warm breath and smell his erotic odor. She shifted slightly away from him.

Adam said, "Your beautiful mouth has a crumb on it." He leaned closer. Before Annabel realized his intention, he licked the side of her mouth with a fast, serpentine flick of his tongue.

His movement took her completely by surprise—and so did her own bodily reaction when he pressed his mouth on hers. Annabel felt his hands against her breasts. She felt a melting warmth spread quickly through her body.

After what they both recognized as token resistance, she slowly fell back upon the grass, feeling that happy warmth down to the tingling tips of her fingers.

Annabel was bewitched by Adam, overwhelmed by the feel of his body crushing hers. Unable to move, she felt the satin-slippery texture of his lips and his slow, hungry kisses.

As Adam tore the gray chiffon from her breasts, Annabel felt her reason drift away, replaced by a passionate longing for the continued hard strength of his body. She wanted him not only to cover her but to envelop her; she wanted to efface herself and melt into him, lose herself in the ecstasy of fusion. Adam lowered his now naked body upon hers and Annabel at last felt his flesh upon her flesh, hard and warm. She smelled the sharp scent of crushed wild thyme beneath her head as he started to move slowly, steadily, and rhythmically.

Afterward, they bathed, silent and naked, in the pool, and then— still naked—they walked, barefoot and hand in hand, through the woods. Often they stopped to kiss and touch, regardless of who might see them, and neither said a word.

Daylight had faded into dusk when they returned to their picnic site. The overturned dish of chicken and the untouched strawberries were now abuzz with wasps.

Annabel never saw the end of *Figaro*.

Chapter·23

Clare stood at the front door, feeling the sun warm her brown arms. The cream climbing rose—appropriately named the New Dawn—which she had planted by the door was in full bloom. A sweetbrier hedge enclosed the garden, and before it grew fragrant, white tobacco flowers, delicate sprays of gypsophila, and very pale pink hydrangeas.

She looked down the herringbone-patterned brick garden path that her visitors were about to tread; the path was edged by herbs: behind the mint were rosemary, thyme, and tarragon (sadly, not doing very well). Then came rows of vegetables, as satisfyingly neat as a sampler, in lines of different-colored greens: cabbages and cauliflowers, lettuces, onions, and carrot tops.

Summer had spilled over into early September. It was so golden a day that Clare had almost decided to hold David's birthday luncheon in the garden, but the buffet meal looked very pretty in the kitchen—a bit like a harvest festival; she had decorated the pink-walled room with branches of elderberry and hawthorn, red berries, and sprays of blackberried brambles. Flat loaves shaped like stooks of wheat had been painted with egg yolk before Clare baked them, so that now they shone; her showpieces were the open tarts: apricot and chestnut, plum and raspberry, peach and pear, and shiny black cherry.

Clare decided to serve drinks before lunch—her homemade lemonade and elderflower wine—under the apple trees. Behind her, she heard David clumping down the uncarpeted wooden staircase and turned to face him. He looked so handsome in the cream silk shirt that was Clare's birthday gift.

In a low voice, he said, "I'm sorry. I'm leaving. Now."

"*You can't leave!* The guests are due, and they're nearly all *your* friends!"

"They know me. They'll understand. I'm sorry. I'm off."

When David was in one of his moods, he would withdraw and treat Clare almost as if she were a stranger. He was always very polite but distant.

These moods differed from David's habitual absentmindedness, which made him unreliable and unpredictable: sometimes he was so absorbed by what he was doing that he lost track of time and forgot to eat or to go to bed—only looking up from his work or his book as dawn filtered through the windows, when he would suddenly realize that he was ravenously hungry and had forgotten to phone Clare.

But when David was in a depression, he would be unable to sit still, impatient, and moody. He would stride restlessly around the kitchen or open the front door. Clare would run to a window and see his long legs hurrying down the brick path to the garden gate, which he sometimes vaulted—in his haste to get away from her, she thought bitterly.

If she tried to stop him from leaving, he became irritable. And if he agreed to stay, he would sit, immobile, in front of the fire for hours, in blank resignation. At some point, he would get up abruptly and leave without a word.

When he was like this, it was impossible to persuade David to do something, for no effort seemed worthwhile to him: he was incapable of reading, of listening to the music he loved, even of eating. He wanted only to be left alone.

At such times, Clare's self-esteem would start to crumble. Her still-fragile newfound self-confidence had been built up by her growing pleasure in her successful bakery but also by David's loving encouragement.

Clare had never probed for further explanation of his moods, but now, as she stood waiting for David's birthday guests, she cried, "This time you *must* tell me! *What do I do wrong?*"

"I've told you before, it's nothing to do with you, Clare. Please let me go. I can't explain at the moment."

Behind them, Josh, in a new pair of jeans, clattered downstairs. He looked from Clare to David and said sharply, "Whatzoop?"

"Nothing, Josh," Clare said. "We're just talking." Josh ran off to climb his favorite apple tree. David fled down the garden path.

Clare's friends were surprised and sorry to hear that David had suddenly developed a migraine.

David's friends—some of whom Clare had never met before—made no comment, but exchanged swift understanding glances and enthusiastically praised Clare's homemade wine.

The following evening, after Clare had put Josh to bed, she heard the front door bang and knew that it was David.

She stayed in the kitchen, her elbows on the pine table and her chin in her hands. "David, I'd give anything to understand your black moods and be able to help."

"I'm sorry. I can't see anyone when I feel like that. I can't work, I can't talk to people. I don't even turn up for business appointments."

"*Why?* What's wrong with you?" Clare asked. Again she felt the bewilderment she had experienced when she first saw her lighthearted, friendly lover—so intuitive and gentle, so naturally in touch with his feelings—change to a morose lump, a heavy, difficult weight that Clare sometimes felt she bore upon her shoulders. Sometimes David's fits of depression lasted several days, and on the rare occasions when he stayed with her, Clare felt mentally drained and physically exhausted once he'd left.

"I've told you before. I get depressions. I feel hemmed in."

"But surely that's when you need a loving friend to cheer you up? To pour you a drink, put on a record, and cook your favorite meal?"

"That sort of loving concern only makes me feel worse. If I see that you're making an effort to cheer me up, it sends me sliding down into the black pit even faster because then I also feel guilty."

Clare said, "Have you thought of seeing a doctor about it?"

"Our family doctor said that I simply needed to snap out of my self-absorption and self-pity. But when I'm depressed"—David shrugged his shoulders in a helpless gesture—"all people, all interests, and all activities tend to shrink and dwindle until they . . . disappear. I can't think or talk or concentrate—or move, sometimes—and I feel as if I'm in a black vacuum. It takes an enormous effort to say 'Yes' or 'No' to anyone. I feel useless, unwanted, and frightened. I expect it sounds melodramatic, but I feel trapped and without hope. When that happens, it feels as if I've been in that state nearly all my life, and that *this* time I won't come out of it."

"But surely *something* must help you when you feel like that?"

"The only thing that helps is time. I just want to be alone, with no one making any demands on me, however slight, while I pray that it will pass. You must understand that *you can't help me.* Nobody can. I only bring other people down with me. I've learned that it's best if I just disappear and sit it out."

"Do the people in your office know?" Clare asked as she struggled to understand what seemed to her a change in character as abrupt, unlikely, and terrifying as that of Mr. Hyde into Dr. Jekyll.

"It's always posed a problem at work. Last time I was fired, I asked my uncle for help." David's uncle had realized that persistence, tenacity, and the medical profession seemed useless in helping David, and so he had helped him to establish a small private country practice, where the pressure was not so great as in London and David could work at his own pace. "My colleagues are understanding and tactfully ignore my symptoms," he went on. "It's the best thing to do."

"Then I will, if that's really what you want," Clare said.

After that talk, she realized that she mustn't try to get too close to David. She sensed that if she wanted him to stay with her, she had to let him feel free to leave. She must learn to trust his love for her and not to question his absences or his sudden departures.

In return, because he was neither possessive nor jealous, David was careful to give Clare the same freedom and privacy she gave him, not realizing that it was the last thing she wanted.

SATURDAY, 21 SEPTEMBER 1968

In David's bedroom, Clare knelt on the window seat, from which she could look down upon a spectacular bird's-eye view of Bath. Below her, the city of golden stone spread like a beautiful, fragile toy replica of classical Greek temples, set in squares and crescents of greenery.

David's house—which he was buying on a mortgage—perched on the rim of the green basin in which Bath nestled. It was bare yet calm and wonderfully comfortable: it was a house in which you could curl up for the winter and almost regret the coming of summer. It was a home.

Beneath David's bedroom, the sitting room contained great quantities of books, piled on the floor as well as stacked on the shelves; these piles overflowed through the door and onto the staircase.

Underneath the sitting room was a large topaz-painted kitchen with a splendid view at either end. Since the terraced house was built on the side of a hill, one entered from the street directly into the kitchen. The walls were covered with pictures: architectural prints hung next to children's paintings; antique views of Bath were beside snapshots of friends; postcards were taped to the walls, as were posters by Matisse and Hockney.

David's offices were on the two lower floors. Beyond the tree-shaded narrow garden, black-and-white Friesian cows grazed in a field. When he was depressed, David often sat at the end of the garden; hunched up, he would stare for hours at the cows.

Hearing David clatter up the stairs, Clare crossed her fingers and hoped he would stay in a good mood for this afternoon's concert at the Assembly Rooms.

David burst into the bedroom. "Time we left!" he said. "You'd better wear a sweater. These late-September days can suddenly turn cold." He opened a drawer, pulled out a green sweater, and threw it to her.

"I think that Bath is the loveliest city in the world," Clare said dreamily as she shut the window.

"Small thanks to the city fathers. When John Wood drew up his scheme for rebuilding the city, the Bath Corporation didn't like it, so poor Mr. Wood was forced to build it bit by bit, starting with Queen Square." David was one of the architects involved in the rebuilding and cleaning of the city, which was slow work: a lot of the old stone was still stained black with the soot from Victorian chimneys and the early railway; there were still bomb sites from the German air raids in 1942. David asserted that even more damage had been done after the war, by the shortsighted city planners who demolished the Georgian and Victorian workmen's cottages and replaced them with ugly apartment blocks.

They walked downhill past a classic semicircle of small, elegant houses with pillared entrances. Clare paused on a stone sidewalk to peer into a bowfront shop. Inside were charming children's clothes.

David gently pulled at her hand. "Come on! You know Josh would hate those rich-kid clothes."

"I wish we'd brought him with us."

"Stop feeling guilty about leaving him for once. He's much better off at the cottage making gingerbread men with Betsy." Betsy, Clare's assistant baker, was staying overnight.

"I can't help feeling guilty about depriving Josh of a lot of things, especially as Christmas approaches."

"I'm going to take you both skiing," David reminded her.

"True. You're wonderful with Josh. But I now realize that no one—however wonderful—can replace a child's own father."

"Divorce is one of the facts of life for modern children."

Clare laughed angrily. "I wish I *could* get a divorce."

Sam would not admit his adultery and refused to divorce Clare for desertion, which he was now able to do because three years had passed since Clare left him. Unless Sam changed his mind, under British law Clare would remain married to him forever: because she had deserted him, she was the guilty party.

David said, "I don't understand why you *can't*."

"No grounds. If you rule out adultery, there's only cruelty—difficult to prove in British courts—or unsound mind. Sam hasn't been continuously in a loony bin for five years, and he hasn't committed rape, sodomy, or bestiality, so—no divorce!"

"Who cares whether you're married or not?" David shrugged his shoulders. "You'd do better to ignore this legal game. Josh is happy enough. You're making enough money from the bakery. You're developing your own ideas and independence."

"Encouraged by you." Clare threw him a grateful smile. David had always helped her—sometimes by kicking her—to think for herself as she built up her bakery business. He had comforted her when she became enmeshed in bureaucratic regulations. He always said that success was built on failure, as any tycoon could tell her. "I wish I didn't need your support so much," Clare said. "I wish I could stand on my own feet."

"You're learning fast. And I need *your* support, perhaps more than you realize." Although he laughed, David was serious. He needed Clare's tenacity and stability to balance his up-in-the-air exultation and down-in-the-dumps gloom. "My passive side likes your passionate, determined, stubborn side," he added. "I like a clear, sharp-witted woman."

"But when I was married to Sam," Clare said, "I ended up a meek doormat. That was why he was so surprised when I got up and walked away."

"That showed your guts," David said.

SUNDAY, 22 SEPTEMBER 1968

Standing next to Annabel at the Nice airport carousel, a drab young woman was identifying luggage to the porter. While she waited for her suitcases, Annabel glanced at the neighboring pile. Twelve navy leather suitcases with maroon bindings had the initials S.K. stamped on them in gold. There were also three Louis Vuittons, one black leather hatbox, a green tapestry carpetbag, eighteen cheap suitcases in different colors, one green plastic garbage bin, one enormous cardboard box held together by string, one child's folding stroller, and two brown trunks— *trunks* on a commercial flight! Each item bore the name Khashoggi daubed in pink nail varnish.

Annabel was grateful for this momentary distraction from her passionate longing for Adam. She felt a wrenching of her gut, a tightening, lurching feeling at the thought of seeing him, or—she dared not think about it—of not seeing him.

For the first time, it occurred to her that Adam might not meet her flight, which was very late. She caught her breath and crossed her fingers. Of *course* Adam would meet her! Although, naturally, they were both cautious: if somebody spotted them together, their secret would slip into the gossip columns.

Annabel no longer cared about Scott's feelings, but Adam had made it clear that, were it publicly known he had seduced the wife of a client, his professional reputation would suffer. Adam had also made it clear that if *that* happened, he would immediately leave Annabel; for the only thing worse than seducing a client's wife was marrying her.

A bitterly disappointed Annabel had protested that Scott *wasn't* Adam's client, but Adam said that this was how it would be perceived. Should Scott sue him for alienation of affections, Adam might as well say goodbye to his business, which was based on a client's trust of his lawyer.

Annabel again felt relieved that she hadn't blurted out her secret to Scott the previous evening, when he appeared with a martini jug in her dressing room.

She had been astonished when Scott poured himself a second martini and then, surprisingly, grumbled about Annabel's departure.

"I've had a tough time at work this week," he said reluctantly, "and I'd like to talk to you about it on the weekend. I need a little reassurance and sympathy."

"Are you complaining?" Annabel asked. "You've no time for *me* these days. Your brilliant career is all that matters."

"Not to you," Scott said. "I feel you don't give a damn about me now. Of course you must visit Elinor, but on the rare occasions when you're actually in this apartment, you always seem too busy with your friends to have any time for me."

Annabel, flustered, snapped, "*I'm* not responsible for Gran's illness!"

"But your trip tomorrow *isn't* to visit Elinor," Scott pointed out. "Why can't Miranda spare the time to superintend this furniture sale at the chateau? Why should *you* be dragged from another continent to do it? I've half a mind to telephone her . . ."

Annabel hurriedly explained that Miranda was holding a seminar—arranged long before Elinor's illness.

When Scott was not mollified, Annabel looked at him from under her eyelashes, pouted charmingly, and said, "Angel will be back in no time."

Scott glared at her. "Cut out that childish, cute behavior—it doesn't work with me anymore. And while we're on the subject, you can also quit crying. Your tears don't make me feel strong and protective; they make me exasperated, annoyed, and resentful." He finished his drink in one gulp. "I'm tired of having a child bride. You no longer seem interested in having a thoughtful conversation, producing a decent meal, or accepting any responsibility. If I say anything that sounds critical, you start crying, as if I'm the world's biggest brute. You are twenty-eight years old, Annabel, and *I* now feel the need to be taken care of, looked after, and loved—for a change."

"Don't blame *me* for your career problems," Annabel had sobbed.

Her reverie was interrupted by the arrival of her suitcases.

•   •   •   •

Although he knew that Annabel expected to be met, Adam did not go to Nice airport. Instead, after switching on the water and heating in the now deserted chateau, he went for a newly fashionable jog in the countryside around Saracen.

Intent on counting his paces and checking his rhythm and breathing, Adam did not notice how the light altered in September so that the far mountains were the same soft mauve as the lavender fields. As he panted along, he did not see the wild figs hanging above hedgerows thick with ripe blackberries. As he checked his pulse rate, Adam failed to smell the delicate scent of conifers and coconut-scented gorse and the acrid, sour, mysterious odor of the ditch. He might as well have been running around a cinder track or pounding lengths in a gym.

Feeling pleasantly exhilarated by his exercise, Adam showered in Elinor's bathroom—something that he'd always wanted to do. He liked to feel really, really, really rich.

He whistled as he toweled himself, then sprinkled half a bottle of invigorating cologne over his body. Through the open window, he saw the sky darken to gray, then slate purple. He had timed his jog nicely.

After an ominous moment of near silence, when only the soft rustling of the ivy on the terrace could be heard, lightning split the sky with sharp brilliance, followed by a mighty clash of thunder.

As rain slashed the chateau, Adam closed the window. He felt snug and safe as he tightened his dressing gown cord. He decided to get some champagne.

Without flowers, noise, or movement, the empty building seemed lifeless. As Adam walked through the entrance hall, his feet echoed on marble from which the antique rugs had been removed for auction. At the end of this week, the furniture would also be taken to Sotheby's. The appraiser was upstairs now, estimating the auction reserve prices.

The drinks cupboard in the beige marble bar was empty, as was the refrigerator, which had been turned off. Adam walked to the kitchen, which still smelled faintly of stale bread; he opened the door to the slate-shelved larder, normally a treasure-house, with gargantuan sausages and smoked hams hung from hooks in the ceiling too high for the cat to reach. There was still a faint smell of bacon, and a lingering peachy odor of summer, but the shelves were empty.

Adam slammed the door and opened the one beyond it, which led to the old dungeon where Elinor kept her wine. In the bulb-lit cellar, the wine racks stood empty.

Eventually Adam found a forgotten bottle of brandy in the television room. As he sipped his drink, he heard a scratching on the glass doors to the terrace. Outside the French windows, a sodden ginger cat was asking to be let in. Supposedly, Fudge had been adopted by Sylvie the cook, who reckoned that otherwise he wouldn't last long among the village toughs of the stray cat pack.

Happy to be home, Fudge curled up on the sofa beside Adam, who flipped through an old magazine, irritated that Annabel was late. How prudent it had been of him not to meet her! It would do Annabel good to feel a little dejected, a little cast down, a little forlorn.

Adam smiled. He supplied Annabel with reassurance. But in order for it to work its magic, she first had to feel unsure of herself.

He could just remember Annabel's childish flirtations with her grandfather, but how she lapsed into terrified submission if Billy slightly raised his voice. *That* was the way to handle her.

Adam liked to get tough with Annabel. When she sensed his disapproval, her lips would tremble with apprehension. Despotic benevolence in his voice, he would then reassure her ("You're so *special*, Annabel"), knowing he could get her to do almost anything for him, if she thought he really believed *that*.

With her, he was truly applying the lessons he had learned from reading Elinor's novels. For Adam knew that Annabel's head was filled with girlish hopes of romance; he knew that she was besotted by him, hungry for him. He guessed that her life now revolved around their clandestine relationship: secretly telephoning him or writing to him, their secret meetings. Adam was almost certain that Annabel longed to marry him—if only he would ask her.

Adam felt a carefully hidden contempt for the emotional dependence of such women, who needed his approval. Miranda was one of the few women he had met who didn't want to experience life parasitically, through some man.

His present situation—two sisters eating out of the palm of his hand and the other one no longer in the running—although somewhat taxing, was only for five more months: Paul Littlejohn needed a little more time than he had originally planned, but by the end of February, Adam would be in Rio.

Had the sisters not fallen so easily into his hands, he suspected he would have had a far harder job persuading them that Saracen should be sold—though if they had not agreed to the sale, it could easily have been proved that selling was to their advantage: when the cash from the sale of the chateau and its contents was invested, the resultant income would increase the trust substantially.

But the sale of Saracen was a clear indication that Elinor would never leave the nursing home, and had the sisters not both been emotionally involved with Adam, the decision to sell it might once again have raised the question of whether the nursing home was the best place for her.

Adam had pointed out to Miranda that it was no longer in their power to remove Elinor. If such a patient wished to be discharged (or should the relatives wish it against medical advice), the Mental Hospital Act provided for compulsory detention of up to twenty-eight days. That would undoubtedly attract the unpleasant attention of the press and gain nothing. A nursing home was not always the best choice for everyone, but in Elinor's case, it provided the finest care possible.

Reluctantly Miranda had agreed that Elinor was being well cared for in luxurious surroundings.

As suddenly as it had started, the rain stopped, and weak sunshine lightened the chateau terrace. In the television room, Adam's thoughts were cut short by footsteps. He looked up at the approach of Mr. Simpson, the furniture appraiser who had been sent from London.

"Excuse me, sir," Mr. Simpson said. "I've found something in Mrs. O'Dare's private library that isn't on the inventory. It's a strongbox—too large and heavy for me to carry."

Adam followed the thin, black-suited figure upstairs and through Elinor's bedroom, where the bed had been stripped and all the furniture labeled.

In the library beyond the bedroom, the bookshelves contained old children's books, tattered paperbacks, and six thousand reference books. On the cheap wooden table before the window stood a battered black tin strongbox.

"It's locked, sir," Mr. Simpson said, "but none of the housekeeper's keys fit."

"Then please break it open," Adam told him. "I should imagine there's a crowbar in the toolbox. Look in the kitchen."

Mr. Simpson hesitated, then firmly said, "I would prefer not to do that, sir, without the written permission of the owner."

Adam, somewhat irritated, went downstairs to call the caretaker, who would have no such scruples.

Ten minutes later, the black lid of the box creaked open.

Adam dismissed the caretaker and Mr. Simpson.

As soon as the door closed behind them, he bent eagerly over the box. But to his exasperation, it appeared to contain only old photographs and childish memorabilia.

Adam rifled through children's paintings and letters; he threw aside faded snapshots, with torn or curling edges, of smiling children in sunbonnets waving spades upon a beach or seated on the backs of fat ponies. At the bottom of the box were bundles of letters in envelopes with an Oxford postmark; they were tied with narrow ivory satin ribbon.

Severely disappointed, Adam was about to bang the lid down and leave the room, when he had a second thought. If Elinor had locked that box and kept the key apart from the normal household keys, then there must be a reason for it. He had better carefully check the contents, item by item.

Swiftly but carefully he sorted out the contents of the box on the wooden tabletop. After about ten minutes, he pounced on an ordinary foolscap envelope, which was sealed. Adam tore it open and pulled out two crumpled sheets of paper.

As he read them, a triumphant smile spread across his face.

Chapter·24

TUESDAY, 31 DECEMBER 1968

Miranda's New Year's Eve ball was, as usual, a great success. Just before midnight, she looked around the scarlet-and-blue-striped tent with satisfaction. Her vision was limited because her face was covered by a golden lion's mask that looked as if it might have been dug from an Inca burial ground; she wore a golden leotard and matching high-heeled sandals; her hair, including a luxurious fall, spread around her head like a flaming lion's mane.

This year's fancy-dress theme was a Fellini circus, and the tent covered Miranda's back garden; inside it, the lighting was low and mysterious; at foot level, swirls of theatrical mist were being pumped upward. Grouped around a revolving central circus ring were two smaller circular tents and three raised platforms, each the size of a small sitting room. The two smaller tents were striped in pale blue and silver; rising from the romantic mist, they looked as if they had last been used at Agincourt. One contained a Gypsy fortune-teller, the other a champagne bar.

A band played on the raised black platform, where three beautiful singers, wearing what looked like silver underwear and Carmen Miranda turbans, gasped the latest Dusty Springfield number. Two other pale-gray-carpeted platforms had been scattered with Louis XVI–style chairs upholstered in pale gray moiré: here guests sat to watch those dancing in the revolving center ring.

Strongmen carrying papier-mâché dumbbells danced with tightrope-walking ballerinas in pastel tutus; skimpily dressed bearded ladies, giants, and dwarfs jounced and bounced, shook, bumped, and twisted. A fairground barker danced with a monkey trainer, whose (real) monkey mournfully sat on her elegant red satin shoulder. An elephant did the twist with a lion tamer. A tiger gyrated with a Nubian slave, naked to the waist in harem trousers and a jeweled turban. The bareback rider in pink had turned up on a gray horse, which had then been led away by her groom.

The women with the best figures wore leotards, tights, and high-heels: an acrobat in silver, a performing panther in black, a contortionist in crimson, a tattooed lady in a white leotard covered with painted tattoos.

Because it was so hot in the tent, the two-headed man had removed his second head: Miranda recognized the Scandinavian prince who had purchased Saracen. Smiling, she moved back to check the midnight-supper buffet.

Inside the house, sackfuls of autumn leaves (which had been sitting in the cellars since October) had been lavishly scattered over the floor, to lend a Sleeping Beauty look to the rooms. Here, too, artificial mist rose from the floor. The furniture of the double drawing room had been replaced by circular tables set with lavender cloths and *eau de Nil* linen napkins. The only light sources were candles in silver candelabras on every table, each draped with fine silk threads shaped like cobwebs.

On her way back to the garden tents, Miranda spotted a bare-chested, turbaned snake charmer in spangled turquoise harem trousers, talking to Mike Grant in the hall.

"Scott!" she cried. "I'm so glad you were able to fly over. Pity you couldn't have been with us for Christmas. . . . It *is* Scott, isn't it? I don't recognize half my guests in their glamorous outfits."

The snake charmer kissed Miranda on the cheek. "Sure it's me. I wouldn't miss this. Where's Annabel?"

"Dancing, I think. Easy to see that you two came as a couple!" Miranda had already admired Annabel's costume: her sister was dressed as a snake. A stuffed emerald satin serpent entwined her green-sequined leotard and tights from her neck to her left ankle. She wore Alan Jones–style, scarlet, four-inch heels.

"What are *you* supposed to be, Mike?" Miranda puzzled. Although the name of an excellent theatrical costumer had been slipped in with the invitations, Mike was wearing black leather motorcycle gear; he carried a bucket.

"I feed the animals," he explained sheepishly.

"No marks for effort," Miranda said tartly. "Look how hard everyone else has tried." She wagged a finger, only half in jest. "If you can't manage something better than that, you won't get asked next year."

Scott said, "Miranda, I'm sure Annabel isn't on the dance floor. I've been looking for her for nearly an hour. Where the hell could she have gone?"

"Perhaps she's down at the swimming pool," Mike suggested.

"No, she won't be there," Miranda said. "I'm not allowing anyone in my new pool this evening. Drunken revelers may jump in and out of the fountains at Trafalgar Square, but I don't want them dripping over my newly decorated house."

As she left for the circus tent, she called over her shoulder, "You're bound to spot Annabel at midnight—we're all going to sing 'Auld Lang Syne' in the circus tent before supper starts—foie gras, wild duck, and quinces baked in a crust!"

"You really should see Miranda's pool," Mike said. "She's turned the entire basement into a Roman bath. Not a new one—one that looks as if it had been built two thousand years ago and has just been excavated and restored. I bet you've never seen anything like it."

"Okay, show me," Scott said.

The two men, drinks in hand, sauntered to the elevator.

"Here for long?" Mike asked.

"No, just to see the New Year in."

Scott also intended to see Adam; he refused to be put off any longer by Adam's excuses. The bottom line was that the guy had promised quarterly accounting—and it wasn't happening. Finally Scott had made it clear to Adam that he was coming to London to pick up those quarterly reports personally—or find out why.

Mike stepped from the elevator and felt to the left for the switch that would light the pool with a dim, eerie radiance. "Hey, the lights are already on! I thought Miranda said that nobody was allowed down here tonight."

Puzzled, he pushed open the cream doors, and Scott saw the beautiful dark green pool. The stone columns were chipped, the vaulted ceiling was crumbling, and the walls looked as if they had been hacked out of rock. What looked like a natural spring trickled down into the far end of the pool. In front of it, before a semicircle of stone pillars, were mattresses covered by cream toweling; on one of these lay a whip and a ringmaster's top hat; on another lay a small pile of green clothing. On an adjoining mattress, a man and woman were passionately locked in a naked embrace.

Mike's clear, gray, wide-set eyes stared. As Mike saw who the man was, he felt disgust rise like bile to his mouth.

And as Scott realized who the woman was, he charged toward the naked couple, yelling, *"You bitch!"*

Mike ran after Scott and grabbed his arm, trying to restrain him. Scott tried to shake Mike off. The two men grappled, until Scott threw a hard punch at Mike, glad of an excuse to hit out, to unleash his violence.

Mike hit Scott hard: as hard as he wanted to hit Adam. How could

Adam do such a bloody cruel thing? How could he have taken such a bloody *stupid* risk—Adam, who had never been seriously involved with a woman?

Scott, clumsy in his harem trousers, grappled again with Mike. They scuffled, grunting, gasping, and swearing, until one of them slipped on the wet stone. Scott's jeweled turban flew off his head and into the pool. Both men followed it.

As Annabel and Adam scrambled to their feet, Annabel grabbed a towel. She was frightened. But she also felt a frisson of excitement. Because now, at least, Scott knew—but Adam would be unable to say that Annabel had told him of their secret. And it had not been her idea to make love by the pool. She and Adam had been dancing on the revolving floor, listening to soft, beguiling music in that dim light. She had felt his warm breath on her ear as she listened to his whispered erotic fantasies. . . . It had been at Adam's suggestion that they came to the pool. No, Adam could *not* blame her for this.

Annabel grabbed her leotard and her scarlet shoes; abandoning her stuffed snake, she fled toward the elevator. She was closely followed by Adam, who didn't bother about a towel.

By the time a furious Scott pulled himself from the pool, the two naked lovers had disappeared. In his dripping harem trousers, Scott ran after them to the elevator.

Mike's leather gear was too waterlogged to allow him to vault from the pool, so he swam clumsily toward the stone steps; as he climbed up, water streamed down his body. Violently he shook water from his hair, and it streamed down his leather back.

He unzipped his jacket, threw it on the floor, and shed the rest of his clothes. Scott had landed a couple of good punches: Mike's ribs felt sore. As he wrapped himself in a towel, another thought occurred to him. If Adam—always so careful—had been caught in a compromising situation with a woman, then Mike knew that must have been what his calculating brother intended. That scene must have been carefully staged. Adam had *planned* to be caught fucking Annabel.

Why?

Toweling his hair, Mike considered. Suppose that Adam had intended Scott to discover his wife's infidelity. How could he have planned that? Simple! Scott—arriving straight from the plane—would naturally have looked for his wife at once.

All Adam needed to do was calculate the earliest time that Scott could arrive from the airport and then, ten minutes before, start fucking Annabel's brains out until they were discovered.

If Scott did not find his wife—then Miranda always had a big "Auld Lang Syne" singsong at her New Year's Eve party. At five minutes to midnight, at the latest, Miranda would expect Annabel to turn up in the tent; should her sister be absent, Miranda would send servants all over the house to find her.

Mike wrapped himself in a cream bath towel and headed for the elevator to get his coat. Why would Adam want to cause trouble between Annabel and her husband? he wondered. There had to be some reason. It was inconceivable that Adam was in love with Annabel, and he was too smart to fuck her for no reason. If he was cited in a divorce, he risked being landed with a woman he didn't want, so there must be a lot at stake. Of course, Annabel was an heiress, but so was Miranda. Why not pick the unattached sister if he was after the money?

No. It had to be some other reason. But what?

Fifteen minutes before midnight, as Miranda was about to send a footman to find Annabel, a maid approached and whispered a message in her ear. Miranda followed her upstairs to a guest bedroom and knocked on the door. "Scott? I hear you fell in the pool!" She laughed.

As he opened the door, Scott growled, "Come inside and lock the door."

"What's happened?" Miranda could see that Scott, who was wearing a bathrobe, was furious. She could also see that he was sober.

"Did you know what was going on, Miranda? Were you in on this? Were you helping them?"

"I don't understand what the hell you're talking about. *What's* going on?"

"I just—Mike and I—just saw Adam with Annabel."

"Oh, I was wondering where she'd got to," Miranda said. "Where was she?"

"They were making love!" Scott shouted. "Adam and Annabel! By your fucking swimming pool!"

Miranda stepped back from his furious face. "There must be . . . You *must* have made a mistake!"

"Ask Mike!" Scott roared. "*He* saw the whole fucking thing as well!"

Miranda made a noise that was half gasp, half groan. She tore off the golden lion's mask that covered her face. She felt as if icy fingers were clawing at her flesh, trying to reach her heart. She seemed to be outside her own body, watching it from a height and a distance: the true Miranda was suspended somewhere near the ceiling, silently howling with pain and rage at this double betrayal. That golden body below her moved, spoke, behaved almost normally, but it felt like a cold, dead thing.

"*Where are they?*" Miranda made a great effort to appear natural.

Scott must on no account guess her pain, her vulnerability, her stupidity. Neither Scott nor anyone else must *ever* guess that she had allowed Adam to creep inside her soul and erode it from within. No one must ever guess her shame.

"They've both left," Scott said, tight-lipped. "One of the security men on the door said that two people wrapped in bathrobes had run out into a waiting Rolls. Couldn't be anyone else. They must have gone to his place. My bitch of a wife wouldn't *dare* take that bastard to our suite at the Ritz."

"Are . . . are you *sure,* Scott?"

"Ask Mike if you don't believe me!" Scott wanted Miranda's comfort, reassurance, and advice—not to be doubted and cross-examined.

Miranda slowly moved to the bedside telephone. There had to be an explanation. Annabel must have thrown herself at Adam. She must have taken him by surprise. He must have been drunk. It must have been a mad, lusty, sexual impulse.

But she could not recall ever having seen Adam drunk.

Miranda dialed an outside number and let it ring for five minutes. "They're not at Adam's house," she said, "or else he isn't answering."

In the silence, both of them imagined what Annabel and Adam might be doing.

Violently angry and hurt, Scott said, "I *never* thought that Annabel . . . She said these trips to England were to see Elinor! . . . *Shit!* What a fool I've been! . . . I wonder how many *others* there have been. She's probably been making a fool of me for years." He shook his head in disbelief. "I would *never* have suspected Annabel of cheating on me!"

Miranda said in a cold voice, "Annabel is governed entirely by self-interest."

Scott spoke wearily. "I'm going back to the Ritz, to try to get some sleep." He wanted to be alone, to curse in a frenzy of impotence, to hammer walls with his fists.

"If Annabel turns up," Miranda said, suddenly anxious, *"don't* do anything rash, Scott. Don't say anything stupid. Let *me* talk to her first. Let me try and find out why this is going on—and how long it's been going on." Her voice was hard.

"Don't worry, I don't want to hit that bitch! I *don't want to touch her!"* Scott said. "And I doubt she'll dare turn up tonight. She'll obviously stay with that bastard." He rubbed his eyes tiredly. "I'll phone you in the morning. As soon as I get hold of Annabel, we're going straight back to New York."

"There are a couple of gossip writers downstairs. I don't want people to start wondering what's happened to me. I'd better go down and attend to my party." Miranda was glad to have some mechanical role to perform; she would smile brightly, move around, check that everyone was happily occupied, sing "Auld Lang Syne."

Usually the last guests lingered until around five in the morning, and usually Miranda longed for that moment, but tonight she dreaded it. Because afterward, she would not be able to avoid thinking. Firmly she pushed away memories of Adam's touch, Adam's smell, Adam's whispered erotic suggestions and the faintly detached way in which he put them into practice.

THURSDAY, 2 JANUARY 1969

Scott telephoned Miranda to tell her that Annabel, after a thirty-six-hour absence, had turned up at the Ritz in a white fox coat and not much else. If Miranda wanted to knock some sense into her sister's head, she'd better get around fast because Annabel was packing. *He* was heading for the bar.

"What are *you* doing here?" Annabel yelled when Miranda walked into her bedroom. She hurled a pile of peach lace into the already crowded suitcase that lay on the bed. "You might as well get out of here, if you think I'm going to listen to one of your lectures!"

"Don't you dare tell me what to do!" Miranda barked.

"I'll do as I please."

"How long has it pleased you to screw Adam?"

"None of your business!"

"Yes it is," Miranda hissed. *"Adam and I have been lovers for over three years."*

"I don't believe you!" Annabel shrieked. She faced her sister.

"The last time we made love was three nights ago."

"I don't believe he loves you! He *couldn't* love you!" Annabel's certainty returned as she fleetingly remembered the last blissful thirty-six hours, most of which had been spent in Adam's bed.

"I don't believe he loves *you!*" Miranda shouted. "If anything, you're a one-night stand for Adam. Has he given you all the trimmings?"

"What the hell do you mean by *that?*"

Miranda looked coldly at her sister. "Does he tickle your nipples with a feather? Does he slowly lick between your toes? Does he run his lips over your entire body, so lightly that there seems to be only a warm space between your skin and his mouth? Does he—"

"Shut up! Shut up! Shut up! *I don't want to hear any more!*" But Annabel longed to know more as uncertainty swept over her again. She stood staring at Miranda.

"Don't you *dare* start crying," Miranda said coldly. "There's *no* reason why Adam and I shouldn't have an affair. But you've deceived your husband—*as well as your sister!*"

"Scott had it coming to him! And I never meant to deceive you. I never *knew* about you!"

"Well, now you do. So take your clammy hands off my man!"

"But he's *not* your man!" Annabel wailed. "If Adam *really* loved you, would he make love to me?" Triumphantly she added, "If he really loves you, then why have you both kept it a secret?"

"None of your damned business," Miranda said with frost in her heart. What a fool she had been to think that Adam loved her enough to marry her: he hadn't even loved her enough to be faithful.

"Yes it is! Adam loves *me!* We're going to be *married!*"

"Has he actually *asked* you to marry him?" Miranda spat.

Annabel hesitated, then spoke the lie with conviction. "Yes."

"Then why doesn't Adam tell me?"

"He said the sensible thing was to wait for the fuss to die down."

Icily Miranda said, "Perhaps we should *both* see Adam together and let him clarify his intentions. Where is he?"

"None of your damned business."

"Oh, *do* stop saying that! If Scott finds Adam—and it shouldn't be difficult—he'll tear him apart."

"Scott won't find Adam," Annabel said. "Scott has to catch the New York plane tonight if he doesn't want to miss a broadcast."

"If Adam is hiding from Scott—which I doubt, by the way—then let's *both* see Adam tomorrow." Miranda looked more casual than she felt. "Where is he?" she asked again.

"I honestly don't know," Annabel lied with equal casualness. "Perhaps he's still at the Savoy. That's where we've been staying."

At the back of Miranda's analytical mind, a half-formed thought almost surfaced: Adam would have had to book well in advance to get a room for New Year's Eve at the Savoy.

But instead of pursuing this logical thought, she let her attention be distracted by the violent passion she felt. Within the past half hour, her love for her sister had turned to jealous hatred. Because Miranda knew that Annabel was right about one thing: If he really loved Miranda, Adam would not have made love to Annabel.

Suddenly Miranda could understand the feelings of someone who kills the person he loves. She certainly wanted to kill Adam—not anonymously with poison, not suddenly with a gun, but by some slow and painful method. She wanted Adam to know that she was responsible for his death. She wanted him to suffer the torment that she felt and would continue to feel.

"I'll find Adam—he won't be able to hide forever." Miranda threw a look of hatred at Annabel, then stormed out of the room.

When Scott returned later, Annabel was sitting on a suitcase that refused to close.

She looked up to find Scott standing just inside the door, looking so furious and so forlorn she wished she could tell him she was sorry she'd hurt him—because she truly was. But because of her guilt, she could not be kind to him.

"Miranda told me her side of the story," Scott growled. "I'd no idea that you could be such an unscrupulous, treacherous *bitch!*"

Coldly Annabel said, "Will you shut this damned thing, or do I have to ring for a porter?"

"Ring, dammit," said Scott. His hurt pride battled with anger and humiliation. "How could you do it to me? How could you do it to your sister?"

"I never knew that Miranda had this . . . this crush on Adam." Annabel glared at Scott and thumbed the bell.

"What the hell has this man *done* to you both?" Scott asked. "Hypnotized you?"

"Adam doesn't put his damned career before everything else! Before his life! Before his wife!"

Scott was suddenly deflated. "Believe me, Annabel, I regret it."

"Adam doesn't take me for granted!"

"So that's how he got to you," Scott said quietly. Adam had given Annabel the attention that Scott had provided when they first met. Scott had underestimated Annabel's loss of self-confidence when her career crumbled. He had briskly attempted to minimize the importance of what had happened to her. But Adam had consoled her with flattery. He had zeroed in on her insecurity, and his honeyed reassurance had clearly repaired the rift in her self-esteem. Scott took two steps toward Annabel. "I never realized I was neglecting you, angel."

"If you knew how I *hate* being called 'angel'!"

"Then why didn't you say so?" Scott yelled. "What does that bastard Adam call you?"

Scott couldn't believe his sense of grief, of loss, almost of mourning. He remembered feeling like this only once before—at his mother's funeral, when much too late he finally realized he had lost something irreplaceable, something that he had never known he valued so much.

Remembering his pain, Scott said, "I can't bear to lose you, Annabel."

"You can't expect *me* to feel the same way." Annabel glared at him again.

"I can't believe that this is happening to *us!*" Scott was usually so astute and observant, yet his wife had been cheating on him for months and he hadn't noticed.

"Why not?" Annabel glared.

"It would have been easy for *me* to screw around at the station. You may laugh, but I believed in absolute commitment. For me, love wasn't just fucking."

"There hasn't been much of *that* lately." Annabel stared impatiently out the window. She couldn't wait to get away.

"It takes two," Scott said. "Remember how often you visited poor Elinor?" He added quietly, "We're both going back to New York together as planned, and we're both going to forget that this ever happened."

Annabel laughed.

Scott's calm shattered. He said sharply, "If you don't, I'll divorce you."

"Go ahead." Annabel laughed again. No more lies. No more cover-ups. No more alibis. No more guilt. She would be free to marry Adam. And if that was the case, she was convinced he would marry her.

Adam wasn't at the Savoy and of course he wouldn't stay in his own home, where she and Scott could badger him, Miranda thought.

Where could that bastard hide, an unexpected guest, for an indefinite period over the holiday season in quiet and comfortable anonymity?

Suddenly she knew where he was hiding. There was one person who would always protect Adam, no matter what he had done.

Twenty minutes later, Miranda rang the bell of the dignified cream house in Eaton Terrace.

When Mike's butler answered the door, she said quietly, "Please tell Mr. Adam Grant that Miss O'Dare is a little early for her appointment."

Once inside the house, instead of waiting in the hall, Miranda silently followed the manservant up the carpeted stairs to the second floor.

The butler paused at a bedroom door. Before he could knock, she had twisted the brass handle, ducked under his arm, and burst into the room.

Seated before the mustard brocade curtains of the bedroom window, Adam was studying a page of figures.

He looked up in surprise. "What are *you* doing here, Miranda?" As he spoke, Adam slipped the sheet of paper between the cushion and the side of the chair so that it was hidden.

"I might ask the same of you!" Miranda said hotly.

"Thank you, Forbes." Adam waited until the door had closed. Then, with apparent sincerity, he said, "I'm sorry you had to find out this way, Miranda. I'm truly sorry I've made such a mess of things for you."

As painfully as if she had just stepped barefoot on a hedgehog, Miranda again felt the destructive spikes of jealousy. Tormented and miserable to the point of frenzy, she burst out, "*Why* did you do it this way, Adam? *That's* what I don't understand. *Do you love Annabel?*"

"I am not going to discuss my feelings for Annabel with you or anyone else," Adam said. He stood up and looked coldly at Miranda.

Her jealousy flared. She flew across the room and lashed out at him with her fists.

Adam easily caught her wrists. Miranda found herself powerless to shake them free. She kicked at his ankle and hit his shinbone. When he winced from the pain, she tried to bite his hands. Adam swiftly shifted his grip so that he held Miranda's face against his chest while firmly grasping her wrists behind her.

She found it difficult to move. Her cheek was pressed against him. Hatred, burning rage, and pain consumed her. "Let me *go*, you bastard!" She twisted upward and managed to clamp her teeth on his chin.

Adam jerked his head back. With satisfaction, Miranda saw blood run from his chin.

Barely concealing the fury in his voice, Adam said, "I'll let you go when I feel like it. You're about to find out who's in control, you careless, stupid little bitch."

"I'd remind you that I'm in control of the company! I'm your boss!"

"I shouldn't be too sure," Adam spat. "Why should you have so large a part of the company that I've done so much to build up!"

"You got a quarter of a million pounds' worth of shares for that! *And* you get a damned good salary! Let me *go!*"

Adam tightened his grip. "I'm sorry to tell you that I not only wished to have *more* of the business but I also wished you to have *less.*"

"*Let me go!*" Miranda desperately tried to pull free of him: her wrists were burning now and tears of pain sprang to her eyes. "By God, I'll fire you, Adam!"

"No. *You can't fire me, Miranda.*"

"I don't know what the hell you mean, Adam, but as soon as I get out of here, I'm going to telephone my solicitors and find out just how quickly I can terminate your contract."

"In that case, Miranda, please remember to tell your solicitors that you no longer have a controlling interest in the company."

"What the hell do you mean?"

"Remembering your extensive knowledge of company law, I'm sure you know that the biggest shareholder virtually controls a company."

"Yes, and that's me."

"You are mistaken, Miranda. *I* now control the biggest shareholding in SUPPLYKITS. Forty-six percent! *And you can't do a thing about it!* You have a choice, of course: you can either leave the company or you can work your ass off to provide me with a splendid income for the rest of my life." In fact, Adam now planned to sell all his shares before leaving for Rio.

"You must be mad," Miranda gasped, still trying to free herself from Adam's grip. She managed to kick him again, and he winced.

"No," he said between gritted teeth, "I'm telling you the truth, my darling. You and your bloody family are about to be wiped out."

Adam quickly twisted Miranda so that her back was against his chest. He then moved backward, toward the door of the room, dragging her with him. She fought wildly against his grip and heard her coat rip as they struggled.

Miranda panted, *"You* can't do anything to my family." She wished she'd thought of kneeing Adam in the groin while she was facing him. She waited until he had to use one hand to open the door, then gave a vicious kick backward and once more hit his leg bone. He grunted with pain—but did not release her.

"You'll find I *can* do something to your family," Adam said, gritting his teeth again as he tightened his hold on Miranda.

"What do you mean?"

But Adam had already said more than he intended. Still gripping Miranda's wrists painfully, he frog-marched her down the wide, maroon-carpeted stairway.

The butler appeared in the hall. He quickly concealed his astonishment and, at Adam's curt request, politely opened the door.

Adam shoved Miranda out, between the elegant Doric columns that guarded the steps to the street.

The front door slammed behind her.

As she clutched a column to steady herself and hailed an approaching taxi, Miranda remembered Adam's parting words.

Exactly *what* could Adam do to her family? She felt a lurch in her stomach, a feeling she had often experienced when he took her in his arms—but this time it was a lurch of fear.

Miranda suddenly remembered that Adam had made the arrangements to set up the Dove Trust. Suppose Buzz was right and Elinor was being deliberately kept in a drug-induced stupor so that Adam could do as he pleased with her money.

"You all right, love?" asked the taxi driver as he stopped at the curb.

Miranda, angry and worried, telephoned for an emergency appointment with Mr. Worthington, senior partner of Swithin, Timmins and Grant.

In his sunny, dusty office, Mr. Worthington reminded her that STG had relinquished control of the Dove Trust, at her grandmother's specific request.

"I appreciate that," Miranda said, "but I've come to ask you to find out what's happening to the trust *now*."

Mr. Worthington said politely, "Regrettably, STG cannot be involved because there's a conflict of interest between the parties concerned—even though Adam Grant and Paul Littlejohn are no longer connected with STG."

"But couldn't you tell me what you *think* might have happened? Off the record?"

Mr. Worthington hesitated. "*Strictly* off the record . . . after what you've told me . . . there *might* be a possibility of embezzlement, arranged so that it is not illegal."

Bitterly Miranda said, "I expect that two international lawyers, who've worked together for years, wouldn't find it difficult to legally defraud a client who trusted them. But can't a trust be broken?"

"Often the reason for setting up a trust is specifically so that it *cannot* be broken," Mr. Worthington said. "Of course, when the trust deeds were originally drawn up, it would have been possible to insert special trust-breaking clauses. But had Adam Grant intended, at that stage, to defraud the beneficiaries, then he would have been careful to insert no such clauses. If I were you, I would immediately get a good lawyer to check the trust deeds."

BOOK·4

Chapter · 25

"What do you want to see me about, Miranda?" As Miranda entered his office, the Earl of Brighton rose from behind a black leather desk. A thin, stooped figure, he unhooked his gold-rimmed half-spectacles from rather large ears and moved forward with a tentative, shambling walk; he looked far more amiable and far less intelligent than he was.

Briefly Miranda told Lord Brighton what Adam had said to her about SUPPLYKITS. She tried to sound calm, reasonable, and business-like, explaining that she was there for one purpose only—to see that Adam did not control the company.

"What's his shareholding?" Lord Brighton asked.

"I went to the registrar myself, James, to check the shareholders. Adam holds only fifteen percent of the shares—the fifteen percent that he bought from me on option and the shares he was entitled to buy at the one-for-three rights issue."

"But Adam might control some of the other shareholders—if he's promised a few big shareholders some special inducement provided they vote with him."

"The biggest single holding belongs to a firm called Highland Croft Holdings. Have you ever heard of them? My broker hasn't."

"No. It's certainly not a publicly quoted company," Lord Brighton said, "but even if Adam *does* control forty-six percent of the shares, as he claims, if there's a real showdown he won't control the company because he needs over fifty percent to do that."

"What can I do? How can I stop Adam controlling the other four or five percent?"

"We need more information," Lord Brighton said.

Miranda hesitated. "Perhaps I should also now tell you, in confidence, that I don't particularly want to control SUPPLYKITS. I'm not interested in acquiring businesses. I'm really interested in only *one* business—KITS." She spoke with determination: "I don't want to be the figurehead of a public company. I want to be the *real* head of my *own* company! Ideally, I'd like to own one hundred percent of the KITS shares."

"So you want to purchase KITS from SUPPLYKITS."

Miranda nodded. "If KITS again became a private company, I could develop the business as *I* wish. I could make long-term plans without constant pressure to provide quick profits. And I wouldn't find my hands tied by some overcautious director who's terrific at pushing figures around on paper but doesn't understand the cosmetics business."

Lord Brighton said, "As chairman, I don't feel that SUPPLYKITS should let you go at this stage."

Miranda played what she hoped was her trump card. "I would only be prepared to stay on as managing director provided I could buy back KITS."

Lord Brighton leaned back in his chair and stared through the window at the river traffic silently drifting on the ocher water of the Thames. Reflectively he said, "We've just had that valuation of KITS."

Miranda smiled. "Leases and stock, less debts, are valued at fourteen thousand pounds."

"That's a very low figure. What about the value of the goodwill?"

Miranda said firmly, "The goodwill of KITS is so bound up with my public image that it'd be difficult for the accountants to put a price on the goodwill if I'm not there. If SUPPLYKITS *dares* to ask me to pay a premium for KITS, then I will immediately resign from SUPPLYKITS."

"Which, as I've said, SUPPLYKITS can't afford at the moment," Lord Brighton said. "As the face of the firm, you are publicly perceived to be responsible for the success of SUPPLYKITS. If you went, the share price would undoubtedly fall. SUPPLYKITS can't afford to lose you or have any rival company acquire your services."

"Exactly, James. But I want to make it clear to *you* that I intend to withdraw gradually from SUPPLYKITS. The company is now established, and my deputy, Alex Stanton, can take over as MD."

"Then I assume you'd like SUPPLYKITS to call an EGM?" An extraordinary general meeting was the only way that such a matter could be decided.

"As fast as possible, please."

"We need to give three weeks' notice of an EGM. Let's hold it on Friday, thirty-first January, which gives us a week extra."

Miranda nodded. Official approval to sell KITS back to her must come from bank, stockbroker, and stock exchange, after which the circular had to be printed and posted to all shareholders.

As he escorted Miranda to the door, Lord Brighton added: "By the way, Adam Grant should be informed as fast as possible. We'll then know his reaction well in advance."

"Could you telephone him, James?"

Lord Brighton nodded. "I could also tactfully bring up that other matter of who holds the controlling interest claimed by Grant. He'll have to give me a truthful answer, evade the question, or lie: any of those possibilities will be interesting."

"If he doesn't control those shares, I can fire him." Miranda was no longer able to maintain her carefully businesslike facade; her voice shook.

"You can't fire Grant just because you feel like doing so," Lord Brighton warned. "He's a director of a public company. Officially, you haven't complained about him—and I'm not sure that you even have the *right* to complain about his behavior: Grant has been very successful at his job, and he's entitled to acquire as many shares as he can—like any other member of the public. Be careful, Miranda, to keep your feelings under control."

"I can still dream," Miranda said. "If you need me for anything, I'll be in Paris early next week for the Cosmetics Safety Conference. At the Ritz, as usual."

When Lord Brighton telephoned, Adam listened in silence as he was told of the purpose of the EGM. Reminded of the book valuation of KITS, he said angrily, "With the greatest respect, that's giving KITS away. The reason KITS is currently worth so little on paper is because it's been our cash cow—we've milked it to finance our expansion in other areas."

"I believe that's one of the things Miranda objects to."

Adam snapped, "What Miranda forgets—or maybe she doesn't—is that in a couple of years, KITS will once again be worth a fortune! So whatever Miranda O'Dare offers for KITS—I'll offer ten percent more."

Lord Brighton telephoned Miranda with this news. He added, "Of course, I'll have to include Grant's counterbid in my letter to the shareholders, but in view of the other considerations, I shall still recommend acceptance of your offer, Miranda. However, the decision doesn't depend on my views—it depends on the votes. And, as interested parties, neither you nor Adam will be allowed to vote, nor will shareholders controlled by either of you."

"Does that mean—assuming Adam's telling the truth about controlling forty-six percent—that the decision will be made by *only the nine percent of outside shareholders?*"

"It does."

"Are Adam and I allowed to lobby the shareholders?"

"Be careful," Lord Brighton warned again. "You don't want to overexcite the press. The share price might drop if it looked as though the directors were squabbling among themselves instead of efficiently running the company."

"Don't worry," Miranda said grimly. "I'll be careful."

"By the way, I checked on Highland Croft Holdings. The company is apparently owned by an offshore holding company, so we can't trace it further. They own four point eight percent of SUPPLYKITS, and there's no way of telling whether those shares are among the percentage that Grant claims to control."

SATURDAY, 4 JANUARY 1969

Although it was past midday, the only light in the room entered through a chink in the mustard brocade curtains.

They lay silent once more, enjoying closeness. Adam felt that he knew the body beside him almost as well as he knew his own feelings, reactions, and needs. And his partner knew precisely what aroused the force of Adam's passion. Slowly each in turn, with the utmost tenderness, softly kissed the other's body and face . . . lips, nose, eyelids . . . and each trembled beneath the other's touch.

Afterward, as they lay side by side and mouth to mouth, their bodies still intertwined, Adam cherished the closeness and subtle tenderness that made him feel the two of them had just fused into one person. For him, it had been an all-encompassing, overwhelming experience of soaring rapture, total understanding, and bliss, emotional as well as physical.

Adam sometimes wondered whether—as he had many times been told—he had lost the capacity to feel, whether it had really been cauterized away before he was old enough to realize it. But he never had such misgivings when he lay enfolded in these arms: here he was always totally involved; he never felt as if, from above, he were dispassionately watching himself manipulate his partner toward spasm.

In these arms, Adam felt as if he were—at last—truly in touch and at peace with himself as he both gave and received. He felt loving and trusting as, in turn, he was loved and trusted. Adam knew this to be true intimacy.

His arms tightened around the smooth shoulders. In the clear, gray, wide-set eyes, so close to his, Adam could see not only his reflection: he could see that this was the person with whom he belonged, the only person with whom he felt at peace, without pretense, and free. He felt tremendous joy.

After seeing Lord Brighton, Miranda spent two sleepless nights thinking about Adam's triple treachery and worrying about the future of SUPPLYKITS and the Dove Trust. She couldn't cancel her trip to Paris, but luckily, she was only billed to make the opening speech at the conference, and for those two days she was determined to forget her problems, and be professional.

On Sunday morning, the sky was cloudy. Gatwick Airport informed Miranda that the cloud base on her route would be around fifteen hundred feet, with a risk of icing at that level. On a more cheerful note, the operator added that there might be a layer of clear sky between three thousand and four thousand feet. Luckily, Miranda had recently acquired her pilot's instrument rating, which permitted her to climb through cloud in weather such as this.

At ten a.m., Miranda's new plane, a pale blue Beechcraft Bonanza, took off from Redhill for Lydd, where she would clear customs.

But the higher the Bonanza climbed, the worse the weather became. That layer of clear sky must be a lot higher than forecast, Miranda thought crossly, realizing that, as she couldn't see through the cloud that now surrounded the plane, she was committed to an instrument flight.

Unfortunately, Gatwick Met had been right about the ice. At four thousand feet, Miranda couldn't raise the tower, or any other airport, because ice had built up on the forward cabin, and when it separated, it damaged the communications radio aerial: the Bonanza had no contact with ground control. Miranda, who had been relying on air traffic control for navigation, could no longer receive instructions from the controller.

The Bonanza's air speed indicator, compass, and all instruments that didn't rely on radio were working. However, Miranda was now flying a very basically equipped airplane in some trouble. In an emergency situation, she would have to continue to follow her last instruction from ground control. She cheered herself up by thinking that ground control could still see her on their radar—and they would know she had a problem, because she wasn't answering them.

Although Miranda knew exactly in which direction she was flying, she did not know her precise position, although she reckoned she was somewhere over the South Downs. So there was no question of putting the plane down, for she risked hitting high ground. She had better stay at four thousand feet and hope for a clear patch of sky below her, which would allow her to see the ground and check her bearings.

Miranda's plan was to descend, slowly and carefully, over the sea near Lydd airport. She hoped that there was no low cloud there, because she then risked hitting the water. A crash landing, in January, in the English Channel would be fatal: she was unlikely to be rescued and wouldn't last twenty minutes in such cold water.

As she flew on in thick, oppressive cloud, Miranda felt increasingly lonely. She cursed herself for having climbed above fifteen hundred feet instead of flying below the cloud base: she should have been more cautious.

After flying for about twenty minutes, she calculated that Lydd lay directly ahead. Firmly pushing anxiety out of her mind, she started a slow descent to three thousand feet . . . two thousand . . . nine hundred . . . Still the Bonanza remained enveloped by white cloud.

Nervously Miranda took the plane down to seven hundred feet . . . then to five hundred: white silence still enshrouded it.

As she peered ahead, straining to see, one of her contact lenses started to irritate her eye. She blinked repeatedly as she went down to four hundred feet . . . then three hundred. Even at this low level, the light was dull and the cloud persisted.

Miranda screwed her eyes up and again peered downward, unsuccessfully searching the opaque cloud below.

At just above two hundred feet, she saw a change in the color of cloud. Yes, it was definitely darker.

Then she saw . . . *the tops of trees.* Although visibility, bad when Miranda started her journey, had since deteriorated, at least she could see where she was going as the Bonanza slowly flew lower.

Now, where was Lydd? Miranda peered at the ground below, hoping to see a town or a road that she could pinpoint on the map that lay on her lap.

She stared, then blinked. She couldn't believe what she saw. It wasn't possible to be so lucky!

Dead ahead of the Bonanza—just visible in the distance—an airport runway bisected the dirty green ground. Miranda felt a wave of relief run, like electricity, through her entire body and out to her fingertips, which started to tingle as her adrenaline level decreased.

She knew exactly where she was! She was approaching the far boundary of the hedged field that lay about a quarter of a mile east of Lydd airport. *She was going to make it!* Her face relaxed a little as she put down her landing gear at just over two hundred feet.

As Miranda adjusted from blind flying on instruments to visual flight, her contact lens again started to irritate her eye. She approached the runway. Her height was now one hundred feet . . . fifty feet, she reckoned.

But because her eye was watering, Miranda miscalculated: she was flying much lower than she thought. Just short of the runway, the Bonanza's landing gear hit the top of the hedge on the airport boundary.

As the nose of the plane jerked abruptly downward, Miranda instinctively corrected by pulling the stick back fast. With crumpled landing gear, the plane skimmed over the ground and leaned to the left; the wing touched ground, and the plane slewed around in a half-circle.

As the left wing buckled, Miranda, who hadn't pulled her seat belt quite tight enough, was thrown forward. Her head hit the top of the instrument panel.

SATURDAY, 25 JANUARY 1969

The thin woman in the violet coat planted a farewell kiss on Adam's cheek and moved away from the restaurant table.

Annabel smiled. "Don't tell me *that* was one of your clients." She leaned across and, with her handkerchief, scrubbed the blackberry lipstick from his cheek.

"No, she's a lingerie buyer for Harvey Nichols. Do you remember Johnny Briar?"

"That man at Lloyds? Your friend who went bankrupt?"

"Yes. He and Nora were divorcing, but she took him back when Johnny had his nervous breakdown." Adam stood up. "I'd better not be late."

"You work too hard," Annabel said seriously. "Who is this client who needs you on Saturday afternoon?"

"An important Jap." Adam blew her a kiss.

Annabel watched him pause for a few words at almost all the pale-yellow-spotlit tables as he worked his way toward the entrance of the fashionable Arethusa Club.

As Annabel ordered more coffee, a man approached her table.

"Roger! How nice to see you. Coffee?" He was an acquaintance from her debutante days, tall but no longer slim, with thinning fair hair. He wore the fashionable art director's uniform: black turtleneck sweater, hipster trousers, and a leather, brass-buckled belt that might have been taken from a cart horse.

"I was sorry to read about Miranda's accident. How is she?" Roger sat down and removed his heavy, horn-rimmed spectacles.

"She's slowly recovering," Annabel said, fighting back tears. She tried not to think about Miranda.

Roger said, "You girls were great fun, and you were all very nice to me."

"*You* were always great fun. And so was Lady Rushleigh, I mean Mrs. Bromley."

"I think Aunt Sonia hoped I'd marry an heiress. But I didn't. I hadn't yet found that I didn't belong in that world, although plenty of people made it plain enough." He smiled ruefully. "Wasn't that Adam Grant who just left?"

"Yes." Annabel brightened at the mention of her beloved's name.

"What's one of my favorite girls doing with a man like that? I know it's none of my business, but, for old time's sake, be careful."

"Be careful of *what,* Roger?"

"Perhaps you don't know Adam as well as I do," Roger said carefully. "We were at prep school together, and schoolboys rarely change. They may turn into art directors and lawyers, but behind the grown-up disguises, basic character doesn't much alter. Did you ever meet Adam's mother, by the way?"

"Yes, although I don't remember her well. She was very severe, very formal, not easy to know; a bit chilling—like the Duchess of Windsor."

"A tough old bird." Roger nodded. "She held the reins in that family. *Her* father was the boss of the business, and she never let anyone forget that. I've always wondered whether Adam inherited his impersonal attitude from her—or whether he had to develop a shell to protect himself from her coldness."

"I've never noticed it." Annabel smiled.

"Surely you've noticed that, like the Ice Queen, Adam's heart is frozen and he cannot feel?"

Annabel said cheerfully, "I think Adam and his heart are wonderful!"

"But unfeeling," Roger repeated earnestly. "Adam doesn't want to feel and he despises anyone who does. He knows that to have feelings would make him vulnerable. *Any* warm impulse of his heart alarms him."

"What are you getting at?" Annabel was puzzled.

Roger started to speak faster: "The nearest Adam gets to feeling *anything* is the pursuit of power. *That's* what excites him. Adam loves money because it brings power. He can rely on money—that's why he can never get enough of it!"

"Does Adam owe you money?" Annabel asked, bewildered and a bit cross.

"Of *course* Adam owes me money—or rather my agency. Adam owes money to everyone," Roger said. "He collected a debt for us from a defaulting client, then invoiced us for rather more than he collected." He gave an unfriendly laugh. "But *that* sort of behavior doesn't worry Adam. After all, he grew up seeing that a shrewd lawyer can get away with anything."

"I don't have anything to do with Adam's business," Annabel said coldly. She stood up to leave.

Roger jumped up and caught hold of her wrist. "I shouldn't be too sure. Adam doesn't touch anything that *isn't* business."

"Let go of my wrist!"

"If you listen to me. I've heard you're very fond of Adam."

"Yes." Annabel's voice was curt.

"Be careful, Annabel. I'd hate to see you hurt. Remember how secretive Adam is. There's a reason for that."

Annabel hesitated. She felt she shouldn't listen to this man abuse Adam, but she also felt an irresistible urge, like Pandora with the box, to hear what he had to say.

"Plenty of people are secretive," she said. "Especially lawyers."

"Adam isn't secretive because he's a cautious lawyer"—Roger shook his head—"but because he's basically selfish. Adam doesn't want to share anything with anyone."

"Why are you telling *me* this?" Annabel asked again, trying to tug her wrist away.

"Because I like you. Because I don't like Adam, and I've good reason for that."

"What makes *you* such an expert on Adam?"

"You should ask him," Roger advised. "And you should remember that Adam has a nasty habit of dumping people when he has no further use for them."

Annabel said, "Perhaps you don't know that Adam and I . . ."

"Of course I know! That's why I'm telling you this. I also know about his affair with Miranda."

That was enough! She was leaving. Annabel again twisted to free herself from his grasp.

"Look, Annabel, I don't want you to be hurt." As Roger released her wrist, he looked at her sadly. "Open those beautiful eyes," he said calmly. "Please! Look at how he's using you, manipulating you. This is not something new; he's always done it—to both women and men. Believe me . . . I know."

In spite of Annabel's fury, she paused. Roger's quiet, consoling voice had the chilling ring of truth.

"I don't believe he's ever really loved anyone," Roger said. "Maybe Miranda, for a while. She's the only woman who *almost* got under Adam's guard. I suspect that was why she lasted so long. Generally Adam likes to make a woman dependent upon him, then dump her straightaway. He uses much the same technique with men."

"With men?" Annabel asked, confusion and indignation in her voice. "What do you mean?"

"Annabel, Adam is bisexual. He likes women *and* men—or maybe, more to the point, he dislikes them both equally. Either way, he seems to be masterly at sex with both. As I said, Annabel, I know."

"Surely you don't mean . . . ? Why, that's preposterous!" Annabel seemed dazed, caught between anger and shock. She stared at Roger and saw long-forgotten pain and rejection in his eyes. Desperately she turned toward the door. How *dare* Roger suggest that Adam and he . . .

Roger hurried behind her. "If you want proof, Adam has one night a week he tries to save for the boys," he said. "He usually goes to the Hilbury Arms—a pub in St. Martin's Lane—on Saturday evenings. That's the big night. And if you decide to go don't bother to show up before nine o'clock—that's when the action starts."

Chapter · 26

Annabel spent an agonized afternoon racked by indecision. She was torn between her need to check on Roger's story and the need to ignore the painful seed of suspicion that he had sown. Finally, at eight o'clock that evening, the need to know won out and she took a cab to St. Martin's Lane.

In a navy mackintosh and with a navy scarf pulled down around her face, Annabel stood on the dark, rain-splashed pavement, which was almost deserted: the theater crowds were now inside, watching the plays.

Annabel looked across the road. The exterior of the Hilbury Arms was dark green; the name was painted on the facade in elaborate gold carnival lettering; the brightly lit, frosted windows looked inviting.

Hands in pockets, feet gradually growing numb from cold, Annabel stood there for over half an hour. She was frightened of her own feelings. Sexual rage and jealousy had swept over her in a violent, scarcely controllable flood of emotion that threatened to engulf her: she felt as crazy and unbalanced as when she first fell in love with Adam. Why on earth was she standing here? This was ridiculous. She kept telling herself that nothing had happened to make her doubt Adam, who was dining with a client. How could she not trust the man she loved? Why did she feel so jealous, after listening to a malicious troublemaker's spiteful gossip?

She should have refused to listen. She should go back to Adam's flat *now*.

But Annabel had to know.

The idea of never knowing the truth was worse than her jealousy. This thought propelled her across the road and through the revolving doors of the Hilbury Arms.

Someone behind Annabel said, "Excuse me," and she was pushed farther inside the pub. Nearly everybody was clustered around the long, curved mahogany bar, although there was plenty of room elsewhere. A pall of cigarette smoke almost blotted out the bitter smell of stale hops. Brass lamps with malachite glass shades hung from a ceiling gingered by smoke. A Billie Holiday recording floated words of sadness and need above the steady babble of voices.

Annabel stared about her. A group of young men in the back corner looked like any suburban boys waiting outside a cinema for their girlfriends. Some of the young men at the far end of the bar looked like art students, in black jeans and turtle sweaters; some wore black paramilitary clothes or black leather jackets; a cluster of good-looking, well-groomed men sitting on barstools might have been actors. One, a Cliff Richard look-alike with a scornful expression, snapped at anyone who drifted up to him. Annabel did not spot any other women.

She sat down shakily just inside the door. Wishing she could be invisible, she listened to the snatches of conversation. "Not much in 'ere tonight, Georgie, let's go to the Coleherne . . ." "I wouldn't mind *that* down the lockup . . ." "Eyes off, sonny, this one's mine." "Fancy a spot of . . ." "I think perhaps you're a little bit interested in my friend George. Right, squire?"

As Billie Holiday's voice continued to moan of love and irony, Adam walked in, passing Annabel without seeing her as she hid in the corner shadows. He bounded toward the bar. The boy who looked like Cliff Richard stared disdainfully at him. Adam eagerly pushed through the crowd to the boy's side. He kissed him on the lips, held him in a long caress.

On trembling legs, Annabel jumped up from her seat and dashed through the door, back into the night. Her hands shook and she felt sick. *"Bastard! Bastard! Bastard!"* she screamed as she ran along the wet pavements and the rain slashed down on her.

S U N D A Y ,   2 6   J A N U A R Y   1 9 6 9

Miranda slowly put her hand to her head, and felt bandages. She opened her eyes, just a crack, and saw a small, cream-colored hospital room filled with flowers.

"My headache seems to have gone," Miranda murmured to the nurse who checked her pulse. When she first recovered consciousness, the worst pain she ever felt had sizzled through her head.

Now Miranda's head seemed filled with clear, pure air. "When can I leave this place?" she whispered.

"Not yet," the nurse said firmly. "You've made good progress in the past two days, but you've had a severe concussion—and it's only been twenty-one days since your accident—"

"*Twenty-one days!*"

"Keep calm—you mustn't get excited. The doctor's instructions were to keep you sedated. You've had ten milligrams of Valium every four hours, which is why you had those swimmy daydreams as you came round, but we've been cutting it down for the last two days. That's why you're more alert this morning."

"Does my office know I'm here?"

The nurse laughed. "Your telephone calls keep our switchboard permanently occupied. Your secretary's staying at the Grand Hotel. She's posted a bodyguard outside this door, to stop the press harassing you. I'm afraid there have been a few silly stories in the tabloids."

"Damn!"

"Your sister Annabel has visited several times and telephones at least twice a day."

"I don't want to see her! Please see she isn't let in!"

"Don't get excited. You needn't see anyone you don't want to see."

"What happened to my plane? Did it catch fire? How did I get out?"

"Your plane didn't catch fire, and it's being repaired. The airport fire-and-rescue team pulled you out: they said you were lucky the door didn't stick. Your secretary has all the newspaper clippings."

"I need a telephone straightaway."

"I'm sorry, not until tomorrow. Doctor's orders."

"If you don't bring me a phone, I'm going to call the bodyguard and have him carry me to one," Miranda said. "I *must* make just a couple of calls."

After further argument, in order to calm the patient's growing agitation, the staff sister agreed that Miranda could have the telephone trolley—for fifteen minutes.

Her secretary wasn't at her hotel, so Miranda dialed Lord Brighton's number.

"Hello . . . no, James, I'm fine. Pay no attention to newspaper stories. I want to know what's happening about the EGM. What's the proxy situation?"

"The proxy votes have started to arrive, but we haven't received as many as I expected. Perhaps the shareholders are going to turn up at the EGM. . . . No, we haven't had proxies from Highland Croft Holdings, but don't let it worry you."

"How can I help worrying, James! Highland Croft Holdings will decide the vote! Their four point eight percent leaves only four point two of other voting shareholders—as Adam and I can't vote the shares we control."

"Perhaps they plan to send a representative to the meeting."

"Or perhaps they're waiting until the last minute, when they'll auction those shares—between me and Adam—for an enormous premium, on condition that Highland Croft votes for the agreed purchaser—who will, of course, not buy until after the EGM."

"That's right. If either you or Adam buys those shares *before* the meeting, then, as interested parties, you won't be able to use the votes."

Grimly Miranda said, "If Adam gets control of that block of shares, then I can kiss KITS goodbye. So *I'll* be forced to buy them, no matter what the price. I'll borrow against my existing shareholding to raise the cash."

"You're clearly recovering," Lord Brighton said. "I made sure no one would trace my query to you, but Highland Croft is *not* prepared to sell."

"They're saying that to drive the price up!"

"There's nothing to be gained by worrying. Don't forget that without you, KITS wouldn't be nearly such an interesting proposition. Adam can't see that because he isn't objective at the moment. I assume he's so used to getting his own way that he's forgotten how to handle himself when he can't."

As Miranda replaced the telephone, a nurse entered. "You have a visitor. She's telephoned every day. A Miss Buzz."

"Buzz! How wonderful!"

"Only ten minutes, mind," the nurse said.

Miranda looked up at the angular figure and burst into tears.

"A fine mess *you're* in!" Buzz took Miranda's hand. "My poor girlie. Ain't seen you cry since you was six years old, when you fell out of the beech tree, remember? There, there . . . tell old Buzz about it."

"Oh, Buzz, everything is such a mess. I thought I was so clever, but I've been so stupid. I've only just realized . . ."

"Don't fret, my girlie. There's nothing that can't wait—"

"No, Buzz! *This can't wait!* . . . I should've listened to you. I think Adam *is* keeping Gran in that place—and he's stealing her money." Briefly Miranda outlined her suspicions.

"So *that's* what he's been up to with all them fancy schemes," Buzz said sourly. "Nell should have put her money in the Woolwich—that's where my salary goes: safely tucked away in a building society. . . . What are we to do, my girl?"

"Can't you get her out of there, Buzz? I don't think we should wait until I'm fit enough, and I don't trust anyone else."

Buzz brightened. "We mustn't let them have any warning. That matron could arrange a compulsory detention order, which'd keep Nell there for another month—while the nursing home tidies up its records, of course."

"Can't you sneak in and get her out somehow?"

"Not me. That matron wouldn't let *me* in again!"

Miranda stopped snuffling as a thought occurred to her. "What's the time? . . . If it's eight in the morning here, then it's late last night in Los Angeles. I'm going to phone Sam—and find out where Clare is."

Instead of the usual operator's delay, within a few minutes Miranda was connected to Sam, to whom she quickly told her story.

Sam said, "I never trusted that bastard Adam. Too smooth and agreeable. That persuasive, masterful air, that total assurance of his—all the things you women liked about him were the things that made me distrust him."

"Maybe you've had more experience with con men."

"Yeah, they're a dime a dozen on the West Coast."

"Do you know where I can find Clare?"

"Sure. I make a point of knowing what she's up to. She's gone skiing with Josh. Klosters, I think. But Clare can't handle this! She's no match for a crooked lawyer."

"Sam, you're so strong, so capable, so experienced, such a know-it-all . . ."

"Let me think. . . . Luckily, we've just finished postproduction work. I can catch a plane tomorrow. First we rescue Elinor, then we go for Adam. I'll be happy to help you do both."

TUESDAY, 28 JANUARY 1969

Still wearing her yellow ski outfit and suede-soled orange socks, Clare looked around her new bakery with satisfaction. David had designed the extension, built onto the side of the kitchen. Next to the two professional ovens were slatted cooling shelves.

A month of Swiss sunshine had tanned Clare's skin, and her aquamarine eyes sparkled. She glowed with health after her first proper holiday in four years; she had enjoyed every minute of it.

Clare returned to the kitchen, pulled a cheese tart from the refrigerator, and put it in the oven to warm for lunch. Through the back window, she could see the new toboggan that David had bought in Klosters. After school, Josh and his gang would take it up on the snow-covered hill behind the cottage.

Clare now had a luxurious, five-hour period before she started to prepare for that night's baking. She wandered into the sitting room and put a record on the stereo David had given her for her thirtieth birthday.

Somewhat guiltily, she enjoyed the peaceful feeling of being alone in the cottage. She sat down and put her feet up on the brass fender before the log fire. As she dreamily watched the crackling flames, she listened to the music and thought—not for the first time—how much luckier she was than Louis XIV. Louis may have been the Sun King and all France may have trembled at his frown, but he couldn't listen to Maria Callas in his bath. Nor could he survey the world from fourteen thousand feet up in the air. And Louis XIV had never had the chance to ski. . . .

The doorbell shrilled.

Clare stood up, thinking, If it's a Jehovah's Witness, I'll scream. She opened the door.

"*Sam! What the hell d'you think you're doing here?*"

"Let me inside and I'll tell you." Sam was shivering. "Miranda called me from the hospital."

"*What's wrong with Miranda?*"

"Everything's okay, but she crashed her plane."

"Was she badly hurt? Where is she? Who's looking after her?"

"Look, could I *please* come inside?" Sam shivered again. "She'll be out of the hospital soon. I spoke to her this morning. You can call her yourself this afternoon. I'm surprised you haven't heard about her crash—it even made the L.A. *Times.*"

After a battery of anxious questions about her sister, Clare explained, "I haven't seen a newspaper for nearly a month. We got back yesterday evening—two days late because of an airport strike. I haven't even read my mail yet."

Clare stood aside ungraciously as Sam stepped into the house; then she led the way to her living room.

"Where's Josh?" Sam asked.

"You can't see him this evening," Clare said curtly. "He's going to tea with a friend and then it's Cubs night."

"I can wait," Sam said, determined to be pleasant. "You look terrific."

Coldly antagonistic, Clare glared at the man who had cheated on her, and who, for almost four years, had refused her a divorce, all the while providing no child support.

"How about some coffee?" Sam suggested, warming his hands at the fire.

"No coffee," Clare said. She wondered what Sam had done to himself: he looked years younger than the last time she'd seen him.

Noticing her surreptitious look, Sam grinned. "Yes, I've taken myself in hand. For my no-flour diet, deduct two years; for no-more-vodka resolution, deduct four years; for exercise bicycle, deduct four years; for new teeth, deduct two years; for smart haircut, deduct one year; for well-cut pants and shirt, deduct two years."

"I'm not interested," Clare said acidly. "Say what you've come to say, and then get out."

Sam said, "You *will* be interested." Briefly he outlined Adam's treachery, Elinor's plight, and the trust problem.

"Are you telling me that Gran has been in a nursing home for nearly a year and my sisters didn't let me know?"

"Don't take it out on me, Clare. I'm the one that's just flown halfway around the world to do something about it."

"Where's Gran? I must see her."

"There's a limo and a driver waiting outside to take you wherever you want to go, but first I have to talk to you. How long is it since you saw Elinor?"

Clare said brusquely, "July 1965, at Saracen."

"You mean you haven't seen Elinor for almost four years?" Sam was astonished.

"I tried," Clare said uneasily. "I wrote to Gran several times, but my letters were always answered by Adam. He said he was sorry to write formally but he had been instructed by his client that she wished no communication to take place . . . that sort of thing."

"I bet Elinor asked Adam to check you were okay. I bet she wanted a reunion. And I bet Adam covered his ass nicely."

"His letters put my back up."

"They were meant to," Sam said. "But how come Buzz didn't get in touch with you, behind Elinor's back—or in front of it?"

Clare, ashamed, said, "Buzz did try. I don't know how she found out where I was, but she turned up one evening, just after I'd moved into my basement flat. I'd had a tough day at the shoe shop—one woman took three hours to buy one pair of shoes. Buzz started telling me to be a good girl and apologize to Gran. I'm afraid I yelled at her and told her fairly forcibly to go. Then she tried to give me money she hid in an envelope—and that convinced me she was really coming from Gran."

"And Buzz never tried to contact you again?" Sam asked.

Clare answered reluctantly: "Yes. . . . She telephoned several times. I'm afraid that I . . . I thought she was Gran's spy, you see? Every time she spoke to me, Buzz said I should think of Josh and not cut off my nose to spite my face and . . . I was determined not to slink back to you with my tail between my legs, as you all thought I would. I was determined to show I could stand on my own feet and live my own life. I wasn't a little girl to be pushed around." She glared at Sam.

He sighed. "Buzz always said you were as stubborn as Elinor . . ."

"If you've come here to—"

Hastily Sam said, "Sorry! But didn't Miranda or Annabel contact you then?"

Clare hesitated, then admitted, "Yes, they did—but with amazing lack of tact! Annabel was feeling sorry for herself on the other side of the Atlantic. And Miranda's face seemed to grin out of every paper I picked up—and everything she was doing was *exactly* what I was trying *not* to do!" Again she glared at Sam. "I don't think you have *any idea* how difficult it was for me—with no employable skills—to earn my own living and look after Josh."

"I promise we'll talk about that after I tell you why I'm here." Sam then outlined Miranda's plan to remove Elinor from the nursing home. Persuasively he ended, "The nursing staff have never seen you, Clare, and they've never seen me, and they can't refuse to let us in if we turn up on the doorstep—on an unexpected business trip to England—with our passports to prove who we are. We're Elinor's blood relatives."

Clare said hesitantly, "Of course I want to see Gran as fast as possible, and I'll do anything to make her happy. But . . . have you any proof of this wild story? You said that Miranda has a concussion. Are you sure she wasn't a bit delirious when she told you this?"

"Don't forget Buzz," Sam reminded her. "She was the first person to become suspicious of Adam *and* of the nursing home, but nobody listened to her. Call Buzz if you like—she's with Miranda."

After she telephoned Buzz, Clare's reticence immediately disappeared. She said, "Eastbourne isn't far from here. Buzz says the best time to remove Gran is probably in the early afternoon, when there are visitors around and the staff won't want to make a fuss. Let's leave now."

Chapter · 27

✹

"I'm still worried . . ." Clare said, seated in the back of Sam's swiftly moving rented Bentley. She had changed from her ski clothes to a respectable navy suit.

"I don't want to push you. The final decision is yours—and so is the responsibility," Sam said firmly. "She isn't *my* grandmother. I know nothing about British medical law, but I *do* know that possession is nine tenths of the law."

Clare stared out at the snow-covered landscape. "I never thought I'd miss her so much. Before her illness, Gran was the rock of our family; she seemed so strong and permanent—always there to look after us. After our . . . disagreement . . . there was a hole in my life. And it will never be filled. I just know it."

Sam said, "Will you stop talking as if Elinor's dead? Now it's *your* turn to look after her. That's all."

Eventually the Bentley turned off the road and passed between snow-encrusted, elaborate back gates and up a curving drive.

Sam glanced at the white columns of the mansion before him. With a note of doubt in his voice, he said, "This place doesn't look like a prison." The mansion looked as immaculately cared for as a rich child's dollhouse. On either side of the building stood snow-capped yew hedges; icicles dripped from the branches of old cedar trees; beyond them, white lawns sloped toward a dismal gray smudge, the English Channel.

In the warm, walnut-paneled entrance hall, Sam felt increasingly uneasy; he and Clare sat on a burgundy brocade sofa while the sandy-haired receptionist went to fetch Matron Braddock.

Matron Braddock entered, wrapped in a navy uniform that made her appear that much more formidable. She did not mention that she had just tried unsuccessfully to contact Mr. Grant by telephone, but instead politely asked Sam for proof of identity. In her charming voice, she explained, "We have to be careful. Many journalists have tried to see Mrs. O'Dare. You'd never believe the lies."

"Yes I would," Sam said, "I work in Hollywood." He produced two passports from his pocket. "We're glad the old lady is being well protected."

Having checked the passports, the matron briefly informed the Shapiros of Elinor's condition, but would give no prognosis or details of her treatment: that could only be discussed with Mrs. O'Dare's doctors.

Clare gasped when she saw her grandmother's gaunt, pale face; white-haired, with eyes closed, Elinor lay motionless on the metal hospital bed.

Clare ran forward and knelt by the bedside. "Gran, Gran darling . . . Can she hear me?" She looked up at the matron.

"She's sleeping," Matron Braddock said. "Her after-lunch nap."

"We'll wait until she wakes up," Clare said decisively. "She looks so frail," she added, fighting tears as she noticed, on the bedside table, silver-framed photographs of Billy, Edward, and the three sisters in their best party dresses at Starlings.

She turned to Sam. "I expect you'll be more comfortable in Gran's sitting room next door, darling, but I want to sit quietly with her."

"Can I offer you afternoon tea?" the matron asked pleasantly.

"Do you have any coffee?" Sam asked equally pleasantly, as he moved toward the interconnecting door. "And can someone ask my driver to bring my briefcase?" He wanted Steve, the driver-cum-bodyguard, to see the layout of the nursing home.

"Mrs. O'Dare might be asleep for quite a long time," the matron warned Clare.

"I don't mind a long wait," Clare said sweetly as she settled in the chair opposite Elinor's bed; behind Clare, the locked glass doors of the French window faced the snowy garden.

Just before four o'clock, Matron Braddock returned.

"I do hope Gran wakes soon," Clare said, "because we'll have to leave shortly. Sam has to get back to our hotel to take his L.A. business calls."

"I don't like to disturb Mrs. O'Dare if it isn't necessary."

"Of course not," Clare reassured her. "We can visit her again before we leave England."

When the coffee tray was removed, Clare rapped on the connecting door, her signal to Sam. He hurried to stand guard in the corridor, ready to loudly ask his way to the john should anyone appear.

Clare gently tried to shake Elinor awake.

She did not respond.

Clare shook harder.

Elinor made no movement.

Clare tried to pull her upright into a sitting position. Elinor's head flopped back, and her arms dangled like a rag doll's.

Quickly Clare rearranged her grandmother, smoothed the bedclothes, and went into the corridor. "Gran's certainly not asleep," she whispered to Sam. "She must be drugged."

"I told Steve to stretch his legs—take a walk around the grounds while it's still light enough to see," Sam said. He looked at his watch. "We'd better start before it gets dark." He joined Clare in the bedroom and pressed Elinor's bedside bell.

When Matron Braddock reappeared, Clare bent over her silent grandmother and kissed her forehead. She and Sam then followed the matron from the room.

As they moved slowly along the corridor toward the entrance hall, the matron looked at Sam. "You've forgotten your briefcase, haven't you? I'll get it for you."

"So I have! Stupid of me. No trouble." Sam turned and moved swiftly back along the corridor.

He snatched up his briefcase and quickly locked both doors leading from Elinor's suite to the corridor, shoving the keys in his pocket. He grabbed some pink blankets from the bureau in the bedroom, pulled aside the high invalid's table on casters that stretched across the end of Elinor's bed, then yanked back the brocade curtains.

Steve's pale face and pale blue eyes appeared outside.

Sam nodded.

Steve pulled up his coat collar, checked his leather driving gloves, walked back ten paces, then charged the window, turning his left shoulder toward it as he reached it.

With loud cracks like pistol shots, the doors caved inward. Glass flew everywhere, and a blast of icy air swept into the bedroom. Steve backed through the shattered doors into the room.

Sam heaved a pink armchair in front of the connecting door to the sitting room and yanked the bedclothes from Elinor's bed.

Steve wrapped Elinor in a pink blanket, threw her over his shoulder in a fireman's lift, and disappeared through the smashed doors into the darkness. He was followed closely by Sam, who couldn't see a thing and didn't know where Steve had parked the car.

Panting, the two men ran through the snow. Steve, the first to reach the Bentley, yanked the back door open and, propping the pink bundle on the back seat, jumped in the driving seat and switched on the ignition and lights. Then he hit the horn three times in fast succession.

Sam threw himself into the back of the car and fell on top of the pink bundle. He leaned across and flung open the far door. Clare should have been running toward it.

But Clare was nowhere to be seen.

Sam panted, "If we're held up, Steve, you take off." He ran through the snow to the front steps of the nursing home, then slowed down to walk calmly through the entrance doors.

In the middle of the hall, Clare was struggling with Matron Braddock. Sam dodged past them, grabbed the screaming receptionist, and flung her at a white-coated male orderly who was running toward the matron. The orderly tried to dodge the outflung arms of the receptionist, lost his footing on the highly polished parquet, and fell to the floor.

Sam threw his right arm around the matron's neck and yanked it backward to pull her away from Clare. The matron gasped and tried to twist her body from Sam's grasp, but she did not let go of Clare.

The orderly scrambled to his feet, leapt forward, and kicked Sam in the kidneys. Sam jerked violently back, pulling the matron with him. As she fell, she released her grip on Clare.

"Get out fast, Clare!" Sam roared.

As Clare scrambled up and ran in stockinged feet toward the glass front door, the orderly raced after her, but she managed to escape. Outside, however, Clare stumbled in the darkness and fell down the stone steps beyond the front door. The man caught up and threw himself upon her.

In the hall, Matron Braddock had twisted so that she was on top of Sam, who was now lying on his back. Fighting like a man, she did her best to gouge his eyes out. Sam managed to pull his right fist back and smash it upward. He felt it strike bone, heard a grunt, and was suddenly able to see again. Half crouched in pain, he staggered toward the front door.

Just beyond the stone steps, the man in the white coat was grappling with Clare. Sam jumped to the bottom of the steps, drew his foot back, and kicked. The man grunted and fell sideways on the snow.

"Get to the car!" Sam yelled, thrusting his hand out to help her.

Together, they ran to the already moving Bentley. Sam shoved Clare into the back, then threw himself on top of her. As they sorted themselves out, the Bentley turned out of the main gates and picked up speed.

"Darling Sam!" Clare flung her arms around him.

The secretary of the Lord Willington Nursing Home did not know how to contact someone on a cruise liner in the Caribbean. She telephoned the travel agent who had arranged Dr. Craig-Dunlop's trip. He advised her to call the cruise liner's London office.

The agitated deputy matron fluttered around the telephone. She said again, "Tell them it's urgent!"

The secretary put her hand over the mouthpiece. "It's not that easy, Sister Parks. We have to contact the *Antigone* through some radio station in Somerset—the main shore-to-ship station. They say it'll take at least a few hours to reach the doctor."

"A few hours!" Nurse Parks twittered.

The secretary explained, "The radio station has to request an emergency appointment with the doctor, giving the callback frequency. Once that's been done, the doctor can speak to you from the ship's radio room. You'll just have to wait, Sister Parks."

In the casualty department of the King Edward VII Hospital, East-bourne, Matron Braddock sat waiting for treatment. Her left arm had been put in a sling to relieve the pressure; it was painful and swelling fast; she couldn't move her fingers. The break was just above the wrist.

The matron's arm throbbed badly, but she decided not to ask for painkillers. She could take more pain than most people, and at the moment, she needed a clear head. As she waited for her arm to be X-rayed, Ivy Braddock carefully considered her position—and her options.

What did she have to lose? A great deal.

Mrs. O'Dare had been removed from the nursing home in what was clearly a carefully planned operation. Mr. Shapiro did not seem the sort of man to let the matter rest, especially since she had hit him: Matron Braddock remembered blood streaming from his mouth.

If the police were called in, she might be arrested. She might even stand trial.

Whether or not she was convicted of helping to restrain a patient for illegal purposes, after the resultant publicity she would certainly never again be able to get another good nursing job in Britain.

The only thing that frightened the matron more than the prospect of discussing Mrs. O'Dare with the police was discussing her with Mr. Grant. Matron Braddock had sensed the violence and vengeance that were part of Mr. Grant's temperament. Of course, he couldn't get any money back from her, but she was frightened of his retribution, whatever it might be.

The matron considered blackmailing Dr. Craig-Dunlop. She rejected this idea only because the doctor was in a position to counter-blackmail her.

There was really only one thing for Matron Ivy Braddock to do.

· · ·

Back in the comforting serenity of Applebank Cottage, Clare sat beside Sam in front of the fire and stared into the flames. She hadn't been able to contact Annabel, but Miranda and Buzz had been thrilled to hear the news of Elinor's rescue. It had been difficult to stop Buzz from traveling over that night to look after her old friend.

Elinor was sleeping in the spare room; Steve, the driver, was staying at the Bath Arms; and Sam—who had insisted on sticking around—said he'd sleep on the living room sofa.

Six-year-old Josh, too excited by the arrival of his father to be able to sleep, kept coming down in his pajamas to ask for a glass of water. Every time he appeared, Clare felt the usual pangs of guilt. Yet again she worried whether Josh would prefer to live alone with a happy mother, or with his father and an unhappy mother.

"Now that the fuss has died down," Sam said, "what happened to *you*?"

"I didn't expect to hear that crash—I suppose you broke the French window. I panicked and started to run toward the front door. That damned matron tried to stop me. I honestly can't remember much about it. I'm sorry—I know I should have waited for the three toots."

Sam grinned. "If you'd just looked surprised, she'd have rushed to investigate and then you could have simply walked out of the front door, as planned."

"Things didn't happen as planned."

"No," Sam said. He paused for a moment before adding, "They almost never do, do they?"

Clare thought how strange it was that the animosity between them had dissolved. For nearly four years, she had bitterly resented Sam's ability to thwart her and been resentful of his power. She remembered Gilda, who had worked with her at the Chelsea shoe shop, saying long ago, "Don't tell *me* you've fallen out of love with that husband of yours! If you had, you'd be indifferent, you wouldn't give a damn about him."

As Sam watched the firelight flicker on Clare's small, neat features, he thought: This is the moment to give it my last try. Aloud he said softly, "I don't know how to say this . . . I want to say I'm sorry I've been such a bastard. I reckoned if I didn't give you any money, and I didn't let you have any evidence, and I didn't let you divorce me, then you'd come back to me."

"That's the way you train dogs, not wives," Clare said tartly.

"Okay. I was wrong. I admit it."

"Thanks," Clare replied bitterly. She added, "I've never understood why you won't let me go. What's the difference between me and your other ex-wives?"

"Josh, for a start."

"I realize that no other man can replace a father—not even a bad one," Clare said, still bitter. "But that's not enough reason to return to you. I have my life to lead. I am not merely Josh's mother."

"I never expected you to be able to manage on your own. I really admire you for that. . . . This bakery is a great idea. You could build it into a chain. Even the name's right." Clare had called her business ABUNDANCE.

Clare said, "I've no intention of building it up into a chain. That's how a man *would* see a successful business! I've looked into men's territory and I didn't like what I saw. I don't want the worry of a big business. I don't want that treadmill! I just want to enjoy my little business and do something useful while I earn my living." She pushed her dark hair out of her eyes and added, "I don't want the sort of life that Miranda leads. It was relatively easy for me to leave for four weeks in Switzerland—but I bet Miranda can't just drop everything and go skiing."

Sam tried a new tack. "I never realized how much I enjoyed being with you—until you'd gone, Clare. And I miss Josh every single goddamn day." Persuasively he continued, "Clare, won't you let me have *one* more chance? Remember that Josh is *our* son, not just yours." He saw Clare wince and pressed on what was clearly her Achilles' heel. "Clare, we *both* should be deciding what's best for Josh."

"You forgot that Josh was your son when it came to paying the bills for him!" Clare cried. "You didn't seem to care *then* what was best for Josh. Don't talk to me of reconciliation. Our marriage clearly wasn't important to you!"

Sam looked into her eyes. "I promise you, Clare, that our marriage *is* important to me. Would I have dropped everything and flown halfway around the world to rescue your grandmother if that weren't the case?"

"I'm grateful. But not that grateful," Clare said. Briefly she remembered. "You had your squalid little adventures, Sam. You thought that what I didn't know wouldn't hurt me. Well, it didn't hurt me, but—I told you before—*it hurt our marriage*. Instead of protecting the ship we were building, you deliberately screwed holes in it—and then looked surprised when it leaked."

"But it hasn't sunk."

"You've been trying to get me into bed ever since we got back here. I remember your tactics. But if you and I made love, it would legally wipe out the last three and a half years. In ten minutes, we would be legally reconciled, so if it didn't work, I'd have to start all over again—and, incidentally, the lawyer's bills would start again. So I can't risk it, even if I wanted to, *which I don't*. I'm in love with another man!"

Clare thought she might as well let him have it between the eyes. "I now have a very happy, steady relationship with a thoughtful, gentle, concerned lover."

Sam said, "And would this thoughtful, gentle, concerned lover of yours have had the guts to smash jaws for your grandmother?"

At seven the next morning, when it was still dark, Josh crept into bed beside Clare and said, "I fink she's woken up."

Clare leapt out of bed and listened outside the spare room door. She heard weak sobbing. She entered and switched on the light.

Elinor turned toward the door, her thin fingers clutching the sheet. "Clare!" she whispered in surprise. "Where am I? How wonderful to see you, dear child."

Clare knelt by the bedside, took the frail blue-veined hands in hers, and kissed them. "You're safe now, darling. This is where I live. You're never going back to that dreadful place again. Buzz is coming to help me look after you."

"Clare, I've missed you so much."

"And I've missed you. I've been stupid and stubborn."

"So have I."

"I'm so sorry, darling Gran. Will you forgive me?"

"If you forgive me."

"Let's not waste any more time, not one more day."

"Not one more day," whispered Elinor as Clare bent to hug her.

Almost weeping, Clare felt she had to explain. "Darling, if you'd answered any of my letters, I would have come rushing to you. I wrote you sad letters, angry letters, and self-pitying letters. But Adam made it clear that you would only see me after I had made a formal apology. I felt more hurt each time he told me."

Elinor whispered, "I wish I'd known. I missed you so. And I missed Josh."

Clare felt remorseful. Elinor had missed three and a half years of the life of her only great-grandchild, who looked so like Daddy Billy's boyhood photos.

Elinor stroked Clare's hair. "But none of it matters now. All that matters is that we're together again."

At ten o'clock, the doctor left Elinor, after prescribing a low dosage of Valium during the next few days while she was weaned from her medication and detoxified.

Just after his departure, Clare answered insistent rings at the front door. Miranda stood on the doorstep, her head still bandaged. Behind her was Buzz.

Speechless, Clare held out her arms to her sister: they hugged in silence.

"How's Nell?" Buzz asked urgently.

"She's going to be fine, especially now that you're both here," Clare said.

After a happy, tearful reunion at Elinor's bedside, they left her to rest.

As the three women drank coffee in the kitchen, Miranda looked puzzled. "Clare darling, I never understood why you were broke. Adam told us you were getting an income from the trust, but that you wouldn't see Gran, and wanted nothing to do with Annabel or me because we sided with Gran."

"Adam told *me* that you and Annabel didn't want to see me," Clare said. "And I didn't get a penny from the trust—my allowance stopped as soon as I left Saracen."

Briefly Miranda wondered how she could ever have allowed herself to care for Adam. She said, "We've got to nail him, fast."

"Sam's on the phone discussing it with some London lawyers."

"I wish I could be more help," Miranda said. "But I'm still getting bad headaches and it's hard for me to concentrate. I'm also having trouble with my memory—I can't remember a thing about my crash."

Hearing a car draw up outside, Clare glanced casually past the pots of geraniums on the window ledge. "What's a London taxi doing here?"

Buzz peered out the window. "Cor, I do believe that's Annabel."

"No, it can't be," Clare said. "Goodness . . . what a wonderful coincidence!"

Miranda darted to the kitchen window and, as Clare ran along the passage to the front door, called angrily to her, "You can't expect *me* to believe this is a coincidence! How *dare* you arrange this!"

Bewildered, Clare turned and said, "What's the matter? I haven't seen Frog for almost four years! I haven't arranged anything."

"Oh, no? Do you expect me to believe that on the first day I see you in over three years, Annabel just *happens* to show up? How dare you try to fix up this clumsy reconciliation behind my back."

"Oh, do shut up, Miranda. I haven't a clue what you're talking about. What *is* your problem?" Clare asked crossly. "Or are you still feeling the effects of your accident?"

"Not at all," Miranda said angrily. "And if you open that door to her, I swear I'm leaving!"

"Stop that! You've always had a flair for dramatics, but this is not the time," Clare said. "Look, I don't know what's happened between the two of you, but you'll just have to sort it out fast. This is too important." She moved forward and opened the front door.

Standing on the doorstep, Annabel burst into tears. "Oh Clare, you *are* here! I was afraid I might have been given an old address. It's so *good* to see you again! I've missed you so!"

"Come inside quickly, darling!" Clare shivered against the cold as she tugged Annabel, babbling happily, along the passage and into the warm kitchen.

Annabel abruptly stopped chattering when she saw Miranda.

Miranda glared. "I don't know how you have the gall to show your face here!"

Annabel sobbed, "Oh, Miranda, you don't know what's happened . . . Adam didn't love me . . ."

"Oh, I knew *that*," Miranda said stonily.

"He didn't love either of us . . ."

"What *are* you talking about?" Clare asked.

Miranda said, "Adam's been having a love affair with me for several years, and with both me *and* Annabel for several months."

"*Both* of you?" Clare looked astonished. "*Adam!* I can't believe it!"

"It's worse than that," Annabel sobbed. "Adam likes *boys,* too!"

The other three women were stunned into silence. Buzz raised her arms in a perplexed gesture.

Then Miranda said contemptuously, "Annabel, you must be out of your mind!"

"No, believe me. I didn't want to accept it either, so I went to a pub where homosexuals hang out. I was told Adam would be there, and he was. I wish . . . I've tried . . . to pretend to myself that I imagined it. *But I know I didn't.* Roger told me Adam's always been like that—so if you don't believe me, ask *him.*"

"Roger who?" Miranda snapped.

"Sonia's nephew. The Roger who taught us all the twist," Annabel said.

Miranda was scornful. "Everyone in London knows that Roger's that way. Plenty of men are. I know some of my friends are *but not Adam.*"

"Yes he is!" Annabel insisted, and again started to cry. "I know how you feel—because I know how I felt. And there was nobody I could talk to about it—nobody I could really trust, who could explain what was going on. I felt so lonely."

"I'm going to phone Roger," Clare decided. "Do you have his number?"

Annabel nodded. Buzz hurried over and hugged her. "My poor lamb."

Clare returned to a silent kitchen. A tearful Annabel sat at the kitchen table staring. From the other side, Miranda scowled suspiciously at Annabel.

"Roger says it's true." Clare spoke quietly. "And I believe him. He and Adam had . . . well . . . a fling some time back. He said he wasn't Adam's first either."

Miranda burst into tears.

Clare said gently, "Annabel, why don't you telephone Scott?"

All the misery she felt was in Annabel's expressive eyes. "I can't . . . I feel . . . too much of a fool." She started to weep again. "I said terrible things to Scott . . . I've made such a fool of myself."

Miranda lifted her head and painfully admitted, "I think we've both made fools of ourselves. But don't be too proud to admit to Scott that you lost your head over a man who doesn't give a damn about you. I know Scott still loves you. Phone him."

Annabel hesitated, then nodded. "All right, I will. But it's five in the morning in New York."

"I should wait a bit, until you're feeling calmer," Clare suggested.

Humbly Annabel said, "Thank you for saying that, Miranda." But she knew she had to say more than that, to start to repair the wound she had slashed in her relationship with Miranda. She knew what she ought to say—but she hesitated. Then Annabel forced herself to say the two words that have, in their time, undoubtedly altered history and the destiny of the human race—two simple words that those who wish to hear them find so easy to expect yet those who wish to say them find so difficult to deliver. Slowly and painfully Annabel said, "I'm sorry, Miranda."

Miranda hesitated, then said, "Thank you. I'm sorry too. Now let's forget it. We've all been hurt by Adam."

"I think we all need a strong cup of tea," Buzz suggested, "before we start repairing the damage Adam's caused. That man had you three exactly where he wanted you!"

As Buzz put the kettle on, Clare said, puzzled, "What I don't understand is why Adam should want to cut me off from my family."

"I think I know," Miranda said. "I also know why he put Gran in that vile place. Adam has been siphoning money away from the trust, using some method that's legal; this has probably taken longer than a straightforward theft. If so, it would explain why Adam separated us and encouraged us to quarrel. He did it to distract us—while he quietly embezzled our money."

"*What?* But I don't understand—if he's stealing the money, why were we sent those huge checks?" Annabel asked.

"What we had was a drop in the ocean, compared to the total,"

Miranda said. "And while Adam was so kindly arranging for us to have as much money as we wanted, it never occurred to us that he was stealing the rest."

The three sisters looked sadly at each other in silence: all felt cheated, humiliated, and angry.

"I feel such a fool," Annabel said quietly.

Clare nodded. "Me too."

"You aren't alone," Miranda said wryly. "I could kick myself when I remember the *acres* of print I've read about my hotshot business brain. How *could* I have been so gullible for so long?" She did not complicate the situation by adding that Adam was fighting her for control of her business.

"I'd better telephone the Bath Arms," Clare said. "We have only one spare room and Gran's sleeping in it. Sam's sleeping on the sitting room sofa."

"And where's Josh?" Miranda asked, suddenly remembering.

"At school," Clare said. She hoped that her son had not forgotten his aunts.

Miranda said, "Does Josh like being in the country? *You* seem a lot less anxious, more relaxed."

"Yes, Josh loves it. And I'm happy with my life."

"We can see you are," Annabel said wistfully.

"You look much better, Annabel," Clare said quickly. "When your face was thinner, it looked elegant, but . . . you look far prettier now."

Miranda nodded. "Clare's right. Sickening to see you look so ravishing without one spot of makeup!"

Annabel wrinkled her tiny nose and said in a pleased voice, "Do you *really* think so?"

When her sisters had taken their baggage to the local inn, Clare told Sam what they had discussed.

"Don't kick yourself too hard," Sam said. "It sounds as if Adam is an experienced con man, and like all of them, he knows how to flatter women and gain their confidence. The bastard's good-looking, charming, sophisticated, and self-assured. He zeroed in on each of your vulnerable areas; he pressed the buttons of your insecurities; he had you all running around in circles, doing exactly what he wanted. Now you must stop reacting and start acting. Now we have to strike back."

Clare said, "Adam doesn't know he's been rumbled. We'd better let him think that we're still quarreling with each other."

"Our weak point there is Annabel. Where does Adam think she's been for the last few days?"

"I've no idea. Ask her."

Later, Annabel explained. "I couldn't face Adam . . . or speak to
him . . . after I saw him with that boy. So I wrote a note, said I was
coming down with flu and didn't want him to catch it, and was going to
a health farm for a week—of course, no health farm would have let me
in with flu, but it was the first lie that jumped into my mind. In fact, I
stayed at the Park Lane and sat in my bedroom shaking and crying, until
I thought to phone Sam's secretary to get Clare's address."

At six o'clock that evening, Clare went to deliver a fresh loaf of bread to
a woman in bed with arthritis. She refused Sam's offer to drive her,
saying that it was only a short trip and she wanted some fresh air. While
she was away, Sam could put Josh to bed.

Josh, who at six considered himself too old to be bathed by his
mother, was thrilled to let Sam bathe him.

When the cork floor of the bathroom was awash with water, Sam,
in his shirtsleeves, went down to the kitchen for a mop. As a key turned
in the front door, he called out, "Clare? I've managed to get Josh *into* the
bath, but it's not so easy to get him out."

Hearing an unexpectedly heavy tread, Sam looked up just as the
best-looking man he had ever seen stooped to avoid the lintel over the
kitchen door.

"Where's Clare?" David asked casually.

"My wife is out," Sam said equally casually. Clare hadn't mentioned that this son of a bitch looked like the hero of a spaghetti western.

The two men stared at each other in silence, like dogs, stiff-legged,
sniffing each other before a fight.

So *this* was why Clare hadn't phoned him as usual yesterday
evening, David thought. When he'd rung her, the line had always been
engaged. The big man with dark curly hair and his shirtsleeves rolled up
over muscular arms seemed more of a charmer than David had expected.
He looked friendly, easy to talk to.

"If you're David, why don't you get the hell out of here?" Sam said,
making the situation clear. He added, "If you want to see my wife, come
back another day. There's a lot going on here." Sam knew that, without
Romeo hanging around, he could operate much more effectively on
Clare. He'd better get the bastard out before she returned.

"As I came to see Clare, I'll wait till she gets back." David had
phoned late that afternoon to find out why he hadn't heard from Clare;
Josh answered and, totally overexcited by the presence of so many
relatives, explained that his daddy had arrived. David had come to see
what was going on.

Sam said, "Clare and I have a lot to talk about. You're in the way."
He took an aggressive step toward David, who did not retreat.

"I'll wait for Clare," David repeated. "If Clare wants me to leave, then she can say so."

They both heard Josh yell from the bathroom, "Dad, where's the *mop!*"

"I'll be up in a minute, son," Sam yelled back. To David he said, "I want you *out* of here, *now!*"

From the darkness outside, both men heard the garden gate wheeze open and the asthmatic twang of a bicycle bell.

Whistling, Clare opened the back door to the kitchen to find Sam and David now staring at each other with the alert, focused, intent expression of two wrestlers about to pounce.

"David! *What's happened?*" Clare exclaimed.

"Nothing yet," Sam said, not taking his eyes off David.

"Why didn't you tell me he was coming?" said David without taking his eyes off Sam.

"Because it's none of your goddamn business!" Sam roared.

"Because I didn't expect him," Clare said. "I tried to ring you this morning, but you were out."

"Does this guy have to stay?" Sam asked.

"Do you want me to go, Clare?" David asked, equally truculent.

"Stop it, both of you!" Clare ordered. "You're behaving like five-year-olds."

"Get the hell out of here," Sam growled to David. "You're in the way. There's no reason for you to stay."

"Yes there is. I want to marry Clare," David said.

"You've never once said so!" Clare cried.

"Clare happens to be married already." Sam glared.

Josh appeared, naked and dripping, in the doorway from the hall. He took no notice of David or Clare but, hero worship imprinted on his face, ran straight to Sam, who swung him up in his arms and hugged him.

"You haven't finished my barf." Josh gave Sam a sloppy kiss.

"Well, will you?" David asked Clare. "Marry me, I mean?"

Hesitantly Clare looked from one man to the other.

Chapter·28

After a restless night, Elinor woke early. Buzz made her a cup of tea and provided a cheerful stream of gossip about her cruise with Bertha Higby.

Then Elinor asked how things were at Saracen.

Buzz hesitated.

Elinor whispered, *"What's happened?"*

Eventually Buzz said, "That Adam, he sold it."

"Sold my home?"

"Someone had to tell you sometime, Nell."

Elinor said nothing, but two tears rolled down her cheeks. Finally she whispered, "What's happened to the staff?"

"Oh, they was well looked after, that I will say! I don't know what's happened to 'em all, because I ain't been back yet."

"At least we're all together again," Elinor murmured. "That's the most important thing."

Buzz comforted her for the next two hours, answering Elinor's halting questions about events of the past year. When it was nearly time for Clare to appear with the breakfast tray, Elinor dried her eyes and tried to look cheerful.

When a smiling Clare arrived, she said, "Annabel and Miranda have gone to London for the day, on business."

"Is it about Adam?"

"Yes."

"He's stolen my money, hasn't he?"

"Don't you tell her no lies," Buzz said.

Hesitantly Clare replied, "It might not all have gone. We don't know yet. But even if it *has* disappeared, you'll still have an income from future book sales."

"If I get any of the money back, I want it divided equally between the five of us," Elinor said weakly. "I should have done that in the first place."

• • •

At about the same time, Dr. Craig-Dunlop, wearing a Paisley silk dressing gown and pajamas, left the stateroom and reported to the radio room, where he was shown how to use the receiver.

The little doctor's black-fringed eyes widened as he listened to the faint but agitated voice of Sister Parks, his deputy matron.

"Calm down, Sister Parks," he said when he could get a word in. "If I understand correctly, some relatives of Mrs. O'Dare have removed her from the nursing home, but you do not know whether or not this was with her consent. It's certainly without *our* consent, and we therefore cannot be responsible for what happens to Mrs. O'Dare. That is our official attitude, Sister Parks." His calm, firm voice obviously reassured her, for she seemed less agitated. "Has Mr. Grant been informed? No? Splendid! As Mrs. O'Dare has been removed by her own relatives, who produced proof of their identity before they did so, I can see no reason to inform Mr. Grant until I return. . . . Yes, naturally I'll come back straightaway."

He thought swiftly. The cruise ship was due to arrive in Jamaica on Friday afternoon, in some thirty hours. God knows how long it would take him to get back to England from Kingston. He might have to hang around until he could get a seat on a plane to New York. There he might have a further long wait: flights to London didn't leave every five minutes. He said, "I'll get back as soon as I can, Sister Parks, but my arrival depends on connections and availability of seats. I won't be there for at least two days—probably longer. I suspect the earliest you'll see me is Sunday evening . . . Yes, the second of February."

When Sister Parks had brought him fully up-to-date, the doctor concluded, "As for Matron Braddock, she did the most extraordinary thing. Completely cleared out her room, went off in a taxi, without a word to anyone, and she left with a broken arm. Perhaps Matron Braddock also had slight concussion after her unfortunate fall. Perhaps officially we had better say that Matron is taking a long-overdue holiday and that we expect her return at the end of the month. There is no need to say more than that to anyone."

He gave a little cough. "Because of Mrs. O'Dare's notoriety, you may hear from newspaper snoopers. Do not speak to strangers, Sister Parks. Tell Patricia to be very careful when she answers my telephone. Give *no* information to *anyone* about Mrs. O'Dare, except for my lawyer. I think it wise to inform him of this exasperating incident as soon as possible, and I would appreciate it if you give him the details. Now I want to speak to Orderly Gibson . . .Well, *get him!*" The doctor started to bite his left thumbnail.

After an aggrieved speech from the orderly, the doctor placated him. "What impudence! It sounds as if you were unduly provoked, Gibson. We will consult my lawyer as soon as I return, regarding assault *and* libel *and* slander. . . . Yes, I promise you. In the meantime, I don't think you should go to the police, or speak to anyone else. After all, *we* mustn't libel or slander anyone. I know that I can rely on your support in this highly embarrassing situation. Do you agree?"

There was silence at the other end of the radiophone.

"I'll make it worth your while," the doctor said wearily.

Silence.

"You'll have a job for life, Gibson."

"Can I have that in writing?" asked the white-coated orderly.

Like many of the legal offices in Lincoln's Inn, that of William Owen, financial specialist lawyer, looked like an overworked headmaster's study. The lawyer sat behind a desk piled high with papers and red box files. He was a bulky man with sallow skin and frizzy gray hair. Next to him sat his consultant accountant, Richard Fraser, who specialized in fraud; he had the pink cheeks and solemn young face of a well-scrubbed choirboy.

Sitting opposite the desk between Annabel and Sam, Miranda felt very tired; her head ached.

Mr. Owen said, "From what you tell me, there are three distinct areas of complaint. Firstly, the seemingly unnecessary detention of your grandmother in the nursing home. Secondly, the possible embezzlement of monies from the trust. Thirdly, the possible purchase of SUPPLYKITS shares by persons at present unknown, upon Adam Grant's instructions, with money that may not rightfully belong to the purchaser but to the Dove Trust."

"Can our grandmother sue the nursing home?" Annabel asked.

Mr. Owen lifted his eyebrows and peered over his spectacles. He did not look optimistic. "Even before I know the full facts, I can tell you that it might take ten years of arduous legal work to be able to reclaim a relatively small amount of money. I probably won't advise such a waste of time and energy."

"What about any embezzlement from the trust?" Miranda asked.

"Surely the trustees must account for all funds?" Annabel added.

Miranda shook her head. "STG warned me that Adam and Paul Littlejohn are probably acting within the law and if that's so, nobody has any power legally to query the actions of the trust."

"But why doesn't Adam have to answer our questions?" Annabel said. "*He* organized the trust."

"If Adam Grant is unwilling to give you information," Mr. Owen replied, "you may, as trust beneficiaries, decide to go to court to seek information about the trust. But to force the information from him through the courts would take a long time."

Richard Fraser leaned forward. "From what you say, it sounds as if this operation was carefully planned, years ago. If so, the money will be accounted for on paper by scurrilous documentation—investments in companies that fail or shares that drop like stones. We'll be able to trace where each sum went when it left the Dove Trust bank accounts. But if fraud is involved, that cash will have quickly been transferred again—to numbered Swiss bank accounts that are untraceable."

William Owen looked over his half-glasses. "Adam Grant is probably the only person who knows where that money is. Undoubtedly, he keeps some written record of what's happening to it—because nobody can keep track of vast sums of money and complicated bank transfers without some record. But I expect his summary is carefully hidden. He probably keeps it in a small unobtrusive notebook—something that he could either carry around with him or leave in a small safe. *If* you could get your hands on it, then we could go to the police—but it's no use going to them without such evidence. Though I do advise you to contact the authorities now, so that they can act immediately should you find any hard evidence."

"Then all we have to do is find that summary?" Annabel asked.

Miranda snapped, "Adam's hardly likely to hand it to us on a plate."

Richard Fraser took the two sisters and Sam to a modern building near Victoria—the fraud squad base—where he introduced them to Detective Inspector Walter Piper; in a navy pin-striped suit and expensive pale blue shirt, he looked more like a young trainee banker than a policeman. He took notes as Miranda told her story. When she had finished, the inspector said, "From what you say, and adding a few guesses based on my experience, we're looking at this sort of situation." Carefully he summarized, "In July 1965, STG set up an offshore Bermuda trust, administered by their associate accountants in Bermuda. The protector of the trust was Paul Littlejohn, a partner of STG. At the same time, Elinor O'Dare signed a general power of attorney in favor of Adam Grant of STG, to be used in event of her illness.

"Unlike Paul Littlejohn, a South African subject living in Bermuda, Grant was based in Britain, subject to British law. So in August 1966, he persuaded Mrs. O'Dare to substitute Paul Littlejohn for himself in the power of attorney held by Grant. Probably a clause in the transfer deed stated that the power of attorney was subject to the law of Bermuda and not British law.

"Mrs. O'Dare also signed papers absolving Adam Grant and STG from any further responsibility for Mrs. O'Dare's affairs.

"In March 1967, Grant left STG to start his own firm. Elinor O'Dare transferred her business from STG to Grant's new office. In February 1968, Paul Littlejohn—who is probably Grant's accomplice— left STG to set up his own firm in Bermuda, to which he transferred the Dove Trust. As the protector, Littlejohn had the power to remove existing trustees and appoint other trustees.

"By February 1968, Mrs. O'Dare had started treatment for paranoia in the Lord Willington Nursing Home. Paul Littlejohn was therefore able to use his power of attorney to strip her of her personal fortune, including a chateau in France. At this point, those two villains would have been able to simply siphon off all funds. Paul Littlejohn controlled the Dove Trust, as well as Mrs. O'Dare's personal fortune, but Adam Grant probably controlled Littlejohn.

"It also appears that Adam Grant, a director of SUPPLYKITS, has acquired control of forty-six percent of the shares of that company, possibly using funds from the Dove Trust. We'll be able to trace back the recent purchases, and if they were paid for with money from the Dove Trust, then those shares rightly belong to the trust. If other trust money has disappeared, then the trust might *also* claim the shares that rightly belong to Grant."

When Inspector Piper was finished, Miranda asked, "Where do we start?"

"Contact Mrs. O'Dare's literary agent, to ensure that no further royalties are forwarded to the Dove Trust until it has been investigated. You can't do anything else until you have proof of illegality."

"Can we prosecute?"

"You can't prosecute unless you find some hard evidence, because in 1966, when your grandmother signed the trust deeds, she also signed papers saying that she no longer wished Adam Grant or STG to handle her affairs and absolved both parties from any future responsibility for her affairs. She also voluntarily signed her application to enter this nursing home. So where's the crime?" The inspector shrugged his shoulders. "But I'll check our records to see whether Mr. Grant has done anything like this before."

Sam asked, "What do we do if we get hard proof?"

"Bring it to us as fast as possible—there's always someone available to take emergency action."

In her pale gray drawing room, Miranda collapsed into an armchair. She was exhausted; she also felt that the white dagger slicing through her head was about to split it in two.

"Help yourselves." She wearily waved her hand toward the drinks tray. "I've been trying to think. I've no idea where Adam might keep a small notebook. It could be *anywhere*."

Sam poured himself a generous whiskey. "Not 'anywhere' because it's very valuable. Where would you hide a twenty-carat, blue-white marquise diamond? *Not anywhere*."

"I doubt he carries it around with him," Miranda mused. "What happens if he takes off his jacket and the notebook falls out? . . . It wouldn't be safe from pickpockets. It wouldn't be safe while he . . . slept."

Annabel volunteered, "Sometimes I fetched things from Adam's pockets—cigarettes, keys, that sort of thing. He'd never have asked me to do such a thing if he kept something secret and precious in his pockets."

"Do you think it might be in a bank vault?" Miranda asked Sam.

"Unlikely," Sam said. "It sounds as if Adam has to keep it handy to make entries."

"He's unlikely to keep it in his SUPPLYKITS office." Miranda continued to think aloud. "We have the usual petty theft problems, so none of the staff are supposed to keep valuables in their desks."

"Maybe he keeps the notebook in an office safe?" Sam asked.

"No, our only safe is in the accountant's office," Miranda said. "And we regard it as a serious burglary risk. We use it as little as possible."

"Adam has his own safe—in his apartment," Annabel volunteered. "It's not particularly secret. It's built into the window wall in his sitting room, and it's hidden by a curtain. . . . Oh my God, I gave him my jewelry to keep safe, and it's still there!"

Miranda smiled grimly. "Maybe. I've also seen that safe. Adam keeps cash in it—but not very much—and a few valuable bits and pieces: his father's gold cigarette case, things like that. Last Christmas I gave him a Cartier watch which he put in that safe. I noticed he never wore it: he always wears that old Omega."

"Maybe the notebook is hidden in his home but not in his safe," Sam said. "It's probably in a private sort of room—his bedroom or bathroom. And it's probably in something immovable rather than something like a briefcase that can be stolen."

Annabel said, "I think I know where it is."

Miranda and Sam looked at her.

"No, really. A couple of weeks ago, when Adam left for work, I was still in bed, doing the newspaper crossword. I wanted an eraser—I'm not very good at crosswords—so I went to that Georgian desk opposite the fireplace. As I pulled the desk flap down, Adam opened the bedroom door—he'd forgotten something. He made a lot of fuss about my going to his desk. But where would you look for an eraser if not in a desk? I wasn't rifling through the drawers, you understand."

"This notebook, or file, wouldn't be lying around in a drawer," Sam said.

"How about a *secret* drawer?" Annabel suggested.

Miranda nodded. "Any good eighteenth-century desk has at least one secret drawer, because they didn't have wall safes then."

"D'you remember Gran showing us how to measure the depth of each desk drawer with a ruler? Any drawer that's shorter than the desk space it seems to occupy probably has a secret compartment behind it."

"There are probably plenty of other hiding places in his bedroom," Sam said. "How can we get in there?"

Miranda said, "You mean . . ."

"Can we break into the house?" Sam asked impatiently. "What staff are there? What burglary precautions?"

"His apartment's on the top two floors of an old house in Cadogan Place," Miranda said. "There are double locks and chains on the front door, sliding steel shutters on the windows. There might be some sort of access to the roof, but I bet it's barred."

In a quiet voice, Annabel said, "There's no need to break in. I still have the keys. Adam thinks I'm at a health farm. As far as he is concerned, our relationship hasn't altered."

"The Trojan horse!" Sam exclaimed, delighted. "When would be the best time for you to get in—when you can be *sure* that Adam won't be there?"

"That's easy," Miranda said triumphantly. "The SUPPLYKITS EGM takes place tomorrow, at nine a.m., at the Connaught Rooms— miles away from Cadogan Place. Adam can't afford to miss that meeting. He has a starring role."

Chapter · 29

Angus Maclayne turned up the collar of his heavy city overcoat and hurried down the steps from the VC10, an hour late. London was almost as cold as New York, he thought, stifling a yawn.

Although eight a.m. in London, it was still only three a.m. New York time. Angus, unable to sleep in the plane, had gone over his notes of the international banking conference that had taken him to New York.

He crunched wearily through the gritty snow to the airport bus, which smelled of stale cigarette smoke. Although he carried only hand baggage to avoid delay, there were too few customs officers, so it was eight forty-five when he hurried to his black Daimler, waiting for him at the terminal entrance: there was still enough time to get to the meeting.

The voice of Maria Callas—*"In mia man' alfin' tu sei"*—throbbed with exultant emotion in Clare's pink kitchen. David, who had eaten little, pushed away his breakfast plate and said, "I wish you'd sit down and talk about this seriously, Clare."

"If people bother to bicycle through the snow for my bread," Clare said, tying her baker's apron, "I'm going to serve them as usual."

"But your damned husband will turn up tonight! I want an answer from you before then!"

Clare looked lovingly at him, but there was also determination in her look. Quietly she said, "I may be able to answer you tonight, but I may not. We've been together now for two years, sharing meals, hopes, concerns; sharing my son, sharing my bed. All that time I've loved you—even when you were in one of your 'difficult' moods, when you didn't want me or anyone else. I have loved you, and you have known it, the whole time. And I've known that you loved me as well, even when it didn't seem that way."

"Then why won't you say you'll marry me?"

"Because all the time we've been together, I've never felt that you were really mine; you've been like some partly domesticated animal—there beside me for months, and then one day—gone! Back to the wilds, or to whatever place your demons drive you. . . . But now you're afraid of losing me, and you don't want that, and I'm very glad. I don't want you to lose me. Nevertheless, I can't accept your ultimatum: there are too many things to be considered. You, and our love for each other, are incredibly important to me, but in the time I've had to wait for you to decide what *you* want to do, I've grown stronger, more sure of myself, increasingly aware of my absolute need *to decide for myself* what's best for me. I need time to make that decision. I can't decide by this evening."

"Fine. How long do you need?"

"I don't know. I may decide by tomorrow, but I may need longer. I might need a week, I might need much longer than that. But I think this is as important as you do—and that's why I'm not going to be rushed into a decision. I hope you'll allow me the time I need, and not put me under pressure. And also I hope you know that I really do love you, David."

"How can I believe that, when you won't say yes?"

"You *know* I love being with you, David; I love doing things with you; I love learning from you. And I simply love sleeping with you." A dreamy look came into her eyes, and she hugged herself. "I can't imagine anything more luxurious than snuggling with you under the patchwork quilt upstairs, knowing that it's snowing outside. Except waking up in the middle of the night and putting my arm out to you—and feeling that wonderful warm lump beside me."

"So how are you going to feel if you wake up and the warm lump beside you turns out to be Sam? You have to decide whether you want me or a square-jawed Superman who gets his way with his fists."

Clare hesitated. At Elinor's rescue, she had secretly found Sam's fight-now-talk-later, he-man side almost irresistible. Now, being fought over by two men made her feel like a medieval damsel with white hands and a wimple. To Clare's surprise and chagrin, two aggressive, battling rivals for her hand made her feel exultant and powerful, sneakily, guiltily thrilled to bits.

Turning away from the oven, she looked intently at David and said, "We're not the only ones concerned."

"Josh likes me—you know he does—and I'm growing very fond of him," David said. "As a matter of fact, I was quite hurt when he—"

"Ran to his dad? Josh ignored *me* as well," Clare said ruefully. "Whether or not *I* think his father deserves it, *Josh loves his father*. And I'm *glad* he's loyal to his father—painful though it is."

"So Josh is going to decide who you'll spend the rest of your life with?" David asked. "What will happen to *you* in twelve years' time when Josh leaves you—with never a backward look—to play in some college band or work his way to India with the rest of his mates? How are you going to feel *then* when you wake up in the dark and feel for the warm lump?"

Clare sat down abruptly. This is what made her decision so difficult. Where did her duty lie? With Josh. And where did her heart lie? With David. But suppose she went back to Sam and it didn't work out? Briefly she recalled what her life had been before David appeared.

No, she preferred not to think of it! Life was never, never, *never* going to be like that again for her. She wasn't going to drop the reins of her own life again. Clare was damned if she was going to be over-influenced by Sam, David, or *anyone*.

Anyway, she told herself, she didn't believe that Sam was going to turn over a new leaf.

But if that wasn't his intention, then why had he bothered to come here? Sam had traveled halfway around the world—no doubt at great inconvenience, for Clare knew how carefully his life was structured—to help solve her family problems and to see her. It certainly looked as if he was serious.

Feeling ambivalent and confused, Clare said, "It's no use. The arguments just go round and round in my mind, until I'm back where I started."

David zipped his windproof wine jacket. From the chair beside him, he picked up his sheepskin gloves and flat tweed cap. "Let me know when you decide."

"You'll be back this evening?" Clare asked anxiously. She pushed back her chair and ran to him.

David hesitated. He knew he ought to say no, that he'd come back only if she agreed to marry him. On the other hand, given David's absence, that bastard Sam would move in as fast as a greased lizard.

He said, "I'll see what the weather's like when I've finished work."

He left without kissing her.

The driver half turned to Angus. "Sorry about this, sir. Looks as if we might be here for some time." The Daimler was stuck in a seemingly immovable traffic jam at Hammersmith Broadway.

Through lightly falling snow, Angus peered impatiently at the conglomeration of honking, static vehicles feeding in from five converging roads. "I'll get to Holborn quicker if I take the underground," he decided. "You go on to the Connaught Rooms and wait for me there."

Carrying his briefcase, Angus slipped and stumbled through translucent brown slush, dodging past cars, lorries, and taxis, toward the blue sign that hung above the station. He was no longer confident of arriving in time for the meeting. He wondered briefly whether to dangle a few fivers in front of one of the motorbike riders who were weaving their way neatly through the traffic. Angus decided against it—better late than never—and hurried to the ticket office.

At a quarter to ten, Adam hurried across the well-swept pavement of Cadogan Place and lowered himself into his black Porsche.

Annabel, wearing a black balaclava and ankle-length wolfskin coat, watched the Porsche dart away and turn left into Pont Street.

She slipped from the inconspicuous gray BMW Sam had hired and stumbled across the wet road toward the old red brick building that seemed suddenly forbidding. When she turned the key in the lock, the black door to the communal entrance hall swung open.

Why shouldn't it? There's no reason why Adam should have changed the locks, Annabel reassured herself as she heaved aside the old-fashioned metal-barred door to the elevator.

And her key also opened the front door to Adam's apartment. Annabel crept into the hall, her wet boots making tracks across the navy carpet.

A dark shape leapt from the floor at her.

She jumped back, alarmed. But it was only Pitch, Adam's huge black cat. He sprang at Annabel's crimson boots, clawing the toes. She bent to stroke his silky head and whisper reassurance, then looked up. The silence seemed threatening.

Ahead was the door to the recently redecorated living room, which stretched the depth of the house with windows at both ends. To Annabel's left was the dining room, and to her right, the kitchen.

Adam's apartment was as handsome, impersonal, and tightly controlled as its owner. His fashionable decorator had done a slick job: The walls were painted in carefully chosen tones of plum, aubergine, and gray blue; the carpet and upholstery were navy. Eastern antiques were mixed with the latest clear-plastic, inflatable armchairs and white pedestal tables.

Suddenly, upstairs, a vacuum whined.

Annabel started. Mrs. Price must be cleaning the bedroom. What a nuisance, she thought—the Georgian desk was there. Annabel had imagined herself going directly to the desk and searching it thoroughly.

Because she reckoned that the desk was the most likely hiding place, she couldn't summon up much enthusiasm for searching elsewhere. But perhaps she should search the living room while Mrs. Price was occupied in the bedroom above it. Or should she just march upstairs, whistling, and use some excuse to get rid of Mrs. Price?

Annabel decided to go straight to the desk. Decisively she turned right, toward the staircase.

At the top of the stairs, she stumbled over Pitch, who crouched, invisible, against the navy-blue carpet. The cat's yellow eyes glared up at her, as if he knew what she was doing and wanted to protect his master's territory.

As Annabel entered the bedroom, she saw the large black backside of Mrs. Price, who was picking bits of white china from the floor. She stood up, turned, and gave a squawk as she saw Annabel. "Oh madam, I'd no idea you were back. Mr. Grant didn't say. That dratted, clumsy cat just knocked over an ashtray!"

"Mr. Grant doesn't know I've returned," Annabel said cheerfully. "It was bitterly cold in Norfolk at the health farm, so I decided to return to town."

"You were lucky to get here, madam. On the early morning news, they said there was blizzards in southeast England."

"Yes, terrible blizzards," Annabel said hastily.

"You must have left very early, madam. Before six. In the dark."

"Yes. But the train arrived on time." Annabel wanted to say, "Go away."

"Shall I unpack for you, madam?"

"I stupidly left my suitcase on the train." Annabel gave an embarrassed laugh and embroidered her lie. "I've already telephoned the lost property office. . . . Luckily, a porter handed it in. I have to go and collect it this afternoon."

"What a nuisance, madam. Would you like me to go for you? Or I could telephone Mr. Grant's secretary. She could have the suitcase picked up."

"You're very kind," Annabel said. "But . . . er . . . er . . . I have to personally sign for it, you see, and produce identification—prove that it's mine." Firmly she added, "What I would like now is a hot bath."

"I haven't finished the bathroom yet, madam."

"Then please leave it until tomorrow. Leave this room as well." Annabel had regained her confidence: Why had she been so frightened?

"Shall I take your boots to dry, madam? They look very wet. They need stuffing with newspaper."

"Thank you. I'll let you have them after my bath."

"Would you care for a cup of tea to warm you up, madam?"

Go away! Go away! Annabel thought, but aloud, said calmly, "No thank you, Mrs. Price, that will be all."

Motionless, Annabel listened as Mrs. Price padded downstairs. Then she ran to the bedroom door and turned the key in the lock. She flung her fur coat on the floor. In the bathroom she shoved the plug in the tub and went through the charade of preparing a bath; while the taps were running, she could take the drawers out without being heard.

Adam's bathroom was above the kitchen, his study above the dining room. His bedroom also ran the width of the house; one end, which overlooked Cadogan Place, was used as a sitting area. Here navy sofas were grouped around a zebra skin before a marble fireplace in which a log fire quietly burned; dark blue shelves on either side of the fireplace held a collection of Thai water jars.

On the opposite wall stood a George III mahogany bureau bookcase. Above four narrow drawers, a sloping desktop could be pulled down to provide a writing surface; above it, a glass-fronted bookcase contained a collection of eighteenth-century drinking glasses.

On trembling legs, Annabel ran toward this splendid piece of furniture.

Miranda wore a plain orange suit, not so short-skirted as the rest of her clothes. She felt nervous but excited. Waiting in the impressive pillared entrance hall of the Connaught Rooms, she had already peeped into the cream hall and seen SUPPLYKITS shareholders sitting in rows, some stamping snow from their shoes, some reading newspapers. The city press had been having a great deal of fun, and there had been a lot of speculation and broad hints—for Miranda's private relationship with Adam was guessed on Fleet Street. Today's headlines had read: SUPPLYKITS BOARDROOM CONTROL BATTLE (*The Times*), IT'S MIRANDA V. ADAM! (*Daily Mail*), NEW BOSS AT SUPPLYKITS? (*Daily Express*), and WHOOPS, IT'S D-DAY FOR CITY SWEETHEART, MIRANDA (*Daily Mirror*).

Miranda, who quite enjoyed a fight, knew that she was about to battle as fiercely as a mother tiger for her wounded cub; the neglected KITS needed all her protection, care, and attention to nurse it back to health.

From behind her, Lord Brighton said, "Nearly time to start—it's five to ten." Together, they moved slowly toward the hall.

"*Miranda!*"

Miranda twisted her head backward as she heard her name shouted.

To her astonishment, she saw the wild red-gold hair and unmistakable Viking-sized figure of Angus Maclayne rushing toward her from the street entrance.

"*Angus!* What are *you* doing here?"

"Thought I'd never make it," he panted. "I'm here to vote."

"But you aren't registered as a shareholder!"

Angus grinned. "Yes I am."

"How? Why?" Miranda puzzled. "I don't understand."

"I've been keeping an eye on your shares. Didn't like it when your holding dipped to forty-five percent and you lost your majority," Angus said. "So I started buying."

"How many shares do you own?" Miranda asked urgently.

"Four point eight, which still won't give you a majority vote. . . . I had hoped to get five point one percent."

"Angus . . . how can you own four point eight percent? Unless . . ."

Angus nodded. "Highland Croft Holdings is indirectly owned by my family."

Miranda flung her arms around him. She mumbled into his still-damp overcoat, "You're *wonderful,* Angus. I love you for thinking of this! Four point eight is all I need!"

Behind her, Lord Brighton coughed. "We should move in."

As Miranda's orange figure appeared on the platform, cameras flashed and a rustle of excitement swept through the hall.

Walking confidently across the platform, Miranda felt exultant. It looked as if she controlled the votes. Behind her back, she crossed her fingers.

Miranda took her seat next to Lord Brighton. She and Adam Grant, sitting on his Lordship's other side, ignored each other.

Annabel could just peer behind the back of the desk, which stood against the wall; nothing was attached to it. She pulled down the sloping top of the central section of the desk. The writing surface, thus revealed, was covered by worn black leather. Centered at the rear was a tiny classical doorway with carved pillars on either side and a pediment above it; on either side of this were pigeonholes, with drawers beneath.

Her hands shaking, Annabel removed each drawer and laid it on the navy-blue carpet—in the order of its removal: she had to be careful to put the drawers back correctly or Adam would immediately spot that someone had been tampering with his desk.

With a tape measure borrowed from Miranda, she measured each drawer: all were the same width and the same depth. Damn!

Annabel closed the sloping top and looked carefully at its beautifully inlaid design of musical instruments. Perhaps if she pressed some part, it would activate a hidden mechanism.

Suddenly she realized that she couldn't hear the bathwater.

She scrambled to her feet and ran toward the bathroom.

The bath had overflowed. Water seeped gently over the navy carpet.

"Damn!" As soon as one drop leaked through the kitchen ceiling,

Mrs. Price would be up with mops and pails; she would see the desk drawers scattered over the carpet.

Annabel sloshed across the carpet. Quickly she turned off the taps and pulled out the plug—her big mistake. She threw all the towels she could see, plus Adam's dressing gown, on the floor and then stamped on the bundle to soak up the water.

Trembling more violently, she ran back to the desk.

Halfway there, she changed her mind and ran back to the bathroom. She turned on the taps above the handbasin, which she did not plug: running taps were still necessary to camouflage any odd noises she might make.

Annabel glanced at her watch. *"Damn!"* Ten-fifteen already. And her knees were knocking.

In the cream-colored assembly hall, the shareholders, quiet but expectant, looked up at Lord Brighton as he outlined the reason for the meeting. Miss Miranda O'Dare wished to regain control of the KITS cosmetics business by separating it from the complex of companies into which her original business had developed. The KITS shops had been losing money since the group went public; therefore, this sale might be no great loss to the holding company.

Should the shareholders agree to the price that their independent assessors had decided was reasonable, Miss O'Dare would pay this price for KITS. Should it be decided that Miss O'Dare could not buy the company, then Miss O'Dare would resign from SUPPLYKITS as soon as her contract expired, in three months.

Mr. Adam Grant had also offered to buy KITS, at ten percent above any price that Miss O'Dare offered to pay.

Lord Brighton concluded his speech by saying that every member of SUPPLYKITS worked hard, but nobody worked harder than Miss O'Dare, KITS' founder. As "the face of the firm," Miss O'Dare was perceived by the public to be responsible for the easy and continued success of the company, and therefore, in his opinion, SUPPLYKITS could not afford to lose Miss O'Dare. They could not afford to lose her services or the publicity generated by Miss O'Dare's presence. Nor could they afford to have any rival company acquire the services of Miss O'Dare. And should she leave, he felt certain, the share price would fall.

For these reasons, Lord Brighton recommended that the shareholders refuse Mr. Adam Grant's offer. He also recommended that they show their appreciation for Miss O'Dare's work by accepting Miss O'Dare's offer and agreeing to sell the cosmetics chain KITS to Miss O'Dare for the independent valuation price of fourteen thousand pounds. Lord Brighton moved that Miss O'Dare's offer be accepted.

• • •

Carefully Annabel ran her hands around each empty drawer space in the desk. She touched the backs, the sides, and the bottoms, hoping to feel a piece of wood move—very, very slightly—when it shouldn't.

"*Ah!*"

At the base of the left-hand bank of drawers, the bottom moved ever so slightly. Annabel pushed it backward, then edged her nails under the base panel.

The thin wooden panel lifted easily.

She had been right to start her search at the desk!

Gently she lifted the panel and pulled it toward her: attached to the end was a box ten inches wide by two inches deep.

Annabel ran her thumb lightly over the top of the box: it yielded. She slid it aside and looked into the secret compartment.

From the second row of seats at the Connaught Rooms, a tall, thin man with a ginger mustache stood up. "Mr. Chairman, I don't go along with what you suggest."

Lord Brighton said, "Do I understand that you object to the company's acceptance of Miss O'Dare's offer to purchase KITS?"

"No, I'm all for that," said the man with the ginger mustache, "but like you said, we all know how hard Miranda—I mean Miss O'Dare— has worked to pay our dividends. Why don't we show a bit *more* appreciation than you suggest? Why don't we *give* KITS to her?"

There was a buzz of noise in the hall. A woman in a beige raincoat quickly stood up and, without addressing the chair, pointed out that Miss O'Dare was well paid for her work; personally, she *expected* Miss O'Dare to work hard for the company; personally, *she* was a canteen manageress, and she *also* worked hard for her pay, and nobody gave *her* gifts worth thousands of pounds. So she opposed the suggestion. She sat down to cries of agreement.

Lord Brighton settled the matter by reminding the meeting that, by law, no proposal of which the shareholders had not been advised by letter could be brought up for consideration.

Annabel stared at the contents of the secret drawer: a battered silver King Edward III sixpence. Clearly, Adam did not know of the existence of this drawer; that sixpence may have lain in it for over two hundred years.

Annabel was bitterly disappointed. She sat back on the heels of her crimson thigh boots and checked her watch. Ten forty-five already. She looked at the desk. Was there any point in searching it further?

She glanced upward. Something *might* be hidden behind the pediment above the doorway in the center of the desk; something *might* be attached to the underside of the base.

Annabel dragged the desk chair closer to the desk and stood on it. Carefully she felt over the top of the bookcase. Her hand came away covered by dirt: obviously, Mrs. Price's feather duster didn't move above eye level.

Then she jumped down from the chair and lay flat on the floor to peer beneath the desk. As she couldn't see clearly, she felt over the entire undersurface; had Adam lodged a notebook there, her fingers would certainly have felt it.

Again disappointed, Annabel sat back on her heels and studied the tiny classical doorway with pillars on either side. She opened it.

Inside were two shelves and, at the top, a very small drawer, too shallow to take anything but visiting cards and rings. Annabel gently withdrew the drawer: it contained only a crumpled old-fashioned white five-pound note.

She bit her lip. She had been so certain that this desk was Adam's hiding place. Before returning the little drawer, she carefully put her hand in the opening and pressed each wooden side; none yielded.

But something didn't feel right.

It was then Annabel realized what she should do.

In the Connaught Rooms, Lord Brighton, as chairman, made sure that anyone who wished to speak was allowed to do so.

Then the votes were taken and counted.

A rustle ran through the room. Reporters flipped their notebooks. Shareholders whispered excitedly to one another. Tension rose.

Adam glared at Miranda, and she glared back.

The shareholders voted in Miranda's favor. The majority was small, but Miranda didn't mind because KITS would be sold back to her for fourteen thousand pounds: the resolution was passed.

But the meeting was not yet finished.

Annabel again studied the little doorway inside the desk. That central structure didn't feel as secure as it should. She took hold of the scrolls of the Ionic pillars on either side of the doorway and tugged them toward her.

She was either about to break a valuable antique or . . .

As Annabel held her breath, the entire little doorway slid to ward her: it was a box unit, measuring about ten inches wide and deep by twelve inches high, and it left a space of the same size in the desk.

Trembling now with excitement, she pushed her hand to the back of this space: there was a little trough in which she could feel several small items.

From it Annabel eagerly withdrew three small, battered black leather notebooks and an envelope.

The black notebooks contained page after page of neat figures in Adam's handwriting. The envelope contained a certificate and a crumpled handwritten letter.

Holding her breath, willing herself to concentrate on what she was doing, Annabel carefully replaced the central section of the desk; then, one by one, she started to replace the little drawers.

Behind her, there was a sudden *crack!*

She jumped and gasped with fright.

But it was only the sound of a smoldering log.

At the SUPPLYKITS EGM, Adam Grant, tight-lipped, stood up. As was appropriate, he offered his resignation from the board of directors of SUPPLYKITS.

Mr. Grant's resignation was accepted.

The meeting was then dissolved. Reporters, wearing unbelted raincoats, rushed toward the platform and a glowing Miranda.

As Annabel crept downstairs, Mrs. Price appeared in the kitchen doorway.

Seeing that Annabel was wearing her fur coat, Mrs. Price said, "Going out again, madam? In *this* weather?" Broom in hand, she advanced to the bottom of the stairs.

"A hair appointment," Annabel said rapidly. "Dare not skip an appointment with Leonard himself, not even in this weather!" Her heart thudded against her black skinny-rib sweater as she added, "I'm afraid I've made rather a mess of the bathroom, Mrs. Price. I'll explain to Mr. Grant that it was my fault."

"Was it the overflow stuck, madam? That's happened to Mr. Grant a couple of times." Now Mrs. Price stood before the front door.

Annabel thought wildly, Get out of my way. *Please! Get away from that front door!* In a worried voice, she said, "Would you mind making *quite* sure I turned all the taps off? I might have left the basin tap running. Awful of me."

Mrs. Price scooted upstairs. She didn't want her kitchen ceiling falling down again.

Annabel flung herself through the front door and waited, trembling, for the elevator, pressing the button anxiously over and over. She couldn't hear it coming up. Damn! Someone must have left it open down below.

She dashed to the end of the passage, clattered down the service stairs, and ran out to the street and headed for Sam's car, parked farther up the road, next to the wrought-iron railings of the garden. Before she reached it, Annabel slipped on the slush and almost fell.

Sam was feeling apprehensive as he waited. Annabel had been in Adam's home for nearly two hours, and there was no way of knowing when the SUPPLYKITS meeting would end. Just then Annabel ran across the road toward him, and Sam could see from her excited face that her search had been successful. He switched on the engine purposefully, and they were gone.

They arrived at the lawyer's office just after midday. Sam and Annabel watched impatiently as the big Rank Xerox dark brown photocopier slowly copied each page of the black notebooks. The machine gave off a slight smell of ozone as the paper went through the heat fuser. Obviously, the copier was one of the older models.

"Can't it go faster?" Annabel asked, then added nervously, "*Must* I take those notebooks back to Adam's apartment?"

"If we want to be safe—yes," Sam said regretfully. "We don't want Adam to realize they're missing. If he suspects that we've enough evidence to put him in jail, he'll immediately whisk off whatever cash is left, remove all evidence, and disappear."

Annabel fidgeted with a fingernail, then remembered that she was supposed to be at the hairdresser. She went to the cracked mirror in the dingy cloakroom and began to comb her hair, flattened by the balaclava, into a thick lion's mane that would rival even that of Baby Jane Holzer. Mrs. Price would definitely see a change.

Heart thudding, Annabel opened Adam's front door. She could hear the news on the radio in the sitting room, which meant that he was in. Her heart sank as she slowly entered the room.

"Where the hell have you been?" Adam asked irritably. A glass of whiskey in one hand, he sat in one of the transparent inflatable armchairs.

"I told you in my note. I've been at the St. Ivory health farm."

"You said *a* health farm. You didn't say which one," Adam said crossly. "Suppose someone had wanted to get in touch with you? Suppose something had happened to your grandmother?"

"I'm so sorry," Annabel said. "I just didn't think . . ." Her voice trailed away.

"Well, hurry up. I've just told Mrs. Price to serve lunch." Adam did not kiss her.

Annabel wondered if she could endure lunch, knowing that proof of her theft was a few feet away, in her scarlet leather shoulder bag. She decided to replace the documents immediately; it would be a risk, but Adam was sitting down with a fresh drink, and she'd be able to do it in three minutes.

"I'll just take off my wet boots," she said.

Taking her bag with her, Annabel hurried upstairs to the bedroom. By the time she reached the top of the stairs, her knees were weak with fear.

She shut the bedroom door, but did not dare lock it. Moving quickly to the desk, she pulled out the sloping desktop.

Slowly she edged out the elaborate central box.

Hands trembling, she opened her bag and replaced the notebooks and envelope, then edged the box back into place and closed the desk flap.

A wave of relief swept over her, only to be replaced by terror as she turned away from the desk.

Adam was standing in the doorway, watching her.

"Looking for stamps?" he asked pleasantly. "Second drawer down on the left-hand side. I've brought you a Campari and soda—tell me if you want more Campari in it. And do hurry down, darling. Mrs. Price is getting tetchy. You know she likes to leave promptly at three o'clock."

"She's had a trying morning. I'm afraid I flooded the bathroom again." With a great effort, Annabel took the drink, and Adam left the room. She collapsed on the sofa and, with shaky hands, tugged her boots off.

Had he seen her?

If so, why hadn't he said anything?

He couldn't have. It was too unbearable to think about.

Downstairs, Adam carefully closed the door of the living room. He needed time to think. There was only one thing Annabel could have been looking for in that desk. Her face told him that she'd found the notebooks. Had she hidden them in her clothes? Or in her purse? Was she about to deliver them to someone outside? Annabel wasn't smart enough to be in this alone. And she certainly wasn't smart enough to understand what was in those notebooks. Someone who did know how important they were had clearly sent Annabel here to steal them . . . and that person must be waiting somewhere outside. Adam could search her purse, he could search her person; he could certainly find and remove the notebooks—but that unknown someone would still come after them.

He had to think clearly, control his momentary panic. Okay—his next move should be to convince Annabel's accomplice that he *didn't* have the notebooks. But how could that be arranged?

Suppose Annabel was given all the space she needed to take anything she wanted out of this house? And then suppose she was mugged—and her purse stolen—before she had a chance to give those notebooks to anyone else? She'd have to be beaten up a little to make the mugging look convincing . . . but the bitch deserved it. . . .

Yes, that was it.

He had to keep calm—there were still a lot of things to work out. He needed to arrange for someone to follow Annabel until she was in a relatively quiet spot where she could be jumped. Maybe he needed two people, in case her accomplice was lurking outside his front door. In that case, they would *both* have to be taken care of. Maybe three men would be needed. . . . Mike would be able to arrange it. God, he hoped he'd be able to get hold of Mike. . . .

And maybe he'd better drop everything and get out of the country without waiting until the rest of the money had been funneled out. Most of the money was out there, waiting for him. . . . He didn't think there was anything the police could hold him for, but then everyone caught in some sharp practice thought that. If he got out fast, he'd be taking no chances. . . . But suppose the airports were already being watched? . . . Steady, steady—no need to panic. *There was no need to worry.* If someone got hold of the notebooks, that someone still wouldn't know *where* the money was, or *how* to get it. No, he had nothing to fear, so long as he kept his head. . . .

Still, it wouldn't be a bad idea to arrange for the notebooks to be "stolen," and to let them rough up that bitch Annabel while they were about it—that would teach the little whore a lesson . . . and if her accomplice was also beaten up, then Adam would discover who he was. Maybe she'd been reconciled to that smart-ass husband of hers—Mr. Hotshot Reporter . . . He'd get them both, mess up both their pretty faces . . . *Yes.*

Now that he'd decided what to do, all that remained was to locate Mike. Obviously, it would take Mike some time to make these arrangements, so he would have to keep Annabel here until Mike's people were in place. But he knew the perfect way to stall Annabel. . . . What better way to kill time than by giving the bitch a fuck she'd never forget?

Adam reached for the telephone. As he listened to the rings, he nervously tugged his hair over his left eye, then jerked his head up to flip it back into place.

"Mike? Thank God I've reached you. I'm in trouble. . . . I knew you would. . . . Look, I need you to take care of someone for me. . . . I promise, I wouldn't ask you if it wasn't absolutely necessary. . . . No, I only want you to frighten someone. . . . Thanks. . . . Right now, as a matter of fact. . . . I'm sorry. . . . Thanks. . . . Well, it's Annabel O'Dare. . . . You bloody well just said you *would!* Mike, I'm sunk if you don't! When I explain later, you'll see there's no alternative for me—short of pushing her out of the window, or jumping myself. . . . No, no, of course I won't!"

Quickly Adam explained that he had just seen Annabel deliberately steal carefully hidden documents that could put him behind bars. "What she's nicked are details of some bank transactions. It won't do her a blind bit of good because she doesn't know where to find the bank account numbers." Adam's voice sounded increasingly desperate as he whispered, "I've *got* to find the bastard she's working with. I've *got* to find out who's after my notebooks . . . and I've *got* to scare Annabel so badly that she'll refuse to do it again—*or* involve the police. . . .

"Why don't *I* frighten her? Because, Mike, it's more frightening if someone else does it. Shows them I have powerful friends. Makes Annabel feel that even if *I'm* put behind bars, she'll still be vulnerable. . . . Yes, of *course* I know it's also safer for me. Look, I want this done by someone else for exactly the same reason Toby Sutch gets other people to do this sort of thing.

"Mike, I swear I *need* you on this. . . . I swear you'll understand when I tell you the whole story. . . . As a matter of fact, I'm scared stiff. If I can't frighten her off, I'll have to leave the country for good. . . . Thanks, Mike. . . . How long will you need to arrange it? . . . Yes, yes, I can keep her here for another couple of hours. Thanks." Triumphantly Adam replaced the receiver.

They ate a pleasant but not very enterprising meal of green pea soup, grilled Dover sole, and a too stiff chocolate mousse, followed by a perfect, ripe Camembert.

Over lunch, Adam chatted agreeably about nothing much: John Lennon's blossoming romance with Yoko Ono; whether the Americans actually would land a man on the moon; whether Golda Meir would be Israel's first woman prime minister; whether Annabel wanted to stay in that evening or dance at Sybilla's.

To Annabel, every minute seemed to stretch to an hour. She felt ashamed, confused—and worried because she knew that she wasn't a very good actress. A screen test in L.A. had once confirmed this.

As he finished his coffee, Adam stared across the table at her elaborate coiffure. He said, "I know you've spent the entire morning at the hairdresser having your hair put up like Marie Antoinette's. But I feel an irresistible impulse to tear it all down."

Smiling, he stood up, walked around to Annabel's seat, drew her chair back for her, took her firmly by the wrist, and led her to the stairs.

It was a quarter to three. Mike had said not before five o'clock, by which time it would be dark.

Chapter · 30

Firmly Adam led Annabel up the stairs. She had no choice but to follow him. She dared not suddenly act out of character: should she seek excuses to avoid going to bed with him, it would be the first time. Adam, whose reactions were as fast and instinctive as those of his damned huge cat, would immediately guess that there was another reason for Annabel's refusal.

He would ask questions, silky smooth and casual at first but gradually becoming sharper, faster, and more pointed. Annabel knew that she would become flustered; she would allow herself to be led into the trap of contradicting herself—and then that many-toothed trap would snap shut! She had watched Adam do this to others—why not to her?

And though the apartment was warm, and Adam's hand was warm, Annabel felt her body chill and the hair prickle on the back of her neck. His strong, insistent fingers firmly clasped her wrist as they climbed the stairs: his hand felt like a handcuff, impossible to unshackle.

Annabel dreaded what was about to happen. She could not bear Adam to touch her, could not bear to think that she had ever *allowed* him to touch her; she could not bear to think that once she had willingly offered her body to him—willingly opened herself, her mind and her affection. Without much hope, she longed for some distraction, some possibility of escape, some means of putting off this humiliation. On the other hand, she was anxious to get this final ordeal finished—and escape.

Adam was now leading her toward his bedroom as he would a call girl—for a little light entertainment on a wintry afternoon. The only way Annabel's situation differed was that the call girl would be paid and would probably feel indifference, for it was something she had chosen to do, and in a way, she would feel wanted.

Of course, Adam would probably prefer a call boy.

Briefly Annabel remembered the moment at the pub when he had given a lingering kiss to that boy and, for the first time, she had seen Adam's emotions not under his usual firm control: she had seen him openly relaxed and happy. Before that moment, she hadn't understood why he had insisted, so successfully, that Miranda keep their long affair a secret—but now she knew what might have happened if those two had become engaged: blackmail. The boy he had kissed was unlikely to be the only one. Annabel supposed that discarded male lovers felt as bruised, battered, and resentful as female ones—and might similarly seek revenge, especially accompanied by wads of cash.

As Adam opened his bedroom door, Annabel felt revulsion and self-disgust. Standing aside to let her enter, he released his grip on her wrist. She smelled his erotic, country smell as she passed before him, and it made her nearly nauseous.

She watched Adam's big black cat jump from the bed and run forward; he rubbed sinuously against Adam's leg. Pitch was as wary and as independent as his master, and Adam was fond of Pitch, primarily because Pitch seemed determined not to be fond of Adam. Pitch might stretch out on the ocelot cover of Adam's bed, but when Adam climbed into the bed, Pitch jumped off.

Outside, against a bleak, pale sky, the witch fingers of the trees in Cadogan Place bent beneath the weight of snow still on their branches. Adam drew the curtains. He said, "I won't switch on the lights." The firelight threw flickering shadows over his thin, taut face, making his dark eyebrows seem longer, more saturnine.

He sat on an armchair and pulled Annabel to him until she stood between his knees. His warm hands slowly traveled up her legs, over sheer black nylon.

Adam said, "You're wearing tights!"

"It's a very cold day." Wearily Annabel thought that she must be the only woman in London not allowed to wear tights when it was snowing. But Adam liked to peel off lace bikinis, suspender belt, high-heeled shoes, and stockings, in that order. Sometimes he did not peel them all off.

"Naughty, naughty." Adam unzipped Annabel's black suede mini-skirt. She felt his hands beneath her black skinny-rib sweater. "Dear me, nothing at all," he said. He pulled up her sweater, and when her face was hidden and her arms trapped, he licked her nipples.

When she was naked except for her black tights, Adam said, "*Don't move!*" He stood up and walked toward the Georgian desk.

Annabel suddenly felt very frightened.

Adam opened a drawer and produced a pair of scissors. He turned and said, "You're shivering! Surely you can't be cold with this roaring log fire?"

"I'm . . . excited," Annabel gulped. She found it difficult to breathe.

Adam returned, sat, and again pulled her to him. "I told you never to wear tights. So I'm cutting these into stockings." He hooked one finger over the waistband and drew it toward him. The scissors flashed in the firelight. Adam pulled at each thigh and snipped until the jagged tights dangled down Annabel's legs.

She felt him stroke her hair.

"You're so silky," he murmured. "Some women are like an old saucepan scourer down there." Adam never let a woman forget that she was not the only one.

Annabel felt him lick her: sick at heart, she felt her body melt, respond.

He looked up and whispered, "You're very tense. Are you frightened?"

"Yes," Annabel breathed truthfully.

"I'm not surprised," Adam said. "You've disobeyed my orders. *Don't move.*"

Again he moved toward the antique desk. And again Annabel felt terrified. Her heart seemed to leap up into the back of her mouth. She swallowed with difficulty. She held her breath. *Was* this some cat-and-mouse game?

Adam returned with a Victorian baby's hairbrush, very soft and backed by ivory.

"First I'll brush your bush, and then you can do it to me." He stroked her pubic hair lightly, slowly, rhythmically.

"Adam . . . Can't we just . . . go to bed?" Annabel had now faced the fact that bed was unavoidable and the sooner she got into it, the sooner she would be able to get out of it.

Adam put down the hairbrush and said, "Of course we're going to bed. Turn around."

Annabel did so.

Adam stood up and pulled the pins from her elaborately disheveled coiffure; he pushed both hands into the long fair strands at the base of her skull and started to shake her hair free.

He said, "Your neck is rigid. You're *very* tense! What's the matter?"

"Nothing," Annabel quavered. "I'm just tired. I know it's only three in the afternoon—but that's just how I feel."

"I know what to do to women who are too tired." He carried her to the bathroom, where he pulled off her shredded tights; together, they stood naked beneath the warm shower. He carefully soaped her body all over, watched her nipples harden. With difficulty, Annabel smiled at him.

Adam played the warm hand spray over each smooth surface and crevice of her body; then he wrapped her in a bathtowel and carried her to his bed.

"A pretty picture," he said, looking at Annabel's plump white body on the ocelot bedspread.

He moved to one of the side tables; they were antique Thai chests with elaborate silver locks, and upon each one, in an eighteen-inch-high pewter holder, stood a huge, thick aubergine candle, which he now lit.

Adam's skilled lovemaking was never mechanical because he was genuinely interested in having a woman at his mercy—hooked on him. He liked to maneuver his women partners into a sexual relationship in which they became increasingly subordinate to him in bed and eventually gave over to him total responsibility for their erotic response.

Unlike most men, Adam had developed his gift of imagination, and put it to use. Fantasy was an important part of his lovemaking because he saw that it excited women. He was adept at playing Rhett Butler, Lewis Carroll or Petruchio; master and slave girl, doctor and nurse, vicar and choirgirl, teacher and schoolgirl.

Adam was especially attractive to the woman who liked the fantasy of being "forced" to have sex with some authority figure: this exonerated her childish feelings of guilt and her wickedness for thinking sexy thoughts. When his partner eventually confided them, Adam always acted out her own fantasies, which aroused her even more.

Whatever their wishes, there were few women who did not stagger, dazed by pleasure, from Adam's long bedroom.

Annabel, however, felt only cold apprehension as, lying on Adam's bed, she watched him go back to the bathroom and return carrying thick white towels. She looked up at his well-muscled body, at the shadow of hair that ran from his neck to his thick penis, and she thought: Oh God, he's going to give me a massage.

She wouldn't be able to get away for at least another hour!

Adam picked up a cut-glass bottle of baby oil; he warmed some in his hands.

It was warm and still in the bedroom. Annabel listened to the soft strains of "The Swans of Tuonela": Sibelius always made her feel as if she were in a cozy, dark hut, in the middle of a quiet, snowy forest, while hungry wolves howled faintly on a distant skyline.

She lay facedown on the bed as Adam started to rub his oiled hands slowly over every inch of her body, movements that were firm but fluid, and never hurt.

Using the entire surface of his hands, keeping his fingers together, he blended each movement into the next. His stroking seemed one smooth and continuous motion as he moved silently from one part of her body to the next, always keeping to the same rhythm and pressure, always repeating each movement three times. Adam smoothed her body until it felt supple as satin. Annabel felt her eyes close and her thoughts drift away. Slowly his hands traveled upward.

Then she felt his tongue on her spine, gently moving up it . . . down . . . and up again.

"Feel better?" Adam's voice caressed her as softly as his hands. Gently he pried her thighs apart and stroked them, first with his fingertips, then with his tongue. He turned her over. As his lips touched her breast, Annabel quivered with pleasure. She breathed, half panting now, as if she had been running.

As his head bent over her, she felt his warm breath just before his lips touched hers; she felt her own lips part before the moist, insistent tip of his tongue; she felt his tongue thrust deep into her mouth. Softly Annabel groaned. It was not only as if Adam were playing her like a fine violin but as if the entire Philharmonic string section were playing arpeggios over every quivering inch of her body, the chords ascending, then descending, in rapid succession, without stop.

Adam knew so well the responses of her body, how to gradually excite her to frenzy, so that she neither knew where she was, or with whom, nor cared who knew it or might observe them.

As she groaned with pleasure, Annabel forgot that this man had clawed and shredded her emotions, had sought to ruin her family and might have succeeded. She knew only that the animal smell of his body, so close to hers, made her lose all grip on reason, and the hard force of that muscular weight against her softness made her forget everything but their swiftly rising passion.

How could I *do* this? Annabel thought fleetingly, and then she did.

Just after four o'clock, Miranda appeared at the offices of Owen and Fraser. The orange suit that she had worn to the EGM was very crumpled; she looked a little dazed and very happy: clearly, Angus had found New York educational, but Miranda was too pleased to feel jealous.

She was shown into a room with a large oval table in the center, strewn with paper. Behind a pile of documents, Sam sat beside Richard Fraser.

"You're late," Sam said crossly. "And so's Annabel. It's after four. God knows why the traffic comes to a standstill all over this island whenever it rains or snows! You'd have thought that by now they'd have all gotten used to the idea that this is normal British weather."

"Sorry, Sam. Everything went as planned at my end." Miranda smirked. "Did Annabel find anything?"

"She found three notebooks in Adam's desk. She left here at one o'clock to put them back where she found them." Sam nodded toward the papers piled on the table. "These are photostats." He did not mention the envelope hidden in his jacket pocket.

With a smile, Richard Fraser said, "We've got what we need to prove your case."

"What have you found?"

"The notebooks contain details of each financial transaction, as Grant moved the money from one bank account to another, until it became untraceable. They clearly show which bank account each sum of money eventually reached."

Sam added, "He seems to have five final bank accounts in which the money accumulates; they are referred to as accounts A, B, C, D, and E. Unfortunately, the notebooks don't give the account numbers or address of the banks; they might all be in a single Swiss bank—or scattered in five different places throughout the world. There's no way of telling from the notebooks."

"Of course," Richard Fraser went on, "Grant could remember the names of the banks and their addresses: it's not difficult to remember that your A account is in Bank Leu, Zurich. But he must have some record of the numbers of these five bank accounts, because without the correct number, you cannot have access to a numbered bank account."

Sam said, "So although we now have hard evidence to convict Adam of embezzlement, we can't get the money back until we find where it is. So there's still a missing bit to our puzzle. Now we've got to look for a list of five numbers."

"I'm glad we can nail the bastard," Miranda said. "But I'm worried about Annabel. What could have happened to her?"

"Her cab's probably stuck in a traffic jam," Sam grunted.

"But if you say she left here around one o'clock, she should have got to Cadogan Place by . . . two at the latest," Miranda calculated. "So she should have been back here by three—no matter how bad the traffic!"

"Maybe someone was there," Sam said. "Maybe Adam turned up, and she hasn't yet been able to put the stuff back in the desk. She said once Adam yelled at her when he saw her open it."

"I suppose we couldn't telephone . . . ?"

"If Adam's not there, then we can. But if he's there—why would you be telephoning him, Miranda? Why would you telephone Annabel? And how could I know that Annabel's there?"

"She might have phoned you."

Sam shook his head. "By now that matron has reported back to Adam," he said, assuming incorrectly. "So he knows how Clare and I took Elinor from the nursing home. We gave our real names and showed our passports. It's clear that we suspect dirty work. So *I* can't exactly telephone him for a friendly chat!"

"Annabel might have had an accident," Miranda worried.

"You women blow a raindrop into a storm," Sam said. "If I telephone the police, they'll think I'm crazy. 'My sister-in-law should have been back an hour ago—so I thought I'd better report her as a missing person.' " Seeing Miranda's dubious expression, he relented and picked up the telephone. "Still, if she's been in an accident, the police'll know about it."

Richard Fraser said, "We've still got work here, Sam. Let Miranda call the police while we finish listing these documents."

Just after five-thirty, Fraser looked up from the boardroom table and said, "It looks as if most of the trust money has been transferred to these five accounts. There seems to be about seventeen percent of the original sum left in the trust."

"How did he manage to shift it?" Miranda asked.

"Most of the money was sent to a Hong Kong firm of investment brokers, who deducted three percent in various ways, then passed the remainder to bank accounts A, B, C, and D. Grant never sent further money to these brokers until the previous amount had been passed to the A, B, C, or D accounts: that's one reason why it's taken a long time to process the money."

"Adam didn't trust them?" Miranda said.

"Why should he?" Fraser replied. "The Hong Kong brokers take a commission of three percent for legally laundering the money. I expect they'll be able to produce 'records' to account for every penny; on paper, it'll look as though they're mighty unlucky stockbrokers: either the firms they invest in go bankrupt, or the stock dives shortly after they've invested in it. Although not *all* the money passed to them has been lost. They still hold some of it—as a stockbroker easily might—in the account referred to as E. I would guess that's a genuine investment account, to give a little plausibility to their cover story."

"The fraud squad should be interested in this Hong Kong outfit," Sam said.

Fraser said laconically, "Probably nothing they can do about it because it's outside U.K. jurisdiction. But I expect they can now pick up Grant." He pulled over the telephone and dialed. "Detective Inspector Piper? . . . The O'Dare case. I'm looking at clear evidence that you can smack him with. I'll need a couple of days to get it in order and check it carefully, but by Monday morning I should have enough for you to act on. . . . The photostats of his account books . . . Yes, all in Grant's handwriting, according to Miss O'Dare. . . . No, we haven't any bank statements yet. . . . I *know* you need to see that the money ends up in a bank statement in Grant's name—but in the meantime, surely you won't let Grant leave the country? There's certainly enough stuff, right in front of me, for you to ask him for help with your inquiries. . . . Okay, I'll bring it straight over to you. . . . Certainly, with one of the family to lodge the complaint."

"Come on, let's go." Sam stood up.

Miranda protested, "It's nearly six o'clock. I'm worried about Annabel—she should have been back here three hours ago! I don't like to leave without her. Can't Detective Inspector Piper do something about finding her?"

Richard Fraser shook his head. "He's fraud squad. And you've already notified the police."

"Look, we're all worried," Sam admitted. "But what can we do except tough it out? And move in on Adam as fast as possible?"

"I'm going round to Adam's place now," Miranda said. "*Don't* try to talk me out of it!"

Sam sighed and turned to Fraser. "You take this stuff to Piper's office. We'll meet you there as soon as possible. I can't let Miranda go by herself."

After the door had shut behind the accountant, Sam said, "Before we leave, I think you should have a swift look at these." He pulled two creased sheets of paper from his pocket and handed them to Miranda.

Miranda scanned the first document. She looked puzzled. "This is my birth certificate. How did *you* get it? Why give it to me now?" She glanced at it again. "Hang on. . . . This *isn't* my birth certificate!"

Mystified, Miranda once again scanned the white sheet of paper, with its royal crest, headed: "Certificate of Birth." She read aloud, " 'Name, Miranda Patricia. Sex, girl. Name of mother, Patricia Doreen Kettle. Name of father, William Montmorency O'Dare. Date of birth, seven November 1941. Place of birth and registration district, St. Pancras. Subdistrict, southwest St. Pancras. Certified to have been compiled from records . . .' "

Miranda looked at Sam.

"This birth certificate says that Daddy Billy was my *father!* What rubbish!"

Sam said nothing.

Miranda looked again at the certificate. "Miranda Patricia O'Dare is *my* name all right, but who is this woman called Patricia Doreen Kettle? *She* isn't my mother! And this isn't my birthday!"

Sam shrugged his shoulders. "Look at the other paper."

The second sheet of paper bore the letterhead of Swithin, Timmins and Grant; it was handwritten and dated 17 March 1942. Slowly

Miranda read: "My dear Elinor, I beg you to do nothing hasty. Miranda is now Billy's only surviving child, and so she might, one day, have a claim to Larkwood, together with the entire estate. Because of this, I advise you on no account to destroy her genuine birth certificate. Yours, in haste, devotedly, Joe."

Miranda looked up and said, "So if these documents aren't forgeries or jokes, I am Daddy Billy's daughter, not his granddaughter. But if this Patricia Doreen Kettle was my mother, then . . . Edward and Jane weren't my parents . . . *and I'm not related to Elinor!*"

Chapter·31

Sam and Miranda hurried from the lawyer's office through lightly falling snow. Miranda impatiently brushed snowflakes from her face and beckoned to her driver, waiting at the opposite curb in her silver Mercedes.

Before the driver could pull over, a taxicab shrieked to a stop in front of her. The driver jumped out and hurried around to open the door for his passenger, but before he could reach it, the door opened.

The passenger collapsed onto the trampled, grimy snow at Miranda's feet.

"Annabel!" Miranda recognized the wolfskin coat and crimson boots. She knelt in the snow beside her sister.

The driver said to Sam, "I wanted to take the lady to St. George's Casualty, guv, but she made me bring 'er 'ere."

Annabel's face was unrecognizable. Her swollen left eyelid was badly torn, leaving the top of her eyeball exposed; the eye was cut and bloody. Her flattened nose was clearly broken. Two front teeth were missing from her open, bleeding mouth.

"What happened?"

"I picked 'er up at the junction of Cadogan Lane and Pont Street. She was staggering about. Matter o' fact, I thought she'd 'ad a bit too much to drink. Then I saw the blood."

"Thank you. She'll be okay with us." Sam thrust notes into his hand.

"Hey, wait a minute, guv. You gotta give me your name and address. Sorry, but we 'ave to report this sort of thing to the police."

The casualty ward doctor bent over Annabel. "Bad bruising on the face . . . left eye cut . . . Looks as if there's a loss of one muscle, which will have to be restitched. The two front teeth can be dealt with later.

Fractured nasal septum . . . Fractured left radius and ulna . . . Fractured fifth, sixth, and seventh ribs on the left side . . . severe abrasion on stomach, chest, and legs." He stood up. "I can't cope with all this. Nurse, please call the emergency eye doctor and get an orthopedic specialist to look at the fractured forearm. Clean her up and get her to the operating theater fast. Give her a normal anesthetic, but with a muscle relaxant."

Sam telephoned C1, the Major Crimes Branch of the Metropolitan Police, from the hospital pay phone. He doubted that Annabel's mugging was a coincidence. If he was right, this case was no longer merely a case of fraud. It was also assault and battery, grievous bodily harm, and attempted—perhaps actual—murder.

After talking to C1, Sam checked his watch: 7:30 p.m. in London meant 2:30 p.m. in New York. He called Scott's office.

Annabel lay in the operating room, her hair tucked beneath a green plastic cap, as the medical team—the ophthalmic surgeon, the orthopedic surgeon, the casualty doctor, the hospital emergency anesthetist, the nursing sister, and two nurses—prepared to go about their business.

After the anesthesia was administered, the orthopedic surgeon cleared up and stitched the abrasions; then Annabel's fractured left arm was gently put back in place and set in plaster, and her ribs strapped back. These matters were dealt with quickly and easily, but the eye operation was a far more delicate matter.

"We're looking at major trauma to the eye," the ophthalmic surgeon said after his initial examination. "I'm going to just clean up initially. She's lost that left eye muscle and may lose her left eye. She's had a nasty laceration, and there's a lot of abrasion as well as damage to the cornea. If I can save the eye, she'll need at least one further major operation, when the bruising and lacerations have subsided. At this stage, I can't say whether her sight will be impaired indefinitely."

The eye operation took over an hour. Afterward, the ophthalmic surgeon removed his gloves and ran his hands over his face wearily. He washed, then again donned his dinner jacket; without being asked, the sister tied his black bow tie. He hurried off.

After Annabel's nose was set, she was given a sedative injection. It was ten p.m. when she was wheeled into a dimly lit ward filled with other recovering emergency patients.

At three in the morning, she became conscious of the pain: it hurt to breathe. She felt such pain in her head that she winced with each labored breath.

Upon hearing her groan, the nurse sitting by her bedside spoke reassuringly. "You're in hospital, Mrs. Svenson. You've had an accident. You're going to be all right. Your family are waiting outside. We had to give you an injection before we tidied you up, and the effects are wearing off now, which is why you're waking up."

"I . . . can't . . . see." Her words were slurred and muffled, almost as though she were drunk.

"That's because your left eye is bandaged, and your right eye is very swollen."

She fed Annabel a little water from a cup with a spout. As the water dribbled into her mouth, Annabel retched. The nurse sponged her lips and continued to soothe her until Annabel drifted into an uneasy sleep.

SATURDAY, 1 FEBRUARY 1969

As soon as Miranda opened her eyes, she reached for the ivory telephone at her bedside.

"It's only seven o'clock. The hospital said you couldn't call before nine," Angus sleepily reminded her.

"I'd forgotten." In the pale winter sunlight, Miranda sighed, then stretched luxuriously. "Well, well, well," she said softly.

"I've been practicing," Angus murmured smugly.

"No more practice needed." Gently she pinched his rather large ear. "I'm a jealous woman."

"So now will you marry me?"

Miranda propped herself on one elbow. "Hold on, darling, give me time to collect my thoughts." She was delighted by his proposal. The big obstacle clearly no longer existed: she would be happy to stay in bed with Angus for the rest of the week, and to live with him for the rest of her life. She was confident that they would live happily ever after, for all the reasons she had originally become engaged to him. But she couldn't think about the future until she had resolved the present. But she wasn't going to risk hurting Angus or herself again by making up her mind in a hurry—although now that it was behind her, she could admit to herself how much she had regretted breaking off their engagement.

By ten a.m., Annabel was vaguely aware of nurses' voices, of squashy rubber-soled shoes treading a rubber floor, china clinking, a radio playing soft music. She could smell antiseptic.

Her right hand was warm. It was being held in somebody else's hand.

Annabel whispered, "Scott?"

"I've been here for over an hour, angel."

"Please . . . don't . . . leave me."

"Never again."

"I'm so . . . sorry."

"So am I!" During his long flight, Scott had been able to think of nothing but Annabel and their marriage. He had eventually decided that there were no innocent partners in a troubled marriage, and if one spouse pointed an accusing finger at the other, it was probably an unrealistic way to solve the problems and save the marriage.

Annabel had not been his wife and partner: he had always expected her to be his second lieutenant, to submerge her individuality to his needs, and to be displayed—Scott's status symbol. He suspected that if she hadn't fallen for that bastard Adam, she'd have fallen for someone else—someone who was prepared to make the effort to make her feel that he cared for her as a person and not as a supportive prop to his self-image as a smart and successful career man.

Scott kissed Annabel's hand. In a frenzied whisper, he told her what he had been longing to say: "I thought my job was a good enough reason to neglect everything else, angel. I didn't mean for it to suck up all my time and energy. Things are going to be different, Annabel. I want to be successful, but I also want my life."

In spite of her woozy state, Annabel could feel his warmth and tenderness. She could feel the difference between Scott's loving attention and the skillful but detached and uninvolved attention she received from Adam.

She whispered, "Scott, I'm so ashamed."

"So am I. In future, I'll be looking after you." He rested his cheek on her arm, which lay on the bedclothes.

"What's . . . happened . . . to me?" Annabel asked.

"A couple of guys mugged you and snatched your purse. The police have to ask you a few things, later. You've got a broken arm and ribs, and . . . they reset your nose. It will look exactly the same—the surgeon swore it would."

"My eyes feel funny."

"They punched your face, angel."

"Are my eyes going to be all right?"

Scott hesitated. "Of course."

"You're such a bad liar, Scott."

After a moment, he said, "Your right eye will be fine."

Annabel's soft sobs hurt her broken ribs.

"You'll certainly be able to see," Scott said. "And it doesn't matter to me . . . Oh Christ, I shouldn't have told you."

"*I want to know.* . . . I don't want to be treated like a child anymore."

"You won't be." Scott again kissed her hand. "In fact, if you still want it . . . I know I've always argued that New York was no place to bring up a child . . . But what the hell—other people do it. Why shouldn't we?"

Annabel stopped crying.

"Can you remember what happened, madam?" the unseen policeman asked quietly.

"Not much," Annabel whispered. "But I'll try."

Just after five o'clock, Annabel had left Adam's home, explaining that she was late for a dress fitting. As she hurried along, her crimson boots occasionally slipped on the slush. She turned left into Pont Street, where she thought she could probably get a cab. There was nobody in sight and very little passing traffic.

Annabel was vaguely aware that a small woman in dark clothes had emerged from the recessed door of a flower shop—already closed for the night—on the corner of Cadogan Lane. As Annabel hurried past, this woman suddenly leapt toward her. Expertly she thrust her left index and middle fingers up Annabel's nostrils, which jerked her head backward. At the same time, the woman hooked her right foot around Annabel's left boot and tugged it forward. Annabel's arms circled wildly as she slipped on the slush.

Desperately she tried to regain her balance but failed. She crashed backward.

From behind, she heard a car draw up. In the light of the streetlamp, she looked up and saw two men with stockings pulled over their heads, flattening their features into terrifying, inhuman shapes.

As the two men jerked Annabel to her feet, twisting her so that she faced the street, she felt the woman grab her red shoulder bag, then saw her jump into the car, take the wheel, and rev the engine.

With a thug on either side of her, Annabel was held in midair. Her elbows pinioned to her body, she was dragged to the rear of an old Morris Minor parked in Cadogan Lane.

As one of her attackers swiftly and roughly searched her, the other hissed, "We've got a message for you. Remember for the future—if you *make* trouble, you *get* trouble!" He drew back his fist, then smashed it in Annabel's jaw.

He continued to hit her with a professional boxer's skill and a steady rhythm as the second man held her more or less upright. Annabel felt agonizing pain in her kidneys; her left ribs seemed to explode. She felt a blow to her chest, then could no longer breathe as her nose was smashed. After the first punch in her eye, she began to lose consciousness.

"Better leave it at that," she heard the second man grunt as she passed out. "You know what happened last time."

In her bronze Reliant Scimitar, Miranda drove Sam to Wiltshire, where Josh was waiting for his dad. Sam had spent the night at the hospital, and felt as stiff and stale as yesterday's bread, but he had promised Josh that he would see him over the weekend. And Miranda wanted to talk to Elinor about the birth certificate.

Jet lag was now catching up with Sam, but Miranda's fast driving over snowy roads in the sports car was sufficiently suspenseful to keep him awake.

Clare waited for them, alone in her kitchen. Elinor and Buzz were having their afternoon nap on the twin beds in the guest room. Josh had happily scuttled off to a Cubs meeting. David, who had to attend the annual meeting of the Kennet and Avon Canal Trust, wasn't due to arrive until evening.

Clare had told David about Annabel's horrific assault, and that she had lost her left eye, but the doctor had warned her not to tell the two older women yet: such a shock might well delay her grandmother's recovery. Although Elinor was still too weak to leave her bed and still spoke in a whisper, she was recovering faster than the doctor had expected; she was responding well to the Parentrovite injections, and her old vitality was returning.

Shortly after three p.m., the Scimitar slid to a halt in front of Applebank Cottage.

Seeing the weary faces of the occupants, Clare asked no questions as she placed the white tureen of mulligatawny soup on the kitchen table.

Sam fell asleep at the table after the cheese omelet and before Clare could serve her apple tart with apricot glazing.

Miranda yawned and said, "I didn't get much sleep last night either. Mind if I have a nap on Josh's bed?" She disappeared.

Clare gently woke Sam and led him upstairs to her bedroom.

At six o'clock, Sam opened his eyes. He could hear faint classical music. The green chintz curtains hadn't yet been closed, and in the firelight, he could see the snow beating silently from the darkness against the windowpanes.

He stretched out a hand, groped for the bedside light, and knocked a brass alarm clock to the floor.

Clare ran upstairs, opened her bedroom door, and flicked on the light switch.

"I'm still a clumsy son of a bitch," Sam said apologetically. He sat up in bed, rubbing his bruised face and black eye.

Clare stared at the crisp black curls that covered his big chest and at the purple bruises inflicted on his arms by Matron Braddock.

"Sit down a minute," Sam said sleepily. He patted the patchwork quilt.

As she perched on the side of the bed, Clare suddenly felt filled with gratitude. "Sam, I can't thank you enough. Maybe we could have done it by ourselves, but . . . you made everything happen so fast. You dealt with that vile nursing home . . . the lawyer . . . the accountant . . . the police . . . the hospital . . . You've been wonderful."

In the firelight, Sam leaned forward and gently kissed the tip of her nose. He put his arms around her, pulled her against his chest, and started kissing her neck. Softly he said, "I have to get back to work the day after tomorrow."

Clare gently pulled away from him, feeling anything but gentle. How *dare* Sam press his advantage and try to seduce her! And yet as she felt indignation rise . . . at the same time . . . although her head was telling her what to do, her body was contradicting the message.

Sam leaned forward, kissed the space between her eyebrows, and tightened his arms around her. Slowly Clare stopped resisting. As she inhaled his familiar acrid odor and remembered the first time she had been aware of his pungent eroticism, she felt as irresistibly drawn to Sam as a pin to a magnet. She remembered how secure she had felt when first encircled by the powerful strength of these muscular, bruised arms. Even as she weakened, she was furious and bewildered. Why didn't she feel this magnetism between herself and David, who was so much better a man than Sam, so much more caring? Why was she even *speaking* to Sam when she knew how hurt David would be if he could see her now?

At this very moment, David was probably collecting Josh from the church hall at Warminster. Tomorrow he was going to help Josh with the work he'd missed, when he was late returning to school after their skiing holiday.

Clare whispered, "I *hate* you, Sam, you manipulative bastard."

"Yes, baby," Sam murmured as he gently kissed her hairline.

"Let me *go*, you bastard," Clare hissed, trying to pull away from him. Sam laughed and kissed her hard on the mouth.

Briefly, Clare tried to remind herself of the way Sam had made her suffer during the past three and a half years, but her memories faded as she felt again the dynamism and protective strength that had first attracted her to him. She didn't want to be independent and sensible; she wanted to lay her head on Sam's hard, hairy chest and feel his arms around her—and know that everything was going to be taken care of by him—just for a few moments.

As her resolve melted and she yielded, somewhere at the back of her head, Clare realized that there was a kernel of truth in Elinor's world of romance.

Later, as Sam slept, Clare lay awake watching the firelight flicker on the ceiling. She felt guilty, treacherous, and miserable.

Just half an hour earlier, after they had made love, she had whispered to Sam, "Why do you *really* want me back? Tell me the truth."

Sam had hugged her hard against his big chest; his crisp, curly hair had tickled her nose as he murmured, "Because I love you."

But Clare knew that the real reasons were not quite so romantic: Sam missed his son, his wife, and family life more than he had ever expected. As a dog becomes accustomed to its basket, Sam had grown used to having Clare around; she made him laugh, she ran his home and his social life, she entertained his clients and took care of all the tedious background trivialities of life; this left Sam free to concentrate on the work he loved.

Clare sighed. Just now Sam had really tried his best. But it had felt as if he was trying. At one point, he had whispered, "What *more* do I have to do? I've been hanging on the chandeliers trying to please you."

And Clare had whispered back, "That's exactly why it isn't going to work, Sam. Because I know you're trying, and so am I. But David and I don't *need* to try."

"What the hell does *he* do that I don't?"

Hesitantly Clare had tried to explain, without hurting Sam. "David accepts me the way I am—the way my body *and* my mind work. David accepts my feelings, so I don't have to twist them to suit his prejudices: he may feel differently—but he isn't going to insist that I agree."

"You mean he's better than me in the sack."

"That just shows you haven't been listening!" Clare felt her indignation grow. "I left you because you didn't *listen* to me, Sam, and you never took me seriously! When I talked to you about something that was important to me, you made the appropriate comments—*but I knew you weren't really hearing me,* because you carried on reading the paper or whatever. That told me that reading the paper was more important than what I had to say!" She sat up in bed. "I felt you weren't really there, that you had removed yourself—to where I couldn't bother you."

"Are you telling me you walked out on me because I didn't *listen* to you?"

In the firelight, Clare lifted her hands in a hopeless gesture. "Sam, you have a conveniently short memory. I left you because I found you in bed with a girl—again."

Sam started to lose his temper. What was the point of bringing up all that again? And if Clare felt so strongly about it—how come they were in bed together? He snapped, "You didn't miss anything. I gave you your orgasms, didn't I? Could one quick fuck in the wrong cunt change so much between *us?*"

Clare snapped back, "Promiscuity devalues the coinage of love." She was adamant. She had learned the hard way that a dishonest sexual relationship could alter a woman's entire life for the worse, because one couldn't separate sex from the rest of reality.

Suddenly Clare knew without a doubt which man she wanted to spend the rest of her life with. Certainly her conscience still told her to take Josh back to his father and let Sam have another chance to prove himself a good husband. But she had already confronted the agonies of conscience over depriving Josh of a father. Why should she endure that again?

And why should she risk going back to Sam? Why should she risk this new, happy life she had struggled so hard to build up—in the hope that he would keep his promise, when he had broken so many promises before?

"I didn't mean that." Sam groped for the words that would reach Clare. "Honey, I'm sorry."

Gently she shook his arm off. She had made her decision, and nothing was going to alter it. Sam was still basically selfish, and David was still basically the unselfish man who had encouraged her to develop her own personality. David was kind and gentle, compassionate and thoughtful. He was a considerate person, and Sam was an inconsiderate person, which is why Sam was a bad lover. Clare remembered that it was this quality in David that had quieted her sexual anxiety. And David's gentle consideration had also lulled the uncertainty within her that had made it difficult for her to stand on her own feet and solve her own problems.

Now as she watched Sam sleep, Clare hoped to God that David would be gentle, compassionate, and understanding when she told him that she had just been to bed with Sam.

At six o'clock that evening, Miranda heard Buzz, in the cottage's only bathroom, singing tunelessly, "All the nice girls love a sailor . . ."

She made a tray of tea and took it up to the guest room. Elinor was sitting in bed pouring Scrabble letters back into the bag.

"I won!" she said triumphantly, then looked anxious. "You don't think Buzz would cheat to let me win?"

"Never," lied Miranda as she poured the tea. She handed a cup to Elinor and said softly, "I have something very important to ask you, Gran. Who is Patricia Kettle?"

With a trembling hand, Elinor slowly put down her cup. "She . . . she had some secretarial job at the War Office." She was clearly making an effort to sound casual. "She was killed in an air raid—sometime in 1943, I think."

"I need to know more than that, darling." Miranda's voice was gentle but determined. She pulled the crumpled birth certificate and Joe Grant's letter from her pocket and handed both to Elinor.

Elinor looked at them sadly. "After all these years . . ." she said. "I suppose . . . you'd better be told what happened." She looked down at her cup of cooling tea, but what she saw was the front room of her home in Earlscourt Square, on Christmas Eve, 1941.

Elinor, wearing the dark green uniform of the Women's Voluntary Service, switched off the wireless. Cheerful news, for a change. In Washington, Churchill was deciding policy with Roosevelt, for after the Japanese surprise attack on the American fleet at Pearl Harbor, the United States had entered the war.

In London, still under threat of German invasion, life seemed to consist either of devastating air raids or of clearing up after them. Like everyone else, Elinor did not get enough sleep, rarely ate a proper meal, and often worked seven days a week, from dawn to long after dark, for the unpaid W.V.S. did any dirty work that seemed to be nobody else's job: they had cared for the exhausted troops evacuated from Dunkirk; they supervised evacuees; they housed and fed the bombed-out; they dislocated their own lives to smooth those of other people.

The O'Dares now lived, ate, and slept in the living room, which arrangement minimized housework, and there was coal only for one fire. On the right of the fireplace opposite the door stood the Morrison shelter—a table-height, four-poster double bed made of iron with metal mesh sides. Inside this shelter slept Clare, nearly three years old, and Annabel, who was a year younger. Elinor also slept in the Morrison, and when there was a raid, Billy left his camp bed to join them.

Objects tended to accumulate along the deep, flat top of the Morrison: Elinor's sewing machine, the notes for her next home-nursing class, a pile of mending, and, tonight, a small Christmas tree that Billy had bought for an exorbitant sum in a pub, and a battered cardboard box.

As Elinor lifted the lid of the box, she smiled with disbelief. Carefully she picked up the golden-haired china angel, with wings of real feathers. "Billy, look! Nothing seems to be broken!" The fragile gold and silver balls, the folded, crinkly multicolored paper bells, the brightly colored, concertina paper chains, lay waiting to be used again on the Christmas tree.

"Why bother with Christmas decorations this year?" Billy asked, from the worn orange-flowered armchair by the fireplace. "The babies won't understand what Christmas is all about. I'm not sure that *I* do. Can't think why you hung up those stockings." He jerked his head to the two red stockings that dangled from the end of the Morrison.

"Stop being an old bear," Elinor said cheerfully. "You're going to play Santa Claus tonight, just as you've always done." She added winningly, "And you're the best-looking Santa in London."

"I always feel a complete fool," Billy grumbled, but he smiled at Elinor and added, "I must admit, girl, you don't look too bad yourself, all things considered. After all, Marjorie is the same age as you, but her skin looks like the Nile Delta."

Although she was past forty, Elinor's looks had worn well and her coloring had not faded. Her creamy skin was unlined; her pink cheeks looked as if she still lived in the country; her blue eyes sparkled; and her hair still waved, honey gold. Of course, her figure had thickened: wartime meals were based on bread and potatoes.

The doorbell rang.

Automatically both adults looked to the window, but the blackout curtains were drawn—no chink of light was showing. So it couldn't be an air-raid warden, about to complain.

Elinor kicked away the sandbag kept at the bottom of the door to cut out drafts. Shivering in the bitter chill of the hall passage, she groped her way to the front door. "Who is it?"

"I'm a friend of Billy," said a woman's voice: it was too dark to see her.

"Come in quickly, out of the cold." After shutting the door, Elinor switched on the hall light and looked at her visitor, who cradled a baby, wrapped in a blanket, in one arm, and carried a small, battered suitcase with the other.

Astonished, Elinor said, "I remember you! Once I saw you speak to my husband in a pub in Whitehall."

It had been on that day Annabel was born. Elinor remembered the distraught face of this girl and her slim-as-a-bulrush, brown-coated figure. She remembered the girl's almost visible aura of depression, her pleading face, and the stooped shoulders that seemed to signal dejection. She remembered that the girl had laid her head on Billy's sleeve. He had roughly shaken her off.

"Who's that?" Billy, clutching the *Daily Telegraph*, opened the front room door.

"Pat! What the hell are you doing *here?*" Billy backed into the room; the woman followed him. To Elinor, he seemed at once startled, truculent, and nervous.

The girl looked at Billy, who wore a shabby knitted cardigan and carpet slippers, no tie. Wearily she said, "You don't look so much of a ladykiller at home, Billy." Her voice was devoid of expression and of hope. "I told you I'd bring her if you didn't turn up." Turning to Elinor, she said abruptly, "It's his." She nodded her head toward the blanket-wrapped bundle in her arms.

"How dare you come here! How dare you make these ridiculous accusations!" Billy blustered.

"Shhhh! You'll wake the girls!" Elinor said automatically as her heart shriveled.

For years, Elinor had subconsciously dreaded just such a scene, had known that Billy would be caught out one day. She was surprised it hadn't happened before. She did not find it difficult to believe the girl, and her words had the surrealist inevitability of a scene déjà vu, although this tired young creature was not the tough, hard-bitten predator Elinor had half expected to appear someday.

Standing in the middle of the room, still clutching the bundle, the young woman started to cry in a soft, hopeless wail. "I *know* Shorty told you I'd had the baby, Billy. He visited me in hospital—brought me two eggs. Every day, I hoped you'd come yourself." She burst into fresh tears. *"Not once!"*

"What the hell do you want?" Billy asked roughly.

"I couldn't stay at the hospital no longer, Billy. I can't go back to the hostel with a baby. I can't go home. My dad would kill me. *I don't know what to do.* Won't you come and look after us, Billy? Remember all those times you promised?"

Billy said, "You have no right to come here and cause trouble between my wife and me."

At his formal tone of voice, the girl's face hardened. She turned to look at Elinor.

Elinor stared back. The threadbare brown coat could not disguise this child's figure; she was clearly unaware of the aura of sexuality that she so strongly projected, and that was probably what had attracted Billy. Elinor was irritatingly aware that her own green W.V.S. uniform made her look dumpy.

The girl said to Billy, "Why do you want to stay with *her?*" She jerked her head toward Elinor.

With a nervous, shaking hand, Elinor pointed to the chimneypiece, upon which stood two silver-framed photographs: Edward, aged seven, and Edward and Jane on their wedding day.

She said, "Billy and I have been married for twenty-three years. That is Billy's son. Billy's granddaughters are sleeping in this room. We are Billy's family, and he will never leave us." Her voice rang with a quiet confidence that she did not feel, although Elinor knew that Billy depended on her strength, ability, and ingenuity to look after him in wartime and still provide him with his home comforts: Billy liked to be looked after; Billy did not want to find himself responsible for this wilting woman-child and her helpless, dependent infant.

"*But you can't dump me!*" Pat Kettle pleaded. "It's your job to look after us, Billy. There's nobody else."

This was a fatal error. Billy took a hesitant step behind Elinor.

"You can't pretend we don't exist!" Miss Kettle wailed. The baby in her arms started to cry. "*Tell me what to do, Billy!* I can't look after a baby and earn my living at the same time!" She looked beseechingly at Billy. "It's *your* baby—whatever you like to think. You *know* I've never been with another man! *I love you, Billy!*" She appealed to Elinor. "*It's his baby as much as mine!* Why should I have all the responsibility? *He's* got a home and someone to look after it—I haven't."

Raising his voice above the baby's yells, Billy said, "I'm not admitting it's mine." He turned to Elinor. "I admit . . . Well, you saw for yourself that she threw herself at me. But it only happened a couple of times. And it . . . was never anything serious. And if it hadn't been for her bloody stupid religion, she could have taken precautions! *That* was her responsibility!"

At this point, the noise woke Annabel, who started to cry. Clare woke up and bawled in sympathy. Billy clapped his hands over his ears and turned away from the two women, toward the window.

Almost incredulous, the girl stared at his rejecting back. "Well, *I* can't cope any longer," she said, and laid the blanket-wrapped baby on top of the Morrison shelter. Then, sobbing, she hurried from the room.

A small, clenched fist thrust up from the wailing, jerking bundle, which rolled toward the edge of the Morrison.

As Elinor jumped forward to stop the baby from falling to the floor, she heard the front door bang.

Defensively Billy said, "Stupid bitch." To break the angry silence, he turned on the wireless. The Andrews Sisters sang cheerfully about the Boogie-Woogie Bugler Boy from Company B.

With the baby in one arm, Elinor switched off the wireless. She glared at Billy. "There's some dried milk in the larder. Make me a jugful. Quickly. This baby is hungry."

She would pretend that this baby was Edward and Jane's third daughter; a six-week baby couldn't be passed off as a ten-month baby, but her new birth date would have to be before Jane's death. So Elinor would have to keep this infant away from the neighbors for a bit; then she would say that the baby had been born prematurely, had been tiny at birth and was still small for her age, and had been kept in hospital for months . . . Luckily, Annabel and Clare were too young to remember anything strange about the arrival of this sister . . . It would be easy to pretend.

"What happened to . . . my mother?" Miranda whispered

"I never saw Miss Kettle again," Elinor said apologetically. "I've no idea whether Billy still carried on with her after that. I doubt she'd have let him. We never spoke of it again."

"She abandoned me. My *mother* abandoned me," Miranda said with disbelief.

"She was very young and clearly at the end of her tether. Be generous," Elinor said.

"No!" Miranda's voice was almost a shriek; her face was ashen white. "Please, I don't want this. I want my sisters and I want you to be . . . *I love you,* Gran! I want to be part of *your* family. You're the one who has always looked after me, the one I've always loved!"

"So you are," Elinor said firmly. She held out her frail arms and pulled Miranda against her. "Some people are born into a family and some people are chosen. I chose you long ago, Miranda, and I love you every bit as much as I love Annabel and Clare." She stroked Miranda's hair. "They are your sisters, and I trust you never to tell them otherwise."

"But then I'll be lying to Clare and Annabel," Miranda cried. "I can't look them in the eyes and know that I'm hiding something so important from them!" She stepped back from Elinor. "I'm not going to lie to them," she said. "I'm not going to deceive them. *And I'm not going to lie to myself!* Then I *really* won't know who I am!" She started to sob. "How can I behave normally, as a sister, if I know I'm lying to them all the time? . . . *You've* always been able to shut your eyes to what you don't want to see, or put on your rose-colored spectacles so that you only see what suits you in life. But *I* want to face up to life, and deal with what's unpleasant, rather than hide or ignore it. I can't live with the people I love, knowing that I'm acting a lie all the time—deceiving them. *I can't do that!* I could never behave naturally with them and I would have no peace of mind—I couldn't stand it. It would always be on my conscience."

"Please, darling," Elinor implored, "you've always been impetuous as well as straightforward. This time please listen to me. Annabel and Clare were too young to know. If I deceived you and your sisters, it was because I love you all very much, and I love you all the same. It's often thought best not to let an orphan know she's adopted, but to raise her as one of the family; that is what I did with you."

"But Gran, you can't imagine how I feel. It's as though someone had suddenly pushed me over a cliff, and I'm falling into a void. I feel rootless. My life is never going to be the same again. I don't belong anywhere. . . ."

"Nonsense. You belong with us, as you always have." Elinor's thin hand stroked Miranda's arm. "Because although this sounds important—*it isn't*. It doesn't change anything: you're still an O'Dare— still one of the family . . . *our* family. What happened was upsetting for me at the time, but if it hadn't happened, then I wouldn't have had my third granddaughter—so I'm glad it did!"

Miranda bit her lower lip. "Nevertheless, I can't keep something like this from my . . . from Clare and Annabel."

"There's a difference between being dishonest and being discreet," Elinor said. "Everyone is morally entitled to guard their privacy to protect themselves; everyone does that, all the time. Nobody blabs their secrets to the world. Sometimes discretion—and I refuse to call it 'dishonesty'—is the best policy."

"But they're not 'the world'! They're . . . my sisters . . . and I want them to know the truth."

"Then I would prefer that you didn't tell them yet. I don't want them to be distressed on your behalf: we've had enough upsets recently in this family. Besides, there's nothing to be gained by telling them the truth. Not now."

Miranda stared at her. "How can *you* judge that? You, who always ran from the truth if it didn't suit you! You, who lied in so many ways—by omission, by insinuation. Gran, you lied to everyone, most especially to yourself. *Why did you do it?*"

Elinor paused before she spoke again; the pain was evident in her voice. "Why does anyone lie? Fear. I was afraid of violence, afraid of the deeper unhappiness—perhaps despair—that I would feel if I had to admit to myself that my life was unhappy; I was afraid of having to face the world alone—every woman's fear—and of being unable to cope. I'm afraid I'm not very brave, Miranda."

Miranda said nothing; her face reflected mute confusion.

Elinor pressed her argument persuasively: "Miranda, you can't see this thing objectively right now—nobody in your position could. So please promise me that you won't say anything to anyone yet."

"Gran, Gran, how can I let you decide anything about this? You're as subjective as I am. *How can I trust your judgement?*"

"I'm only asking you to give yourself time, to think more calmly about the matter."

After reflection, Miranda nodded her head slowly. "All right. I'll agree to that."

"And should you eventually decide that they should be told, then let *me* tell them. . . ." Elinor persisted.

"Okay," Miranda responded wearily.

"And let *me* choose the time and the place to tell them. Just promise me that, darling."

With great reluctance, Miranda said, "Yes, if that's what you want."

Elinor sighed with relief. She had managed to postpone this unhappy matter, but what was more important was that she had managed quickly to persuade Miranda that this hurtful revelation was of no consequence—and that was certainly true.

Miranda threw her head back and stared unhappily at her grandmother. "There's another thing I also feel ashamed about. All my life I've howled for my fair share of whatever was going—I felt it was my moral right. I felt cheated when I was left out of something because I was the youngest. I even insisted that I was morally entitled to inherit one third of all your money. I always made a point of *that!* And now I realize I'm not entitled to a single penny! Adam knew that. Why else would he have my birth certificate? It gave him proof I wasn't entitled to any of the Dove Trust. Oh, Gran, I've been such a greedy little bitch! How could you stand me?"

"Hush, darling. I don't want to hear any more of this nonsense. The youngest child often feels left out, and I always understood how you felt. All *any* child is entitled to is a good education and perhaps a start in life, and luckily I was able to give you that. As to the rest . . . Who knows whether I'm going to have *any* money to leave anybody? But we're none of us going to be homeless and starving. And, anyway, that's not what matters right now." She tightened her arms around Miranda, and Miranda felt like a little girl again, being comforted in Elinor's arms.

Then Elinor slowly said, "Perhaps I *also* need that peace of mind of which you spoke."

Chapter · 32

Mike wore his black leathers with the jacket unzipped; he stood, legs astride, before the pine log fire in Adam's study. His face was white, and his clear, wide-apart gray eyes reflected his fury—and his horror.

Adam brandished the *Evening Standard*. " '*Society beauty loses eye*'!" he shouted. "I told you to *scare* her—not half kill her! You can't hush up this sort of thing, you know!"

"I'm just as worried as you are. How do you suppose *I* feel?" Mike had rarely seen his brother so angry. Bad-tempered, yes, but not this towering fury. Unlike Mike, whose self-control could easily snap if he was sufficiently provoked, Adam usually kept his feelings under tight control.

"How the hell did it happen?"

"These people aren't always controllable—*you* know that, Adam! One of the reasons they do it is because they *enjoy* it. They don't *want* to stop."

Adam roared, "You didn't even get my notebooks back!"

"There were *no* notebooks in Annabel's purse, just the usual junk," Mike again insisted. "Her clothes were searched as well—they found nothing."

Adam didn't bother to mention that the notebooks were upstairs in his desk, as usual. He felt chagrined that he hadn't checked on them before having Annabel beaten up. He had a sudden thought. "I'd better make sure that Elinor doesn't find out about this! Of course she doesn't read the papers, but there's a TV stuck in front of her bloody bed! It could mean trouble!" As he spoke, he snatched up the telephone and dialed the long-distance operator.

When connected, Adam brusquely addressed the receptionist: "Get me Matron Braddock. . . . What do you *mean*, she's resigned? . . . Then give me Dr. Craig-Dunlop!"

The receptionist stammered, "Dr. Craig-Dunlop is cruising in the Caribbean, on his winter vacation."

"When will he return?" Adam's voice was harsh.

"Dr. Craig-Dunlop has already left the cruise ship," quavered the receptionist. "He's flying back to Britain as fast as he can. I'll telephone your office as soon as he arrives, Mr. Grant."

Adam could have kicked himself. He should have checked on Elinor every single goddamn day. Why hadn't the doctor told him that he was going on a cruise? Why hadn't someone told him that the matron was leaving? My God, if you wanted anything done, you had to do it yourself.

Sharply he asked, "And in the meantime, *who* is in charge of the nursing home? . . . Then tell the assistant matron that I want to speak to her immediately. . . . To discuss one of her patients, of course. . . . Mrs. O'Dare."

The receptionist stammered, "We have strict instructions not to talk about Mrs. O'Dare."

Adam was almost speechless with anger. "*I* am Mrs. O'Dare's lawyer!" His voice dropped as, carefully, he asked, "Is Mrs. O'Dare dead?"

There was a long pause.

"Well, is she or isn't she?" Adam growled, his anxiety once more surfacing.

"No. Mrs. O'Dare hasn't passed away," said the receptionist reluctantly. "But I can't tell you more than that."

Clearly there was a lot more to be told. Something odd was happening at the Lord Willington, and Adam was sure he would get more information from this stupid bitch at the desk than from the assistant matron. He barked, "I'm coming down to Eastbourne immediately unless you tell me what's happened to Mrs. O'Dare."

The terrified receptionist didn't want this bullying lawyer yelling at her in person. She blurted out, "That wouldn't do any good—Mrs. O'Dare's no longer here!"

"*What do you mean, she isn't there?*" Adam bellowed.

Prudently the receptionist pulled the line from the switchboard.

Adam turned to Mike. "I've been cut off. Deliberately, I suspect. I wonder what the *hell* is happening."

Mike was astonished by the speed with which his brother's interest had switched from the frightening problem of Annabel's injuries to trouble at Elinor's nursing home. Why should it matter so much to Adam where Elinor was? And it was obvious that Adam had hoped she was dead. *Why?*

The answer had to be money, Mike figured. He'd probably rigged her will—something like that. What a cold-blooded bastard his brother was.

Adam tapped a finger against his teeth as he considered what to do. He decided, "I'd better get down to the nursing home and check what's happened." He looked at his watch. "Six o'clock." Snatching up the telephone, he said, "The quickest way to Eastbourne is by train. When's the next express?"

Having gained this information, Adam turned to Mike. "You can take me to Victoria Station on your bike!" he ordered. "The next train leaves in fifteen minutes, so get going, you lazy bastard!"

Mike stared, surprised. Normally Adam would never deign to ride a motorbike. He didn't understand why Mike chose to drive a bike—like a greaser—when he had a perfectly good, new E-Type that could go far faster than all his two-wheeled monsters. Adam didn't seem to realize that a motorbike was no longer a poor man's transport method: Bikes were dangerous and exciting. A man who rode a bike was a man ready for action. And even the most expensive Ferrari was a vanishing dot in the rearview mirror of a fast bike.

But apparently, Adam did realize that during the rush hour, no transport was faster for weaving in and out of London traffic than a motorbike.

"Come *on!*" Adam urged brusquely, hurrying toward the door. In the hall, he pulled on his overcoat and waited impatiently as Mike buckled his German officer's black leather trench coat—liberated from the original owner by their uncle, in Munich, in 1945. "Hurry!" Adam snapped.

Both brothers clattered down the back stairs rather than wait for the slow, wheezing elevator. As he did so, Mike fastened his helmet strap and pulled on his leather gloves: if he came off, he preferred to sacrifice the leather and not his skin.

Outside, it was already dark. The weak morning sunshine had dissolved the slush, and the roads were now dry.

"For Christ's sake, *get moving!*" Adam snarled.

The bike didn't start at Mike's first kick.

"Mike the Bike!" Adam jeered. Even Adam knew that only legendary racer Mike Hailwood was known as Mike the Bike. He also knew that his brother didn't like to be teased about his bikes.

Mike, on edge after hearing the bad news about Annabel, turned his head and said, "Don't take your bloody bad temper out on me!"

"I'll say whatever I bloody well like to you, and you'll bloody well do whatever I tell you to do!" Adam yelled.

As always, Mike was bewildered by Adam's abrupt change of mood. He understood the hard shell into which Adam retreated when the world became too threatening; he also understood the depth of feeling in Adam that lay hidden from the rest of the world. But Mike never understood why his brother always chose to vent his vile moods on him—of all people.

Mike kicked the starter again. The bike merely coughed.

"Why doesn't this fucking machine *work?*" Adam screamed. He kicked the side panel.

"Don't kick my bike," Mike growled. After years of being at Adam's mercy, being humiliated by him, being the recipient of his bad-tempered kicks and snarls, Mike was finally pushed to violent action. He decided it was time that Adam stopped treating him like a dog. It was time—more than time—that he taught Adam a lesson. He would show him that he *wasn't* always in the superior position. *For once, Mike would be in control.* He was going to give Adam the fright of his life.

The black Egli Vincent with the nickel-plated frame started on the third kick. Listening to the thundering noise from the throbbing 1,000cc V twin, Mike smiled to himself. The Vincent engine was tuned to Black Lightning Specification, capable of doing a hundred and forty miles an hour.

Mike turned from Cadogan Place, then left onto Pont Street. With a roar, the bike shot ahead into Belgrave Square, a central garden encircled by cream, classical buildings.

"Hey!" Half deafened by the noise from the exhaust, Adam yelled over Mike's shoulder, *"This is a one-way street! You just turned the wrong way!"*

Mike smiled. He knew that at this time of night, there was never much traffic in Belgrave Square.

The Egli tore at increasing speed around the black-spiked railings that surrounded the central garden.

"What the fuck do you think you're doing?" Adam screamed into the wind.

His brother's terrified reaction made Mike grin. The euphoria went right to his head, like a glass of fizzing champagne on an empty stomach. His bike throbbed beneath him, leaping ahead.

The harsh wind on Adam's face forced tears from the corners of his eyes. The buildings were leaning out at him. No, the bike was leaning in. He felt dizzy and frightened. As the Egli swerved to avoid a sedate limousine, Adam screamed, and his arms tightened around Mike's waist.

Mike laughed. He could still hear an enraged horn behind them as, with a thunder of exhaust, he slid out of Belgrave Square. He knew it seemed to Adam that he was handling the Egli with violence—even savagery; Adam probably thought that he wasn't completely in charge of his machine, though Mike knew that he was.

Leaving the square, Mike should have turned right, toward Victoria Station. Instead, he turned left.

"This isn't the way to Victoria Station! Where the fuck do you think you're going?" The wind flung Adam's words back into his mouth.

At this point, Adam seriously considered throwing himself from the Egli, but that would be even more dangerous, with all the traffic, on this dark night, than clinging to his brother.

As the bike picked up speed, Mike felt increasingly exhilarated. Adam, who never spared a thought for other people, now knew what it felt like to be at someone else's mercy, to endure violence, to be terrified.

Ahead of the Egli loomed a high triumphal arch with elaborate gates. Mike headed toward these closed gates, as if to smash straight into them.

Adam screamed.

At the last minute, the Egli swerved.

Now, to Adam's left, shadowed trees threatened him from beneath old-fashioned lamplight; to his right loomed the spike-topped walls of Buckingham Palace.

"Lean in with me!" Mike yelled over his shoulder.

The Egli started to slalom. In terrifying fashion, the gleaming monster wove in and out of the moving vehicles. The shrieks of protesting horns could be heard even above the howl of the bike. Adam ducked his head behind Mike's body and clung to him, concentrating simply on staying alive and thinking only from one moment to the next.

With a powerful roar, the bike zoomed around the statue in front of Buckingham Palace and up the Mall, where Mike took the Egli up to maximum speed.

Adam's cheeks were forcibly drawn back, and his breath torn from his mouth. The crenellated walls of St. James's Palace blurred past on his left. In front of the Egli, traffic lights were red.

Mike did not reduce speed.

Adam shut his eyes.

Just as the Egli reached the lights, they switched to amber. The Egli roared on, at full throttle.

Adam, surprised to find himself still alive, opened his eyes to see, ahead, the stately gray curve of Admiralty Arch.

With a squeal of tires, Mike viciously decelerated, turning into Trafalgar Square. Briefly the Egli's front wheel left the ground.

Adam's brain began functioning again as the bike slowed down.

"What do I have to do to get you to stop? What do you want?" he yelled to a background cacophony of loud bangs as the engine backfired on the overrun, and flames flashed from the exhaust.

Mike swung the bike to the right, calling over his shoulder, "Ten percent of what you're getting from the Dove Trust."

"Bugger that!" yelled Adam. *"No!"*

Mike grinned. So he had guessed correctly. Adam *was* milking the trust. He flicked his wrist and the speed increased.

They were circling Trafalgar Square now. In the square, the base of Nelson's Column was guarded by four enormous bronze lions in a semicircle of iron posts. Behind this were two pools, their fountains of bronze mermaids and dolphins floodlit from below. Naturally, no tourists or slick-selling touts were hanging about after dark in the cold, but there was plenty of traffic around the square. The Egli thundered past weary, double-decker, red buses and licorice-black taxis.

Adam again wondered whether it was more dangerous to stay on the bike or hurl himself off. He half decided to throw himself off, knowing that Mike would have to slow down when he turned right—*if* he turned right—at the top of the square.

But as the Egli climbed uphill toward the top, Adam saw the row of posts that protected the stone steps leading down into the square; to hit one of those iron guards with his head would mean a funeral march.

He decided to hang on tight and remember what a good driver Mike was—although it was no use thinking that Mike wouldn't put himself at risk, because a biker did that all the time.

Mike swerved to the right. The Egli dodged between two posts.

Adam—beyond screaming—gurgled hoarsely as the motorbike slithered down the shallow steps to the square.

A crowd of pigeons fluttered into the air as the Egli bounced from the steps, then passed the ornamental pools, thundered past the dark, crouching lions, and bumped onto the road again.

Again Mike flicked the bike to the right. Dear God, Adam thought. He's going to do that nightmare stunt *again!*

He leaned forward and yelled into Mike's ear, *"All right! Ten percent. You win!"*

Mike grinned into the wind. He knew Adam wouldn't give him a penny, but Mike wasn't serious about the money. He didn't want it. What he wanted was to be in control and have Adam begging for mercy—just once.

"You're sure you *really* want to give me ten percent?" Mike teased over his shoulder as the Egli again circled the square.

"Yes!"

"Sure?"

"Yes! Yes!"

"I don't believe you!" Mike's laugh was torn by the wind. He was really enjoying this ride.

As the Egli tore past the top of the square for the second time, it continued straight ahead. Like a howling black and silver bullet, the motorbike shot past the policeman at the traffic lights. Then Mike turned left, into the Strand.

On Adam's right shone the lights of Charing Cross Station. The bike's acceleration made him feel nauseous. He hoped he wouldn't vomit . . .

Hell, what did it matter if he did?

The first set of lights were green.

The second set of lights were green.

Adam's heart thudded against his chest as the Egli thundered toward the third set of traffic lights, where the road was divided by central iron railings.

The third set of lights were green.

As the bike charged on, Adam ducked his head and glimpsed the silvery metal portico of the Savoy Hotel. Top-hatted porters in green uniform stood before revolving doors.

Mike slammed the bike to the left, curved around the island of the Aldwych, then drove back toward the Savoy.

At this point, the downpour that had been threatening all afternoon suddenly started. Mike immediately slowed down.

Adam, relieved, hunched his back, but couldn't prevent the rain from streaming down the back of his neck. He dared not let go with one hand to turn up his coat collar. He would *kill* Mike when he finally stopped!

As they approached the brilliantly lit cul-de-sac where the Savoy Hotel stood, the traffic lights changed to green, which allowed the Egli right-of-way.

Not noticing that the lights had changed, a majestic maroon Bentley slowly drew out of the cul-de-sac onto the main road.

Mike hurriedly swerved to the right to avoid the tank-tough Bentley. He then swerved again to avoid the central line of iron railings that divided the road.

In front of the Egli, an Italian businessman had just paid his taxi fare. Without looking, from force of habit he mistakenly opened the right-hand passenger door.

The Egli charged into the open door of the taxi.

The door ripped from its hinges. The plump Italian was flung back into the interior of the cab, with a broken thumb. Mike and Adam were hurled into the air over the door of the taxi.

Head-on, Adam crashed into an ornate pale blue lamppost. He was thrown backward onto the pavement.

The Egli slid down the Strand on its left side, the footrest and handlebars raising a shower of sparks from the road.

After that, nothing seemed to happen for a long time.

Mike lay on his back in the road, between the cab and his bike. As he tried to sit up, pain shot through his left arm and leg, and he fell back. He clapped his right arm to his left and touched shredded flesh and sticky blood: the arm of his jacket had been ripped off. He fumbled for his left thigh and felt the shredded remains of his trouser leg. But his kneecap was still there. He tried again, unsuccessfully, to bend his knee.

Slowly Mike lifted his head and looked around. The Egli lay on its left side, wheels still spinning. "Shit!" At least his broken leg would mend, but he realized that his irreplaceable bike was a write-off.

As rain streamed down on him, he painfully pulled himself up on his right elbow. Where was Adam? He twisted his body to the right so that he could see behind him.

About seven feet behind, Adam lay, inert, on the road.

In spite of the rain, passersby with coat collars turned up gathered on the pavement. A woman screamed, "Someone get the police!" A man in black bowler hat and fashionable overcoat hurried toward Mike, who was now crawling down the middle of the road.

Mike shook his head to the offer of help; with gritted teeth, he inched his way toward his brother. Soon he was near enough to see that the top of Adam's head was missing and his neck lolled at an odd angle. Blood and dark splotches of brain splattered the pavement.

With hoarse groans, Mike started to cry.

A policeman came up to him and draped his black rain cape over Mike, but Mike shook it off. When the ambulance arrived, he was huddled by the side of the road, hugging Adam in his arms and rocking him back and forth. Tears ran down his filthy, bloodied, torn face.

The two paramedics gently pried Mike's arms away from Adam's body. One said, "It's all right, mate, we'll look after him now."

"Be careful of him," Mike said through sobs. "He's my *brother*."

"Course we will, mate. Leave him to us."

Rain slashed down as the two paramedics slid Adam onto the stretcher. As they lifted him, his left arm flopped over the side, and Mike glimpsed a gleam of gold.

"His watch! I'd better look after his watch for him," he said. Adam was fond of that watch for some reason. He'd never forgive Mike if someone nicked it on the way to the hospital.

The paramedics glanced at each other. The poor sod couldn't accept that his brother was a goner. The policeman unstrapped the Omega watch, replaced Adam's arm on the stretcher, and handed the watch down to Mike. "They'll be right back for you, sir," he said. Once again he covered Mike with his black rain cape.

Mike glanced at the watch and turned it over. In the light of the streetlamp that had killed his brother he noticed five lines of figures engraved on the back of it.

Mike felt sick; then he felt faint. He put the watch down beside him on the stone curb and flopped on the pavement. He still hoped that this scene was as unreal as it seemed to him. He still hoped that he would have the chance to tell Adam how sorry he was for trying to frighten him.

When the paramedics returned to load Mike on the stretcher, he forgot about the watch. It lay under the lamplight, on the blood-streaked curbstone, and the raindrops fell softly upon it.

Chapter · 33

— decorative element —

TUESDAY, 1 APRIL 1969

"Darling Gran, may I phone you back?" Miranda looked at the pile of folders on her desk. "I have a directors' meeting in ten minutes, and Adam left so much to straighten out—as if I hadn't enough work!"

"I hope you're allowing enough time for the wedding preparations," Elinor reminded her anxiously.

"Oh, Angus is organizing our wedding. I'm not allowed to do a thing. He won't even tell me where we're going on our honeymoon. Even the doctor who gave me my shots wouldn't tell me. Just smiled as he said, 'This one's anticholera—you can't be too careful in Brighton.'"

"I can't help wishing that you and Clare were having a double wedding."

"You know Clare and David would hate a grand wedding. And besides, you're only allowed your *first* wedding in church." Miranda glanced at her watch. "Darling, can't this wait until I see you on Saturday?"

"I had the feeling that you might be so busy you'd cancel Saturday. I'm really just calling to make sure you don't."

"I must admit I thought of it. I reckon I could almost catch up, given an uninterrupted working weekend."

"Not this weekend," Elinor said firmly. "You promised to drive Annabel down here, and it's the last time we'll all be together for goodness knows how long. Scott arrives on Monday to take her for her final checkup at St. George's, and then they're both flying back to New York."

"Well, if you insist," Miranda said reluctantly, "I *will* be there."

"I do, Miranda," Elinor said. "This is important. I have something to tell you all, something I should have told you long ago. It's a story . . . a rather special story."

"Darling, you've been telling stories for forty—"

"I know," Elinor's quiet voice interrupted, "but this is *my* story, Miranda, and I can't live alone with it any longer."

A touch of *Wuthering Heights,* Miranda thought, sighing. "I may be the first bride to walk down the aisle of St. Margaret's, Westminster, with a briefcase in her hand, but of course I'll come if it's important to you."

SATURDAY, 5 APRIL 1969

"Only another five minutes," Miranda said as she swung the Reliant Scimitar off the main road toward Clare's cottage. She added, "Now remember, Annabel, in front of Gran, you *don't* mind wearing that eye patch."

"Of course not. I adore wearing the goddamn thing. It gives me an air of mystery, like the man in the Hathaway shirt ads." Annabel paused. "Actually, you know, I do rather like the eye patch because it reminds me that I'm *not* as I was before. Oh, I know the plastic surgeon has promised me the scars will go away, and I know the glass eye will look every bit as natural as the one I lost, but in an odd way, that mugging freed me. It's freed me to be myself—and I'm only just starting to find out who I am, because up to now I've hidden behind an eight-by-ten glossy print. And you know what? So far my real self has been *quite* a surprise to me."

"We're all proud of the new, grown-up Annabel—especially Gran."

"She certainly seems back to normal—tough as old boots."

"Buzz says she wakes up happy every morning, just because she's not in that grim nursing home."

"I still don't understand why she won't sue that awful doctor," Annabel said.

"Craig-Dunlop is bound to have covered himself legally, and it would just drag on and on in the courts, as Mr. Owen told us," Miranda reminded her. "It's much better for Gran to try and forget the whole thing, and look forward to something pleasant. She and Buzz are planning a trip to the south of France. They want to find a small farmhouse, where they can start a new life and put this behind them."

"Oh, I wish we all could." Annabel sighed. "There are just so many unanswered questions. I suppose Adam's watch hasn't turned up yet?"

"No. One of the ambulance paramedics remembers a policeman unstrapping it from Adam's wrist and handing it to Mike, but since then there's been so sign of it. Mike probably dropped it on the street, which means anything could have happened to it. Someone may have walked off with it, or it might have been destroyed, in which case some Swiss bank will hang on to all that money! I can't bear to think of it!"

"I don't understand why our lawyers are offering that huge reward, especially since nobody's even certain that those bank account numbers were engraved on the back of the watch. It's only guesswork by Angus."

"I'd bet on it. Those numbers *must* be written down somewhere," Miranda said. "The detectives found nothing in Adam's home or office. Besides, it really is more than guesswork by Angus. He says that those numbers have to be written down somewhere. Some people engrave them on backs of signet rings, or maybe inside a pocket watch. We've checked all of Adam's jewelry and found nothing. No, it must be that watch; he was always so protective of it. And who knows? Maybe it'll turn up."

"I suppose we should be grateful that Adam didn't get *all* Gran's money," Annabel said ruefully.

"No, there's still about seventeen percent left in the trust—a little over one and a half million pounds," Miranda replied. "Plus, the lawyers think the trust will be awarded all of Adam's shares in SUPPLYKITS in lieu of the money he so clearly stole: the trust will then own forty-six percent of the company, which is worth about two and a half million pounds. Plus, the royalties on Gran's novels keep coming in, so there really is plenty. In American dollars, what's left in the trust should total at least ten million."

"That's all well and good," said Annabel, "but I *still* don't understand why the trust wasn't protected, when we were told it was insured for millions."

"Because Adam was careful to do nothing overtly illegal," Miranda explained, yet again. "His taking money from the trust and squirreling it away in some secret place was obviously not Gran's intent, but the fact remains that she gave him her power of attorney, a document that virtually said, 'I hereby authorize Adam Grant to do anything he likes with everything I own.' "

"I wonder whether Adam would have been able to get away with it if he'd been dealing with men, not women," Annabel mused.

"Probably not," Miranda said. "God knows men aren't any smarter, but most of them are brought up to be self-reliant, to look after themselves more, and not to always be so dependent . . . and trusting."

After lunch, when Josh had gone out to play, Elinor looked at the expectant faces around the table and knew that there would never be a better moment to tell them.

Quietly, she related the truth of Miranda's parentage.

"The dirty dog," Buzz said.

Clare looked at Miranda's wary face and slowly said, "It doesn't alter anything between us, you know."

Annabel added, "Of course not."

Then they all started talking at once. Everyone hugged Miranda.

Eventually, Elinor said, "At first I didn't want you to know about this . . . unpleasantness, but Miranda insisted, and when she did I realized there was something else you had to be told." She took a deep breath, "You all think I don't want to talk about what happened with Adam—but I *do*. All my life, I've allowed myself to ignore the lessons I should have learned and to forget the ones I should have remembered. Well, *not this time!* I can't. I can't go on pretending that bad things don't happen, that the happy ending will always come along. Not after this. Not after I've seen my family almost destroyed. All because I couldn't deal with reality and always, always refused to face unpleasant facts. I now see that if, ostrich-like, you pretend not to see your own problems, then you can't solve them."

An astonished silence greeted this firm speech: Elinor had clearly regained her old strength.

"Don't be too hard on yourself, Gran," Annabel said. "We've survived."

"Only just! You and I could have been killed! I almost lost my reason, not to mention most of my money. *Your* money. Miranda lost control of her business. Buzz found herself with no home and no income. And Clare was almost lost to me forever. *How did I let that happen?*"

"Don't blame yourself, Nell," Buzz said. "*Nobody* noticed what was happening because Adam was a con man, and nobody spots a successful con man—until it's too late. And he was very good—he could have fooled anyone."

Elinor slowly shook her head. "I mustn't hide behind excuses. Not this time, and not ever again. I could have stopped all this before it started, and *I know why I didn't.*"

Everyone stared at Elinor.

"You see, I didn't trust myself to handle my own problems," she explained. "If any man said, 'This isn't the sort of thing that a woman understands,' then I immediately decided that I didn't understand it, and let him handle it."

Gently Clare said, "Gran, I'm so pleased that you can finally admit this."

"I always expected a man to look after me," Elinor went on. "I always believed that a man would know best. Now I know how wrong I was, and I regret it. It's harmed all of you."

"Nonsense, darling!" Annabel cried. "You've never hurt us. And you've always given us everything we needed."

Elinor looked around the table. "Yes, everything. Except the truth. *That's* why Annabel and Miranda expected a perfect Prince Charming.

I now realize that happiness is not hoping for protection by an illusory, perfect man, but in discovering the surprising strength of one's imperfect self—that inner core, the 'real me' that every woman senses. Only Clare always said I confused romance with reality. When she fought me, I was determined not to let her win. . . . I *couldn't* let her win, because losing would mean tearing down the facade that I'd carefully erected to conceal the truth of my life—most especially from myself—because my reality was so painful."

"Surely not after Daddy Billy died?" Annabel asked.

"*Especially* after Billy died." Elinor paused, then continued quietly: "It's time I also told you the truth about Billy's death, time I stopped remembering a fake life and started to live a real one . . . in the real world."

Elinor paused again. She knew it would take all her ability as a storyteller and all her strength as a survivor to tell this, her most difficult story, because she had lived the lie for so long that she had almost come to believe it. But now the truth had to be told—without sentiment, without romance.

"On the day Billy died," Elinor began, "I'd visited my publishers in London. They'd called me there for press interviews, but there was also another reason they wanted to see me. When I arrived at their office, I found that Joe Grant was also there. Unsavory stories were being spread, stories that threatened my good name and ultimately threatened my growing success as a writer. Apparently, they were being spread by Billy—silly rumors to get him attention and sympathy rather than harming me. For the most part, no one had paid attention to them.

"However, the latest story was not so easily dismissed. It didn't come from Billy, but it involved him, and it was ugly. It seems he had bothered a young girl . . . No, that's not quite it." She hesitated, determined to tell the story straight. "It seems he had *molested* a young girl, or at least attempted to do so. Apparently Billy offered to photograph her, then tried to take off her clothes. Afterwards, when the girl made trouble and threatened to contact me through my publisher, Billy confessed to Joe Grant, who tried to hush up the situation; he decided I had better be warned. In fact I already knew. Maybe not about this one, but there had been others. I had even once confronted Billy. He denied it, of course. And of course I tried hard to believe him."

In the silence of her kitchen, Clare said, "Gran, does that matter now? It all happened so long ago . . ."

"It mattered then," Elinor said, "because I knew I would have to speak to Billy about it. I had to make him realize his danger—the danger for all of us. But in order to do that, he would have to admit his folly to me, and to himself. I knew it would be almost impossible, but I *had* to try.

I was too depressed to talk to him when I got back from London that evening, and anyway, he wasn't home when I returned, exhausted, at ten—an hour before the pubs closed. Neither was Buzz." She looked at her friend. "Remember, you were spending your summer holiday with us at Starlings and had gone to a church whist party that night? So I went straight to bed. But I was woken just before midnight . . ." Elinor's eyes closed.

She could almost hear the slow, ponderous stumbling as Billy pulled himself up the stairs, and the high-pitched, unearthly sound that had wakened her. She had leapt from her bed and run to the landing. A disheveled Billy stood halfway up the stairs. His right hand clutched the fluffy white nursery cat by its hind legs; it was the cat's anguished, terrified howls that had roused Elinor. Billy's other hand was stretched out to Annabel, who stood frozen in fright only a few steps above him.

Annabel said quietly, "Yes, I remember. Daddy Billy was tormenting Snowball. And you pulled me away and told me to go back to bed and stay there. I heard noises, but I was too frightened to leave my bed again."

"That's what I wanted," Elinor said. "What happened next was my secret and I thought that if no one ever knew about it, then it wouldn't be true, that it never really happened, you see.

"But it did happen, of course. As soon as Annabel was gone, I grabbed the cat from Billy's hand. As I did, he reached out, clutching at me. His hand caught in the lace on my nightgown, and he pulled me toward him. I smelled the brandy on his breath. I felt his anger, his belligerence; I knew in that moment that I had to be free of him. I couldn't live with his lies and my disgust and the fear—always the fear. Fear that he would hurt you girls. Fear that others would know the truth. And perhaps the worst fear was that he would be taken away from me and imprisoned.

"In that moment, I made up my mind. With all my strength, I pushed him away from me, down the stairs. The lace on my nightgown tore as he fell backward, but he didn't manage to pull me with him. I watched as he stumbled and grasped for a hold but missed it. I watched his bloodshot eyes as they opened wide with the realization that I wanted him to die. For a moment, I almost felt sorry for him. For a moment, I thought of the wonderful man I had fallen in love with, and regretted what I had done. But it was too late." Elinor paused once more, remembering how Billy had crashed downstairs, turned a final half-somersault, then landed on his back, his eyes closed.

She shook her head sadly. "I had seen plenty of dead men; I was sure he was dead. I didn't want to touch him. I decided that the sensible thing to do was to leave him lying in the hall. I remember that my mind was very clear, that for once in my life, I felt completely in control. I decided to forget reality and rewrite the entire scene in my mind, then memorize it according to my new script, hoping that in time it would be the only version I'd remember."

Elinor recalled that she had stared at Billy and felt relief, fresh as a sea breeze playing around her head. She had drawn a deep breath and allowed herself the luxury of her true feelings; for just a few moments, she allowed herself to hate Billy for what he had done to their marriage . . .

Miranda leaned back in her chair and shook her head, still trying to understand why it was so important for them all to hear this story. Puzzled, she asked, "So you just went back to bed?"

Elinor shook her head again and said with difficulty, "No. As I looked at Billy . . . his eyelids slowly opened." Once again she forced herself to remember the terror she had felt as Billy's pouchy, red-veined eyes glared maliciously at her. "Just you wait," he croaked, and then started to vomit. As she stared down at him, Elinor, horrified, also thought of the many times she had had to clean up Billy's mess before someone else saw it. She remembered the many times she had dutifully tended him and served him.

And for one bewildering moment, Billy's malicious stare reminded her of something else, something buried—fragments of a memory she had thought long forgotten. Her head felt as if a storm were raging inside it, whirling her thoughts around like fluttering and panicking birds. For as Billy's eyes stared up at her, Elinor felt again the total despair and helplessness she had felt when her father looked at her with the same contemptuous malevolence.

Violent rage suddenly consumed her. She wanted to howl to primitive gods, for she felt cheated: she had grasped at release, she had acted in vengeance, she had been granted her freedom—but now it was being snatched back . . .

"What *did* you do, Gran?" Miranda persisted.

Elinor started, blinked, and looked in a dazed way at the four faces around the kitchen table. She said quietly, "I ran upstairs and grabbed a pillow from my bed. Then I rushed downstairs and . . . I held it over Billy's face." The pillow had hidden Billy's angry eyes as he heaved in protest. When his body started to jerk and writhe in its final struggle, Elinor called on a reserve of strength she had never known she possessed, holding the pillow over his face with the entire weight of her body. Gradually Billy heaved less, until only his arms, protruding beyond the pillow, twitched occasionally. Eventually all movement ceased.

Elinor said, "I don't know how long I stayed that way. I remember I didn't remove the pillow until the grandfather clock struck one." She had stood up wearily, her body suddenly drained of all strength, and looked with distaste at the vomit-smeared pillowcase. She removed it from the pillow; she would have to wash it. She felt perfectly calm.

Clare's kitchen was completely still as the women sat in stunned silence.

Finally Elinor spoke again. "I was terrified that Annabel might have heard something, might even have seen me . . . do it."

"No," Annabel said, "I saw nothing. I just remember that you brought Snowball up to my bedroom, and the gardener took him to the vet the next morning."

"After I put Snowball in your bed, I stayed until you fell asleep," Elinor said. "Luckily, Buzz hadn't wakened—her bedroom was at the far end of the house, over the kitchen quarters. I remember very clearly the calm with which I sprinkled a bottle of brandy over Billy's body, washed the pillow, then repaired the tear in my nightgown as best I could.

"I lay in bed, awake nearly all night, terrified of what I had done, longing to wake Buzz but afraid to involve her in what was . . . a murder."

Elinor looked slowly around the room, her eyes resting briefly on each face, searching for some reaction.

Clare thought fleetingly of the silver-framed photograph at Elinor's bedside and wondered how, every night, Gran could have slept beside that smiling face, knowing that she had killed him. Then Clare realized suddenly that the bright-eyed young man in that photograph was the perfect husband Gran chose to remember; her carefully crafted fantasy had blanked out the debauched, middle-aged drunkard—the bully she had murdered.

Buzz said, "I can't say I'm sorry, Nell. Billy was a vicious blighter; he tried to bugger up everything you tried to do for them kids. In my view, he died because you had to protect them—from him."

"That's what I tell myself," Elinor murmured. "But I also know that I . . . did what I did . . . to protect *myself.*"

"I still reckon Billy deserved it," Buzz said firmly.

"Poor darling," Annabel said. "You must have been scared stiff."

"No," Elinor said. "At first I was too angry to be scared. I didn't care if they caught me—although, in those days, you were hanged for murder. Later, of course, I *was* frightened, and that fear has never really left me. I'd tremble and my heart would thump every time I saw Sergeant Watson bicycle up the drive on what, thank God, always turned out to be some trivial matter." She looked at Buzz. "I longed to talk to you about it. I never dared. I was terrified of telling anyone. But I've always wondered whether . . ."

Slowly Buzz nodded. "Yes. I knew."

"How?"

"I got back fairly early from the church social and was asleep before eleven, so I woke at six that morning and went downstairs to get a cup of tea. I actually found Billy before the maid came downstairs. And I saw the one thing you had overlooked—a piece of your lace nightgown still clutched in Billy's hand. I pried it loose and burned it, so no one would ever know."

Miranda said urgently, "Why are you telling us this now, Gran, after keeping your secret for so many years? As you once told me, everyone is morally entitled to guard their privacy to protect themselves."

Elinor looked levelly at her. "Because I want you all to see—and see me acknowledge—the danger of self-deception. And perhaps I can only truly admit this to myself, and absolve myself, by telling you—who have seen how destructive it was for us all. That—and my deference.

"I hope each of you now understands how important it is to trust yourself and stand up for yourself; I should have done so earlier. I should have confronted Billy or left him; I would have managed somehow, I would have stood on my own two feet—but I didn't trust myself to try." She looked around the table, then said earnestly, "If, at the beginning, I'd made it clear to Billy that I wasn't going to put up with his self-indulgent ill-treatment, then perhaps it wouldn't have escalated—as bad behavior always does when it's unchecked."

"I know what you mean," Clare said, thinking of Sam.

Buzz said soothingly, "Well, now we all know what happened, I see no reason ever to mention it again. It's all in the past."

"The past is always a part of the present," Elinor said. "And these three must never forget it."

Clare pushed her chair back, hurried around the table to her grandmother, and hugged her. "I'm proud of you for facing the truth at last."

Earnestly Miranda said, "*I'm* proud of you, Gran, because you've always fought and survived, all your life. Although you've never believed it, you've *always* been capable of looking after yourself. You never needed anyone to protect you, Gran—you only thought you did."

After a moment, Annabel said hopefully, "And now we've all learned to stand on our own two feet, haven't we?"

Miranda sighed. "It was an expensive experience."

Quietly Elinor said, "All profitable experience is expensive."

"Not as expensive as the folly of misplaced trust," Clare said.

"Talking of which," Miranda said ruefully, "there's certainly one thing that we've all learned at last . . ."

"Oh yes," Clare sent her a wry smile. "We've finally realized that . . . Daddy doesn't know best."

Epilogue

Liberty: freedom from arbitrary or
despotic control; the power to do as
one pleases; the power of choice;
independence; the quality or state of
being free.

Acknowledgments

As always there are many people whom I wish to thank for their kind help in getting this book before your eyes, and the person to whom I'm most grateful is my kind and considerate "Mission Control," Nikki Manwaring.

In New York, I much appreciated the hard work of Michael Korda, Chuck Adams, Jack McKeown, Sandi Gelles-Cole, Victoria Meyer, Frank Metz, and Sandi Mendelson. I am also, as always, grateful to my agents, Morton Janklow and Anne Sibbald.

I must also thank the Laurey Girls Agency, who took so much trouble to obtain temporary typists who could read my handwriting (in particular I appreciated the charm and ability of Maria Dubow), Ronald Colon, who provided the typewriters, and Anthony J. Barbaro for his banking expertise.

I am also grateful to Judy Licht, Paul Smirnoff, John Parsons, Judy Tygard, Christine Tomlinson, Bob O'Brien, Carol Ann Sullivan and Catherine O'Shea of TV Channel 5.

In Los Angeles I must thank Bill Haber, Joanne Brough and Judy Hilsinger; in Canada, Richard Pearce.

In Britain, as always I am grateful for the patience, understanding and cheerful support of my British publishers, William Armstrong and Peter Carson, as well as George Sharp and Jacqueline Graham-Pelham; I would also like to thank Debbie Gill, Jenny Page and Dido Armstrong for their help.

In Monaco, I would like Nikki Manwaring, Nicole Proetta and Kristina Gonzales de Linares to know how much I appreciated their organization, typing, enthusiasm, attention to detail and general support. I am also very grateful to Roselyn Haudberg, Jane Dubuisson, Suzanne Proetta, Mary George, Paula Whittam, Eva Cleydon and Diego Gonzales de Linares for their help in producing the manuscript.

I was lucky enough to have the final manuscript read and criticized by Geraldine Cooke, Pete Williams and Dr. Georges Sandulescu.

I must also thank Maurice Baird Smith, who taught Miranda to fly, and Gill Brooks of the Cannes Flying School; Ariane Davies-Gilbert, who gave Elinor her Elizabethan candied flower recipe; Elizabeth Barker, who was Miranda's stockbroker; Wendy Williams who designed the garden at Starlings; Ian Melrose who advised Mike on his motor-bikes; Alexander Plunket Greene who gambled with Adam, and Annie Trehearne who advised Miranda on fashion and publicity.

For professional advice on legal matters, I am indebted to Sir Patrick Lawrence, Charles Chatwin, John Dewhurst, Charles Doughty and William Easun. For advice on accounting and finance I am grateful to Richard MacLellan, Stephen Ainsworth and Peter Alexander; for advice on Lloyds I am grateful to David Larner; for advice on business procedure I was lucky enough to be helped by Jennifer d'Abo and Jonathan Bevan.

For advice on fraud, I much appreciated the advice, sagacity and wit of Walter (Wally) White of the Fraud Squad. For medical information I am grateful to Dr. John Cardwell, Dr. Dennis Friedman, Dr. Jonathan Gould, Dr. Margaret Reinhardt and Marion Symes.

For technical information on World War I (including advice on nurses' underwear) I am most grateful to Malcolm Brown, as well as the Imperial War Museum and the RAF Museum at Hendon. I am also grateful to Trevor Williams and John Bryant of the League Against Cruel Sports and Nick Symes for his musical advice.

Others who have helped are Sharon Flynn of Rank Xerox, Diane Kane of British Airways, Claude Laughier and Geoff Osman.

As always, I am indebted to my son Sebastian Conran for esoteric information on such subjects as old motor coaches and atom bombs, vintage motor bikes and Hong Kong massage parlors; and to my son Jasper Conran for fashion advice, criticism and moral support.

Finally I would like also to thank Isabel Carr, Julia de Biere, Elizabeth Chatwin and Patrick Seale for their advice and encouragement. I would also like particularly to thank Bettina Culham (who typed my first novel) and Vanessa Gayle (who typed my second novel), who have kept an eye on me ever since.